VALUE-AT-RISK

Theory and Practice

VALUE-AT-RISK

Theory and Practice

GLYN A. HOLTON
Contingency Analysis, Boston

ACADEMIC PRESS
An imprint of Elsevier Science
Amsterdam Boston London New York Oxford Paris
San Diego San Francisco Singapore Sydney Tokyo

This book is printed on acid-free paper. ♾

Academic Press
An imprint of Elsevier Science
525 B Street, Suite 1900, San Diego, California 92101-4495, USA
http://www.academicpress.com

Academic Press
84 Theobald's Road, London WC1X 8RR, UK
http://www.academicpress.com

Library of Congress Catalog Card Number: 2003100453

International Standard Book Number: 0-12-354010-0

Printed in the United States of America
03 04 05 06 07 9 8 7 6 5 4 3 2 1

To the memory of
Elizabeth Anne Carlson

Contents

Part I
Overview

Chapter 3
Probability

Part I

Overview

Chapter 0

Preface

0.1. WHAT WE'RE ABOUT

A watershed in the history of value-at-risk (VaR) was the publication of JP Morgan's *RiskMetrics Technical Document*. Writing in the third edition of that document, Guldimann (1995) identified three practical methods for calculating VaR:

- the parametric method,
- the historical simulation method, and
- the structured Monte Carlo method;

and so, the "methods" approach for describing VaR was born. Explaining VaR as comprising three "methods" is simple, intuitive and direct. The "methods" approach has been widely adopted by authors of books and research papers. Variations on the three basic "methods" abound, but only one truly new "method" has been introduced since 1995. This might be termed the "quadratic method." Rouvinez (1997) ultimately published it.

For some time, I have felt that the top-down "methods" approach for explaining VaR was flawed. It is like explaining options pricing theory by presenting the Black–Scholes (1973), Merton (1973), and Black (1976) option pricing formulas. As an alternative, a bottom-up description might start with arbitrage pricing, stochastic calculus and replicating portfolios. Top-down explanations are appealing because they go directly to results, but they lead nowhere after that. Bottom-up explanations build a foundation for deeper understanding and further research. I have felt that VaR required such a foundation.

In writing this book, I faced three challenges:

- Although I perceived that VaR needed the firm foundation of a bottom-up explanation, I had no idea what form this should take. I was starting out with a blank sheet of paper.
- More fundamental than this were certain philosophical questions relating to the subjective nature of risk and how to justify attaching a number to—measuring—a subjective notion.
- Finally, I had to decide how technical to make the book.

I addressed the first challenge with hard work. I wrote and discarded hundreds of pages. Of three preliminary chapters I wrote in 1997, hardly a trace remains. Through all this work, a flexible bottom-up framework for understanding VaR gradually emerged.

To address the philosophical issues, I turned to the libraries around Boston. I read philosophical treatises by David Hume and Rudolf Carnap. I delved into the literature on subjective probabilities. I found what I was looking for in the Operationalism of Percy Bridgman. Little of this is mentioned explicitly in the following chapters, but the spirit of Operationalism permeates the entire book.

To settle on a suitable level of mathematics, I considered both the mathematics employed by sophisticated VaR measures and the level of mathematical knowledge that might reasonably be assumed of practitioners. There was somewhat of a gap between the two. The mathematics of VaR is like the proverbial river that is a mile wide but an inch deep. There is a tremendous amount of it—calculus, linear algebra, probability, statistics, time series analysis, numerical methods—but most is not particularly deep. I decided to assume basic knowledge of calculus, linear algebra, and probability, but to fill in the rest.

0.2. CONTENTS OVERVIEW

The book is divided into three parts. The first contains this Preface and Chapter 1. Chapter 1 introduces the bottom-up framework employed throughout the remainder of the book. It explains important notation and terminology. It is a roadmap for subsequent chapters. On its own, Chapter 1 offers a nice introduction to VaR.

Part 2 covers essential mathematics. Starting with Chapter 2, it reviews a number of useful techniques of applied mathematics. Chapter 3 covers topics in probability theory. Assuming familiarity with basic concepts, it delves into more specialized topics, such as mixed-normal distributions, principal component analysis, the Cornish–Fisher expansion and the inversion theorem. Chapter 4 discusses basic notions from classical statistics and time series analysis. The statistics is important for a subsequent discussion of the Monte Carlo method in Chapter 5.

To avoid seeming "cookbookish," I have treated the math as a stand-alone topic and, for the most part, have resisted the temptation to immediately illustrate concepts with VaR applications. This should serve readers well, since much of the math can be used in VaR measures in different ways. Most of it is invaluable for financial applications unrelated to VaR, so it is worth learning in its own right. However, Part 2 is focused. Only topics that will be relevant later in the book are covered.

Part 3 is a bottom-up explanation of how to design VaR measures. Chapter 6 discusses issues relating to the gathering and processing of historical market data. Chapter 7 covers inference procedures. Chapters 8 and 9 cover mapping procedures. Chapter 10 closes with transformation procedures. The discussion is practical, detailing how to implement scalable production VaR systems. A number of techniques are presented for the first time in book form. Among these are:

- the mathematics of quadratic transformations;
- variance reduction techniques applicable to VaR measures; and
- essential remapping techniques.

There are practical examples throughout Part 3. Some are drawn from actual VaR measures I have implemented.

Inevitably, there is much a book cannot include. General discussions of financial risk management are outside the scope of the book. Techniques that complement VaR, such as stress testing, are also excluded.

I had hoped to include a discussion of quasi-Monte Carlo methods. Time and space limitations prevented me from doing so in anything but a cursory manner, so I decided to not do so at all. Still, the book is written with quasi-Monte Carlo methods in mind. Although it does not do so explicitly, it provides plenty of guidance for anyone familiar with quasi-Monte Carlo methods to apply them with VaR measures. A practical issue is the high dimensionality of most VaR applications. Chapter 9 on remappings details techniques for reducing those dimensionalities.

Backtesting of VaR measures is an important topic that raises certain philosophical issues. If risk is subjective, what does it mean for a measure of risk to be "right" or "wrong"; "good" or "bad"; "accurate" or "inaccurate"? I felt that a treatment of backtesting should confront such philosophical issues. To avoid writing a philosophical treatise, I have saved the discussion for another day.

Some authors use the term "value-at-risk" to refer to any probabilistic measure of financial risk, so they speak of VaR measures of credit risk or VaR measures of operational risk. Other authors, including myself, are less extravagant. In this book, VaR encompasses only measures of market risk. Some of the techniques covered can be applied to other risks, but I would not call the resulting measures "VaR measures."

It has become fashionable to caution users that VaR has certain limitations. Doing so is to state the obvious. All tools have limitations. For example, screw drivers are limited by the fact that they cannot drive nails. This book describes how to design, implement, and use VaR measures. It forgoes earnest suggestions of how VaR might not be used.

0.3. AUDIENCE

Through my consulting and training practice, I have worked with hundreds of practitioners—risk managers, traders, regulators, managers, software developers and consultants—representing the capital, commodity, and energy markets. This exposure has helped me understand practitioners' needs, as well as the hurdles they face in understanding, implementing, and using VaR. It has also given me a clear sense of what mathematical knowledge it is reasonable to assume in my writing. The book's primary audience is practitioners who need to implement VaR systems or otherwise require an intimate knowledge of how production VaR systems (should) work. This includes auditors, consultants and regulators. It includes many financial engineers.

The book's bottom-up approach, rigor and treatment of advanced topics will appeal to researchers. My hope is that it will spur further research by clarifying the state of the art and by identifying areas that require further study.

Finally, the book is suitable for students. It offers practical mathematics they can "sink their teeth into." Exercises offer opportunities for practice. References for further reading are indicated at the ends of chapters.

0.4. HOW TO READ THE BOOK

Read this chapter and especially the discussion of notation. Then proceed to Chapter 1. Depending upon your math skills, some of the quantitative examples may be a bit intimidating. Skim them and move on. You can return later.

Part 2 covers essential mathematics that is anticipated in Part 1 and used extensively in Part 3. If you need to review basic calculus, linear algebra, or probability, there are references at the ends of Chapters 2 and 3. It is not essential that you master all of Part 2 before proceeding to Part 3. Some readers may want to skim the material and refer back to it as necessary.

Don't attempt Part 3 until you have mastered Chapter 1. If you have difficulty with the mathematics of Chapter 1, learn that mathematics in Part 2, and then reread Chapter 1 before proceeding to Part 3. Part 3 has a lot of technical depth. You may want to read it twice. Go quickly through the material the first time to get an overview of how it all fits together. Read it more carefully the second time to gain deeper understanding.

Exercises are an essential part of the text. I encourage readers to work through as many as time permits. Doing so will accelerate learning and provide insights that are difficult to achieve through reading alone. Most exercises can be performed with pencil and paper or a spreadsheet. For a few, more sophisticated analytical software will be useful. Such exercises are indicated with a symbol ▦. I had hoped to provide solutions to all exercises. Space limitations made it infeasible to do so in the book itself, so I have posted complete solutions on the Internet at

http://www.contingencyanalysis.com

There are various ways the book can be used in a classroom setting. If students have strong quantitative skills, the book can be covered in a single semester. Focus on Parts 1 and 3. Students can refer to the mathematics of Part 2 on their own as needed.

If students need to develop their quantitative skills, you might design a two-semester financial mathematics course that uses VaR to motivate topics. Cover Part 1 carefully, referring forward to the mathematics of Part 2 as necessary. Then cover highlights of Part 2. Finally, go through the chapters of Part 3 sequentially, referring back to mathematics in Part 2 as needed. You can design the course so that all the material of Part 2 is covered at some point, with much of it motivated by specific applications from Parts 1 and 3.

0.5. NOTATION AND TERMINOLOGY

Currencies are indicated with standard codes. Where applicable, millions are indicated as MM. For example, 3.5 million Japanese yen is indicated: JPY 3.5MM. Currency codes used in the book are shown in Exhibit 0.1.

Code	Currency	Code	Currency
AUD	Australian dollar	JPY	Japanese yen
CAD	Canadian dollar	NOK	Norwegian krone
CHF	Swiss franc	PHP	Philippine peso
DKK	Danish krone	SEK	Swedish krona
EUR	European euro	SGD	Singapore dollar
GBP	British pound	THB	Thailand bath
GRD	Greek drachma	TWD	Taiwan dolla
HKD	Hong Kong dollar	USD	United States dollar
IDR	Indonesian rupiah		

Exhibit 0.1 Currency codes.

Exchange rates are indicated as fractions, so an exchange rate of 1.62 USD/GBP indicates that one British pound is worth 1.62 US dollars. Acronyms used include those shown in Exhibit 0.2.

BBA	British Bankers Association
CAD	Capital Adequacy Directive
CBOT	Chicago Board Of Trade
CDF	cumulative distribution function (distribution function)
CME	Chicago Mercantile Exchange
CSCE	Coffee, Sugar and Cocoa Exchange
EICG	explicit inversive congruential generator
ETL	expected tail loss
ICG	inversive congruential generator
IID	independent and identically distributed
IPE	International Petroleum Exchange
LCG	linear congruential generator
Libor	London Interbank Offered Rate
LIFFE	London International Financial Futures and Options Exchange
LME	London Metals Exchange
MGF	moment generating function
ML	maximum likelihood
MRG	multiple recursive generator
MSE	mean squared error
NYBOT	New York Board of Trade
NYMEX	New York Mercantile Exchange
NYSE	New York Stock Exchange
OTC	over the counter
P&L	profit and loss
PDF	probability density function
PF	probability function
RAROC	risk-adjusted return on capital
RORAC	return on risk-adjusted capital
SEC	Securities and Exchange Commission
TSE	Toronto Stock Exchange
UNCR	Uniform Net Capital Rule
VaR	Value-at-Risk
WCE	Winnipeg Commodities Exchange

Exhibit 0.2 Acronyms.

VaR draws on many branches of mathematics. Each offers its own notation conventions. Because these conflict, it is impossible to observe them all simultaneously. I have developed a system of notation that consistently presents financial concepts related to calculus, linear algebra, probability, statistics, time series analysis, and numerical methods. It draws on existing conventions as much as possible. It is employed uniformly throughout the book.

Random quantities are indicated with capital English letters. If they are random variables—that is, univariate—they are italic nonbold: Q, R, S, X, etc. If they are multivariate in some sense—random vectors, random matrices, stochastic processes—they are italic bold: $\boldsymbol{Q}, \boldsymbol{R}, \boldsymbol{S}, \boldsymbol{X}$, etc. Nonrandom quantities are indicated with lowercase italic letters. These are nonbold for scalars: q, r, s, x, etc. They are bold for vectors, matrices, or time series: $\boldsymbol{q}$, $\boldsymbol{r}$, $\boldsymbol{s}$, $\boldsymbol{x}$, etc.[1]

[1] An exception to this notation is the (nonrandom) identity matrix. Bowing to convention, I denote it $\boldsymbol{I}$.

With this notation, if a random variable is denoted X, a specific realization of that random variable may be denoted x. Such notational correspondence between random quantities and realizations of those random quantities is employed throughout the book.

Components of vectors or matrices are distinguished with subscripts. Consider the random vector

$$\boldsymbol{Q} = \begin{pmatrix} Q_1 \\ Q_2 \\ Q_3 \end{pmatrix}, \qquad [0.1]$$

or the matrix

$$\boldsymbol{c} = \begin{pmatrix} c_{1,1} & c_{1,2} \\ c_{2,1} & c_{2,2} \end{pmatrix}. \qquad [0.2]$$

Time also enters the equation. To avoid confusion, I do not indicate time with subscripts. Instead, I use superscripts that precede the rest of the symbol. For example, the AUD Libor curve evolves over time. We may represent its value at time t as

$${}^{t}\boldsymbol{R} = \begin{pmatrix} {}^{t}R_1 \\ {}^{t}R_2 \\ {}^{t}R_3 \\ {}^{t}R_4 \\ {}^{t}R_5 \\ \vdots \\ {}^{t}R_{15} \end{pmatrix} \sim \begin{pmatrix} \text{spot-next AUD Libor} \\ \text{1-week AUD Libor} \\ \text{2-week AUD Libor} \\ \text{1-month AUD Libor} \\ \text{2-month AUD Libor} \\ \vdots \\ \text{12-month AUD Libor} \end{pmatrix}. \qquad [0.3]$$

The value at time 3 of 1-month AUD Libor is ${}^{3}R_4$. The entire curve at time 1 is denoted ${}^{1}\boldsymbol{R}$. The univariate stochastic process representing 1-week AUD Libor over time is represented $\boldsymbol{R}_2$. The 15-dimensional stochastic process representing the entire curve over time is denoted $\boldsymbol{R}$. Time 0 is generally considered the current time. At time 0, current and past Libor curves are known. As non-random quantities, they are represented with lowercase letters: $\ldots, {}^{-3}\boldsymbol{r}, {}^{-2}\boldsymbol{r}, {}^{-1}\boldsymbol{r}, {}^{0}\boldsymbol{r}$. If time is measured in days, yesterday's value of 12-month AUD Libor is denoted ${}^{-1}r_{15}$.

The advantage of using preceding superscripts to denote time is clarity. By keeping time and component indices physically separate, my notation ensures one will never be confused for the other. Use of preceding superscripts is unconventional, but not without precedent. Actuarial notation makes extensive use of preceding superscripts.

Much other notation is standardized, as will become evident as the book unfolds. Frequently occurring notation is summarized in Exhibit 0.3. See Sections 1.8, 2.2, and 4.5 for more detailed explanations.

log	natural logarithm
$n!$	factorial of an integer n, which is given by the product: $n! = 1 \cdot 2 \cdot 3 \cdot \ldots \cdot (n-1) \cdot n$
$U(a, b)$	uniform distribution on the interval (a, b)
$U_n(\Omega)$	n-dimensional uniform distribution on the region Ω
$N(\mu, \sigma^2)$	normal distribution with mean μ and variance σ^2
$\Lambda(\mu, \sigma^2)$	lognormal distribution with mean μ and variance σ^2
$\chi^2(\nu, \delta^2)$	chi-squared distribution with ν degrees of freedom and non-centrality parameter δ^2
$N_n(\boldsymbol{\mu}, \boldsymbol{\Sigma})$	joint-normal distribution with mean vector $\boldsymbol{\mu}$ and covariance matrix $\boldsymbol{\Sigma}$
${}^1P$	random variable for a portfolio's value at time 1
${}^0p$	portfolio value at time 0
$({}^0p, {}^1P)$	a portfolio
${}^1L$	random variable for portfolio loss: ${}^0p - {}^1P$
${}^1\boldsymbol{R}$	random vector of key factors (key vector)
${}^0\boldsymbol{r}$	vector of key factor values at time 0
${}^1\boldsymbol{S}$	random vector of asset values at time 1 (asset vector)
${}^0\boldsymbol{s}$	vector of asset values at time 0
${}^1\boldsymbol{Q}$, ${}^1\dot{\boldsymbol{Q}}$ or ${}^1\ddot{\boldsymbol{Q}}$	frequently used to indicate risk vectors that are not key vectors
$E(\,)$	unconditional expected value
${}^tE(\,)$	expected value conditional on information available at time t
$std(\,)$	unconditional standard deviation
${}^tstd(\,)$	standard deviation conditional on information available at time t
$var(\,)$	unconditional variance
${}^tvar(\,)$	variance conditional on information available at time t
${}^t\mu$	unconditional mean of the time t term of a stochastic process
${}^{t\|t-k}\mu$	mean of the time t term of a stochastic process conditional on information available at time $t-k$
${}^t\boldsymbol{\Sigma}$	unconditional covariance matrix of the time t term of a stochastic process

Exhibit 0.3 Frequently used notation.

${}^{t\|t-k}\boldsymbol{\Sigma}$	covariance matrix of the time t term of a stochastic process conditional on information available at time $t-k$
θ	frequently used to denote a portfolio mapping function
φ	frequently used to denote a (non-portfolio) mapping function
$\boldsymbol{\omega}$	portfolio holdings
${}^{t}\phi(\,)$	unconditional PDF of the time t term of a stochastic process
${}^{t\|t-k}\phi(\,)$	PDF of the time t term of a stochastic process conditional on information available at time $t-k$
${}^{t}\Phi(\,)$	unconditional PDF of the time t term of a stochastic process
${}^{t\|t-k}\Phi(\,)$	PDF of the time t term of a stochastic process conditional on information available at time $t-k$
$\sim$	sometimes placed above notation to indicate a remapping; for example, ${}^{1}\widetilde{P} = \widetilde{\theta}({}^{1}\widetilde{\boldsymbol{R}})$ denotes a remapping of ${}^{1}P = \theta({}^{1}\boldsymbol{R})$.
	indicates that analytic software more sophisticated than a spreadsheet may be useful in solving an exercise

Exhibit 0.3 *Continued.*

0.6. ACKNOWLEDGMENTS

Many people have contributed to this project over the years. Early encouragement came from Oliver Wells and Ruth McMullen. My perceptions of VaR have been shaped by clients and participants in the Financial Risk Management Discussion Group (http://www.riskchat.com). In e-mail correspondence, Emmanuel Fruchard generously elaborated on his own published research. Humberto De Luigi taught me much about the coffee and cocoa markets while we worked together on a VaR implementation. Pierre L'Ecuyer kindly shared his insights on the state of the art for pseudorandom number generators. Ken Garbade and Till Guldimann generously contributed their recollections on the history of VaR measures.

The manuscript benefited from several rounds of anonymous reviews. Anonymity was not perfectly preserved, so I am able to thank directly: Kevin Dowd, Roza Galeeva, Mario Melchiori, Peter Moles, Arcady Novosyolov, Lisa Rister, and Kevin Weber.

My editor, Scott Bentley of Academic Press, has been tremendously patient with missed deadlines and early manuscript drafts that seemed unrelated to popular conceptions of VaR. Converting a manuscript into a book requires concerted efforts of many people. Staff at Elsevier and contractors has included Waseem Andrabi, Nishith Arora, Debby Bicher, Mike Early, Kirsten Funk, Brock Hanke,

Kristin Landon, Keith Roberts, and Jane Stark. Suzanne Rogers has designed a wonderful cover. Nancy Zachor and Diane Grossman managed the entire process and kept us on schedule. Mara Conner and Jennifer Pursley have been pivotal in planning publicity. Working with everyone has been a pleasure. Results speak for themselves.

My friends have been enormously supportive. I have missed countless outings and get-togethers so I could work on "the book." Still, they never stopped inviting. Thank you all.

Glyn A. Holton
Contingency Analysis
December 3, 2002

Chapter 1

Value-at-Risk

1.1. HISTORY

The term "value-at-risk" (VaR) did not enter the financial lexicon until the early 1990s, but the origins of VaR measures go further back. These can be traced to capital requirements for US securities firms of the early 20th century, starting with an informal capital test the New York Stock Exchange (NYSE) first applied to member firms around 1922.

Regulatory VaR Measures

The original NYSE rule[1] required firms to hold capital equal to 10% of assets comprising proprietary positions and customer receivables. By 1929, this had developed into a requirement that firms hold capital equal to:

- 5% of customer debits;
- 10% (minimum) on proprietary holdings in government of municipal bonds;
- 30% on proprietary holdings in other liquid securities; and
- 100% on proprietary holdings in all other securities.

Over time, regulators took over responsibility for setting capital requirements. In 1975, the US Securities and Exchange Commission (SEC) established a Uniform Net Capital Rule (UNCR) for US broker-dealers trading non-exempt securities. This included a system of "haircuts" that were applied to a firm's capital as a safeguard against market losses that might arise during the time it would take to

[1] See Dale (1996), pp. 60–61 and Molinari and Kibler (1983), footnote 41.

liquidate positions. Financial assets were divided into 12 categories such as government debt, corporate debt, convertible securities, and preferred stock. Some of these were further broken down into subcategories primarily according to maturity. To reflect hedging effects, long and short positions were netted within subcategories, but only limited netting was permitted across subcategories. An additional haircut was applied to any concentrated position in a single asset.

Volatility in US interest rates motivated the SEC to update these haircuts in 1980. The new haircuts were based upon a statistical analysis of historical market data. They were intended to reflect a .95-quantile of the amount of money a firm might lose over a 1-month liquidation period.[2] Although crude, the SEC's system of haircuts was a VaR measure.

Later, additional regulatory VaR measures were implemented for banks or securities firms, including:

- the UK Securities and Futures Authority 1992 "portfolio" VaR measure;
- Europe's 1993 Capital Adequacy Directive (CAD) "building-block" VaR measure; and
- the Basle Committee's[3] 1996 VaR measure based largely upon the CAD building-block measure.

In 1996, the Basle Committee approved the limited use of proprietary VaR measures for calculating bank capital requirements. In this and other ways, regulatory initiatives helped motivate the development of proprietary VaR measures.

Proprietary VaR Measures

Tracing the historical development of proprietary VaR measures is difficult because they were used by firms for internal purposes. They were not published and were rarely mentioned in the literature. One interesting document is a letter from Stephen C. Francis (1985) of Fischer, Francis, Trees & Watts to the Federal Reserve Bank of New York. He indicates that their proprietary VaR measure was similar to the SEC's UNCR but employed more asset categories, including 27 categories for cash market US Treasuries alone. He notes:

---

[2] See Dale (1996), p. 78.

[3] The Basle Committee on Banking Supervision is a standing committee comprising representatives from central banks and regulatory authorities. Over time, the focus of the committee has evolved, embracing initiatives designed to define roles of regulators in cross-jurisdictional situations; ensure that international banks or bank holding companies do not escape comprehensive supervision by some "home" regulatory authority; and promote uniform capital requirements so banks from different countries may compete with one another on a "level playing field." Although the Basle Committee's recommendations lack force of law, G-10 countries are implicitly bound to implement its recommendations as national laws.

> We find no difficulty utilizing on an essentially manual basis the larger number of categories, and indeed believe it necessary to capturing accurately our gross and net risk exposures.

Working at Bankers Trust, Garbade (1986) describes sophisticated VaR measures for fixed income markets that employed linear and principal component remappings to simplify computations. These may have been influenced by, but were different from, an internal VaR measure Bankers Trust implemented around 1983 for use with its risk-adjusted return on capital (RAROC) system of internal capital allocation.

Garbade today recollects[4] efforts within Bankers Trust to improve existing VaR measures following the stock market crash of 1987. During the crash, Treasury interest rates fell sharply while stock prices plummeted. Such correlated market moves are often observed during periods of market turmoil. They have motivated suggestions that correlations become more extreme during periods of elevated market volatility. Within Bankers Trust, there were several efforts to model this phenomena with mixed normal distributions. These comprised two joint-normal distributions. One was likely to be drawn from and had modest standard deviations and correlations. The other was less likely to be drawn from and had more extreme standard deviations and correlations. Using time-series methods available at the time, the researchers were unable to fit a reasonable model to available market data. They concluded that their inability to do so indicated a significant shortcoming of VaR measures then in use.

At about the same time, Chase Manhattan Bank was developing a Monte Carlo based VaR measure for use with its return on risk-adjusted capital (RORAC) internal capital allocation system. Citibank was implementing another VaR measure, also for capital allocation, which measured what the bank referred to as "potential loss amount" or PLA.[5]

A 1993 survey conducted by Price Waterhouse for the Group of 30[6] found that, at that time, among 80 responding derivatives dealers, 30% were using VaR to support market risk limits. Another 10% planned to do so.

Portfolio Theory

Directly or indirectly, regulatory and proprietary VaR measures were influenced by portfolio theory. Markowitz (1952) and Roy (1952) independently published VaR measures to support portfolio optimization. In 1952, processing power was inadequate to support practical use of such schemes, but Markowitz's ideas

---

[4]Personal correspondence with the author.

[5]These VaR measures are described by Chew (1993).

[6]Founded in 1978, the Group of 30 is a nonprofit organization of senior executives, regulators, and academics. Through meetings and publications, it seeks to deepen understanding of international economic and financial issues. Results of the Price Waterhouse study are reported in Group of 30 (1994).

spawned work by more theoretically inclined researchers. Papers by Tobin (1958), Treynor (1961), Sharpe (1963, 1964), Lintner (1965), and Mossin (1966) contributed to the emerging portfolio theory. The VaR measures they employed were best suited for equity portfolios. There were few alternative asset categories, and applying VaR to these would have raised a number of modeling issues. Real estate cannot be marked to market with any frequency, making VaR inapplicable. Applying VaR to either debt instruments or futures contracts entails modeling term structures. Also, debt instruments raise issues of credit spreads. Futures that were traded at the time were primarily for agricultural products, which raise seasonality issues. Schrock (1971) and Dusak (1973) describe simple VaR measures for futures portfolios, but neither addresses term structure or seasonality issues.

Lietaer (1971) describes a practical VaR measure for foreign exchange risk. He wrote during the waning days of fixed exchange rates when risk manifested itself as currency devaluations. Since World War II, most currencies had devalued at some point; many had done so several times. Governments were secretive about planned devaluations, so corporations maintained ongoing hedges. Lietaer (1971) proposes a sophisticated procedure for optimizing such hedges. It incorporates a VaR measure with a variance of market value VaR metric. It assumes devaluations occur randomly, with the conditional magnitude of a devaluation being normally distributed. Computations are simplified using a modification of Sharpe's (1963) diagonal model. Lietaer's work may be the first instance of the Monte Carlo method being employed in a VaR measure.

Emergence of Risk Management

In 1990, risk management was novel. Many financial firms lacked an independent risk management function. This concept was practically unheard of in nonfinancial firms. The term "risk management" was not new. It had long been used to describe techniques for addressing property and casualty contingencies. Doherty (2000) traces such usage to the 1960s and 1970s when organizations were exploring alternatives to insurance, including:

- risk reduction through safety, quality control, and hazard education; and
- alternative risk financing, including self-insurance and captive insurance.

Such techniques, together with traditional insurance, were collectively referred to as risk management.

More recently, derivative dealers had been promoting "risk management" as the use of derivatives to hedge or customize market-risk exposures. For this reason, derivative instruments were sometimes called "risk management products."

The new "risk management" that evolved during the 1990s is different from either of the earlier forms. It tends to view derivatives as a problem as much as a solution. It focuses on reporting, oversight, and segregation of duties within organizations.

On January 30, 1992, Gerald Corrigan, President of the New York Federal Reserve, addressed the New York Bankers Association. His comments set a tone for the new risk management:[7]

> ... the interest rate swap market now totals several trillion dollars. Given the sheer size of the market, I have to ask myself how it is possible that so many holders of fixed or variable rate obligations want to shift those obligations from one form to the other. Since I have a great deal of difficulty in answering that question, I then have to ask myself whether some of the specific purposes for which swaps are now being used may be quite at odds with an appropriately conservative view of the purpose of a swap, thereby introducing new elements of risk or distortion into the marketplace—including possible distortions to the balance sheets and income statements of financial and nonfinancial institutions alike.
>
> I hope this sounds like a warning, because it is. Off-balance sheet activities have a role, but they must be managed and controlled carefully, and they must be understood by top management as well as by traders and rocket scientists.

With concerns about derivatives increasing, Paul Volker, Chairman of the Group of 30, approached Dennis Weatherstone, Chairman of JP Morgan, and asked him to lead a study of derivatives industry practices. Weatherstone formed an international steering committee and a working group of senior managers from derivatives dealers; end users; and related legal, accounting, and academic disciplines. They produced a 68-page report, which the Group of 30 published in July 1993. Entitled *Derivatives: Practices and Principles*, it has come to be known as the *G-30 Report*. It describes then-current derivatives use by dealers and end-users. The heart of the study is a set of 20 recommendations to help dealers and end-users manage their derivatives activities. Topics addressed include:

- the role of boards and senior management,
- the implementation of independent risk management functions, and
- the various risks that derivatives transactions entail.

With regard to the market risk faced by derivatives dealers, the report recommends that portfolios be marked-to-market daily, and that risk be assessed with both VaR and stress testing. It recommends that end-users of derivatives adopt similar practices as appropriate for their own needs.

Although the *G-30 Report* focuses on derivatives, most of its recommendations are applicable to the risks associated with other traded instruments. For this reason, the report largely came to define the new risk management of the 1990s. The report is also interesting, as it seems to be the first published document to use the term "value-at-risk." Alternative names, such as "capital-at-risk" and "dollars-at-risk" were also used for a time and appeared earlier in the literature.[8]

---

[7]This incident is documented in Shirreff (1992). See Corrigan (1992) for a full text of the speech.

[8]The name "dollars-at-risk" appears as early as Mark (1991), and "capital-at-risk" as early as Wilson (1992).

Still, VaR remained a specialized tool known primarily to risk managers at financial firms. This changed in 1994 when JP Morgan introduced its free RiskMetrics service.

RiskMetrics

During the late 1980s, JP Morgan developed a firm-wide VaR system. This modeled several hundred key factors. A covariance matrix was updated quarterly from historical data. Each day, trading units would report by e-mail their positions' deltas with respect to each of the key factors. These were aggregated to express the combined portfolio's value as a linear polynomial of the risk factors. From this, the standard deviation of portfolio value was calculated. Various VaR metrics were employed. One of these was 1-day 95% USD VaR, which was calculated using an assumption that the portfolio's value was normally distributed.

With this VaR measure, JP Morgan replaced a cumbersome system of notional market risk limits with a simple system of VaR limits. Starting in 1990, VaR numbers were combined with P&L's in a report for each day's 4:15 PM Treasury meeting in New York. Those reports, with comments from the Treasury Group, were forwarded to Chairman Weatherstone.

One of the architects of the new VaR measure was Till Guldimann. His career with JP Morgan had positioned him to help develop and then promote the VaR measure within the firm. During the mid 1980s, he was responsible for the firm's asset/liability analysis. Working with other professionals, he developed concepts that would be used in the VaR measure. Later as chairman of the firm's market risk committee, he promoted the VaR measure internally. As fate would have it, Guldimann's next position placed him in a role to promote the VaR measure outside the firm.

In 1990 Guldimann took responsibility for Global Research, overseeing research activities to support marketing to institutional clients. In that capacity he managed an annual research conference for clients. In 1993, risk management was the conference theme. Guldimann gave the keynote address and arranged for a demonstration of JP Morgan's VaR system. The demonstration generated considerable interest. Clients asked if they might purchase or lease the system. Since JP Morgan was not a software vendor, they were disinclined to comply. Guldimann proposed an alternative. The firm would provide clients with the means to implement their own systems. JP Morgan would publish a methodology, distribute the necessary covariance matrix, and encourage software vendors to develop compatible software.

Guldimann formed a small team to develop something for the next year's research conference. The service they developed was called **RiskMetrics**.

It comprised a detailed technical document as well as a covariance matrix for several hundred key factors, which was updated daily. Both were distributed without charge over the Internet. The service was rolled out with considerable fanfare in October 1994. A public relations firm placed ads and articles in the financial press. Representatives of JP Morgan went on a multi-city tour to promote the service. Software vendors, who had received advance notice, started promoting compatible software.[9]

Publicized Losses

Timing for the release of RiskMetrics was excellent, as it came during a period of publicized financial losses. In February 1993, Japan's Showa Shell Sekiyu oil company reported a USD 1050MM loss from speculating on exchange rates. In December of that year, MG Refining and Marketing, a US subsidiary of Germany's Metallgesellschaft AG, reported a loss of USD 1300MM from failed hedging of long-dated oil supply commitments.

In 1994, there was a litany of losses. China's state sponsored CITIC conglomerate and Chile's state-owned Codelco copper corporation lost USD 40MM and USD 207MM trading metals on the London Metals Exchange (LME). US companies Gibson Greetings, Mead, Proctor & Gamble, and Air Products and Chemicals all reported losses from differential swaps transacted with Bankers Trust. Japan's Kashima Oil lost USD 1500MM speculating on exchange rates. California's Orange County announced losses from repos and other transactions that would total USD 1700MM. These are just a few of the losses publicized during 1994.

The litany continued into 1995. A notable example is Japan's Daiwa Bank. One of its US-based bond traders had secretly accumulated losses of USD 1100MM over a 10 year period. What grabbed the world's attention, though, was the dramatic failure of Britain's Barings PLC in February 1995. Nick Leeson, a young trader based at its Singapore office, lost USD 1400MM from unauthorized Nikkei futures and options positions. Barings had been founded in 1762. It had financed Britain's participation in the Napoleonic wars. It had financed America's Louisiana purchase and construction of the Erie Canal. Following its collapse, Barings was sold to Dutch bank ING for the price of one GBP.

By the mid-1990s, regulatory initiatives, concerns about OTC derivatives, the release of RiskMetrics, and publicized losses had created a flurry of interest in the new risk management and related techniques. Today, "value-at-risk" is not quite a household word, but it is familiar to most professionals working in wholesale financial, energy, and commodities markets.

---

[9]The above discussion of RiskMetrics is based upon Guldimann (2000), the author's own recollections, and private correspondence with Till Guldimann.

1.2. MEASURES

A **measure** is an operation that assigns a value to something. There are measures of length, temperature, mass, time, speed, strength, aptitude, etc. Assigned values are usually numbers, but can be elements of any ordered set. Shoe widths are sometimes assigned values from the ordered set {A, B, C, D, E}. We distinguish between:

- a **measure**, which is the operation that assigns the value, and
- a **metric**, which is an interpretation of the value.

A highway patrolman points a Doppler radar at an approaching automobile. The radar transmits microwaves, which are reflected off the auto and return to the radar. By comparing the wavelength of the transmitted microwaves to that of the reflected microwaves, the radar generates a number, which it displays. This entire process is a measure. An interpretation of that number—speed in miles/hour—is a metric.

Questionnaires are mailed to a diverse sample of 5000 households throughout the United States. They ask questions relating to:

1. business conditions in the household's area;
2. anticipated business conditions in 6 months;
3. job availability in the area;
4. anticipated job availability in 6 months; and
5. anticipated family income in 6 months.

Approximately 3500 households respond. Responses are seasonally adjusted. A statistical formula is applied to the set of responses to produce a number. This process is a measure. The Conference Board interprets the number as "consumer confidence," a unitless quantity. The interpretation is a metric.

Let's consider our first exercise. Solutions for all exercises are available online at http://www.contingencyanalysis.com.

Exercises

1.1 Describe a measure and corresponding metric that might be used in weather forecasting.

1.3. RISK MEASURES

Risk has two components:

- exposure, and
- uncertainty.

If we swim in shark-infested waters, we are *exposed* to bodily injury or death from a shark attack. We are *uncertain* because we don't know if we will be attacked. Being both exposed and uncertain, we face risk.

A **risk measure** is a measure that is applied to risks. A **risk metric** is an interpretation of such a measure. Risk metrics typically take one of three forms:

- those that quantify exposure;
- those that quantify uncertainty;
- those that quantify exposure and uncertainty in some combined manner.

Probability of rain is a risk metric that only quantifies uncertainty. It does not address our exposure to rain, which depends upon whether or not we have outdoor plans.

Credit exposure is a risk metric that only quantifies exposure. It indicates how much money we might lose if a counterparty were to default. It says nothing about our uncertainty as to whether or not the counterparty will default.

Risk metrics that quantify uncertainty—either alone or in combination with exposure—are usually probabilistic. Many summarize risk with a parameter of some probability distribution. Standard deviation of tomorrow's spot price of copper is a risk metric that quantifies uncertainty. It does so with a standard deviation. Average highway deaths per passenger-mile is a risk metric that quantifies uncertainty and exposure. We may interpret it as reflecting the mean of a probability distribution.

Exercises

1.2 Give an example of a situation that entails uncertainty but not exposure, and hence no risk.

1.3 Give an example of a situation that entails exposure but not uncertainty, and hence no risk.

1.4 In our example of the deaths per passenger-mile risk metric, for what random variable's probability distribution may we interpret it as reflecting a mean?

1.5 Give three examples of risk metrics that quantify financial risks. Choose one that quantifies exposure. Choose one that quantifies uncertainty. Choose one that quantifies uncertainty combined with exposure.

1.4. MARKET RISK

Business activities entail a variety of risks. For convenience, we distinguish between different categories of risk: market risk, credit risk, liquidity risk, etc. Although such categorization is convenient, it is only informal. Usage and definitions vary. Boundaries between categories are blurred. A loss due to widening credit spreads may reasonably be called a market loss or a credit loss, so market risk and credit risk overlap. Liquidity risk compounds other risks, such as market risk and credit risk. It cannot be divorced from the risks it compounds.

For our purposes, it is convenient to distinguish between market risk and business risk. **Market risk** is exposure to the uncertain market value of a portfolio.

A trader holds a portfolio of commodity forwards. She knows what its market value is today, but she is uncertain as to its market value a week from today. She faces market risk. **Business risk** is exposure to uncertainty in economic value that cannot be marked-to-market. The distinction between market risk and business risk parallels the distinction between market-value accounting and book-value accounting. Suppose a New England electricity wholesaler is long a forward contract for on-peak electricity delivered over the next 12 months. There is an active forward market for such electricity, so the contract can be marked to market daily. Daily profits and losses on the contract reflect market risk. Suppose the firm also owns a power plant with an expected useful life of 30 years. Power plants change hands infrequently, and electricity forward curves don't exist out to 30 years. The plant cannot be marked to market on a regular basis. In the absence of market values, market risk is not a meaningful notion. Uncertainty in the economic value of the power plant represents business risk.

Most risk metrics apply to a specific category of risks. There are market risk measures, credit risk measures, etc. Note that we do not categorize risk measures according to the specific operations those measures entail. We characterize them according to the risk metrics they are intended to support.

Gamma—as used by options traders—is a metric of market risk. There are various operations by which we might calculate gamma. We might:

- use a closed form solution related to the Black-Scholes formula;
- value the portfolio at three different underlier values and interpolate a quadratic polynomial; etc.

Each method defines a risk measure. We categorize them all as measures of gamma, not based upon the specific operations that define them, but simply because they all support gamma as a risk metric.

Exercises

1.6 Describe two different risk measures, both of which support duration as a risk metric.

1.5. VALUE-AT-RISK

Value-at-risk (VaR) is a category of market risk measures. As with any category of risk measures, we define VaR in terms of the risk metrics the measure supports.

Suppose a portfolio were to remain untraded for a certain period—say from the current time 0 to some future time 1. The portfolio's market value ${}^0p$ at the start of the period is known. Its market value ${}^1P$ at the end of the period is unknown. It is a random variable. As a random variable, we may assign it a probability distribution conditional upon information available at time 0. We might quantify the portfolio's market risk with some real-valued parameter of that conditional distribution.

Formally, a **VaR metric** is a real-valued function of:

- the distribution of ${}^1P$ conditional on information available at time 0; and
- the portfolio's current value ${}^0p$.

Standard deviation of ${}^1P$, conditional on information available at time 0, is a VaR metric:

$$ {}^0std({}^1P). \tag{1.1} $$

Conditional standard deviation of a portfolio's simple return ${}^1Z$ is a VaR metric:

$$ {}^0std({}^1Z) = {}^0std\left(\frac{{}^1P - {}^0p}{{}^0p}\right) = \frac{{}^0std({}^1P - {}^0p)}{{}^0p} = \frac{{}^0std({}^1P)}{{}^0p}. \tag{1.2} $$

If we define **portfolio loss** as

$$ {}^1L = {}^0p - {}^1P, \tag{1.3} $$

then the conditional standard deviation of ${}^1L$ is also a VaR metric:

$$ {}^0std({}^1L) = {}^0std({}^0p - {}^1P) = {}^0std({}^1P). \tag{1.4} $$

Quantiles of portfolio loss make intuitively appealing VaR metrics. If the conditional .95-quantile of ${}^1L$ is GBP 2.6MM, then such a portfolio can be expected to lose less than GBP 2.6MM on 19 days out of 20.

The functions that define VaR metrics can be fairly elaborate. An **expected tail loss** (ETL) VaR metric indicates a portfolio's expected loss conditional on that loss exceeding some specified quantile of loss.[10]

To fully specify a VaR metric, we must indicate three things:

- the period of time—1 day, 2 weeks, 1 month, etc.—between time 0 and time 1; this is the **horizon**;
- the function of ${}^0p$ and the conditional distribution of ${}^1P$;
- the currency in which ${}^0p$ and ${}^1P$ are denominated; this is the **base currency**.

Note that we always measure time in units equal to the length of the VaR horizon, so the VaR horizon always starts at time 0 and ends at time 1. We adopt a convention for naming VaR metrics:

1. The metric's name is given as the horizon, function, and currency, in that order, followed by "VaR."

[10]See Dowd (2002) for more on ETL metrics.

2. If the horizon is expressed in days without qualification, these are understood to be trading days.
3. If the function is a quantile of loss, it is indicated simply as a percentage.

For example, we may speak of a portfolio's:

- 1-day standard deviation of simple return USD VaR,
- 2-week 95% JPY VaR, or
- 1-week 90% ETL GBP VaR, etc.

Recall that risk measures are categorized according to the metrics they support. Having defined VaR metrics, we define VaR as the category of risk measures that support VaR metrics. If a risk measure supports a metric that is a VaR metric, then the measure is a **VaR measure**. If we apply a VaR measure to a portfolio, the value obtained is called a **VaR measurement** or, less precisely, the **portfolio's VaR**.

A VaR measure is just an operation—some set of computations—designed to support a VaR metric. To design a VaR measure, we generally have some financial model in mind. Models take many forms, embracing certain assumptions and drawing on fields such as portfolio theory, financial engineering, or time series analysis. Such models are the assumptions and logic that motivate a VaR measure. We call them **VaR models**.

Finally, to use a VaR measure, we must implement it. We must secure necessary inputs, code the measure as software, and install the software on computers and related hardware. The result is a **VaR implementation**.

Exercises

1.7 Which of the following represent VaR metrics:
   1. conditional variance of a portfolio's USD market value 1 week from today;
   2. conditional standard deviation of a portfolio's JPY net cash flow over the next month.
   3. beta, as defined by Sharpe's (1964) Capital Asset Pricing Model, conditional on information available at time 0.

1.8 Using the naming convention indicated in the text, name the following VaR metrics:
   1. the conditional standard deviation of a portfolio's market value, measured in AUD, 1 week from today;
   2. the conditional standard deviation of a portfolio's USD simple return over the next 3 trading days;
   3. the conditional 99% quantile of a portfolio's loss, measured in GBP, over the next day.

1.9 Consider a 1-day standard deviation of simple return JPY VaR metric. A portfolio's return is a unitless quantity; so is its conditional standard deviation of return. Must we specify a base currency (JPY) for this VaR metric? Couldn't we just call it a 1-day standard deviation of simple return VaR metric?

1.6. RISK LIMITS

VaR measures are used for a variety of tasks, including oversight, capital calculations, and portfolio optimization. The quintessential application is VaR limits.

Risk limits are a device for authorizing specific forms of risk taking. A pension fund hires an outside investment manager to invest some of its assets in intermediate corporate bonds. The fund wants the manager to take risk on its behalf, but it has a specific form of risk in mind. It doesn't want the manager investing in equities, precious metals, or cocoa futures. It communicates its intentions with contractually binding investment guidelines. These specify acceptable investments. They also specify risk limits, such as requirements that:

- the portfolio's duration always be less than 7 years;
- all bonds have a credit rating of BBB or better.

The first is an example of a market risk limit; the second of a credit risk limit.

When an organization authorizes a risk limit for risk-taking activities, it must specify three things:

1. a risk metric,
2. a risk measure that supports the metric, and
3. the limit—a value for the risk metric that is not to be exceeded.

At any point in time, a limit's **utilization** is the actual amount of risk being taken, as quantified by the risk measure. Any instance where utilization exceeds the risk limit is called a **limit violation.**

A bank's corporate lending department is authorized to lend to a specific counterparty subject to a credit exposure limit of GBP 10MM. For this purpose, the bank measures credit exposure as the sum amount of outstanding loans and loan commitments to the counterparty. The lending department lends the counterparty GBP 8MM, causing its utilization of the limit to be GBP 8MM. Since the limit is GBP 10MM, the lending department has remaining authority to lend up to GBP 2MM to the counterparty.

A metals trading firm authorizes a trader to take gold price risk subject to a 2000 troy ounce delta limit. Using a specified measure of delta, his portfolio's delta is calculated at 4:30 PM each trading day. Utilization is calculated as the absolute value of the portfolio's delta.

Market Risk Limits

For monitoring market risk, many organizations segment portfolios in some manner. They may do so by trader and trading desk. Commodities trading firms may do so by delivery point and geographic region. A hierarchy of market risk limits is typically specified to parallel such segmentation, with each segment of the portfolio having its own limits. Limits generally increase in size as you move up the hierarchy—from traders to desks to the overall portfolio; or from individual delivery points to geographic regions to the overall portfolio.

Exhibit 1.1 illustrates how a hierarchy of market risk limits might be implemented for a trading unit. A risk metric is selected, and risk limits are specified based upon this. Each limit is depicted with a cylinder. The height of the cylinder corresponds to the size of the limit. The trading unit has three trading desks, each with its own limit. There are also limits for individual traders, but only those for trading desk A are shown. The extent to which each cylinder is shaded black corresponds to the utilization of that limit. Trader A3 is utilizing almost all his limit. Trader A4 is utilizing little of hers.

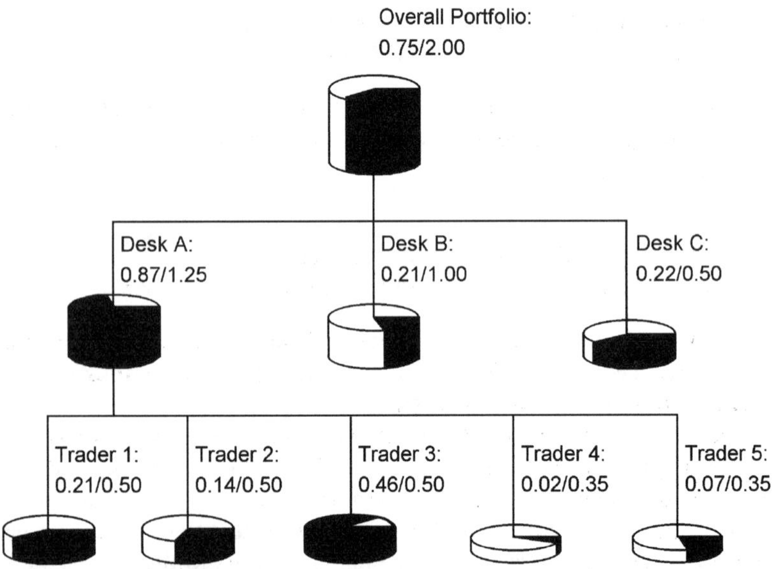

Exhibit 1.1 A hierarchy of market risk limits is illustrated for a hypothetical trading unit. A risk metric—VaR, delta, etc.—is chosen. Risk limits are specified for the portfolio and subportfolios based upon this. The limits are depicted with cylinders. The height of each cylinder corresponds to the size of the limit. The degree to which it is shaded black indicates current utilization of the limit. Fractions next to each cylinder indicate utilization and limit size. Units are not indicated here, as these will depend upon the particular risk metric used. Individual traders have limits, but only those for traders on desk A are indicated in the exhibit.

For such a hierarchy of risk limits to work, an organization must have a suitable risk measure to calculate utilization of each risk limit on an ongoing basis. Below, we describe three types of market risk limits, culminating with VaR limits.

Stop-Loss Limits

A stop-loss limit indicates an amount of money that a portfolio's single-period market loss should not exceed. Various periods may be used, and sometimes multiple stop-loss limits are specified for different periods. A trader might be given the following stop-loss limits:

- 1-day EUR 0.5MM,
- 1-week EUR 1.0MM,
- 1-month EUR 3.0MM.

A limit violation occurs whenever a portfolio's single-period market loss exceeds a stop-loss limit. In such an event, a trader is usually required to hedge material exposures—hence the name **stop-loss limit**.

Stop-loss limits have shortcomings. Single-period market loss is a retrospective risk metric. It only indicates risk after the financial consequences of that risk have been realized. Also, it provides an inconsistent indication of risk. If a portfolio suffers a large loss over a given period, this is a clear indication of risk. If the portfolio does not suffer a large loss, this does not indicate an absence of risk! Another problem is that traders cannot control the specific losses they incur, so it is difficult to hold traders accountable for isolated stop-loss limit violations. However, the existence of stop-loss limits does motivate traders to manage portfolios in such a manner as to avoid limit violations.

Despite their shortcomings, stop-loss limits are simple and convenient to use. Non-specialists easily understand stop-loss limits. A single risk metric can be applied consistently across an entire hierarchy of limits. Calculating utilization is as simple as marking a portfolio to market. Finally, because portfolio loss encompasses all sources of market risk, just one or a handful of limits is required for each portfolio or sub-portfolio. For these reasons, stop-loss limits are widely implemented by trading organizations.

Exposure Limits

Exposure limits are limits based upon an exposure risk metric. For limiting market risk, common metrics include: duration, convexity, delta, gamma, and vega. Crude exposure limits may also be based upon notional amounts. These are called **notional limits**. Many exposure metrics can take on positive or negative values, so utilization may be defined as the absolute value of exposure.

Exposure limits address many of the shortcomings of stop-loss limits. They are prospective. Exposure limits indicate risk before its financial consequences are realized. Also, exposure metrics provide a reasonably consistent indication of risk. For the most part, traders can be held accountable for exposure limit violations because they largely control their portfolio's exposures. There are rare exceptions. A sudden market rise may cause a positive-gamma portfolio's delta to increase, resulting in an unintended delta limit violation.

For the most part, utilization of exposure limits is easy to calculate. There may be analytic formulas for certain exposure metrics. At worst, a portfolio must be valued under multiple market scenarios with some form of interpolation applied to assess exposure.

Exposure limits pose a number of problems. A hierarchy of exposure limits will depend upon numerous risk metrics. Not only is delta different from gamma, but crude oil delta is different from natural gas delta. Because a portfolio or subportfolio can have multiple exposures, it will require multiple exposure limits. An equity derivatives trader might have delta, gamma, and vega limits for each of 1000 equities—for a total of 3000 exposure limits.

Exposure limits are ineffective in contexts where spread trading, cross-hedging, or similar strategies minimize risk by taking offsetting positions in correlated assets. Large exposure limits are required in order to accommodate each of the offsetting positions. Because they cannot ensure reasonable hedging, the exposure limits allow for net risk far in excess of that required by the intended hedging strategy.

With the exception of notional limits, non-specialists do not easily understand exposure limits. It is difficult to know what might be a reasonable delta limit for an electricity trading desk if you don't have both:

- a technical understanding of what delta means, and
- practical familiarity with the typical size of market fluctuations in the electricity market.

This, and the sheer number of exposure limits that are often required, makes it difficult for managers to establish effective hierarchies of exposure limits.

VaR Limits

VaR limits combine many of the advantages of exposure limits and stop-loss limits. Like exposure metrics, VaR metrics are prospective. They indicate risk before its economic consequences are realized. Also like exposure metrics, VaR metrics provide a reasonably consistent indication of risk. Finally, as long as utilization is calculated for traders in a timely and ongoing manner, it is reasonable to hold them accountable for limit violations. As with exposure limits, there are rare exceptions. Consider a trader with a negative gamma position. While she is responsible for hedging the position on an ongoing basis, it is possible that a sudden move in the underlier will cause an unanticipated spike in VaR.

As with stop-loss limits, non-specialists intuitively understand VaR metrics. If a portfolio has 1-day 90% USD VaR of 7.5MM, a non-specialist understands that such a portfolio will lose less than USD 7.5MM an average of 9 days out of 10.

With VaR limits, a single metric, such as 1-day 99% USD VaR, can be applied consistently across an entire hierarchy of limits. In theory, VaR encompasses all sources of market risk. Just one limit is required for each portfolio or sub-portfolio.

VaR aggregates across assets. Depending upon the sophistication of a VaR measure, it can reflect even the most complex hedging or diversification effects. Accordingly, VaR limits are perfect for limiting risk with spread trading, cross-hedging, or similar trading strategies.

VaR limits have one significant drawback: utilization may be computationally expensive to calculate. For many portfolios, VaR is easy to calculate. It can often be done in real time on a single processor. For other portfolios, it may take minutes or hours to calculate, even with parallel processors.

Comparison

Exhibit 1.2 summarizes the strengths and weakness of stop-loss, exposure, and VaR limits. VaR limits are attractive in almost all respects. Their only significant drawback is the computational expense of calculating VaR for certain portfolios.

Characteristic	Stop-loss Limits	Exposure Limits	VaR Limits
A single metric applies across a hierarchy of limits.	✓		✓
One or few limits required per portfolio or sub-portfolio.	✓		✓
Can aggregate across exposures.	✓		✓
Easily understood by non-specialists.	✓		✓
Addresses risk prospectively.		✓	✓
Utilization provides a consistent indication of risk.		✓	✓
Traders can be held accountable for limit violations.		✓	✓
Utilization is easy to calculate.	✓	✓	

Exhibit 1.2 Characteristics of stop-loss, exposure, and VaR limits are compared. See the text for clarifications of specific issues.

1.7. EXAMPLES

Let's consider some examples of VaR measures. These will introduce basic concepts and standard notation. They will also illustrate a framework for thinking about VaR measures, which we shall formalize in Section 1.8.

Example: The Leavens VaR Measure

Leavens (1945) published a paper describing the benefits of diversification. He accompanied his explanations with a simple example. This is the earliest known published VaR measure.

Measure time t in appropriate units. Let time $t = 0$ be the current time. Leavens considers a portfolio of 10 bonds over some horizon [0, 1]. Each bond will either mature at time 1 for USD 1000 or default and be worthless. Events of default are assumed independent. Accordingly, the portfolio's market value ${}^1P$ at time 1 is given by

$$ {}^1P = \sum_{i=1}^{10} {}^1S_i \qquad [1.5] $$

where the ${}^1S_i$ represent the individual bonds' accumulated values at time 1. Let's express this relationship in matrix notation. Let ${}^1\boldsymbol{S}$ be a random vector with components ${}^1S_i$. Let $\boldsymbol{\omega}$ be a row vector whose components are the portfolio's holdings in each bond. Since the portfolio holds one of each, $\boldsymbol{\omega}$ has a particularly simple form:

$$ \boldsymbol{\omega} = (1 \quad 1 \quad 1 \quad 1 \quad 1 \quad 1 \quad 1 \quad 1 \quad 1 \quad 1). \qquad [1.6] $$

With this matrix notation, [1.5] becomes the product:

$$ {}^1P = \boldsymbol{\omega}\,{}^1\boldsymbol{S}. \qquad [1.7] $$

Let ${}^{1|0}\phi_i$ denote the probability function, conditional on information available at time 0, of the ith bond's value at time 1:

$$ {}^{1|0}\phi_i({}^1s_i) = \begin{cases} 0.9 & \text{for } {}^1s_i = 1000 \\ 0.1 & \text{for } {}^1s_i = 0 \end{cases}. \qquad [1.8] $$

Measured in USD 1000s, the portfolio's value ${}^1P$ has a binomial distribution with parameters $n = 10$ and $p = 0.9$. The probability function is graphed in Exhibit 1.3:

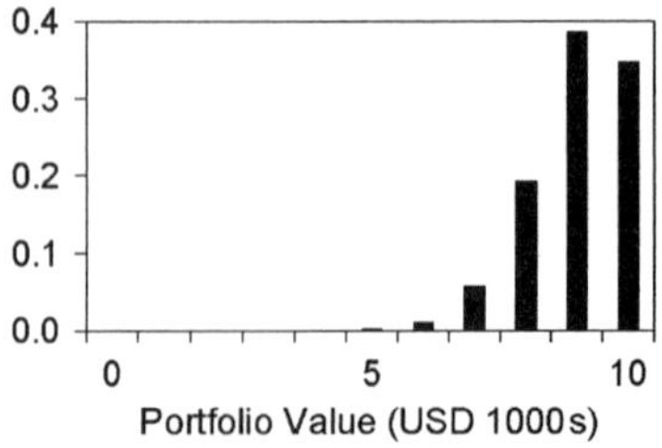

Exhibit 1.3 The market value (measured in USD 1000s) of Leavens' bond portfolio has a binomial distribution with parameters 10 and 0.9.

Writing for a non-technical audience, Leavens does not explicitly identify a VaR metric, but he speaks repeatedly of the "spread between probable losses and gains." He seems to have the standard deviation of portfolio market value in mind. Based upon this metric, his portfolio has a VaR of USD 948.69.

Our next two examples are more technical. Many readers will find them simple. Other readers—those whose mathematical background is not so strong—may find them more challenging. A note for each group:

- For the first group, the examples may tell you things you already know, but in a new way. They introduce notation and a framework for thinking about VaR that will be employed throughout the text. At points, explanations may appear more involved than the immediate problem requires. Embrace this complexity. The framework we start to develop in the examples will be invaluable in later chapters when we consider more complicated VaR measures.
- For the second group, you do not need to master the examples on a first reading. Don't think of them as a main course. They are not even an appetizer. We are taking you back into the kitchen to sample a recipe or two. Don't linger. Taste and move on. In Chapters 2 through 5, we will step back and explain the mathematics used in the examples—and used in VaR measures generally. A purpose of the examples is to provide practical motivation for those upcoming discussions.

There is a useful formula that we will use in the next two examples. We introduce it here for use in the examples, but will cover it again in more detail in Section 3.5.

Let $\boldsymbol{X}$ be a random vector with covariance matrix $\boldsymbol{\Sigma}$. Define random variable Y as a linear polynomial

$$Y = \boldsymbol{bX} + a \qquad [1.9]$$

of $\boldsymbol{X}$, where $\boldsymbol{b}$ is an n-dimensional row vector and a is a scalar. The variance of Y is given by

$$var(Y) = \boldsymbol{b\Sigma b}', \qquad [1.10]$$

where a prime $'$ indicates transposition. Formula [1.10] is a quintessential formula for describing how correlated risks combine, but there is a caveat. It only applies if Y is a linear polynomial of $\boldsymbol{X}$.

Example: Industrial Metals

Today is June 30, 2000. A US metals merchant has a portfolio of unsold physical positions in several industrial metals. We wish to calculate the portfolio's 1-week

90% USD VaR. Measure time t in weeks. Specify the random vector

$$
{}^1\boldsymbol{S} = \begin{pmatrix} {}^1S_1 \\ {}^1S_2 \\ {}^1S_3 \\ {}^1S_4 \\ {}^1S_5 \\ {}^1S_6 \end{pmatrix} \sim \begin{pmatrix} \text{accumulated value of a ton of aluminum} \\ \text{accumulated value of a ton of copper} \\ \text{accumulated value of a ton of lead} \\ \text{accumulated value of a ton of nickel} \\ \text{accumulated value of a ton of tin} \\ \text{accumulated value of a ton of zinc} \end{pmatrix} \qquad [1.11]
$$

where accumulated values are in USD and reflect the value of a ton of metal accumulated from time 0 to time 1. Accumulated value might reflect price changes, cost of financing, warehousing, and insurance. For simplicity, we consider only price changes in this example.

Current values in USD/ton for the respective metals are

$$
{}^0\boldsymbol{s} = \begin{pmatrix} {}^0s_1 \\ {}^0s_2 \\ {}^0s_3 \\ {}^0s_4 \\ {}^0s_5 \\ {}^0s_6 \end{pmatrix} = \begin{pmatrix} 1516.0 \\ 1719.5 \\ 476.0 \\ 7945.0 \\ 5715.0 \\ 1165.0 \end{pmatrix}. \qquad [1.12]
$$

The portfolio's holdings are:

- 1000 tons of aluminum,
- 2000 tons of copper,
- 500 tons of lead,
- 250 tons of nickel,
- 1000 tons of tin, and
- 100 tons of zinc,

which we represent with a row vector:

$$
\boldsymbol{\omega} = (1000 \quad 2000 \quad 500 \quad 250 \quad 1000 \quad 100). \qquad [1.13]
$$

The portfolio's current value is

$$
{}^0p = \boldsymbol{\omega}\,{}^0\boldsymbol{s} = 13.011\text{MM}. \qquad [1.14]
$$

Its future value ${}^1P$ is random:

$$
{}^1P = \boldsymbol{\omega}\,{}^1\boldsymbol{S}. \qquad [1.15]
$$

We call this relationship a **portfolio mapping**. We represent it schematically as

$$
{}^1P \xleftarrow{\boldsymbol{\omega}} {}^1\boldsymbol{S}. \qquad [1.16]
$$

Let ${}^{1|0}\sigma$ and ${}^{1|0}\boldsymbol{\Sigma}$ be the standard deviation of ${}^1P$ and the covariance matrix of ${}^1\boldsymbol{S}$, both conditional on information available at time 0. Let's apply [1.10]. By

[1.15], ${}^1P$ is a linear polynomial of ${}^1\mathbf{S}$, so:[11]

$$ {}^{1|0}\sigma = \sqrt{\boldsymbol{\omega}\,{}^{1|0}\boldsymbol{\Sigma}\boldsymbol{\omega}'}. \qquad [1.17] $$

We know $\boldsymbol{\omega}$. We need ${}^{1|0}\boldsymbol{\Sigma}$ to obtain ${}^{1|0}\sigma$. Exhibit 1.4 indicates historical metals price data.

Date	Time t	Aluminum ${}^ts_1$	Copper ${}^ts_2$	Lead ${}^ts_3$	Nickel ${}^ts_4$	Tin ${}^ts_5$	Zinc ${}^ts_6$
12/10/99	–29	1,516.0	1,719.5	476.0	7,945.0	5,715.0	1,165.0
12/17/99	–28	1,580.5	1,796.0	482.0	8,155.0	5,730.0	1,216.0
12/24/99	–27	1,609.0	1,834.0	474.0	8,380.0	5,700.0	1,200.0
12/30/99	–26	1,630.5	1,846.0	478.0	8,450.0	6,105.0	1,239.0
⋮	⋮	⋮	⋮	⋮	⋮	⋮	⋮
5/12/00	–7	1,455.0	1,808.5	418.0	10,040.0	5,490.0	1,170.5
5/19/00	–6	1,498.0	1,815.0	403.0	10,600.0	5,480.0	1,156.0
5/26/00	–5	1,464.0	1,793.5	432.0	10,435.0	5,405.0	1,158.0
6/2/00	–4	1,464.0	1,770.0	423.0	10,020.0	5,440.0	1,118.5
6/9/00	–3	1,456.5	1,722.5	421.0	8,480.0	5,450.0	1,099.0
6/16/00	–2	1,555.0	1,768.0	422.0	8,230.0	5,525.0	1,125.5
6/23/00	–1	1,544.5	1,767.0	416.0	7,925.0	5,515.0	1,124.0
6/30/00	0	1,564.0	1,773.5	440.5	8,245.0	5,465.0	1,148.0

Exhibit 1.4 Thirty weekly historical prices for the indicated metals. All prices are in USD per ton. Source: London Metals Exchange (LME).

Applying time-series methods described in Chapter 4, we construct

$$ {}^{1|0}\boldsymbol{\Sigma} = \begin{pmatrix} 1{,}709 & 1{,}227 & 8 & 3{,}557 & 774 & 275 \\ 1{,}227 & 1{,}746 & 65 & 6{,}274 & 574 & 469 \\ 8 & 65 & 128 & -270 & -49 & 69 \\ 3{,}557 & 6{,}274 & -270 & 137{,}361 & -2{,}459 & 1{,}764 \\ 774 & 574 & -49 & -2{,}459 & 13{,}621 & 952 \\ 275 & 469 & 69 & 1{,}764 & 952 & 544 \end{pmatrix}. \qquad [1.18] $$

Substituting [1.13] and [1.18] into [1.17], we conclude that ${}^1P$ has conditional standard deviation ${}^{1|0}\sigma$ of 0.217MM USD.

Let ${}^{1|0}\Phi_{{}^1L}$ denote the cumulative distribution function (CDF) of portfolio loss ${}^1L$ conditional on information available at time 0. Its inverse ${}^{1|0}\Phi^{-1}_{{}^1L}$ provides quantiles of ${}^1L$. Our VaR metric is 1-week 90% USD VaR, so we seek the .90-quantile, ${}^{1|0}\Phi^{-1}_{{}^1L}(.90)$, of portfolio loss ${}^1L$.

We don't have an expression for ${}^{1|0}\Phi_{{}^1L}$. All we have is a conditional standard deviation ${}^{1|0}\sigma$ for ${}^1P$. We need additional assumptions or information. A simple solution is to assume that ${}^1P$ is conditionally normal with mean ${}^{1|0}\mu = {}^0p =$ 13.011MM. Since a normal distribution is fully specified by a mean and standard deviation, we have now specified a conditional CDF, ${}^{1|0}\Phi_{{}^1P}$, for ${}^1P$.

[11] Recall that standard deviation is the square root of variance.

The .90-quantile of portfolio loss is

$$ {}^{1|0}\Phi^{-1}_{{}^1L}(.90) = {}^0p - {}^{1|0}\Phi^{-1}_{{}^1P}(.10). \qquad [1.19]$$

A property of normal distributions is that a .10-quantile occurs 1.282 standard deviations below its mean,[12] so

$$ {}^{1|0}\Phi^{-1}_{{}^1P}(.10) = {}^{1|0}\mu - 1.282\,{}^{1|0}\sigma = {}^0p - 1.282\,{}^{1|0}\sigma. \qquad [1.20]$$

Substituting [1.20] into [1.19]:

$$ {}^{1|0}\Phi^{-1}_{{}^1L}(.90) = 1.282\,{}^{1|0}\sigma = 0.278\text{MM}. \qquad [1.21]$$

The portfolio's 1-week 90% USD VaR is USD 0.278MM. Note that ${}^0p$ dropped out of the calculations entirely, so we did not actually need to calculate its value in [1.14].

Example: Australian Equities

Our next example is ostensibly similar to the last. As we work through it, a number of issues will arise. These will motivate different approaches for a solution.

Today is March 9, 2000. A British trader holds a portfolio of Australian stocks. We wish to calculate the portfolio's 1-day 95% GBP VaR. The portfolio's current value ${}^0p$ is GBP 0.198MM. Let ${}^1P$ represent its value tomorrow. Define the random vector

$$ {}^1\boldsymbol{S} = \begin{pmatrix} {}^1S_1 \\ {}^1S_2 \\ {}^1S_3 \end{pmatrix} \sim \begin{pmatrix} \text{GBP accumulated value of a share of National Australia Bank} \\ \text{GBP accumulated value of a share of Westpac Banking Corp.} \\ \text{GBP accumulated value of a share of Goodman Fielder} \end{pmatrix}. \qquad [1.22]$$

Accumulated values reflect price changes, dividends, and changes in the GBP/AUD exchange rate since time 0. The portfolio's holdings are:

- 10,000 shares of National Australia Bank,
- 30,000 shares of Westpac Banking Corp.,
- −15,000 shares of Goodman Fielder (short position),

which we represent with a row vector

$$ \boldsymbol{\omega} = (10{,}000 \quad 30{,}000 \quad -15{,}000). \qquad [1.23]$$

The portfolio's future value ${}^1P$ is a linear polynomial of ${}^1\boldsymbol{S}$:

$$ {}^1P = \boldsymbol{\omega}\,{}^1\boldsymbol{S}. \qquad [1.24]$$

We face a minor problem. In the last example, we used historical data to construct a covariance matrix for ${}^1\boldsymbol{S}$. In the present example, components of ${}^1\boldsymbol{S}$ are

[12] See Section 3.9.

denominated in GBP, but any historical data for Australian stocks will be denominated in AUD. We solve the problem with a change of variables ${}^1\boldsymbol{S} = \varphi({}^1\boldsymbol{R})$:

$$ {}^1\boldsymbol{S} = \varphi({}^1\boldsymbol{R}) = {}^1R_4 \begin{pmatrix} {}^1R_1 \\ {}^1R_2 \\ {}^1R_3 \end{pmatrix}, \qquad [1.25] $$

where

$$ {}^1\boldsymbol{R} = \begin{pmatrix} {}^1R_1 \\ {}^1R_2 \\ {}^1R_3 \\ {}^1R_4 \end{pmatrix} \sim \begin{pmatrix} \text{AUD accumulated value of a share of National Australia Bank} \\ \text{AUD accumulated value of a share of Westpac Banking Corp.} \\ \text{AUD accumulated value of a share of Goodman Fielder} \\ \text{GBP/AUD exchange rate} \end{pmatrix}. \qquad [1.26] $$

Composing $\boldsymbol{\omega}$ with φ we obtain a function $\theta = \boldsymbol{\omega} \circ \varphi$ that relates ${}^1P$ to ${}^1\boldsymbol{R}$:

$$ {}^1P = \theta({}^1\boldsymbol{R}) = {}^1R_4\left(10000\,{}^1R_1 + 30000\,{}^1R_2 - 15000\,{}^1R_3\right). \qquad [1.27] $$

This is a quadratic polynomial—the exchange rate ${}^1R_4$ combines multiplicatively with the accumulated values ${}^1R_1$, ${}^1R_2$, ${}^1R_3$. It is our portfolio mapping, and we represent it schematically as

$$ \overbrace{{}^1P \xleftarrow{\ \omega\ } {}^1S \xleftarrow{\ \varphi\ } {}^1\boldsymbol{R}}^{\theta}. \qquad [1.28] $$

Exhibit 1.5 provides historical data for ${}^1\boldsymbol{R}$.

Date	Time	National Australia Bank	Westpac Banking Corp.	Goodman Fielder	GBP/AUD
	t	${}^tr_1$	${}^tr_2$	${}^tr_3$	${}^tr_4$
1/10/00	–42	22.200	10.207	1.400	0.4007
1/11/00	–41	21.800	10.215	1.410	0.3990
1/12/00	–40	21.630	10.220	1.380	0.3995
1/13/00	–39	21.430	10.310	1.370	0.4057
⋮	⋮	⋮	⋮	⋮	⋮
2/29/00	–7	21.400	10.400	1.170	0.3901
3/1/00	–6	22.106	10.767	1.184	0.3828
3/2/00	–5	22.273	10.580	1.200	0.3855
3/3/00	–4	21.442	10.410	1.170	0.3847
3/6/00	–3	20.950	10.410	1.140	0.3824
3/7/00	–2	21.340	10.414	1.080	0.3826
3/8/00	–1	20.830	10.500	1.130	0.3844
3/9/00	0	20.080	10.800	1.150	0.3892

Exhibit 1.5 Two months of historical data for the GBP/AUD exchange rate and AUD prices for the indicated stocks. None of the stocks had ex-dividend dates during the period indicated. Source: Federal Reserve Bank of Chicago and Dow Jones.

Using time-series methods described in Chapter 4, we construct a conditional covariance matrix for ${}^{1}\boldsymbol{R}$:

$$
{}^{1|0}\boldsymbol{\Sigma} = \begin{pmatrix} .156644 & .030382 & -.000135 & -.000213 \\ .030382 & .029574 & .000157 & .000053 \\ -.000135 & .000157 & .000739 & -.000010 \\ -.000213 & .000053 & -.000010 & .000015 \end{pmatrix}. \qquad [1.29]
$$

Now we face another problem. We have a portfolio mapping ${}^{1}P = \theta({}^{1}\boldsymbol{R})$ that expresses ${}^{1}P$ as a quadratic polynomial of ${}^{1}\boldsymbol{R}$, and we have a conditional covariance matrix ${}^{1|0}\boldsymbol{\Sigma}$ for ${}^{1}\boldsymbol{R}$. This is similar to the previous example where we had a portfolio mapping ${}^{1}P = \boldsymbol{\omega}\,{}^{1}\boldsymbol{S}$ that expressed ${}^{1}P$ as a linear polynomial of ${}^{1}\boldsymbol{S}$, and we had a covariance matrix ${}^{1|0}\boldsymbol{\Sigma}$ for ${}^{1}\boldsymbol{S}$. Critically, in the previous example, our portfolio mapping was linear. Now it is quadratic. In the previous example, we could apply [1.10] to obtain the conditional standard deviation of ${}^{1}P$. Now we cannot.

Nonlinear portfolio mappings pose a recurring challenge for measuring VaR. There are various solutions, including:

- apply the Monte Carlo method to approximate the desired quantile;
- approximate the quadratic polynomial θ with a linear polynomial $\widetilde{\theta}$ and then apply [1.10] as before;
- assume ${}^{1}\boldsymbol{R}$ is conditionally joint-normal and apply probabilistic techniques appropriate for quadratic polynomials of joint-normal random vectors.

Each is a standard solution used frequently in VaR measures. Each has advantages and disadvantages. We will study them all in later chapters. For now, we briefly describe how each is used to calculate VaR for this Australian equities example.

EXAMPLE: AUSTRALIAN EQUITIES (MONTE CARLO TRANSFORMATION). We discuss the Monte Carlo method formally in Chapter 5. For now, an intuitive treatment will suffice. We assume ${}^{1}\boldsymbol{R}$ is joint-normal with mean vector ${}^{1|0}\boldsymbol{\mu} = {}^{0}\boldsymbol{r}$ and covariance matrix ${}^{1|0}\boldsymbol{\Sigma}$ given by [1.29]. Based upon these assumptions, we "randomly" generate 10,000 realizations, ${}^{1}\boldsymbol{r}^{[1]}, {}^{1}\boldsymbol{r}^{[2]}, \ldots, {}^{1}\boldsymbol{r}^{[10{,}000]}$, of ${}^{1}\boldsymbol{R}$. We set

$$
{}^{1}p^{[k]} = \theta\left({}^{1}\boldsymbol{r}^{[k]}\right) \qquad [1.30]
$$

for each k, constructing 10,000 realizations ${}^{1}p^{[1]}, {}^{1}p^{[2]}, \ldots, {}^{1}p^{[10{,}000]}$ of ${}^{1}P$. Results are indicated in Exhibit 1.6.

k	National Australia Bank $^1r_1^{[k]}$	Westpac Banking Corp. $^1r_2^{[k]}$	Goodman Fielder $^1r_3^{[k]}$	GBP/AUD $^1r_4^{[k]}$	Portfolio $^1p^{[k]}$
1	20.290	10.913	1.150	0.3823	196,135
2	19.392	10.333	1.153	0.3870	188,327
3	20.088	10.744	1.164	0.3917	198,117
4	20.620	11.083	1.124	0.3920	204,538
5	19.660	10.811	1.154	0.3909	196,855
6	19.973	10.806	1.162	0.3823	193,639
7	19.732	10.867	1.158	0.3902	197,437
8	19.655	10.925	1.200	0.3889	196,902
9	20.101	10.886	1.122	0.3909	199,665
10	21.136	11.064	1.129	0.3801	200,037
11	19.968	10.839	1.180	0.3881	196,804
12	20.112	10.750	1.119	0.3906	197,961
⋮	⋮	⋮	⋮	⋮	⋮
9998	20.240	10.565	1.166	0.3846	193,033
9999	19.531	10.378	1.186	0.3930	192,149
10000	20.078	11.215	1.154	0.3936	204,619

Exhibit 1.6 Results of the Monte Carlo analysis.

Realizations $^1p^{[k]}$ of ^1P are summarized with a histogram in Exhibit 1.7. We may approximate any parameter of ^1P with the corresponding sample parameter of the realizations.

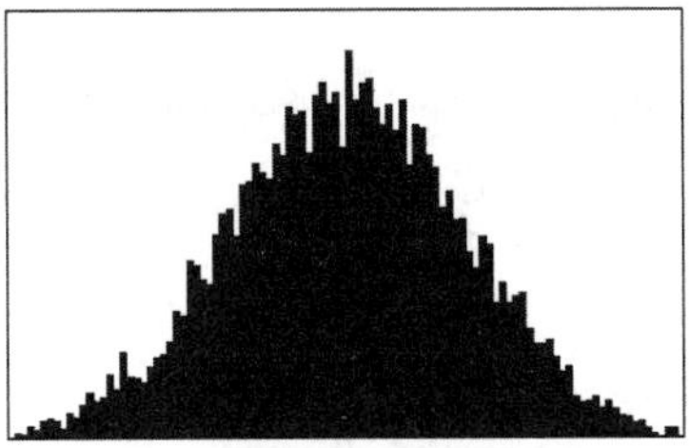

Exhibit 1.7 Histogram of realizations $^1p^{[k]}$ of the portfolio's value ^1P.

The sample .05-quantile of our realizations $^1p^{[k]}$ is USD 191,614. We use this as an approximation of the .05-quantile, $^{1|0}\Phi^{-1}_{^1P}(.05)$, of ^1P. The .95-quantile of portfolio loss is:

$$^{1|0}\Phi^{-1}_{^1L}(.95) = {}^0p - {}^{1|0}\Phi^{-1}_{^1P}(.05) \quad [1.31]$$

$$\approx 197{,}539 - 191{,}614 \quad [1.32]$$

$$= 5925. \quad [1.33]$$

The portfolio's 1-day 95% GBP VaR is approximately GBP 5925.

EXAMPLE: AUSTRALIAN EQUITIES (LINEAR REMAPPING). As an alternative solution, let's approximate θ with a linear polynomial $\widetilde{\theta}$ based upon the gradient[13] of θ. We must choose a point at which to take the gradient. A reasonable choice is ${}^{0}E({}^{1}\boldsymbol{R})$, which is the expected value of ${}^{1}\boldsymbol{R}$ conditional on information available at time 0. Let's assume ${}^{0}E({}^{1}\boldsymbol{R}) = {}^{0}\boldsymbol{r}$. We define

$$ {}^{1}\widetilde{P} = \widetilde{\theta}({}^{1}\boldsymbol{R}) = \theta({}^{0}\boldsymbol{r}) + \nabla\theta({}^{0}\boldsymbol{r})'[{}^{1}\boldsymbol{R} - {}^{0}\boldsymbol{r}]. \qquad [1.34] $$

Our approximation ${}^{1}\widetilde{P} = \widetilde{\theta}({}^{1}\boldsymbol{R})$ of the portfolio mapping ${}^{1}P = \theta({}^{1}\boldsymbol{R})$ is an example of a **portfolio remapping**. We obtain ${}^{0}\boldsymbol{r} = (20.080, 10.800, 1.150, 0.3892)$ from Exhibit 1.5 and evaluate

$$ \theta({}^{0}\boldsymbol{r}) = 197{,}539 \qquad [1.35] $$

and

$$ \nabla\theta({}^{0}\boldsymbol{r}) = \begin{pmatrix} 3{,}892 \\ 11{,}676 \\ -5{,}838 \\ 507{,}550 \end{pmatrix}. \qquad [1.36] $$

Our remapping [1.34] is

$$ {}^{1}\widetilde{P} = \theta({}^{0}\boldsymbol{r}) + \nabla\theta({}^{0}\boldsymbol{r})'[{}^{1}\boldsymbol{R} - {}^{0}\boldsymbol{r}] \qquad [1.37] $$

$$ = \nabla\theta({}^{0}\boldsymbol{r})'{}^{1}\boldsymbol{R} + [\theta({}^{0}\boldsymbol{r}) - \nabla\theta({}^{0}\boldsymbol{r})'{}^{0}\boldsymbol{r}] \qquad [1.38] $$

$$ = \nabla\theta({}^{0}\boldsymbol{r})'{}^{1}\boldsymbol{R} - 197{,}538. \qquad [1.39] $$

The portfolio remapping is represented schematically as

$$ \begin{array}{ccccc} & & \overbrace{\hphantom{xxxxxxxxxx}}^{\theta} & & \\ {}^{1}P & \xleftarrow{\ \omega\ } & {}^{1}\boldsymbol{S} & \xleftarrow{\ \varphi\ } & {}^{1}\boldsymbol{R} \\ \uparrow & & & & \\ {}^{1}\widetilde{P} & & \xleftarrow{\qquad \widetilde{\theta} \qquad} & & {}^{1}\boldsymbol{R} \end{array} \qquad [1.40] $$

The upper part of the schematic is precisely schematic [1.28], indicating the original portfolio mapping ${}^{1}P = \theta({}^{1}\boldsymbol{R})$. The lower part indicates the remapping ${}^{1}\widetilde{P} = \widetilde{\theta}({}^{1}\boldsymbol{R})$. In such schematics, vertical arrows indicate approximations. ${}^{1}\widetilde{P}$ approximates ${}^{1}P$.

Because [1.39] is a linear polynomial, we can apply [1.10] to obtain the conditional standard deviation ${}^{1|0}\widetilde{\sigma}$ of ${}^{1}\widetilde{P}$:

$$ {}^{1|0}\widetilde{\sigma} = \sqrt{\nabla\theta({}^{0}\boldsymbol{r})'\,{}^{1|0}\boldsymbol{\Sigma}\,\nabla\theta({}^{0}\boldsymbol{r})} = 3572. \qquad [1.41] $$

[13]Gradient approximations are discussed in Section 2.3.

Assume ${}^1\tilde{P}$ is conditionally normal with this standard deviation ${}^{1|0}\tilde{\sigma}$ and mean ${}^{1|0}\tilde{\mu} = {}^0p$. The .05-quantile of a normal distribution occurs 1.645 standard deviations below its mean, so

$$^{1|0}\Phi^{-1}_{{}^1\tilde{P}}(.05) = {}^{1|0}\tilde{\mu} - 1.645\,{}^{1|0}\tilde{\sigma} = 191{,}662, \qquad [1.42]$$

and the .95-quantile of portfolio loss is

$$^{1|0}\Phi^{-1}_{{}^1\tilde{L}}(.95) = {}^0p - {}^{1|0}\Phi^{-1}_{{}^1\tilde{P}}(.05) = 5876. \qquad [1.43]$$

The portfolio's 1-day 95% GBP VaR is approximately GBP 5876. This result compares favorably with our previous result of GBP 5925, which we obtained with the Monte Carlo method.

EXAMPLE: AUSTRALIAN EQUITIES (QUADRATIC TRANSFORMATION). For a third approach to calculating VaR for our Australian equities portfolio, assume that ${}^1\boldsymbol{R}$ is joint-normal with conditional mean vector ${}^0E({}^1\boldsymbol{R}) = {}^0\boldsymbol{r}$ and covariance matrix ${}^{1|0}\boldsymbol{\Sigma}$ obtained previously. Our original portfolio mapping ${}^1P = \theta({}^1\boldsymbol{R})$ defines ${}^1P$ as a quadratic polynomial of a conditionally joint-normal random vector ${}^1\boldsymbol{R}$. As we will discuss in Chapter 3, any real-valued quadratic polynomial of a joint-normal random vector can be expressed as a linear polynomial of independent normal and chi-squared random variables. In this case, the expression takes the form

$$^1P = -15.02X_1 + 14.63X_2, \qquad [1.44]$$

where X_1 and X_2 are independent chi-squared random variables, each with 1 degree of freedom and respective non-centrality parameters of 674.2 and 14,195.[14] This is not an approximation. The representation is exact.

There are various ways to extract a quantile of portfolio loss from a representation such as [1.44]. Two approaches that we shall discuss in Chapter 3 are:

1. approximate the desired quantile using the Cornish-Fisher (1937) expansion, and
2. invert the characteristic function of ${}^1P$ using numerical integration.

Applying the first approach to our Australian equities portfolio yields an approximate 1-day 95% GBP VaR of GBP 5854.

EXERCISES

1.10 Using a spreadsheet, extend Leavens' analysis to a bond portfolio that holds 20 bonds.
   a. Graph the resulting probability function for ${}^1P$.
   b. Based upon Leavens' "spread between probable losses and gains" VaR metric, what is the VaR of the portfolio?

[14]The chi-squared distribution is discussed in Section 3.9.

1.11 Using only the information provided in the example, which of the following VaR metrics could we evaluate for Leavens' bond portfolio:
   a. 95% quantile of loss;
   b. variance of portfolio value;
   c. standard deviation of simple return.

1.12 This exercise is based upon an equity example in Harry Markowitz's 1959 book *Portfolio Selection*. Suppose today is January 1, 1955. Measure time t in years and define:

$$^{1}\mathbf{S} = \begin{pmatrix} ^{1}S_1 \\ ^{1}S_2 \\ \vdots \\ ^{1}S_7 \end{pmatrix} \sim \begin{pmatrix} \text{accumulated value of 1 USD in AT\&T} \\ \text{accumulated value of 1 USD in American Tobacco} \\ \vdots \\ \text{accumulated value of 1 USD in Firestone} \end{pmatrix}. \qquad [1.45]$$

Each accumulated value represents the value at time 1 of an investment worth 1 USD at time 0 in the indicated stock. Accumulated values include price changes and dividends. Consider a portfolio with holdings

$$\boldsymbol{\omega} = (10{,}000 \quad 5{,}000 \quad -1{,}000 \quad 2{,}000 \quad -5{,}000 \quad 1{,}000 \quad 6{,}000). \qquad [1.46]$$

Based upon data provided by Markowitz, we construct a conditional covariance matrix $^{1|0}\boldsymbol{\Sigma}$ for $^{1}\mathbf{S}$:

$$^{1|0}\boldsymbol{\Sigma} = \begin{pmatrix} 0.0147 & 0.0215 & 0.0080 & 0.0145 & 0.0100 & 0.0254 & 0.0244 \\ 0.0215 & 0.0534 & 0.0162 & 0.0243 & 0.0322 & 0.0400 & 0.0490 \\ 0.0080 & 0.0162 & 0.1279 & 0.0209 & 0.0128 & 0.1015 & 0.0515 \\ 0.0145 & 0.0243 & 0.0209 & 0.0288 & 0.0113 & 0.0291 & 0.0208 \\ 0.0100 & 0.0322 & 0.0128 & 0.0113 & 0.0413 & 0.0296 & 0.0290 \\ 0.0254 & 0.0400 & 0.1015 & 0.0291 & 0.0296 & 0.1467 & 0.0900 \\ 0.0244 & 0.0490 & 0.0515 & 0.0208 & 0.0290 & 0.0900 & 0.0955 \end{pmatrix}. \qquad [1.47]$$

Calculate the portfolio's 1-year 90% USD VaR according to the following steps:

a. Value the vector $^{0}\mathbf{s}$. (Hint: Based upon how the problem has been presented, the answer is trivial.)
b. Using the formula $^{0}p = \boldsymbol{\omega}\,^{0}\mathbf{s}$, value ^{0}p.
c. Specify a portfolio mapping that defines ^{1}P as a linear polynomial of $^{1}\mathbf{S}$.
d. Draw a schematic for your portfolio mapping.
e. Determine the conditional standard deviation $^{1|0}\sigma$ of ^{1}P using [1.10].
f. Assume ^{1}P is normally distributed with conditional mean $^{1|0}\mu = {}^{0}p$ and conditional standard deviation obtained in part (e). Calculate the

.10-quantile of ${}^{1}P$ with the formula

$$ {}^{1|0}\Phi^{-1}_{{}^{1}P}(.10) = {}^{1|0}\mu - 1.282\,{}^{1|0}\sigma. \qquad [1.48]$$

g. Calculate the portfolio's 1-year 90% USD VaR as

$$ {}^{1|0}\Phi^{-1}_{{}^{1}L}(.90) = {}^{0}p - {}^{1|0}\Phi^{-1}_{{}^{1}P}(.10). \qquad [1.49]$$

1.8. VaR MEASURES

In the previous section, we described several VaR measures. Despite a disparity in modeling techniques, our treatment was standardized. Certain concepts recurred. You are now familiar with notation such as: $\boldsymbol{\omega}$, ${}^{1}P$, θ, ${}^{1}\boldsymbol{S}$, ${}^{1}\boldsymbol{R}$, and ${}^{1|0}\boldsymbol{\Sigma}$.

We have many VaR measures to consider. Before long, we will stop describing entire VaR measures and start describing stand-alone components of VaR measures—much as auto enthusiasts might discuss types of brakes or fuel injectors without having a particular automobile in mind. In this sense, our discussions will have a "building block" quality. We don't want every VaR measure to be a unique monolith standing on its own. Instead, we will treat them as modular. Avoiding the top-down approach of discussing Toyotas, Fords, and Mercedes, we will take a bottom-up approach, discussing fuel injectors, suspension systems, and brakes. To this end, we must identify the essential components that make up any VaR measure. In doing so, we will lay out a framework for much of this book.

RISK FACTORS

A **risk factor** is any random variable ${}^{1}Q_i$ whose value will be realized during the interval (0,1] and will affect the market value of a portfolio at time 1. A **risk vector** ${}^{1}\boldsymbol{Q}$ is a random vector of risk factors. If a risk vector reflects a future value of some time series, we may speak of its **current value** ${}^{0}\boldsymbol{q}$ or **historical values** ${}^{0}\boldsymbol{q}$, ${}^{-1}\boldsymbol{q}$, ${}^{-2}\boldsymbol{q}$, ${}^{-3}\boldsymbol{q}$, . . .

One particular risk factor and two risk vectors play important roles in VaR measures. We give them special names and notation. These are:

- the portfolio's future value ${}^{1}P$;
- the asset vector ${}^{1}\boldsymbol{S}$; and
- the key vector ${}^{1}\boldsymbol{R}$.

The **portfolio's future value** ${}^{1}P$ represents the market value at time 1 of the portfolio for which VaR is to be measured. The portfolio is assumed fixed in the sense that it will not be traded during the period [0, 1], and no assets will be added or withdrawn. This does not preclude traders or portfolio managers from trading!

It simply means that a VaR measure quantifies the market risk of a portfolio based upon its composition at time 0. The VaR measure can recognize changes in the portfolio's composition during the period [0, 1] due to planned events such as options expiring, dividends being paid, or scheduled payments being made on a swap.

We are interested in the portfolio's current value ${}^0p$ only if a VaR metric depends upon it. We generally do not consider or attempt to define prior historical portfolio values. Asset vector ${}^1\boldsymbol{S}$ has **asset values** ${}^1S_i$ as components. These represent accumulated values of specific assets that may make up a portfolio. Realizations ${}^1s_i$ may be negative, so our definition recognizes no accounting distinction between assets and liabilities. Accumulated value is denominated in the base currency employed by the VaR metric. It may reflect such variables as capital gains, dividends, coupons, margin payments, reinvestment income, storage costs, insurance, financing, changes in exchange rates, leasing income, etc.

Mathematically, we define a **portfolio** as a pair $({}^0p, {}^1P)$, where the constant ${}^0p$ is the portfolio's current value, and the random variable ${}^1P$ is the portfolio's future value. Similarly, we mathematically define an **asset** as a pair $({}^0s_i, {}^1S_i)$, where ${}^0s_i$ is the asset's current value, and ${}^1S_i$ is the asset's future value.

We have considerable leeway in how we select what financial instruments to represent with assets. This may affect VaR results. Consider an investor who borrows EUR 100,000 and invests it in Hoechst stock. We might model the portfolio three different ways:

1. as comprising holdings in two assets whose values ${}^1S_1$ and ${}^1S_2$ represent the accumulated values of the stock and the financing, respectively;
2. as comprising a single asset whose value ${}^1S_1$ represents the accumulated value of the stock less the accumulated value of its financing;
3. as comprising a single asset whose value ${}^1S_1$ represents the accumulated value of the stock.

The first two representations are financially equivalent. One approach (probably the first) will be computationally easier to work with, but both will result in the same VaR. The third representation is different. It excludes financing from the portfolio. With it, the random variable ${}^1P$ represents something different than it does with the first two approaches.

As we shall see, every VaR measure must directly characterize a conditional probability distribution for some vector of risk factors, such as prices, interest rates, spreads, or implied volatilities. Those risk factors ${}^1R_i$ are called **key factors**. They are the components of the **key vector** ${}^1\boldsymbol{R}$. Occasionally, we use asset values ${}^1S_i$ as key factors. This was the case in our examples of Leavens' VaR measure and the VaR measure for industrial metals. We explore the role of key factors in more detail shortly.

HOLDINGS

When we design a VaR measure, we must decide what financial assets to represent with mathematical assets $({}^0s_i,\ {}^1S_i)$. We might measure equity positions in shares or round lots. In Exercise 1.12, we measured them as the number of USD held in a given stock at time 0. Positions in cocoa might be measured in pounds, bags, or tons. The choice of units is largely arbitrary, but it must be explicit if we are to define portfolio holdings.

A portfolio's **holdings** is a row vector $\boldsymbol{\omega}$ indicating the number ω_i of units held by the portfolio in each asset.

MAPPINGS

In mathematics, a mapping is a function. The words are synonyms. In the context of VaR, we reserve the word "mapping" for functions relating specific risk vectors to one another. If ${}^1\boldsymbol{Q}$ and ${}^1\dot{\boldsymbol{Q}}$ are risk vectors, a **mapping** is a functional relationship:

$$ {}^1\boldsymbol{Q} = \varphi({}^1\dot{\boldsymbol{Q}}). \qquad [1.50] $$

We call φ the **mapping function**.

A **portfolio mapping** is a mapping that defines a portfolio's value ${}^1P$ as a function of some risk vector ${}^1\boldsymbol{Q}$:

$$ {}^1P = \varphi({}^1\boldsymbol{Q}). \qquad [1.51] $$

Portfolio mappings play a simple but inevitable role in VaR measures. Let's focus on two of our earlier examples: Leavens' VaR measure and our Australian equities VaR measures.

To calculate a portfolio's VaR, we must calculate the value of some function—VaR metric—of ${}^0p$ and the conditional distribution of ${}^1P$. We interpret ${}^1P$ as the portfolio's market value at time 1, but this is not a definition. Mathematically, there are two ways we may define the random variable ${}^1P$:

1. we can directly specify a conditional distribution for ${}^1P$;
2. we can define ${}^1P$ as a function of some random vector.

The first approach is hardly feasible. Portfolios and financial markets tend to be complicated, so it is difficult to directly specify a conditional distribution for ${}^1P$. Inevitably, we define ${}^1P$ using the second approach—which leads to portfolio mappings. Both the Leavens and Australian equities VaR measures define ${}^1P$ as a function of some asset vector ${}^1\boldsymbol{S}$:

$$ {}^1P = \boldsymbol{\omega}\,{}^1\boldsymbol{S}. \qquad [1.52] $$

We interpret ${}^1\boldsymbol{S}$ as a vector of accumulated values, but this is not a definition. To complete our definition of ${}^1P$, we must mathematically define ${}^1\boldsymbol{S}$. As with ${}^1P$, there are two ways to define ${}^1\boldsymbol{S}$:

1. we can directly specify a conditional distribution for ${}^1\boldsymbol{S}$;
2. we can define ${}^1\boldsymbol{S}$ as a function of some other random vector.

At this point, Leavens uses the first approach. He specifies a conditional distribution for ${}^1\boldsymbol{S}$ and uses this to infer a binomial distribution for ${}^1P$. We schematically represent Leavens' portfolio mapping as

$$ {}^1P \xleftarrow{\boldsymbol{\omega}} {}^1\boldsymbol{S}. \qquad [1.53] $$

The Australian equities VaR measures don't stop there. Rather than directly specify a joint distribution for ${}^1\boldsymbol{S}$, they define ${}^1\boldsymbol{S}$ as a mapping of another random vector ${}^1\boldsymbol{R}$. We schematically represent the resulting portfolio mapping as

$$ \overbrace{{}^1P \xleftarrow{\boldsymbol{\omega}} {}^1\boldsymbol{S} \xleftarrow{\varphi}}^{\theta} {}^1\boldsymbol{R}. \qquad [1.54] $$

No matter how many mappings are composed, ultimately ${}^1P$ must be defined as a function of some random vector for which we directly characterize a joint distribution. That random vector is the key vector ${}^1\boldsymbol{R}$. We denote the mapping function that relates ${}^1P$ to its key vector ${}^1\boldsymbol{R}$ with θ. Accordingly, the notation

$$ {}^1P = \theta({}^1\boldsymbol{R}) \qquad [1.55] $$

recurs frequently in this text. An exception is if asset values are used as key factors. In this case, the relationship is

$$ {}^1P = \boldsymbol{\omega}\,{}^1\boldsymbol{S}, \qquad [1.56] $$

and ${}^1\boldsymbol{S}$ plays the dual role of asset vector and key vector.

Here, we have described not only portfolio mappings, but also a general procedure for constructing them. Portfolio mappings constructed in this manner—starting with asset vector ${}^1\boldsymbol{S}$ and holdings $\boldsymbol{\omega}$, and perhaps mapping ${}^1\boldsymbol{S}$ to some key vector ${}^1\boldsymbol{R}$—are called **primary mappings**. The name distinguishes them from portfolio mappings constructed as remappings. All portfolio mappings stem from primary mappings. They either are left in that form, or are approximated using one or more remappings. We discuss primary mappings in Chapter 8.

Inference

In order to characterize a distribution for ${}^1P$ conditional on information available at time 0, we must characterize a conditional distribution for ${}^1\boldsymbol{R}$. We do so with an **inference procedure**. It is not always necessary to fully specify a distribution. We require only information sufficient to value our chosen VaR metric. Some inference procedures characterize the conditional distribution of ${}^1\boldsymbol{R}$ with just a covariance matrix. We say an inference procedure is **complete** if it fully specifies a conditional distribution for ${}^1\boldsymbol{R}$. Otherwise it is **incomplete**.

Inference procedures take various forms. Leavens (1945) simply makes up a distribution suitable for his example. In practice, techniques of time series analysis are employed—in conjunction with financial theory—to obtain a reasonable characterization. We discuss inference procedures in Chapter 7.

TRANSFORMATIONS

A **transformation procedure**—or **transformation**—characterizes a conditional distribution for ${}^1P$ and uses this characterization to value a desired VaR metric. Recall that risk comprises two components:

- exposure, and
- uncertainty.

A portfolio mapping ${}^1P = \theta({}^1\boldsymbol{R})$ incorporates both. The characterization of a conditional distribution of ${}^1\boldsymbol{R}$ reflects our uncertainty. The mapping function θ reflects our exposure. The challenge for a transformation procedure is to combine both components to characterize a conditional distribution for ${}^1P$. To intuitively understand what this entails, consider some simple examples.

A portfolio's value depends upon a single normally distributed key factor ${}^1R_1$. The mapping function θ is a linear polynomial. The situation is depicted in Exhibit 1.8:

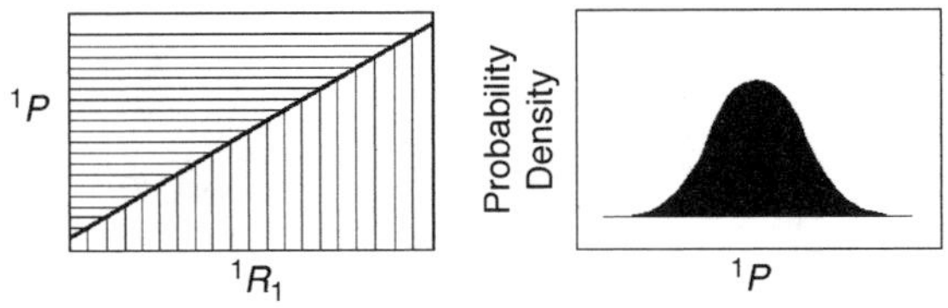

Exhibit 1.8 A linear mapping function θ is applied to a key factor ${}^1R_1$. This is illustrated intuitively by mapping evenly spaced realizations for ${}^1R_1$ through the mapping function. The output values for ${}^1P$ are also evenly spaced, indicating that the mapping function causes no distortion. Since ${}^1R_1$ is conditionally normal, so is ${}^1P$.

The graph on the left depicts the mapping function θ. Evenly spaced realizations for ${}^1R_1$ have been mapped into corresponding realizations for ${}^1P$. The resulting realizations of ${}^1P$ are also evenly spaced, indicating that θ imparts no distortions. Since ${}^1R_1$ is conditionally normal, ${}^1P$ will also be conditionally normal, as illustrated in the graph on the right.

For our second example, consider a portfolio comprising a single call option with a conditionally normal key factor ${}^1R_1$ as its underlier. To avoid a need for additional key factors, treat applicable interest rates and implied volatilities as constant.

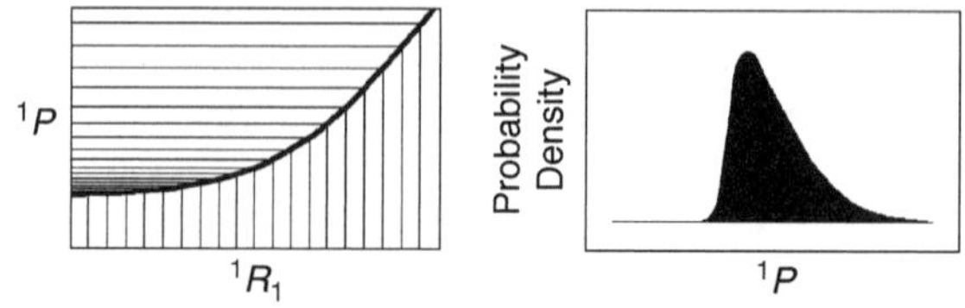

Exhibit 1.9 A nonlinear mapping function θ is applied to a conditionally normal key factor ${}^1R_1$. The result is a conditionally non-normal portfolio value ${}^1P$. This is illustrated intuitively by mapping evenly spaced realizations for ${}^1R_1$ through the mapping function. The corresponding values for ${}^1P$ are not evenly spaced, reflecting how the mapping function distorts the distribution of ${}^1P$.

In Exhibit 1.9, the left graph depicts the familiar "hockey stick" mapping function of a call option. Evenly spaced realizations for ${}^1R_1$ do not map into evenly spaced realizations for ${}^1P$, so the mapping function causes distortions. Since ${}^1R_1$ is conditionally normal, the resulting distribution of ${}^1P$ is conditionally non-normal, as illustrated on the right.

Our third example considers a long-short options position applied to a short position in the underlier. The mapping function θ, which is illustrated in the left graph of Exhibit 1.10, causes realizations of ${}^1P$ to cluster in two regions. If the underlier ${}^1R_1$ is conditionally normal, ${}^1P$ will have the dramatically non-normal conditional distribution shown on the right.

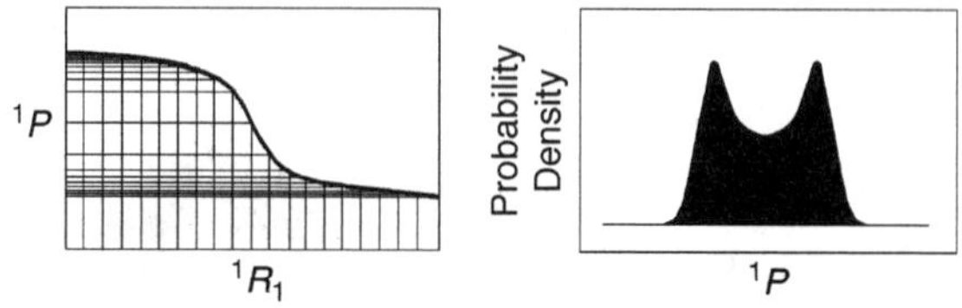

Exhibit 1.10 A long-short options position can result in a bimodal distribution for ${}^1P$.

These are simple examples, especially since each entails a single key factor. Practical VaR measures often entail 100 or more key factors. If a portfolio holds complex instruments such as exotic derivatives or mortgage-backed securities, a mapping function can be extremely complex. Such issues can make it difficult to design a practical transformation procedure.

We say a transformation procedure is **complete** if its characterization of the conditional distribution for ${}^1P$ is sufficiently general to support any practical VaR metric. Otherwise, the transformation procedure is **incomplete**. For example, if a transformation characterizes the conditional distribution of ${}^1P$ with a mean and a standard deviation, it is incomplete. If it characterizes it as conditionally normal with a specified mean and standard deviation, it is complete. We call a VaR measure **complete** or **incomplete** according to whether its transformation procedure is complete.

In our examples of Section 1.7, we illustrated three types of transformations:

1. linear transformations,
2. quadratic transformations, and
3. Monte Carlo transformations.

The first applies if a portfolio mapping function θ is a linear polynomial. The second applies if θ is a quadratic polynomial and ${}^1\boldsymbol{R}$ is joint-normal. The third applies quite generally and is one example of a category of transformations called numerical transformations. We discuss transformation procedures in Chapter 10.

Remappings

All the VaR measures we have considered so far entail modest calculations. They apply to small portfolios that are easy to value. When we develop VaR measures for real portfolios, this will change.

Every VaR measure employs—explicitly or implicitly—a primary mapping ${}^1P = \theta({}^1\boldsymbol{R})$. Primary mappings can be complicated. This occurs for two reasons:

1. The mapping function θ may be complicated—Mapping functions are formulas for marking-to-market a portfolio as of time 1. They are constructed using techniques of financial engineering. All the computational challenges that arise with financial engineering can arise with θ.
2. The key vector ${}^1\boldsymbol{R}$ may be complicated—VaR measures are sometimes implemented with 1000 or more key factors ${}^1R_i$. Also, the joint distribution of ${}^1\boldsymbol{R}$ may be difficult to work with.

Such complexity can make it difficult to directly apply a transformation procedure. This is especially true if both a primary mapping and a transformation procedure employ the Monte Carlo method—resulting in nested Monte Carlo analyses.

Consider a portfolio holding 300 exotic derivatives, each of which can only be valued using the Monte Carlo method. The primary mapping has the form

$$\overbrace{{}^1P \xleftarrow{\omega} {}^1\boldsymbol{S} \xleftarrow{\varphi} {}^1\boldsymbol{R}}^{\theta}, \qquad [1.57]$$

where key factors ${}^1R_i$ represent values for underliers, implied volatilities, and discount factors. Valuing the mapping ${}^1\boldsymbol{S} = \varphi({}^1\boldsymbol{R})$ for a specific realization ${}^1\boldsymbol{r}^{[k]}$ requires 300 Monte Carlo analyses, one for each derivative's value: ${}^1s_i^{[k]} = \varphi_i({}^1\boldsymbol{r}^{[k]})$. Valuing a realization ${}^1p^{[k]}$ of ${}^1P$ based upon one realization ${}^1\boldsymbol{r}^{[k]}$ entails performing all 300 of these Monte Carlo analyses.

Suppose we employ a Monte Carlo transformation procedure to calculate the portfolio's VaR. This will nest the 300 valuation Monte Carlo analyses within the Monte Carlo transformation. The Monte Carlo transformation might calculate 10,000 realizations ${}^1p^{[k]}$. Since each entails 300 valuation Monte Carlo analyses, the entire analysis will entail 10,000(300) = 3,000,000 Monte Carlo analyses. This is a staggering computational load.

To make a transformation less computationally expensive, we might replace a primary mapping ${}^1P = \theta({}^1\boldsymbol{R})$ with an approximation ${}^1\widetilde{P} = \widetilde{\theta}({}^1\widetilde{\boldsymbol{R}})$, which we call a remapping. In our (second) Australian equities example, we considered a simple remapping. The above example of nested Monte Carlo analyses illustrates an extreme case. Here, a remapping would be crucial.

Formally, a remapping is an approximation of a risk vector ${}^1\boldsymbol{Q}$ with some other risk vector ${}^1\widetilde{\boldsymbol{Q}}$. We describe remappings more generally in Chapter 9. For now, we are interested in remappings ${}^1\widetilde{P}$ of ${}^1P$. If we have a portfolio mapping ${}^1P = \theta({}^1\boldsymbol{R})$, such remappings may take three forms:

1. A **function remapping** approximates ${}^1P = \theta({}^1\boldsymbol{R})$ by replacing θ with an approximate mapping function $\widetilde{\theta}$, so ${}^1\widetilde{P} = \widetilde{\theta}({}^1\boldsymbol{R})$.
2. A **variables remapping** approximates ${}^1P = \theta({}^1\boldsymbol{R})$ by replacing ${}^1\boldsymbol{R}$ with alternative key vector ${}^1\widetilde{\boldsymbol{R}}$, so ${}^1\widetilde{P} = \theta({}^1\widetilde{\boldsymbol{R}})$.
3. A **dual remapping** approximates ${}^1P = \theta({}^1\boldsymbol{R})$ by replacing both θ and ${}^1\boldsymbol{R}$, so ${}^1\widetilde{P} = \widetilde{\theta}({}^1\widetilde{\boldsymbol{R}})$.

The first and third forms are most common. Many function remappings approximate a portfolio mapping function θ with a linear or quadratic polynomial $\widetilde{\theta}$ to facilitate use of a linear or quadratic transformation. Many dual remappings replace a high-dimensional ${}^1\boldsymbol{R}$ with a lower dimensional ${}^1\widetilde{\boldsymbol{R}}$. Principal component analysis, which we discuss in Chapter 3, can be useful for this purpose. Remappings may be applied to primary mappings or to other remappings—approximating approximations.

Function and dual remappings entail a change of key factors. This raises an important issue. Key factors are specific to a portfolio. Portfolio $({}^0p, {}^1P)$ has key vector ${}^1\boldsymbol{R}$. A remapped portfolio $({}^0\widetilde{p}, {}^1\widetilde{P})$ may have the same key vector ${}^1\boldsymbol{R}$ (as is the case with a function remapping) or it may have a different key vector ${}^1\widetilde{\boldsymbol{R}}$. We discuss remappings in Chapter 9.

Summary

Recall our definition of measure from Section 1.2:

A measure is an operation that assigns a value to something.

A VaR measure is an operation that assigns a value to a portfolio. That operation comprises various procedures, which we have defined above. Exhibit 1.11 relates these to one another in a general schematic.

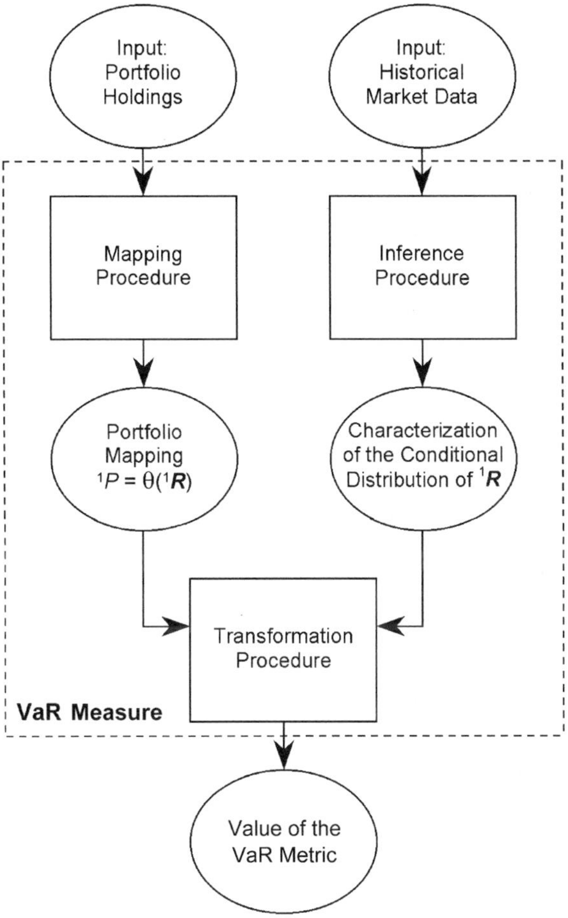

Exhibit 1.11 VaR measures follow a common general scheme, which is depicted here. Procedures are indicated with rectangles; inputs and outputs for procedures are indicated with ovals.

Specific VaR measures vary in certain respects, but all conform generally to the scheme of Exhibit 1.11. They accept both a portfolio's holdings and historical market data as inputs. A **mapping procedure** specifies a portfolio mapping function θ, which may reflect a primary portfolio mapping or a portfolio remapping. An **inference procedure** characterizes a conditional distribution for $^1\boldsymbol{R}$. It generally employs techniques of time-series analysis.

The outputs of the mapping and inference procedures reflect the two components of risk. The mapping function θ reflects exposure. The characterization of the conditional distribution of $^1\boldsymbol{R}$ reflects uncertainty. A transformation procedure combines these two components to somehow characterize the conditional distribution of ${}^1P$. It then uses that characterization to determine a value for the desired VaR metric, which is the output for the VaR measure.

To characterize the conditional distribution of ${}^1P$, the transformation procedure may employ results from probability theory as well as methods of numerical integration, such as the Monte Carlo method. The characterization may take many forms—a probability density function (PDF), a characteristic function, certain parameters of the distribution of ${}^1P$, a realization of a sample[15] from the distribution of ${}^1P$, etc. If the characterization is sufficiently general to calculate any practical VaR metric, we say the transformation is **complete**. Otherwise, it is **incomplete**. We call a VaR measure **complete** or **incomplete** according to whether or not its transformation procedure is complete.

EXERCISES

1.13 Below are informal descriptions of three portfolio mappings and three schematics of portfolio mappings. Match each description with the corresponding schematic.

a. Portfolio value depends upon key factors ${}^1R_i$ representing exchange rates, implied volatilities, and interest rates in various currencies.

b. A stock portfolio is modeled as a function of individual stocks' single-period returns. For simplicity, all return pairs are assumed to have the same correlation.

c. A portfolio holds options and futures on gold. Its market value is approximated as a quadratic polynomial of applicable risk factors.

Schematic 1:

$$\begin{array}{l} \overbrace{{}^1P \xleftarrow{\;\omega\;} {}^1\boldsymbol{S} \xleftarrow{\;\varphi\;} {}^1\boldsymbol{R}}^{\theta} \\ \uparrow \\ {}^1\tilde{P} \xleftarrow{\qquad\tilde{\theta}\qquad} {}^1\boldsymbol{R} \end{array} \qquad [1.58]$$

Schematic 2:

$$\overbrace{{}^1P \xleftarrow{\;\omega\;} {}^1\boldsymbol{S} \xleftarrow{\;\varphi\;} {}^1\boldsymbol{R}}^{\theta} \qquad [1.59]$$

[15] As obtained with a Monte Carlo transformation.

Schematic 3:

$$\overbrace{{}^1P \xleftarrow{\omega} {}^1\boldsymbol{S} \xleftarrow{\varphi} {}^1\boldsymbol{R}}^{\theta} \qquad [1.60]$$
$$\begin{array}{ccc} \uparrow & \uparrow & \uparrow \end{array}$$
$${}^1\tilde{P} \xleftarrow{\omega} {}^1\tilde{\boldsymbol{S}} \xleftarrow{\varphi} {}^1\tilde{\boldsymbol{R}}$$

1.14 Exhibit 1.12 illustrates three portfolio mapping functions θ for portfolios whose values ${}^1P$ depend upon a single key factor ${}^1R_1$. As we did in Exhibits 1.8, 1.9, and 1.10, sketch what each conditional PDF of ${}^1P$ might look like assuming ${}^1R_1$ is conditionally normal with its mean at the mid-point of each graph.

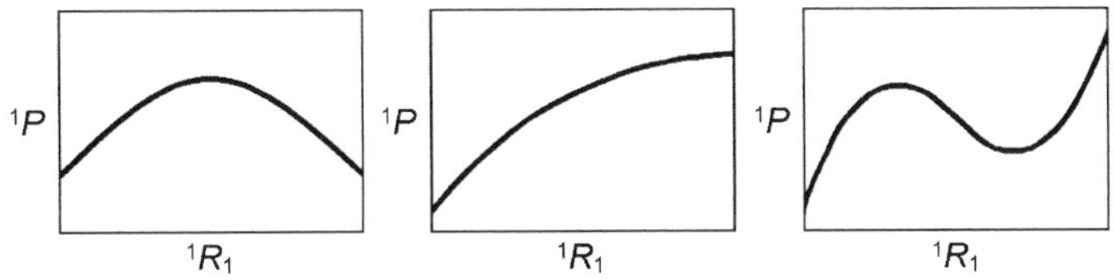

Exhibit 1.12 Portfolio mapping functions θ for Exercise 1.14.

1.15 Describe portfolios whose mapping functions might appear like those of the previous exercise.

1.9. FURTHER READING

For more information on the origins of regulatory VaR measures, see Dale (1996) and Molinari and Kibler (1983). Bernstein (1992) and Markowitz (1999) describe the origins of VaR measures in the context of portfolio theory. See Guldimann (2000) for the history of RiskMetrics. Our discussion of measures is largely operational; see Lad (1996). The classic text—and still one of the best—on financial risk management is the Group of 30 (1993) report. See also Culp (2001). For market risk management specifically, see Goldman Sachs and SBC Warburg Dillon Read (1998). For an alternative treatment of VaR measures, see Morgan Guaranty (1996), Dowd (2002), or Marrison (2002).

Part II

Essential Mathematics

Chapter 2

Mathematical Preliminaries

2.1. MOTIVATION

In this chapter, we describe a number of techniques of applied mathematics. Some may already be familiar to you. All will play a role in subsequent discussions of VaR. This opening section places them in that context.

Recall Section 1.8, which described a framework for modeling VaR. It includes a general schematic describing VaR measures, which we reproduce in Exhibit 2.1.

A mapping procedure specifies a primary portfolio mapping ${}^{1}P = \theta({}^{1}\boldsymbol{R})$. Sometimes, the mapping function θ or key vector ${}^{1}\boldsymbol{R}$ is computationally expensive to work with, making the subsequent application of a transformation procedure impractical. A solution is to replace the primary mapping with an approximation ${}^{1}\widetilde{P} = \widetilde{\theta}({}^{1}\widetilde{\boldsymbol{R}})$, which we call a portfolio remapping. There are many ways this might be done. Several are described in Chapter 9. In anticipation of that discussion, the present chapter covers a variety of techniques that are useful for constructing approximations. These include:

- gradient and gradient-Hessian approximations,
- ordinary interpolation,
- ordinary least squares.

Principal component analysis offers another technique of approximation. It is probabilistic, so we discuss it in Chapter 3. The present chapter covers eigenvalues and eigenvectors, which anticipate that discussion.

We considered Monte Carlo transformations in Section 1.7. That discussion was largely intuitive. To apply variance reduction techniques within Monte Carlo

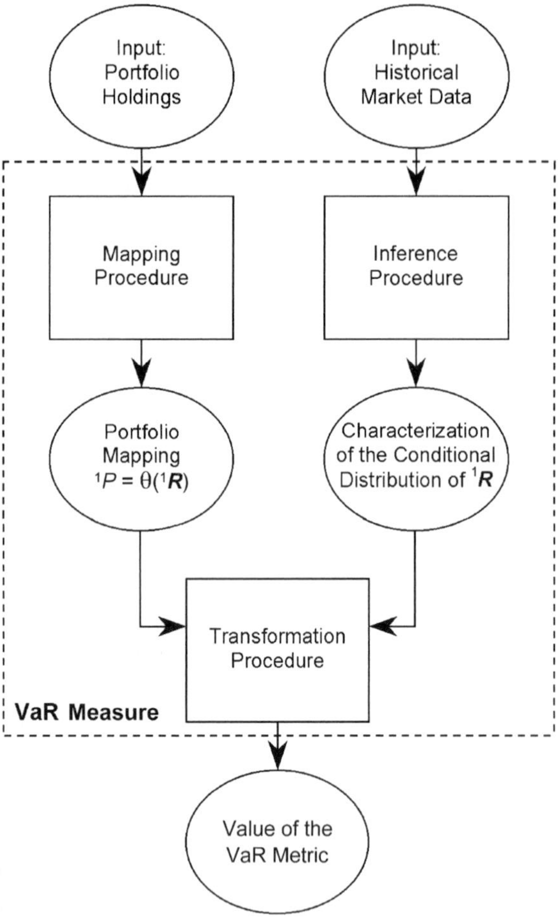

Exhibit 2.1 A reproduction of Exhibit 1.11, which is a general schematic for VaR measures. The techniques of applied mathematics described in this chapter are employed throughout the remainder of the book. They are especially important for discussions of mapping procedures in Chapter 9 and transformation procedures in Chapter 10.

transformations, we will need a more formal understanding of the Monte Carlo method. That more formal understanding will come in the context of numerical integration. In anticipation of that discussion, the present chapter discusses the famous change-of-variables formula for definite integrals as well as deterministic techniques of numerical integration in one and multiple dimensions. One of those techniques—the trapezoidal rule—will be employed with quadratic transformations in Chapter 10.

Other topics covered in this chapter are:

- the Cholesky factorization, which allows us to take the "square root" of a covariance matrix in Chapter 3;
- cubic splines, which offer an alternative to ordinary interpolation for modeling term structures in Chapter 6;
- complex numbers, which are used to define characteristic functions in Chapter 3; and
- Newton's method, which is a practical tool for solving nonlinear equations.

2.2. NOTATION AND TERMINOLOGY

We indicate that an element a is contained in a set A with the notation $a \in A$. We indicate that a set B is a subset of A with the notation $B \subset A$. If $B \subset A$ and $A \subset B$, the sets A and B are equal, $A = B$. We denote the union and intersection of two sets A_1 and A_2 as $A_1 \cup A_2$ and $A_1 \cap A_2$, respectively.

We use the following notation to indicate familiar sets of numbers:

- $\mathbb{N}$: natural numbers $\{1, 2, 3, \ldots\}$;
- $\mathbb{Z}$: integers $\{\ldots, -2, -1, 0, 1, 2, \ldots\}$;
- $\mathbb{R}$: real numbers.

In Section 2.5, we introduce the set of complex numbers, which we denote:

- $\mathbb{C}$: complex numbers.

We may indicate the elements of a set by listing them between brackets. The set of natural numbers less than 5 can be expressed $\{1, 2, 3, 4\}$. Shorthand notion for a set $\{x_1, x_2, \ldots, x_n\}$ is simply $\{x_i\}$, which is read "the set of x_i." We may use the notation $\{x \in A\text{: property}\}$ to indicate the subset of A whose elements satisfy the indicated property. In this manner, the set of natural numbers less than 5 is expressed $\{x \in \mathbb{N}\text{: } x < 5\}$. If the set A is evident from context, the notation may be simplified as $\{x\text{: property}\}$.

We denote intervals of real numbers with parentheses or braces, depending upon whether or not end points are included. The interval (2, 3) is the set $\{x \in \mathbb{R}\text{: } 2 < x < 3\}$. The interval [5, 10) is the set $\{x \in \mathbb{R}\text{: } 5 \leq x < 10\}$.

Cartesian Products

An **ordered pair** is a set containing two elements with an ordering that identifies one element as being "first" and the other element as being "second." The set {yellow, red} equals the set {red, yellow}, but the ordered pair (yellow, red) does not equal the ordered pair (red, yellow). Similarly, an ***n*-tuple** is an ordered set containing n elements. As in our example, we indicate ordered pairs and ordered

n-tuples with parentheses () to distinguish them from sets, which we indicate with brackets {}.[1]

Let A and B be sets. The **Cartesian product** $A \times B$ is the set of ordered pairs (a, b) where $a \in A$ and $b \in B$. More generally, let $A_1, A_2, \ldots A_n$ be n sets. The Cartesian product $A_1 \times A_2 \times \cdots \times A_n$ is the set of n-tuples $(a_1, a_2, \ldots, a_n)$ where $a_i \in A_i$. Shorthand notation for the Cartesian product of a set with itself is $A^2 = A \times A$, or more generally, $A^n = A \times A \times \cdots \times A$. In this manner, $\mathbb{R}^2$ represents two-dimensional space and $\mathbb{R}^n$ represents n-dimensional space.

Vectors

We assume familiarity with vectors, which are elements of—n-tuples or "points" in—$\mathbb{R}^n$. We distinguish between column vectors and row vectors. Unless stated otherwise, all vectors are assumed to be column vectors. There are two different notations used for vectors. One is **matrix notation**, which indicates column vectors $\boldsymbol{x}$ and row vectors $\boldsymbol{y}$ as

$$\boldsymbol{x} = \begin{pmatrix} x_1 \\ x_2 \\ \vdots \\ x_n \end{pmatrix} \quad \text{and} \quad \boldsymbol{y} = (y_1 \quad y_2 \quad \ldots \quad y_n). \qquad [2.1]$$

More compact is n-tuple notation, which we have already introduced. This indicates the same column and row vectors as

$$\boldsymbol{x} = (x_1, x_2, \ldots, x_n) \quad \text{and} \quad \boldsymbol{y} = (y_1, y_2, \ldots, y_n)'. \qquad [2.2]$$

A distinguishing characteristic is that n-tuple notation employs commas whereas matrix notation does not. With either notation, we may use a prime $'$ to indicate transposition. We denote a zero vector $(0, 0, \ldots, 0)$ as $\boldsymbol{0}$.

The **norm** or **length** $\|\boldsymbol{x}\|$ of a vector $\boldsymbol{x}$ is defined as

$$\|\boldsymbol{x}\| = \sqrt{x_1^2 + x_2^2 + \cdots + x_n^2}. \qquad [2.3]$$

In one dimension, length reduces to absolute value, which we denote $|x|$.

Matrices

We assume familiarity with matrices. We indicate a zero matrix as $\boldsymbol{0}$ and an identity matrix as $\boldsymbol{I}$. As with vectors, we indicate matrix transposition with a prime $'$, so $\boldsymbol{h}'$ is the transpose of $\boldsymbol{h}$. We denote a matrix inverse as $\boldsymbol{h}^{-1}$ and a determinant

---

[1] It should be apparent from context when parentheses are being used to indicate an interval as opposed to an ordered pair.

as $|\boldsymbol{h}|$. Components of matrices are assumed to be real numbers unless stated otherwise. Matrix addition and matrix multiplication require that matrices have compatible dimensions. Such compatibility is assumed whenever we apply these operations.

FUNCTIONS

Notation to indicate that a function f maps elements of a set A to elements of a set B is:

$$f\colon A \to B. \tag{2.4}$$

A is the function's domain; B contains its range. We are primarily interested in three types of functions:

- functions from $\mathbb{R}$ to $\mathbb{R}$,
- functions from $\mathbb{R}^n$ to $\mathbb{R}$,
- functions from $\mathbb{R}^n$ to $\mathbb{R}^m$.

We call functions of the first form **real**—they map real numbers to real numbers. The natural logarithm function is a real function, which we denote *log*. We do not employ the logarithm base 10. If a function f has an inverse, we denote this f^{-1}. The derivative of a real function f may be indicated with differential notation or simply as f'.[2] We indicate the value of a function f at a particular point a as either $f(a)$ or $f|_a$.

Consider $f\colon \mathbb{R}^p \to \mathbb{R}^m$ and $g\colon \mathbb{R}^n \to \mathbb{R}^p$. The **composition** of f and g is the function $f \circ g$ from $\mathbb{R}^n$ to $\mathbb{R}^m$ defined as

$$f \circ g(x) = f(g(x)). \tag{2.5}$$

The **gradient** ∇f and **Hessian** $\nabla^2 f$ of a function $f\colon \mathbb{R}^n \to \mathbb{R}$ are the vector of its first partial derivatives and matrix of its second partial derivatives:

$$\nabla f = \begin{pmatrix} \dfrac{\partial f}{\partial x_1} \\ \dfrac{\partial f}{\partial x_2} \\ \vdots \\ \dfrac{\partial f}{\partial x_n} \end{pmatrix} \quad \text{and} \quad \nabla^2 f = \begin{pmatrix} \dfrac{\partial^2 f}{\partial x_1^2} & \dfrac{\partial^2 f}{\partial x_1 \partial x_2} & \cdots & \dfrac{\partial^2 f}{\partial x_1 \partial x_n} \\ \dfrac{\partial^2 f}{\partial x_2 \partial x_1} & \dfrac{\partial^2 f}{\partial x_2^2} & & \dfrac{\partial^2 f}{\partial x_2 \partial x_n} \\ \vdots & & \ddots & \vdots \\ \dfrac{\partial^2 f}{\partial x_n \partial x_1} & \dfrac{\partial^2 f}{\partial x_n \partial x_2} & \cdots & \dfrac{\partial^2 f}{\partial x_n^2} \end{pmatrix}. \tag{2.6}$$

The Hessian is symmetric if the second partials are continuous.

[2] It should be clear from context whether a prime indicates differentiation of a function as opposed to transposition of a vector or matrix.

The Jacobian Jf of a function $f\colon \mathbb{R}^n \to \mathbb{R}^m$ is the matrix of its first partial derivatives.

$$Jf = \begin{pmatrix} \frac{\partial f_1}{\partial x_1} & \frac{\partial f_1}{\partial x_2} & \cdots & \frac{\partial f_1}{\partial x_n} \\ \frac{\partial f_2}{\partial x_1} & \frac{\partial f_2}{\partial x_2} & & \frac{\partial f_2}{\partial x_n} \\ \vdots & & \ddots & \vdots \\ \frac{\partial f_m}{\partial x_1} & \frac{\partial f_m}{\partial x_2} & \cdots & \frac{\partial f_m}{\partial x_n} \end{pmatrix}. \qquad [2.7]$$

Note that the Hessian of a function $f\colon \mathbb{R}^n \to \mathbb{R}$ is the Jacobian of its gradient.

POLYNOMIALS

A polynomial from $\mathbb{R}$ to $\mathbb{R}$ is **linear** if it has form

$$p(x) = bx + a \qquad [2.8]$$

with a and b scalars. It is **quadratic** if it has form:

$$p(x) = cx^2 + bx + a \qquad [2.9]$$

with a, b and c scalars. These notions generalize to higher dimensions. A polynomial from $\mathbb{R}^n$ to $\mathbb{R}$ is **linear** if it has form

$$p(\boldsymbol{x}) = \boldsymbol{bx} + a \qquad [2.10]$$

with $\boldsymbol{b}$ an n-dimensional row vector and a a scalar. It is **quadratic** if it has form

$$p(\boldsymbol{x}) = \boldsymbol{x}'\boldsymbol{cx} + \boldsymbol{bx} + a \qquad [2.11]$$

with $\boldsymbol{c}$ an $n \times n$ matrix, $\boldsymbol{b}$ an n-dimensional row vector and a a scalar. Without loss of generality, we always assume $\boldsymbol{c}$ is symmetric. For example, the quadratic polynomial

$$p(x_1, x_2, x_3) = 2x_1^2 - 6x_1x_2 + 5x_1x_3 + x_2 + 17 \qquad [2.12]$$

can be expressed in form [2.11] with

$$\boldsymbol{c} = \begin{pmatrix} 2 & -3 & 2.5 \\ -3 & 0 & 0 \\ 2.5 & 0 & 0 \end{pmatrix}, \qquad [2.13]$$

$$\boldsymbol{b} = (0 \quad 1 \quad 0), \qquad [2.14]$$

and

$$a = 17. \qquad [2.15]$$

2.3. GRADIENT AND GRADIENT-HESSIAN APPROXIMATIONS

Polynomials are frequently used to locally approximate functions. There are various ways this may be done. We consider here several forms of differential approximation.

UNIVARIATE APPROXIMATIONS

Consider a function $f\colon \mathbb{R} \to \mathbb{R}$ that is differentiable in an open interval about some point $x^{[0]} \in \mathbb{R}$. The linear polynomial

$$p_1(x) = f\left(x^{[0]}\right) + f'\left(x^{[0]}\right)\left(x - x^{[0]}\right) \qquad [2.16]$$

provides a good approximation for f, at least in a small interval about $x^{[0]}$. This is because:

- p_1 equals f at $x^{[0]}$ and
- p_1 has the same first derivative as f at $x^{[0]}$.

If f is twice differentiable in an open interval about $x^{[0]}$, we can improve the approximation with a quadratic polynomial:

$$p_2(x) = f\left(x^{[0]}\right) + f'\left(x^{[0]}\right)\left(x - x^{[0]}\right) + \frac{f''\left(x^{[0]}\right)}{2}\left(x - x^{[0]}\right)^2. \qquad [2.17]$$

Consider the function

$$f(x) = 3e^x - e^{2x}, \qquad [2.18]$$

which has first and second derivatives

$$f'(x) = 3e^x - 2e^{2x}, \qquad [2.19]$$

$$f''(x) = 3e^x - 4e^{2x} \qquad [2.20]$$

on $\mathbb{R}$. Let's construct a linear polynomial approximation for f about the point $x^{[0]} = 0$. Applying [2.16], we obtain

$$p_1(x) = (3e^0 - e^0) + (3e^0 - 2e^0)(x - 0) \qquad [2.21]$$

$$= x + 2. \qquad [2.22]$$

This is graphed in Exhibit 2.2

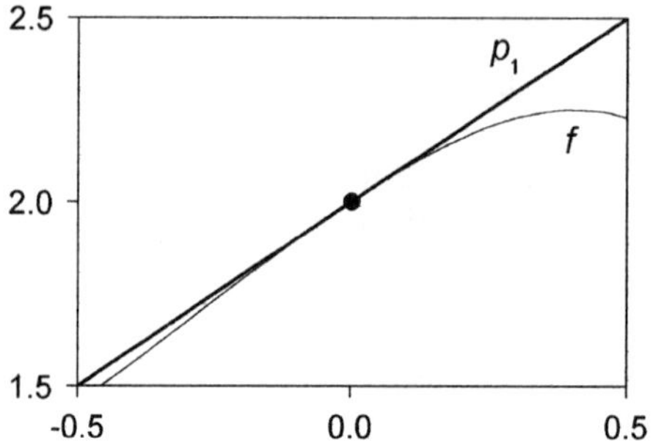

Exhibit 2.2 Comparison of function f and linear polynomial p_1.

We can improve the approximation, at least for values of x close to 0, with a quadratic polynomial. Applying [2.17] at $x^{[0]} = 0$, we obtain

$$p_2(x) = (3e^0 - e^0) + (3e^0 - 2e^0)(x - 0) + \frac{(3e^0 - 4e^0)}{2}(x - 0)^2 \quad [2.23]$$

$$= -\frac{x^2}{2} + x + 2. \quad [2.24]$$

This is graphed in Exhibit 2.3.

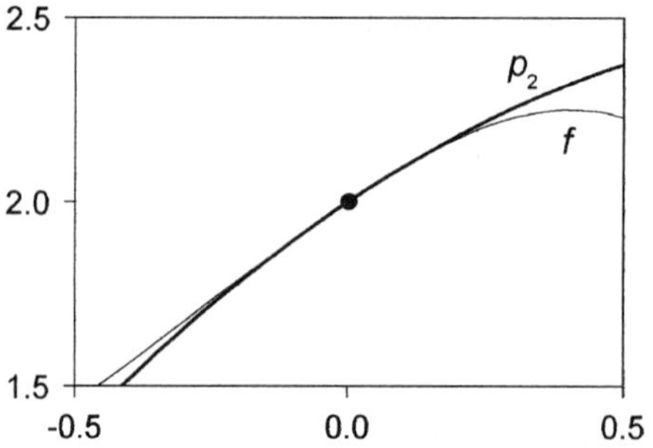

Exhibit 2.3 Comparison of function f and quadratic polynomial p_2.

Multivariate Approximations

Polynomial approximations [2.16] and [2.17] generalize to multiple dimensions. For $f\colon \mathbb{R}^n \to \mathbb{R}$, gradients replace first derivatives and Hessians replace second derivatives, so linear polynomial [2.16] and quadratic polynomial [2.17] become

$$p_1(\boldsymbol{x}) = f\left(\boldsymbol{x}^{[0]}\right) + \nabla f\left(\boldsymbol{x}^{[0]}\right)'\left(\boldsymbol{x} - \boldsymbol{x}^{[0]}\right), \quad [2.25]$$

$$p_2(\boldsymbol{x}) = f\left(\boldsymbol{x}^{[0]}\right) + \nabla f\left(\boldsymbol{x}^{[0]}\right)'\left(\boldsymbol{x} - \boldsymbol{x}^{[0]}\right) + \frac{1}{2}\left(\boldsymbol{x} - \boldsymbol{x}^{[0]}\right)'\nabla^2 f\left(\boldsymbol{x}^{[0]}\right)\left(\boldsymbol{x} - \boldsymbol{x}^{[0]}\right). \quad [2.26]$$

We call these **gradient approximations** and **gradient-Hessian approximations**, respectively.

Consider the function

$$f(x_1, x_2) = e^{x_1 x_2}, \qquad [2.27]$$

which has gradient and Hessian

$$\nabla f = \begin{pmatrix} x_2 e^{x_1 x_2} \\ x_1 e^{x_1 x_2} \end{pmatrix}, \qquad [2.28]$$

$$\nabla^2 f = \begin{pmatrix} x_2^2 e^{x_1 x_2} & e^{x_1 x_2} + x_1 x_2 e^{x_1 x_2} \\ e^{x_1 x_2} + x_1 x_2 e^{x_1 x_2} & x_1^2 e^{x_1 x_2} \end{pmatrix}. \qquad [2.29]$$

Let's construct a gradient-Hessian approximation about the point (0,1). Applying [2.26], we obtain

$$p_2(x_1, x_2) = 1 + (1 \quad 0)\begin{pmatrix} x_1 - 0 \\ x_2 - 1 \end{pmatrix} + \frac{1}{2}(x_1 - 0 \quad x_2 - 1)\begin{pmatrix} 1 & 1 \\ 1 & 0 \end{pmatrix}\begin{pmatrix} x_1 - 0 \\ x_2 - 1 \end{pmatrix} \qquad [2.30]$$

$$= \frac{1}{2}x_1^2 + x_1 x_2 + 1. \qquad [2.31]$$

Taylor Polynomials

The linear and quadratic polynomial approximations discussed in this section are examples of a more general concept called **Taylor polynomials**. Consider a function $f\colon \mathbb{R} \to \mathbb{R}$ whose first m derivatives exist in an open interval about a point $x^{[0]} \in \mathbb{R}$. The polynomial

$$p_m(x) = f\left(x^{[0]}\right) + \frac{f'\left(x^{[0]}\right)}{1!}\left(x - x^{[0]}\right) + \frac{f''\left(x^{[0]}\right)}{2!}\left(x - x^{[0]}\right)^2$$
$$+ \cdots + + \frac{f^{(m)}\left(x^{[0]}\right)}{m!}\left(x - x^{[0]}\right)^m \qquad [2.32]$$

is called the mth-order Taylor polynomial of f about the point $x^{[0]}$. It provides a good approximation for f, at least in a small interval about $x^{[0]}$. If all derivatives exist for f in an open interval about $x^{[0]}$, we may consider the limiting polynomial as m approaches infinity. This is called the **Taylor series** expansion of f about the point $x^{[0]}$. In some cases—but not all!—a function equals its Taylor series expansions on $\mathbb{R}$. For example, functions e^x and $sin(x)$ both equal their Taylor series expansions about the point $x^{[0]} = 0$:

$$e^x = 1 + x + \frac{x^2}{2!} + \frac{x^3}{3!} + \frac{x^4}{4!} + \cdots \qquad [2.33]$$

$$sin(x) = x - \frac{x^3}{3!} + \frac{x^5}{5!} - \frac{x^7}{7!} \cdots \qquad [2.34]$$

Taylor polynomials and Taylor series generalize to higher dimensions.

Exercises

2.1 Apply [2.17] to construct a quadratic polynomial approximation for the function $f(x) = xe^x$ about the point $x^{[0]} = 0$.

2.2 Apply [2.26] to construct a quadratic polynomial approximation for the function $f(x_1, x_2) = x_1 e^{x_2}$ about the point $\boldsymbol{x}^{[0]} = (0, 0)$.

2.3 Construct the Taylor series expansion for the function $log(1 + x)$ about the point $x^{[0]} = 0$.

2.4. ORDINARY INTERPOLATION

Interpolation is any procedure for fitting a function to a set of points in such a manner that the function intercepts each of the points. Consider m points ($\boldsymbol{x}^{[k]}$, $y^{[k]}$) where $\boldsymbol{x}^{[k]} \in \mathbb{R}^n$, $y^{[k]} \in \mathbb{R}$, and the $\boldsymbol{x}^{[k]}$ are distinct. We wish to construct a function $f: \mathbb{R}^n \to \mathbb{R}$ such that $y^{[k]} = f(\boldsymbol{x}^{[k]})$ for all k. There are various solutions to this problem. We consider an approach called **ordinary interpolation**.[3] This is applicable to a wide range of interpolation functions. Later, we will consider another approach that uses cubic splines as interpolation functions.

Example: Linear Interpolation. Between two points, $(x^{[1]}, y^{[1]})$ and $(x^{[2]}, y^{[2]})$ with $x^{[1]} \neq x^{[2]}$, we may interpolate a linear polynomial of the form

$$f(x) = \beta_2 x + \beta_1. \quad [2.35]$$

Consider points (2, 1) and (5, 3). These and an interpolated linear polynomial are graphed in Exhibit 2.4

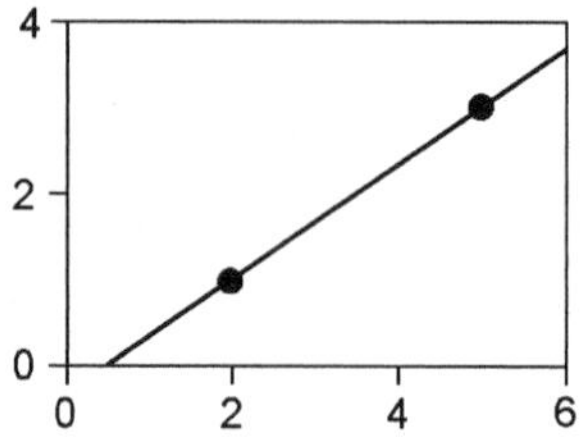

Exhibit 2.4 The two points (2, 1) and (5, 3) and an interpolated linear polynomial.

To solve for the interpolated polynomial, we must determine constants β_1 and β_2. If the linear polynomial is to intercept (2, 1) and (5, 3), it must satisfy

$$f(2) = \beta_2 2 + \beta_1 = 1, \quad [2.36]$$

$$f(5) = \beta_2 5 + \beta_1 = 3. \quad [2.37]$$

[3] Our name reflects the method's similarity to the method of ordinary least squares. See Exercise 2.16.

This is a system of two linear equations in two unknowns. We express it in matrix form:

$$\begin{pmatrix} 2 & 1 \\ 5 & 1 \end{pmatrix} \begin{pmatrix} \beta_2 \\ \beta_1 \end{pmatrix} = \begin{pmatrix} 1 \\ 3 \end{pmatrix}. \qquad [2.38]$$

Solving, we obtain $\beta_1 = -1/3$ and $\beta_2 = 2/3$, so our interpolated polynomial is

$$f(x) = 2x/3 - 1/3. \qquad [2.39]$$

EXAMPLE: QUADRATIC INTERPOLATION. Suppose we want to interpolate a quadratic polynomial between the five points $(\boldsymbol{x}^{[k]}, y^{[k]})$ of Exhibit 2.5.

k	$(x_1^{[k]}, x_2^{[k]})$	$y^{[k]}$
1	(1, 1)	2
2	(2, 3)	2
3	(2, 5)	5
4	(4, 2)	1
5	(5, 5)	6

Exhibit 2.5 Five points through which we wish to interpolate a quadratic polynomial.

The general form for a quadratic polynomial from $\mathbb{R}^2$ to $\mathbb{R}$ is

$$f(x_1, x_2) = \beta_6 x_1 x_2 + \beta_5 x_1^2 + \beta_4 x_2^2 + \beta_3 x_1 + \beta_2 x_2 + \beta_1. \qquad [2.40]$$

Solving for the six constants β_j based upon the five points $(\boldsymbol{x}^{[k]}, y^{[k]})$ of Exhibit 2.5 would entail a system of five equations in six unknowns. Such a system is likely to have infinitely many solutions. To obtain a unique solution, we may consider a less general form of quadratic polynomial than [2.40]. We might require $\beta_5 = \beta_4$ or set $\beta_1 = 0$, etc. For this example, let's interpolate a quadratic polynomial with zero cross term, $\beta_6 = 0$. Our polynomial then has form

$$f(x_1, x_2) = \beta_5 x_1^2 + \beta_4 x_2^2 + \beta_3 x_1 + \beta_2 x_2 + \beta_1. \qquad [2.41]$$

We require that this polynomial intercept each of our five points. This renders a system of five equations in five unknowns, which we express in matrix notation as

$$\begin{pmatrix} 1 & 1 & 1 & 1 & 1 \\ 4 & 9 & 2 & 3 & 1 \\ 4 & 25 & 2 & 5 & 1 \\ 16 & 4 & 4 & 2 & 1 \\ 25 & 25 & 5 & 5 & 1 \end{pmatrix} \begin{pmatrix} \beta_5 \\ \beta_4 \\ \beta_3 \\ \beta_2 \\ \beta_1 \end{pmatrix} = \begin{pmatrix} 2 \\ 2 \\ 5 \\ 1 \\ 6 \end{pmatrix}. \qquad [2.42]$$

Solving, we obtain

$$f(x_1, x_2) = 0.4048x_1^2 + 0.2143x_2^2 - 2.500x_1 - 0.2143x_2 + 4.095. \quad [2.43]$$

This and the five points are graphed in Exhibit 2.6

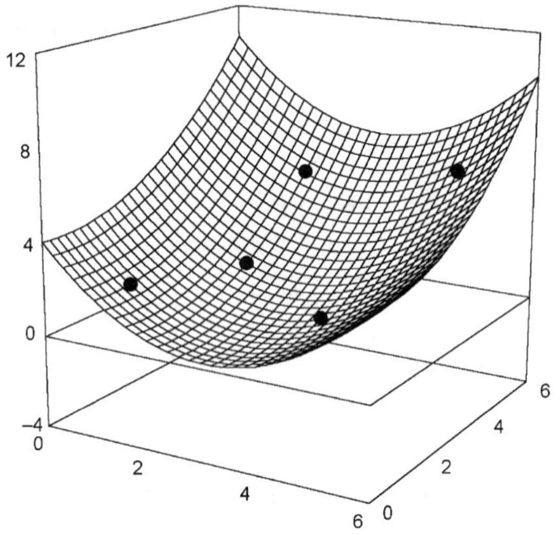

Exhibit 2.6 A quadratic polynomial of form [2.41] is interpolated between the points of Exhibit 2.5.

Methodology

We now formalize the interpolation procedure illustrated in our two examples. The examples used polynomials as interpolation functions f. The following discussion extends the procedure to a broader range of interpolating functions.

Consider m points $(\boldsymbol{x}^{[k]}, y^{[k]})$ where $\boldsymbol{x}^{[k]} \in \mathbb{R}^n$, $y^{[k]} \in \mathbb{R}$ and the $\boldsymbol{x}^{[k]}$ are distinct. We wish to interpolate a function $f: \mathbb{R}^n \to \mathbb{R}$ of the form

$$f(\boldsymbol{x}) = \beta_m f_m(\boldsymbol{x}) + \beta_{m-1} f_{m-1}(\boldsymbol{x}) + \cdots + \beta_1 f_1(\boldsymbol{x}) \quad [2.44]$$

in such a manner that f intercepts each of the points. Functions $f_j: \mathbb{R}^n \to \mathbb{R}$ can take any form. In our above quadratic example, they were:

- $f_1(\boldsymbol{x}) = 1$,
- $f_2(\boldsymbol{x}) = x_2$,
- $f_3(\boldsymbol{x}) = x_1$,
- $f_4(\boldsymbol{x}) = x_2^2$,
- $f_5(\boldsymbol{x}) = x_1^2$,

but exponentials, roots, logarithms, and other functions are permissible. Let's express our problem with matrices. Define

$$\boldsymbol{\beta} = \begin{pmatrix} \beta_1 \\ \beta_2 \\ \vdots \\ \beta_m \end{pmatrix}. \qquad [2.45]$$

This is unknown. It is what we want to solve for. Define $\boldsymbol{f}$ as the $m \times m$ matrix comprising values of each function f_j evaluated at each point $\boldsymbol{x}^{[k]}$:

$$\boldsymbol{f} = \begin{pmatrix} f_1(\boldsymbol{x}^{[1]}) & f_2(\boldsymbol{x}^{[1]}) & \cdots & f_m(\boldsymbol{x}^{[1]}) \\ f_1(\boldsymbol{x}^{[2]}) & f_2(\boldsymbol{x}^{[2]}) & & f_m(\boldsymbol{x}^{[2]}) \\ \vdots & & \ddots & \vdots \\ f_1(\boldsymbol{x}^{[m]}) & f_2(\boldsymbol{x}^{[m]}) & \cdots & f_m(\boldsymbol{x}^{[m]}) \end{pmatrix}. \qquad [2.46]$$

Define the vector

$$\boldsymbol{y} = \begin{pmatrix} y^{[1]} \\ y^{[2]} \\ \vdots \\ y^{[m]} \end{pmatrix}. \qquad [2.47]$$

Both the matrix $\boldsymbol{f}$ and vector $\boldsymbol{y}$ are constants. They are known. Our requirement that f intercept each point $(\boldsymbol{x}^{[k]}, y^{[k]})$ yields the equation

$$\boldsymbol{f}\boldsymbol{\beta} = \boldsymbol{y}. \qquad [2.48]$$

If the matrix $\boldsymbol{f}$ is invertible, this has the unique solution

$$\boldsymbol{\beta} = \boldsymbol{f}^{-1}\boldsymbol{y}. \qquad [2.49]$$

Exercises

2.4 Consider three points $(x^{[k]}, y^{[k]}) = (1,2), (4,2), (5,3)$. Interpolate a quadratic polynomial of the form

$$f(x) = \beta_3 x^2 + \beta_2 x + \beta_1. \qquad [2.50]$$

2.5 Interpolate a function $f: \mathbb{R}^2 \to \mathbb{R}$ of the form

$$f(\boldsymbol{x}) = \beta_2 exp(x_1 + x_2) + \beta_1 exp(x_1 - x_2) \qquad [2.51]$$

such that $f(1, 0) = 1$ and $f(1, 1) = 1$.

2.5. COMPLEX NUMBERS

Many people find **complex numbers** disturbing. Before delving into their mathematics, let's consider why we might be interested in these constructs.

Complex numbers act much like a bridge between two villages that are located on opposite sides of a river. If the nearest ford is 10 miles upstream, a bridge may provide a direct path between the two villages. In traveling between the two villages, we might take the ford or the bridge. Either way, our destination is the same.

Similarly, we may have a mathematical problem that is expressed entirely with real numbers and has a solution that depends only on real numbers. However, using complex numbers to reach that solution may provide a convenient shortcut compared to techniques that only involve real numbers. We use the complex numbers to bridge the gap between the problem and its solution. Doing so does not change the solution. It merely provides a convenient means—a bridge—for obtaining the solution.

THE NUMBER i

The real numbers contain no solution to the equation $x^2 = -1$. We remedy this by extending the real numbers through the inclusion of an "imaginary" number i that satisfies

$$i^2 = -1. \qquad [2.52]$$

As with any number, we can add, multiply, take roots and perform other operations with this new number i. Multiplying i by 5 results in the number $5i$. Adding 3 to this yields $3 + 5i$. Squaring this yields $9 + 30i + 25i^2$.

At this point, imaginary numbers may be starting to seem like a Pandora's box. By adding a single number i to $\mathbb{R}$, we have actually added many numbers, and the expressions for these numbers seem to be getting more and more complicated. What would happen now if we were to divide our number $9 + 30i + 25i^2$ into 7?

In fact, such concerns are unfounded. Although the addition of i to $\mathbb{R}$ does add many numbers to $\mathbb{R}$, expressions for these numbers always simplify to the form

$$a + bi, \qquad [2.53]$$

where a and b are real. For example, using [2.52], we can simplify our number $9 + 30i + 25i^2$ as follows:

$$9 + 30i + 25i^2 = 9 + 30i + 25(-1) = -16 + 30i, \qquad [2.54]$$

which has the form [2.53].

We call the set of numbers of the form [2.53] the **complex numbers** and denote this set $\mathbb{C}$. Given a complex number $z = a + bi$, we call the real number a the **real part** of z. We call the real number b the **imaginary part** of z. This motivates the *Re* and *Im* functions that map a complex number $z = a + bi$ to its real and imaginary parts a and b, respectively:

$$Re(a + bi) = a, \qquad [2.55]$$

$$Im(a + bi) = b. \qquad [2.56]$$

Complex Operations

Operations on complex numbers are extensions of the familiar operations on real numbers. Indeed, we have already performed complex addition and multiplication. We now formally define the operations of complex addition, subtraction, multiplication, division, and the taking of square roots. Let $a + bi$ and $c + di$ be complex numbers where $a, b, c, d \in \mathbb{R}$. Then

$$(a + bi) + (c + di) = (a + c) + (b + d)i, \qquad [2.57]$$

$$(a + bi) - (c + di) = (a - c) + (b - d)i, \qquad [2.58]$$

$$(a + bi)(c + di) = (ac - bd) + (ad + bc)i, \qquad [2.59]$$

$$\frac{a + bi}{c + di} = \frac{(ac + bd)}{c^2 + d^2} + i\frac{(bc - ad)}{c^2 + d^2} \quad c + di \neq 0, \qquad [2.60]$$

$$\sqrt{a + bi} = \pm\left(\sqrt{\frac{a + \sqrt{a^2 + b^2}}{2}} + i\frac{b}{|b|}\sqrt{\frac{-a + \sqrt{a^2 + b^2}}{2}}\right). \qquad [2.61]$$

With the exception of 0, every number has two square roots. For example, the square roots of 4 are 2 and -2. The square roots of -1 are i and $-i$.

In formulas [2.57] through [2.61], we observe several things. First, the formulas reduce to the corresponding operations for real numbers if they are applied to real numbers. Also, the right side of each formula is always defined and corresponds to a complex number of the form [2.53]. The only exception is division by zero, which is undefined with regard to real as well as complex numbers.[4]

Recall that we were motivated to introduce complex numbers by the equation $x^2 = -1$, which has no solution in $\mathbb{R}$. Is it possible that there is an equation $x^2 = a + bi$ that has no solution in $\mathbb{C}$? If this were the case, we might feel compelled to extend the complex numbers through the addition of still another

[4]In [2.61], if $b = 0$, set $b/|b| = 0$.

"imaginary" number to solve this new equation. Because the right side of [2.61] is always defined, this will never happen.

We can make a more sweeping statement. Consider a polynomial equation of the form

$$w_n z^n + \cdots + w_2 z^2 + w_1 z + w_0 = 0 \qquad [2.62]$$

where the $w_i \in \mathbb{C}$ are constants. Every such equation has exactly n solutions $z \in \mathbb{C}$, including repeated solutions.[5] This is an important result. It is called the **fundamental theorem of algebra**.

Complex Functions

We extend the exponential function to $\mathbb{C}$ with

$$e^{a+bi} = e^a cos(b) + i e^a sin(b). \qquad [2.63]$$

This is the famous Euler's formula that links the exponential function with the sine and cosine functions. We extend the sine and cosine functions to $\mathbb{C}$ with

$$sin(z) = \frac{e^{zi} - e^{-zi}}{2i}, \qquad [2.64]$$

$$cos(z) = \frac{e^{zi} + e^{-zi}}{2}. \qquad [2.65]$$

Exercises

2.6 Express the following in $a + bi$ form:
- a. $(5 + 3i)(2 - i)$,
- b. $5/(2 + i)$,
- c. e^i.

2.6. EIGENVALUES AND EIGENVECTORS

Consider a square matrix $\boldsymbol{c}$. If:

$$\boldsymbol{c}\boldsymbol{v} = \lambda \boldsymbol{v} \qquad [2.66]$$

for some scalar λ and some vector $\boldsymbol{v} \neq \boldsymbol{0}$, then we call λ an **eigenvalue** and $\boldsymbol{v}$ an **eigenvector** of $\boldsymbol{c}$. This means that an eigenvector of a matrix is any vector for

[5] Consider the equation $z^2 + 4z + 5 = 0$. Factoring the left side, we obtain $(z+2+i)(z+2-i) = 0$, indicating the two solutions $z = -2 - i$ and $z = -2 + i$. Now consider the equation $z^2 - 4z + 10 = 6$. Subtracting 6 from both sides and factoring, we obtain $(z - 2)(z - 2) = 0$. This has two solutions, but they coincide. We say that the equation has the repeated solution $z = 2$.

which multiplying by the matrix is not different from multiplying by a scalar (the eigenvalue).

Suppose λ is an eigenvalue and $\boldsymbol{v}$ is a corresponding eigenvector of $\boldsymbol{c}$. For any scalar a, the vector $a\boldsymbol{v}$ is also an eigenvector corresponding to eigenvalue λ. This follows because

$$\boldsymbol{c}(a\boldsymbol{v}) = a(\boldsymbol{c}\boldsymbol{v}) = a(\lambda\boldsymbol{v}) = \lambda(a\boldsymbol{v}). \qquad [2.67]$$

Accordingly, eigenvectors are uniquely determined only up to scalar multiplication. If a set of eigenvectors are linearly independent, we say they are **distinct**.

To determine eigenvalues and eigenvectors of a matrix, we focus first on the eigenvalues. Rearranging [2.66], we obtain

$$(\boldsymbol{c} - \lambda\boldsymbol{I})\boldsymbol{v} = \boldsymbol{0}, \qquad [2.68]$$

where $\boldsymbol{I}$ is the identity matrix. This equation will hold for some nonzero vector $\boldsymbol{v}$ if and only if the matrix $(\boldsymbol{c} - \lambda\boldsymbol{I})$ is singular. Accordingly, we seek values λ for which the matrix $(\boldsymbol{c} - \lambda\boldsymbol{I})$ has a determinant of 0.

Consider matrix

$$\boldsymbol{c} = \begin{pmatrix} 2 & 0 & 1 \\ 0 & 0 & 1 \\ 0 & 3 & 2 \end{pmatrix}, \qquad [2.69]$$

for which

$$(\boldsymbol{c} - \lambda\boldsymbol{I}) = \begin{pmatrix} 2-\lambda & 0 & 1 \\ 0 & -\lambda & 1 \\ 0 & 3 & 2-\lambda \end{pmatrix}. \qquad [2.70]$$

This has determinant

$$(2-\lambda)(-\lambda)(2-\lambda) - 3(2-\lambda) = -\lambda^3 - 4\lambda^2 + \lambda + 6, \qquad [2.71]$$

which is a third-order polynomial. It has roots $\lambda = -1, 2$, and 3. We find corresponding eigenvectors $\boldsymbol{v}$ by substituting the eigenvalues into [2.68] and solving. For example, with $\lambda = -1$, [2.68] becomes:

$$\begin{pmatrix} 3 & 0 & 1 \\ 0 & 1 & 1 \\ 0 & 3 & 3 \end{pmatrix} \begin{pmatrix} v_1 \\ v_2 \\ v_3 \end{pmatrix} = \begin{pmatrix} 0 \\ 0 \\ 0 \end{pmatrix}. \qquad [2.72]$$

By inspection, a solution is $\boldsymbol{v} = (1, 3, -3)$. Obviously, any multiple of this is also a solution. We repeat the same analysis for the other eigenvalues. Results are indicated in Exhibit 2.7.

Eigenvalue	Eigenvector
−1	(−1, −3, 3)
2	(1, 0, 0)
3	(3, 1, 3)

Exhibit 2.7 Eigenvalues and eigenvectors of matrix [2.69].

The approach we employed in our example is useful for deriving an important result. Consider an arbitrary $n \times n$ matrix $\boldsymbol{c}$. To find its eigenvalues, we construct the determinant of $(\boldsymbol{c} - \lambda\boldsymbol{I})$ and set it equal to 0. This results in an nth-order polynomial equation. By the fundamental theorem of algebra, it has n solutions. We conclude that every matrix has n eigenvalues. Of course, some may be complex. Others may be repeated.

In practical applications, eigenvalues are not calculated in this manner. Although setting the determinant of $(\boldsymbol{c} - \lambda\boldsymbol{I})$ equal to 0 and solving is theoretically useful, there are more efficient algorithms, which are implemented in various software packages. See Strang (1988).

Eigenvalues have a number of convenient properties. A matrix and its transpose both have the same eigenvalues. If λ is an eigenvalue of a nonsingular matrix, then $1/\lambda$ is an eigenvalue of its inverse. The product of the eigenvalues of a matrix equals its determinant.

Intuitive Example

Consider an intuitive example. A sphere of unit radius is positioned at the center of a three-dimensional coordinate system. It is rotating about the x_3-axis. The matrix:

$$\boldsymbol{c} = \begin{pmatrix} .7071 & .7071 & 0 \\ -.7071 & .7071 & 0 \\ 0 & 0 & 1 \end{pmatrix} \qquad [2.73]$$

describes a one-eighth (45°) rotation of the sphere. For example, multiplying $\boldsymbol{c}$ by the vector (1, 0, 0) yields the vector (.7071, .7071, 0), which is rotated 45°. This is depicted in Exhibit 2.8.

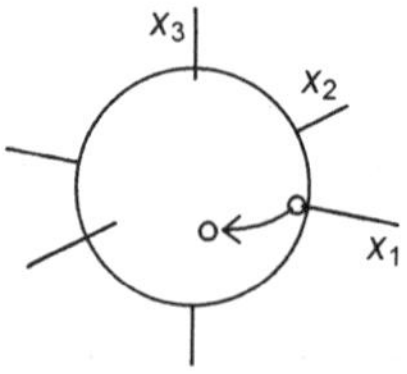

Exhibit 2.8 The matrix $\boldsymbol{c}$ rotates points 45° about the x_3-axis. This is illustrated for the point (1, 0, 0), which it transforms into the point (.7071, .7071, 0).

Intuitively, what might we expect to be an eigenvector of the matrix $\boldsymbol{c}$? Is there a point on the unit sphere that a 45° rotation transforms into a multiple of itself? Of course! Consider the point at the north pole. It is the point (0, 0, 1), and it is transformed into itself. We conclude that an eigenvector of $\boldsymbol{c}$ is the vector (0, 0, 1). The corresponding eigenvalue is 1. Because it is a 3×3 matrix, $\boldsymbol{c}$ has two other eigenvalues, but they are both complex numbers.

Exercises

2.7 Find the eigenvalues and eigenvectors of the matrix

$$\begin{pmatrix} 3 & 1 \\ 2 & 2 \end{pmatrix}. \qquad [2.74]$$

2.8 Prove that the eigenvalues of a diagonal matrix are its diagonal elements.

2.9 Use one of the stated properties of eigenvalues to prove that a matrix is singular if and only if it has 0 as one of its eigenvalues.

2.7. CHOLESKY FACTORIZATION

If we think of matrices as multi-dimensional generalizations of numbers, we may draw useful analogies between numbers and matrices. Not least of these is an analogy between positive numbers and positive definite matrices. Just as we can take square roots of positive numbers, so can we take "square roots" of positive definite matrices.

Positive Definite Matrices

A real symmetric matrix $\boldsymbol{x}$ is said to be:

- **positive definite** if $\boldsymbol{bxb}' > 0$ for all row vectors $\boldsymbol{b} \neq \boldsymbol{0}$;
- **positive semidefinite** if $\boldsymbol{bxb}' \geq 0$ for all row vectors $\boldsymbol{b}$;
- **negative definite** if $\boldsymbol{bxb}' < 0$ for all row vectors $\boldsymbol{b} \neq \boldsymbol{0}$;
- **negative semidefinite** if $\boldsymbol{bxb}' \leq 0$ for all row vectors $\boldsymbol{b}$;
- **indefinite** if none of the above hold.

These definitions may seem abstruse, but they lead to an intuitively appealing result. A symmetric matrix $\boldsymbol{x}$ is:

- positive definite if all its eigenvalues are real and positive;
- positive semidefinite if all its eigenvalues are real and nonnegative;
- negative definite if all its eigenvalues are real and negative;
- negative semidefinite if all its eigenvalues are real and nonpositive;
- indefinite if none of the above hold.

It is useful to think of positive definite matrices as analogous to positive numbers and positive semidefinite matrices as analogous to nonnegative numbers. The essential difference between semidefinite matrices and their definite analogues is that the former can be singular whereas the latter cannot. This follows because a matrix is singular if and only if it has a 0 eigenvalue.

Matrix "Square Roots"

Nonnegative numbers have real square roots. Negative numbers do not. An analogous result holds for matrices. Any positive semidefinite matrix $\boldsymbol{h}$ can be factored in the form $\boldsymbol{h} = \boldsymbol{k}\boldsymbol{k}'$ for some real square matrix $\boldsymbol{k}$, which we may think of as a matrix square root of $\boldsymbol{h}$. The matrix $\boldsymbol{k}$ is not unique, so multiple factorizations of a given matrix $\boldsymbol{h}$ are possible. This is analogous to the fact that square roots of positive numbers are not unique either. If $\boldsymbol{h}$ is ***nonsingular*** (positive definite), $\boldsymbol{k}$ will be ***nonsingular***. If $\boldsymbol{h}$ is singular, $\boldsymbol{k}$ will be singular.

Cholesky Factorization

A particularly easy factorization $\boldsymbol{h} = \boldsymbol{k}\boldsymbol{k}'$ to perform is one known as the **Cholesky factorization**. Any positive semidefinite matrix has a factorization of the form $\boldsymbol{h} = \boldsymbol{g}\boldsymbol{g}'$ where $\boldsymbol{g}$ is a lower triangular matrix. Solving for $\boldsymbol{g}$ is straightforward. Suppose we wish to factor the positive definite matrix

$$\begin{pmatrix} 4 & -2 & -6 \\ -2 & 10 & 9 \\ -6 & 9 & 14 \end{pmatrix}. \qquad [2.75]$$

A Cholesky factorization takes the form

$$\begin{pmatrix} 4 & -2 & -6 \\ -2 & 10 & 9 \\ -6 & 9 & 14 \end{pmatrix} = \begin{pmatrix} g_{1,1} & 0 & 0 \\ g_{2,1} & g_{2,2} & 0 \\ g_{3,1} & g_{3,2} & g_{3,3} \end{pmatrix} \begin{pmatrix} g_{1,1} & g_{2,1} & g_{3,1} \\ 0 & g_{2,2} & g_{3,2} \\ 0 & 0 & g_{3,3} \end{pmatrix}. \qquad [2.76]$$

By inspection, $g_{1,1}^2 = 4$, so we set $g_{1,1} = 2$. Also by inspection, $g_{1,1}g_{2,1} = -2$. Since we already have $g_{1,1} = 2$, we conclude $g_{2,1} = -1$. Proceeding in this manner, we obtain a matrix $\boldsymbol{g}$ in 6 steps:

1. $g_{1,1}^2 = 4 \Rightarrow g_{1,1} = \sqrt{4} = 2,$
2. $g_{1,1}g_{2,1} = -2 \Rightarrow g_{2,1} = \dfrac{-2}{g_{1,1}} = -1,$
3. $g_{1,1}g_{3,1} = -6 \Rightarrow g_{3,1} = \dfrac{-6}{g_{1,1}} = -3,$
4. $g_{2,1}^2 + g_{2,2}^2 = 10 \Rightarrow g_{2,2} = \sqrt{9} = 3,$

5. $g_{2,1}g_{3,1} + g_{2,2}g_{3,2} = 9 \Rightarrow g_{3,2} = \dfrac{6}{g_{2,2}} = 2,$
6. $g_{3,1}^2 + g_{3,2}^2 + g_{3,3}^2 = 14 \Rightarrow g_{3,3} = \sqrt{1} = 1.$

Our Cholesky matrix is

$$g = \begin{pmatrix} 2 & 0 & 0 \\ -1 & 3 & 0 \\ -3 & 2 & 1 \end{pmatrix}. \qquad [2.77]$$

The above example illustrates a **Cholesky algorithm**, which generalizes for higher dimensional matrices. Our algorithm entails two types of calculations:

1. Calculating diagonal elements $g_{i,i}$ (steps 1, 4, and 6) entails taking a square root.
2. Calculating off-diagonal elements $g_{i,j}$, $i > j$ (steps 2, 3, and 5) entails dividing some number by the last-calculated diagonal element.

For a positive definite matrix $\boldsymbol{h}$, all diagonal elements $g_{i,i}$ will be nonzero. Solving for each entails taking the square root of a nonnegative number. We may take either the positive or negative root. Standard practice is to take only positive roots. Defined in this manner, the Cholesky matrix of a positive definite matrix is unique.

The same algorithm applies for singular positive semidefinite matrices $\boldsymbol{h}$, but the result is not generally called a Cholesky matrix. This is just an issue of terminology. When the algorithm is applied to the singular $\boldsymbol{h}$, at least one diagonal element $g_{i,i}$ equals 0. If only the last diagonal element $g_{n,n}$ equals 0, we can obtain $\boldsymbol{g}$ as we did in our example. If some other diagonal element $g_{i,i}$ equals 0, off-diagonal element $g_{i+1,i}$ will be indeterminate. We can set such indeterminate values equal to any value within an interval $[-a, a]$, for some $a \geq 0$.

Consider the matrix

$$\begin{pmatrix} 4 & 2 & -2 \\ 2 & 1 & -1 \\ -2 & -1 & 10 \end{pmatrix}. \qquad [2.78]$$

Performing the first four steps of our algorithm above, we obtain

$$\begin{pmatrix} 4 & 2 & -2 \\ 2 & 1 & -1 \\ -2 & -1 & 10 \end{pmatrix} = \begin{pmatrix} 2 & 0 & 0 \\ 1 & 0 & 0 \\ -1 & g_{3,2} & g_{3,3} \end{pmatrix} \begin{pmatrix} 2 & 1 & -1 \\ 0 & 0 & g_{3,2} \\ 0 & 0 & g_{3,3} \end{pmatrix}. \qquad [2.79]$$

In the fifth step, we multiply the second row of $\boldsymbol{g}$ by the third column of $\boldsymbol{g}'$ to obtain

$$g_{2,1}g_{3,1} + g_{2,2}g_{3,2} = -1. \qquad [2.80]$$

We already know $g_{2,1} = 1$, $g_{3,1} = -1$, and $g_{2,2} = 0$, so we have

$$(1)(-1) + 0g_{3,2} = -1, \qquad [2.81]$$

$$\Rightarrow 0g_{3,2} = 0, \qquad [2.82]$$

which provides us with no means of determining $g_{3,2}$. It is indeterminate, so we set it equal to a variable x and proceed with the algorithm. We obtain

$$g = \begin{pmatrix} 2 & 0 & 0 \\ 1 & 0 & 0 \\ -1 & x & \sqrt{9-x^2} \end{pmatrix}. \qquad [2.83]$$

For the element $g_{3,3}$ to be real, we can set x equal to any value in the interval $[-3, 3]$. The interval of acceptable values for indeterminate components will vary, but it will always include 0. For this reason, it is standard practice to set all indeterminate values equal to 0. With this selection, we obtain

$$g = \begin{pmatrix} 2 & 0 & 0 \\ 1 & 0 & 0 \\ -1 & 0 & 3 \end{pmatrix}. \qquad [2.84]$$

We can leave $\boldsymbol{g}$ in this form, or we can delete the second column, which contains only 0's. The resulting 3×2 matrix provides a valid factorization of $\boldsymbol{h}$ since

$$\boldsymbol{h} = \begin{pmatrix} 2 & 0 & 0 \\ 1 & 0 & 0 \\ -1 & 0 & 3 \end{pmatrix} \begin{pmatrix} 2 & 1 & -1 \\ 0 & 0 & 0 \\ 0 & 0 & 3 \end{pmatrix} = \begin{pmatrix} 2 & 0 \\ 1 & 0 \\ -1 & 3 \end{pmatrix} \begin{pmatrix} 2 & 1 & -1 \\ 0 & 0 & 3 \end{pmatrix}. \qquad [2.85]$$

If a symmetric matrix $\boldsymbol{h}$ is not positive semidefinite, our Cholesky algorithm will, at some point, attempt to take a square root of a negative number and fail. Accordingly, the Cholesky algorithm is a means of testing if a matrix is positive semidefinite.

Computational Issues

In exact arithmetic, our Cholesky algorithm will run to completion with all diagonal elements $g_{i,i} > 0$ if and only if the matrix $\boldsymbol{h}$ is positive definite. It will run to completion with all diagonal elements $g_{i,i} \geq 0$ and at least one diagonal element $g_{i,i} = 0$ if and only if the matrix $\boldsymbol{h}$ is singular positive semidefinite.

Things are more complicated if arithmetic is performed with rounding, as is done on a computer. Off-diagonal elements are obtained by dividing by diagonal elements. If a diagonal element is close to 0, any roundoff error may be magnified in such a division. For example, if a diagonal element should be .00000001, but roundoff error causes it to be calculated as .00000002, division by this number will yield an off-diagonal element that is half of what it should be.

An algorithm is said to be **unstable** if roundoff error can be magnified in this way or if it can cause the algorithm to fail. The Cholesky algorithm is unstable for singular positive semidefinite matrices $\boldsymbol{h}$. It is also unstable for positive definite matrices $\boldsymbol{h}$ that have one or more eigenvalues close to 0.

Exercises

2.10 Identify all factorizations of the following matrices that are obtainable with our Cholesky algorithm. Take only positive square roots when selecting nonzero diagonal elements $g_{i,i}$. In each case, is the original matrix positive definite, singular positive semidefinite, or neither of these?

a.

$$\begin{pmatrix} 9 & -3 & 3 \\ -3 & 2 & 1 \\ 3 & 1 & 6 \end{pmatrix}, \qquad [2.86]$$

b.

$$\begin{pmatrix} 4 & -2 & 2 \\ -2 & 1 & -1 \\ 2 & -1 & 5 \end{pmatrix}, \qquad [2.87]$$

c.

$$\begin{pmatrix} 1 & 2 & -1 \\ 2 & 5 & 1 \\ -1 & 1 & 10 \end{pmatrix}. \qquad [2.88]$$

2.8. MINIMIZING A QUADRATIC POLYNOMIAL

In this section, we consider how to minimize quadratic polynomials. This problem is equivalent to that of maximizing a polynomial, since any maximum of a quadratic polynomial p occurs at a minimum of the quadratic polynomial $-p$.

Recall from elementary calculus that any minimum on $\mathbb{R}$ of a differentiable function $f\colon \mathbb{R} \to \mathbb{R}$ occurs at a point x at which $f'(x) = 0$. Generalizing to multiple dimensions, any minimum on $\mathbb{R}^n$ of a differentiable function $f\colon \mathbb{R}^n \to \mathbb{R}$ occurs at a point $\boldsymbol{x}$ at which $\nabla f(\boldsymbol{x}) = 0$.

A quadratic polynomial $p\colon \mathbb{R} \to \mathbb{R}$

$$p(x) = cx^2 + bx + a \qquad [2.89]$$

has a unique minimum if and only if c is positive, in which case the minimum occurs at the point

$$x = -\frac{1}{2}c^{-1}b. \qquad [2.90]$$

This generalizes in a very intuitive manner to multiple dimensions. A quadratic polynomial $p\colon \mathbb{R}^n \to \mathbb{R}$

$$p(\boldsymbol{x}) = \boldsymbol{x}'\boldsymbol{c}\boldsymbol{x} + \boldsymbol{b}\boldsymbol{x} + a, \qquad [2.91]$$

has a unique minimum if and only if $\boldsymbol{c}$ is positive definite, in which case the minimum occurs at the point

$$\boldsymbol{x} = -\frac{1}{2}\boldsymbol{c}^{-1}\boldsymbol{b}'. \qquad [2.92]$$

Compare [2.92] with [2.90]. This is another situation in which positive definite matrices play a role analogous to positive numbers. To understand our result more intuitively, consider Exhibit 2.9. It shows graphs for three quadratic polynomials of the form [2.91] from $\mathbb{R}^2$ to $\mathbb{R}$. The first one has a positive definite matrix $\boldsymbol{c}$. Both of its eigenvalues are positive, and the polynomial has a minimum. The second polynomial has a matrix $\boldsymbol{c}$ with mixed eigenvalues. One is positive and the other is negative. The polynomial has a saddle shape, so it has neither a maximum nor a minimum. The third polynomial has a negative definite matrix $\boldsymbol{c}$. Both of its eigenvalues are negative, and the polynomial has a maximum.

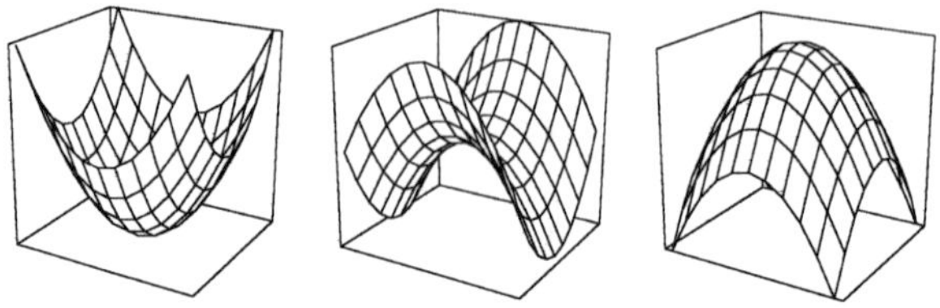

Exhibit 2.9 Three quadratic polynomials from $\mathbb{R}^2$ to $\mathbb{R}$ are graphed. The first has a positive definite matrix $\boldsymbol{c}$. It achieves a minimum. The second has matrix $\boldsymbol{c}$ with mixed eigenvalues—one is positive and the other is negative. It achieves neither a maximum nor a minimum. The third has a negative definite matrix $\boldsymbol{c}$. It achieves a maximum.

Exercises

2.11 Similar to the graphs of Exhibit 2.9, sketch a graph for a quadratic polynomial from $\mathbb{R}^2$ to $\mathbb{R}$ that has a positive semidefinite matrix $\boldsymbol{c}$. (Hint: Depending upon your solution, your polynomial will either have no minima or infinitely many.)

2.12 Repeat Exercise 2.11 assuming $\boldsymbol{c}$ is negative semidefinite.

2.13 Consider the quadratic polynomial $p: \mathbb{R}^3 \to \mathbb{R}$:

$$p(\boldsymbol{x}) = x_1^2 + x_2^2 + 2x_3^2 + 2x_1x_3 + 4x_2 + 5. \qquad [2.93]$$

a. Express the polynomial in matrix form [2.91]. Make sure your matrix $\boldsymbol{c}$ is symmetric.
b. Apply the Cholesky algorithm to determine if your matrix $\boldsymbol{c}$ is positive definite.
c. Solve for the point $\boldsymbol{x}$ indicated by [2.92].

d. What is the polynomial's value at the point $\boldsymbol{x}$ obtained in item (c)?
e. Is your solution a maximum, minimum, or saddle point?

2.9. ORDINARY LEAST SQUARES

The method of **least squares** is an alternative to interpolation for fitting a function to a set of points. Unlike interpolation, it does not require the fitted function to intersect each point. The method of least squares is probably best known for its use in statistical regression, but it is used in many contexts unrelated to statistics. The method encompasses many techniques. We present a fairly general approach called **ordinary least squares.**

EXAMPLE. Suppose researchers gather 10 data points $(x^{[k]}, y^{[k]})$ related to some phenomenon. We interpolate a ninth-order polynomial based upon the data. See Exhibits 2.10 and 2.11:

k	$x^{[k]}$	$y^{[k]}$
1	1.1	2.14
2	1.4	2.60
3	2.5	1.15
4	2.7	1.19
5	3.2	1.88
6	3.6	1.55
7	4.1	2.65
8	4.3	3.80
9	4.5	4.46
10	4.9	6.35

Exhibit 2.10 Ten example points.

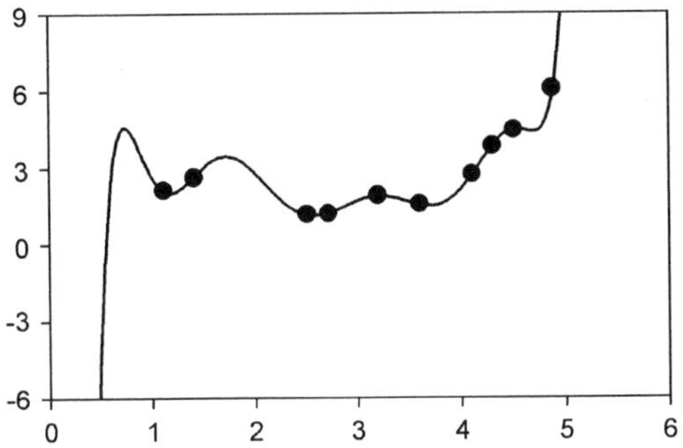

Exhibit 2.11 Interpolated ninth-order polynomial.

Because the polynomial is forced to intercept every point, it weaves up and down. In some applications, data may reflect random errors or other sources of "noise." Forcing a curve to pass through each point causes its shape to reflect such noise as much as any underlying process that generated the data. We say the interpolated function is **overfit** to the data. As an alternative, we may fit a curve to data without requiring that it intercept each point. A quadratic polynomial fit in this manner to the data of Exhibit 2.10 is illustrated in Exhibit 2.12

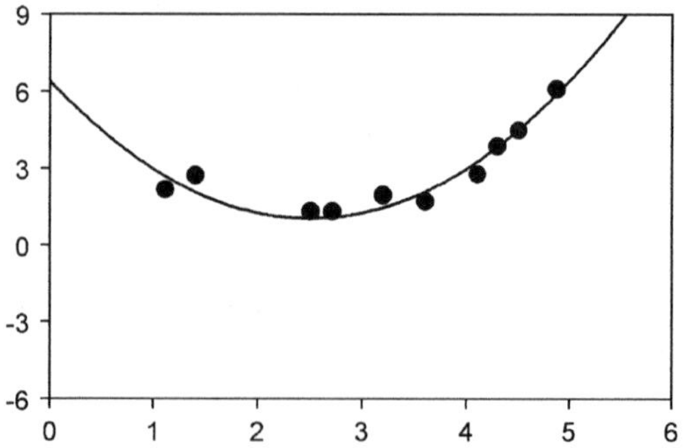

Exhibit 2.12 A quadratic polynomial fit to the data of Exhibit 2.10 using the method of ordinary least squares.

The polynomial of Exhibit 2.12 was constructed with the method of ordinary least squares. The form of the polynomial was specified as

$$f(x) = \beta_3 x^2 + \beta_2 x + \beta_1, \tag{2.94}$$

and the constants β_1, β_2, and β_3 were determined in such a manner as to minimize the sum of squares

$$\sum_{k=1}^{10} [f(x^{[k]}) - y^{[k]}]^2. \tag{2.95}$$

Ordinary Least Squares

Consider l points $(\boldsymbol{x}^{[k]}, y^{[k]})$ where $\boldsymbol{x}^{[k]} \in \mathbb{R}^n$, and $y^{[k]} \in \mathbb{R}$. We wish to fit a function $f: \mathbb{R}^n \to \mathbb{R}$ of form

$$f(\boldsymbol{x}) = \beta_m f_m(\boldsymbol{x}) + \beta_{m-1} f_{m-1}(\boldsymbol{x}) + \cdots + \beta_1 f_1(\boldsymbol{x}) \tag{2.96}$$

to the data in such a manner as to minimize the sum of squares

$$\sum_{k=1}^{l} [f(\boldsymbol{x}^{[k]}) - y^{[k]}]^2. \tag{2.97}$$

As with the interpolation methodology of Section 2.4, functions $f_j\colon \mathbb{R}^n \to \mathbb{R}$ can take any form. Unlike the interpolation methodology, we require that the number m of functions be less than the number l of points.

Let's express our problem with matrices. Define

$$\boldsymbol{\beta} = \begin{pmatrix} \beta_1 \\ \beta_2 \\ \vdots \\ \beta_m \end{pmatrix}. \qquad [2.98]$$

This is unknown. It is what we want to solve for. Define $\boldsymbol{f}$ as the $l \times m$ matrix comprising values of each function f_j evaluated at each point $\boldsymbol{x}^{[k]}$:

$$\boldsymbol{f} = \begin{pmatrix} f_1(\boldsymbol{x}^{[1]}) & f_2(\boldsymbol{x}^{[1]}) & \cdots & f_m(\boldsymbol{x}^{[1]}) \\ f_1(\boldsymbol{x}^{[2]}) & f_2(\boldsymbol{x}^{[2]}) & & f_m(\boldsymbol{x}^{[2]}) \\ \vdots & & \ddots & \vdots \\ f_1(\boldsymbol{x}^{[l]}) & f_2(\boldsymbol{x}^{[l]}) & \cdots & f_m(\boldsymbol{x}^{[l]}) \end{pmatrix}. \qquad [2.99]$$

Define the vector

$$\boldsymbol{y} = \begin{pmatrix} y^{[1]} \\ y^{[2]} \\ \vdots \\ y^{[l]} \end{pmatrix}. \qquad [2.100]$$

Both the matrix $\boldsymbol{f}$ and vector $\boldsymbol{y}$ are constants. They are known. We express sum-of-squares formula [2.97] as

$$\sum_{k=1}^{l} \left(f(\boldsymbol{x}^{[k]}) - y^{[k]}\right)^2 = (\boldsymbol{f}\boldsymbol{\beta} - \boldsymbol{y})'(\boldsymbol{f}\boldsymbol{\beta} - \boldsymbol{y}) \qquad [2.101]$$

$$= \boldsymbol{\beta}'\boldsymbol{f}'\boldsymbol{f}\boldsymbol{\beta} - 2\boldsymbol{y}'\boldsymbol{f}\boldsymbol{\beta} + \boldsymbol{y}'\boldsymbol{y}. \qquad [2.102]$$

This is a quadratic polynomial in $\boldsymbol{\beta}$ of the form [2.91], with $\boldsymbol{c} = \boldsymbol{f}'\boldsymbol{f}$. It can be shown that, for any matrix $\boldsymbol{h}$ that has independent columns, the product $\boldsymbol{h}'\boldsymbol{h}$ is positive definite. This is analogous to the fact that the square of any nonzero real number is a positive number. Accordingly, as long as $\boldsymbol{f}$ has linearly independent columns, our sum-of-squares formula [2.97] has a unique minimum. By [2.92], this occurs for

$$\boldsymbol{\beta} = -\frac{1}{2}(\boldsymbol{f}'\boldsymbol{f})^{-1}(-2\boldsymbol{y}'\boldsymbol{f})' = (\boldsymbol{f}'\boldsymbol{f})^{-1}\boldsymbol{f}'\boldsymbol{y}. \qquad [2.103]$$

EXAMPLE (*Continued*). Continuing with our example of fitting a quadratic polynomial to the data of Exhibit 2.10, we seek a polynomial

$$f(x) = \beta_3 f_3(x) + \beta_2 f_2(x) + \beta_1 f_1(x), \quad [2.104]$$

where

- $f_1(x) = 1$,
- $f_2(x) = x$,
- $f_3(x) = x^2$.

Let

$$\boldsymbol{\beta} = \begin{pmatrix} \beta_1 \\ \beta_2 \\ \beta_3 \end{pmatrix}. \quad [2.105]$$

We have

$$\boldsymbol{f} = \begin{pmatrix} f_1(x^{[1]}) & f_2(x^{[1]}) & f_3(x^{[1]}) \\ f_1(x^{[2]}) & f_2(x^{[2]}) & f_3(x^{[2]}) \\ & \vdots & \\ f_1(x^{[10]}) & f_2(x^{[10]}) & f_3(x^{[10]}) \end{pmatrix} = \begin{pmatrix} 1 & 1.1 & 1.21 \\ 1 & 1.4 & 1.96 \\ & \vdots & \\ 1 & 4.9 & 24.01 \end{pmatrix} \quad [2.106]$$

and

$$\boldsymbol{y} = \begin{pmatrix} y^{[1]} \\ y^{[2]} \\ \vdots \\ y^{[10]} \end{pmatrix} = \begin{pmatrix} 2.14 \\ 2.60 \\ \vdots \\ 6.35 \end{pmatrix}. \quad [2.107]$$

Applying [2.103], we obtain

$$\boldsymbol{\beta} = \begin{pmatrix} 6.367 \\ -4.277 \\ 0.856 \end{pmatrix}, \quad [2.108]$$

and our quadratic polynomial is

$$f(x) = 0.856x^2 - 4.277x + 6.367, \quad [2.109]$$

which was graphed in Exhibit 2.12.

Exercises

2.14 Use ordinary least squares to fit a linear polynomial

$$f(x) = \beta_2 x + \beta_1 \qquad [2.110]$$

to the five points indicated in Exhibit 2.13.

k	$x^{[k]}$	$y^{[k]}$
1	1	13
2	2	10
3	3	11
4	4	8
5	5	6

Exhibit 2.13 Point set for Exercise 2.14.

2.15 Use ordinary least squares to fit a function of the form

$$f(\mathbf{x}) = \beta_2 \, log(x_1 x_2) + \beta_1 \qquad [2.111]$$

to the five points indicated in Exhibit 2.14.

k	$(x_1^{[k]}, x_2^{[k]})$	$y^{[k]}$
1	(1, 4)	0.55
2	(2, 3)	2.17
3	(2, 5)	4.31
4	(4, 2)	3.32
5	(6, 3)	6.51

Exhibit 2.14 Point set for Exercise 2.15.

2.16 Prove that, if the number m of functions f_j equals the number l of points $(\mathbf{x}^{[k]}, y^{[k]})$, then the least squares solution [2.103] reduces to the interpolation solution [2.49]. In this regard, ordinary least squares is a generalization of ordinary interpolation.

2.10. CUBIC SPLINE INTERPOLATION

The method of least squares provides, among other things, an alternative to ordinary interpolation that avoids the problem of overfitting. Another alternative is spline interpolation, which encompasses a range of interpolation techniques that reduce the effects of overfitting. The method of cubic spline interpolation presented here is widely used in finance. It applies only in one dimension, but is useful for modeling yield curves, forward curves, and other term structures.

A **cubic spline** is a function $f(x): \mathbb{R} \to \mathbb{R}$ constructed by piecing together cubic polynomials $p_k(x)$ on different intervals $[x^{[k]}, x^{[k+1]}]$. It has the form

$$f(x) = \begin{cases} p_1(x) & x^{[1]} \leq x < x^{[2]}, \\ p_2(x) & x^{[2]} \leq x < x^{[3]}, \\ \vdots & \vdots \\ p_{m-1}(x) & x^{[m-1]} \leq x \leq x^{[m]}. \end{cases} \qquad [2.112]$$

Consider points $(x^{[1]}, y^{[1]}), (x^{[2]}, y^{[2]}), \ldots, (x^{[m]}, y^{[m]})$, with $x^{[1]} < x^{[2]} \cdots < x^{[m]}$. We construct a cubic spline by interpolating a cubic polynomial p_k between each pair of consecutive points $(x^{[k]}, y^{[k]})$ and $(x^{[k+1]}, y^{[k+1]})$ according to the following constraints:

1. Each polynomial passes through its respective end points:
$$p_k\left(x^{[k]}\right) = y^{[k]} \quad \text{and} \quad p_k\left(x^{[k+1]}\right) = y^{[k+1]}. \qquad [2.113]$$
2. First derivatives match at interior points:
$$\frac{d}{dx} p_k\left(x^{[k+1]}\right) = \frac{d}{dx} p_{k+1}\left(x^{[k+1]}\right). \qquad [2.114]$$
3. Second derivatives match at interior points:
$$\frac{d^2}{dx^2} p_k\left(x^{[k+1]}\right) = \frac{d^2}{dx^2} p_{k+1}\left(x^{[k+1]}\right). \qquad [2.115]$$
4. Second derivatives vanish at the end points:
$$\frac{d^2}{dx^2} p_1\left(x^{[1]}\right) = 0 \quad \text{and} \quad \frac{d^2}{dx^2} p_{m-1}\left(x^{[m]}\right) = 0. \qquad [2.116]$$

The above conditions specify a system of linear equations that can be solved for the cubic spline. In practice, it makes little sense to fit a cubic spline to fewer than five points. However, for the purpose of illustration, let's interpolate a cubic spline between just three points.

Consider the points $(x^{[k]}, y^{[k]}) = (1, 1), (2, 5), (3, 4)$. We seek to fit a cubic polynomial on the interval $[1, 2]$ and another cubic polynomial on the interval $[2, 3]$. These take the forms

$$p_1(x) = \delta_1 x^3 + \gamma_1 x^2 + \beta_1 x + \alpha_1, \qquad [2.117]$$

$$p_2(x) = \delta_2 x^3 + \gamma_2 x^2 + \beta_2 x + \alpha_2. \qquad [2.118]$$

Our first condition requires

$$p_1(1) = 1, \qquad [2.119]$$

$$p_1(2) = 5, \qquad [2.120]$$

$$p_2(2) = 5, \qquad [2.121]$$

$$p_2(3) = 4. \qquad [2.122]$$

The second condition requires

$$p_1'(2) = p_2'(2). \quad [2.123]$$

The third condition requires

$$p_1''(2) = p_2''(2). \quad [2.124]$$

Finally, the last condition requires

$$p_1''(1) = 0, \quad [2.125]$$

$$p_2''(3) = 0. \quad [2.126]$$

We have eight equations in eight unknowns. These can be expressed as

$$\begin{pmatrix} 1 & 1 & 1 & 1 & 0 & 0 & 0 & 0 \\ 8 & 4 & 2 & 1 & 0 & 0 & 0 & 0 \\ 0 & 0 & 0 & 0 & 8 & 4 & 2 & 1 \\ 0 & 0 & 0 & 0 & 27 & 9 & 3 & 1 \\ 12 & 4 & 1 & 0 & -12 & -4 & -1 & 0 \\ 12 & 2 & 0 & 0 & -12 & -2 & 0 & 0 \\ 6 & 2 & 0 & 0 & 0 & 0 & 0 & 0 \\ 0 & 0 & 0 & 0 & 18 & 2 & 0 & 0 \end{pmatrix} \begin{pmatrix} \delta_1 \\ \gamma_1 \\ \beta_1 \\ \alpha_1 \\ \delta_2 \\ \gamma_2 \\ \beta_2 \\ \alpha_2 \end{pmatrix} = \begin{pmatrix} 1 \\ 5 \\ 5 \\ 4 \\ 0 \\ 0 \\ 0 \\ 0 \end{pmatrix}, \quad [2.127]$$

which we solve to obtain

$$\begin{pmatrix} \delta_1 \\ \gamma_1 \\ \beta_1 \\ \alpha_1 \\ \delta_2 \\ \gamma_2 \\ \beta_2 \\ \alpha_2 \end{pmatrix} = \begin{pmatrix} -1.25 \\ 3.75 \\ 1.50 \\ -3.00 \\ 1.25 \\ -11.25 \\ 31.50 \\ -23.00 \end{pmatrix}. \quad [2.128]$$

Our two polynomials are

$$p_1(x) = -1.25x^3 + 3.75x^2 + 1.50x + -3.00, \quad [2.129]$$

$$p_2(x) = 1.25x^3 + -11.25x^2 + 31.50x + -23.00. \quad [2.130]$$

The cubic spline, along with the three points upon which it is based, is shown in Exhibit 2.15:

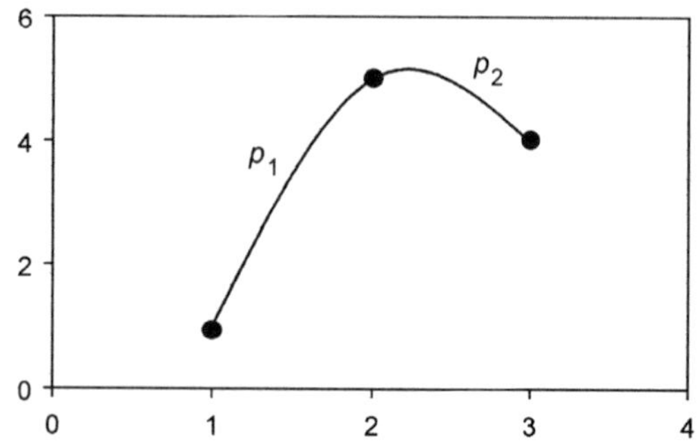

Exhibit 2.15 A cubic spline interpolated between the points $(x^{[k]}, y^{[k]}) = (1, 1), (2, 5), (3, 4)$ is constructed from two cubic polynomials p_1 and p_2.

Exercises

2.17 Interpolate a cubic spline between the three points (0, 1), (2, 2), and (4, 0).

2.11. FINITE DIFFERENCE APPROXIMATIONS OF DERIVATIVES

Suppose the derivative of a function $f: \mathbb{R} \to \mathbb{R}$ is needed at a specific point $x^{[0]}$. If an analytic expression for f' is unavailable, the derivative can be approximated based upon a **finite difference**:

$$\left.\frac{df}{dx}\right|_{x^{[0]}} \approx \frac{f\left(x^{[0]} + h/2\right) - f\left(x^{[0]} - h/2\right)}{h}. \qquad [2.131]$$

The scalar h should be small, but not so small that roundoff error distorts the result. Often, the value $f(x^{[0]})$ is already known. If valuing f at two additional points will be computationally expensive, one valuation can be avoided by using the alternative approximation:

$$\left.\frac{df}{dx}\right|_{x^{[0]}} \approx \frac{f\left(x^{[0]} + h\right) - f\left(x^{[0]}\right)}{h}. \qquad [2.132]$$

We call [2.131] a central approximation and [2.132] a forward approximation. These generalize to multiple dimensions. A partial derivative of a function $f: \mathbb{R}^n \to \mathbb{R}$ can be approximated at point $\boldsymbol{x}^{[0]}$ with a central approximation:

$$\left.\frac{\partial f}{\partial x_i}\right|_{\boldsymbol{x}^{[0]}} \approx \frac{f\left(\boldsymbol{x}^{[0]} + \boldsymbol{e}_i h/2\right) - f\left(\boldsymbol{x}^{[0]} - \boldsymbol{e}_i h/2\right)}{h}, \qquad [2.133]$$

where $\boldsymbol{e}_i$ is a vector whose only nonzero component is its ith component, which equals 1. The corresponding forward approximation is

$$\left.\frac{\partial f}{\partial x_i}\right|_{\boldsymbol{x}^{[0]}} \approx \frac{f\left(\boldsymbol{x}^{[0]} + \boldsymbol{e}_i h\right) - f\left(\boldsymbol{x}^{[0]}\right)}{h}. \qquad [2.134]$$

Exercises

2.18 Consider $f\colon \mathbb{R}^2 \to \mathbb{R}^2$:

$$f(\boldsymbol{x}) = (exp(x_1 x_2), 3x_2). \qquad [2.135]$$

Value the Jacobian matrix of f at $\boldsymbol{x} = (1, 1)$ three different ways:
a. analytically,
b. with a central approximation,
c. with a forward approximation.
In items (b) and (c), use $h = .00001$.

2.12. NEWTON'S METHOD

Newton's method is a numerical technique for solving equations of the form

$$f(\boldsymbol{x}) = \boldsymbol{0}, \qquad [2.136]$$

where $f\colon \mathbb{R}^n \to \mathbb{R}^n$ is differentiable. It starts with an initial guess or "seed" value $\boldsymbol{x}^{[1]}$, which the user supplies. Based upon this, the procedure recursively generates a sequence of values $\boldsymbol{x}^{[2]}, \boldsymbol{x}^{[3]}, \boldsymbol{x}^{[4]}, \ldots$, which should converge to a solution.

Univariate Newton's Method

In the univariate case, we consider $f\colon \mathbb{R} \to \mathbb{R}$ and seek a value x such that

$$f(x) = 0. \qquad [2.137]$$

If f is nonlinear, this may be difficult to solve directly. However, we can fit a linear polynomial approximation $\tilde{f}$ to f and easily solve

$$\tilde{f}(x) = 0. \qquad [2.138]$$

The solution approximates a solution to the original equation [2.137]. The quality of the approximation depends upon how we construct $\tilde{f}$. Newton's method repeats this process recursively, at each step improving its approximation $\tilde{f}$ of f until the solution for [2.138] comes sufficiently close to a solution for [2.137].

Start with seed value $x^{[1]}$. Fit a tangent-line approximation $\tilde{f}^{[1]}$ to f:

$$\tilde{f}^{[1]}(x) = f\left(x^{[1]}\right) + f'\left(x^{[1]}\right)\left(x - x^{[1]}\right), \qquad [2.139]$$

and select $x^{[2]}$ as the solution to

$$\tilde{f}^{[1]}(x) = 0. \qquad [2.140]$$

This is illustrated in Exhibit 2.16.

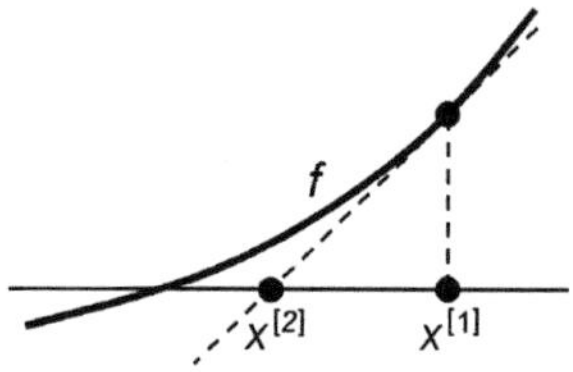

Exhibit 2.16 Value $x^{[2]}$ is obtained from seed value $x^{[1]}$ by fitting a tangent line approximation $\tilde{f}^{[1]}$ to f and setting $x^{[2]}$ equal to the solution of $\tilde{f}^{[1]}(x^{[2]}) = 0$.

Repeat the process at $x^{[2]}$ to obtain $\tilde{f}^{[2]}$ and $x^{[3]}$. Subsequent $\tilde{f}^{[k]}$ and $x^{[k+1]}$ are obtained recursively in this manner. In general

$$\tilde{f}^{[k]}(x) = f\left(x^{[k]}\right) + f'\left(x^{[k]}\right)\left(x - x^{[k]}\right). \qquad [2.141]$$

Setting this equal to 0 and solving for $x^{[k+1]}$ yields

$$x^{[k+1]} = x^{[k]} - \frac{f\left(x^{[k]}\right)}{f'\left(x^{[k]}\right)}. \qquad [2.142]$$

This is the general recursive formula for the univariate Newton's method.

EXAMPLE: UNIVARIATE NEWTON'S METHOD. Consider the equation

$$x^8 + 5x - 10 = 0. \qquad [2.143]$$

In this case,

$$f(x) = x^8 + 5x - 10, \qquad [2.144]$$

and

$$f'(x) = 8x^7 + 5. \qquad [2.145]$$

Starting with seed value $x^{[1]} = 1$, apply [2.142] recursively. Results are indicated in Exhibit 2.17. Equation [2.143] has solution $x = 1.19089$.

k	$x^{[k]}$	$f(x^{[k]})$
1	1.00000	-4.00000
2	1.30769	5.09001
3	1.21889	0.96637
4	1.19275	0.06010
5	1.19090	0.00028
6	1.19089	0.00000

Exhibit 2.17 Results of applying Newton's method to solve Equation [2.143].

Caveats

The univariate Newton's method is easy to implement and usually converges rapidly. In theory, it can fail. This will happen if $f'(x^{[k]}) = 0$ for some k or if f has an inconvenient shape. Such a circumstance is depicted in Exhibit 2.18. These problems may be solved by starting at a different seed value $x^{[1]}$.

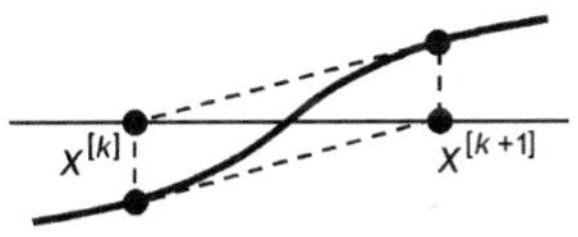

Exhibit 2.18 It is possible for Newton's method to fail to converge to a solution. In this example, it enters a continual loop.

Equation [2.137] need not have any solutions, so failure of Newton's method to converge may indicate that no solutions exist. Alternatively, [2.137] may have multiple solutions. For any given seed value, Newton's method will find only one solution. Starting with other seed values may allow us to find others, but Newton's method may converge to the same solution found with the first seed value. In this situation, Newton's method must be supplemented with other analyses to ensure all solutions are found. Suitable analyses will depend upon the form of Equation [2.137].

Secant Method

If an analytic expression for the derivative of f is unavailable, it can be approximated using finite differences. Another alternative is the **secant method**, which is a modification of Newton's method. Using the same general approach as Newton's method, it replaces tangent lines with secant lines interpolated between consecutive points $x^{[k]}$ and $x^{[k+1]}$, as illustrated in Exhibit 2.19:

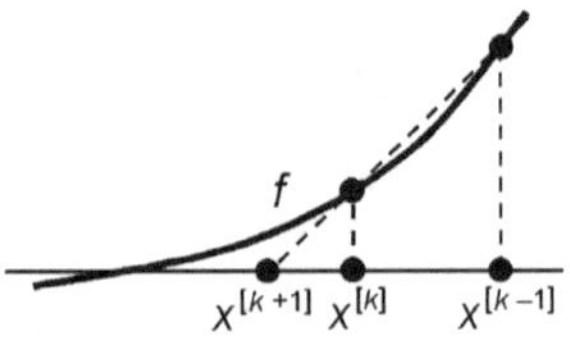

Exhibit 2.19 The secant method is similar to Newton's method, but it replaces tangent lines with secant lines.

In recursive formula [2.142] of Newton's method, the derivative $f'(x^{[k]})$ is replaced with the secant line slope

$$\frac{f\left(x^{[k]}\right) - f\left(x^{[k-1]}\right)}{x^{[k]} - x^{[k-1]}}. \qquad [2.146]$$

Given values $x^{[k-1]}$ and $x^{[k]}$, subsequent value $x^{[k+1]}$ is obtained as

$$x^{[k+1]} = x^{[k]} - \frac{f\left(x^{[k]}\right)\left[x^{[k]} - x^{[k-1]}\right]}{f\left(x^{[k]}\right) - f\left(x^{[k-1]}\right)}. \qquad [2.147]$$

The secant method is initialized with two seed values $x^{[1]}$ and $x^{[2]}$. The function f need not be differentiable. As long as it is continuous and reasonably well behaved, the secant method generally performs well, but convergence issues similar to those with Newton's method arise.

Multivariate Newton's Method

Newton's method generalizes naturally to multiple dimensions. We seek a solution $\boldsymbol{x}$ for

$$f(\boldsymbol{x}) = \boldsymbol{0} \qquad [2.148]$$

where $f\colon \mathbb{R}^n \to \mathbb{R}^n$ is differentiable. Start with seed value $\boldsymbol{x}^{[1]}$, and recursively obtain subsequent values $\boldsymbol{x}^{[2]}, \boldsymbol{x}^{[3]}, \boldsymbol{x}^{[4]}, \ldots$ as follows. At each value $\boldsymbol{x}^{[k]}$, construct Jacobian approximation $\tilde{f}^{[k]}$ for f:

$$\tilde{f}^{[k]}(\boldsymbol{x}) = f\left(\boldsymbol{x}^{[k]}\right) + Jf\left(\boldsymbol{x}^{[k]}\right)\left(\boldsymbol{x} - \boldsymbol{x}^{[k]}\right), \qquad [2.149]$$

and select $\boldsymbol{x}^{[k+1]}$ as the solution to

$$\tilde{f}^{[k]}(\boldsymbol{x}) = \boldsymbol{0}. \qquad [2.150]$$

Substituting [2.149] into [2.150] and setting $\boldsymbol{x} = \boldsymbol{x}^{[k+1]}$ yields the recursive equation

$$\boldsymbol{x}^{[k+1]} = \boldsymbol{x}^{[k]} - \left[Jf\left(\boldsymbol{x}^{[k]}\right)\right]^{-1} f\left(\boldsymbol{x}^{[k]}\right), \qquad [2.151]$$

which generalizes [2.142].

Newton's method entails similar convergence issues in multiple dimensions as in a single dimension. Just as the univariate method fails if $f'(x^{[k]}) = 0$, so will the multivariate method fail if $Jf(\boldsymbol{x}^{[k]})$ is singular. Issues of no solution or multiple solutions also arise.

If an analytic formula for the Jacobian of f is unavailable, there is a generalization of the secant method called **Broyden's method**. See Dennis and Schnabel (1983) or Burden and Faires (1993). A simpler solution is to apply Newton's method using finite differences to approximate the Jacobian matrix.

Line Searches

For Newton's method, define the kth **step length** as $\|\boldsymbol{x}^{[k+1]} - \boldsymbol{x}^{[k]}\|$. By construction, $\widetilde{f}^{[k]}$ tends to approximate f best near $\boldsymbol{x}^{[k]}$, so small step lengths are desirable. It is the nature of Newton's method that step lengths tend to decrease as it approaches a solution. For this reason, convergence is excellent close to a solution, but can be poor further from a solution. Line searches are a technique for selectively shortening step lengths during the first few iterations of Newton's method. They are invaluable in situations where a seed value $\boldsymbol{x}^{[1]}$ may be some distance from a solution.

Suppose we are performing Newton's method on a function $f\colon \mathbb{R}^2 \to \mathbb{R}^2$. Newton's method has just determined point $\boldsymbol{x}^{[k]}$. It and subsequent point $\boldsymbol{x}^{[k+1]}$ are plotted in Exhibit 2.20, which is a topographical graph. It indicates contour lines on which $\|f(\boldsymbol{x})\|$ is constant.

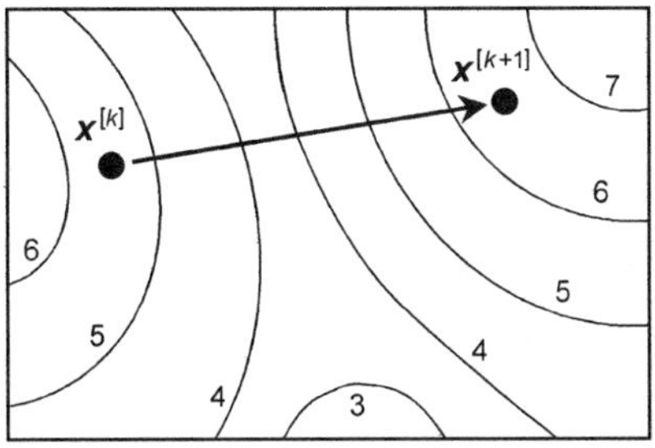

Exhibit 2.20 A topographical graph of the norm $\|f(\boldsymbol{x})\|$ for $f\colon \mathbb{R}^2 \to \mathbb{R}^2$. Numbers next to contour lines indicate the value of $\|f(\boldsymbol{x})\|$ on those lines. In the example, an iteration of Newton's method causes the norm of f to increase going from $\boldsymbol{x}^{[k]}$ to $\boldsymbol{x}^{[k+1]}$. As illustrated, this is due to the large step size.

Since our goal is to find a value $\boldsymbol{x}$ such that $f(\boldsymbol{x}) = 0$, we expect the norm $\|f(\boldsymbol{x}^{[k]})\|$ to diminish with each iteration of Newton's method. In the specific iteration illustrated in Exhibit 2.20, this does not happen. Moving along the line that connects $\boldsymbol{x}^{[k]}$ and $\boldsymbol{x}^{[k+1]}$, the norm $\|f(\boldsymbol{x})\|$ initially does decrease—from over 5 to less than 4. By the time we reach $\boldsymbol{x}^{[k+1]}$, however, it has risen again to exceed 6. The step length is too long. We may address the problem by searching backwards along the line between $\boldsymbol{x}^{[k]}$ and $\boldsymbol{x}^{[k+1]}$ to find a more suitable value to use in place of $\boldsymbol{x}^{[k+1]}$. This is called a **line search**. Line searches are performed in various ways. They raise two questions:

1. When should we use them?
2. How should we perform them?

When Newton's method is close to a solution, it doesn't make sense to perform line searches. Convergence will be rapid anyway, so there is no need to encumber the process. Since we have no way of knowing if Newton's method is near a solution, we need some criteria to determine at which iterations to perform a line search. A simple criterion is to require:[6]

$$\left\| f\left(\boldsymbol{x}^{[k+1]}\right) \right\| < \left\| f\left(\boldsymbol{x}^{[k]}\right) \right\| \qquad [2.152]$$

and perform a line search if the criterion is not met.

If a line search is called for, it is performed by approximating f with a quadratic polynomial on the line between $\boldsymbol{x}^{[k]}$ and $\boldsymbol{x}^{[k+1]}$. Define $g\colon \mathbb{R} \to \mathbb{R}$ as the restriction of $\| f \|$ to that line:

$$g(\lambda) = \left\| f\left([1-\lambda]\boldsymbol{x}^{[k]} + \lambda \boldsymbol{x}^{[k+1]}\right) \right\|, \quad \lambda \in [0, 1]. \qquad [2.153]$$

We have

$$g(0) = \left\| f\left(\boldsymbol{x}^{[k]}\right) \right\|, \qquad [2.154]$$

$$g'(0) = \frac{-\left\| f\left(\boldsymbol{x}^{[k]}\right) \right\|}{\left\| \boldsymbol{x}^{[k+1]} - \boldsymbol{x}^{[k]} \right\|}, \qquad [2.155]$$

$$g(1) = \left\| f\left(\boldsymbol{x}^{[k+1]}\right) \right\|, \qquad [2.156]$$

and from these construct quadratic approximation $\widetilde{g}$ for g:

$$\widetilde{g}(\lambda) = [g(1) - g(0) - g'(0)]\lambda^2 + g'(0)\lambda + g(0). \qquad [2.157]$$

This is minimized at

$$\lambda = \frac{-g'(0)}{2[g(1) - g(0) - g'(0)]}. \qquad [2.158]$$

We set

$$\lambda^* = max\left(\frac{-g'(0)}{2[g(1) - g(0) - g'(0)]}, 0.1\right), \qquad [2.159]$$

[6]See Dennis and Schnabel (1983) for a more sophisticated solution.

which satisfies

$$\lambda^* \in [0.1, 0.5]. \qquad [2.160]$$

Let $\boldsymbol{x}^*$ be the value for $\boldsymbol{x}$ corresponding to λ^*

$$\boldsymbol{x}^* = [1 - \lambda^*]\boldsymbol{x}^{[k]} + \lambda^* \boldsymbol{x}^{[k+1]}. \qquad [2.161]$$

Replace the unacceptable value for $\boldsymbol{x}^{[k+1]}$ with $\boldsymbol{x}^*$. We are not yet done because our new value $\boldsymbol{x}^{[k+1]}$ was obtained with quadratic approximation [2.157] and a minimum bound of 0.1 for λ^*, so it may also fail criterion [2.152]. If it satisfies the criterion, proceed to the next iteration of Newton's method. Otherwise, perform another line search based upon $\boldsymbol{x}^{[k]}$ and the new $\boldsymbol{x}^{[k+1]}$.

Line searches may be ineffective if components f_i of f have different magnitudes in a neighborhood of a solution. Consider a function $f\colon \mathbb{R}^2 \to \mathbb{R}^2$ whose components f_1 and f_2 have magnitudes on the order of 10^6 and 10^{-4} near a solution. Then $\| f \|$ will be dominated by the value of f_1, causing criterion [2.152] to largely ignore convergence with regard to f_2. This problem can usually be solved with scaling. Define the function

$$\dot{f}(\boldsymbol{x}) = (f_1(\boldsymbol{x})/a_1,\ f_2(\boldsymbol{x})/a_2, \ldots, f_n(\boldsymbol{x})/a_n), \qquad [2.162]$$

where the a_i are selected so that the components of $\dot{f}$ all have similar magnitudes in a neighborhood of a solution. Then apply Newton's method with line searches to solve

$$\dot{f}(\boldsymbol{x}) = 0. \qquad [2.163]$$

Exercises

2.19 Use Newton's method with seed value $x^{[1]} = 0$ to solve the equation:

$$e^x - 3x^2 = 0. \qquad [2.164]$$

2.20 Use the secant method with seed values $x^{[1]} = 0$ and $x^{[2]} = 1$ to solve the same equation as in the previous exercise.

2.21 Use Newton's method with line searches to solve $f(\boldsymbol{x}) = 0$, where $f\colon \mathbb{R}^2 \to \mathbb{R}^2$ is defined as

$$f(\boldsymbol{x}) = \left(x_1^2 x_2^3 - x_1 x_2^3 - 1,\ x_1^3 - x_1 x_2^3 - 4\right). \qquad [2.165]$$

Use seed value $\boldsymbol{x}^{[1]} = (1, 1)$. Do not use scaling.

2.13. CHANGE OF VARIABLES FORMULA

The most basic arithmetic operation is addition. Integral calculus generalizes this operation with the definite integral, which is a generalized sum. Definite integrals will play an important role in our discussions of value-at-risk (VaR). Indeed, the task of calculating a portfolio's VaR is largely one of valuing a definite integral.

Definite integrals can often be simplified through a judicious change of variables. If an integral is to be valued using numerical techniques, a change of variables may be essential to avoid a singularity or to convert an unbounded region of integration into one that is bounded. The notion of changing variables is as old as addition itself. It is easier to count eggs in dozens than to count them individually.

For a one-dimensional integral over an interval $[a, b]$, an invertible, continuously differentiable change of variables $x = g(u)$ yields

$$\int_a^b f(x)dx = \int_{g^{-1}(a)}^{g^{-1}(b)} f(g(u))g'(u)du. \qquad [2.166]$$

For example:

$$\int_3^5 \left(x + \frac{1}{x}\right)dx = \int_{\sqrt{3}}^{\sqrt{5}} \left(u^2 + \frac{1}{u^2}\right)2u\,du. \qquad [2.167]$$

Generalizing to multiple dimensions, consider integrable function $f\colon \mathbb{R}^n \to \mathbb{R}$ and invertible, continuously differentiable change of variables $g\colon \mathbb{R}^n \to \mathbb{R}^n$ Then

$$\int_\Omega f(\boldsymbol{x})d\boldsymbol{x} = \int_{g^{-1}(\Omega)} f(g(\boldsymbol{u}))\,|Jg(\boldsymbol{u})|d\boldsymbol{u}, \qquad [2.168]$$

where $\Omega \subset \mathbb{R}^n$, and $|Jg(\boldsymbol{u})|$ is the determinant of the Jacobian of g. Consider integral:

$$\int_\Omega exp\left(\frac{x_1 - x_2}{x_1 + x_2}\right)dx_1dx_2, \qquad [2.169]$$

where the region Ω is indicated in Exhibit 2.21.

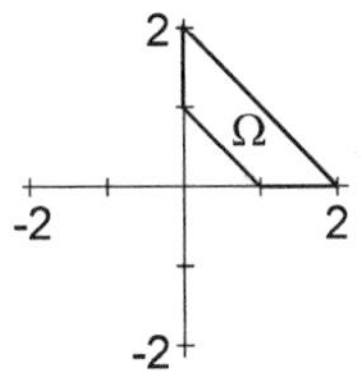

Exhibit 2.21 The region Ω is bounded by the four lines $x_1 = 0$, $x_2 = 0$, $x_2 = 1 - x_1$, and $x_2 = 2 - x_1$.

Integral [2.169] is difficult to solve directly, but consider the change of variables $\boldsymbol{x} = g(\boldsymbol{u})$ defined by

$$(x_1, x_2) = (g_1(\boldsymbol{u}), g_2(\boldsymbol{u})) = \left(\frac{u_2 + u_1}{2}, \frac{u_2 - u_1}{2}\right). \qquad [2.170]$$

The Jacobian determinant of g is

$$|Jg(\boldsymbol{u})| = \begin{vmatrix} \dfrac{\partial g_1}{\partial u_1} & \dfrac{\partial g_1}{\partial u_2} \\ \dfrac{\partial g_2}{\partial u_1} & \dfrac{\partial g_2}{\partial u_2} \end{vmatrix} = \begin{vmatrix} 1/2 & 1/2 \\ -1/2 & 1/2 \end{vmatrix} = 1/2, \qquad [2.171]$$

so, by [2.168], the integral becomes

$$\int_{g^{-1}(\Omega)} exp\left(\frac{u_1}{u_2}\right)\frac{1}{2}du_1du_2. \qquad [2.172]$$

Region $g^{-1}(\Omega)$ is indicated in Exhibit 2.22. It has twice the area of the original region Ω, so it should come as no surprise that the Jacobian determinant introduces an offsetting scaling factor of 1/2 into integral [2.172]. Region $g^{-1}(\Omega)$ has a

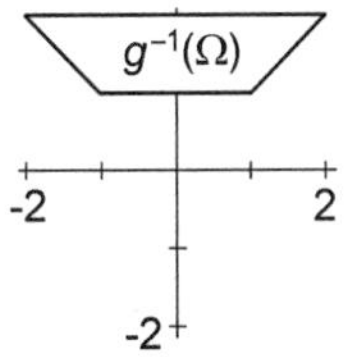

Exhibit 2.22 The region $g^{-1}(\Omega)$ is bounded by the four lines $u_2 = 1$, $u_2 = 2$, $u_2 = u_1$, and $u_2 = -u_1$.

convenient shape, which allows us to represent the integral as

$$\int_{1}^{2}\int_{-u_2}^{u_2} exp\left(\frac{u_1}{u_2}\right)\frac{1}{2}du_1du_2. \quad [2.173]$$

This is easily valued as 0.8146.

Exercises

2.22 Use change of variables $x = g(u) = \sqrt{(u-1)/5}$ to value the integral

$$\int_{1}^{2}\frac{x}{(5x^2+1)}dx. \quad [2.174]$$

2.23 Consider the integral

$$\int_{-1}^{0}\int_{2x_2+2}^{x_2+2}\left(x_2^2 - x_1x_2 - x_1 + 2x_2 + 1\right)dx_1dx_2. \quad [2.175]$$

a. Solve the integral directly.
b. Solve the integral using the change of variables $\boldsymbol{x} = g(\boldsymbol{u})$ defined by

$$(x_1, x_2) = (g_1(\boldsymbol{u}), g_2(\boldsymbol{u})) = (u_1 + 2u_2, u_1 - 1). \quad [2.176]$$

(Hint: Sketch the regions of integration Ω and $g^{-1}(\Omega)$.)

2.14. NUMERICAL INTEGRATION IN ONE DIMENSION

The fundamental theorem of calculus provides an explicit formula for the value of a definite integral. Let f be a real-valued function with antiderivative F, both defined on some open interval that contains points a and b. Then

$$\int_{a}^{b} f(x)dx = F(b) - F(a). \quad [2.177]$$

If we lack an expression for the anti-derivative F, we cannot apply the fundamental theorem of calculus, but the integral can be valued using numerical methods of integration. In this section, we consider techniques based upon Riemann sums or generalizations of Riemann sums.

Riemann Sums

Assume $f\colon \mathbb{R} \to \mathbb{R}$ is Riemann integrable. We want to evaluate the definite integral

$$\int_a^b f(x)dx \qquad [2.178]$$

for some $a, b \in \mathbb{R}$. With the method of Riemann sums we approximate the integral by dividing the interval $[a, b]$ into m subintervals and approximating f with a constant function on each subinterval.

For any positive integer m, we define a **partition** P of $[a, b]$ as $m + 1$ points $x^{[0]} < x^{[1]} < \cdots < x^{[m]}$, where $x^{[0]} = a$, $x^{[m]} = b$ and consecutive $x^{[k]}$ are spaced a constant length $\Delta x = (b - a)/m$ apart. We approximate our definite integral [2.178] with a Riemann sum:

$$\int_a^b f(x)dx \approx \sum_{k=1}^{m} f\left(x^{[k]}\right)\Delta x. \qquad [2.179]$$

Example: Riemann Sums. As will be discussed in Chapter 3, a standard normal random variable has a probability of being between 0 and 1 that is given by the integral

$$\int_0^1 \frac{e^{-x^2/2}}{\sqrt{2\pi}}dx. \qquad [2.180]$$

There are more efficient ways this might be evaluated, but let's approximate a solution with a Riemann sum. Setting $m = 10$, our subinterval length Δx is .10. Computations are presented in Exhibit 2.23.

$x^{[k]}$ [1]	$\phi(x^{[k]})$ [2]	Δx [3]	$\phi(x^{[k]})\Delta x$ [2][3]
0.0	–		–
0.1	0.396953	0.1	0.039695
0.2	0.391043	0.1	0.039104
0.3	0.381388	0.1	0.038139
0.4	0.368270	0.1	0.036827
0.5	0.352065	0.1	0.035207
0.6	0.333225	0.1	0.033322
0.7	0.312254	0.1	0.031225
0.8	0.289692	0.1	0.028969
0.9	0.266085	0.1	0.026609
1.0	0.241971	0.1	0.024197
Total			0.333294

Exhibit 2.23 Calculations to approximate [2.180] using a Riemann sum with $m = 10$.

We are approximating the integral by summing the areas of 10 rectangles. This is illustrated in Exhibit 2.24.

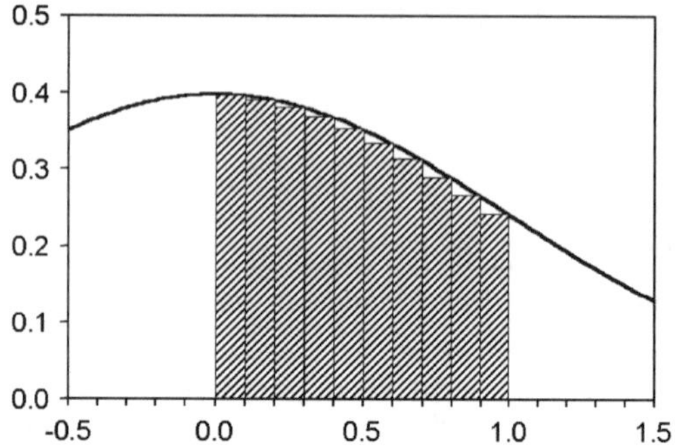

Exhibit 2.24 Graphical depiction of our Riemann sum calculations.

We can improve our approximation by valuing the Riemann sum [2.179] for a greater value m. Results for selected values of m are shown in Exhibit 2.25.

m	Riemann Sum
10	.333294
20	.337370
30	.338706
40	.339370
50	.339767
100	.340558
1000	.341266

Exhibit 2.25 Approximation [2.179] for [2.180] improves as m increases.

Trapezoidal Rule

The **trapezoidal rule** is a form of numerical integration that works in the same manner as Riemann sums. Instead of approximating f with a constant function on each subinterval of $[a, b]$, it does so with a linear polynomial. The region under that linear polynomial is a trapezoid.

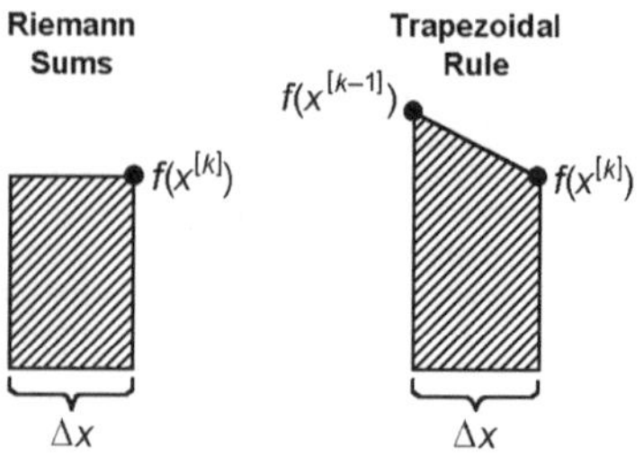

Exhibit 2.26 The trapezoidal rule employs trapezoids instead of the rectangles employed by Riemann sums.

On each sub-interval $[x^{[k-1]}, x^{[k]}]$, the trapezoid has area

$$\frac{1}{2}\left[f\left(x^{[k-1]}\right) + f\left(x^{[k]}\right)\right]\Delta x. \qquad [2.181]$$

Summing these areas across all the sub-intervals, we obtain an approximation for the definite integral:

$$\int_a^b f(x)dx \approx \sum_{k=1}^{m} \frac{1}{2}\left[f\left(x^{[k-1]}\right) + f\left(x^{[k]}\right)\right]\Delta x \qquad [2.182]$$

$$= \left(\frac{1}{2}f\left(x^{[0]}\right) + \sum_{k=1}^{m-1} f\left(x^{[k]}\right) + \frac{1}{2}f\left(x^{[m]}\right)\right)\Delta x. \qquad [2.183]$$

EXAMPLE: TRAPEZOIDAL RULE. Let's apply the trapezoidal rule to the same integral [2.180] to which we applied Riemann sums. We apply the trapezoidal rule [2.183] with $m = 10$, so our subinterval length Δx is .10. Our calculations are presented in Exhibit 2.27, and the work is illustrated graphically in Exhibit 2.28:

$x^{[k]}$ [1]	$\phi(x^{[k]})$ [2]	Weight [3]	Δx [4]	Product [2][3][4]
0.0	0.398942	0.5	0.1	0.019947
0.1	0.396953	1.0	0.1	0.039695
0.2	0.391043	1.0	0.1	0.039104
0.3	0.381388	1.0	0.1	0.038139
0.4	0.368270	1.0	0.1	0.036827
0.5	0.352065	1.0	0.1	0.035207
0.6	0.333225	1.0	0.1	0.033322
0.7	0.312254	1.0	0.1	0.031225
0.8	0.289692	1.0	0.1	0.028969
0.9	0.266085	1.0	0.1	0.026609
1.0	0.241971	0.5	0.1	0.012099
Total				0.341143

Exhibit 2.27 Calculations to approximate [2.180] using the trapezoidal rule with $m = 10$.

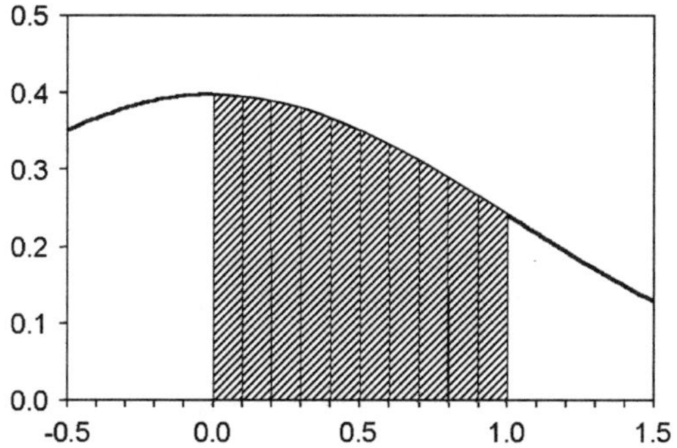

Exhibit 2.28 Graphical depiction of our trapezoidal rule calculations.

We can improve our approximation by increasing m. Results for selected values are shown in Exhibit 2.29. In this example, the trapezoidal rule achieves with $m = 20$ a result superior to that obtained by Riemann sums with $m = 1000$.

m	Trapezoidal Rule
10	.341143
20	.341294
30	.341322
40	.341332
50	.341337
100	.341343
1000	.341345

Exhibit 2.29 Example results are excellent for the trapezoidal rule, even with modest values of *m*.

Simpson's Rule

Simpson's rule is a third method of numerical integration. Instead of approximating f with constant functions or linear polynomials, it does so with quadratic polynomials. To evaluate an integral [2.178], we select a partition $P$of the interval $[a, b]$ for some even number m. On each pair of consecutive subintervals, the area under f is approximated with the area under a quadratic polynomial.

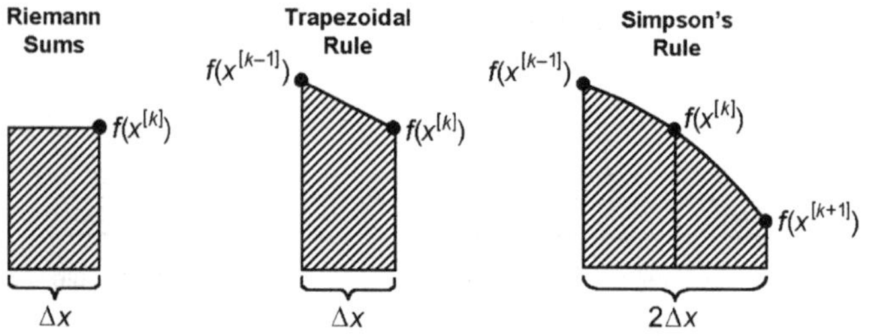

Exhibit 2.30 The method of Riemann sums approximates *f* with constant functions on each subinterval. The trapezoidal rule approximates *f* with a linear polynomial on each subinterval. Simpson's rule approximates *f* with a quadratic polynomial on each pair of consecutive subintervals.

On each pair of sub-intervals, $[x^{[k-1]}, x^{[k]}]$ and $[x^{[k]}, x^{[k+1]}]$, the area under the indicated quadratic polynomial is found by integration to be

$$\frac{\Delta x}{3}\left[f\left(x^{[k-1]}\right) + 4f\left(x^{[k]}\right) + f\left(x^{[k+1]}\right)\right]. \qquad [2.184]$$

Summing across pairs of sub-intervals, we obtain the formula for Simpson's rule:

$$\int_a^b f(x)dx \approx \frac{\Delta x}{3}\left[f\left(x^{[0]}\right) + 4f\left(x^{[1]}\right) + 2f\left(x^{[2]}\right) + 4f\left(x^{[3]}\right) + \cdots + 2f\left(x^{[m-2]}\right) + 4f\left(x^{[m-1]}\right) + f\left(x^{[m]}\right)\right]. \quad [2.185]$$

EXAMPLE: SIMPSON'S RULE. We apply Simpson's rule [2.185] to the same integral [2.180] as in our previous examples. Setting $m = 10$, our subinterval length Δx is .10. Our calculations are presented in Exhibit 2.31.

$x^{[k]}$ [1]	$\phi(x^{[k]})$ [2]	Weight [3]	Δx [4]	Product [2][3][4]
0.0	0.398942	1/3	0.1	0.013298
0.1	0.396953	4/3	0.1	0.052927
0.2	0.391043	2/3	0.1	0.026070
0.3	0.381388	4/3	0.1	0.050852
0.4	0.368270	2/3	0.1	0.024551
0.5	0.352065	4/3	0.1	0.046942
0.6	0.333225	2/3	0.1	0.022215
0.7	0.312254	4/3	0.1	0.041634
0.8	0.289692	2/3	0.1	0.019313
0.9	0.266085	4/3	0.1	0.035478
1.0	0.241971	1/3	0.1	0.008066
Total				0.341345

Exhibit 2.31 Calculations to approximate [2.180] using Simpson's rule with $m = 10$.

With $m = 10$, we obtain the same result that we obtained for $m = 1000$ using the trapezoidal rule. Simpson's rule does not always outperform so dramatically. In Section 3.16, we will consider an application for which the trapezoidal rule routinely outperforms Simpson's rule.

EXERCISES

2.24 Evaluate the integral

$$\int_1^2 \frac{1}{x}\,dx \quad [2.186]$$

four different ways:

a. analytically;
b. with a Riemann sum using $m = 10$;
c. with the trapezoidal rule using $m = 10$;
d. with Simpson's rule using $m = 10$.

2.15. NUMERICAL INTEGRATION IN MULTIPLE DIMENSIONS

In this section, we extend Riemann sums, the trapezoidal rule, and Simpson's rule to multidimensional integrals of the form:

$$\int_{\Omega} f(\boldsymbol{x})d\boldsymbol{x} = \int_{a_n}^{b_n} \cdots \int_{a_2}^{b_2} \int_{a_1}^{b_1} f(x_1, x_2, \ldots, x_n)dx_1 dx_2 \cdots dx_n. \qquad [2.187]$$

We first define quadrature rules, which are a generalized form of numerical integration. We then present the product rule that constructs quadrature rules for multiple-dimensional integrals from quadrature rules for one-dimensional integrals.

Quadrature

We have defined a partition P as a set of equally spaced points in $\mathbb{R}$. We now define a partition more generally as a set of equally spaced points in $\mathbb{R}^n$. Let $\Omega = [a_1, b_1] \times [a_2, b_2] \times \cdots \times [a_n, b_n]$ be a rectangular region of $\mathbb{R}^n$. Let $P_1, P_2, \ldots, P_n$ be one-dimensional partitions of the respective intervals $[a_1, b_1]$, $[a_2, b_2], \ldots, [a_n, b_n]$ for constants $m_1, m_2, \ldots, m_n$. We define a partition P of Ω as the set $P_1 \times P_2 \times \cdots \times P_n$ of n-dimensional points $\boldsymbol{x}^{[k_1,k_2,\ldots,k_n]}$. This is illustrated for a two-dimensional partition in Exhibit 2.32.

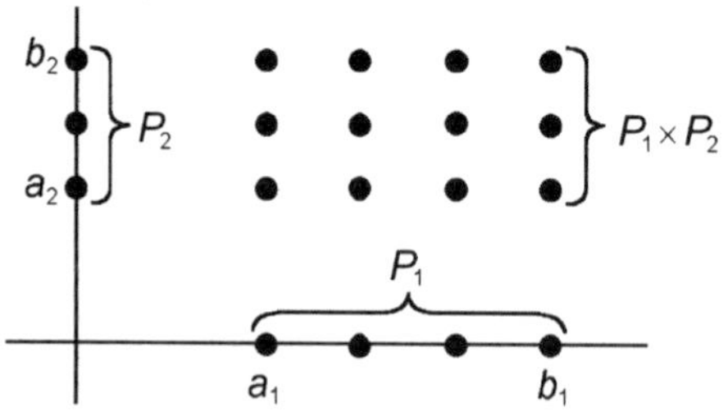

Exhibit 2.32 A two-dimensional partition $P = P_1 \times P_2$ of the region $\Omega = [a_1, b_1] \times [a_2, b_2]$ is constructed from two one-dimensional partitions P_1 and P_2.

A **quadrature rule** $W(P)$ is a general rule for approximating integrals on Ω. For any partition P of Ω, the quadrature rule specifies a set W of weights $w^{[k_1,k_2,\ldots,k_n]}$ whose sum equals the area of Ω:

$$\sum_{k_n=0}^{m_n} \cdots \sum_{k_2=0}^{m_2} \sum_{k_1=0}^{m_1} w^{[k_1,k_2,\ldots,k_n]} = (b_1 - a_1)(b_2 - a_2) \cdots (b_n - a_n). \quad [2.188]$$

The quadrature rule must specify weight in such a manner that, for any function f that is Riemann integrable on Ω,

$$\lim_{min(m_i)\to\infty} \sum_{k_n=0}^{m_n} \cdots \sum_{k_2=0}^{m_2} \sum_{k_1=0}^{m_1} w^{[k_1,k_2,\ldots,k_n]} f\left(\boldsymbol{x}^{[k_1,k_2,\ldots,k_n]}\right) = \int_{\Omega} f(\boldsymbol{x})d\boldsymbol{x}. \quad [2.189]$$

For any partition P, a quadrature rule yields the approximation

$$\int_{\Omega} f(\boldsymbol{x})d\boldsymbol{x} \approx \sum_{k_n=0}^{m_n} \cdots \sum_{k_2=0}^{m_2} \sum_{k_1=0}^{m_1} w^{[k_1,k_2,\ldots,k_n]} f\left(\boldsymbol{x}^{[k_1,k_2,\ldots,k_n]}\right). \quad [2.190]$$

Riemann sums, the trapezoidal rule, and Simpson's rule are all examples of one-dimensional quadrature rules. For any partition P, they assign weights of, respectively,

$$W = \{0, \Delta x_m, \Delta x_m, \Delta x_m, \ldots, \Delta x_m\}, \quad [2.191]$$

$$W = \left\{\frac{\Delta x_m}{2}, \Delta x_m, \Delta x_m, \ldots, \Delta x_m, \frac{\Delta x_m}{2}\right\}, \quad [2.192]$$

$$W = \left\{\frac{\Delta x_m}{3}, \frac{4\Delta x_m}{3}, \frac{2\Delta x_m}{3}, \frac{4\Delta x_m}{3}, \ldots, \frac{2\Delta x_m}{3}, \frac{4\Delta x_m}{3}, \frac{\Delta x_m}{3}\right\}. \quad [2.193]$$

The Product Rule

Suppose we have one-dimensional quadrature rules $W_i(P_i)$ for each of n intervals $[a_i, b_i]$. Let $\Omega = [a_1, b_1] \times [a_2, b_2] \times \cdots \times [a_n, b_n]$. It can be shown that for partition $P = P_1 \times P_2 \times \cdots \times P_n$, we can specify a quadrature rule $W(P)$ by setting all weights equal to the product

$$w^{[k_1,k_2,\ldots,k_n]} = w_1^{[k_1]} w_2^{[k_2]} \cdots w_n^{[k_n]}. \quad [2.194]$$

EXAMPLE: PRODUCT RULE. As will be discussed in Chapter 3, a two-dimensional joint-normal random vector $\boldsymbol{X}$ with mean vector and covariance matrix:

$$\begin{pmatrix}1\\0\end{pmatrix}, \quad \begin{pmatrix}1 & 1\\1 & 2\end{pmatrix} \quad [2.195]$$

has a probability of both $X_1 \in [2, 4]$ and $X_2 \in [0, 3]$ given by the integral

$$\int_0^3 \int_2^4 \frac{exp\left(-x_1^2 - x_2^2/2 + x_1x_2 + 2x_1 - x_2 - 1\right)}{2\pi} d\boldsymbol{x}. \quad [2.196]$$

Let's use Simpson's rule and the product rule to approximate this integral. We define partitions P_1 and P_2 of the intervals [2, 4] and [0, 3] for $m_1 = m_2 = 4$:

$$P_1 = \{2.00, 2.50, 3.00, 3.50, 4.00\}, \quad [2.197]$$

$$P_2 = \{0.00, 0.75, 1.50, 2.25, 3.00\}. \quad [2.198]$$

We use Simpson's rule to define quadrature rules

$$W(P_1) = \{1/6, 4/6, 2/6, 4/6, 1/6\}, \quad [2.199]$$

$$W(P_2) = \{1/4, 4/4, 2/4, 4/4, 1/4\}. \quad [2.200]$$

We define the partition $P = P_1 \times P_2$ and apply the product rule to define a quadrature rule $W(P)$. Calculations are presented in Exhibit 2.33.

k_1	k_2	$w^{[k_1]}$	$w^{[k_2]}$	$w^{[k_1,k_2]}$	$\boldsymbol{x}^{[k_1,k_2]}$	$f(\boldsymbol{x}^{[k_1,k_2]})$	$w^{[k_1,k_2]}f(\boldsymbol{x}^{[k_1,k_2]})$
[1]	[2]	[3]	[4]	[5]=[3][4]	[6]	[7]	[8]=[5][7]
0	0	1/6	1/4	1/24	(2.00, 0.00)	0.058550	0.002440
0	1	1/6	4/4	4/24	(2.00, 0.75)	0.093562	0.015594
0	2	1/6	2/4	2/24	(2.00, 1.50)	0.085190	0.007099
0	3	1/6	4/4	4/24	(2.00, 2.25)	0.044196	0.007366
0	4	1/6	1/4	1/24	(2.00, 3.00)	0.013064	0.000544
1	0	4/6	1/4	4/24	(2.50, 0.00)	0.016775	0.002796
1	1	4/6	4/4	16/24	(2.50, 0.75)	0.039003	0.026002
1	2	4/6	2/4	8/24	(2.50, 1.50)	0.051670	0.017223
1	3	4/6	4/4	16/24	(2.50, 2.25)	0.039003	0.026002
1	4	4/6	1/4	4/24	(2.50, 3.00)	0.016775	0.002796
2	0	2/6	1/4	2/24	(3.00, 0.00)	0.002915	0.000243
2	1	2/6	4/4	8/24	(3.00, 0.75)	0.009861	0.003287
2	2	2/6	2/4	4/24	(3.00, 1.50)	0.019008	0.003168
2	3	2/6	4/4	8/24	(3.00, 2.25)	0.020877	0.006959
2	4	2/6	1/4	2/24	(3.00, 3.00)	0.013064	0.001089
3	0	4/6	1/4	4/24	(3.50, 0.00)	0.000307	0.000051
3	1	4/6	4/4	16/24	(3.50, 0.75)	0.001512	0.001008
3	2	4/6	2/4	8/24	(3.50, 1.50)	0.004241	0.001414
3	3	4/6	4/4	16/24	(3.50, 2.25)	0.006778	0.004518
3	4	4/6	1/4	4/24	(3.50, 3.00)	0.006171	0.001029
4	0	1/6	1/4	1/24	(4.00, 0.00)	0.000020	0.000001
4	1	1/6	4/4	4/24	(4.00, 0.75)	0.000141	0.000023
4	2	1/6	2/4	2/24	(4.00, 1.50)	0.000574	0.000048
4	3	1/6	4/4	4/24	(4.00, 2.25)	0.001335	0.000222
4	4	1/6	1/4	1/24	(4.00, 3.00)	0.001768	0.000074
							0.130995

Exhibit 2.33 Calculations for our approximation of the integral [2.196].

Curse of Dimensionality

A problem with using quadrature to solve multidimensional integrals is the fact that the number of points in a partition grows exponentially with the dimensions of the integral. Because the computational expense of valuing [2.190] is directly proportional to the number of points in the partition, that computational expense also grows exponentially.

Consider a partition $P = P_1 \times P_2 \times \cdots \times P_n$, where each component partition P_i has $m+1$ points (m subintervals). The overall partition P then has $(m+1)^n$ points. Suppose we set $m + 1 = 10$ and an integral has three dimensions. Valuing the integral using quadrature entails a sum [2.190] of $10^3 = 1000$ values. Now suppose the integral has 12 dimensions. Valuing this will entail a sum [2.190] of $10^{12} =$ 1,000,000,000,000 values. This is a staggering number of calculations, but things can get far worse. Applications abound that involve integrals of 50, 100, 1000, or even more dimensions. Valuing such integrals using quadrature entails calculations that are beyond the processing power of any computer.

This problem is known as the **curse of dimensionality**. It means that quadrature can only be applied to integrals that have a modest number of dimensions. It is a significant problem for us because the task of a VaR measure's transformation procedure is essentially one of solving a multidimensional integral. Integrals encountered in practical VaR applications routinely exceed 50 dimensions.

Exercises

2.25 Evaluate the integral

$$\int_3^5 \int_1^2 x_1 x_2^3 \, dx_1 dx_2 \qquad [2.201]$$

two different ways:

a. analytically;
b. with quadrature using the product rule and Simpson's rule. Use $m_i = 6$ for each component partition.

2.16. FURTHER READING

To review calculus topics assumed in this chapter, see Thomas and Finney (1996) or any other elementary text that covers the subject in multiple dimensions. For linear algebra, Strang (1988) is a practical introduction. See Ortega (1987) for a more advanced treatment. Apostol (1969) offers a sophisticated introduction to both calculus and linear algebra. For information on the Cholesky and related factorizations, see Golub and Van Loan (1996) and Gentle (1998). Burden and Faires (1993) covers various numerical techniques. See Dennis and Schnabel (1983) for Newton's method in multiple dimensions. For quadrature, see Evans and Swartz (2000).

Chapter 3

Probability

3.1. MOTIVATION

VaR measures are inherently probabilistic. A central question that VaR addresses is this: If a portfolio comprises holdings in various instruments, how is its market risk determined by theirs? In the parlance of probability, the question becomes: If a random variable is defined as a function of other random variables, how is its distribution determined by theirs?

As it relates to market risk, the question is addressed in Chapter 10, which discusses transformation procedures. That chapter draws on various techniques from this chapter, including:

- techniques for characterizing the distribution of a linear polynomial of a random vector;
- techniques for characterizing the distribution of a quadratic polynomial of a random vector;
- the central limit theorem;
- the inversion theorem.

Concepts from the present chapter underlie statistics and time series analysis, which are the topics of Chapter 4. They, in turn, are used in Chapter 7 to design inference procedures.

Finally, the present chapter describes principal component analysis, which is used in Chapter 9 with a category of portfolio remappings called, transparently, "principal component remappings."

3.2. PREREQUISITES

We assume familiarity with basic notation and concepts from probability. If E is an event, we denote its probability $Pr(E)$. You should be familiar with **random variables** and **random vectors**. A random vector $\boldsymbol{X}$ can be thought of as an n-dimensional vector of random variables X_i all defined on the same sample space. When we present general definitions or results for random vectors, these also apply to random variables.

It is important to distinguish between a random vector $\boldsymbol{X}$ and a realization of that random vector, which we may denote $\boldsymbol{x}$. The **realization** is an element of the range of the random vector.

You should be familiar with **discrete** and **continuous** distributions for random vectors. You should be comfortable working with **probability functions** (PFs), **probability density functions** (PDFs), and **cumulative distribution functions** (CDFs). You should be familiar with **joint distributions**, **conditional distributions**, and **marginal distributions**.

We may think of random vectors as being "equivalent" in several senses. We distinguish between two of these. Random vectors $\boldsymbol{X}$ and $\boldsymbol{Y}$ are **equal**, denoted $\boldsymbol{X} = \boldsymbol{Y}$, if they both take on the same value with probability 1. If $\boldsymbol{X}$ and $\boldsymbol{Y}$ simply have the same probability distribution, we denote this relationship $\boldsymbol{X} \sim \boldsymbol{Y}$. We also use the symbol $\sim$ to indicate what a random variable represents, say: $X \sim$ tomorrow's 3-month USD Libor rate.

You should know what it means for two or more components of a random vector $\boldsymbol{X}$ to be **independent**. In particular, if n components X_i are independent, their joint CDF and marginal CDFs satisfy:

$$\Phi(x_1, x_2, \ldots, x_n) = \Phi_1(x_1)\Phi_2(x_2)\cdots\Phi_n(x_n). \quad [3.1]$$

for all $x_1, x_2, \ldots, x_n \in \mathbb{R}$. Similarly, their joint PDF and marginal PDFs satisfy:

$$\phi(x_1, x_2, \ldots, x_n) = \phi_1(x_1)\phi_2(x_2)\cdots\phi_n(x_n). \quad [3.2]$$

for all $x_1, x_2, \ldots, x_n \in \mathbb{R}$.[1]

3.3. PARAMETERS

Parameters describe random vectors much as we might use height or age to describe a person. Formally, a **parameter** is a function that is applied to a random vector's probability distribution. It may take on real, vector, or matrix values. A standard deviation, mean vector, or covariance matrix are all examples

[1]For technical reasons, we should qualify [3.2] and say that it may fail to hold on a set of values for $\boldsymbol{X}$ of probability 0.

of parameters. In this section, we describe parameters for random variables. In Section 3.4, we extend the discussion to parameters for random vectors.

Expectation

Let X be a random variable. We denote the **expected value**, **expectation**, or **mean** of X as either μ or $E(X)$. If X is discrete, we define its expectation as

$$E(X) = \sum_x x\phi(x), \qquad [3.3]$$

where ϕ is the PF of X. If X is continuous, we replace the summation with an integral and define

$$E(X) = \int_{-\infty}^{\infty} x\phi(x)dx, \qquad [3.4]$$

where ϕ is the PDF of X.

Expectation is used to define a number of other parameters, but first we must discuss expectations of functions of random variables.

Expectation of a Function of a Random Variable

Suppose X is a random variable and f is a function from $\mathbb{R}$ to $\mathbb{R}$. Then $f(X)$ is a new random variable[2] whose probability distribution we can, at least in theory, infer from that of X. We do not need the probability distribution of $f(X)$ in order to determine the expectation $E[f(X)]$. This can be obtained directly from the probability distribution of X using the formula

$$E[f(X)] = \sum_x f(x)\phi(x) \qquad [3.5]$$

or

$$E[f(X)] = \int_{-\infty}^{\infty} f(x)\phi(x)dx, \qquad [3.6]$$

depending upon whether X is discrete or continuous. In a sense, [3.5] and [3.6] are generalizations of [3.3] and [3.4].

[2] Technically, f must be measurable for $f(X)$ to be a random variable.

Variance and Standard Deviation

Variance is a parameter that measures how dispersed a random variable's probability distribution is. In Exhibit 3.1, two PDFs have a mean of 0. The one on the left is more dispersed than the one on the right. It has a higher variance.

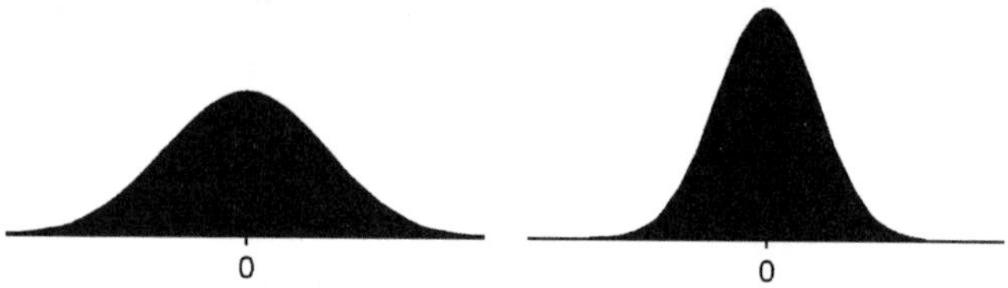

Exhibit 3.1 These graphs illustrate the notion of variance. Both PDFs have an expectation of 0, but the one on the left is more dispersed than the one on the right. It has a higher variance.

The **variance**, denoted σ^2 or $var(X)$, of a random variable X is defined as an expectation of a function of X:

$$var(X) = E[(X - \mu)^2]. \qquad [3.7]$$

Standard deviation, denoted σ or $std(X)$, is the positive square-root of variance.

Skewness

Skew or **skewness** is a measure of asymmetry in a random variable's probability distribution. Both PDFs in Exhibit 3.2 have the same mean and standard deviation. The one on the left is positively skewed. The one on the right is negatively skewed.

Exhibit 3.2 These graphs illustrate the notion of skewness. Both PDFs have the same mean and variance. The one on the left is positively skewed. The one on the right is negatively skewed.

The skewness of a random variable X is denoted η_1 or $skew(X)$. It is defined as

$$skew(X) = \frac{E[(X - \mu)^3]}{\sigma^3}. \qquad [3.8]$$

Kurtosis

Kurtosis is another parameter that describes the shape of a random variable's probability distribution. Consider the two PDFs in Exhibit 3.3. Both have a mean and skewness of 0. Which would you say has the greater standard deviation? It is impossible to say. The distribution on the right is more peaked at the center, which might lead us to believe that it has a lower standard deviation. It has fatter tails, which might lead us to believe that it has a greater standard deviation. If the effect of the peakedness exactly offsets that of the fat tails, the two distributions may have the same standard deviation. The different shapes of the two distributions illustrates kurtosis. The distribution on the right has a greater kurtosis than the distribution on the left.

Exhibit 3.3 These graphs illustrate the notion of kurtosis. The PDF on the right has higher kurtosis than the PDF on the left. It is more peaked at the center, and it has fatter tails.

The **kurtosis** of a random variable X is denoted η_2 or $kurt(X)$.[3] It is defined as

$$kurt(X) = \frac{E[(X - \mu)^4]}{\sigma^4}. \qquad [3.9]$$

If a distribution's kurtosis is greater than 3, it is said to be **leptokurtic**. If its kurtosis is less than 3, it is said to be **platykurtic**. Leptokurtosis is associated with distributions that are simultaneously "peaked" and have "fat tails." Platykurtosis is associated with distributions that are simultaneously less peaked and have thinner tails. In Exhibit 3.3, the distribution on the left is platykurtic. The one on the right is leptokurtic.

Quantiles

Consider a random variable X with CDF Φ. A q-quantile of X is any value x such that $Pr(X \leq x) = q$. A q-quantile need not exist. If it does exist, it need not be unique.[4] In most VaR applications, all q-quantiles exist and are unique for

[3]The use of subscripts in the notation η_1 and η_2 for skewness and kurtosis is unfortunate because it can lead to confusion if subscripts are also employed to distinguish between different random variables. We use the notation because it is well established.

[4]We could force uniqueness by defining the q-quantile as the supremum of all values satisfying the definition provided in the text.

$q \in (0, 1)$. In such cases, a q-quantile is a parameter and equals the inverse CDF evaluated at q. For this reason, we denote a q-quantile as $\Phi^{-1}(q)$.

MOMENTS

For any positive integer k, the kth **moment** of a random variable X is defined as

$$\mu'_k = E(X^k). \tag{3.10}$$

Its kth **central moment** is defined as

$$\mu_k = E[(X - \mu)^k], \tag{3.11}$$

where $\mu = E(X)$. Based upon our earlier definitions, the expectation and variance of a random variable are its first moment and second central moment. Its skewness and kurtosis are scaled third and fourth central moments.

For any $n > 0$, a random variable's first n moments convey the same information as its first n central moments—each can be derived from the other. See Exercise 3.15.

We say a random variable X is **bounded** if there exists a number a such that $Pr(|X| > a) = 0$. If a random variable is bounded, all its moments exist. If it is unbounded, specific moments may or may not exist. However, if the kth moment of X exists, then all moments of order less than k must also exist.

EXERCISES

3.1 PDFs for two continuous random variables are illustrated in Exhibit 3.4. Assume probability density is 0 for both distributions outside the graphed regions. Where possible, indicate which random variable has the greater:
   a. expectation,
   b. standard deviation,
   c. skewness,
   d. kurtosis, and
   e. .25-quantile.

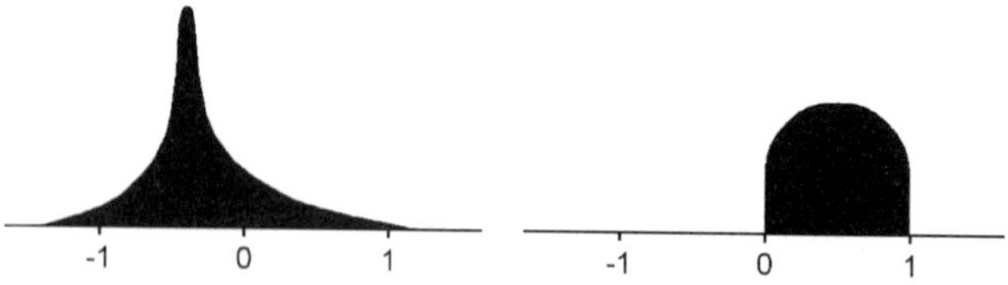

Exhibit 3.4 PDFs for two continuous random variables.

3.2 Consider a discrete random variable Y, which represents the number of "heads" that will be obtained in three flips of a fair coin. It has PF

$$\phi(y) = \begin{cases} 0.125 & y = 0 \text{ or } 3 \\ 0.375 & y = 1 \text{ or } 2. \\ 0 & \text{otherwise} \end{cases} \qquad [3.12]$$

a. Calculate the mean of Y.
b. Calculate the variance of Y.
c. Calculate the standard deviation of Y.
d. Calculate the skewness of Y.
e. Calculate the kurtosis of Y.
f. Calculate a .10 quantile of Y.
g. Calculate a .875 quantile of Y.

3.3 Consider a continuous random variable Z with PDF

$$\phi(z) = \begin{cases} 0.5 & 1 < z < 3 \\ 0 & \text{otherwise} \end{cases}. \qquad [3.13]$$

a. Calculate the mean of Z.
b. Calculate the variance of Z.
c. Calculate the standard deviation of Z.
d. Calculate the skewness of Z.
e. Calculate the kurtosis of Z.
f. Calculate a .10-quantile of Z.
g. Calculate a .875-quantile of Z.

3.4 Consider the random variable $W = Z^2$, where Z is defined as in the previous exercise.
a. Calculate the mean of W.
b. Calculate the variance of W.
c. Calculate the standard deviation of W.

3.5 True or false: If a continuous random variable X has a symmetric distribution, $\phi(x - \mu) = \phi(-x - \mu)$, it must have 0 skewness.

3.6 In general, for any random variable X and any constant b, $E(bX) = bE(X)$. Prove this result for the case X is discrete.

3.7 In general, for any random variable X and any constant a, $E(X + a) = E(X) + a$. Prove this result for the case X is continuous.

3.8 In general, for any random variable X and any constant b, $std(bX) = |b|std(X)$, where $|b|$ indicates the absolute value of b. Prove this result for the case X is discrete. Use your result from Exercise 3.6.

3.9 In general, for any random variable X and any constant a, $std(X + a) = std(X)$. Prove this result for the case X is continuous. Use your result from Exercise 3.7.

3.4. PARAMETERS OF RANDOM VECTORS

The **expectation** of an n-dimensional random vector $\boldsymbol{X}$ is a vector which we denote either $\boldsymbol{\mu}$ or $E(\boldsymbol{X})$. Its components are the expectations of the marginal distributions of the X_i:

$$E(\boldsymbol{X}) = \begin{pmatrix} E(X_1) \\ E(X_2) \\ \vdots \\ E(X_n) \end{pmatrix} = \begin{pmatrix} \mu_1 \\ \mu_2 \\ \vdots \\ \mu_n \end{pmatrix}. \qquad [3.14]$$

Expectation of a Function of a Random Vector

Let $\boldsymbol{X}$ be an n-dimensional random vector and f a function from $\mathbb{R}^n$ to $\mathbb{R}$ that defines a random variable $f(\boldsymbol{X})$. We may generalize [3.5] and [3.6] to calculate the mean of $f(\boldsymbol{X})$. If $\boldsymbol{X}$ is discrete with PF ϕ, we have

$$E[f(\boldsymbol{X})] = \sum_{\boldsymbol{x}} f(\boldsymbol{x})\phi(\boldsymbol{x}). \qquad [3.15]$$

If $\boldsymbol{X}$ is continuous with PDF ϕ, this becomes

$$E[f(\boldsymbol{X})] = \int_{\mathbb{R}^n} f(\boldsymbol{x})\phi(\boldsymbol{x})d\boldsymbol{x} \qquad [3.16]$$

$$= \int_{-\infty}^{\infty}\int_{-\infty}^{\infty}\cdots\int_{-\infty}^{\infty} f(x_1, x_2, \ldots, x_n)\phi(x_1, x_2, \ldots, x_n)dx_1dx_2\cdots dx_n. \qquad [3.17]$$

Joint Moments

Joint moments generalize moments. Let X_i and X_j be components of a random vector. We define their (k, l) **joint moment** as

$$E\left[X_i^k X_j^l\right]. \qquad [3.18]$$

We define their (k, l) **joint central moment** as

$$E[(X_i - \mu_i)^k (X_j - \mu_j)^l]. \qquad [3.19]$$

We define the $\boldsymbol{n}^{\text{th}}$ **moments** of a random vector $\boldsymbol{X}$ as all its joint moments $E[X_i^k X_j^l]$ for which $k + l = n$. We define its $\boldsymbol{n}^{\text{th}}$**central moments** as all its joint central moments $E[(X_i - \mu_i)^k (X_j - \mu_j)^l]$ for which $k + l = n$.

COVARIANCE

We are primarily interested in the (1, 1) joint central moment, which we call **covariance**. For the ith and j^{th} components of $\boldsymbol{X}$, we denote covariance $\Sigma_{i,j}$ or $cov(X_i, X_j)$. By definition, covariance is symmetric, with $\Sigma_{i,j} = \Sigma_{j,i}$. Also, the covariance of any component X_i with itself is that component's variance:

$$\Sigma_{i,i} = E[(X_i - \mu_i)(X_i - \mu_i)] = E[(X_i - \mu_i)^2] = \sigma_i^2. \qquad [3.20]$$

We summarize all the covariances of a random vector $\boldsymbol{X}$ with a **covariance matrix**:

$$\boldsymbol{\Sigma} = \begin{pmatrix} \Sigma_{1,1} & \Sigma_{1,2} & \Sigma_{1,3} & \cdots & \Sigma_{1,n} \\ \Sigma_{2,1} & \Sigma_{2,2} & \Sigma_{2,3} & & \\ \Sigma_{3,1} & \Sigma_{3,2} & \Sigma_{3,3} & & \vdots \\ \vdots & & & \ddots & \\ \Sigma_{n,1} & & \cdots & & \Sigma_{n,n} \end{pmatrix}. \qquad [3.21]$$

By the symmetry property of covariances, the covariance matrix is symmetric. Intuitively, covariance is a metric of the tendency of two components of a random vector to vary together, or co-vary. The magnitude of a covariance depends upon the standard deviations of the two components. To obtain a more direct metric of how two components co-vary, we scale covariance to obtain **correlation**.

CORRELATION

The **correlation**, $\rho_{i,j}$ or $cor(X_i, X_j)$, of the ith and j^{th} components of a random vector $\boldsymbol{X}$ is defined as

$$\rho_{i,j} = \frac{cov(X_i, X_j)}{\sigma_i \sigma_j}. \qquad [3.22]$$

By construction, a correlation is always a number between -1 and 1. Correlation inherits the symmetry property of covariance: $\rho_{i,j} = \rho_{j,i}$. From [3.20] and [3.22], $\rho_{i,i} = 1$, which indicates that a random variable co-varies perfectly with itself. If X_i and X_j are independent, their correlation is 0. The converse is not true. As with covariances, we can summarize all the correlations of a random vector $\boldsymbol{X}$ with a symmetric **correlation matrix**:

$$\boldsymbol{\rho} = \begin{pmatrix} \rho_{1,1} & \rho_{1,2} & \rho_{1,3} & \cdots & \rho_{1,n} \\ \rho_{2,1} & \rho_{2,2} & \rho_{2,3} & & \\ \rho_{3,1} & \rho_{3,2} & \rho_{3,3} & & \vdots \\ \vdots & & & \ddots & \\ \rho_{n,1} & & \cdots & & \rho_{n,n} \end{pmatrix}. \qquad [3.23]$$

Exercises

3.10 Use [3.17] to prove that, if the components X_1 and X_2 of a two-dimensional random vector $\boldsymbol{X}$ are independent, then

$$E(X_1X_2) = E(X_1)E(X_2). \qquad [3.24]$$

3.11 Consider the two-dimensional discrete random vector $\boldsymbol{Q}$ with PF

$$\phi(\boldsymbol{q}) = \begin{cases} 0.3 & \boldsymbol{q} = (1,0) \\ 0.1 & \boldsymbol{q} = (1,3) \\ 0.2 & \boldsymbol{q} = (2,1) \\ 0.1 & \boldsymbol{q} = (0,3) \\ 0.3 & \boldsymbol{q} = (3,2) \end{cases}. \qquad [3.25]$$

Calculate $\rho_{1,2}$.

3.12 Give an example of a two-dimensional random vector whose components have 0 covariance but are not independent.

3.5. LINEAR POLYNOMIALS OF RANDOM VECTORS

We now consider formula [1.10], which we used in some of the examples of Chapter 1. Let $\boldsymbol{X}$ be a random vector with mean vector $\boldsymbol{\mu}$ and covariance matrix $\boldsymbol{\Sigma}$. Define random variable Y as a linear polynomial

$$Y = \boldsymbol{bX} + a \qquad [3.26]$$

of $\boldsymbol{X}$, where $\boldsymbol{b}$ is an n-dimensional row vector and $a \in \mathbb{R}$. The mean and variance of Y are given by

$$E(Y) = \boldsymbol{b\mu} + a, \qquad [3.27]$$

$$var(Y) = \boldsymbol{b\Sigma b}'. \qquad [3.28]$$

Formulas [3.27] and [3.28] are general. They require no additional assumptions about $\boldsymbol{X}$ whatsoever.

Vector Linear Polynomials

Formulas [3.27] and [3.28] generalize for vector-valued polynomials. Let $\boldsymbol{Y}$ be an m-dimensional random vector defined as a linear polynomial

$$\boldsymbol{Y} = \boldsymbol{bX} + \boldsymbol{a} \qquad [3.29]$$

of an n-dimensional random vector $\boldsymbol{X}$. Here, $\boldsymbol{b}$ is an $m \times n$ matrix and $\boldsymbol{a}$ is an m-dimensional vector. If $\boldsymbol{X}$ has mean vector $\boldsymbol{\mu}_X$ and covariance matrix $\boldsymbol{\Sigma}_X$, then $\boldsymbol{Y}$

has mean vector and covariance matrix

$$\boldsymbol{\mu}_Y = \boldsymbol{b}\boldsymbol{\mu}_X + \boldsymbol{a}, \qquad [3.30]$$

$$\boldsymbol{\Sigma}_Y = \boldsymbol{b}\boldsymbol{\Sigma}_X\boldsymbol{b}'. \qquad [3.31]$$

Exercises

3.13 Suppose $\boldsymbol{X}$ is a three-dimensional random vector with the parameters shown in Exhibit 3.5. Let $Y = 10 + X_1 + 3X_2 - 2X_3$. Calculate the mean and standard deviation of Y using [3.27] and [3.28].

Component	Mean	Standard Deviation	Correlations		
			X_1	X_2	X_3
X_1	–4	1.1	1.0		
X_2	0	0.7	0.3	1.0	
X_3	5	0.4	0.1	–0.2	1.0

Exhibit 3.5 Assumptions for Exercise 3.13.

3.14 Suppose a random variable Z is equal to the sum of two other random variables A and B which are related by the functional relationship $B = A^2 - 2A - 4$. Both A and B have a standard deviation of 3. Their correlation is 0.25. What is the standard deviation of Z?

3.15 Use [3.27] to prove that, in general:

$$var(X) = E(X^2) - E(X)^2. \qquad [3.32]$$

3.16 Consider a three-dimensional random vector $\boldsymbol{X}$. Its first two components, X_1 and X_2, are uncorrelated. They have standard deviations of 5 and 4, respectively. If $X_3 = 2X_1 - 3X_2$, what is the correlation between X_1 and X_3?

3.6. PROPERTIES OF COVARIANCE MATRICES

Covariance matrices are always positive semidefinite. To see why, let $\boldsymbol{X}$ be any random vector with covariance matrix $\boldsymbol{\Sigma}$, and let $\boldsymbol{b}$ be any constant row vector. Define the random variable

$$Y = \boldsymbol{b}\boldsymbol{X}. \qquad [3.33]$$

By [3.28], the variance of Y is

$$var(Y) = \boldsymbol{b}\boldsymbol{\Sigma}\boldsymbol{b}'. \qquad [3.34]$$

The variance of any random variable Y must be nonnegative, so expression [3.34] is nonnegative. Recall from Section 2.7 that a symmetric matrix $\boldsymbol{\Sigma}$ is positive semidefinite if $\boldsymbol{b}\boldsymbol{\Sigma}\boldsymbol{b}' \geq 0$ for all row vectors $\boldsymbol{b}$. A covariance matrix is necessarily symmetric, so we conclude that all covariance matrices $\boldsymbol{\Sigma}$ are positive semidefinite.

We shall call a random vector **nonsingular** or **singular** according to whether its covariance matrix is positive definite or singular positive semidefinite.

Singular Random Vectors

Suppose random vector $\boldsymbol{X}$ is singular with covariance matrix $\boldsymbol{\Sigma}$. There exists a row vector $\boldsymbol{b} \neq \boldsymbol{0}$ such that $\boldsymbol{b}\boldsymbol{\Sigma}\boldsymbol{b}' = 0$. Consider the random variable $\boldsymbol{bX}$. By [3.28],

$$var(\boldsymbol{bX}) = \boldsymbol{b}\boldsymbol{\Sigma}\boldsymbol{b}' = 0. \qquad [3.35]$$

Since random variable $\boldsymbol{bX}$ has 0 variance, it must equal some constant a. This argument is reversible, so we conclude that a random vector $\boldsymbol{X}$ is singular if and only if there exists a row vector $\boldsymbol{b} \neq \boldsymbol{0}$ and a constant a such that

$$\boldsymbol{bX} = a. \qquad [3.36]$$

Dispensing with matrix notation, this becomes

$$b_n X_n + \cdots + b_2 X_2 + b_1 X_1 = a. \qquad [3.37]$$

Since $\boldsymbol{b} \neq \boldsymbol{0}$, at least one component b_i is nonzero. Without loss of generality, assume $b_1 \neq 0$. Rearranging [3.37], we obtain

$$X_1 = \left(-\frac{b_n}{b_1}\right)X_n + \cdots + \left(-\frac{b_2}{b_1}\right)X_2 + a, \qquad [3.38]$$

which expresses component X_1 as a linear polynomial of the other components X_i. We conclude that a random vector $\boldsymbol{X}$ is singular if and only if one of its components is a linear polynomial of the other components. In this sense, a singular covariance matrix indicates that at least one component of a random vector is extraneous.

If one component of $\boldsymbol{X}$ is a linear polynomial of the rest, then all realizations of $\boldsymbol{X}$ must fall in a plane within $\mathbb{R}^n$, where $m < n$. The random vector $\boldsymbol{X}$ can be thought of as an m-dimensional random vector sitting in a plane within $\mathbb{R}^n$. This is illustrated with realizations of a singular two-dimensional random vector $\boldsymbol{X}$ in Exhibit 3.6.

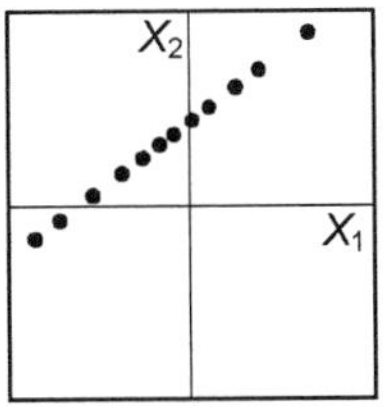

Exhibit 3.6 Realizations of a singular two-dimensional random vector $\boldsymbol{X}$. Component X_2 is a linear polynomial of component X_1.

If a random vector $\boldsymbol{X}$ is singular, but the plane it sits in is not aligned with the coordinate system of $\mathbb{R}^n$, we may not immediately realize that it is singular from its covariance matrix $\boldsymbol{\Sigma}$. A simple test for singularity is to calculate the determinant $|\boldsymbol{\Sigma}|$ of the covariance matrix. If this equals 0, $\boldsymbol{X}$ is singular.

Once we know that $\boldsymbol{X}$ is singular, we can apply a change of variables to eliminate extraneous components X_i and transform $\boldsymbol{X}$ into an equivalent m-dimensional random vector $\boldsymbol{Y}$, $m < n$. The change of variables will do this by transforming (rotating, shifting, etc.) the plane that realizations of $\boldsymbol{X}$ sit in so that it aligns with the coordinate system of $\mathbb{R}^n$. Such a change of variables is obtained with a linear polynomial of the form:

$$\boldsymbol{X} = \boldsymbol{kY} + \boldsymbol{d}. \qquad [3.39]$$

Consider a three-dimensional random vector $\boldsymbol{X}$ with mean vector and covariance matrix

$$\boldsymbol{\mu}_X = \begin{pmatrix} 1 \\ 1 \\ 3 \end{pmatrix} \quad \text{and} \quad \boldsymbol{\Sigma}_X = \begin{pmatrix} 25 & 8 & 10 \\ 8 & 4 & 2 \\ 10 & 2 & 5 \end{pmatrix}. \qquad [3.40]$$

We note that $\boldsymbol{\Sigma}$ has determinant $|\boldsymbol{\Sigma}| = 0$, so it is singular. We propose to transform $\boldsymbol{X}$ into an equivalent two-dimensional random vector $\boldsymbol{Y}$ using a linear polynomial of the form [3.39]. For convenience, let's find a transformation such that $\boldsymbol{Y}$ will have mean vector $\boldsymbol{0}$ and covariance matrix $\boldsymbol{I}$:

$$\boldsymbol{\mu}_Y = \begin{pmatrix} 0 \\ 0 \end{pmatrix} \quad \text{and} \quad \boldsymbol{\Sigma}_Y = \begin{pmatrix} 1 & 0 \\ 0 & 1 \end{pmatrix}. \qquad [3.41]$$

We first solve for $\boldsymbol{k}$. By [3.31]:

$$\boldsymbol{\Sigma}_X = \boldsymbol{k\Sigma}_Y\boldsymbol{k}' = \boldsymbol{kIk}' = \boldsymbol{kk}', \qquad [3.42]$$

so we seek a factorization $\boldsymbol{\Sigma}_X = \boldsymbol{kk}'$. Applying the Cholesky factorization and discarding an extraneous column of 0's, as described in Section 2.7, we obtain:

$$\boldsymbol{k} = \begin{pmatrix} 5.0 & 0.0 \\ 1.6 & 1.2 \\ 2.0 & -1.0 \end{pmatrix}. \qquad [3.43]$$

Solving next for $\boldsymbol{d}$, by [3.30]:

$$\boldsymbol{\mu}_X = \boldsymbol{k}\boldsymbol{\mu}_Y + \boldsymbol{d}, \qquad [3.44]$$

$$\Rightarrow \boldsymbol{d} = \boldsymbol{\mu}_X - \boldsymbol{k}\boldsymbol{\mu}_Y \qquad [3.45]$$

$$= \boldsymbol{\mu}_X - \boldsymbol{k}\boldsymbol{0} \qquad [3.46]$$

$$= \boldsymbol{\mu}_X. \qquad [3.47]$$

Accordingly, our transformation is

$$\begin{pmatrix} X_1 \\ X_2 \\ X_3 \end{pmatrix} = \begin{pmatrix} 5.0 & 0.0 \\ 1.6 & 1.2 \\ 2.0 & -1.0 \end{pmatrix} \begin{pmatrix} Y_1 \\ Y_2 \end{pmatrix} + \begin{pmatrix} 1 \\ 1 \\ 3 \end{pmatrix}. \qquad [3.48]$$

Exhibit 3.7 illustrates how this change of variables transforms the plane in which $\boldsymbol{X}$ sits so that it aligns with the coordinate system of $\mathbb{R}^2$.

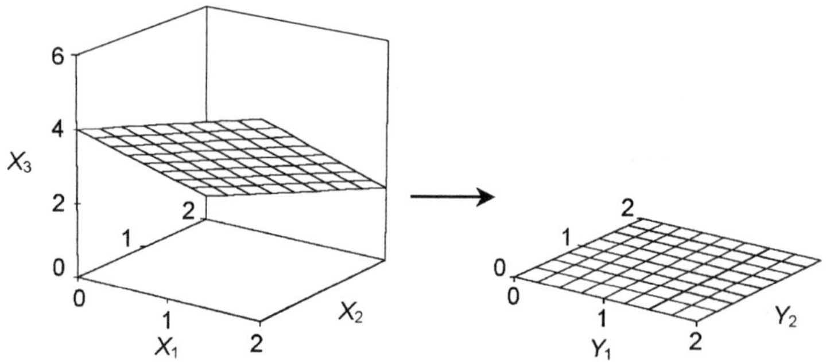

Exhibit 3.7 Our change of variables transforms the plane that realizations of $\boldsymbol{X}$ sit in so that it aligns with the coordinate system of $\mathbb{R}^2$. The third extraneous component of $\boldsymbol{X}$ "drops out."

Multicollinear Random Vectors

Suppose we are analyzing the risk in a natural gas trading portfolio. Random variables represent tomorrow's values for each price the portfolio is exposed to. The portfolio holds New York Mercantile Exchange (NYMEX) Henry Hub futures out to 24 months, so there are 24 futures prices. It also has forward positions out to 18 months for 30 delivery points, for another 540 prices. In total, our model depends upon a vector of 564 random variables!

Based upon a time series analysis of historical price data, we construct a 564 × 564 covariance matrix for our random vector of prices. Gazing at the 318,096 variances and covariances of our matrix, we wonder: Do we really need all these numbers?

Intuitively, we know that the random variables are interdependent. Prices for 6-month and 7-month Transco Zone 2 delivery are highly correlated. So are

3-month prices for adjacent Transco Zones 1 and 2. Because of such interdependencies, it is conceivable that our random vector is singular, but this is probably not the case. Singularity arises infrequently in applications. A more common situation is "almost" singularity, which is known as **multicollinearity**.

We illustrate with two four-dimensional random vectors. Random vector $\boldsymbol{X}$ is singular. Its first three components X_1, X_2, and X_3 are uncorrelated, each with mean 0 and standard deviation 1. The fourth component X_4 equals $X_1 + X_2 + X_3$. The covariance matrix for $\boldsymbol{X}$ is

$$\boldsymbol{\Sigma}_X = \begin{pmatrix} 1 & 0 & 0 & 1 \\ 0 & 1 & 0 & 1 \\ 0 & 0 & 1 & 1 \\ 1 & 1 & 1 & 3 \end{pmatrix}. \qquad [3.49]$$

Random vector $\mathbf{Z}$ is multicollinear. Like $\boldsymbol{X}$, its first three components Z_1, Z_2, and Z_3 are uncorrelated, each with mean 0 and standard deviation 1. The fourth component Z_4 equals $Z_1 + Z_2 + Z_3 + E$, where E is a "noise" random variable that is uncorrelated with Z_1, Z_2, and Z_3 and has mean 0 and standard deviation .001. Except for the addition of "noise" E, our random vector $\mathbf{Z}$ is identical to our random vector $\boldsymbol{X}$. Its covariance matrix is

$$\boldsymbol{\Sigma}_Z = \begin{pmatrix} 1 & 0 & 0 & 1 \\ 0 & 1 & 0 & 1 \\ 0 & 0 & 1 & 1 \\ 1 & 1 & 1 & 3.000001 \end{pmatrix}. \qquad [3.50]$$

The covariance matrix of $\boldsymbol{X}$ is singular. It has determinant 0. The covariance matrix of $\mathbf{Z}$ is not singular, but with a determinant of .000001, it is "almost" singular. The random variable Z_4 is almost a linear polynomial of Z_1, Z_2, and Z_3, but not quite. We added just enough random "noise" to make it linearly independent. We say a random vector is **multicollinear** if it is "almost" singular in this sense.

Realizations of a multicollinear random vector tend to cluster near a plane within $\mathbb{R}^n$. They don't all lie in that plane, but they "almost" do. This is illustrated with realizations of a two-dimensional multicollinear random vector $\mathbf{Z}$ in Exhibit 3.8.

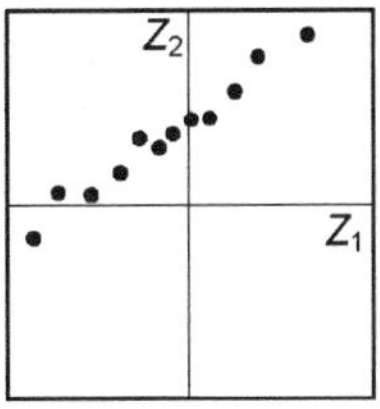

Exhibit 3.8 Realizations of a multicollinear two-dimensional random vector **Z**. Component Z_2 is "almost" a linear polynomial of component Z_1.

We may think of a random vector $\mathbf{Z}$ as being "almost" singular if its covariance matrix has a determinant $|\boldsymbol{\Sigma}_{\mathbf{Z}}|$ close to 0. In practical applications, the magnitude of this determinant will depend upon the units in which components of $\mathbf{Z}$ are measured. A more reasonable test for multicollinearity is to consider the determinant $|\boldsymbol{\rho}_{\mathbf{Z}}|$ of the correlation matrix of $\mathbf{Z}$. This determinant will always be in the interval [0, 1]. If it is close to 0, this is an indication of multicollinearity. Obviously, if it equals 0, $\mathbf{Z}$ is singular.

As we have seen, the dimensionality of a singular random vector $\mathbf{X}$ can be reduced with a simple change of variables. No information is lost, as we only eliminate extraneous random variables. Multicollinearity is more problematic. Reducing the dimensionality of a multicollinear random vector $\mathbf{Z}$ requires an approximation that somehow identifies and discards minor randomness that is preventing the covariance matrix from being singular.

This is the situation we face with our natural gas portfolio. We feel confident that the natural gas market can reasonably be modeled with less than 564 random variables, but we can't arbitrarily discard random variables! If our covariance matrix isn't singular, how can we replace our 564 random variables with a smaller set that conveys essentially the same information? Principal component analysis will provide a solution.

Exercises

3.17 Below are described four three-dimensional random vectors: $\mathbf{W}$, $\mathbf{V}$, $\mathbf{X}$, and $\mathbf{Y}$. Assuming their second moments exist, which of the random vectors has a singular covariance matrix?

a. Components V_1 and V_2 are independent. Component $V_3 = 2V_1 - 5V_2 + 1$.

b. Components W_1 and W_2 are independent. Component $W_3 = W_1 - log(W_2)$.

c. Components X_1, X_2, and X_3 represent next year's total returns for three different companies' common stocks.

d. Components Y_1 and Y_2 represent tomorrow's prices for the nearby 3-month Treasury bill and 3-month Eurodollar futures. Component Y_3 represents tomorrow's price difference between those two futures.

3.18 True or false:

a. A covariance matrix is singular if and only if it is positive definite.

b. A covariance matrix is nonsingular if and only if it is positive semidefinite.

c. Every random vector has a positive semidefinite covariance matrix.

3.19 Which of the following covariance matrices $\boldsymbol{\Sigma}$ are singular? Which are multicollinear?

a.

$$\begin{pmatrix} 1.21 & 2.31 & 1.32 \\ 2.31 & 4.41 & 2.52 \\ 1.32 & 2.52 & 2.65 \end{pmatrix} \qquad [3.51]$$

b.

$$\begin{pmatrix} 1.69 & 1.82 & 0.91 \\ 1.82 & 1.97 & 0.98 \\ 0.91 & 0.98 & 0.58 \end{pmatrix} \qquad [3.52]$$

c.

$$\begin{pmatrix} 8.19 & 1.20 & 1.68 \\ 1.20 & 2.68 & 2.24 \\ 1.68 & 2.24 & 6.40 \end{pmatrix} \qquad [3.53]$$

3.20 Consider a singular random vector $\boldsymbol{X}$ with mean vector and covariance matrix

$$\boldsymbol{\mu}_X = \begin{pmatrix} 1 \\ 0 \\ -2 \end{pmatrix} \quad \text{and} \quad \boldsymbol{\Sigma}_X = \begin{pmatrix} 1 & 2 & -1 \\ 2 & 13 & 1 \\ -1 & 1 & 2 \end{pmatrix}. \qquad [3.54]$$

Transform $\boldsymbol{X}$ into an equivalent two-dimensional random vector $\boldsymbol{Y}$ with mean vector $\boldsymbol{0}$ and covariance matrix $\boldsymbol{I}$:

$$\boldsymbol{\mu}_Y = \begin{pmatrix} 0 \\ 0 \end{pmatrix} \quad \text{and} \quad \boldsymbol{\Sigma}_Y = \begin{pmatrix} 1 & 0 \\ 0 & 1 \end{pmatrix}. \qquad [3.55]$$

3.7. PRINCIPAL COMPONENT ANALYSIS

With principal component analysis, we transform a random vector $\boldsymbol{Z}$ with correlated components Z_i into a random vector $\boldsymbol{D}$ with uncorrelated components D_i. This is called an **orthogonalization** of $\boldsymbol{Z}$.

Principal component analysis can be performed on any random vector $\boldsymbol{Z}$ whose second moments exist, but it is most useful with multicollinear random vectors. Principal component analysis takes the plane in which realizations of a multicollinear random vector "almost" sit and aligns it with the coordinate system of $\mathbb{R}^n$.

The components of $\boldsymbol{D}$ that are perpendicular to the transformed plane have small, almost trivial standard deviations. Discarding these components provides a lower-dimensional approximate representation for $\boldsymbol{Z}$. This is illustrated with realizations of a multicollinear two-dimensional random vector $\boldsymbol{Z}$ in Exhibit 3.9:

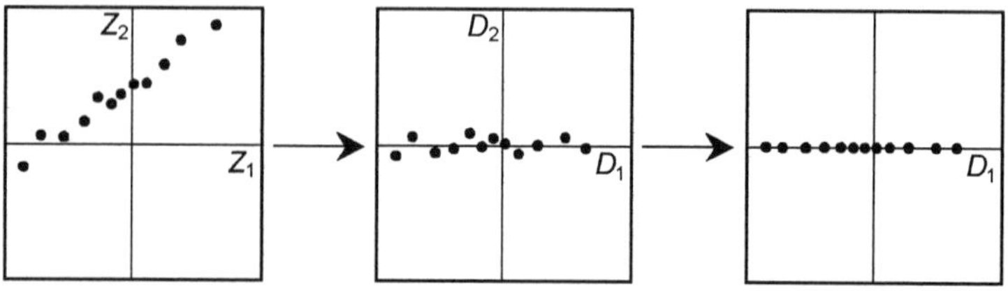

Exhibit 3.9 Principal component analysis can be used to reduce the dimensionality of a multicollinear random vector. Realizations for a multicollinear two-dimensional random vector $\boldsymbol{Z}$ are illustrated in the left graph. Principal component analysis transforms $\boldsymbol{Z}$ into an equivalent multicollinear random vector $\boldsymbol{D}$ that is aligned with the coordinate system of $\mathbb{R}^2$. Realizations of $\boldsymbol{D}$ are shown in the middle graph. Discarding the second component D_2 of $\boldsymbol{D}$ transforms $\boldsymbol{D}$ into a one-dimensional approximate representation of the two-dimensional $\boldsymbol{Z}$. Realizations of this representation are shown in the right graph.

EXAMPLE: EUROPEAN CURRENCIES. Suppose today is June 30, 2000. We consider a random vector $\boldsymbol{Z}$ whose components represent the simple price returns that specific European currencies will realize versus the US dollar (USD) over the upcoming trading day:

$$\boldsymbol{Z} = \begin{pmatrix} Z_1 \\ Z_2 \\ Z_3 \\ Z_4 \\ Z_5 \\ Z_6 \\ Z_7 \end{pmatrix} \sim \begin{pmatrix} \text{Swiss franc (CHF) price return} \\ \text{Danish krone (DKK) price return} \\ \text{Euro (EUR) price return} \\ \text{British pound (GBP) price return} \\ \text{Greek drachma (GRD) price return} \\ \text{Norwegian krone (NOK) price return} \\ \text{Swedish krona (SEK) price return} \end{pmatrix}. \qquad [3.56]$$

Exhibit 3.10 graphs 18 months of daily exchange-rate data drawn from the period immediately following the launch of the new EUR currency. In our data, the EUR weakens following its launch, and the remaining European currencies—those that did not join the EUR on January 1, 1999—weaken in sympathy. All the currencies track the EUR, but the GBP does so the least. It is less correlated with the EUR and loses value more slowly.

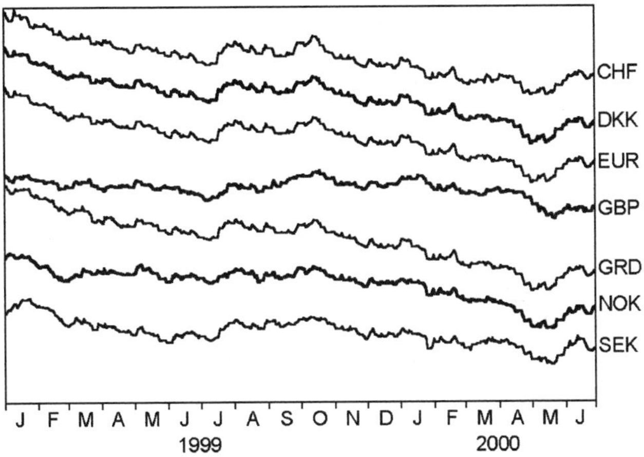

Exhibit 3.10 Historical exchange rates versus the USD for the period January 1, 1999 through June 30, 2000. Exchange rates are presented as USD/unit of currency, so a rising curve indicates a strengthening currency. Exchange rates are individually scaled so they all fit on the graph.

We assume $\boldsymbol{\mu}_Z = \mathbf{0}$.[5] Based upon a time series analysis of the historical price data, we construct a covariance matrix for $\mathbf{Z}$

$$\boldsymbol{\Sigma}_Z = \begin{pmatrix} .00004256 & .00003912 & .00003900 & .00001737 & .00003776 & .00002726 & .00002735 \\ .00003912 & .00003994 & .00003929 & .00001602 & .00003865 & .00002829 & .00002848 \\ .00003900 & .00003929 & .00003935 & .00001599 & .00003829 & .00002793 & .00002810 \\ .00001737 & .00001602 & .00001599 & .00002105 & .00001524 & .00001256 & .00001175 \\ .00003776 & .00003865 & .00003829 & .00001524 & .00003961 & .00002782 & .00002805 \\ .00002726 & .00002829 & .00002793 & .00001256 & .00002782 & .00002959 & .00002603 \\ .00002735 & .00002848 & .00002810 & .00001175 & .00002805 & .00002603 & .00003220 \end{pmatrix}. \quad [3.57]$$

The corresponding correlation matrix is:

$$\boldsymbol{\rho}_Z = \begin{pmatrix} 1 & .9488 & .9530 & .5804 & .9197 & .7682 & .7388 \\ .9488 & 1 & .9911 & .5523 & .9717 & .8229 & .7940 \\ .9530 & .9911 & 1 & .5554 & .9698 & .8184 & .7894 \\ .5804 & .5523 & .5554 & 1 & .5276 & .5031 & .4512 \\ .9197 & .9717 & .9698 & .5276 & 1 & .8124 & .7855 \\ .7682 & .8229 & .8184 & .5031 & .8124 & 1 & .8434 \\ .7388 & .7940 & .7894 & .4512 & .7855 & .8434 & 1 \end{pmatrix}. \quad [3.58]$$

The correlations are all positive. Several exceed 0.90. The one between DKK and EUR exceeds 0.99. The smallest is a respectable 0.45 between GBP and SEK.

[5] An alternative would be to derive a mean vector based upon interest rate parity.

With such pronounced interdependencies between its components, we expect $\boldsymbol{Z}$ to be multicollinear, and it is. The correlation matrix has determinant $|\boldsymbol{\rho}| = .0000045$.

To define principal components of $\boldsymbol{Z}$, we calculate orthonormal[6] eigenvectors $\boldsymbol{v}_i$ of the covariance matrix $\boldsymbol{\Sigma}$ of $\boldsymbol{Z}$. We arrange these as the columns of a matrix:

$$\boldsymbol{v} = \begin{pmatrix} .4331 & -.2211 & -.2704 & .1110 & .7702 & -.2897 & -.0306 \\ .4323 & -.0401 & -.2237 & -.0083 & -.1764 & .4874 & -.7020 \\ .4288 & -.0566 & -.2312 & -.0005 & -.1269 & .4873 & .7112 \\ .1929 & -.7592 & .6074 & .0542 & -.1208 & .0005 & -.0013 \\ .4245 & .0026 & -.2402 & -.0362 & -.5658 & -.6635 & .0198 \\ .3324 & .3361 & .4134 & -.7622 & .1549 & -.0261 & .0057 \\ .3373 & .5070 & .4753 & .6343 & .0270 & -.0118 & .0048 \end{pmatrix}. \qquad [3.59]$$

The eigenvectors are graphed in Exhibit 3.11. Corresponding eigenvalues λ_i are also indicated.

The eigenvectors may be thought of as "modes of fluctuation" of random vector $\boldsymbol{Z}$. We observed in our historical data a tendency for the European currencies to move together. This is reflected in the first eigenvector. It describes a broad move in all the currencies, with the GBP participating about half as much as the other currencies. The second eigenvector has the GBP moving in opposition to the NOK and SEK, with the CHF moving modestly with the GBP. The third eigenvector describes the GBP, NOK, and SEK moving together in opposition to the other currencies. The remaining eigenvectors describe other "modes of fluctuation."

If the eigenvectors $\boldsymbol{v}_i$ are modes of fluctuations of $\boldsymbol{Z}$, then $\boldsymbol{Z}$ is a random combination of those modes of fluctuation:

$$\boldsymbol{Z} = D_1\boldsymbol{v}_1 + D_2\boldsymbol{v}_2 + \cdots + D_7\boldsymbol{v}_7 = \boldsymbol{vD}. \qquad [3.60]$$

The D_i are the principal components of $\boldsymbol{Z}$. They are random variables that define each mode of fluctuation's random contribution to $\boldsymbol{Z}$. The D_i are uncorrelated with variances equal to the eigenvalues of their corresponding eigenvectors. The vector $\boldsymbol{D}$ of principal components has mean $\boldsymbol{\mu}_D = \boldsymbol{0}$ and covariance matrix

$$\boldsymbol{\Sigma}_D = \begin{pmatrix} .00020719 & 0 & 0 & 0 & 0 & 0 & 0 \\ 0 & .00001469 & 0 & 0 & 0 & 0 & 0 \\ 0 & 0 & .00001305 & 0 & 0 & 0 & 0 \\ 0 & 0 & 0 & .00000471 & 0 & 0 & 0 \\ 0 & 0 & 0 & 0 & .00000315 & 0 & 0 \\ 0 & 0 & 0 & 0 & 0 & .00000117 & 0 \\ 0 & 0 & 0 & 0 & 0 & 0 & .00000035 \end{pmatrix}. \qquad [3.61]$$

[6]A set of vectors is **orthonormal** if they are orthogonal and normalized (of length 1).

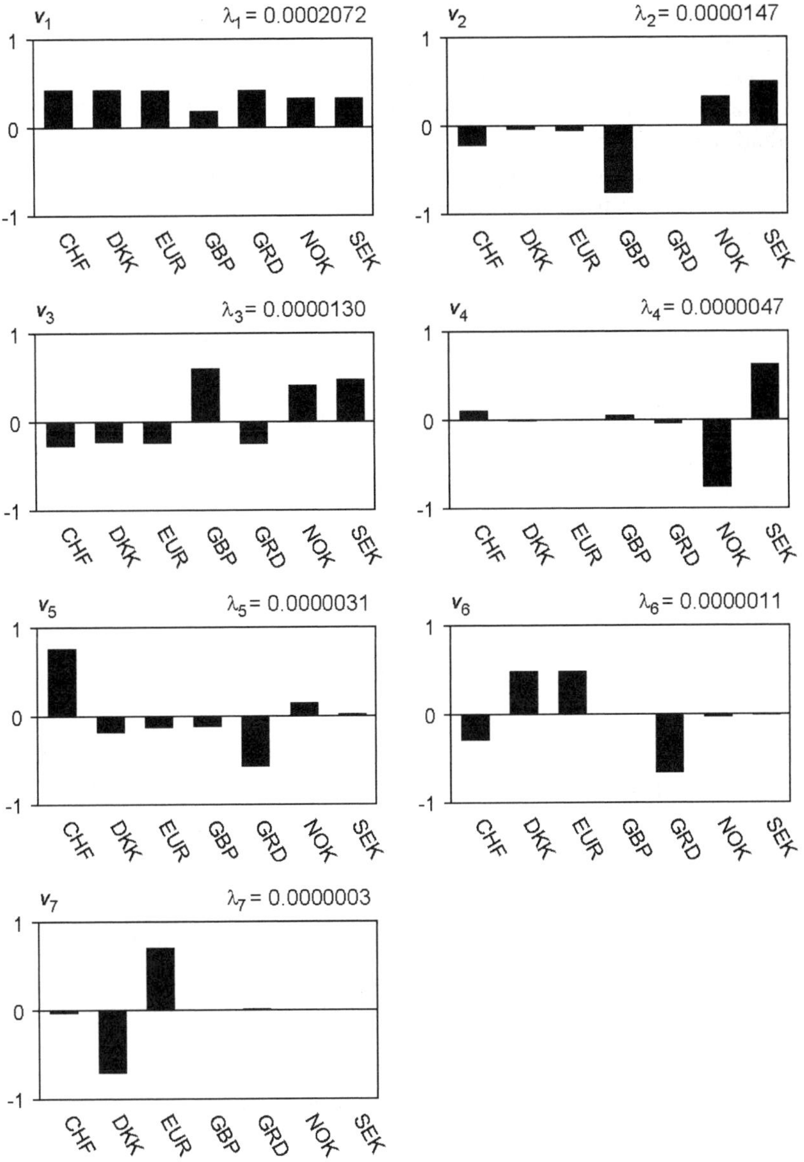

Exhibit 3.11 Eigenvectors $\mathbf{v}_i$ of covariance matrix [3.57]. Corresponding eigenvalues λ_i are also indicated.

We have ordered our principal components according to their variances. From our covariance matrix $\mathbf{\Sigma}_D$, we see that the first three principal components are more significant than the rest. The last two principal components, D_6 and D_7, have variances that are less than 1% of the variance of D_1. Their contribution to random vector $\mathbf{Z}$ is trivial.

We can approximate $\mathbf{Z}$ by discarding from [3.60] insignificant principal components. The more we discard, the simpler—and cruder!—will be our approximation. If we want to be aggressive in our approximation, we can discard the contributions of the last four principal components, and approximate $\mathbf{Z}$ with just the first three. A more accurate approximation can be obtained by discarding only the last two. For this example, we pursue the more aggressive course. We define

$$\widetilde{\mathbf{Z}} = D_1\mathbf{v}_1 + D_2\mathbf{v}_2 + D_3\mathbf{v}_3. \qquad [3.62]$$

and approximate $\mathbf{Z}$ with $\widetilde{\mathbf{Z}}$. Like $\mathbf{Z}$, $\widetilde{\mathbf{Z}}$ has mean vector $\mathbf{0}$. Its covariance matrix is obtained from [3.61] and [3.62] using [3.31]:

$$\mathbf{\Sigma}_{\widetilde{\mathbf{Z}}} = \begin{pmatrix} .00004054 & .00003971 & .00003948 & .00001763 & .00003893 & .00002728 & .00002694 \\ .00003971 & .00003940 & .00003912 & .00001595 & .00003872 & .00002837 & .00002853 \\ .00003948 & .00003912 & .00003884 & .00001594 & .00003844 & .00002800 & .00002811 \\ .00001763 & .00001595 & .00001594 & .00002099 & .00001503 & .00001281 & .00001159 \\ .00003893 & .00003872 & .00003844 & .00001503 & .00003809 & .00002795 & .00002820 \\ .00002728 & .00002837 & .00002800 & .00001281 & .00002795 & .00002678 & .00002830 \\ .00002694 & .00002853 & .00002811 & .00001159 & .00002820 & .00002830 & .00003030 \end{pmatrix}. \qquad [3.63]$$

Comparing this covariance matrix with [3.57], you can judge for yourself the quality of our approximation.

Principal Components

Our example informally introduced principal components. Now let's formalize them. Consider an n-dimensional random vector $\mathbf{Z}$ with mean $\boldsymbol{\mu}_{\mathbf{Z}}$ and nonsingular covariance matrix $\mathbf{\Sigma}_{\mathbf{Z}}$. We construct principal components in such a manner that the first accounts for as much of the variability of $\mathbf{Z}$ as possible. The second accounts for as much of the remaining variability of $\mathbf{Z}$ as possible, and so on.

Specifically, the first principal component D_1 is defined as

$$D_1 = \mathbf{v}_1'(\mathbf{Z} - \boldsymbol{\mu}_{\mathbf{Z}}), \qquad [3.64]$$

where $\mathbf{v}_1$ has unit length and is selected to maximize the variance of D_1. This is achieved by setting $\mathbf{v}_1$ equal to the normalized first eigenvector of $\mathbf{\Sigma}_{\mathbf{Z}}$—the eigenvector with the largest eigenvalue. In this case, the variance of D_1 equals that eigenvalue, λ_1.

The second principal component D_2 is defined as

$$D_2 = \mathbf{v}_2'(\mathbf{Z} - \boldsymbol{\mu}_{\mathbf{Z}}), \qquad [3.65]$$

where $\boldsymbol{v}_2$ is selected from the set of all n-dimensional unit vectors that are orthogonal to $\boldsymbol{v}_1$ in such a manner as to maximize the variance of D_2. This is achieved by setting $\boldsymbol{v}_2$ equal to the normalized second eigenvector of $\boldsymbol{\Sigma}_Z$—the eigenvector with the second largest eigenvalue. The variance of D_2 equals that eigenvalue, λ_2.

Proceeding in this manner, we define the remaining principal components. There will be m principal components D_i, each one corresponding to a normalized eigenvector $\boldsymbol{v}_i$ of $\boldsymbol{\Sigma}_Z$. We can represent

$$\boldsymbol{Z} = D_1\boldsymbol{v}_1 + D_2\boldsymbol{v}_2 + \cdots + D_m\boldsymbol{v}_m + \boldsymbol{\mu}_Z = \boldsymbol{vD} + \boldsymbol{\mu}_Z. \qquad [3.66]$$

The vector of principal components $\boldsymbol{D}$ has mean $\boldsymbol{\mu}_D = \boldsymbol{0}$ and covariance matrix

$$\boldsymbol{\Sigma}_D = \begin{pmatrix} \lambda_1 & 0 & \cdots & 0 \\ 0 & \lambda_2 & & \vdots \\ \vdots & & \ddots & 0 \\ 0 & 0 & \cdots & \lambda_m \end{pmatrix}. \qquad [3.67]$$

If $\boldsymbol{\Sigma}_Z$ is nonsingular, the number m of principal components equals the dimensionality n of $\boldsymbol{Z}$. If $\boldsymbol{\Sigma}_Z$ is singular, some of its eigenvalues will equal 0, and the number m of principal components will be less than the dimensionality n of $\boldsymbol{\Sigma}_Z$. In this case, [3.66] will have reduced the dimensionality of the singular $\boldsymbol{Z}$ in the same manner as that described in Section 3.6.

Choice of Weights

Principal component analysis is best performed on random variables whose standard deviations are reflective of their relative significance for an application. This is because principal component analysis depends upon both the correlations between random variables and the standard deviations of those random variables. If we were to change the standard deviations of a set of random variables but leave their correlations the same, this would change their principal components. In a sense, principal component analysis uses standard deviation as a metric of significance. If one random variable has a standard deviation that far exceeds the rest, that random variable will dominate the first eigenvector.

Unfortunately, there may be no correspondence between a random variable's standard deviation and its significance. Standard deviations depend upon the units in which a random variable is measured. Suppose a random variable reflects the time it takes for some event to occur, and if the random variable is measured in days, it has a standard deviation of 13.5. If the standard deviation is measured in hours, it is 324. Measured in minutes, it becomes 19,440. Certainly, the 19,440 standard deviation is no more significant than the 13.5 standard deviation, but principal component analysis will treat it as more significant!

If we use principal components only to orthogonalize a random vector, this will not be a problem. No information is lost. It will be a problem if principal components are discarded to form an approximation. In this case, information is lost. Before we discard principal components that appear "insignificant," we should make sure that they truly are insignificant.

There are various solutions to this problem. We might insist that all random variables be measured in the same units, but this is not always feasible. If one random variable represents temperature and another represents volume, these are fundamentally different quantities. Also, identical units do not necessarily correspond to identical significance. Suppose we are analyzing blood samples for lead, and we have a random variable for each component of the blood. All components are measured in parts per million (ppm). Measured in ppm, the standard deviation of lead will be trivial compared to standard deviations for other constituents of the blood. Yet, the lead component is the most important random variable!

Alternatively, we might apply principal component analysis to normalized random variables:

$$Z_i^* = \frac{Z_i}{\sigma_i}. \qquad [3.68]$$

With this approach, we effectively apply principal component analysis to the random variables' correlation matrix. This represents a different weighting from that obtained by measuring all random variables in identical units, but not necessarily a better one.

Any solution may be reasonable in certain contexts and unreasonable in others. Each one weights the random variables in some manner. There is no objective way to assign weights, just as there is no objective way to assign "significance." Weights and "significance" can and should vary from one application to another. When we use principal components to reduce the dimensionality of a random vector, there is subjectivity in the process.

Exercises

3.21 Consider a random vector $\mathbf{Z}$ with mean and covariance matrix

$$\boldsymbol{\mu}_Z = \begin{pmatrix} 2.1 \\ 0.4 \\ 1.6 \end{pmatrix} \quad \text{and} \quad \boldsymbol{\Sigma}_Z = \begin{pmatrix} 13.82 & 10.73 & 12.21 \\ 10.73 & 16.82 & 1.74 \\ 12.21 & 1.74 & 18.18 \end{pmatrix}. \qquad [3.69]$$

a. Calculate the determinant of the corresponding correlation matrix.
b. Is $\mathbf{Z}$ singular, multicollinear, or neither of these?
c. ▦[7] Calculate the eigenvalues and eigenvectors of $\boldsymbol{\Sigma}_Z$.

[7]The symbol ▦ indicates that this is a computationally involved problem that may require computing tools more sophisticated than a spreadsheet.

d. Represent $\mathbf{Z}$ in terms of its principal components as in [3.66].
e. What is the covariance matrix $\boldsymbol{\Sigma}_D$ of the vector of principal components $\boldsymbol{D}$?
f. Construct an approximation $\widetilde{\mathbf{Z}}$ for $\mathbf{Z}$ based on the first two principal components of $\mathbf{Z}$.
g. Construct the covariance matrix of $\widetilde{\mathbf{Z}}$. Compare your result with the covariance matrix of $\mathbf{Z}$.

3.8. UNIFORM AND RELATED DISTRIBUTIONS

Until now, we have avoided mentioning any standard families of distributions such as the uniform, normal, or chi-squared families of distributions. This has been intentional. All the results we have discussed so far are general and assume no particular distributions. We emphasized this fact by not incorporating any standard distributions into the discussion. Let's reiterate. Formulas [3.30] and [3.31] for the mean and variance of a linear polynomial of a random vector are entirely general. So are principal component analysis, the fact that covariance matrices are positive semidefinite, and every other result we have presented so far. None assumes any particular distribution.

To construct probabilistic models, it is useful to consider standard families of distributions. We assume passing familiarity with a variety of distributions. See Evans et al. (1993) for summary information on important distributions. For our purposes, uniform distributions play a particularly important role, as do normal and related distributions. We review important properties of these in this and the next section. The distributions we consider in this section, along with a shorthand notation for each, are the:

1. uniform distribution: $U(a, b)$,
2. multivariate uniform distribution: $U_n(\Omega)$.

Uniform Distribution

A **uniform distribution** has constant probability density on an interval (a, b) and zero probability density elsewhere. The distribution is specified by two parameters: the end points a and b. We denote the distribution $U(a, b)$. Its PDF is

$$\phi(x) = \begin{cases} \dfrac{1}{b-a} & a < x < b, \\ 0 & \text{otherwise}, \end{cases} \qquad [3.70]$$

which is illustrated in Exhibit 3.12

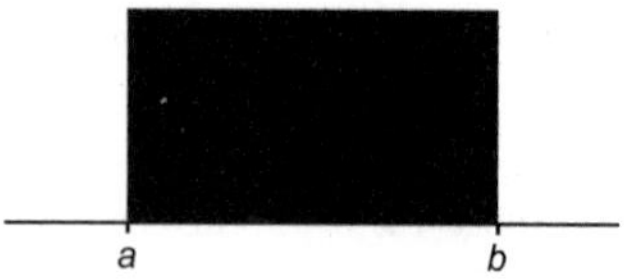

Exhibit 3.12 PDF of a uniform distribution $U(a, b)$.

A $U(a, b)$ random variable has CDF and inverse CDF:

$$\Phi(x) = \frac{x-a}{b-a} \qquad a < x < b, \tag{3.71}$$

$$\Phi^{-1}(q) = a + (b-a)q \quad 0 < q < 1. \tag{3.72}$$

The expectation, standard deviation, skewness, and kurtosis of a $U(a, b)$ random variable are:

$$\mu = \frac{a+b}{2}, \tag{3.73}$$

$$\sigma = \frac{b-a}{2\sqrt{3}}, \tag{3.74}$$

$$\eta_1 = 0, \tag{3.75}$$

$$\eta_2 = \frac{9}{5}. \tag{3.76}$$

Multivariate Uniform Distribution

Let $\Omega \subset \mathbb{R}^n$ be a bounded region with volume (area) $v(\Omega)$. The **multivariate uniform** distribution on Ω is denoted $U_n(\Omega)$ and has PDF

$$\phi(\boldsymbol{x}) = \begin{cases} \dfrac{1}{v(\Omega)} & \text{if } \boldsymbol{x} \in \Omega \\ 0 & \text{if } \boldsymbol{x} \notin \Omega \end{cases}. \tag{3.77}$$

In applications, the distribution $U_n((0, 1)^n)$ often arises. If $\boldsymbol{X} \sim U_n((0, 1)^n)$, its components X_i are independent random variables, each with marginal distribution $U(0, 1)$.

Exercises

3.22 Answer the following questions:

a. If $U \sim U(0, 1)$, how is $V = 1 - U$ distributed?

b. If $U \sim U(0, 1)$, how is $W = bU + a$ distributed for arbitrary constants a, b?

3.23 Suppose $\boldsymbol{U} \sim U_n((0, 1)^n)$. What is $Pr(U_i > 0.5 \text{ for all } i)$?

3.24 Suppose $\boldsymbol{V} \sim U_n(\Omega)$ where the region Ω is indicated in Exhibit 3.13.

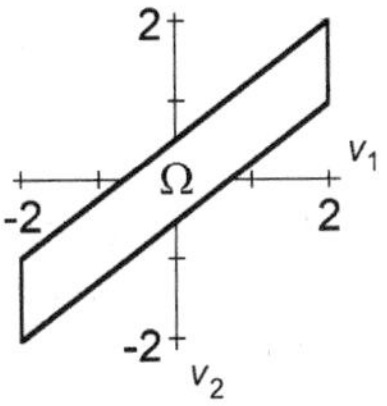

Exhibit 3.13 Region Ω for Exercise 3.24.

a. Is component V_1 marginally uniformly distributed?
b. Is component V_2 marginally uniformly distributed?
c. Are components V_1 and V_2 independent?

3.9. NORMAL AND RELATED DISTRIBUTIONS

We now consider normal and related distributions. Particular families we consider, along with shorthand notation for each, are:

1. normal: $N(\mu, \sigma^2)$,
2. lognormal: $\Lambda(\mu, \sigma^2)$,
3. chi-squared: $\chi^2(\nu, \delta^2)$,
4. joint-normal: $N_n(\boldsymbol{\mu}, \boldsymbol{\Sigma})$.

Normal Distributions

A **normal distribution** is specified by two parameters: a mean μ and variance σ^2. We denote it $N(\mu, \sigma^2)$. Its PDF is

$$\phi(x) = \frac{exp\left(-\frac{1}{2}\left(\frac{x-\mu}{\sigma}\right)^2\right)}{\sigma\sqrt{2\pi}}. \qquad [3.78]$$

This is graphed in Exhibit 3.14:

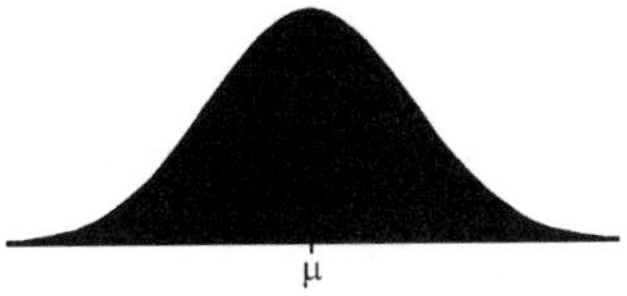

Exhibit 3.14 PDF of a normal distribution.

Irrespective of its mean or standard deviation, every normal distribution has skewness and kurtosis

$$\eta_1 = 0, \quad [3.79]$$

$$\eta_2 = 3. \quad [3.80]$$

With a kurtosis of 3, normal distributions fall precisely between platykurtosis and leptokurtosis. Distributions that have lower kurtosis than a normal distribution are platykurtic. Those that have higher kurtosis are leptokurtic.

A linear polynomial of a normal random variable is also normal. If $X \sim N(\mu, \sigma^2)$, then

$$bX + a \sim N(b\mu + a, (b\sigma)^2). \quad [3.81]$$

for any constants $a, b \in \mathbb{R}$. This means that any $N(\mu, \sigma^2)$ random variable X can be expressed as a linear polynomial of some $N(0, 1)$ random variable Z:

$$X = \sigma Z + \mu. \quad [3.82]$$

We call $N(0, 1)$ the **standard normal distribution**.

It has been proven that there is no closed-form expression for the CDF Φ of a normal distribution. The function exists. It simply cannot be expressed in terms of other standard functions. In practice, it and its inverse Φ^{-1} are approximated to many decimal places using computer algorithms. See Patel (1996).

Based upon [3.82], it follows that any quantile of an $N(\mu, \sigma^2)$ distribution occurs a distance from its mean μ that is a fixed multiple of σ. For example, the .90-quantile $\Phi_Z^{-1}(.90)$ of a standard normal variable Z is obtained from a standard normal table as 1.282. For any $N(\mu, \sigma^2)$ random variable X, the .90-quantile $\Phi_X^{-1}(.90)$ occurs 1.282 standard deviations σ above its mean μ because, by [3.82],

$$.90 = Pr(Z \leq 1.282) \quad [3.83]$$

$$= Pr((X - \mu)/\sigma \leq 1.282) \quad [3.84]$$

$$= Pr(X \leq 1.282\sigma + \mu). \quad [3.85]$$

The result is independent of the values of μ and σ. Accordingly, the .90-quantile of any $N(\mu, \sigma^2)$ random variable is 1.282 standard deviations σ greater than its mean μ. Results for other quantiles are shown in Exhibit 3.15:

q	$\Phi_X^{-1}(q)$
.50	μ
.90	$\mu + 1.282\sigma$
.95	$\mu + 1.645\sigma$
.975	$\mu + 1.960\sigma$
.99	$\mu + 2.326\sigma$

Exhibit 3.15 Selected quantiles of an $N(\mu, \sigma^2)$ distribution.

Because a normal distribution is symmetrical about its mean, the .10, .05, .025, and .01 quantiles can be obtained by replacing plus signs with minus signs in Exhibit 3.15.

Lognormal Distributions

A random variable X is **lognormally distributed** if the natural logarithm of X is normally distributed. A lognormal distribution may be specified by its mean μ and variance σ^2. Alternatively, it may be specified by the mean m and variance s^2 of the normally distributed $log(X)$. We denote a lognormal distribution $\Lambda(\mu, \sigma^2)$, but its PDF is most easily expressed in terms of m and s:

$$\phi(x) = \begin{cases} \dfrac{exp\left(-\dfrac{1}{2}\left(\dfrac{log(x) - m}{s}\right)^2\right)}{xs\sqrt{2\pi}} & x > 0 \\ 0 & \text{otherwise} \end{cases} \quad . \tag{3.86}$$

A lognormal distribution is illustrated in Exhibit 3.16.

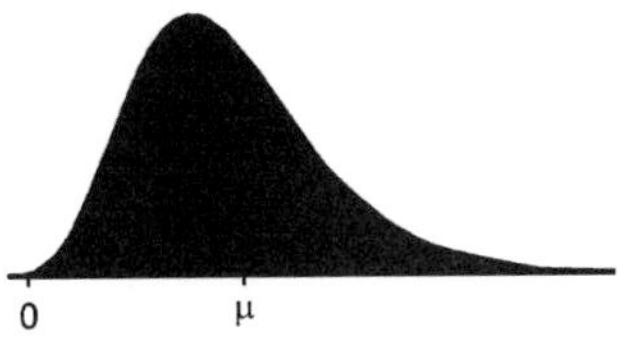

Exhibit 3.16 The PDF of a lognormal distribution.

The expectation, standard deviation, skewness, and kurtosis of a lognormal distribution are, in terms of m and s,

$$\mu = exp([2m + s^2]/2), \tag{3.87}$$

$$\sigma = \sqrt{exp[2m + 2s^2] - exp[2m + s^2]}, \tag{3.88}$$

$$\eta_1 = [exp(s^2) + 2]\sqrt{exp(s^2) - 1}, \tag{3.89}$$

$$\eta_2 = exp(4s^2) + 2exp(3s^2) + 3exp(2s^2) - 3. \tag{3.90}$$

If we know μ and σ instead of m and s, we can convert between these with

$$m = log\left(\frac{\mu^2}{\sqrt{\sigma^2 + \mu^2}}\right), \tag{3.91}$$

$$s = \sqrt{log[(\sigma/\mu)^2 + 1]}. \tag{3.92}$$

The reverse conversion is provided by [3.87] and [3.88].

As with the normal distribution, the CDF of a lognormal distribution exists but cannot be expressed in terms of standard functions. It can be valued using a standard normal table. Let $X \sim \Lambda(\mu, \sigma^2)$ with corresponding parameters m and s. Then $X = exp(sZ + m)$ for some $Z \sim N(0, 1)$. Denote the CDFs of X and Z as Φ_X and Φ_Z. By [3.82] and the definition of the lognormal distribution:

$$\Phi_X(x) = Pr(X \leq x) \quad [3.93]$$

$$= Pr(log(X) \leq log(x)) \quad [3.94]$$

$$= Pr(sZ + m \leq log(x)) \quad [3.95]$$

$$= Pr\left(Z \leq \frac{log(x) - m}{s}\right) \quad [3.96]$$

$$= \Phi_Z\left(\frac{log(x) - m}{s}\right), \quad [3.97]$$

which can be looked up in a standard normal table. Note that step [3.94] depends critically on the monotonicity of the *log* function. As indicated in Exhibit 3.17, $a \leq b$ if and only if $log(a) \leq log(b)$.

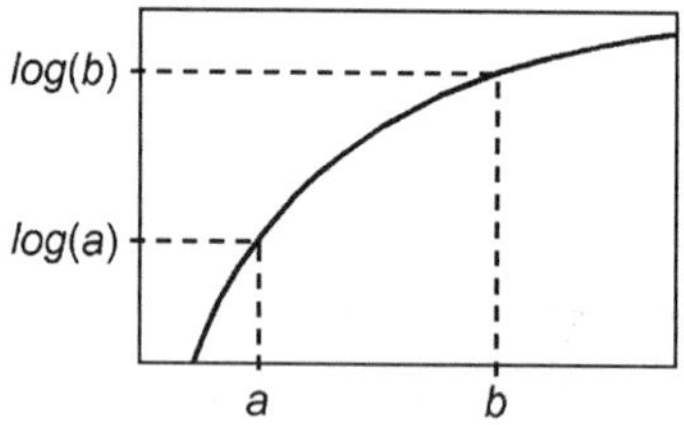

Exhibit 3.17 Because the *log* function is monotone, $a \leq b$ if and only if $log(a) \leq log(b)$.

Chi-Squared Distributions

Suppose Z is a standard normal random variable. How is Z^2 distributed? The answer is a chi-squared distribution. More generally, let $Z_1, Z_2, \ldots Z_\nu$ be ν independent standard normal random variables, and let $\delta_1, \delta_2, \ldots \delta_\nu$ be constants. Then the random variable

$$X = (Z_1 + \delta_1)^2 + (Z_2 + \delta_2)^2 + \cdots + (Z_\nu + \delta_\nu)^2 \quad [3.98]$$

has a chi-squared distribution with ν **degrees of freedom** and **noncentrality parameter**[8]

$$\delta^2 = \sum_{i=1}^{\nu} \delta_i^2. \quad [3.99]$$

[8]Treatment of the noncentrality parameter is not standardized in the literature. Some authors define the parameter as in [3.99] but denote it simply δ. Others define the parameter differently, for example, taking a square root in [3.99] or dividing the sum by 2.

We denote a chi-squared distribution $\chi^2(\nu, \delta^2)$. If $\delta^2 = 0$, the distribution is said to be **centrally chi-squared**. Otherwise, it is said to be **noncentrally chi-squared**. The PDF for a central chi-squared distribution is

$$\phi(x) = \begin{cases} \dfrac{x^{(\nu-2)/2} exp(-x/2)}{2^{\nu/2}\Gamma(\nu/2)} & x > 0, \\ 0 & \text{otherwise.} \end{cases} \quad [3.100]$$

For noncentral chi-squared distributions, this generalizes to

$$\phi(x) = \begin{cases} \dfrac{exp[-(x+\delta^2)/2]}{2^{\nu/2}} \displaystyle\sum_{j=0}^{\infty} \dfrac{x^{j-1+\nu/2}\delta^{2j}}{\Gamma(j+\nu/2)2^{2j}j!} & x > 0, \\ 0 & \text{otherwise,} \end{cases} \quad [3.101]$$

where $\Gamma(\,)$ denotes the gamma function[9]

$$\Gamma(y) = \int_0^{\infty} e^{-z} z^{y-1} dz. \quad [3.102]$$

The PDF of a chi-squared distribution is illustrated in Exhibit 3.18.

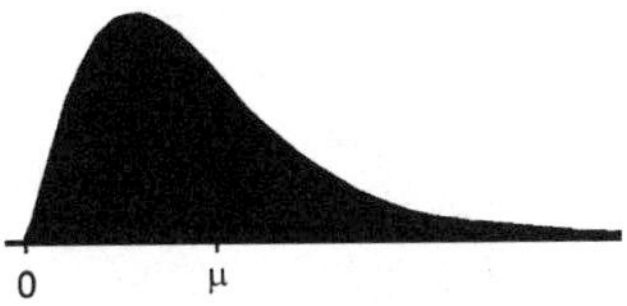

Exhibit 3.18 PDF of a chi-squared distribution.

The expectation, standard deviation, skewness, and kurtosis of a chi-squared distribution are

$$\mu = \nu + \delta^2, \quad [3.103]$$

$$\sigma = \sqrt{2(\nu + 2\delta^2)}, \quad [3.104]$$

$$\eta_1 = \frac{2^{3/2}(\nu + 3\delta^2)}{(\nu + 2\delta^2)^{3/2}}, \quad [3.105]$$

$$\eta_2 = 3 + \frac{12(\nu + 4\delta^2)}{(\nu + 2\delta^2)^2}. \quad [3.106]$$

[9] The gamma function is defined for any $y > 0$. It is related to the factorial function by $\Gamma(y) = (y-1)!$ for $y \in \mathbb{N}$.

Joint-Normal Distributions

Let $\boldsymbol{X}$ be an n-dimensional random vector with mean vector $\boldsymbol{\mu}$ and covariance matrix $\boldsymbol{\Sigma}$. Suppose the marginal distribution of each component X_i is normal. Let Y be a random variable defined as a linear polynomial

$$Y = \boldsymbol{b}\boldsymbol{X} + a \qquad [3.107]$$

of $\boldsymbol{X}$. Based upon [3.27] and [3.28], we can calculate the mean μ_Y and standard deviation σ_Y of Y. Knowing only that the marginal distributions of the X_i are normal, there is little more that we can say about the distribution of Y. However, there is an additional condition that we can impose upon $\boldsymbol{X}$ that will cause Y to be normally distributed. That condition is joint-normality.

The definition of joint-normality is almost trivial. A random vector $\boldsymbol{X}$ is said to be **joint-normal** if every nontrivial linear polynomial Y of $\boldsymbol{X}$ is normal. We denote the n-dimensional joint-normal distribution with mean vector $\boldsymbol{\mu}$ and covariance matrix $\boldsymbol{\Sigma}$ as $N_n(\boldsymbol{\mu}, \boldsymbol{\Sigma})$. If $\boldsymbol{\Sigma}$ is positive definite, it has PDF

$$\phi(\boldsymbol{x}) = \frac{exp\left(-\frac{1}{2}(\boldsymbol{x}-\boldsymbol{\mu})'\boldsymbol{\Sigma}^{-1}(\boldsymbol{x}-\boldsymbol{\mu})\right)}{\sqrt{(2\pi)^n\,|\boldsymbol{\Sigma}|}}, \qquad [3.108]$$

where $|\boldsymbol{\Sigma}|$ is the determinant of $\boldsymbol{\Sigma}$. Exhibit 3.19 illustrates a joint-normal distribution in two random variables X_1 and X_2. If we define $Y = X_1 + X_2$, then Y is normal.

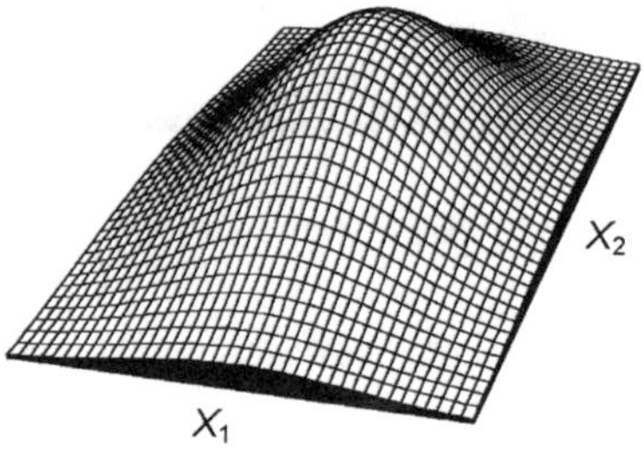

Exhibit 3.19 The PDF of a joint-normal distribution.

Now let's illustrate how a random vector may fail to be joint-normal despite each of its components being marginally normal.[10] Let $\boldsymbol{X}$ be a two-dimensional random vector with components X_1 and X_2. Let X_1 and Z be independent $N(0, 1)$ random variables, and define $X_2 = sign(X_1)|Z|$.[11] In this case, both X_1 and X_2

[10] See Stoyanov (1987) for more counterexamples relating to the joint-normal distribution.

[11] The *sign* function is defined as:

$$sign(x) = \begin{cases} 1 & x \geq 0 \\ -1 & x < 0 \end{cases}.$$

are $N(0, 1)$, but the vector $\boldsymbol{X}$, whose PDF is illustrated in Exhibit 3.20, is not joint-normal. In this case, the random variable $Y = X_1 + X_2$ is not normal. Instead, it has the PDF illustrated in Exhibit 3.21.

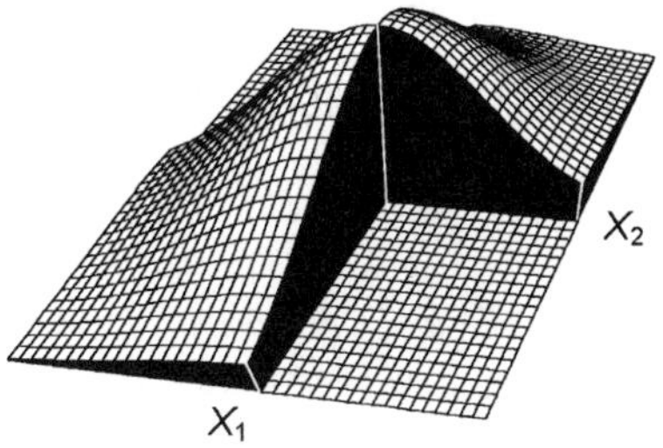

Exhibit 3.20 This PDF illustrates how a random vector $\boldsymbol{X}$ can have two components that are both marginally normal but not be joint-normal.

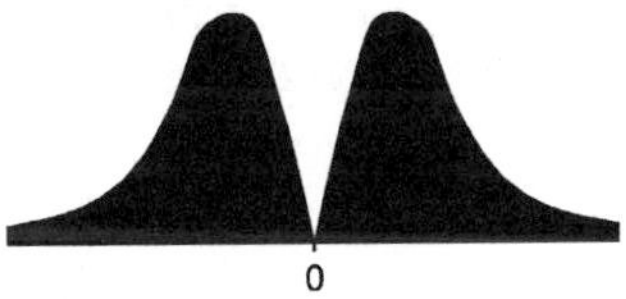

Exhibit 3.21 The PDF of $Y = X_1 + X_2$ is illustrated where X_1 and X_2 are components of random vector $\boldsymbol{X}$, whose PDF is illustrated in Exhibit 3.20. This example illustrates that a linear polynomial of normal random variables need not be normal.

A random vector is joint-normal with uncorrelated components if and only if the components are independent normal random variables.

A property of joint-normal distributions is the fact that marginal distributions and conditional distributions are either normal (if they are univariate) or joint-normal (if they are multivariate). Specifically, let $\boldsymbol{X} \sim N_n(\boldsymbol{\mu}, \boldsymbol{\Sigma})$. Select k components. Without loss of generality, suppose these are the first k components X_1, X_2, ... X_k. Let $\boldsymbol{X}_1$ be a k-dimensional vector comprising these components, and let $\boldsymbol{X}_2$ be an $(n-k)$-dimensional vector of the remaining components. These partition $\boldsymbol{X}$, $\boldsymbol{\mu}$, and $\boldsymbol{\Sigma}$ into sub-vectors and sub-matrices as follows

$$\boldsymbol{X} = \begin{pmatrix} \boldsymbol{X}_1 \\ \boldsymbol{X}_2 \end{pmatrix}, \quad \boldsymbol{\mu} = \begin{pmatrix} \boldsymbol{\mu}_1 \\ \boldsymbol{\mu}_2 \end{pmatrix}, \quad \boldsymbol{\Sigma} = \begin{pmatrix} \boldsymbol{\Sigma}_{1,1} & \boldsymbol{\Sigma}_{1,2} \\ \boldsymbol{\Sigma}_{2,1} & \boldsymbol{\Sigma}_{2,2} \end{pmatrix}. \qquad [3.109]$$

The marginal distribution of $\boldsymbol{X}_1$ is $N_k(\boldsymbol{\mu}_1, \boldsymbol{\Sigma}_{1,1})$ and that of $\boldsymbol{X}_2$ is $N_{n-k}(\boldsymbol{\mu}_2, \boldsymbol{\Sigma}_{2,2})$. If $\boldsymbol{\Sigma}_{2,2}$ is positive definite, the conditional distribution of $\boldsymbol{X}_1$, given that $\boldsymbol{X}_2 = \boldsymbol{x}_2$, is

$$N_k\left(\boldsymbol{\mu}_1 + \boldsymbol{\Sigma}_{1,2}\boldsymbol{\Sigma}_{2,2}^{-1}(\boldsymbol{x}_2 - \boldsymbol{\mu}_2), \boldsymbol{\Sigma}_{1,1} - \boldsymbol{\Sigma}_{1,2}\boldsymbol{\Sigma}_{2,2}^{-1}\boldsymbol{\Sigma}_{2,1}\right). \qquad [3.110]$$

If $\boldsymbol{X} \sim N_n(\boldsymbol{\mu}, \boldsymbol{\Sigma})$, $\boldsymbol{b}$ is a constant $m \times n$ matrix, and $\boldsymbol{a}$ is an m-dimensional constant vector, then

$$\boldsymbol{bX} + \boldsymbol{a} \sim N_m(\boldsymbol{b\mu} + \boldsymbol{a}, \boldsymbol{b\Sigma b}'). \qquad [3.111]$$

This generalizes property [3.81] of one-dimensional normal distributions.

Exercises

3.25 Answer the following questions. If the answer is some nonstandard distribution or cannot be determined from the information provided, say so.
   a. If $N \sim N(1, 4)$, how is $M = 3N + 5$ distributed?
   b. If $L \sim \Lambda(1, 3)$, how is $G = log(L)$ distributed?
   c. If $N \sim N(2, 6)$, how is $E = e^N$ distributed?
   d. If $N_1 \sim N(0, 9)$ and $N_2 \sim N(2, 1)$ have correlation 0.3, how is $M = N_1 + 3N_2$ distributed?
   e. If $N_1 \sim N(1, 1)$ and $N_2 \sim N(0, 4)$ are independent, how is $M = 2N_1 + N_2$ distributed?
   f. If $N \sim N(0, 1)$, how is $H = N^2$ distributed?
   g. If $N_1 \sim N(0, 1)$ and $N_2 \sim N(0, 1)$ are independent, how is $H = N_1^2 + (N_2 + 5)^2$ distributed?
   h. If $X \sim \chi^2(1, 0)$, how is $C = \sqrt{X}$ distributed?

3.26 Suppose $Z \sim N(0, 1)$. Use a standard normal table to determine $Pr(Z \leq 1.15)$.

3.27 Suppose $Z \sim N(0, 1)$. Use a standard normal table to determine $Pr(Z \leq -0.51)$. (Hint: Use the symmetry of the normal distribution to find a solution.)

3.28 Suppose $X \sim N(5, 7)$. Use a standard normal table to determine $Pr(X \leq 8)$.

3.29 Suppose $X \sim N(2, .09)$. Use a standard normal table to determine the .90 quantile $\Phi^{-1}(.90)$ of X.

3.30 Suppose $X \sim N(100, 36)$. Use a standard normal table to determine the .15 quantile $\Phi^{-1}(.15)$ of X.

3.31 Suppose $X \sim N(\mu, \sigma^2)$. Use a standard normal table to determine the .10, .70, and .80 quantiles of X.

3.32 Suppose $X \sim \Lambda(1.1, .0625)$. Use a standard normal table to determine $Pr(X \leq .9)$.

3.33 Suppose $X \sim \Lambda(1.05, 0.01)$. Use a standard normal table to determine the .75 quantile $\Phi^{-1}(.75)$ of X.

3.10. MIXTURES OF DISTRIBUTIONS

Consider an experiment. You will flip a fair coin. If it comes up heads, you will draw a number from an $N(0, 4)$ distribution.[12] If it comes up tails, you will draw the number from an $N(0, 9)$ distribution. The number X that results from your experiment has a **mixed normal distribution** with PDF

$$\phi(x) = \frac{1}{2}\frac{exp(-x^2/8)}{2\sqrt{2\pi}} + \frac{1}{2}\frac{exp(-x^2/18)}{3\sqrt{2\pi}}. \qquad [3.112]$$

This is the weighted average of the PDFs of the two normal distributions. More generally, consider m random variables X_k, each with PDF ϕ_k. Define m weights $\xi_k > 0$ that sum to 1. Then the random variable X that has PDF

$$\phi(x) = \sum_{k=1}^{m} \xi_k \phi_k(x) \qquad [3.113]$$

is said to have a **mixed distribution**.

Parameters of Mixed Distributions

Consider a random variable X with a mixed distribution as described above. The X_k have means μ_k and standard deviations σ_k. Then X has mean μ and standard deviation σ given by

$$\mu = \sum_{k=1}^{m} \xi_k \mu_k, \qquad [3.114]$$

$$\sigma = \sqrt{\left(\sum_{k=1}^{m} \xi_k E\left(X_k^2\right)\right) - \mu^2} = \sqrt{\left(\sum_{k=1}^{m} \xi_k \left(\sigma_k^2 + \mu_k^2\right)\right) - \mu^2}. \qquad [3.115]$$

Calculating a q-quantile of X requires that we solve a nonlinear system of equations, which can be done with Newton's method. The q-quantile is that value x such that

$$\Phi_X(x) = \sum_{k=1}^{m} \xi_k \Phi_{X_k}(x) = q, \qquad [3.116]$$

so we seek probabilities $q_1, q_2, \ldots, q_m$ such that

$$\sum_{k=1}^{m} \xi_k q_k = q, \qquad [3.117]$$

[12] We discuss random variate generation in Chapter 5.

while

$$\Phi_{X_1}^{-1}(q_1) = \Phi_{X_2}^{-1}(q_2) = \cdots = \Phi_{X_m}^{-1}(q_m). \quad [3.118]$$

The desired q-quantile x of X then equals any of—all of—these:

$$x = \Phi_X^{-1}(q) = \Phi_{X_k}^{-1}(q_k). \quad [3.119]$$

These conditions are motivated for the case $m = 2$ in Exhibit 3.22.

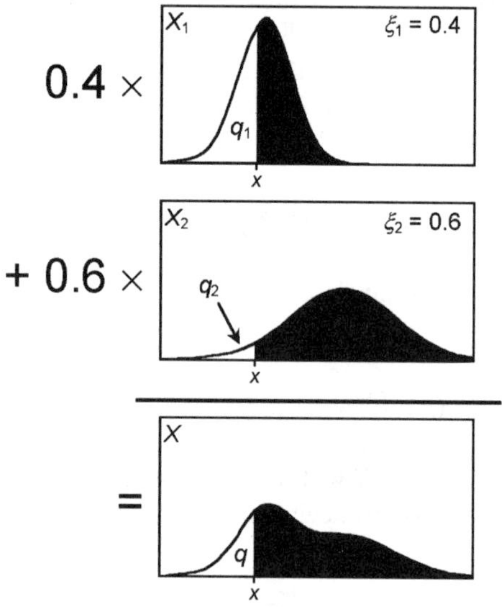

Exhibit 3.22 Random variable X is a mixture of normal random variables X_1 and X_2. Respective weights are $\xi_1 = 0.4$ and $\xi_2 = 0.6$. To find a q-quantile of X, we must find probabilities q_1 and q_2 such that $\xi_1 q_1 + \xi_2 q_2 = q$ while $\Phi_{X_1}^{-1}(q_1) = \Phi_{X_2}^{-1}(q_2)$.

Mixed-Normal Distributions

Since a normal distribution is defined by a mean and standard deviation, a mixed-normal distribution $N^m(\boldsymbol{\mu}, \boldsymbol{\sigma}^2, \boldsymbol{\xi})$ is defined with a vector $\boldsymbol{\mu}$ of means, a vector $\boldsymbol{\sigma}^2$ of variances, and a vector $\boldsymbol{\xi}$ of weights:

$$\boldsymbol{\mu} = \begin{pmatrix} \mu_1 \\ \mu_2 \\ \vdots \\ \mu_m \end{pmatrix}, \quad \boldsymbol{\sigma}^2 = \begin{pmatrix} \sigma_1^2 \\ \sigma_2^2 \\ \vdots \\ \sigma_m^2 \end{pmatrix}, \quad \boldsymbol{\xi} = \begin{pmatrix} \xi_1 \\ \xi_2 \\ \vdots \\ \xi_m \end{pmatrix}, \quad [3.120]$$

where the weights $\xi_k > 0$ sum to 1.

Mixed-normal distributions are useful for modeling multimodal or leptokurtic distributions. Exhibit 3.23 illustrates PDFs for two mixed-normal distributions.

The first is weighted 0.6 in an $N(-1, 1)$ distribution and 0.4 in an $N(2, 1)$ distribution to achieve a bimodal distribution. The second is evenly weighted in $N(0, 1)$ and $N(0, 9)$ distributions to achieve a leptokurtic distribution.

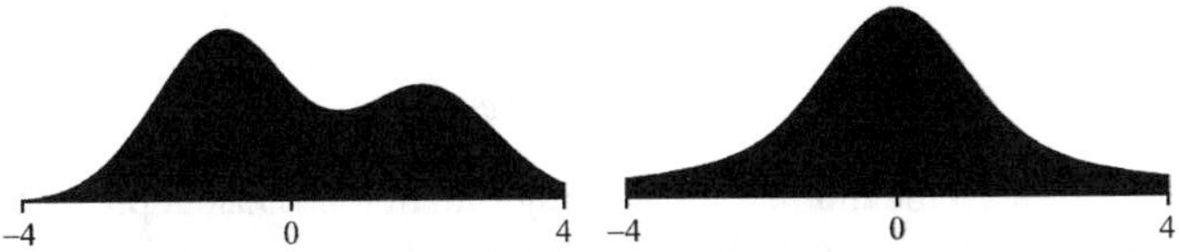

Exhibit 3.23 PDFs for two mixed normal distributions are illustrated. The first is weighted 0.6 in an $N(-1, 1)$ distribution and 0.4 in an $N(2, 1)$ distribution to achieve a bimodal distribution. The second is evenly weighted in $N(0, 1)$ and $N(0, 9)$ distributions to achieve a leptokurtic distribution.

Mixed Joint-Normal Distributions

While our discussion of mixed distributions has focused on random variables, similar concepts generalize for random vectors.

Market professionals often observe that market correlations seem exaggerated during large market swings. This phenomenon can be modeled with a mixture of joint-normal distributions—one with low variances and modest correlations and the other with high variances and more extreme correlations.

Consider vectors of n-dimensional mean vectors, $n \times n$ covariance matrices, and scalar weights:

$$\mu = \begin{pmatrix} \mu_1 \\ \mu_2 \\ \vdots \\ \mu_m \end{pmatrix}, \quad \Sigma = \begin{pmatrix} \Sigma_1 \\ \Sigma_2 \\ \vdots \\ \Sigma_m \end{pmatrix}, \quad \xi = \begin{pmatrix} \xi_1 \\ \xi_2 \\ \vdots \\ \xi_m \end{pmatrix}, \qquad [3.121]$$

where the weights $\xi_k > 0$ sum to 1. These define a **mixed joint-normal distribution** $N_n^m(\mu, \Sigma, \xi)$ with PDF

$$\phi(x) = \sum_{k=1}^{m} \xi_k \phi_k(x), \qquad [3.122]$$

where $\phi_k(x) \sim N_n(\mu_k, \Sigma_k)$.

Exercises

3.34 Derive formulas [3.114] and [3.115].

3.35 Consider random variable $X \sim N^2(\mu, \sigma^2, \xi)$, where:

$$\mu = \begin{pmatrix} -1 \\ 1 \end{pmatrix}, \quad \sigma^2 = \begin{pmatrix} 4 \\ 9 \end{pmatrix}, \quad \xi = \begin{pmatrix} 0.3 \\ 0.7 \end{pmatrix}. \qquad [3.123]$$

Calculate the mean, standard deviation, and .25-quantile of X.

3.11. MOMENT-GENERATING FUNCTIONS

The **moment-generating function** (MGF) of a random variable X is defined as:

$$M_X(w) = E(e^{wX}) \quad [3.124]$$

for $w \in \mathbb{R}$. We call it the moment-generating function because it provides a means of calculating the moments of X. If the MGF is finite on an open interval about $w = 0$, then all the moments of X exist and the kth moment of X equals the kth derivative with respect to w of the MGF evaluated at $w=0$. Heuristically, we motivate this result by applying the Taylor series expansion for the exponential function in our definition [3.124]:

$$M_X(w) = E\left(1 + wx + \frac{(wx)^2}{2!} + \frac{(wx)^3}{3!} + \frac{(wx)^4}{4!} + \cdots\right). \quad [3.125]$$

If $M_X(w)$ is finite on some interval about the point $w = 0$, it can be shown that the expectation of the sum equals the sum of the expectations

$$M_X(w) = 1 + E(wX) + E\left(\frac{(wX)^2}{2!}\right) + E\left(\frac{(wX)^3}{3!}\right) + E\left(\frac{(wX)^4}{4!}\right) + \cdots \quad [3.126]$$

$$= 1 + wE(X) + \frac{w^2E(X^2)}{2!} + \frac{w^3E(X^3)}{3!} + \frac{w^4E(X^4)}{4!} + \cdots \quad [3.127]$$

You may confirm that the kth derivative of [3.127] with respect to w evaluating at $w = 0$ yields the kth moment $E(X^k)$.

Let X be a random variable and $a, b \in \mathbb{R}$. Define a new random variable $Y = bX + a$. By definition [3.124], the MGF for the new random variable is related to the MGF of X by

$$M_Y(w) = e^{aw} M_X(bw). \quad [3.128]$$

More generally, suppose $\boldsymbol{X}$ is an n-dimensional random vector with independent components X_i; $\boldsymbol{b}$ is an n-dimensional row vector $(b_1\ b_2\ \ldots\ b_n)$, and $a \in \mathbb{R}$. Define the random variable $Y = \boldsymbol{bX} + a$. The MGF of Y is

$$M_Y(w) = e^{aw} M_{X_1}(b_1w) M_{X_2}(b_2w) \cdots M_{X_n}(b_nw). \quad [3.129]$$

A uniform, $U(a, b)$, random variable has MGF

$$M(w) = \frac{e^{bw} - e^{aw}}{w(b-a)}. \quad [3.130]$$

Those of $N(\mu, \sigma^2)$ or $\chi^2(\nu, \delta^2)$ random variables are, respectively,

$$M(w) = exp\left(\mu w + \frac{\sigma^2 w^2}{2}\right), \qquad [3.131]$$

$$M(w) = \frac{exp[\delta^2 w/(1-2w)]}{(1-2w)^{\nu/2}}, \quad w < 1/2. \qquad [3.132]$$

The MGF for a lognormal random variable is derived by Leipnik (1991). It is complicated, so we do not present it here.

Exercises

3.36 ▦ Consider a two-dimensional random vector $\boldsymbol{Z}$, whose components are independent and both have $U(0, 1)$ marginal PDFs. Let $Y = Z_1 + Z_2$. Use moment-generating functions to calculate $E(Y^2)$.

3.12. QUADRATIC POLYNOMIALS OF JOINT-NORMAL RANDOM VECTORS

Formulas [3.27] and [3.28] provide general expressions for the mean and variance of a linear polynomial of a random vector. What about the mean and variance of a quadratic polynomial of a random vector? Unfortunately, no general formulas exist. However, if we restrict our attention to quadratic polynomials of a joint-normal random vector, there are expressions for the mean, variance, and all moments. To obtain these, we generalize an earlier result regarding chi-squared distributions.

Simplified Representation

In Section 3.9, we saw that the specific form [3.98] of a quadratic polynomial of a joint standard normal random vector has a chi-squared distribution. Generalizing this, we shall demonstrate that *any* quadratic polynomial of *any* joint-normal random vector can be expressed as a linear polynomial of independent chi-squared and normal random variables. Specifically, let $\boldsymbol{X} \sim N_m(\boldsymbol{\mu}, \boldsymbol{\Sigma})$ with $\boldsymbol{\Sigma}$ positive-definite.[13] Define Y as a quadratic polynomial of $\boldsymbol{X}$:

$$Y = \boldsymbol{X}'\boldsymbol{c}\boldsymbol{X} + \boldsymbol{b}\boldsymbol{X} + a. \qquad [3.133]$$

---

[13] We lose no generality by assuming $\boldsymbol{\Sigma}$ is positive-definite. If $\boldsymbol{\Sigma}$ were singular, we could perform dimensional reduction as described in Section 3.6 to obtain a positive-definite joint-normal random vector.

Let z be the Cholesky matrix of $\boldsymbol{\Sigma}$, and define $\boldsymbol{u}$ as a square matrix whose rows comprise orthonormal eigenvectors of $\boldsymbol{z}'\boldsymbol{c}\boldsymbol{z}$. By construction, $\boldsymbol{u}$ is orthogonal: $\boldsymbol{u}^{-1} = \boldsymbol{u}'$. Define the change of variables

$$\dot{\boldsymbol{X}} = \boldsymbol{u}\boldsymbol{z}^{-1}(\boldsymbol{X} - \boldsymbol{\mu}). \qquad [3.134]$$

Then, by [3.30] and [3.31], $\dot{\boldsymbol{X}}$ is joint-normal with mean vector

$$E(\dot{\boldsymbol{X}}) = E[\boldsymbol{u}\boldsymbol{z}^{-1}(\boldsymbol{X} - \boldsymbol{\mu})] \qquad [3.135]$$

$$= \boldsymbol{u}\boldsymbol{z}^{-1}(E[\boldsymbol{X}] - \boldsymbol{\mu}) \qquad [3.136]$$

$$= \boldsymbol{u}\boldsymbol{z}^{-1}(\boldsymbol{0}) \qquad [3.137]$$

$$= \boldsymbol{0} \qquad [3.138]$$

and covariance matrix $\dot{\boldsymbol{\Sigma}}$

$$\dot{\boldsymbol{\Sigma}} = (\boldsymbol{u}\boldsymbol{z}^{-1})\boldsymbol{\Sigma}(\boldsymbol{u}\boldsymbol{z}^{-1})' \qquad [3.139]$$

$$= \boldsymbol{u}\boldsymbol{z}^{-1}\boldsymbol{\Sigma}(\boldsymbol{z}')^{-1}\boldsymbol{u}' \qquad [3.140]$$

$$= \boldsymbol{u}\boldsymbol{I}\boldsymbol{u}' \qquad [3.141]$$

$$= \boldsymbol{I}. \qquad [3.142]$$

Accordingly, $\dot{\boldsymbol{X}} \sim N_m(\boldsymbol{0}, \boldsymbol{I})$. Applying our change of variables [3.134]:

$$Y = \boldsymbol{X}'\boldsymbol{c}\boldsymbol{X} + \boldsymbol{b}\boldsymbol{X} + a \qquad [3.143]$$

$$= (\boldsymbol{z}\boldsymbol{u}^{-1}\dot{\boldsymbol{X}} + \boldsymbol{\mu})'\boldsymbol{c}(\boldsymbol{z}\boldsymbol{u}^{-1}\dot{\boldsymbol{X}} + \boldsymbol{\mu}) + \boldsymbol{b}(\boldsymbol{z}\boldsymbol{u}^{-1}\dot{\boldsymbol{X}} + \boldsymbol{\mu}) + a \qquad [3.144]$$

$$= \dot{\boldsymbol{X}}'(\boldsymbol{u}\boldsymbol{z}'\boldsymbol{c}\boldsymbol{z}\boldsymbol{u}')\dot{\boldsymbol{X}} + [(2\boldsymbol{\mu}'\boldsymbol{c} + \boldsymbol{b})\boldsymbol{z}\boldsymbol{u}']\dot{\boldsymbol{X}} + (\boldsymbol{\mu}'\boldsymbol{c}\boldsymbol{\mu} + \boldsymbol{b}\boldsymbol{\mu} + a), \qquad [3.145]$$

so Y has form

$$Y = \dot{\boldsymbol{X}}'\dot{\boldsymbol{c}}\dot{\boldsymbol{X}} + \dot{\boldsymbol{b}}\dot{\boldsymbol{X}} + \dot{a}, \qquad [3.146]$$

where

$$\dot{\boldsymbol{c}} = \boldsymbol{u}\boldsymbol{z}'\boldsymbol{c}\boldsymbol{z}\boldsymbol{u}', \qquad [3.147]$$

$$\dot{\boldsymbol{b}} = (2\boldsymbol{\mu}'\boldsymbol{c} + \boldsymbol{b})\boldsymbol{z}\boldsymbol{u}', \qquad [3.148]$$

$$\dot{a} = \boldsymbol{\mu}'\boldsymbol{c}\boldsymbol{\mu} + \boldsymbol{b}\boldsymbol{\mu} + a. \qquad [3.149]$$

Recall that we defined $\boldsymbol{u}$ as a matrix whose rows comprise orthonormal eigenvectors of $\boldsymbol{z}'\boldsymbol{c}\boldsymbol{z}$. This means, by the spectral theorem of linear algebra, that the matrix $\dot{\boldsymbol{c}}$ is diagonal with diagonal elements equal to the eigenvalues of $\boldsymbol{z}'\boldsymbol{c}\boldsymbol{z}$. Consequently, Y depends upon no cross terms of the form $\dot{c}_{i,j}\dot{X}_i\dot{X}_j$. We can write [3.145] as

$$Y = \sum_{i=1}^{m} \left(\dot{c}_{i,i}\dot{X}_i^2 + \dot{b}_i\dot{X}_i\right) + \dot{a}, \qquad [3.150]$$

and conclude that Y depends upon each of the variables $\dot{X}_i$ in one of four ways:

- No dependence: $\dot{c}_{i,i} = 0$ and $\dot{b}_i = 0$.
- Linear dependence: $\dot{c}_{i,i} = 0$ and $\dot{b}_i \neq 0$, so Y depends upon a term $\dot{b}_i \dot{X}_i$.
- Central quadratic dependence: $\dot{c}_{i,i} \neq 0$ and $\dot{b}_i = 0$, so Y depends upon a term $\dot{c}_{i,i} \dot{X}_i^2$.
- Noncentral quadratic dependence: $\dot{c}_{i,i} \neq 0$ and $\dot{b}_i \neq 0$, so Y depends upon a term $\dot{c}_{i,i} \dot{X}_i^2 + \dot{b}_i \dot{X}_i$.

In the last case, "completing the squares" results in a dependence of the form

$$\dot{c}_{i,i} \left(\dot{X}_i + \frac{\dot{b}_i}{2\dot{c}_{i,i}} \right)^2 . \qquad [3.151]$$

Y is a linear polynomial of independent random variables, each of which is standard normal, central chi-squared with one degree of freedom, or noncentral chi-squared with one degree of freedom and noncentrality parameter $(\dot{b}_i / 2\dot{c}_{i,i})^2$.

Since a linear polynomial of independent normal random variables is itself normal, all normal terms can be combined into one. A general expression for Y is

$$Y = \left(\sum_{k=1}^{n} \gamma_k Q_k \right) + \beta Q_0 + \alpha \qquad [3.152]$$

where the Q_k are chi-squared with one degree of freedom, noncentrality parameters are obtainable from [3.151], and Q_0 is standard normal. The constants γ_k, β, and α can be calculated directly from the terms $\dot{\boldsymbol{c}}$, $\dot{\boldsymbol{b}}$, and $\dot{a}$.

EXAMPLE. Consider random vector $\boldsymbol{X} \sim N_3(\boldsymbol{\mu}, \boldsymbol{\Sigma})$ with

$$\boldsymbol{\mu} = \begin{pmatrix} 1 \\ -1 \\ 0 \end{pmatrix} \quad \text{and} \quad \boldsymbol{\Sigma} = \begin{pmatrix} 2 & 0 & 1 \\ 0 & 1 & 2 \\ 1 & 2 & 5 \end{pmatrix}. \qquad [3.153]$$

Let

$$Y = \boldsymbol{X}'\boldsymbol{c}\boldsymbol{X} + \boldsymbol{b}\boldsymbol{X} + a, \qquad [3.154]$$

where

$$\boldsymbol{c} = \begin{pmatrix} 3 & 6 & -3 \\ 6 & 16 & -6 \\ -3 & -6 & 3 \end{pmatrix}, \qquad [3.155]$$

$$\boldsymbol{b} = (18 \quad 32 \quad -12), \qquad [3.156]$$

$$a = 12. \qquad [3.157]$$

We wish to express Y as a linear polynomial of independent chi-squared and normal random variables. To do so, we construct the Cholesky matrix z of $\boldsymbol{\Sigma}$,

$$z = \begin{pmatrix} 1.4142 & 0.0000 & 0.0000 \\ 0.0000 & 1.0000 & 0.0000 \\ 0.7071 & 2.0000 & 0.7071 \end{pmatrix}, \qquad [3.158]$$

and a matrix $\boldsymbol{u}$ with rows equal to orthonormal eigenvectors of $z'\boldsymbol{c}z$:

$$\boldsymbol{u} = \begin{pmatrix} 0.0000 & 1.0000 & 0.0000 \\ 0.7071 & 0.0000 & -0.7071 \\ 0.7071 & 0.0000 & 0.7071 \end{pmatrix}. \qquad [3.159]$$

We define the change of variables $\dot{\boldsymbol{X}} \sim N_3(\boldsymbol{0}, \boldsymbol{I})$ for $\boldsymbol{X}$

$$\dot{\boldsymbol{X}} = \boldsymbol{u}z^{-1}(\boldsymbol{X} - \boldsymbol{\mu}), \qquad [3.160]$$

and obtain

$$Y = \dot{\boldsymbol{X}}'\dot{\boldsymbol{c}}\dot{\boldsymbol{X}} + \dot{\boldsymbol{b}}\dot{\boldsymbol{X}} + \dot{a}, \qquad [3.161]$$

where

$$\dot{\boldsymbol{c}} = \boldsymbol{u}z'\boldsymbol{c}z\boldsymbol{u}' = \begin{pmatrix} 4 & 0 & 0 \\ 0 & 3 & 0 \\ 0 & 0 & 0 \end{pmatrix}, \qquad [3.162]$$

$$\dot{\boldsymbol{b}} = (2\boldsymbol{\mu}'\boldsymbol{c} + \boldsymbol{b})z\boldsymbol{u}' = (0 \quad 12 \quad 6), \qquad [3.163]$$

$$\dot{a} = \boldsymbol{\mu}'\boldsymbol{c}\boldsymbol{\mu} + \boldsymbol{b}\boldsymbol{\mu} + a = 5. \qquad [3.164]$$

Multiplying [3.161] out:

$$Y = 4\dot{X}_1^2 + 3\dot{X}_2^2 + 12\dot{X}_2 + 6\dot{X}_3 + 5. \qquad [3.165]$$

We complete the squares for terms involving $\dot{X}_2$ to obtain

$$Y = 4\dot{X}_1^2 + 3(\dot{X}_2 + 2)^2 + 6\dot{X}_3 - 7. \qquad [3.166]$$

We have expressed Y as a linear polynomial of three independent random variables:

- $\dot{X}_1^2 \sim \chi^2(1, 0)$,
- $(\dot{X}_2 + 2)^2 \sim \chi^2(1, 4)$,
- $\dot{X}_3 \sim N(0, 1)$.

Moments

We have seen that a random variable Y that is a quadratic polynomial of a random vector $\boldsymbol{X} \sim N_m(\boldsymbol{\mu}, \boldsymbol{\Sigma})$ can be expressed as a linear polynomial of independent chi-squared and normal random variables. Based upon this representation, we may apply [3.129] to obtain the MGF of Y. From this, we can calculate the moments of Y. The details of the derivation are covered by Mathai and Provost (1992). Results, based upon notation introduced earlier in this section, are as follows.

Define, for positive integers k,

$$g^{[k]} = \begin{cases} \boldsymbol{\mu}'\boldsymbol{c}\boldsymbol{\mu} + \boldsymbol{b}\boldsymbol{\mu} + a + \sum_{j=1}^{m} \dot{c}_{j,j} & k = 0, \\ \dfrac{(k+1)!}{2} \sum_{j=1}^{m} \dot{b}_j^2 (2\dot{c}_{j,j})^{k-1} + \dfrac{k!}{2} \sum_{j=1}^{m} (2\dot{c}_{j,j})^{k+1} & k > 0, \end{cases} \qquad [3.167]$$

where any undefined term 0^0 is set equal to 0. The rth moment of Y is given by[14]

$$E(Y^r) = \sum_{r_1=0}^{r-1} \left[\binom{r-1}{r_1} g^{[r-1-r_1]} \sum_{r_2=0}^{r_1-1} \left[\binom{r_1-1}{r_2} g^{[r_1-1-r_2]} \times \sum_{r_3=0}^{r_2-1} \left[\binom{r_2-1}{r_3} g^{[r_2-1-r_3]} \cdots \right]\right]\right], \qquad [3.168]$$

where any empty product is interpreted as equaling 1. Based upon [3.168],

$$E(Y) = g^{[0]}, \qquad [3.169]$$

$$E(Y^2) = g^{[1]} + \binom{1}{1} g^{[0]} E(Y), \qquad [3.170]$$

$$E(Y^3) = g^{[2]} + \binom{2}{1} g^{[1]} E(Y) + \binom{2}{2} g^{[0]} E(Y^2), \qquad [3.171]$$

$$E(Y^4) = g^{[3]} + \binom{3}{1} g^{[2]} E(Y) + \binom{3}{2} g^{[1]} E(Y^2) + \binom{3}{3} g^{[0]} E(Y^3), \qquad [3.172]$$

$$E(Y^5) = g^{[4]} + \binom{4}{1} g^{[3]} E(Y) + \binom{4}{2} g^{[2]} E(Y^2) + \binom{4}{3} g^{[1]} E(Y^3) + \binom{4}{4} g^{[0]} E(Y^4), \qquad [3.173]$$

and so forth according to a similar pattern.

EXAMPLE. Consider the random variable Y defined by [3.154] in our last example. Let's calculate its first five moments. Based upon results from that example, we calculate values for $g^{[k]}$ as indicated in Exhibit 3.24. Moments of Y are calculated from these by [3.169] through [3.173]. Results are indicated in Exhibit 3.25.

---

[14]We employ the notation $\binom{a}{b} = \frac{a!}{b!(a-b)!}$.

k	$g^{[k]}$
0	12
1	230
2	3,320
3	78,384
4	2,352,768

Exhibit 3.24 Using formula [3.167], $g^{[k]}$ values are calculated for the random variable Y defined by [3.154]. Inputs for the calculations are obtained from [3.153], [3.155], [3.156], [3.157], [3.162], and [3.163].

r	$E(Y^r)$
1	12
2	374
3	13,328
4	615,900
5	33,217,840

Exhibit 3.25 Moments of portfolio value are indicated for the random variable Y defined by [3.154]. Computations are performed according to [3.169] through [3.173]. Inputs are the values of Exhibit 3.24.

Other Parameters

We can calculate any central moment of Y. This is simply a matter of multiplying out the formula for the desired central moment and substituting in values for moments. Consider the third central moment:

$$\mu_3 = E[(Y-\mu)^3] \quad [3.174]$$

$$= E[Y^3 - 3Y^2\mu + 3Y\mu^2 - \mu^3] \quad [3.175]$$

$$= E(Y^3) - 3E(Y^2)\mu + 3E(Y)\mu^2 - \mu^3 \quad [3.176]$$

$$= E(Y^3) - 3E(Y^2)\mu + 2\mu^3. \quad [3.177]$$

where $\mu = E(Y)$. The variance of Y is, by our result from Exercise 3.15,

$$\sigma^2 = E(Y^2) - E(Y)^2. \quad [3.178]$$

The skewness η_1 and kurtosis η_2 are obtained as

$$\eta_1 = \frac{E[(Y-\mu)^3]}{\sigma^3} = \frac{E(Y^3) - 3\mu E(Y^2) + 3\mu^2 E(Y) - \mu^3}{\sigma^3}, \quad [3.179]$$

$$\eta_2 = \frac{E[(Y-\mu)^4]}{\sigma^4} = \frac{E(Y^4) - 4\mu E(Y^3) + 6\mu^2 E(Y^2) - 4\mu^3 E(Y) + \mu^4}{\sigma^4}. \quad [3.180]$$

Quantiles of Y can be approximated using the Cornish-Fisher (1937) expansion, which we discuss in the next section. They can be calculated exactly using the inversion theorem that we discuss in Section 3.15.

Exercises

3.37 ▦ Consider random vector $\boldsymbol{X} \sim N_3(\boldsymbol{\mu}, \boldsymbol{\Sigma})$ with

$$\boldsymbol{\mu} = \begin{pmatrix} 1 \\ -1 \\ 0 \end{pmatrix} \quad \text{and} \quad \boldsymbol{\Sigma} = \begin{pmatrix} 5 & 0 & 2 \\ 0 & 1 & 2 \\ 2 & 2 & 5 \end{pmatrix}. \qquad [3.181]$$

Let

$$Y = \boldsymbol{X}'\boldsymbol{c}\boldsymbol{X} + \boldsymbol{b}\boldsymbol{X} + a, \qquad [3.182]$$

where

$$\boldsymbol{c} = \begin{pmatrix} 2 & 8 & -4 \\ 8 & 31 & -16 \\ -4 & -16 & 8 \end{pmatrix}, \qquad [3.183]$$

$$\boldsymbol{b} = (20 \quad 90 \quad -43), \qquad [3.184]$$

$$a = 29. \qquad [3.185]$$

Express Y as a linear polynomial of independent chi-squared and normal random variables.

3.38 Calculate the mean and standard deviation of the random variable Y of the previous exercise.

3.13. THE CORNISH-FISHER EXPANSION

The **cumulants** of a random variable X are conceptually similar to its moments. They are defined, somewhat abstrusely, as those values κ_r such that the identity

$$exp\left(\sum_{r=1}^{\infty} \frac{\kappa_r t^r}{r!}\right) = \sum_{r=0}^{\infty} \frac{E(X^r)t^r}{r!} \qquad [3.186]$$

holds for all t. Cumulants of a random variable X can—see Stuart and Ord (1994)—be expressed in terms of its mean $\mu = E(X)$ and central moments $\mu_r = E[(X-\mu)^r]$. Expressions for the first five cumulants are

$$\kappa_1 = \mu, \qquad [3.187]$$

$$\kappa_2 = \mu_2, \qquad [3.188]$$

$$\kappa_3 = \mu_3, \qquad [3.189]$$

$$\kappa_4 = \mu_4 - 3\mu_2^2, \qquad [3.190]$$

$$\kappa_5 = \mu_5 - 10\mu_3\mu_2. \qquad [3.191]$$

Suppose X has mean 0 and standard deviation 1. Cornish and Fisher (1937) provide an expansion for approximating the q-quantile, $\Phi_X^{-1}(q)$, of X based upon its cumulants. Using the first five cumulants, the expansion is

$$\begin{aligned}\Phi_X^{-1}(q) \approx \Phi_Z^{-1}(q) &+ \frac{\Phi_Z^{-1}(q)^2 - 1}{6}\kappa_3 + \frac{\Phi_Z^{-1}(q)^3 - 3\Phi_Z^{-1}(q)}{24}\kappa_4 \\ &- \frac{2\Phi_Z^{-1}(q)^3 - 5\Phi_Z^{-1}(q)}{36}\kappa_3^2 + \frac{\Phi_Z^{-1}(q)^4 - 6\Phi_Z^{-1}(q)^2 + 3}{120}\kappa_5 \\ &- \frac{\Phi_Z^{-1}(q)^4 - 5\Phi_Z^{-1}(q)^2 + 2}{24}\kappa_3\kappa_4 + \frac{12\Phi_Z^{-1}(q)^4 - 53\Phi_Z^{-1}(q)^2 + 17}{324}\kappa_3^3,\end{aligned} \quad [3.192]$$

where $\Phi_Z^{-1}(q)$ is the q-quantile of $Z \sim N(0, 1)$. Although [3.192] applies only if X has mean 0 and standard deviation 1, we can still use it to approximate quantiles if X has some other mean μ and standard deviation σ. Simply define the **normalization** of X as

$$X^* = \frac{X - \mu}{\sigma}, \quad [3.193]$$

which has mean 0 and standard deviation 1. Central moments of X^* can be calculated from central moments of X with

$$\mu_r^* = \frac{\mu_r}{\sigma^r}, \quad [3.194]$$

where $\sigma = \sqrt{\mu_2}$ is the standard deviation of X. Apply the Cornish-Fisher expansion to obtain the q-quantile x^* of X^*. The corresponding q-quantile x of X is then

$$x = x^*\sigma + \mu. \quad [3.195]$$

EXAMPLE. Let's use the Cornish-Fisher expansion to approximate the .10-quantile of the random variable Y defined by [3.154] in our earlier example. From the first five moments of Y provided in Exhibit 3.25, we calculate the central moments of Y and the central moments and cumulants of the normalization Y^* of Y. Results are indicated in Exhibit 3.26.

r	μ_r	μ_r^*	κ_r^*
1	0	0.00000	0.00000
2	230	1.00000	1.00000
3	3,320	0.95180	0.95180
4	237,084	4.48174	1.48174
5	9,988,768	12.45066	2.93265

Exhibit 3.26 Central moments of Y, central moments of Y^*, and cumulants of Y^* are calculated from formulas [3.11], [3.194], and [3.187] through [3.191].

Applying the Cornish-Fisher expansion [3.192] yields the .10-quantile of Y^* as –1.123. Applying [3.195], we obtain the .10-quantile of Y as –5.029.

Exercises

3.39 Using a spreadsheet and inputs from Exhibit 3.26, reproduce the results from the example of this section.

3.14. CENTRAL LIMIT THEOREM

The normal distribution is useful for modeling various random quantities, such as people's heights, asset returns, and test scores. This is no coincidence. If a process is additive—reflecting the combined influence of multiple random occurrences—the result is likely to be approximately normal. This follows from the **central limit theorem**.

Let $\boldsymbol{X}$ be an n-dimensional random vector with independent and identically distributed (IID) components X_i. It doesn't matter what their common distribution is as long as its mean μ and standard deviation σ exist. Let $\overline{X}_n$ be the random variable equal to the average of the X_i. By [3.27] and [3.28], $\overline{X}_n$ has mean μ and standard deviation $\sigma/\sqrt{n}$. Accordingly, the normalized average

$$\overline{X}_n^* = \frac{\overline{X}_n - \mu}{\sigma/\sqrt{n}} \qquad [3.196]$$

has mean 0 and standard deviation 1. The central limit theorem tells us $\overline{X}_n^*$ is approximately $N(0, 1)$. Specifically, it states that, for any constant x,

$$\lim_{n\to\infty} Pr\left(\overline{X}_n^* \leq x\right) = \Phi(x), \qquad [3.197]$$

where $\Phi(x)$ is the CDF of the standard normal distribution.

Exhibit 3.27 illustrates the PDF for the profit and loss (P&L) that will be realized by purchasing and holding for 1 month EUR 30,000 of a particular at-the-money 3-month call option on Euribor futures. The limited downside risk of the options strategy is evident in the skewed P&L distribution. It has skewness 0.96 and kurtosis 3.90.

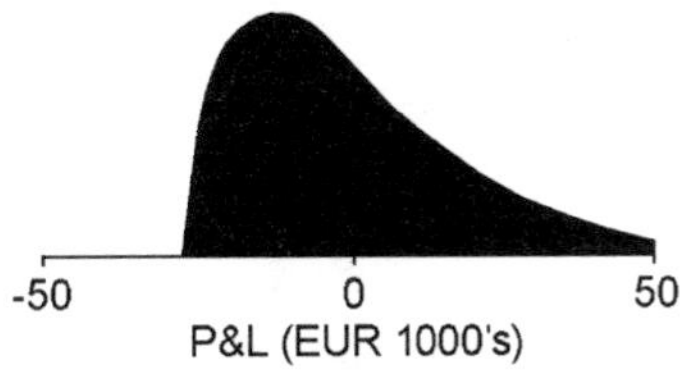

Exhibit 3.27 PDF for the P&L that will be realized by purchasing EUR 30,000 of at-the-money 3-month call options on Euribor futures and holding the position for 1 month. The PDF is based upon market conditions on May 1, 2000.

Suppose random changes in Euribor are independent from one month to the next. We repeat our options strategy every month for 18 months. At the start of every month, we purchase at-the-money 3-month options and liquidate them at the end of the month. Repeating this process for 18 consecutive months yields a total P&L for the 18 months whose PDF is graphed in Exhibit 3.28.[15]

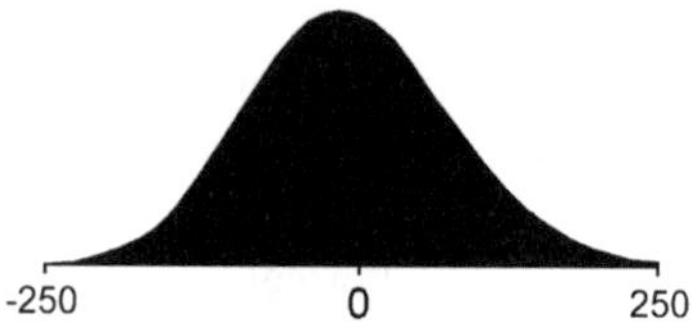

Exhibit 3.28 PDF for the P&L that will be realized by rolling 3-month call options monthly for 18 months.

The P&L distribution for the 18-month strategy is not skewed like that of the 1-month strategy. It does not afford the same protection against downside risk. With skewness of just 0.23, kurtosis of 3.05, and a familiar "bell" shape, it is almost normal. Rolling options for 18 months offers a P&L distribution that is little different from that which could be obtained by just holding the underlying futures.

Our example illustrates the central limit theorem. With the 1-month strategy, we randomly draw a P&L from the probability distribution of Exhibit 3.27. With our 18-month strategy, we independently draw from that distribution 18 times. The 18-month P&L is the sum of these.

There are many versions of the central limit theorem.[16] Several of these place additional restrictions on the X_i but do not require that they be identically distributed. The additional restrictions vary, but are generally designed to prevent one or a handful of random variables from dominating the average, which might happen if one random variable has a standard deviation far greater than the rest.

In Exhibit 3.29, probability distributions are illustrated for five independent random variables X_i. All five distributions have mean 0 and standard deviation 1 and are dramatically non-normal. They were selected arbitrarily, but their normalized average $\overline{X}_5^*$ is approximately normal.

[15]This and the analysis of Exhibit 3.27 were performed with the Monte Carlo method, which we describe in Chapter 5.

[16]See Spanos (1999) for a detailed discussion including historical notes.

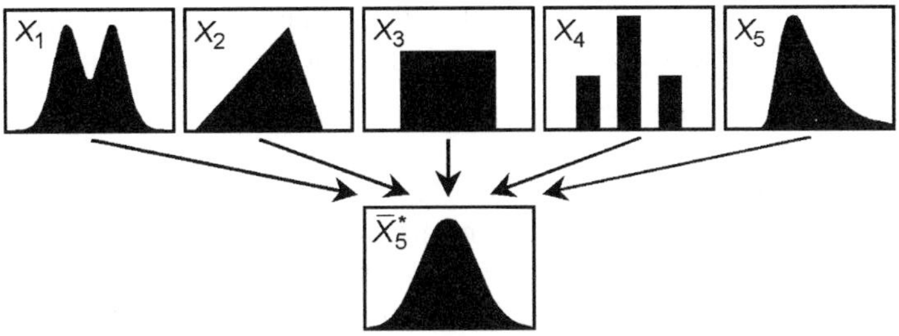

Exhibit 3.29 The central limit theorem is illustrated in the case of five arbitrarily selected independent random variables. Random variables X_1, X_2, X_3, and X_5 are continuous, so their PDFs are shown; X_4 is discrete, so its PF is shown. The normalized average $\overline{X}_5^*$ is approximately $N(0, 1)$. All graphs indicate the interval $[-3, 3]$ on the x-axis.

Exhibit 3.30 provides summary information on the distributions of Exhibit 3.29.

Random Variable	Mean	Standard Deviation	Skewness	Kurtosis	Description
X_1	0.00	1.00	0.00	1.89	continuous
X_2	0.00	1.00	-0.41	2.41	continuous
X_3	0.00	1.00	0.00	1.80	continuous
X_4	0.00	1.00	0.00	2.00	discrete
X_5	0.00	1.00	1.62	7.89	continuous
$\overline{X}_5^*$	0.00	1.00	0.11	3.03	continuous

Exhibit 3.30 Summary information on the distributions of Exhibit 3.29. All distributions were constructed with mean 0 and standard deviation 1. This was done primarily to standardize the graphs in Exhibit 3.29, but having uniform standard deviations does aid convergence to a normal distribution.

Other versions of the central limit theorem modestly weaken the independence assumption for the X_i. The central limit theorem generalizes to multiple dimensions.

Exercises

3.40 Let $\overline{X}_n^*$ be the normalized average of n independent $U(-1, 1)$ random variables. Based upon your intuition:

a. How large do you think n must be for the PDF of $\overline{X}_n^*$ to have the same general shape as the PDF of a standard normal distribution?

b. How large do you think n must be for the kurtosis of $\overline{X}_n^*$ to match the 3.0 kurtosis of a normal distribution to one decimal place?

3.41 Suppose Y equals a sum of 20 independent random variables. One is $U(-10, 10)$. The rest are $U(-1, 1)$. Is Y approximately normal?

3.42 To gain insight into the last exercise, use your intuition to sketch the PDFs of:

a. a $U(-10, 10)$ random variable;
b. a sum of a $U(-10, 10)$ and 1 independent $U(-1, 1)$ random variables;
c. a sum of a $U(-10, 10)$ and 2 independent $U(-1, 1)$ random variables;
d. a sum of a $U(-10, 10)$ and 3 independent $U(-1, 1)$ random variables.

3.15. THE INVERSION THEOREM

Much of this chapter has been devoted to studying linear polynomials of random vectors. Results have included:

- formulas [3.30] and [3.31] for calculating the means and covariances of linear polynomials of random vectors;
- the use of moment-generating functions to calculate moments of linear polynomials of independent random variables;
- the definition that a linear polynomial of a joint-normal random vector is normal;
- the fact that a quadratic polynomial of a joint-normal random vector can be expressed as a linear polynomial of independent chi-squared and normal random variables;
- the central limit theorem describing certain linear polynomials of random variables as being approximately normal.

In this section, we present an inversion theorem, which is primarily of theoretical interest. We shall use it for the practical purpose of evaluating the CDF of a linear polynomial of independent random variables.

IMAGINARY RANDOM VARIABLES

To define characteristic functions, we must extend the notion of random variables into the complex plane. Let U_1 and U_2 be real random variables, and let $i = \sqrt{-1}$. Then

$$U = U_1 + iU_2 \qquad [3.198]$$

is a **complex random variable**. We define its expectation as

$$E(U) = E(U_1) + iE(U_2). \qquad [3.199]$$

Characteristic Functions

Characteristic functions are similar to MGFs. We define the **characteristic function** of a random variable X as

$$\Psi(w) = E(e^{iwX}), \quad [3.200]$$

where w is real and $i = \sqrt{-1}$. If X is continuous,

$$\Psi(w) = E(e^{iwX}) = \int_{-\infty}^{\infty} \phi(x)e^{iwx}dx. \quad [3.201]$$

If $\boldsymbol{X}$ is a random vector with independent components X_i, and Y is a linear polynomial of $\boldsymbol{X}$

$$Y = \boldsymbol{bX} + a \quad [3.202]$$

with $\boldsymbol{b}$ and a a real row vector and scalar, then, analogous to [3.129] for MGFs,

$$\Psi_Y(w) = e^{aiw}\Psi_{X_1}(b_1 w)\Psi_{X_2}(b_2 w)\cdots\Psi_{X_n}(b_n w). \quad [3.203]$$

A uniform, $U(a, b)$, random variable has characteristic function

$$\Psi(w) = \frac{e^{ibw} - e^{iaw}}{iw(b-a)}. \quad [3.204]$$

Characteristic functions for $N(\mu, \sigma^2)$ and $\chi^2(\nu, \delta^2)$ random variables are, respectively,

$$\Psi(w) = exp\left(i\mu w - \frac{\sigma^2 w^2}{2}\right), \quad [3.205]$$

$$\Psi(w) = \frac{exp[\delta^2 iw/(1-2iw)]}{(1-2iw)^{\nu/2}}. \quad [3.206]$$

The characteristic function for a lognormal random variable is derived by Leipnik (1991). It is complicated, so we do not present it here.

Inversion Theorem

The CDF of a random variable is uniquely determined by its characteristic function. If two random variables have the same characteristic function, they have the same CDF. An **inversion theorem** provides the CDF of a random variable X in terms of its characteristic function:

$$\Phi(x) = \frac{1}{2} + \frac{1}{2\pi}\int_{0}^{\infty} \frac{\Psi(-w)e^{ixw} - \Psi(w)e^{-ixw}}{iw}dw. \quad [3.207]$$

Exercises

3.43 Determine the characteristic function for the following random variables:
a. $X \sim N(1, 4)$;
b. $Y = 3Q + R + 5$, where $Q \sim U(0, 1)$ and $R \sim \chi^2(2, 1)$ are independent;
c. $Z = X_1^2 + X_2^2$, where $X_1 \sim X_2 \sim N(0, 1)$ are independent.

3.44 Use the characteristic function [3.205] of the normal distribution and [3.203] to prove that, if $X_1 \sim N(\mu_1, \sigma_1^2)$ and $X_2 \sim N(\mu_2, \sigma_2^2)$ are independent, then

$$X_1 + X_2 \sim N(\mu_1 + \mu_2, \sigma_1^2 + \sigma_2^2). \quad [3.208]$$

3.16. QUANTILES OF QUADRATIC POLYNOMIALS OF JOINT-NORMAL RANDOM VECTORS

Consider a random variable Y that is a quadratic polynomial of a joint-normal random vector $\boldsymbol{X}$. We can approximate its quantiles using the Cornish-Fisher expansion. Alternatively, if exact quantiles are required, we may employ the inversion theorem in a manner described by Imhof (1961) and Davies (1973). This provides the CDF of Y. From this, we can calculate quantiles.

The CDF of a Quadratic Polynomial of a Joint-Normal Random Vector

As described in Section 3.12, express Y as a linear polynomial of independent random variables,

$$Y = \left(\sum_{k=1}^{m} \gamma_k Q_k \right) + \beta Q_0 + \alpha, \quad [3.209]$$

where $Q_0 \sim N(0, 1)$ and $Q_k \sim \chi^2(1, \delta_k^2)$ for $k > 0$. Based upon this representation, the characteristic function of Y is calculated from [3.203], [3.205], and [3.206] as

$$\Psi(w) = \frac{exp\left(iw\alpha - \dfrac{w^2\beta^2}{2} + iw \displaystyle\sum_{k=1}^{m} \frac{\gamma_k \delta_k^2}{1 - 2iw\gamma_k} \right)}{\displaystyle\prod_{k=1}^{m} \sqrt{1 - 2iw\gamma_k}}. \quad [3.210]$$

Inversion theorem [3.207] provides an expression for the CDF of Y in terms of this characteristic function

$$\Phi(y) = \frac{1}{2} + \frac{1}{2\pi}\int_{0}^{\infty} \frac{\Psi(-w)e^{iyw} - \Psi(w)e^{-iyw}}{iw} dw, \qquad [3.211]$$

but it involves an integral that is not amenable to standard techniques of numerical integration, such as the trapezoidal rule or Simpson's rule. Employing the algebra of complex numbers, the theorem can be reformulated as

$$\Phi(y) = \frac{1}{2} - \frac{1}{\pi}\int_{0}^{\infty} \frac{Im(e^{-iwy}\Psi(w))}{w} dw. \qquad [3.212]$$

Substituting characteristic function [3.210] into [3.212] and simplifying yields

$$\Phi(y) = \frac{1}{2} - \frac{1}{\pi}\int_{0}^{\infty} \frac{e^{A} sin(B + C)}{D} dw, \qquad [3.213]$$

where

$$A = -\frac{w^2}{2}\left(\beta^2 + 4\sum_{k=1}^{m} \frac{\gamma_k^2\delta_k^2}{1 + 4\gamma_k^2 w^2}\right), \qquad [3.214]$$

$$B = w\left(\alpha - y + \sum_{k=1}^{m} \frac{\gamma_k\delta_k^2}{1 + 4\gamma_k^2 w^2}\right), \qquad [3.215]$$

$$C = \frac{1}{2}\sum_{k=1}^{m} tan^{-1}(2\gamma_k w), \qquad [3.216]$$

$$D = w\left(\prod_{k=1}^{m} \left(1 + 4\gamma_k^2 w^2\right)\right)^{1/4}, \qquad [3.217]$$

and tan^{-1} denotes the inverse tangent function with output in radians. The integral in [3.213] appears cumbersome, but it entails no imaginary numbers and its integrand is easily evaluated by a computer. To solve the integral numerically, two problems must be addressed:

- The integrand has form $0/0$ as w approaches 0.
- The interval of integration is unbounded.

To solve the first problem, we apply l'Hôpital's rule to obtain[17]

$$\lim_{w \to 0} \frac{e^{A} sin(B + C)}{D} = \alpha - y + \sum_{k=1}^{m} \gamma_k\left(\delta_k^2 + 1\right). \qquad [3.218]$$

[17] I am indebted to Arcady Novosyolov for this simplification.

We solve the second problem with the approximation

$$\int_0^\infty \frac{e^A sin(B+C)}{D} dw \approx \int_0^u \frac{e^A sin(B+C)}{D} dw, \qquad [3.219]$$

where $u < \infty$ is chosen sufficiently large. Valuing this integral is one instance where the trapezoidal rule provides consistently superior results to Simpson's rule. By selecting an appropriate value for u, we can make the error in approximation [3.219] arbitrarily small. The solution is essentially exact.

Quantiles of a Quadratic Polynomial of a Joint-Normal Random Vector

Since we can evaluate the CDF $\Phi(y)$ of Y, we can now calculate any q-quantile of Y. Consider a specific value q. We seek that value y such that $\Phi(y) = q$. We might find this by evaluating Φ at a range of values for y and finding which one yields a probability closest to q. A faster and more systematic approach is to use the secant method of Section 2.12.

The secant method requires two seed values $y^{[1]}$ and $y^{[2]}$. Subsequent values $y^{[3]}, y^{[4]}, y^{[5]}, \ldots$ are obtained with the recursive equation

$$y^{[i]} = y^{[i-1]} - \frac{\left[\Phi\left(y^{[i-1]}\right) - q\right]\left(y^{[i-1]} - y^{[i-2]}\right)}{\Phi\left(y^{[i-1]}\right) - \Phi\left(y^{[i-2]}\right)}. \qquad [3.220]$$

The resulting sequence of values should converge to the q-quantile y of Y.

Example. Consider again the random variable Y that is a quadratic polynomial of a joint-normal random vector $\boldsymbol{X}$ as defined by [3.154]. We have considered this random variable in several examples. Let's find its .10-quantile.

Based upon representation [3.166] and formula [3.213], we can use the trapezoidal rule to evaluate $\Phi(y)$ at any point y. For this purpose, we use approximation [3.219] with $u = 1$. We partition $[0, u]$ into 500 subintervals to apply the trapezoidal rule. Consider seed values $y^{[1]} = 0$ and $y^{[2]} = 1$. Applying the trapezoidal rule to each, we obtain

- $\Phi(0) = 0.21752$,
- $\Phi(1) = 0.24546$.

Applying the secant method, we obtain the results indicated in Exhibit 3.31.

The .10-quantile of Y is -5.004, which is exact to the number of decimal places shown. Compare this with the -5.029 approximation we obtained for the same quantile using the Cornish-Fisher expansion in Section 3.13.

i	$y^{[i]}$	$\Phi(y^{[i]})$
1	0.000	0.21752
2	1.000	0.24546
3	−4.207	0.11565
4	−4.835	0.10322
5	−4.997	0.10013
6	−5.004	0.10000

Exhibit 3.31 Results of applying the secant method to evaluate the .10-quantile of Y. Each iteration requires the evaluation of Φ using the trapezoidal rule.

Exercises

3.45 ▦ Independently reproduce the results of the example of this section.

3.17. FURTHER READING

DeGroot (1986) covers basic probability theory. Feller (1968, 1971) is a more advanced treatment. Spanos (1999) is a formal text with a detailed treatment of the central limit theorem. See Johnson (1998) for an elementary discussion of principal component analysis. Multicollinearity is discussed in econometrics texts, typically in relation to regression analysis. Judge *et al.* (1988) offers an alternative treatment relating to principal component analysis. See Mathai and Provost (1992) for quadratic polynomials of joint-normal random vectors. Stuart and Ord (1994) offers an authoritative if somewhat inaccessible treatment of various topics, including the Cornish-Fisher expansion, characteristic functions, and the inversion theorem.

Chapter 4

Statistics and Time Series Analysis

4.1. MOTIVATION

In Section 1.3, we described risk as having two components: exposure and uncertainty. To quantify a portfolio's market risk, a VaR measure must describe both of these. Its mapping procedure describes exposure. Its inference procedure describes uncertainty.

In Chapter 2, we discussed various techniques of applied mathematics. Most of these will be employed in Chapter 9 to support mapping procedures. In the present chapter, we describe techniques from statistics and time series analysis. These will be used to support inference procedures, which we describe in Chapter 7.

The discussions of statistics—especially the notions of samples and estimators—will also play an important role in our development of the Monte Carlo method in Chapter 5.

4.2. FROM PROBABILITY TO STATISTICS

In the last chapter, we considered probability theory, which is the mathematics of probability distributions. Given a characterization of a distribution—usually a PF, PDF, or CDF—we may infer certain probabilities. This is probability.

Things become more complicated when we attempt to apply probability to practical problems. We soon realize that probability offers no guidance as to how we might construct distributions. It tells us what to do with them, but not where they come from!

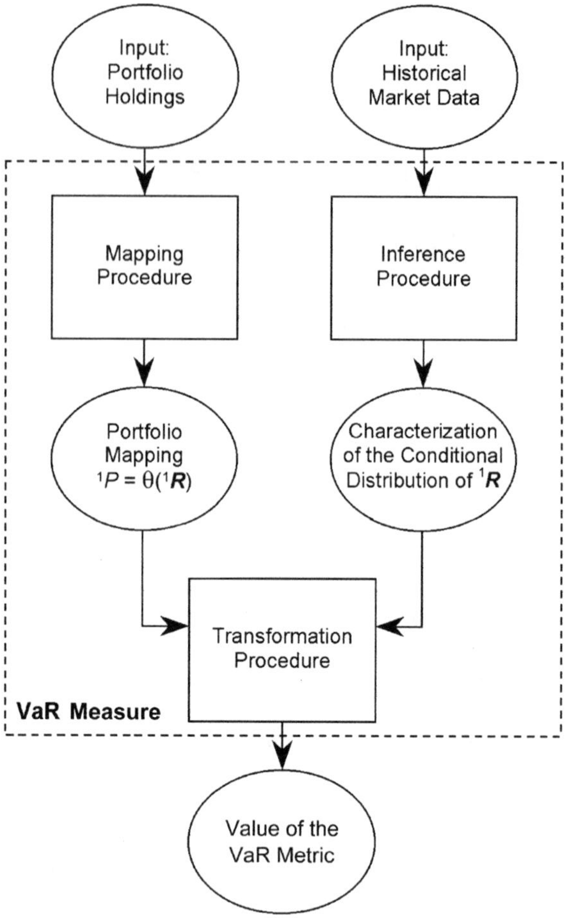

Exhibit 4.1 A reproduction of Exhibit 1.11, which is a general schematic for VaR measures. The statistical and time-series methods described in the present chapter underlie inference procedures. Statistics is also important for our discussion of the Monte Carlo method in Chapter 5.

Before we construct distributions, we must decide what we want them to represent. What should probabilities signify? This is another question that probability does not address. According to probability theory, probabilities are numbers satisfying certain axioms. Any interpretation of those numbers is our own.

Over the years, many interpretations have been proposed for probabilities. We may broadly describe these as falling into two categories:

- objective interpretations, and
- subjective interpretations.

According to objective interpretations, probabilities are real. They exist independently of us. We can deduce or approximate them through logic or careful observation. According to the competing subjective interpretations, there are no true probabilities for us to deduce or approximate. We construct probabilities to reflect our perceptions.

Although philosophers may debate the merits of objective or subjective interpretations, we shall find it convenient to embrace either, depending upon our application. When we discuss the Monte Carlo method in Chapter 5, we shall perceive the underlying probabilities as largely objective. When we discuss the modeling of financial markets in Chapter 7, we shall perceive them as more subjective.[1]

There are various ways probabilities are inferred or assigned:

1. symmetry—we ascribe each of 52 cards an equal probability of being drawn;
2. personal judgement—we look at the sky and contemplate the probability of rain;
3. data analysis—we repeat an experiment a number of times and analyze the results.

Statistics is a body of techniques for inferring or assigning probabilities based on data. Objective and subjective interpretations of probability support competing statistical traditions. Both arose during the 20th century. The objectivist tradition, called **classical statistics**, developed from the works of Karl Pearson and Ronald A. Fisher. The subjectivist tradition, called **Bayesian statistics**, developed from the works of Bruno de Finetti and Leonard J. Savage.

In this book, we employ the methods and terminology of classical statistics, irrespective of whether we perceive specific probabilities as objective or subjective. We do so for expedience only: readers are likely to be more familiar with classical statistics.

4.3. ESTIMATION

Although statistics is employed for various purposes, we are primarily interested in using it to estimate parameters of distributions, which is the topic of this section.

SAMPLES

Many people have an intuitive understanding of samples that does not conform to the technical definition, which is quite formal. We shall use samples extensively in this book, so it is worth embracing the formality of the technical definition.

[1] See Holton (1997).

Observations are made, resulting in a body of data $\{\boldsymbol{x}^{[1]}, \boldsymbol{x}^{[2]}, \ldots, \boldsymbol{x}^{[m]}\}$. We perceive the data as "randomly generated." Depending upon our application, we may apply some statistical formula to the data. The question that concerns us now is: how do we justify whatever statistical formula we use? The answer is: probability theory. We construct a probabilistic model for our data and use it to justify the formula.

Consider a random vector $\boldsymbol{X}$. A realization of $\boldsymbol{X}$ is a vector $\boldsymbol{x}$ in the range of $\boldsymbol{X}$. We might treat our data $\{\boldsymbol{x}^{[1]}, \boldsymbol{x}^{[2]}, \ldots, \boldsymbol{x}^{[m]}\}$ as a set of m realizations of $\boldsymbol{X}$, but this model is not useful. A more useful model is to consider a set of m independent random vectors $\{\boldsymbol{X}^{[1]}, \boldsymbol{X}^{[2]}, \ldots, \boldsymbol{X}^{[m]}\}$, each with the same distribution as $\boldsymbol{X}$. We say the $\boldsymbol{X}^{[k]}$ are **IID**—independent and identically distributed. We treat each value $\boldsymbol{x}^{[k]}$ in our data as a realization of the corresponding random vector $\boldsymbol{X}^{[k]}$. We call the set of random vectors $\{\boldsymbol{X}^{[1]}, \boldsymbol{X}^{[2]}, \ldots, \boldsymbol{X}^{[m]}\}$ a **sample**. We call m the **sample size** and the set of values $\{\boldsymbol{x}^{[1]}, \boldsymbol{x}^{[2]}, \ldots, \boldsymbol{x}^{[m]}\}$ a **realization of the sample**.

Estimators

Represent some observable phenomenon with a random variable X. The distribution of X is known except for the value of some parameter θ. We observe the phenomenon m times, compiling numerical data $\{x^{[1]}, x^{[2]}, \ldots, x^{[m]}\}$, which we treat as a realization of a sample $\{X^{[1]}, X^{[2]}, \ldots, X^{[m]}\}$. We wish to use the data to estimate the parameter θ of the distribution of X.

If we, in some manner, estimate a parameter θ, we obtain a quantity

$$\hat{\theta} = \theta + e, \qquad [4.1]$$

where the error e is a realization of some random variable E.

Suppose we wish to estimate the mean μ of X. Consider two very different notions:

$$h = \mu + e = \frac{1}{m}\sum_{k=1}^{m} x^{[k]}, \qquad [4.2]$$

$$H = \mu + E = \frac{1}{m}\sum_{k=1}^{m} X^{[k]}. \qquad [4.3]$$

The first is a number. It is an estimate h for μ. The second is a random variable. It is an estimator H for μ. Formally, an **estimator** is a function of a sample. **Estimates** are obtained from estimators by substituting a realization $\{x^{[1]}, x^{[2]}, \ldots, x^{[m]}\}$ for the sample $\{X^{[1]}, X^{[2]}, \ldots, X^{[m]}\}$. Estimators are random variables. Estimates are realizations of estimators.

Because estimators are random variables, they have probability distributions. We prefer that an estimator have a mean equal to the parameter being estimated and a standard deviation as small as possible. This leads to the notions of bias and standard error, which we describe shortly. First, let's consider a category of estimators.

Sample Estimators

Data is often summarized with summary statistics, such as the sample mean. Summary statistics can be used as estimators, in which case they are called **sample estimators**. Sample estimators for a mean or variance are[2]

$$\overline{X} = \frac{1}{m}\sum_{k=1}^{m} X^{[k]}, \qquad [4.4]$$

$$S^2 = \frac{1}{m}\sum_{k=1}^{m} \left(X^{[k]} - \overline{X}\right)^2. \qquad [4.5]$$

We have already used the sample mean as an estimator in [4.3]. Sample estimators for skewness, kurtosis, quantiles, and other parameters are defined similarly.

Bias

The **bias** of an estimator H is the expected value of the estimator less the value θ being estimated:

$$\text{bias} = E(H) - \theta. \qquad [4.6]$$

If an estimator has a zero bias, we say it is **unbiased**. Otherwise, it is **biased**. Let's calculate the bias of the sample mean estimator [4.4]:

$$E(\overline{X}) - \mu = E\left(\frac{1}{m}\sum_{k=1}^{m} X^{[k]}\right) - \mu \qquad [4.7]$$

$$= \left(\frac{1}{m}\sum_{k=1}^{m} E\left(X^{[k]}\right)\right) - \mu \qquad [4.8]$$

$$= \left(\frac{1}{m}\sum_{k=1}^{m} \mu\right) - \mu \qquad [4.9]$$

---

[2]Usage of the term "sample variance" is inconsistent. Some authors define estimator [4.27] as the sample variance.

$$= \mu - \mu \qquad [4.10]$$

$$= 0, \qquad [4.11]$$

where μ is the mean $E(X)$ being estimated. The sample mean estimator is unbiased.

Standard Error

The **standard error** of an estimator is its standard deviation:

$$\text{standard error} = std(H) = \sqrt{E([H - E(H)]^2)}. \qquad [4.12]$$

Let's calculate the standard error of the sample mean estimator [4.4]:

$$std\left(\overline{X}\right) = std\left(\frac{1}{m}\sum_{k=1}^{m} X^{[k]}\right) \qquad [4.13]$$

$$= \frac{1}{m} std\left(\sum_{k=1}^{m} X^{[k]}\right) \qquad [4.14]$$

$$= \frac{1}{m}\sqrt{\sum_{k=1}^{m} std\left(X^{[k]}\right)^2} \qquad [4.15]$$

$$= \frac{1}{m}\sqrt{\sum_{k=1}^{m} \sigma^2} \qquad [4.16]$$

$$= \frac{1}{m}\sqrt{m\sigma^2} \qquad [4.17]$$

$$= \frac{\sigma}{\sqrt{m}}, \qquad [4.18]$$

where σ is the standard deviation $std(X)$ being estimated. We don't know the standard deviation σ of X, but we can approximate the standard error based upon some estimated value s for σ. Irrespective of the value of σ, the standard error decreases with the square root of the sample size m. Quadrupling the sample size halves the standard error.

Mean Squared Error

We seek estimators that are unbiased and have minimal standard error. Sometimes these goals are incompatible. Consider Exhibit 4.2, which indicates PDFs for two estimators of a parameter θ. One is unbiased. The other is biased but has a lower standard error. Which estimator should we use?

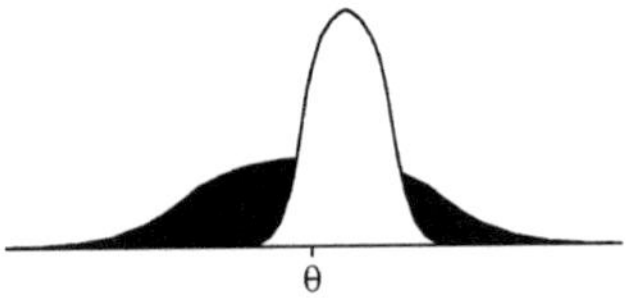

Exhibit 4.2 PDFs are indicated for two estimators of a parameter θ. One is unbiased. The other is biased but has lower standard error.

Mean squared error (MSE) combines the notions of bias and standard error. It is defined as

$$\text{MSE} = E([H - \theta]^2) = (\text{standard error})^2 + (\text{bias})^2. \quad [4.19]$$

Since we have already determined the bias and standard error of estimator [4.4], calculating its mean squared error is easy:

$$E([\overline{X} - \mu]^2) = (\text{standard error})^2 + (\text{bias})^2 \quad [4.20]$$

$$= \left(\frac{\sigma}{\sqrt{m}}\right)^2 + 0^2 \quad [4.21]$$

$$= \frac{\sigma^2}{m}. \quad [4.22]$$

Faced with alternative estimators for a given parameter, it is generally reasonable to use the one with the smallest MSE.

Random Vectors

So far, we have considered estimators for random variables. This discussion generalizes for random vectors. Our earlier definitions of estimator and sample estimator generalize without modification. Samples may comprise random vectors. Parameters may comprise vectors or matrices. For example, we might estimate a random vector's mean vector and covariance matrix, both of which are non-scalar parameters. The notions of bias, standard error, and MSE are defined for estimators of scalar parameters, but analogous issues arise with estimators of non-scalar parameters.

Exercises

4.1 What is the difference between a sample and a realization of a sample?

4.2 Consider the data of Exhibit 4.3:

k	$x^{[k]}$	k	$x^{[k]}$	k	$x^{[k]}$	k	$x^{[k]}$	k	$x^{[k]}$
1	9.91	11	3.86	21	8.00	31	12.51	41	3.15
2	11.41	12	9.65	22	11.68	32	3.51	42	6.86
3	7.34	13	8.59	23	10.25	33	1.61	43	5.18
4	6.23	14	4.74	24	8.30	34	0.84	44	9.28
5	0.64	15	6.30	25	12.06	35	5.69	45	8.88
6	2.82	16	7.36	26	9.19	36	1.52	46	3.82
7	6.35	17	6.57	27	0.42	37	11.47	47	9.66
8	5.91	18	6.26	28	5.29	38	0.21	48	2.59
9	12.48	19	13.69	29	7.55	39	1.39	49	7.99
10	14.66	20	4.71	30	12.58	40	3.82	50	11.25

Exhibit 4.3 Data for Exercise 4.2.

Treat the data as a realization $\{x^{[1]}, x^{[2]}, \ldots, x^{[50]}\}$ of a sample $\{X^{[1]}, X^{[2]}, \ldots, X^{[50]}\}$ for $X \sim U(0, \theta)$. We wish to estimate the unknown parameter θ. Consider two estimators:

$$H_1 = max\left(X^{[1]}, X^{[2]}, \ldots, X^{[50]}\right), \qquad [4.23]$$

$$H_2 = \frac{2}{50}\sum_{k=1}^{50} X^{[k]}. \qquad [4.24]$$

a. Make sure you understand both estimators. Describe in your own words why each is reasonable.
b. Using the data, estimate θ based upon each of the estimators.
c. In light of the fact that $x^{[10]} = 14.66$, did both estimators produce reasonable estimates for the upper bound θ of the interval $[0, \theta]$?
d. Are the estimators biased or unbiased?

4.3 In this exercise, you will demonstrate that sample variance estimator [4.5] is biased but that alternative estimator [4.27] is unbiased.

a. First prove a technical result that will be needed for the derivations. Prove that, given any set of numbers $\{x^{[1]}, x^{[2]}, \ldots, x^{[m]}\}$ whose average is $\bar{x}$:

$$\sum_{k=1}^{m}\left(x^{[k]} - \bar{x}\right)^2 = \left(\sum_{k=1}^{m} x^{[k]^2}\right) - m\bar{x}^2. \qquad [4.25]$$

b. Derive a formula for the bias of estimator [4.5].
c. Modify your derivation from (b) to obtain a formula for the bias of [4.27].

4.4 Suppose a distribution has known mean μ (perhaps obtained by some symmetry argument) but unknown variance σ^2. Calculate the bias of the following estimator for σ^2:

$$H = \frac{1}{m}\sum_{k=1}^{m}\left(X^{[k]} - \mu\right)^2. \qquad [4.26]$$

4.4. MAXIMUM LIKELIHOOD ESTIMATORS

Estimators can be constructed in various ways, and there is some controversy as to which is most suitable in any given situation. There is considerable literature on the use of unbiased estimators, but biased estimators are sometimes more appropriate. Consider two estimators for variance:

$$\frac{1}{m-1}\sum_{k=1}^{m}\left(X^{[k]}-\overline{X}\right)^2, \qquad [4.27]$$

$$\frac{1}{m+1}\sum_{k=1}^{m}\left(X^{[k]}-\overline{X}\right)^2. \qquad [4.28]$$

The first is widely used because it is unbiased. However, if X is known to be normal, the second has a lower MSE than either the first or sample estimator [4.5]. Sometimes unbiased estimators have disturbing properties or are downright nonsensical. Indeed, there are circumstances where unbiased estimators do not exist. As an alternative, it might seem appropriate to seek estimators with minimal MSE, but there is no systematic way to identify such estimators.

ML Estimators

Maximum likelihood (ML) is an approach to constructing estimators that is widely applicable. The resulting **ML estimators** are not always optimal in terms of bias or MSE, but they tend to be good estimators nonetheless. ML estimators are attractive because they exist and can be easily identified in most situations. Unlike sample estimators, which make no use of an assumed underlying distribution, ML estimators fully utilize such information.

Consider a sample $\{\boldsymbol{X}^{[1]}, \boldsymbol{X}^{[2]}, \ldots, \boldsymbol{X}^{[m]}\}$ whose underlying distribution is known except for some parameter θ. To emphasize this θ dependence, we denote the PDF of $\boldsymbol{X}$ as $\phi(\boldsymbol{x}|\theta)$. Because the random vectors that comprise a sample are independent, the PDF for the entire sample is

$$\phi_m\left(\boldsymbol{x}^{[1]}, \boldsymbol{x}^{[2]}, \ldots, \boldsymbol{x}^{[m]}|\theta\right) = \phi\left(\boldsymbol{x}^{[1]}|\theta\right)\phi\left(\boldsymbol{x}^{[2]}|\theta\right)\cdots\phi\left(\boldsymbol{x}^{[m]}|\theta\right). \qquad [4.29]$$

For any realization $\{\boldsymbol{x}^{[1]}, \boldsymbol{x}^{[2]}, \ldots, \boldsymbol{x}^{[m]}\}$, the sample PDF ϕ_m is then a function of θ. We call this the **likelihood function** and denote it $L(\theta|\boldsymbol{x}^{[1]}, \boldsymbol{x}^{[2]}, \ldots, \boldsymbol{x}^{[m]})$ or simply $L(\theta)$. Mathematically, $L(\theta|\boldsymbol{x}^{[1]}, \boldsymbol{x}^{[2]}, \ldots, \boldsymbol{x}^{[m]})$ is identical to $\phi_m(\boldsymbol{x}^{[1]}, \boldsymbol{x}^{[2]}, \ldots, \boldsymbol{x}^{[m]}|\theta)$. The new name and notation merely indicate a different perspective. We think of ϕ_m as a function of a realization dependent upon a parameter. We think of L as a function of a parameter dependent upon a realization. We define the **ML estimate** of θ as that value h that maximizes the value of the likelihood function. It is the value for θ that associates the maximum probability density with the data set $\{\boldsymbol{x}^{[1]}, \boldsymbol{x}^{[2]}, \ldots, \boldsymbol{x}^{[m]}\}$.

ML Estimates of Scalar Parameters

Given a differentiable likelihood function $L(\theta)$ of a scalar parameter θ, solving for an ML estimate is a simple application of calculus. Standard techniques for maximizing differentiable functions apply. We take the derivative of the likelihood function and set it equal to 0:

$$\frac{dL}{d\theta} = 0. \qquad [4.30]$$

Roots of this equation are investigated to determine which maximizes $L(\theta)$. If θ is restricted to some region Ω, values on the boundary of Ω must also be investigated. For example, if θ represents a variance, then $\Omega = [0, \infty)$, and it is conceivable that the likelihood function is maximized at $\theta = 0$.

It is often convenient to maximize the logarithm of the likelihood function, which is called the **log-likelihood function**. To see why, compare

$$L(\theta) = \phi(\boldsymbol{x}^{[1]}|\theta)\phi(\boldsymbol{x}^{[2]}|\theta)\cdots\phi(\boldsymbol{x}^{[m]}|\theta) \qquad [4.31]$$

with

$$log[L(\theta)] = log[\phi(\boldsymbol{x}^{[1]}|\theta)] + log[\phi(\boldsymbol{x}^{[2]}|\theta)] + \cdots + log[\phi(\boldsymbol{x}^{[m]}|\theta)]. \qquad [4.32]$$

Because the latter is a sum, its derivative is easier to work with. The logarithm function is strictly increasing, so any value h that maximizes L will also maximize $log[L]$. In some cases, an analytic solution for the roots of the equation

$$\frac{d}{d\theta} log(L) = 0 \qquad [4.33]$$

can be found. Alternatively, numerical techniques such as Newton's method must be applied.

It is possible that the log-likelihood function will fail to achieve a maximum on Ω or it may achieve a maximum at multiple points. In either circumstance, review your assumptions either to determine what is preventing the log-likelihood function from achieving a maximum or to indicate some criteria for selecting one of several maxima as your estimate.

ML Estimates of Non-Scalar Parameters

The foregoing technique generalizes for estimating vector-valued parameters θ, but gradients replace derivatives. We may attempt to directly maximize the likelihood function, solving

$$\nabla L(\theta) = \mathbf{0}, \qquad [4.34]$$

or work with the log-likelihood function, solving

$$\nabla log[L(\theta)] = \mathbf{0}. \qquad [4.35]$$

Again, this can sometimes be solved analytically, but numerical solutions are often necessary. Similar issues of existence and uniqueness arise.

A matrix-valued parameter θ may be estimated similarly. Simply arrange the components of the matrix into a vector and proceed accordingly.

EXAMPLE: MIXED NORMAL DISTRIBUTION. Consider the data of Exhibit 4.4. We treat the data as a realization of a sample for a mixed normal distribution $N^2(\mu, \boldsymbol{\sigma}^2, \boldsymbol{\omega})$ with:

$$\boldsymbol{\sigma}^2 = \begin{pmatrix} 1 \\ 1 \end{pmatrix} \quad \text{and} \quad \boldsymbol{\omega} = \begin{pmatrix} 0.5 \\ 0.5 \end{pmatrix}. \qquad [4.36]$$

k	$x^{[k]}$	k	$x^{[k]}$	k	$x^{[k]}$	k	$x^{[k]}$
1	1.85	6	−1.98	11	−1.29	16	2.20
2	1.49	7	1.34	12	−0.14	17	0.20
3	−1.52	8	0.69	13	1.96	18	0.53
4	3.35	9	−1.94	14	1.92	19	3.09
5	−1.08	10	2.32	15	−2.58	20	−1.97

Exhibit 4.4 Example data.

We shall use the data to construct an ML estimate for the unknown mean vector

$$\mu = \begin{pmatrix} \mu_1 \\ \mu_2 \end{pmatrix}. \qquad [4.37]$$

The PDF $\phi(x|\mu)$ of the mixed normal distribution is

$$\phi(x|\mu) = \frac{1}{\sqrt{8\pi}}\left(exp\left(\frac{-(x-\mu_1)^2}{2}\right) + exp\left(\frac{-(x-\mu_2)^2}{2}\right)\right), \qquad [4.38]$$

which has gradient

$$\nabla\phi(x|\mu) = \left(\frac{(x-\mu_1)}{\sqrt{8\pi}}exp\left(\frac{-(x-\mu_1)^2}{2}\right), \frac{(x-\mu_2)}{\sqrt{8\pi}}exp\left(\frac{-(x-\mu_2)^2}{2}\right)\right). \qquad [4.39]$$

Based upon our data, the log-likelihood function $log(L(\mu))$ is

$$log(L(\mu)) = log(\phi(1.85|\mu)) + log(\phi(1.49|\mu)) + \cdots + log(\phi(-1.97|\mu)). \qquad [4.40]$$

Its gradient is

$$\nabla log(L(\mu)) = \frac{\nabla\phi(1.85|\mu)}{\phi(1.85|\mu)} + \frac{\nabla\phi(1.49|\mu)}{\phi(1.49|\mu)} + \cdots + \frac{\nabla\phi(-1.97|\mu)}{\phi(-1.97|\mu)}. \qquad [4.41]$$

To maximize the log-likelihood function, we set [4.41] equal to **0** and solve for $\boldsymbol{\mu}$ using Newton's method. There is a saddle point at $\boldsymbol{\mu} = (0.4212, 0.4212)$. The global maximum we seek occurs at $\boldsymbol{\mu} = (-1.3616, 1.8513)$.

EXERCISES

4.5 Reproduce the results of the example of this section. Use different seed values with Newton's method to locate both the saddle point and global maximum.

4.5. STOCHASTIC PROCESSES

Measure time t in appropriate units—days, months, years. A **time series** is a series $\{{}^{-\alpha}\boldsymbol{x}, \ldots, {}^{-1}\boldsymbol{x}, {}^{0}\boldsymbol{x}\}$ of n-dimensional vectors observed over a period of time $[-\alpha, 0]$. The natural number n is called the **dimensionality** of the time series. If $n = 1$, the time series is **univariate**; otherwise it is **multivariate**. Vectors ${}^{t}\boldsymbol{x}$ are recorded with a frequency corresponding to a single unit of time. These concepts are illustrated in Exhibits 4.5 and 4.6 with a two-dimensional time series of daily high and low temperatures at the summit of Mt. Washington during the month of January 2000.

Date	t	${}^{t}x_1$	${}^{t}x_2$	Date	t	${}^{t}x_1$	${}^{t}x_2$
1/1/00	–30	8	–4	1/17/00	–14	10	–30
1/2/00	–29	20	5	1/18/00	–13	–1	–30
1/3/00	–28	36	19	1/19/00	–12	4	–10
1/4/00	–27	36	15	1/20/00	–11	1	–9
1/5/00	–26	39	5	1/21/00	–10	7	–5
1/6/00	–25	17	–18	1/22/00	–9	–2	–30
1/7/00	–24	13	–14	1/23/00	–8	–13	–31
1/8/00	–23	15	–2	1/24/00	–7	13	–13
1/9/00	–22	13	–4	1/25/00	–6	20	3
1/10/00	–21	21	12	1/26/00	–5	27	9
1/11/00	–20	24	14	1/27/00	–4	28	0
1/12/00	–19	21	7	1/28/00	–3	6	–13
1/13/00	–18	15	–6	1/29/00	–2	6	–14
1/14/00	–17	8	–28	1/30/00	–1	17	–3
1/15/00	–16	–21	–31	1/31/00	0	22	13
1/16/00	–15	1	–28				

Exhibit 4.5 Daily high and low temperatures at the summit of Mt. Washington during the month of January 2000. Temperatures are in degrees Fahrenheit. Time $t = -30$ corresponds to January 1, 2000. Source: Mt. Washington Observatory.

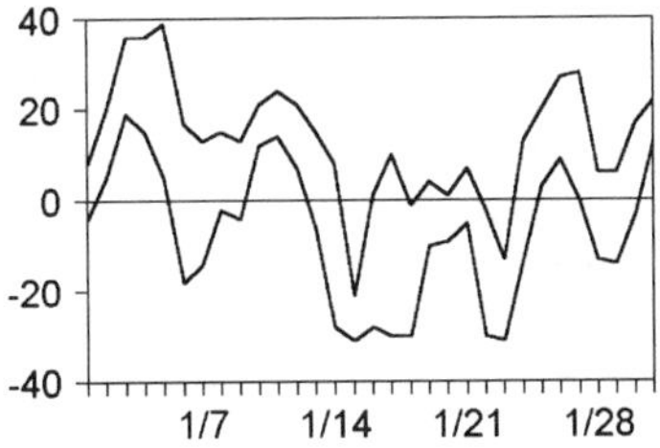

Exhibit 4.6 Graph of daily high and low temperature data from Exhibit 4.5.

Often, each value ${}^t\boldsymbol{x}$ of a time series $\boldsymbol{x}$ corresponds to an observation made precisely at time t, but this is not always the case. In our Mt. Washington example, each day's high and low temperatures ${}^t x_1$ and ${}^t x_2$ are realized at different times during a given day, but we associate them both with the specific integer point in time t.

Presumably, the process that generated a time series will continue into the future. We are interested in future values, which we treat as random. To model these, we specify a model called a stochastic process based upon the time series. A **stochastic process**—or **process**—is a sequence of random vectors ${}^t\mathbf{X}$ with t taking on integer values.[3] Values t extend back to $-\infty$ and forward to ∞. Modeling all these terms may seem excessive, especially for practical work. We do so as a mathematical convenience. It saves us having to artificially model some initial or terminal behavior for the process.

Given a time series $\{{}^{-\alpha}\boldsymbol{x}, \ldots, {}^{-1}\boldsymbol{x}, {}^{0}\boldsymbol{x}\}$, we construct a stochastic process $\{\ldots, {}^{-1}\boldsymbol{X}, {}^{0}\boldsymbol{X}, {}^{1}\boldsymbol{X}, \ldots\}$ by treating the time series as a single realization of the corresponding segment $\{{}^{-\alpha}\boldsymbol{X}, \ldots, {}^{-1}\boldsymbol{X}, {}^{0}\boldsymbol{X}\}$ of the stochastic process. We apply statistical techniques to specify a stochastic process that is consistent with such a realization. The undertaking is called **time series analysis**.

Conditional Versus Unconditional Distributions

Time series analysis is different from statistical estimation. Statistical estimators apply to realizations $\{\boldsymbol{x}^{[1]}, \ldots, \boldsymbol{x}^{[m-1]}, \boldsymbol{x}^{[m]}\}$ of samples $\{\boldsymbol{X}^{[1]}, \ldots, \boldsymbol{X}^{[m-1]}, \boldsymbol{X}^{[m]}\}$. Time series analysis applies to realizations $\{{}^{-\alpha}\boldsymbol{x}, \ldots, {}^{-1}\boldsymbol{x}, {}^{0}\boldsymbol{x}\}$ of segments of stochastic processes $\{{}^{-\alpha}\boldsymbol{X}, \ldots, {}^{-1}\boldsymbol{X}, {}^{0}\boldsymbol{X}\}$. A segment of a stochastic process is *not* a sample. It lacks an important property of samples. The random vectors $\boldsymbol{X}^{[k]}$ that make up a sample are IID. The random vectors ${}^t\boldsymbol{X}$ that make up a segment of a stochastic process may not be. This should be obvious from our Mt.

[3]We consider only discrete processes. With continuous processes, t takes on real values.

Washington example. Temperatures follow trends. Cold days tend to follow cold days; warm days tend to follow warm days. Clearly, the random vectors $^{t}\boldsymbol{X}$ in that example are not independent. They are also not identically distributed, since temperatures follow seasonal patterns.

Since terms $^{t}\boldsymbol{X}$ of a process need not be independent, we must distinguish between conditional and unconditional distributions of terms. The conditional distribution of $^{t}\boldsymbol{X}$ as of time $t-k$ is its distribution conditional on all values $^{t-k}\boldsymbol{x}$, $^{t-k-1}\boldsymbol{x}$, $^{t-k-2}\boldsymbol{x}$, ... Usually, we don't need to know all preceding values. Only a handful of the most recent values may be relevant, but this depends upon the particular process.

Consider a somewhat contrived process $\boldsymbol{Y}$. All terms ^{t}Y are equal,

$$\ldots = {}^{t-2}Y = {}^{t-1}Y = {}^{t}Y = {}^{t+1}Y = {}^{t+2}Y \ldots, \qquad [4.42]$$

and are $U(0, 1)$. Two realizations of the process are illustrated in Exhibit 4.7.

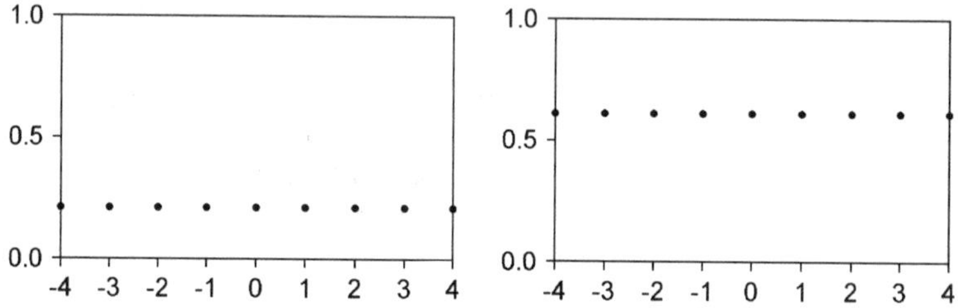

Exhibit 4.7 Terms of the process $\boldsymbol{Y}$ are equal and $U(0, 1)$. Two realizations are depicted.

In this example, ^{1}Y has unconditional distribution $U(0, 1)$, but its distribution conditional on information at time 0 is degenerate, with $^{1}Y = {}^{0}y$.

We indicate the conditional expectation of a term ^{t}X as of time $t-k$ as $^{t-k}E(^{t}X)$. We indicate the unconditional expectation as simply $E(^{t}X)$. Standard deviations, variances, skewnesses, and kurtoses are treated similarly. For example, the unconditional standard deviation of ^{1}X is denoted $std(^{1}X)$. Conditional on information available at time 0, it is denoted $^{0}std(^{1}X)$.

Conditional parameters, such as a mean or standard deviation conditional on information available through time $t-k$, can also be indicated as $^{t|t-k}\mu$ or $^{t|t-k}\sigma$. Corresponding unconditional parameters are indicated $^{t}\mu$ or $^{t}\sigma$. Conditional or unconditional CDFs and PDFs are indicated similarly: $^{t|t-k}\Phi$ and $^{t|t-k}\phi$ or $^{t}\Phi$ and $^{t}\phi$.

In Chapter 3, we introduced shorthand notation for certain families of probability distributions. For example, we used notations $N(\mu, \sigma^2)$ and $U(a, b)$ to indicate univariate normal and uniform distributions. We modify this notation with superscripts to distinguish conditional distributions from unconditional distributions.

For example, if ${}^{t}X$ is uniformly distributed conditional on information available at time $t - k$, we indicate this ${}^{t}X \sim {}^{t-k}U(a, b)$. If ${}^{t}X$ is unconditionally normal, no superscript is needed to indicate this: ${}^{t}X \sim N(\mu, \sigma^2)$.

Correlations

If the terms of a process were IID, only unconditional correlations between components of each term $cor({}^{t}X_i, {}^{t}X_j)$ could be nonzero. Absent an IID condition, two other types of unconditional correlations arise. There are correlations between corresponding components of two terms lagged a period k apart, $cor({}^{t}X_i, {}^{t-k}X_i)$. These are called **autocorrelations** with lag k. There are also correlations between distinct components of terms lagged a period k apart, $cor({}^{t}X_i, {}^{t-k}X_j)$. These are called **cross correlations** with lag k.

Stationarity

To fully specify a stochastic process, we must specify—explicitly or implicitly—a joint distribution for all components ${}^{t}X_i$ of all terms ${}^{t}\mathbf{X}$. This entails specifying infinitely many parameters. To reduce this to a manageable—and finite!—number of distinct parameters, we assume some sort of homogeneity across terms. A simple solution is to assume that terms are IID. This reduces the task of specifying a stochastic process to that of specifying the joint distribution of the components of a single term. Of course, this solution defeats the purpose of time series analysis. We introduced stochastic processes as having non-IID terms specifically because we wanted to model temporal dependencies in time series.

An alternative and widely used solution is to consider only processes that have some form of stationarity. A process is said to be **strictly stationary** if the unconditional joint distribution of any segment $\{{}^{t}\mathbf{X}, {}^{t+1}\mathbf{X}, \ldots, {}^{t+m}\mathbf{X}\}$ is identical to the unconditional joint distribution of any other segment $\{{}^{t+k}\mathbf{X}, {}^{t+k+1}\mathbf{X}, \ldots, {}^{t+k+m}\mathbf{X}\}$ of the same length. Note the similarity of this definition to the IID condition, which we rejected earlier. That approach requires that unconditional distributions of terms be identical. Strict stationarity requires that unconditional distributions of segments be identical. Strict stationarity is appealing because it affords a form of homogeneity across terms without requiring that terms be independent.

A more widely used solution is to consider processes that are covariance stationary. A process is said to be **covariance stationary**—or simply **stationary**—if the unconditional distribution of any segment $\{{}^{t}\mathbf{X}, {}^{t+1}\mathbf{X}, \ldots, {}^{t+m}\mathbf{X}\}$ has means, standard deviations, and correlations that are identical to the corresponding means, standard deviations, and correlations of the unconditional distribution of any other segment $\{{}^{t+k}\boldsymbol{X}, {}^{t+k+1}\boldsymbol{X}, \ldots, {}^{t+k+m}\boldsymbol{X}\}$ of the same length. Correlations include autocorrelations and cross correlations.

Note that covariance stationarity requires that all first and second moments exist whereas strict stationarity does not. In this one respect, covariance stationarity is a stronger condition.

In applications, a stationarity assumption is not always reasonable. For example, a time series may rise over time, making a constant unconditional mean assumption unreasonable. Every situation is unique, but a solution that often works is to transform a time series in some manner to make it compatible with a stationarity assumption. Transformations take various forms to address different departures from stationarity.

Differencing

One technique is to take differences of one or more components of the time series. With differencing, we transform a time series $\boldsymbol{x}$ into a time series $\dot{\boldsymbol{x}}$ by replacing suitable components ${}^{t}x_i$ with differences:

$$ {}^{t}\dot{x}_i = {}^{t}x_i - {}^{t-1}x_i. \qquad [4.43] $$

Not all components may need to be differenced. For those components ${}^{t}x_j$ that don't require it, we merely set

$$ {}^{t}\dot{x}_i = {}^{t}x_i. \qquad [4.44] $$

Although differencing is widely used in economic applications, it may fail to address nonstationarities in financial time series. Consider a stock's price. Differences in a stock's price tend to be proportional to the stock's price. If the unconditional mean of a stock's price increases with time, so will the unconditional mean of differences in the stock's price. We may solve this problem by taking returns instead of differences.

Returns

In finance, a **return** is a metric of economic benefit from holding assets. If an asset's value is EUR 50 one day and EUR 55 the next day, we might say the asset had a 1-day 10% return. Let's extend this notion to quantities other than asset values. If an interest rate rises one day from .050 to .055, it is reasonable to say that the interest rate had a 1-day 10% return. In this context, return is no longer a metric of economic benefit, but merely a metric of change in a time series. Suppose the temperature at the summit of Mt. Washington rises over a day from 50°F to 55°F: isn't it reasonable to say that the temperature had a 1-day 10% return? Accordingly, we treat returns as a purely mathematical notion.

Consider univariate time series $\boldsymbol{x} = \{{}^{-\alpha}x, \ldots, {}^{-2}x, {}^{-1}x, {}^{0}x\}$. We define two metrics of return. The **simple return** of $\boldsymbol{x}$ over the period $[t-1, t]$ is

$$ {}^{t}z_{simple} = \frac{{}^{t}x - {}^{t-1}x}{{}^{t-1}x}. \qquad [4.45] $$

The **log return** of $\boldsymbol{x}$ over the period $[t-1, t]$ is

$$ {}^{t}z_{log} = log\left(\frac{{}^{t}x}{{}^{t-1}x}\right). \qquad [4.46] $$

For small returns, these two metrics closely approximate each other. Both are widely used in finance. Each has advantages and disadvantages. Simple returns are appealing because they combine linearly across positions. If a portfolio is equally invested in two assets whose values experience respective simple returns of .08 and $-.02$ over a given period, the portfolio experiences a .03 simple return over the period, but this would not be true with log returns. On the other hand, log returns combine linearly over time. If a portfolio experiences a .05 log return followed by a $-.04$ log return, its log return over the entire period is .01. This would not be true with simple returns.

A shortcoming of returns is the fact that their calculation entails division. If a time series can take on the value 0, returns may be poorly behaved or undefined. An example might be a component of a time series representing the spread between spot prices of gold and platinum. At various times, this spread has been positive, negative, and even zero. For such components of time series, differencing may be used instead of returns.

HETEROSKEDASTICITY

A stochastic process $\boldsymbol{X}$ is **homoskedastic** if unconditional covariance matrices ${}^{t}\boldsymbol{\Sigma}$ of terms ${}^{t}\boldsymbol{X}$ are constant. It is **heteroskedastic** if they are not constant. A process is **conditionally homoskedastic** if conditional covariance matrices ${}^{t|t-1}\boldsymbol{\Sigma}$ for terms ${}^{t}\boldsymbol{X}$ are constant. It is **conditionally heteroskedastic** if they are not.

These distinctions are easy to grasp intuitively with a picture. Exhibit 4.8 depicts realizations for two processes. The realization on the left exhibits constant standard deviations consistent with homoskedasticity and conditional homoskedasticity. The one on the right exhibits nonconstant standard deviations consistent with heteroskedasticity or conditional heteroskedasticity.

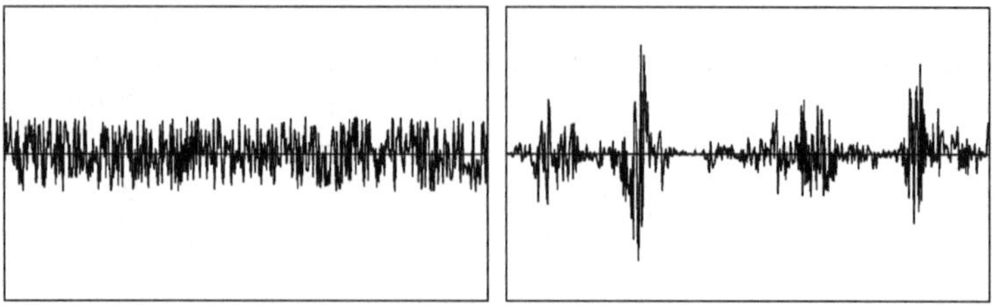

Exhibit 4.8 Realizations for two processes. The realization on the left exhibits constant standard deviations consistent with homoskedasticity and conditional homoskedasticity. The one on the right exhibits nonconstant standard deviations consistent with heteroskedasticity or conditional heteroskedasticity.

Financial markets experience random periods of high and low volatility. For this reason, conditionally heteroskedastic processes are widely used in financial applications.

Exercises

4.6 What is the difference between a time series and a stochastic process?

4.7 In our Mt. Washington example, each recorded high temperature ${}^{t}x_1$ is associated with the specific integer point in time t, but might have been realized at any point during a 24-hour period. Give two examples of financial time series:
1. one for which values ${}^{t}x$ are actually realized at a specific time t, and
2. another for which values ${}^{t}x$ may be realized at any time in an interval that we associate with time t.

4.8 Consider the process $\boldsymbol{Y}$, which we described earlier (all terms ${}^{t}Y$ are equal and are unconditionally $U(0, 1)$; two realizations are indicated in Exhibit 4.7).
1. Is $\boldsymbol{Y}$ stationary?
2. Is it unconditionally homoskedastic?
3. Is it conditionally homoskedastic?
4. What is the unconditional standard deviation ${}^{1}\sigma$?
5. What is the conditional standard deviation ${}^{1|0}\sigma$?

4.9 Explain in your own words the difference between covariance stationarity and homoskedasticity. Does covariance stationarity imply homoskedasticity? Does covariance stationarity imply conditional homoskedasticity?

4.10 Suppose $\boldsymbol{x}$ is a time series with ${}^{-1}x = 100$.
1. Calculate ${}^{0}x$ if ${}^{0}z_{simple} = 0.05$.
2. Calculate ${}^{0}x$ if ${}^{0}z_{log} = 0.05$.

4.11 Exhibit 4.9 indicates values for a time series $\boldsymbol{x}$. Complete the table by calculating the corresponding differences, simple returns, and log returns for the time series.

t	${}^{t}x$	${}^{t}x - {}^{t-1}x$	${}^{t}z_{simple}$	${}^{t}z_{log}$
-9	3.0			
-8	3.5			
-7	2.5			
-6	1.5			
-5	0.5			
-4	-0.5			
-3	-1.5			
-2	0.0			
-1	0.1			
0	1.5			

Exhibit 4.9 Values are indicated for a time series $\boldsymbol{x}$. The table is to be completed for Exercise 4.11.

4.12 For a strictly positive (${}^{t}x > 0$ for all t) univariate time series $\boldsymbol{x}$, what is the range of values possible for:
1. the simple returns ${}^{t}z_{simple}$ of $\boldsymbol{x}$?
2. the log returns ${}^{t}z_{log}$ of $\boldsymbol{x}$?

4.13 Treating ${}^{t}z_{log}$ as a function of ${}^{t}x$, construct a first-order Taylor polynomial for ${}^{t}z_{log}$. Do so about the point ${}^{t-1}x$. Simplifying the result, what do you obtain?

4.6. WHITE NOISE, AUTOREGRESSIVE, AND MOVING-AVERAGE PROCESSES

In this section, we consider several models, which are commonly used for specifying stationary conditionally homoskedastic processes.

White Noise

A stochastic process

$$\ldots, {}^{t-2}\mathbf{W}, {}^{t-1}\mathbf{W}, {}^{t}\mathbf{W}, {}^{t+1}\mathbf{W}, \ldots \qquad [4.47]$$

is said to be **white noise** if unconditional expectations satisfy

$$E({}^{t}\mathbf{W}) = \mathbf{0}, \qquad [4.48]$$

$$E({}^{t}\mathbf{W}\,{}^{t+k}\mathbf{W}') = \begin{cases} \mathbf{\Sigma} & k = 0, \\ \mathbf{0} & k \neq 0, \end{cases} \qquad [4.49]$$

for some constant covariance matrix $\boldsymbol{\Sigma}$. Condition [4.49] does not require that the ${}^{t}\boldsymbol{W}$ be independent. If we make this stronger assumption, the process is called **independent white noise**. If we further assume the ${}^{t}\boldsymbol{W}$ are joint normal, it is called **Gaussian white noise**.[4] A realization of a univariate Gaussian white noise with variance 1 is graphed in Exhibit 4.10.

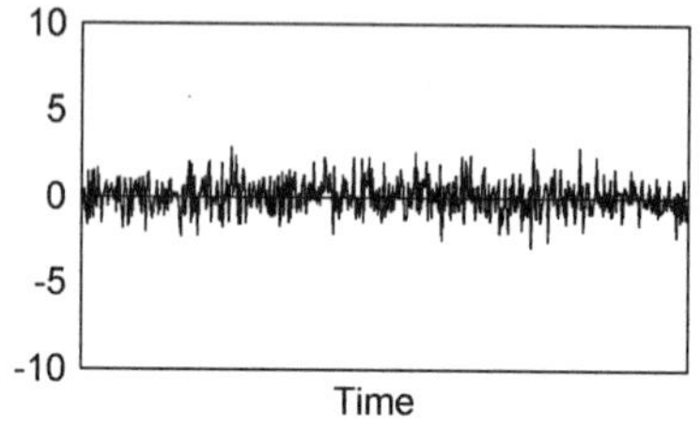

Exhibit 4.10 A realization of a univariate Gaussian white noise with variance 1.

Moving-Average Processes

An n-dimensional **moving-average process** of order q, MA(q), has form

$$ {}^{t}\boldsymbol{X} = \boldsymbol{a} + {}^{t}\boldsymbol{W} + \sum_{k=1}^{q} \boldsymbol{\beta}_k \, {}^{t-k}\boldsymbol{W}, \qquad [4.50] $$

where $\boldsymbol{a}$ is an n-dimensional vector, the $\boldsymbol{\beta}_k$ are $n \times n$ matrices, and $\boldsymbol{W}$ is n-dimensional white noise. The coefficients $\boldsymbol{\beta}_k$ of [4.50] induce autocorrelations in an MA process. In applications, MA(1) and MA(2) processes are common.

Exhibit 4.11 indicates a realization of the univariate MA(2) process

$$ {}^{t}X = 1 + {}^{t}W + .50\ {}^{t-1}W + .25\ {}^{t-2}W, \qquad [4.51] $$

where $\boldsymbol{W}$ is variance 1 Gaussian white noise.

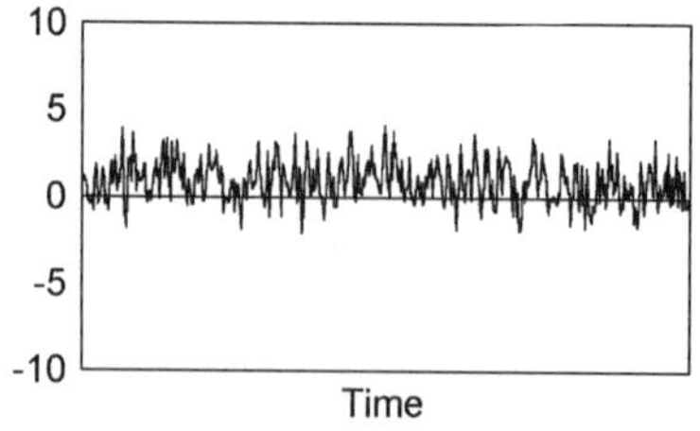

Exhibit 4.11 A realization of the MA(2) process [4.51].

[4] Usage of the term "white noise" is not uniform. Some authors use the term to mean Gaussian white noise.

Autoregressive Processes

An n-dimensional **autoregressive process** of order p, AR(p), has form

$$ {}^{t}\boldsymbol{X} = \boldsymbol{a} + \sum_{k=1}^{p} \boldsymbol{b}_k \, {}^{t-k}\boldsymbol{X} + {}^{t}\boldsymbol{W}, \qquad [4.52] $$

where $\boldsymbol{a}$ is an n-dimensional vector, the $\boldsymbol{b}_k$ are $n \times n$ matrices, and $\boldsymbol{W}$ is n-dimensional white noise. The name "autoregressive" indicates that [4.52] defines a regression of ${}^{t}\boldsymbol{X}$ on its own past values. In applications, AR(1) and AR(2) processes are common.

Exhibit 4.12 indicates a realization of the univariate AR(2) process

$$ {}^{t}X = 1 + .80 \, {}^{t-1}X - .10 \, {}^{t-2}X + {}^{t}W, \qquad [4.53] $$

where $\boldsymbol{W}$ is variance 1 Gaussian white noise.

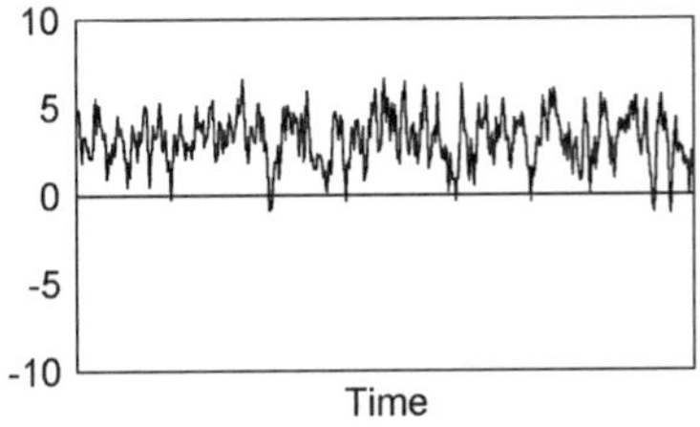

Exhibit 4.12 A realization of the AR(2) process [4.53].

Autoregressive Moving-Average Processes

An n-dimensional **autoregressive moving-average process** of orders p and q, ARMA(p, q), has form

$$ {}^{t}\boldsymbol{X} = \boldsymbol{a} + {}^{t}\boldsymbol{W} + \sum_{k=1}^{q} \boldsymbol{\beta}_k \, {}^{t-k}\boldsymbol{W} + \sum_{k=1}^{p} \boldsymbol{b}_k \, {}^{t-k}\boldsymbol{X}. \qquad [4.54] $$

As the name suggests, it combines an AR(p) model with an MA(q) model of the same dimension n. In applications, ARMA(1,1) processes are common.

Exhibit 4.13 indicates a realization of the univariate ARMA(1,1) process

$$ {}^{t}X = 1 + {}^{t}W + .50 \, {}^{t-1}W + .50 \, {}^{t-1}X, \qquad [4.55] $$

where $\boldsymbol{W}$ is variance 1 Gaussian white noise.

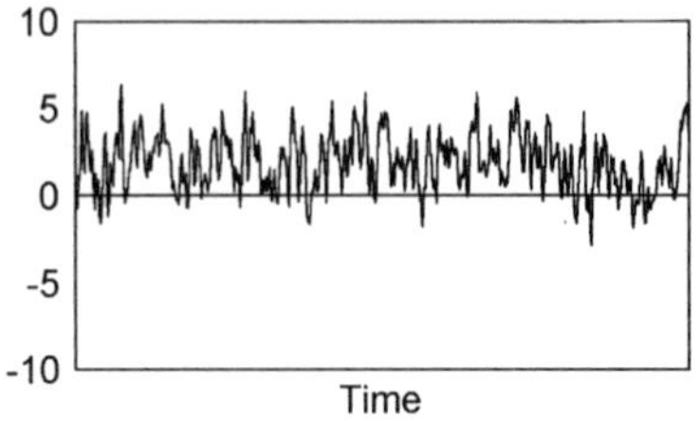

Exhibit 4.13 A realization of the ARMA(1,1) process [4.55].

Properties

As generally implemented, the models of this section are stationary and conditionally homoskedastic, but nothing in our definitions requires this. A white noise can be conditionally heteroskedastic. Any nontrivial MA, AR, or ARMA model based upon such a white noise will also be conditionally heteroskedastic.

MA processes are necessarily stationary, although some choices of coefficient matrices $\boldsymbol{\beta}_k$ will cause components to oscillate. AR and ARMA processes need not be stationary. Depending upon coefficient matrices $\boldsymbol{b}_k$, components can increase or decrease without bound. They may also oscillate wildly. If an AR or ARMA process does not exhibit such behaviors, it is generally stationary. See Hamilton (1994) for necessary and sufficient conditions for covariance stationarity.

Estimation

Stochastic processes are estimated from time series using techniques of statistical estimation as appropriate. In the case of a Gaussian white noise $\boldsymbol{W}$, terms are IID. We may treat a segment $\{{}^{-\alpha}\boldsymbol{W}, \ldots, {}^{-1}\boldsymbol{W}, {}^{0}\boldsymbol{W}\}$ of the stochastic processes as a sample, and employ sample estimators to estimate the constant covariance matrix of terms ${}^{t}\boldsymbol{W}$. Estimation for other processes may be more difficult. ML estimators are widely used for this purpose. Consider an example.

t	${}^{t}x$	t	${}^{t}x$	t	${}^{t}x$	t	${}^{t}x$
–31	0.99	–23	0.89	–15	–1.20	–7	1.80
–30	5.72	–22	1.26	–14	1.38	–6	5.13
–29	2.77	–21	–0.93	–13	3.19	–5	0.33
–28	0.83	–20	–0.50	–12	–1.44	–4	0.42
–27	2.42	–19	–1.20	–11	0.55	–3	0.70
–26	0.44	–18	3.10	–10	4.48	–2	0.47
–25	5.21	–17	0.84	–9	3.49	–1	–5.12
–24	3.09	–16	–1.62	–8	4.00	0	–2.26

Exhibit 4.14 Example time series.

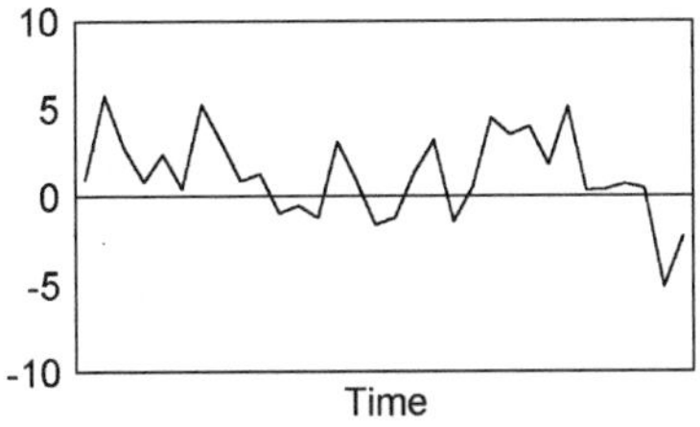

Exhibit 4.15 Graph of the time series of Exhibit 4.14.

Exhibit 4.14 indicates a time series, which is graphed in Exhibit 4.15. We treat the time series as a realization of a segment of a univariate stationary AR(1) process:

$$^{t}X = a + b_1\,{}^{t-1}X + {}^{t}W, \qquad [4.56]$$

where $\boldsymbol{W}$ is Gaussian white noise, ${}^{t}W \sim N(0, \sigma^2)$. Parameters that need to be estimated are a, b_1, and σ. Let $\theta = (a, b_1, \sigma)$. Let ${}^{t}\phi({}^{t}x|\theta)$ be the PDF of ${}^{t}X$ conditional only on θ, and let ${}^{t|t-1}\phi({}^{t}x|\theta, {}^{t-1}x)$ be the PDF of ${}^{t}X$ conditional on both θ and the previous value ${}^{t-1}x$. With ${}^{t}W$ normal, it can be shown that ${}^{t}X$ is both conditionally and unconditionally normal. It has unconditional mean

$$E({}^{t}X) = a + b_1 E({}^{t}X) \Rightarrow E({}^{t}X) = \frac{a}{1 - b_1}. \qquad [4.57]$$

By [3.32], it has unconditional variance

$$E([{}^{t}X - E({}^{t}X)]^2) = E({}^{t}X^2) - E({}^{t}X)^2 \qquad [4.58]$$

$$= E([a + b_1\,{}^{t-1}X + {}^{t}W]^2) - E({}^{t}X)^2 \qquad [4.59]$$

$$= \frac{\sigma^2}{1 - b_1^2}. \qquad [4.60]$$

Accordingly

$${}^{t}\phi({}^{t}x|\theta) \sim N\left(\frac{a}{1 - b_1}, \frac{\sigma^2}{1 - b_1^2}\right). \qquad [4.61]$$

Similarly, we conclude

$${}^{t|t-1}\phi({}^{t}x|\theta, {}^{t-1}x) \sim N(a + b_1\,{}^{t-1}x, \sigma^2). \qquad [4.62]$$

Since terms ${}^{t}X$ are dependent, the likelihood function employs conditional probability densities ${}^{t|t-1}\phi({}^{t}x|\theta, {}^{t-1}x)$ for all but the first term:

$$L(\theta) = {}^{-31}\phi({}^{-31}x|\theta)\; {}^{-30|-31}\phi({}^{-30}x|\theta, {}^{-31}x) \cdots {}^{0|-1}\phi({}^{0}x|\theta, {}^{-1}x). \qquad [4.63]$$

The log-likelihood function is

$$log[L(\theta)] = log[{}^{-31}\phi({}^{-31}x|\theta)] + \sum_{t=-30}^{0} log[{}^{t|t-1}\phi({}^{t}x|\theta, {}^{t-1}x)]. \quad [4.64]$$

Substituting in time series values from Exhibit 4.14, this becomes

$$log[{}^{-31}\phi(0.99|\theta)] + log[{}^{-30|-31}\phi(5.72|\theta, 0.99)] + \cdots$$
$$+ log[{}^{0|-1}\phi(-2.26|\theta, -5.12)]. \quad [4.65]$$

We take the gradient of the log-likelihood function and set it equal to **0**. Applying Newton's method, we estimate $\theta = (a, b_1, \sigma)$ as (0.82, 0.31, 1.50).

Exercises

4.14 Exhibit 4.16 indicates a realization of 50 consecutive terms of a variance 1 Gaussian white noise.[5]

0.293	0.317	0.047	–0.286	–1.237
–0.554	0.535	–1.640	–0.899	–0.704
–1.886	0.271	0.418	1.651	0.078
0.528	1.013	2.296	0.086	1.471
–0.580	–1.776	–2.217	0.502	–1.104
–1.211	0.205	0.110	0.011	0.778
–1.036	1.195	–1.169	–0.162	–0.504
–0.679	–1.366	0.885	–0.476	1.644
–1.665	0.129	2.882	0.978	0.054
–0.396	0.685	1.403	–0.009	0.918

Exhibit 4.16 Realization of 50 consecutive terms of a variance 1 Gaussian white noise for use in Exercise 4.14 and subsequent exercises.

Use this to generate a corresponding realization of the MA(2) process

$${}^{t}X = -2 + {}^{t}W + .60\,{}^{t-1}W + .30\,{}^{t-2}W, \quad [4.66]$$

where ${}^{t}W$ is a variance 1 Gaussian white noise.

4.15 Use the white noise realization of Exhibit 4.16 to generate and graph a realization of the AR(2) process

$${}^{t}X = 2 + .70\,{}^{t-1}X - .10\,{}^{t-2}X + {}^{t}W, \quad [4.67]$$

where ${}^{t}W$ is a variance 1 Gaussian white noise. Initialize the realization with terms ${}^{0}x = {}^{1}x = 0$.

[5] Such a realization can be constructed using techniques of random variate generation described in Chapter 5.

4.16 Use the white noise realization of Exhibit 4.16 to generate and graph a realization of the ARMA(1,1) process

$$ {}^{t}X = 2 + {}^{t}W - .25\,{}^{t-1}W + .50\,{}^{t-1}X, \qquad [4.68] $$

where ${}^{t}W$ is a variance 1 Gaussian white noise. Initialize the realization with term ${}^{0}x = 0$.

4.17 Derive expressions for the unconditional and conditional means, $E({}^{t}\boldsymbol{X})$ and ${}^{t-1}E({}^{t}\boldsymbol{X})$, of an MA($q$) process [4.50].

4.18 Derive expressions for the unconditional and conditional means, $E({}^{t}\boldsymbol{X})$ and ${}^{t-1}E({}^{t}\boldsymbol{X})$, of an AR($p$) process [4.52], assuming they exist.

4.7. GARCH PROCESSES

Engle (1982) proposes **autoregressive conditional heteroskedastic** (ARCH) processes. These are univariate conditionally heteroskedastic white noises. An ARCH(q) process $\boldsymbol{W}$ has conditional distribution

$$ {}^{t}W \sim {}^{t-1}N(0, {}^{t|t-1}\sigma^2), \qquad [4.69] $$

$$ {}^{t|t-1}\sigma^2 = a + \sum_{k=1}^{q} \beta_k\, {}^{t-k}W^2. \qquad [4.70] $$

Bollerslev (1986) extends the model by allowing ${}^{t|t-1}\sigma^2$ to also depend on its own past values. His **generalized ARCH**, or GARCH(p,q), process has form

$$ {}^{t}W \sim {}^{t-1}N(0, {}^{t|t-1}\sigma^2), \qquad [4.71] $$

$$ {}^{t|t-1}\sigma^2 = a + \sum_{k=1}^{q} \beta_k\, {}^{t-k}W^2 + \sum_{k=1}^{p} b_k\, {}^{t-k|t-k-1}\sigma^2. \qquad [4.72] $$

See Hamilton (1994) for stationarity conditions. In applications, GARCH(1,1) processes are common. Exhibit 4.17 indicates a realization of the GARCH(1,1) process

$$ {}^{t}W \sim {}^{t-1}N(0, {}^{t|t-1}\sigma^2), \qquad [4.73] $$

$$ {}^{t|t-1}\sigma^2 = .05 + .50\,{}^{t-1}W^2 + .50\,{}^{t-1|t-2}\sigma^2. \qquad [4.74] $$

GARCH processes are often estimated by maximum likelihood.

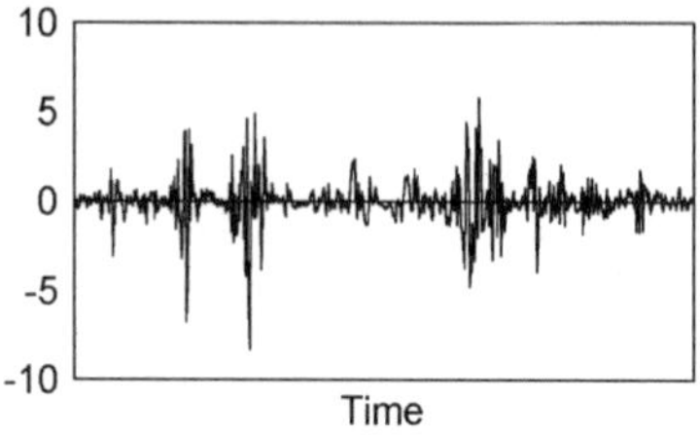

Exhibit 4.17 A realization of the GARCH(1,1) process [4.73].

There have been many attempts to generalize GARCH models to multiple dimensions. Attempts include:

- the vech and BEKK models of Engle and Kroner (1995),
- CCC-GARCH of Bollerslev (1990),
- orthogonal GARCH of Ding (1994), Alexander and Chibumba (1997), and Klaassen (2000), and
- DCC-GARCH of Engle (2000), and Engle and Sheppard (2001).

With some of these approaches, the number of parameters that must be specified becomes unmanageable as dimensionality n increases. With some, estimation requires considerable user intervention or entails other challenges. Some require assumptions that are difficult to reconcile with phenomena to be modeled. This is an area of ongoing research. To illustrate general techniques, we present two of the above models.

CCC-GARCH

Bollerslev (1990) proposes an n-dimensional GARCH model that comprises n univariate GARCH processes ${}^{t}W_i$ related to one another with a constant conditional correlation matrix $\boldsymbol{\rho}$. We call this the **constant conditional correlation** GARCH or CCC-GARCH model. It has form

$$ {}^{t}\mathbf{W} \sim {}^{t-1}N_n(\mathbf{0}, {}^{t|t-1}\mathbf{\Sigma}), \qquad [4.75]$$

$$ {}^{t|t-1}\mathbf{\Sigma} = {}^{t|t-1}\boldsymbol{\sigma}\boldsymbol{\rho}\,{}^{t|t-1}\boldsymbol{\sigma}, \qquad [4.76]$$

where $\boldsymbol{\rho}$ is a correlation matrix, and

$$ {}^{t|t-1}\boldsymbol{\sigma} = \begin{pmatrix} \sqrt{{}^{t|t-1}\sigma_1^2} & 0 & \cdots & 0 \\ 0 & \sqrt{{}^{t|t-1}\sigma_2^2} & & 0 \\ \vdots & & \ddots & \vdots \\ 0 & 0 & \cdots & \sqrt{{}^{t|t-1}\sigma_n^2} \end{pmatrix}, \qquad [4.77]$$

with conditional variances ${}^{t|t-1}\sigma_i^2$ modeled as with a univariate GARCH(p, q) process:

$$ {}^{t|t-1}\sigma_i^2 = a_i + \sum_{k=1}^{q} \beta_{i,k}\, {}^{t-k}W_i^2 + \sum_{k=1}^{p} b_{i,k}\, {}^{t-k|t-k-1}\sigma_i^2. \qquad [4.78] $$

These may be estimated using maximum likelihood.

Orthogonal GARCH

Ding (1994), Alexander and Chibumba (1997), and Klaassen (2000) propose an n-dimensional GARCH model based upon the principal components of a constant unconditional covariance matrix $\boldsymbol{\Sigma}$ of ${}^t\boldsymbol{W}$. Set

$$ {}^t\boldsymbol{W} = \boldsymbol{v}\, {}^t\boldsymbol{D}, \qquad [4.79] $$

where $\boldsymbol{v}$ is an $n \times n$ matrix with columns equal to orthonormal eigenvectors of $\boldsymbol{\Sigma}$. The ${}^tD_i$ are modeled as conditionally uncorrelated univariate GARCH(p, q) processes:

$$ {}^tD_i \sim {}^{t-1}N\left(0, {}^{t|t-1}\sigma_i^2\right), \qquad [4.80] $$

$$ {}^{t|t-1}\sigma_i^2 = a_i + \sum_{k=1}^{q} \beta_{i,k}\, {}^{t-k}D_i^2 + \sum_{k=1}^{p} b_{i,k}\, {}^{t-k|t-k-1}\sigma_i^2. \qquad [4.81] $$

By construction, the ${}^tD_i$ are necessarily unconditionally uncorrelated. The model makes a simplifying assumption that they are also conditionally uncorrelated. Essentially, orthogonal GARCH is CCC-GARCH with a change of coordinates. Instead of assuming that ${}^t\boldsymbol{W}$ has a conditional correlation matrix that is constant over time, it assumes that ${}^t\boldsymbol{D}$ does.

An orthogonal GARCH process is estimated from a time series $\{{}^{-\alpha}\boldsymbol{w}, \ldots, {}^{-1}\boldsymbol{w}, {}^{0}\boldsymbol{w}\}$ by first constructing the unconditional covariance matrix $\boldsymbol{\Sigma}$. This can be set equal to the data's sample covariance matrix. From this, construct $\boldsymbol{v}$. Decompose data points:

$$ {}^t\boldsymbol{w} = \boldsymbol{v}\, {}^t\boldsymbol{d} \qquad [4.82] $$

to obtain a time series $\{{}^{-\alpha}d_i, \ldots, {}^{-1}d_i, {}^{0}d_i\}$ for each i. Univariate GARCH(p, q) processes [4.80] are estimated from these using a separate maximum likelihood analysis for each.

Properties

Both CCC-GARCH and orthogonal GARCH model time-varying standard deviations well. Where they fall short is in modeling time-varying correlations.

CCC-GARCH assumes a constant conditional correlation matrix. Orthogonal GARCH offers a nonconstant conditional correlation matrix, but the stochastic behavior of that correlation matrix is not modeled directly. It is an artifact of the model, and results are sometimes unreasonable.

4.8. REGIME-SWITCHING PROCESSES

A stochastic process is said to be **regime-switching** if its behavior is determined by different models—different regimes—during different periods. We are interested in processes that switch randomly between regimes.

Consider an n-dimensional white noise $\boldsymbol{W}$ constructed with m joint-normal regimes. Let stochastic process $\boldsymbol{Z}$ indicate the regime in force at any time t, so terms ${}^{t}Z$ are random variables taking on values in the set $\{1, 2, \ldots, m\}$. $\boldsymbol{Z}$ is defined as a **Markov process**, which has constant probabilities of switching from one regime to another. These transition probabilities are indicated with a matrix:

$$\boldsymbol{p} = \begin{pmatrix} p_{1,1} & p_{1,2} & \cdots & p_{1,m} \\ p_{2,1} & p_{2,2} & & p_{2,m} \\ \vdots & & \ddots & \vdots \\ p_{m,1} & p_{m,2} & \cdots & p_{m,m} \end{pmatrix}. \qquad [4.83]$$

Component $p_{i,j}$ indicates the probability of transitioning from regime j in force at any time $t-1$ to regime i at time t. Each column sums to 1. At any time $t-1$, the regime that will be in force at time t is uncertain, so ${}^{t}\boldsymbol{W}$ is conditionally mixed joint-normal,

$${}^{t}\boldsymbol{W} \sim {}^{t-1}N_n^m(\boldsymbol{\mu}, \boldsymbol{\Sigma}, {}^{t}\boldsymbol{\xi}), \qquad [4.84]$$

where

$$\boldsymbol{\mu} = \begin{pmatrix} \boldsymbol{0} \\ \boldsymbol{0} \\ \vdots \\ \boldsymbol{0} \end{pmatrix}, \quad \boldsymbol{\Sigma} = \begin{pmatrix} \boldsymbol{\Sigma}_1 \\ \boldsymbol{\Sigma}_2 \\ \vdots \\ \boldsymbol{\Sigma}_m \end{pmatrix}, \quad {}^{t}\boldsymbol{\xi} = \begin{pmatrix} p_{1,{}^{t-1}z} \\ p_{2,{}^{t-1}z} \\ \vdots \\ p_{m,{}^{t-1}z} \end{pmatrix}. \qquad [4.85]$$

Exhibit 4.18 indicates a realization of the univariate three-regime process

$${}^{t}\boldsymbol{W} \sim {}^{t-1}N^3(\boldsymbol{\mu}, \boldsymbol{\sigma}^2, {}^{t}\boldsymbol{\xi}), \qquad [4.86]$$

$${}^{t}z \in \{1, 2, 3\}, \qquad [4.87]$$

$$\boldsymbol{\mu} = \begin{pmatrix} 0 \\ 0 \\ 0 \end{pmatrix}, \quad \boldsymbol{\sigma}^2 = \begin{pmatrix} 0.75 \\ 1.50 \\ 3.00 \end{pmatrix}, \quad {}^t\xi = \begin{pmatrix} p_{1,^{t-1}z} \\ p_{2,^{t-1}z} \\ p_{3,^{t-1}z} \end{pmatrix}, \tag{4.88}$$

$$p = \begin{pmatrix} .95 & .25 & .10 \\ .05 & .74 & .20 \\ .00 & .01 & .70 \end{pmatrix}. \tag{4.89}$$

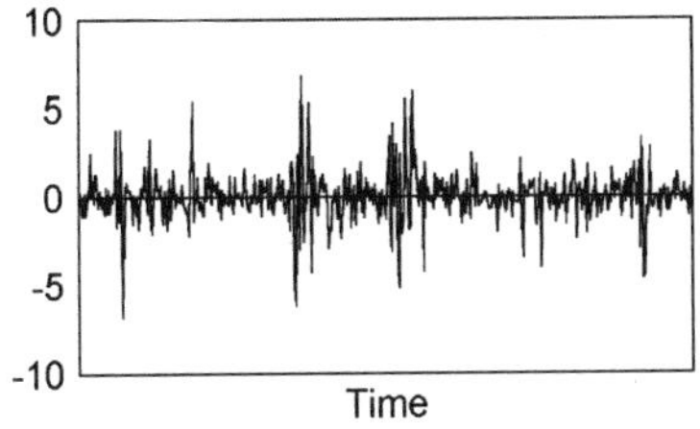

Exhibit 4.18 A realization of regime-switching process [4.86].

See Goldfeld and Quandt (1973) and Hamilton (1993) for estimation techniques.

Properties

Regime-switching models offer an alternative to GARCH processes for modeling conditional heteroskedasticity. In the multivariate case, covariance matrices directly specify any relationship between correlations and standard deviations. As dimensionality n increases, the number of parameters that must be specified for a completely general model becomes unmanageable. Research is ongoing.

4.9. FURTHER READING

DeGroot (1986) and Hogg and Craig (1995) offer nice introductory treatments of statistics. Franses (1998) is an accessible introduction to time series analysis. Harvey (1993) is more advanced. Hamilton (1994) is the definitive reference.

Chapter 5

Monte Carlo Method

5.1. MOTIVATION

Most financial professionals have some familiarity with the Monte Carlo method. Many learn of it as a tool financial engineers use for pricing derivatives. We have already given, in Chapter 1, an intuitive description of how it is employed with VaR measures. Such intuitive familiarity is an inadequate foundation if we are to implement practical VaR measures based on the Monte Carlo method.

Many VaR measures that employ the Monte Carlo method take hours to run, even with parallel processing. Run times are dramatically improved with variance reduction techniques, which we apply to VaR measures in Chapter 10. To understand how these work, we need a formal understanding of the Monte Carlo method.

The purpose of this chapter is to replace intuitive familiarity with formal understanding. We place the Monte Carlo method in its (nonfinancial) historical context. We then consider two applications of the Monte Carlo method. Both applications can be expressed as definite integrals, which leads us to consider the Monte Carlo method as an alternative technique of numerical integration. This perception sets the stage for variance reduction techniques, which we introduce at the end of the chapter.

A secondary purpose of the chapter is to describe standard techniques for generating pseudorandom numbers. Many generators that come packaged with software are unsuitable for the high-dimensional analyses that some VaR measures entail. We clarify this problem and offer guidance in selecting appropriate generators.

5.2. THE MONTE CARLO METHOD

In Section 2.15, we considered quadrature rules for numerical integration. These suffer from the curse of dimensionality, so they are useless for evaluating high-dimensional integrals. The Monte Carlo method is a technique of numerical integration that overcomes this curse. It is as applicable to a 500-dimensional integral as it is to a one-dimensional integral.

STANISLAW ULAM

Credit for inventing the Monte Carlo method often goes to Stanislaw Ulam, a Polish-born mathematician who worked for John von Neumann on the United States' Manhattan Project during World War II. Ulam is primarily known for designing the hydrogen bomb with Edward Teller in 1951.[1] He conceived of the Monte Carlo method in 1946 while pondering the probability of winning a game of solitaire.[2] After attempting to solve this problem with pure combinatorial calculations, he wondered if it might be simpler to play multiple hands of solitaire and observe the frequency of wins. This lead Ulam to consider how problems of neutron diffusion and other questions of mathematical physics might be represented in a form interpretable as a succession of random operations.

The Monte Carlo method, as it is understood today, encompasses any technique of statistical sampling employed to approximate solutions to quantitative problems. Ulam did not invent statistical sampling. This had been employed to solve quantitative problems before,[3] with physical processes such as dice tosses or card draws being used to generate realizations of samples. Ulam's contribution was to recognize the potential for the newly invented electronic computer to automate such sampling. Working with John von Neumann and Nicholas Metropolis, he developed algorithms for computer implementations as well as exploring means of transforming nonrandom problems into random forms that would facilitate their solution via statistical sampling.[4,5] This work transformed statistical sampling from a mathematical curiosity to a formal methodology applicable to a wide

[1]Ulam and Teller were fierce rivals during their tenure at Los Alamos. Rota (1987) indicates that Ulam's significant contribution to the design of the hydrogen bomb resulted coincidentally from his efforts to prove Teller's design infeasible.

[2]This incident is described in Eckhardt (1987).

[3]W. S. Gossett, who published under the pen name "Student," randomly sampled from height and middle-finger measurements of 3000 criminals to simulate two correlated normal random variables. He discusses this methodology in both Student (1908a) and Student (1908b).

[4]Laplace had previously described the potential for statistical sampling to approximate solutions to nonrandom problems, including the valuation of definite integrals. See Chapter V of his *Théorie Analytique des Probabilités* and a 1781 memoir, both available in his collected works published between 1878 and 1912.

[5]See Eckhardt (1987) and Metropolis (1987) for historical accounts of this early work.

variety of problems. It was Metropolis who named the new methodology after the casinos of Monte Carlo. Ulam and Metropolis published the first paper on the Monte Carlo method in 1949.[6]

EXAMPLE: APPROXIMATING π. More than 200 years before Metropolis coined the name "Monte Carlo method," George-Louis Leclerc (Comte de Buffon) communicated several problems to the Academy of Sciences in Paris, including the following.[7] If a needle of length l is dropped at random on the middle of a horizontal surface ruled with parallel lines a distance $d > l$ apart, what is the probability that the needle will cross one of the lines? Today, this is known as the problem of Buffon's needle. To solve it, consider Exhibit 5.1.

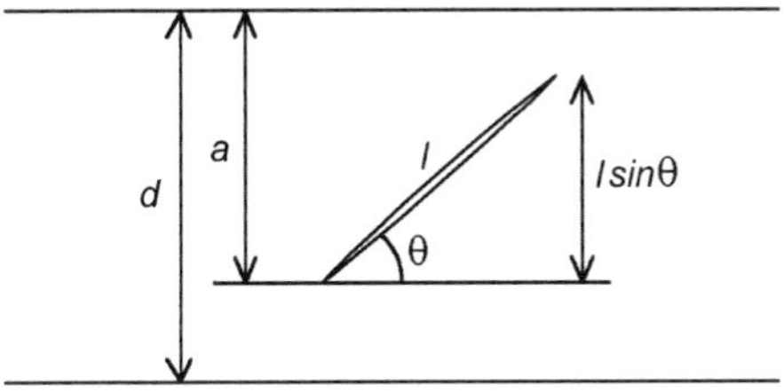

Exhibit 5.1 To derive the probability of a needle crossing a line, we describe the positioning of the needle relative to nearby lines with a random vector that has components $a \in [0,d)$ and $\theta \in [0,\pi)$.

The positioning of the needle relative to nearby lines is described by a random vector with components $a \in [0, d)$ and $\theta \in [0, \pi)$. The random vector (a,θ) is uniformly distributed on the region $[0, d) \times [0, \pi)$. Accordingly, it has PDF

$$\phi(a,\theta) = \begin{cases} \frac{1}{\pi d} & (a,\theta) \in [0,d) \times [0,\pi), \\ 0 & \text{otherwise,} \end{cases} \qquad [5.1]$$

Let X be a random variable for the number of lines crossed in a single drop of the needle. With $d > l$, a line will be crossed if and only if $a < l sin\theta$, so we have:

$$Pr(X = 1) = \int_0^{\pi} \int_0^{l sin\theta} \phi(a,\theta) da\, d\theta \qquad [5.2]$$

$$= \int_0^{\pi} \int_0^{l sin\theta} \frac{1}{\pi d} da\, d\theta \qquad [5.3]$$

$$= \frac{2l}{\pi d}. \qquad [5.4]$$

[6]Metropolis and Ulam (1949).

[7]Buffon communicated this problem to the Academy in 1733. See Todhunter (1865) for a historical account of Buffon's work.

In this solution, Pierre-Simon Laplace perceived[8] an amusing, if inefficient, means of approximating the number π. Suppose Buffon's experiment is performed with m tosses of the needle. During those tosses the needle is observed to cross a line C times. We have

$$E\left(\frac{C}{m}\right) = Pr(X = 1), \tag{5.5}$$

so the ratio C/m is an unbiased estimator for $Pr(X = 1)$. Substituting this in [5.4] yields an estimator for π:

$$\frac{m}{C}\left(\frac{2l}{d}\right). \tag{5.6}$$

In 1864, Captain O. C. Fox performed this experiment three times to occupy himself while recovering from wounds.[9] His results are shown in Exhibit 5.2.

m	c	l (inches)	d (inches)	Surface	π Approximation
500	236	3	4	stationary	3.1780
530	253	3	4	rotated	3.1423
590	939	5	2	rotated	3.1416

Exhibit 5.2 Results of Fox's needle-dropping experiments.

Fox's results illustrate two important issues for the Monte Carlo method.

1. After obtaining a poor approximation for π in his first experiment, Fox modified his subsequent experiments by applying a slight rotary motion to the ruled surface between drops. He did this to eliminate any bias arising from his position while dropping the needle. His approximations in subsequent experiments were markedly improved. This same need to eliminate bias exists today with computer implementations of the Monte Carlo method, although biases now arise from inappropriate pseudorandom number generators instead of posture.
2. In his third experiment, Fox used a 5-inch needle and spaced the lines on the surface just 2 inches apart. Now, the needle could cross as many as three lines in a single toss. In 590 tosses, Fox obtained 939 line crossings. Doing so entailed little more effort than his first two experiments, but it yielded a better approximation for π.[10] Fox's innovation was a precursor of today's variance reduction techniques.

[8] See Chapter V of his *Théorie Analytique des Probabilités*, available in his collected works published between 1878 and 1912.

[9] Fox's experiment is reported by Hall (1873).

[10] The approximation may be too good. Gridgeman (1960) documents a number of historical implementations of the needle dropping experiment. He includes a statistical analysis of the plausibility of Fox's reported results.

EXAMPLE: APPROXIMATING A STANDARD DEVIATION. Suppose $X \sim N(0, 1)$, and consider the function

$$f(x) = \frac{4x}{x^2 + 1}, \qquad [5.7]$$

which is graphed in Exhibit 5.3.

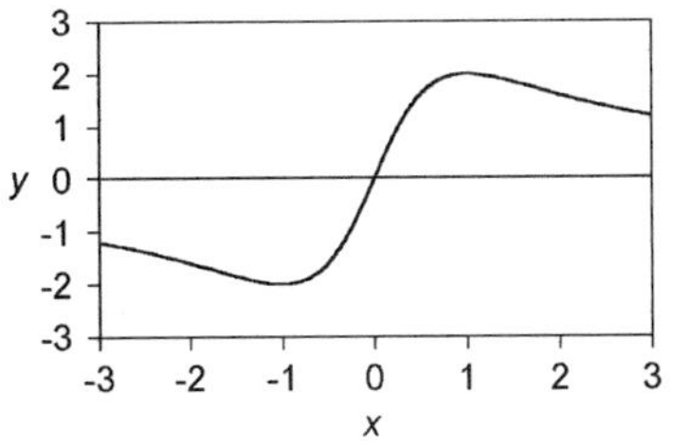

Exhibit 5.3 Graph of the function *f*.

We use this function to define a new random variable $Y = f(X)$. Although X is unbounded, we see in Exhibit 5.3 that Y is bounded, so the mean μ of Y must exist. We also see that f is symmetrical through the origin. Based upon this, and the symmetry of the standard normal distribution, we infer that the mean μ of Y is 0.

Suppose we need to determine the variance σ^2 of Y. Because Y is bounded, this also must exist. Analytically solving for σ^2 is a difficult problem, but we can easily approximate a solution with the Monte Carlo method. We define a sample $\{X^{[1]}, X^{[2]}, \ldots, X^{[100]}\}$ for X, and construct a realization $\{x^{[1]}, x^{[2]}, \ldots, x^{[100]}\}$ for this. We will discuss algorithms for doing so shortly. Our realization is indicated in Exhibit 5.4, and is plotted as a histogram in Exhibit 5.5.

0.23002	–0.46834	0.64139	–0.08692	–0.15508
0.82457	–2.09127	–2.43988	–0.86112	1.68951
–0.24670	0.27326	0.75721	0.80790	–1.29161
1.36672	1.78588	2.36952	–0.27323	–1.41296
0.86917	–0.06726	–0.62629	0.67229	0.83437
–1.34663	–0.61277	0.30748	0.14596	0.84569
2.96975	0.67757	–0.84644	1.50476	–0.06666
–0.52096	1.38464	–0.53059	–2.01150	–0.38679
1.66196	–0.32325	1.16994	–0.89059	0.46550
–0.51023	0.81236	–1.22809	–0.19939	–1.18054
2.21762	–0.50815	–1.52396	–1.99767	0.39806
–0.45419	1.10424	1.05993	–1.31552	–0.04703
–0.52572	0.23828	0.61519	0.24278	0.16820
0.82893	–0.31305	–1.43708	1.87178	1.73266
–0.05739	0.17749	0.24117	–1.49394	–0.73508
–0.38452	1.06686	0.04340	0.14024	–0.67774
–0.41968	1.85422	0.52743	–0.40165	0.58535
0.80286	1.78565	–1.99099	–0.06844	1.21061
–1.82357	–0.66618	0.12124	–0.63079	–1.46235
0.39613	0.59384	0.10556	–1.73320	2.01235

Exhibit 5.4 A realization of a sample $\{X^{[1]}, X^{[2]}, \ldots, X^{[100]}\}$ for X.

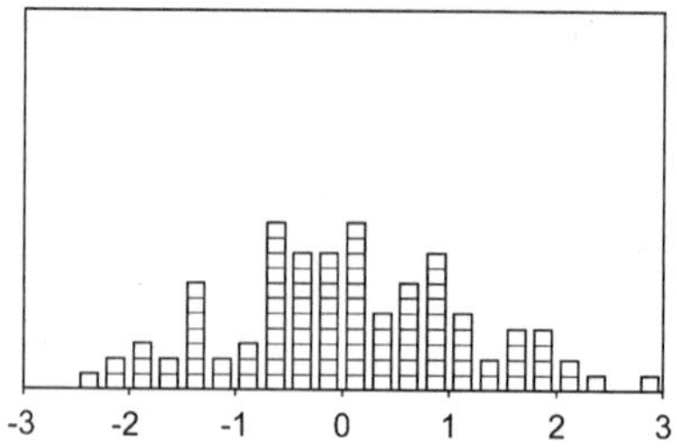

Exhibit 5.5 Histogram of the realization $\{x^{[1]}, x^{[2]}, \ldots, x^{[100]}\}$.

Based upon each value $x^{[k]}$, we calculate the corresponding value $y^{[k]} = f(x^{[k]})$. Results comprise a realization $\{y^{[1]}, y^{[2]}, \ldots, y^{[100]}\}$ of a sample $\{Y^{[1]}, Y^{[2]}, \ldots, Y^{[100]}\}$ for Y and are indicated in Exhibits 5.6 and 5.7.

0.87384	−1.53637	1.81776	−0.34509	−0.60574
1.96336	−1.55675	−1.40364	−1.97785	1.75331
−0.93020	1.01709	1.92507	1.95534	−1.93626
1.90622	1.70515	1.43290	−1.01701	−1.88618
1.98050	−0.26782	−1.79938	1.85207	1.96765
−1.91458	−1.78197	1.12369	0.57167	1.97224
1.20974	1.85750	−1.97252	1.84390	−0.26547
−1.63901	1.89857	−1.65613	−1.59449	−1.34581
1.76705	−1.17068	1.97562	−1.98665	1.53039
−1.61935	1.95758	−1.95852	−0.76707	−1.97276
1.49894	−1.61546	−1.83474	−1.60112	1.37446
−1.50608	1.99021	1.99662	−1.92708	−0.18770
−1.64754	0.90191	1.78515	0.91705	0.65427
1.96531	−1.14045	−1.87535	1.66249	1.73175
−0.22883	0.68828	0.91166	−1.84902	−1.90887
−1.33996	1.99582	0.17329	0.55013	−1.85768
−1.42733	1.67117	1.65056	−1.38343	1.74389
1.95274	1.70527	−1.60433	−0.27250	1.96402
−1.68638	−1.84563	0.47793	−1.80497	−1.86377
1.36962	1.75608	0.41758	−1.73148	1.59408

Exhibit 5.6 Values $y^{[k]} = \frac{4x^{[k]}}{x^{[k]2}+1}$.

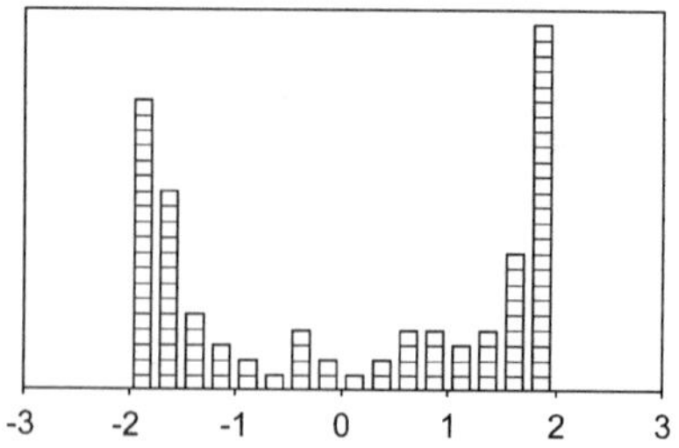

Exhibit 5.7 Histogram of values $y^{[k]}$.

We apply sample estimator [4.26] to the $y^{[k]}$ to obtain an approximate value for the variance σ^2 of Y:

$$\frac{1}{m}\sum_{k=1}^{m}\left(y^{[k]}-\mu\right)^2=\frac{1}{100}\sum_{k=1}^{100}y^{[k]^2}=2.47. \qquad [5.8]$$

5.3. REALIZATIONS OF SAMPLES

Computer implementations of the Monte Carlo method employ realizations of samples to solve problems. We introduced samples and their realizations in Chapter 4. There, we would obtain data from some experiment and model it as a realization $\{\boldsymbol{x}^{[1]}, \boldsymbol{x}^{[2]}, \ldots, \boldsymbol{x}^{[m]}\}$ of a sample $\{\boldsymbol{X}^{[1]}, \boldsymbol{X}^{[2]}, \ldots, \boldsymbol{X}^{[m]}\}$. This allowed us to make inferences about the unknown distribution of a random vector $\boldsymbol{X}$.

In a Monte Carlo application, we know the distribution of $\boldsymbol{X}$, but must somehow construct a realization $\{\boldsymbol{x}^{[1]}, \boldsymbol{x}^{[2]}, \ldots, \boldsymbol{x}^{[m]}\}$ for use in the analysis. Historically, realizations were constructed with some physical process such as tossing dice or drawing cards. Today, computer implementations of the Monte Carlo method employ algorithms that generate realizations.

To avoid biasing our results, we want a realization to be, in some sense, "random." This cannot be formalized. The notion of a random variable is well defined. The notion of a random number is not. We may consider a finite sequence of numbers to be random if it is obtained in such a manner that the numbers are uncertain to us prior to their being obtained. For Monte Carlo work, this intuitive conception is not useful. Uncertainty is immaterial to the success of a Monte Carlo analysis. What is important is that the realization be statistically consistent with the sample $\{\boldsymbol{X}^{[1]}, \boldsymbol{X}^{[2]}, \ldots, \boldsymbol{X}^{[m]}\}$. There are numerous—indeed, infinitely many—empirical tests for statistical consistency that we might perform. Examples include:

- the sample mean of $\{\boldsymbol{x}^{[1]}, \boldsymbol{x}^{[2]}, \ldots, \boldsymbol{x}^{[m]}\}$ should be close to the mean of $\boldsymbol{X}$;
- the sample covariance matrix of $\{\boldsymbol{x}^{[1]}, \boldsymbol{x}^{[2]}, \ldots, \boldsymbol{x}^{[m]}\}$ should be close to the covariance matrix of $\boldsymbol{X}$;
- to satisfy the IID condition, sample autocorrelations between lagged values of a given component, $x_i^{[j]}$ and $x_i^{[j-k]}$, should be approximately 0 for any integer k.

We might call a realization $\{\boldsymbol{x}^{[1]}, \boldsymbol{x}^{[2]}, \ldots, \boldsymbol{x}^{[m]}\}$ "random" if it passed every conceivable empirical test, but this definition is empty. There are infinitely many tests we might perform. For a continuously distributed random vector $\boldsymbol{X}$, no realization of a finite sample could pass them all![11] To avoid such theoretical and even

[11] In constructing a realization of a sample of size m, we have m degrees of freedom. These allow us to simultaneously satisfy m independent conditions. However, the existence of infinitely many possible tests means there are infinitely many conditions to satisfy. With a continuous distribution, infinitely many of the tests will be independent.

philosophical issues related to defining randomness, we define instead a notion called pseudorandomness. We say that a realization of a sample is **pseudorandom** if it passes certain empirical tests deemed important by the user. Actual tests will depend upon the nature of the intended Monte Carlo analysis as well as the user's ability or inclination to perform tests. The important test—whether a realization causes the Monte Carlo analysis to yield a reasonable value for the quantity being estimated—is likely to be infeasible to perform.

Our initial discussions of the Monte Carlo method will focus on numbers $u^{[k]}$ that are pseudorandom for a $U(0, 1)$ distribution. We call these **pseudorandom numbers**. We will also employ pseudorandom vectors $\boldsymbol{u}^{[k]}$ for distribution $U_n((0, 1)^n)$. These may be constructed by generating n pseudorandom numbers $u^{[i]}$ and setting the components $u_i^{[k]}$ of $\boldsymbol{u}^{[k]}$ equal to the respective pseudorandom numbers $u^{[i]}$:

$$\boldsymbol{u}^{[k]} = \begin{pmatrix} u_1^{[k]} \\ u_2^{[k]} \\ \vdots \\ u_n^{[k]} \end{pmatrix} = \begin{pmatrix} u^{[1]} \\ u^{[2]} \\ \vdots \\ u^{[n]} \end{pmatrix}. \qquad [5.9]$$

Later, we will discuss numbers that are pseudorandom, but for distributions other than $U(0, 1)$. We call these **pseudorandom variates**. We apply the term **pseudorandom vector** to any vector that is pseudorandom irrespective of distribution.

Exercises

5.1 Empirical tests for pseudorandomness are usually applied to large sequences of numbers—perhaps 100,000 numbers or more. For practice, let's apply some empirical tests to the short sequence of numbers in Exhibit 5.8.

k	$u^{[k]}$	k	$u^{[k]}$	k	$u^{[k]}$	k	$u^{[k]}$
1	0.778	11	0.899	21	0.098	31	0.740
2	0.688	12	0.159	22	0.042	32	0.727
3	0.831	13	0.570	23	0.171	33	0.162
4	0.680	14	0.278	24	0.130	34	0.628
5	0.780	15	0.551	25	0.369	35	0.797
6	0.449	16	0.595	26	0.195	36	0.525
7	0.725	17	0.024	27	0.656	37	0.754
8	0.175	18	0.640	28	0.534	38	0.882
9	0.629	19	0.036	29	0.965	39	0.850
10	0.006	20	0.457	30	0.340	40	0.320

Exhibit 5.8 An ordered set of numbers.

a. Propose five empirical tests for pseudorandom numbers.
b. Apply your tests to the ordered set of Exhibit 5.8.
c. What conclusions do you draw?

5.4. PSEUDORANDOM NUMBERS

Pseudorandom numbers may come from various sources. On computers, they are usually specified by deterministic algorithms called **pseudorandom number generators**. A pseudorandom number generator works by accepting one or more **seed values**. These may be specified by the user or drawn from an internal clock or other routine running on the computer. The pseudorandom number generator then calculates numbers recursively based on these.

Researchers devote considerable effort to designing generators whose output passes empirical tests for pseudorandomness. This saves users the trouble of performing empirical tests every time they use pseudorandom numbers from these generators. Of course, there is no perfect pseudorandom number generator. No matter how sophisticated a generator may be, it is possible to design an empirical test that its output will fail. It is useful to keep this in mind when selecting a generator for any application. A poor choice of generator can introduce a bias in Monte Carlo results. Such bias is a separate error from the standard error associated with statistical estimation. Using larger sample sizes cannot eliminate it. The problem is with the generator, or more specifically, an incompatibility between the generator and the application. Gärtner (1999) describes an actual Monte Carlo analysis that was performed using a well-known linear congruential generator.[12] The results were a little too interesting. Subsequent analysis revealed the pseudorandom numbers to be correlated with the application.

LINEAR CONGRUENTIAL GENERATORS

Today, the most widely used pseudorandom number generators are **linear congruential generators** (LCGs). Introduced by Lehmer (1951), these are specified with nonnegative integers η, a, and c.[13] An integer seed value $z^{[0]}$ is selected, $0 \leq z^{[0]} < \eta$, and a sequence of integers $z^{[k]}$ is obtained recursively with the formula

$$z^{[k]} = az^{[k-1]} + c \ (\mathrm{mod}\ \eta). \qquad [5.10]$$

[12]The particular generator used in this analysis was the so-called DRAND48 linear congruential generator, which has parameters $\eta = 2^{48}$, $a = 25{,}214{,}903{,}917$ and $c = 0$. We discuss linear congruential generators below.

[13]Lehmer (1951) considers the case $c = 0$. Obviously, if $c = 0$ and $z^{[k-1]} = 0$, then all subsequent values $z^{[k]}, z^{[k+1]}, z^{[k+2]}, \ldots$ will equal 0. This will never happen as long as 0 is not used as a seed and η is not divisible by a.

The modular notation "mod" indicates that $z^{[k]}$ is the remainder after dividing the quantity $az^{[k-1]} + c$ by η. A sequence of pseudorandom numbers $u^{[k]}$ is obtained by dividing the $z^{[k]}$ by η:

$$u^{[k]} = z^{[k]}/\eta. \qquad [5.11]$$

Consider the simplistic generator

$$z^{[k]} = 3z^{[k-1]} + 1 \text{ (mod 7)}. \qquad [5.12]$$

Starting with a seed $z^{[0]} = 4$, we calculate a sequence of pseudorandom numbers in Exhibit 5.9.

k	$az^{[k-1]} + c$	$z^{[k]}$	$u^{[k]}$
0		4	0.57142857
1	13	6	0.85714286
2	19	5	0.71428571
3	16	2	0.28571429
4	7	0	0.00000000
5	1	1	0.14285714
6	4	4	0.57142857
7	13	6	0.85714286
8	19	5	0.71428571
9	16	2	0.28571429
⋮	⋮	⋮	⋮

Exhibit 5.9 Numbers generated by LCG [5.12], starting with a seed value of 4.

These illustrate three important properties of LCGs:

- They are periodic. Because the integers $z^{[k]}$ are nonnegative and bounded by η, the sequence of pseudorandom numbers must repeat in a continual loop of period $\leq \eta$.
- Their pseudorandom numbers always fall on a lattice. In our example, the lattice has a spacing between numbers that is a multiple of $1/7$. More generally, Marsaglia (1968) demonstrates that n-tuples of consecutive numbers from LCGs always fall on sets of parallel planes in n-dimensional space.
- They may generate 0 as a pseudorandom number. Our definition of pseudorandom numbers requires that the numbers be in the open interval (0, 1).

Periodicity is a property of all pseudorandom number generators. It is addressed by using a generator whose period exceeds the number of pseudorandom numbers required for an application. An LCG's period can be as high as η, but many have lower periods. We call a pseudorandom number generator whose period is the maximum possible for its form a **full-period generator**.

A lattice structure may or may not be a problem, depending upon how closely the planes are spaced and the nature of the intended Monte Carlo application. Exhibit 5.10 illustrates two-dimensional lattice structures for two LCGs:

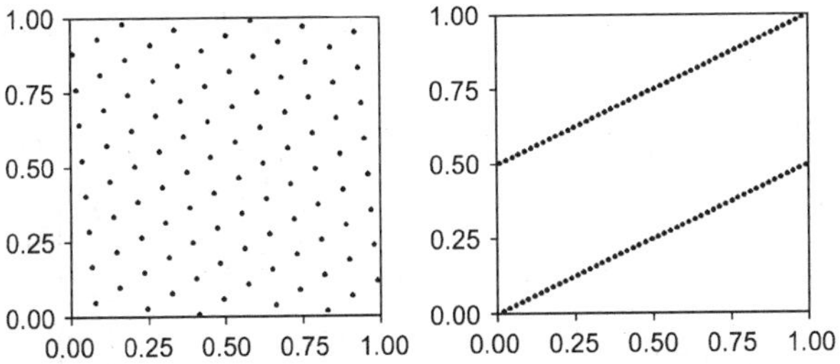

Exhibit 5.10 Sets of all points $(x^{[k]}, x^{[k+1]})$ generated by the LCGs: $z^{[k]} = 89z^{[k-1]}$ (mod 101) and $z^{[k]} = 51z^{[k-1]}$ (mod 101).

Because they have low periods, neither of these generators would be used in practice, but they illustrate how lattice structures can vary from very good to very bad.

An LCG has a different lattice structure for each dimension. It may have excellent lattice structures in certain dimensions but poor lattice structures in others. A classic example is the so-called RANDU[14] generator:

$$z^{[k]} = 65{,}539z^{[k-1]} \bmod 2^{31}. \qquad [5.13]$$

This was widely adopted during the 1960s because computer implementations of the generator ran quickly. Division by 2^{31} was easy on binary computers just as division by 100 is easy with decimal numbers. A simple trick made it easy to multiply by 65,539. Unfortunately, RANDU was a mistake. We know today that its two-dimensional lattice is good, but not its three-dimensional lattice. All 3-tuples generated by RANDU fall on just 15 parallel planes. This discovery cast doubt on Monte Carlo results obtained during the 1960s and 1970s with this generator.

Another issue with LCGs is the fact that correlations between pseudorandom numbers separated by large lags may be strong.

A number of LCGs have been adopted as default generators in various operating systems and software packages. An example is the LCG

$$z^{[k]} = 16{,}807z^{[k-1]} \bmod (2^{31} - 1). \qquad [5.14]$$

This was first proposed by Lewis, Goodman, and Miller (1969) for the IBM System/360. Based upon its performance on empirical tests as well as its ease of implementation, Park and Miller (1988) proposed it as a minimal standard against which other generators might be compared. This LCG was incorporated into operating systems for personal computers and Macintosh computers, as well as the IMSL subroutine library, MATLAB, and a number of simulation packages.

[14]This is the name given to the generator in IBM's System/360 Scientific Subroutine Package, Version III, Programmer's Manual, 1968.

Exhibit 5.11 illustrates a sample of 2-tuples from the generator as well as its two-dimensional lattice structure:

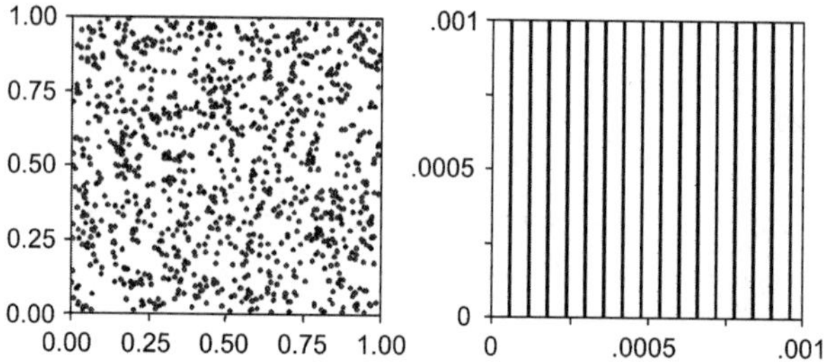

Exhibit 5.11 The left chart illustrates 1000 points ($x^{[2k]}$, $x^{[2k+1]}$) formed from 2000 consecutive numbers generated with [5.14] using seed 1234. The right chart shows the lattice structure of all points ($x^{[k]}$, $x^{[k+1]}$), within the indicated region, for the same generator. The lines appear vertical, but are actually tilted slightly to the right. Note the change of scale in the right chart.

Multiple-Recursive Generators

In practical Monte Carlo work, we use only a small subsequence of the numbers generated by a pseudorandom number generator. It might seem sufficient for the generator's period to exceed the number of pseudorandom numbers used by only a few orders of magnitude, but this is not the case. In Section 5.5, we will see that it is desirable to employ pseudorandom number generators with extremely high periods, even for applications that use only a few pseudorandom numbers.

In theory, through judicious selection of the parameters η, a, and c, an LCG can be made to have a period of any order of magnitude. In practice, we choose parameters so that

$$a(\eta - 1) + c < 2^{53}. \quad [5.15]$$

This ensures that all calculations performed by the LCG can, with suitable coding,[15] be performed in floating-point form without rounding on 32-bit computers. This restriction limits the maximal period η that can be achieved with LCGs. Higher period LCGs may be implemented with multiple-precision arithmetic, but this is computationally inefficient. An alternative is to explore generalizations of LCGs that have high periods but can still be implemented with single-precision floating-point arithmetic. The most popular of these are **multiple-recursive generators** (MRGs) defined by

$$z^{[k]} = a_1 z^{[k-1]} + a_2 z^{[k-2]} + \cdots + a_m z^{[k-m]} \pmod{\eta}, \quad [5.16]$$

$$u^{[k]} = z^{[k]}/\eta. \quad [5.17]$$

[15] See, for example, Park and Miller (1988).

for some positive integer k, positive integers $a_1, a_2, \ldots, a_m$, and seed values $z^{[0]}$, $z^{[1]}, \ldots, z^{[k-1]}$. Through judicious selection of parameters, an MRG can have a period as high as $\eta^k - 1$. As a generalization of LCGs, MRGs share many of the same properties. They have similar lattice structures, and certain MRGs exhibit strong correlations between pseudorandom numbers separated by large lags.

L'Ecuyer, Blouin, and Couture (1993) performed an extensive search for good MRGs. One that they found is

$$z^{[k]} = 1{,}071{,}064 z^{[k-1]} + 2{,}113{,}664 z^{[k-7]} \bmod (2^{31} - 19). \qquad [5.18]$$

This can be efficiently implemented on a 32-bit computer. It has period $\eta^7 - 1 \approx 2^{217}$ and exhibits generally good lattice properties for dimensions up to 20.

Inversive Generators

We call LCGs and MRGs linear generators because they are defined by the linear modular polynomials [5.10] and [5.16]. As we have seen, such generators may suffer from poor lattice structures or strong correlations between pseudorandom numbers separated by large lags. Such problems can be avoided with **nonlinear generators**, an interesting category of which uses **modular inversion** to generate pseudorandom numbers.

We say that an integer $\bar{b}$, $0 \leq \bar{b} < \eta$, is the **inverse** of an integer b mod η if $b\bar{b} = 1 \bmod \eta$ for $b \neq 0$ and $\bar{b} = 0$ for $b = 0$. If η is prime, the modular inverse $\bar{b}$ is uniquely defined for any integer b. Modular inverses can be calculated using Fermat's little theorem. This states that, if η is prime, and $0 < b < \eta$,[16] then

$$b^{\eta-1} = 1 \pmod{\eta}. \qquad [5.19]$$

From this, it follows that the modular inverse $\bar{b}$ of b is given by

$$\bar{b} = b^{\eta-2} \pmod{\eta}. \qquad [5.20]$$

The integer $b^{\eta-2}$ can be calculated by multiplying b by itself $\eta - 2$ times, but for large η, it is worth simplifying this calculation. With the **square and multiply** method, we calculate $b^{\eta-2}$ by calculating each quantity $b, b^2, b^4, b^8, \ldots, b^{2^\alpha}$, where 2^α is the largest power of 2 for which $2^\alpha \leq \eta - 1$. With repeated squaring, all terms are obtained with just α multiplications. Then $b^{\eta-2}$ is obtained by multiplying certain of the terms together. For example, b^{45} can be obtained as the product of b, b^4, b^8, and b^{32}.

[16] More generally, all that is required is that b not be divisible by η.

A form of inversive pseudorandom number generator, first proposed by Eichenauer and Lehn (1986), is the **inversive congruential generator** (ICG):

$$z^{[k]} = a\overline{z^{[k-1]}} + c \pmod{\eta}, \tag{5.21}$$

$$u^{[k]} = z^{[k]}/\eta. \tag{5.22}$$

ICGs have been investigated for η a power of 2 or η a prime. The latter case performs best. In particular, ICGs with prime η yield pseudorandom numbers that have no lattice structures. Also, for prime η, ICGs can have periods as large as η. A simple ICG with period η is

$$z^{[k]} = \overline{z^{[k-1]}} + 1 \bmod (2^{31} - 1). \tag{5.23}$$

A different form of inversive generator is the **explicit inversive congruential generator** (EICG) proposed by Eichenauer-Herrmann (1993) as

$$z^{[k]} = \overline{a(k + k_0) + c} \pmod{\eta}, \tag{5.24}$$

$$u^{[k]} = z^{[k]}/\eta \tag{5.25}$$

where η is prime, a is an integer, $0 < a < \eta$, and k_0 is a seed value. EICGs exhibit no lattice structures and always have period η. Also, jumping ahead to a specific point in a sequence of EICG numbers is as easy as advancing to another seed value. An example of an EICG is

$$z^{[k]} = \overline{(k + k_0)} \bmod (2^{48} - 59). \tag{5.26}$$

Inversive generators, both ICGs and EICGs, are attractive because most forms exhibit no lattice structures. They do exhibit certain nonlinear patterns, but these are less likely to bias an application. Also, full-period inversive generators tend to be insensitive to choice of parameters. By comparison, with linear generators, it is necessary to carefully choose parameters to ensure good statistical properties.

A drawback of inversive generators is computational inefficiency. Because they must perform modular inversion, they tend to run more slowly than linear generators. Also, inversive generators with long periods must be implemented with multiple precision. Just as we introduced MRGs to address this problem for LCGs, there are similar avenues to address the problem with inversive generators. These are less developed than such methods for linear generators.

For the foregoing reasons, practitioners tend to reserve inversive generators for validating analyses performed with more traditional linear generators. Every generator has empirical tests it will fail. For this reason, it is a good idea to occasionally verify Monte Carlo results obtained using one generator by performing the same analysis with a second generator that has very different properties. The nonlinear properties of inversive generators make them excellent tools for verifying results obtained with linear generators.

5.5. TESTING PSEUDORANDOM NUMBER GENERATORS

There are various tests that may be applied to pseudorandom number generators. Although some tests are not easily categorized, it is convenient to describe tests as being either:

- empirical, or
- theoretical.

We have already discussed **empirical tests** in Section 5.3. These are statistical tests that are applied to subsequences of the numbers produced by a generator. For a given subsequence, a particular sample statistic is calculated, and the result is assessed for consistency with a $U(0, 1)$ sample. In Section 5.3, we mentioned empirical tests for sample mean, sample covariance matrix, and sample autocorrelations. More sophisticated empirical tests assess independence, equidistribution, or recurring patterns either in the numbers or in n-tuples of the numbers. Empirical tests often have beguiling names such as the **poker test**, **birthday test**, or **coupon collector's test**.

Theoretical tests consider the formula that defines a generator, often employing advanced mathematical techniques to infer its properties. In this sense, theoretical tests characterize the entire sequence of numbers produced by a generator. Theoretical tests assess such things as period, lattice structures, uniformity, or correlations—often the same notions assessed by empirical tests, but for a generator's entire period. Theoretical tests are limited since the full-period performance of a generator may be different from the behavior of a subsequence of numbers from that generator used in a particular application. For example, the lattice structure of an LCG is a property of that generator's entire period. It exhibits a uniformity that is not apparent in reasonably sized subsequences from the same LCG. Despite such limitations, certain theoretical tests have proven to be consistent predictors of a generator's performance on empirical tests. We call these tests **figures of merit**. Two important figures of merit are the spectral test and discrepancy.

The Spectral Test

For pseudorandom number generators with lattice structures, an important theoretical test is the **spectral test** of Coveyou and MacPherson (1967). This can be interpreted in different ways. The most intuitive interpretation is that it measures, in a given dimension, the spacing between the parallel planes of the lattice. For LCGs, MRGs, and other generators with lattice structures, the spectral test is the quintessential figure of merit. Speaking of such generators, Knuth (1997) notes:

> Not only do all good generators pass this test, all generators now known to be bad actually *fail* it. Thus it is by far the most powerful test known, and it deserves particular attention.

It is not sufficient to perform the spectral test in just a few dimensions. As we saw with the infamous RANDU generator, it is possible for a generator to have good lattice structures in certain dimensions, but very poor lattice structures in others. In particular, if vectors are to be formed from consecutive n-tuples of pseudorandom numbers, it is desirable to apply the spectral test to the generator in n dimensions to confirm that the vectors will not fall on just a few widely spaced planes in that dimensionality.

A drawback of the spectral test is its computational complexity. The number of calculations needed to perform the spectral test increases exponentially[17] with the dimension being considered. For this reason, it is impossible to directly assess high-dimensional lattice structures.

Discrepancy

A standard empirical test is the **equidistribution test**, or its generalization to multiple dimensions, which we call the **serial test**. In one dimension, we divide the unit interval [0, 1] into a equal subintervals. We then test the uniformity of a finite sequence of m numbers by determining how many of them fall into each subinterval. A perfectly equidistributed set of numbers might have an equal number of values occurring in each bucket, but we would not expect such perfect equidistribution from a $U[0, 1)$ sample. We would not consider 1000 numbers to be particularly random if we divided the unit interval into 200 equal buckets and found that exactly 5 of the numbers fell into each of the 200 buckets. Instead, we would expect some random variability in the number of occurrences in each bucket. The equidistribution test looks for such variability and assesses whether it is consistent with that of a $U[0, 1)$ sample.

A limitation of the equidistribution test is the fact that results depend upon the particular number a of subintervals employed. It is convenient to have a measure of equidistribution that does not depend upon this number of subintervals. **Discrepancy** is such a measure. Because its definition is technical, we shall not present it. Interested readers may consult Niederreiter (1992).

A drawback of discrepancy is its computational complexity. The number of calculations required to calculate discrepancy for m n-dimensional points increases with either m or n in proportion with m^n. For this reason, it is impractical to apply discrepancy as an empirical test. Instead, researchers employ it as a theoretical

---

[17] Knuth (1997, p. 103) indicates that the number of calculations for dimension n is on the order of 3^n. Fincke and Pohst (1985) provide a more detailed complexity analysis.

test, using mathematical arguments to determine upper and lower bounds for the discrepancies of generators.

Period

Period is not usually considered a figure of merit because its predictive ability is limited. Certainly, there are generators with high periods that fail empirical tests miserably. However, it is reasonable to discuss period along with standard figures of merit because, among generators that do exhibit good behavior on empirical tests, performance does correlate with period. This is especially true of linear generators such as LCGs and MRGs. The best LCGs with periods of around 2^{32} have noticeably inferior properties compared to the best LCGs with periods of around 2^{48}. These, in turn, are noticeably inferior to the best LCGs with periods of around 2^{64}. Accordingly, the best linear generators tend to have very high periods.

Another reason to consider period is the need to employ a generator whose period exceeds the number of pseudorandom numbers required by an intended application. Every application is unique, but a rule of thumb is that a generator should have a period well in excess of the square of the number of pseudorandom numbers required for the application. Today, many operating systems and software packages employ default generators that are LCGs with periods less than 2^{32}. Accordingly, such default generators are inappropriate for use in applications that require more than, say, $2^{15} = 32{,}768$ pseudorandom numbers. Many VaR applications require more pseudorandom numbers than this.

For inversive generators, extremely long periods are not as necessary. Empirical work indicates it is sufficient for an inversive generator's period to exceed the number of pseudorandom numbers required by a few orders of magnitude.

5.6. IMPLEMENTING PSEUDORANDOM NUMBER GENERATORS

There are a number of practical considerations for implementing pseudorandom number generators.

The Number 0

Some pseudorandom number generators can include the number 0 in a sequence of pseudorandom numbers. This happened in our simplistic example of an LCG in Exhibit 5.9, and it will happen with many standard generators if precautions are not taken. The occurrence of a 0 pseudorandom number is a problem for some applications, including any that entail division by pseudorandom numbers.

A solution is to convert any pseudorandom number that equals 0 to a very small number such as .00000001. A similar but more sophisticated solution applicable with LCGs is to set all pseudorandom numbers $u^{[k]}$ equal to $z^{[k]}/(\eta + 1)$ instead of $z^{[k]}/\eta$, while setting $u^{[k]} = \eta/(\eta + 1)$ whenever $z^{[k]}$ equals 0. Analogous approaches can be applied with other generators. Another solution is to judiciously select seed values. If an application calls for m pseudorandom numbers, it is easy to check seed values in advance to ensure that the first m pseudorandom numbers generated from those seeds do not include 0. Suitable seed values can be stored for future use. Note that many large-period generators realize 0 multiple times during a single period. Therefore, this solution will only work if the maximum spacing between consecutive 0 values exceeds m. Another solution is to let pseudorandom numbers equal 0, but to incorporate exception-handling code into applications. Finally, we might only use generators that do not include 0 in their full period of numbers.

It is also possible for a generator to produce a pseudorandom number of 1. Such generators are less common and a pseudorandom number of 1 is less likely to crash an application than is 0. However, this problem will arise, and similar solutions to those proposed for 0 apply.

Integer Calculations

All the pseudorandom number generators we have considered work with integers $z^{[k]}$ and convert these through division to pseudorandom numbers $u^{[k]}$ only as a last step. The primary reason for this is portability. If intermediate calculations employed noninteger numbers, calculations would involve rounding. Because different computers may round numbers differently, output from a pseudorandom number generator would vary depending upon which computer it was run on. Such uncertain output would make empirical testing of generators machine-dependent. It would render theoretical testing pointless.

Integer calculations solve the problem of rounding, but they pose the equivalent problem of integer overflow. To work properly, a generator's integer calculations must be exact, without any overflow of numbers. Such overflow might degrade the randomness and/or period of a generator. As we have already indicated, there are various solutions for this problem, including:

- employing specialized coding techniques;
- using generators such as MRGs that employ small integers in all their calculations; and
- implementing generators using multiple precision.

Optimized algorithms or actual code have been published for many standard random number generators. Whenever possible it is a good idea to base implementations on these.

Implementation Verification

Every implementation of a pseudorandom number generator should be verified. This usually takes place when the implementation is first coded, but it should also happen whenever the code is ported to a new computer system. Systems vary with regard to the maximum single-precision integer they can represent without overflow, so an implementation that works on one system may fail on another.

Choosing a Generator

The worst way to choose a pseudorandom number generator is by default—simply using one that is packaged with software. Many standard generators, including the widely used LCG [5.14], have periods that are inadequate for some VaR calculations. Don't attempt to design your own generator or to improve upon some standard generator, as results will be unpredictable. The literature documents high-quality generators that have been exhaustively tested and are recommended by experts. Use them.

Despite their limitations, it is best to use linear generators such as LCGs and MRGs. These have been studied for a long time and are well understood. Inversive generators have much appeal, but are still fairly new. Reserve them for verification purposes.

Because of their high periods, MRGs are appealing. MRG [5.18] should work well for many VaR applications. As mentioned previously, its lattice pattern is known to be good for dimensions up to 20. Heuristically, we may expect it to perform well at even higher dimensions. Some VaR applications have dimensions in excess of 100. While no linear generator's lattice pattern has ever been tested for such high dimensions, a generalized MRG recommended by L'Ecuyer (1999) should perform well.

5.7. BREAKING THE CURSE OF DIMENSIONALITY

The Monte Carlo method is an application of statistical inference. As such, it entails the familiar standard error associated with all statistical inferences. So far, we have discussed the Monte Carlo method in a largely intuitive manner. If we are to assess its standard error or discuss techniques of reducing this error, we need to formalize the Monte Carlo method. We do so in this section.

In Section 5.2, we considered two examples of the Monte Carlo method. Estimating π is a deterministic problem. Estimating the variance of a random variable Y is probabilistic. Although statistical in nature, the Monte Carlo method was just as applicable to the deterministic problem as it was to the probabilistic one. Let's take another look at those two examples. Observe that both may be represented as definite integrals. Fox's needle dropping was an elaborate means of estimating the integral

$$\int_0^{\pi}\int_0^{l\sin\theta}\frac{1}{\pi d}da\,d\theta. \qquad [5.27]$$

Our estimation of the variance σ^2 of the random variable Y was actually an estimate of the definite integral

$$\int_{-\infty}^{\infty}(y-\mu)^2\phi_Y(y)dy = \int_{-\infty}^{\infty}(f(x)-0)^2\,\phi_X(x)dx = \int_{-\infty}^{\infty}\left(\frac{4x}{x^2+1}\right)^2\frac{e^{-x^2/2}}{\sqrt{2\pi}}dx. \qquad [5.28]$$

Crude Monte Carlo Estimator

All Monte Carlo analyses entail selecting a realization $\{\boldsymbol{x}^{[1]},\boldsymbol{x}^{[2]},\ldots,\boldsymbol{x}^{[m]}\}$ of some sample $\{\boldsymbol{X}^{[1]},\boldsymbol{X}^{[2]},\ldots,\boldsymbol{X}^{[m]}\}$ and applying some function to estimate some quantity ψ. Accordingly, a Monte Carlo analysis represents a statistical estimator:

$$H(\boldsymbol{X}^{[1]},\boldsymbol{X}^{[2]},\ldots,\boldsymbol{X}^{[m]}), \qquad [5.29]$$

which we call a **Monte Carlo estimator**. Hammersley and Handscomb (1964)[18] provide an interesting proof that, at least in a trivial sense, all Monte Carlo computations can be viewed as approximations to definite integrals. This result is too general for practical work, but it motivates us to explore the Monte Carlo method from the standpoint of numerical integration. Suppose we need to evaluate a multidimensional definite integral of the form

$$\psi = \int_{(0,1)^n} f(\boldsymbol{u})d\boldsymbol{u}, \qquad [5.30]$$

where f is bounded on the region of integration. In practical applications, integrals can usually be converted to this form through a suitable change of variables.

This is a nonrandom problem, but the Monte Carlo method approximates a solution by introducing a random vector $\boldsymbol{U}$ that is $U_n((0,1)^n)$. Applying the function f to $\boldsymbol{U}$, we obtain a random variable $f(\boldsymbol{U})$. By [3.16] its expectation is

$$E[f(\boldsymbol{U})] = \int_{\mathbb{R}^n} f(\boldsymbol{u})\phi(\boldsymbol{u})d\boldsymbol{u} = \int_{(0,1)^n} f(\boldsymbol{u})d\boldsymbol{u}. \qquad [5.31]$$

[18]See Hammersley and Handscomb (1964), p. 50.

Comparing this expression for $E[f(\boldsymbol{U})]$ with our original integral [5.30], we obtain a probabilistic expression for that non-probabilistic integral,

$$\psi = E[f(\boldsymbol{U})], \tag{5.32}$$

so random variable $f(\boldsymbol{U})$ has mean ψ and some standard deviation σ. We define

$$H = f\left(\boldsymbol{U}^{[1]}\right) \tag{5.33}$$

as an unbiased estimator for ψ with standard error σ. This is a little unconventional, since [5.33] is an estimator that depends upon a sample $\{\boldsymbol{U}^{[1]}\}$ of size 1, but it is a valid estimator nonetheless.

To estimate ψ with a standard error lower than σ, let's generalize our estimator to accommodate a larger sample $\{\boldsymbol{U}^{[1]}, \boldsymbol{U}^{[2]}, \ldots, \boldsymbol{U}^{[m]}\}$. Applying the function f to each of these yields m IID random variables, $f(\boldsymbol{U}^{[1]}), f(\boldsymbol{U}^{[2]}), \ldots, f(\boldsymbol{U}^{[m]})$, each with expectation ψ and standard deviation σ. By [3.27] and [3.28], the generalization

$$H = \frac{1}{m}\sum_{k=1}^{m} f\left(\boldsymbol{U}^{[k]}\right) \tag{5.34}$$

of [5.33] is an unbiased estimator for ψ with standard error

$$\frac{\sigma}{\sqrt{m}}. \tag{5.35}$$

If we have a realization $\{\boldsymbol{u}^{[1]}, \boldsymbol{u}^{[2]}, \ldots, \boldsymbol{u}^{[m]}\}$ for our sample, we may estimate ψ as

$$h = \frac{1}{m}\sum_{k=1}^{m} f\left(\boldsymbol{u}^{[k]}\right). \tag{5.36}$$

We call [5.34] the **crude Monte Carlo estimator** for ψ.

Implications of Standard Error

It is important to distinguish between the **error**

$$H - \psi \tag{5.37}$$

and standard error

$$std(H) = \frac{\sigma}{\sqrt{m}} \tag{5.38}$$

of the crude Monte Carlo estimator H. The former is a random variable. The latter is a parameter of that random variable. Since

$$std(H) = std(H - \psi), \tag{5.39}$$

standard error is the standard deviation of error.

Formula [5.38] for standard error is important because neither its numerator σ nor its denominator $\sqrt{m}$ depends upon the dimensionality n of the integral ψ. The crude Monte Carlo estimator is a technique of numerical integration that is not subject to the curse of dimensionality.

The formula for standard error places no bounds on error. It only describes error probabilistically with a standard deviation. For a large sample size m, the central limit theorem applies, so error will be approximately normally distributed with mean 0 and standard deviation equal to the standard error. Error will exceed standard error approximately 32% of the time. It will exceed twice the standard error approximately 4.5% of the time.

Exercises

5.2 A crude Monte Carlo estimator of some quantity ψ has a standard error of 7.5 when a sample size $m = 1000$ is used. What sample size should be used to achieve a standard error of 2?

5.3 Consider the definite integral

$$\int_{-1}^{1} e^x dx. \qquad [5.40]$$

a. Evaluate the integral analytically.
b. Use change of variables formula [2.166] and change of variables

$$x = 2u - 1 \qquad [5.41]$$

to convert the integral to form [5.30].
c. Estimate the integral from part (b) with a crude Monte Carlo estimator four times, using samples of size 1, 10, 100, and 1000.
d. Estimate the standard errors of your four estimators in parts (c).

5.4 Consider the definite integral

$$\int_{\Omega} f(\boldsymbol{x}) = \int_{1}^{2}\int_{0}^{1}\int_{-1}^{1} \frac{x_1 x_2^2}{x_3} dx_1\, dx_2\, dx_3. \qquad [5.42]$$

a. Evaluate the integral analytically.
b. Implement a change of variables $\boldsymbol{u}$ for $\boldsymbol{x}$ to convert the integral to form [5.30].
c. Estimate the integral from part (b) with a crude Monte Carlo estimator four times, using samples of size 1, 10, 100, and 1000.
d. Estimate the standard errors of your four estimators in parts (c).

5.8. PSEUDORANDOM VARIATES

In this section, we consider how to construct pseudorandom variates $x^{[k]}$ from pseudorandom numbers $u^{[k]}$. We also consider how to construct joint-normal pseudorandom vectors $\boldsymbol{x}^{[k]}$ from $U_n((0, 1)^n)$ pseudorandom vectors $\boldsymbol{u}^{[k]}$. We then consider how to use these with a crude Monte Carlo estimator.

Consider a random vector $\boldsymbol{X}$ with some specified distribution. Conceptually, we may construct pseudorandom vectors $\boldsymbol{x}^{[k]}$ from pseudorandom vectors $\boldsymbol{u}^{[k]} \sim U_n((0, 1)^n)$ by selecting a function $g\colon \mathbb{R}^n \to \mathbb{R}^n$ that is probability preserving in the sense that $\boldsymbol{X}$ has the same distribution as $g(\boldsymbol{U})$ for $\boldsymbol{U} \sim U_n((0, 1)^n)$. We then set

$$\boldsymbol{x}^{[k]} = g\left(\boldsymbol{u}^{[k]}\right). \qquad [5.43]$$

Inverse Transform Method

Suppose X has CDF Φ with inverse Φ^{-1}. Then Φ^{-1} is probability preserving in the foregoing sense. We set $g = \Phi^{-1}$ and generate pseudorandom variates from pseudorandom numbers using [5.43]. This is called the **inverse transform** method of pseudorandom variate generation.

An $N(0, 1)$ pseudorandom variate $x^{[k]}$ can be obtained from a pseudorandom number $u^{[k]}$ with this method. We apply the inverse standard normal CDF Φ^{-1} to a pseudorandom number $u^{[k]}$ to obtain $x^{[k]}$. The transformation is illustrated in Exhibit 5.12 with evenly spaced values used as a proxy for pseudorandom numbers.

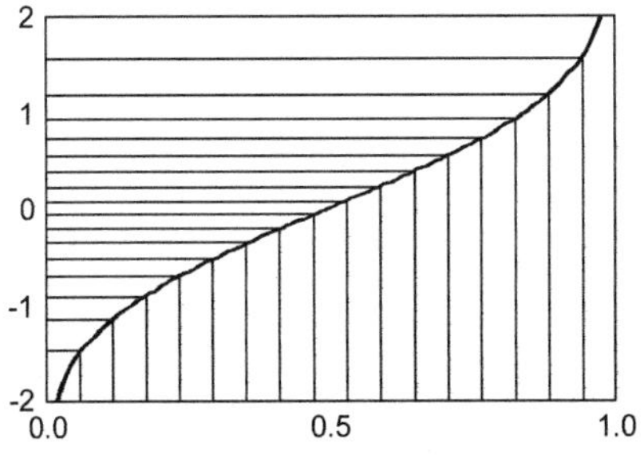

Exhibit 5.12 The inverse CDF of the standard normal distribution maps $U(0, 1)$ pseudorandom numbers into $N(0, 1)$ pseudorandom variates. Note how evenly spaced points are mapped into points that cluster around 0 and trail off in either direction.

By [3.82], an $N(\mu, \sigma^2)$ pseudorandom variate $y^{[k]}$ can be obtained from an $N(0, 1)$ pseudorandom variate $x^{[k]}$ by setting

$$y^{[k]} = \sigma x^{[k]} + \mu. \qquad [5.44]$$

By definition, a random variable Y is lognormal if $log(Y)$ is normal. Correspondingly, if X is normal, e^X is lognormal. To generate a $\Lambda(\mu, \sigma^2)$ pseudorandom variate $y^{[k]}$, we apply [3.91] and [3.92] to determine the mean m and standard deviation s of the corresponding $N(m, s^2)$ distribution. We generate an $N(m, s^2)$ pseudorandom variate $x^{[k]}$ and set $y^{[k]} = e^{x^{[k]}}$.

These techniques for constructing normal and lognormal variates are widely used. Because they require the evaluation of the inverse CDF of the standard normal distribution for each pseudorandom variate generated, they are computationally expensive. If a large number of pseudorandom variates are required, it is worth exploring computationally more efficient algorithms. See Fishman (1996).

Joint-Normal Pseudorandom Vectors

An $N_n(\mathbf{0}, \boldsymbol{I})$ pseudorandom vector $\boldsymbol{x}^{[k]}$ can be obtained by generating n $N(0, 1)$ pseudorandom variates $x^{[i]}$, and setting each component $x_i^{[k]}$ equal to one of them:

$$\boldsymbol{x}^{[k]} = \begin{pmatrix} x_1^{[k]} \\ x_2^{[k]} \\ \vdots \\ x_n^{[k]} \end{pmatrix} = \begin{pmatrix} x^{[1]} \\ x^{[2]} \\ \vdots \\ x^{[n]} \end{pmatrix} \qquad [5.45]$$

By [3.111], we can construct an $N_n(\boldsymbol{\mu}, \boldsymbol{\Sigma})$ pseudorandom vector $\boldsymbol{y}^{[k]}$ from an $N_n(\mathbf{0}, \boldsymbol{I})$ pseudorandom vector $\boldsymbol{x}^{[k]}$ by setting

$$\boldsymbol{y}^{[k]} = \boldsymbol{k}\boldsymbol{x}^{[k]} + \boldsymbol{\mu} \qquad [5.46]$$

where $\boldsymbol{k}$ is the Cholesky matrix of $\boldsymbol{\Sigma}$.

Generalizing the Crude Monte Carlo Estimator

A Monte Carlo estimator need not employ a $U_n((0, 1)^n)$ sample. We saw this in Section 5.2 where we estimated the variance of a random variable Y that was a function of an $N(0, 1)$ random variable X. For that example, it was computationally convenient—and intuitively appealing—to directly model a realization $\{x^{[1]}, x^{[2]}, \ldots, x^{[m]}\}$ of a sample $\{X^{[1]}, X^{[2]}, \ldots, X^{[m]}\}$ for the non-uniform random variable X. Another example was in Section 1.7, where we used the Monte Carlo method to estimate the VaR of a portfolio. There, we directly modeled a realization $\{{}^1\boldsymbol{r}^{[1]}, {}^1\boldsymbol{r}^{[2]}, \ldots, {}^1\boldsymbol{r}^{[m]}\}$ of a sample $\{{}^1\boldsymbol{R}^{[1]}, {}^1\boldsymbol{R}^{[2]}, \ldots, {}^1\boldsymbol{R}^{[m]}\}$ for ${}^1\boldsymbol{R}$.

Such estimators are no different from the crude Monte Carlo estimator [5.34]. They simply incorporate a change of variables. As the intuitive nature of our earlier examples illustrates, such changes of variables can simplify problems that are inherently probabilistic.

Consider an n-dimensional random vector $\boldsymbol{X}$ with PDF ϕ. We need to calculate the expected value of $E(q(\boldsymbol{X}))$ for some function $q\colon \mathbb{R}^n \to \mathbb{R}$. By [3.16], the expectation equals

$$E(q(\boldsymbol{X})) = \int_{\mathbb{R}^n} q(\boldsymbol{x})\phi(\boldsymbol{x})d\boldsymbol{x} \qquad [5.47]$$

To estimate the integral with the crude Monte Carlo estimator [5.34], we must convert the area of integration from $\mathbb{R}^n$ to $(0, 1)^n$. We do so with a differentiable function $g\colon (0, 1)^n \to \mathbb{R}^n$. By change of variables formula [2.168], the integral becomes

$$E(q(\boldsymbol{X})) = \int_{(0,1)^n} q(g(\boldsymbol{u}))\phi(g(\boldsymbol{u}))\,|Jg(\boldsymbol{u})|\,d\boldsymbol{u}. \qquad [5.48]$$

We obtain crude Monte Carlo estimator

$$\frac{1}{m}\sum_{k=1}^{m} q\left(g\left(\boldsymbol{u}^{[k]}\right)\right)\phi\left(g\left(\boldsymbol{u}^{[k]}\right)\right)\left|Jg\left(\boldsymbol{u}^{[k]}\right)\right|. \qquad [5.49]$$

This change of variables can be accomplished with any differentiable function $g\colon (0, 1)^n \to \mathbb{R}^n$, but suppose we employ a function g that is probability preserving in the sense defined earlier in this section. In this case, two things happen. First, using [2.168], it can be shown that

$$|Jg(\boldsymbol{u})| = \frac{1}{\phi(g(\boldsymbol{u}))}, \qquad [5.50]$$

so the crude Monte Carlo estimator [5.49] becomes

$$\frac{1}{m}\sum_{k=1}^{m} q\left(g\left(\boldsymbol{u}^{[k]}\right)\right). \qquad [5.51]$$

Second, as indicated by [5.43], if $\boldsymbol{u}^{[k]}$ is a $U_n((0, 1)^n)$ pseudorandom vector, $g(\boldsymbol{u}^{[k]})$ is a pseudorandom vector $\boldsymbol{x}^{[k]}$ for $\boldsymbol{X}$. Substituting this into [5.51] yields the highly intuitive Monte Carlo estimator

$$\frac{1}{m}\sum_{k=1}^{m} q\left(\boldsymbol{x}^{[k]}\right). \qquad [5.52]$$

To estimate $E(q(\boldsymbol{X}))$, all we need do is generate pseudorandom vectors $\boldsymbol{x}^{[k]}$, apply q to each, and average the results. The foregoing derivation demonstrates that this intuitive Monte Carlo estimator is nothing more than a crude Monte Carlo estimator with a change of variables.

Exercises

5.5 Use pseudorandom number $u^{[1]} = .983467$ to generate an $N(1, 4)$ pseudorandom variate $x^{[1]}$.

5.6 Use pseudorandom number $u^{[1]} = .762415$ to generate a $\Lambda(1, 9)$ pseudorandom variate $y^{[1]}$.

5.7 Use $U_3((0, 1)^3)$ pseudorandom vector

$$\boldsymbol{u}^{[1]} = \begin{pmatrix} .194385 \\ .843852 \\ .665872 \end{pmatrix} \qquad [5.53]$$

to generate an $N_3(\boldsymbol{\mu}, \boldsymbol{\Sigma})$ pseudorandom vector, where

$$\boldsymbol{\mu} = \begin{pmatrix} 1 \\ 0 \\ 3 \end{pmatrix}, \quad \text{and} \quad \boldsymbol{\Sigma} = \begin{pmatrix} 4 & 0 & 2 \\ 0 & 1 & 1 \\ 2 & 1 & 9 \end{pmatrix}. \qquad [5.54]$$

5.9. VARIANCE REDUCTION

We have considered two techniques of numerical integration: quadrature and the Monte Carlo method. Quadrature is deterministic. The Monte Carlo method is random. We may reduce the standard error of a Monte Carlo estimator by making it more deterministic. Variance reduction techniques are one way of doing this. These encompass a variety of methods that make an estimator more deterministic by incorporating additional information about a problem.

Control Variates

Consider crude Monte Carlo estimator

$$\frac{1}{m}\sum_{k=1}^{m} f\left(\boldsymbol{U}^{[k]}\right) \qquad [5.55]$$

for some quantity $\psi = E[f(\boldsymbol{U})]$, $\boldsymbol{U} \sim U_n((0, 1)^n)$. Let ξ be a function from $\mathbb{R}^n$ to $\mathbb{R}$ for which the mean

$$\mu_\xi = E[\xi(\boldsymbol{U})] \qquad [5.56]$$

is known. We shall refer to the random variable $\xi(\boldsymbol{U})$ as a **control variate**.

Consider the random variable $f^*(\boldsymbol{U})$ based upon this control variate,

$$f^*(\boldsymbol{U}) = f(\boldsymbol{U}) - c[\xi(\boldsymbol{U}) - \mu_\xi], \qquad [5.57]$$

for some constant c. This is an unbiased estimator for ψ because

$$E[f^*(\boldsymbol{U})] = E[f(\boldsymbol{U}) - c[\xi(\boldsymbol{U}) - \mu_\xi]] \quad [5.58]$$

$$= E[f(\boldsymbol{U})] - c[E[\xi(\boldsymbol{U})] - \mu_\xi] \quad [5.59]$$

$$= \psi - c[\mu_\xi - \mu_\xi] \quad [5.60]$$

$$= \psi. \quad [5.61]$$

Accordingly, we can estimate ψ with the Monte Carlo estimator

$$\frac{1}{m}\sum_{k=1}^{m} f^*(\boldsymbol{U}^{[k]}) = \frac{1}{m}\sum_{k=1}^{m}\left(f(\boldsymbol{U}^{[k]}) - c\left[\xi(\boldsymbol{U}^{[k]}) - \mu_\xi\right]\right). \quad [5.62]$$

This will have a lower standard error than [5.55] if the standard deviation σ^* of $f^*(\boldsymbol{U})$ is smaller than the standard deviation σ of $f(\boldsymbol{U})$. This will happen if $\xi(\boldsymbol{U})$ has a high correlation ρ with the random variable $f(\boldsymbol{U})$, in which case random variables $c\xi(\boldsymbol{U})$ and $f(\boldsymbol{U})$ will tend to offset each other in [5.62]. We formalize this observation by calculating

$$\sigma^* = std[f(\boldsymbol{U}) - c[\xi(\boldsymbol{U}) - \mu_\xi]] \quad [5.63]$$

$$= std[f(\boldsymbol{U}) - c\xi(\boldsymbol{U})] \quad [5.64]$$

$$= \sqrt{\sigma^2 + c^2\sigma_\xi^2 - 2c\sigma\sigma_\xi\rho}, \quad [5.65]$$

where σ_ξ is the standard deviation of $\xi(\boldsymbol{U})$. Accordingly, σ^* will be smaller than σ if

$$\rho > \frac{c\sigma_\xi}{2\sigma}. \quad [5.66]$$

It can be shown that σ^* is minimized by setting

$$c = \frac{\sigma\rho}{\sigma_\xi}, \quad [5.67]$$

in which case, from [5.65],

$$\sigma^* = \sigma\sqrt{1 - \rho^2}. \quad [5.68]$$

Often, ρ and σ_ξ are unknown, which makes determining the optimal value [5.67] for c problematic. We can estimate ρ and σ_ξ with a separate Monte Carlo analysis. Alternatively, if ξ closely approximates f, c might simply be set equal to 1.

EXAMPLE: CONTROL VARIATES. Suppose

$$f(\boldsymbol{u}) = exp\left[\left(u_1^2 + u_2^2\right)/2\right], \quad [5.69]$$

and consider the definite integral

$$\psi = \int_{(0,1)^2} f(\boldsymbol{u})d\boldsymbol{u}. \quad [5.70]$$

This has crude Monte Carlo estimator

$$\frac{1}{m}\sum_{k=1}^{m} f\left(U^{[k]}\right) = \frac{1}{m}\sum_{k=1}^{m} exp\left[\left(U_1^{[k]^2} + U_2^{[k]^2}\right)/2\right]. \quad [5.71]$$

We may reduce its standard error with the control variate

$$\xi(U) = 1 + \left(U_1^2 + U_2^2\right)/2. \quad [5.72]$$

Here, ξ is a second-order Taylor approximation for f. We easily obtain the mean μ_ξ of $\xi(U)$:

$$\mu_\xi = E[\xi(U)] = \int_0^1\int_0^1 \left(1 + \left(u_1^2 + u_2^2\right)/2\right)du_1\, du_2 = \int_0^1 \left(7/6 + u_2^2/2\right)du_2 = 4/3. \quad [5.73]$$

We set $c = 1$ and obtain

$$f^*(U) = f(U) - [\xi(U) - \mu_\xi] = exp\left[\left(U_1^2 + U_2^2\right)/2\right] - \left(U_1^2 + U_2^2\right)/2 + 1/3. \quad [5.74]$$

Our control-variate Monte Carlo estimator is

$$\frac{1}{m}\sum_{k=1}^{m} f^*\left(U^{[k]}\right) = \frac{1}{m}\sum_{k=1}^{m}\left(exp\left[\left(U_1^{[k]^2} + U_2^{[k]^2}\right)/2\right] - \left(U_1^{[k]^2} + U_2^{[k]^2}\right)/2 + 1/3\right). \quad [5.75]$$

To compare the performance of this estimator with that of the crude estimator [5.71], we set $m = 100$ and select a realization for $\{U^{[1]}, U^{[2]}, \ldots, U^{[100]}\}$, which is presented with a histogram in Exhibit 5.13.

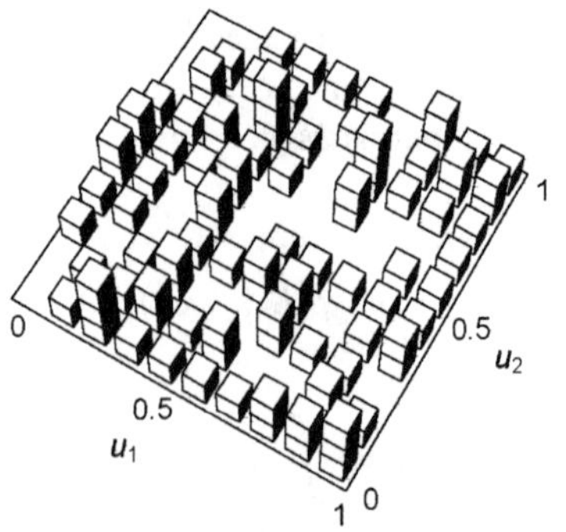

Exhibit 5.13 Histogram of a realization of $\{U^{[1]}, U^{[2]}, \ldots, U^{[100]}\}$.

We value the functions f and f^* at each point. Results are presented as histograms in Exhibit 5.14.

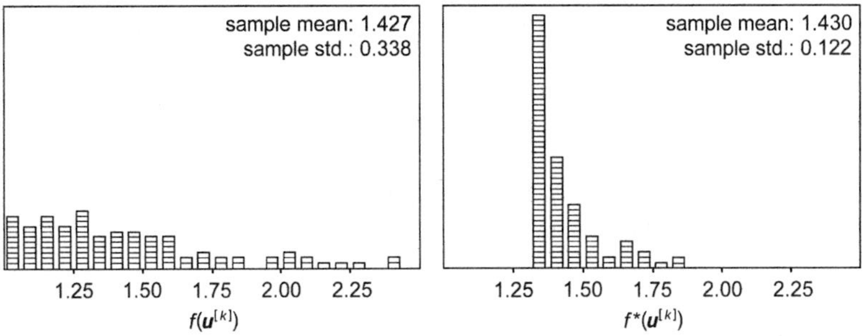

Exhibit 5.14 Values $f(\boldsymbol{u}^{[k]})$ (left) and $f^*(\boldsymbol{u}^{[k]})$ (right) obtained as described in the text.

Sample means are 1.427 and 1.430, respectively, so estimators [5.71] and [5.75] have yielded similar estimates for ψ. However, the sample standard deviations are 0.338 and 0.122, respectively, so values $f(\boldsymbol{u}^{[k]})$ have a substantially higher sample standard deviation than values $f^*(\boldsymbol{u}^{[k]})$. We can use these sample standard deviations to estimate the standard errors of our two estimators. The sample standard deviation 0.338 is an estimate for the standard deviation σ of $f(\boldsymbol{U})$. The sample standard deviation 0.122 is an estimate for the standard deviation σ^* of $f^*(\boldsymbol{U})$. Substituting these into [5.35], we estimate the standard errors of our Monte Carlo estimators as 0.0338 and 0.0122, respectively. Variance reduction using a control variate reduced standard error.

To place this variance reduction in perspective, consider how much we would need to increase the sample size m for crude Monte Carlo estimator [5.71] to achieve the same reduction in standard error. We set [5.35] equal to 0.0122 and substitute our sample standard deviation 0.338 for σ. We obtain

$$\frac{0.338}{\sqrt{m}} = 0.0122 \quad \Rightarrow \quad m = 768. \qquad [5.76]$$

In this particular example, our control variate estimator [5.75] accomplishes with a sample of size 100 what the crude estimator [5.71] would accomplish with a sample of size 768.

In any application, the variance reduction achieved with a particular control variate $\xi(\boldsymbol{U})$ depends critically upon the correlation ρ between $\xi(\boldsymbol{U})$ and $f(\boldsymbol{U})$. Suppose we employ the optimal value for c given by [5.67], and consider the ratio of the standard error for a crude estimator [5.55] with that of a control variate estimator [5.62]. By [5.68], this is

$$\frac{\dfrac{\sigma}{\sqrt{m}}}{\dfrac{\sigma^*}{\sqrt{m}}} = \frac{\sigma}{\sigma^*} = \frac{1}{\sqrt{1-\rho^2}} \qquad [5.77]$$

If $\xi(\boldsymbol{U})$ and $f(\boldsymbol{U})$ have a correlation of $\rho = .9$, standard error is reduced by a factor of $1/2.3$. If the correlation is .99, that factor increases to $1/7.1$. In the example we just presented, the correlation was actually .992, but we only reduced standard error by a factor of $1/2.8$ because we set $c = 1$ instead of determining an optimal value.

Control Variates Generalized

Our development of control variates assumes that a crude Monte Carlo estimator can be represented as a sum:

$$\frac{1}{m}\sum_{k=1}^{m} f(\boldsymbol{U}^{[k]}). \qquad [5.78]$$

In theory, this is always possible. In practice, it may be inconvenient. Consider a crude Monte Carlo estimator for a q-quantile of a random variable $f(\boldsymbol{U})$. If $\{f(\boldsymbol{u}^{[1]}), f(\boldsymbol{u}^{[2]}), \ldots, f(\boldsymbol{u}^{[m]})\}$ is a realization of a sample, we estimate the q-quantile of $f(\boldsymbol{U})$ by selecting that value $f(\boldsymbol{u}^{[k]})$ such that qm of the values are less than or equal to it. With some effort, this computation may be represented as a sum, but doing so is inconvenient. Such a representation is not necessary for applying a control variate.

Suppose $\xi(\boldsymbol{U})$ is a control variate for $f(\boldsymbol{U})$, as defined earlier. We wish to estimate some parameter ψ of $f(\boldsymbol{U})$. Suppose the corresponding parameter $\widetilde{\psi}$ of $\xi(\boldsymbol{U})$ is known. Let

$$H\left(f(\boldsymbol{U}^{[1]}), f(\boldsymbol{U}^{[2]}), \ldots, f(\boldsymbol{U}^{[m]})\right) \qquad [5.79]$$

be an estimator for ψ. Define a corresponding estimator

$$\widetilde{H} = H\left(\xi(\boldsymbol{U}^{[1]}), \xi(\boldsymbol{U}^{[2]}), \ldots, \xi(\boldsymbol{U}^{[m]})\right), \qquad [5.80]$$

which is an estimator for $\widetilde{\psi}$. Define a control variate estimator for ψ as

$$H - c[\widetilde{H} - \widetilde{\psi}]. \qquad [5.81]$$

We shall use this form of control variate estimator in Chapter 10 for estimating portfolio VaR. Note the similarity between this estimator and control variate estimator [5.62], which we developed earlier. Indeed, if H represents an average

$$\widetilde{\psi} = E(\widetilde{H}) = \mu_{\xi}, \qquad [5.82]$$

and control variate estimator [5.81] reduces to control variate estimator [5.62]:

$$H - c[\widetilde{H} - \widetilde{\psi}] = \frac{1}{m}\sum_{k=1}^{m} f(\boldsymbol{U}^{[k]}) - c\left[\frac{1}{m}\sum_{k=1}^{m}\xi(\boldsymbol{U}^{[k]}) - \mu_{\xi}\right]. \qquad [5.83]$$

$$= \frac{1}{m}\sum_{k=1}^{m}\left(f(\boldsymbol{U}^{[k]}) - c[\xi(\boldsymbol{U}^{[k]}) - \mu_{\xi}]\right). \qquad [5.84]$$

We shall call $\widetilde{H}$ a control variate for H. If the correlation between $\widetilde{H}$ and H is difficult to estimate, we may simply set $c = 1$.

Stratified Sampling

Consider crude Monte Carlo estimator

$$\frac{1}{m}\sum_{k=1}^{m} f(\boldsymbol{U}^{[k]}) \qquad [5.85]$$

for some quantity $\psi = E[f(\boldsymbol{U})]$, $\boldsymbol{U} \sim U_n((0, 1)^n)$. Stratify the region $(0, 1)^n$ into w disjoint subregions:

$$(0, 1)^n = \Omega_1 \cup \Omega_2 \cup \cdots \cup \Omega_w. \qquad [5.86]$$

Define w random vectors $\boldsymbol{X}_j \sim U_n(\Omega_j)$. Then $f(\boldsymbol{U})$ can be represented as a mixture, in the sense of Section 3.10, of the $f(\boldsymbol{X}_j)$ using weights $p_j = Pr(\boldsymbol{X} \in \Omega_j)$. Consequently

$$\psi = E[f(\boldsymbol{U})] = p_1 E[f(\boldsymbol{X}_1)] + p_2 E[f(\boldsymbol{X}_2)] + \cdots + p_w E[f(\boldsymbol{X}_w)]. \qquad [5.87]$$

With the method of stratified sampling, we apply a separate Monte Carlo estimator for each expectation $E[f(\boldsymbol{X}_j)]$ and use the probabilities p_j to take the probability-weighted mean. The result is an unbiased estimator

$$p_1 \frac{\sum_{k=1}^{m_1} f(\boldsymbol{X}_1^{[k]})}{m_1} + p_2 \frac{\sum_{k=1}^{m_2} f(\boldsymbol{X}_2^{[k]})}{m_2} + \cdots + p_w \frac{\sum_{k=1}^{m_w} f(\boldsymbol{X}_w^{[k]})}{m_w}, \qquad [5.88]$$

where m_j is the sample size employed on subregion Ω_j. The standard error for stratified sampling is:

$$\sqrt{\sum_{j=1}^{w} \frac{p_j^2 \sigma_j^2}{m_j}} \qquad [5.89]$$

where σ_j is the standard deviation of $f(\boldsymbol{X}_j)$. This formula suggests that, when partitioning $(0, 1)^n$, we do so in a manner that minimizes the terms $p_j\sigma_j$. Consider Exhibit 5.15. This depicts a function f on an interval $(0, 1)$, which has been partitioned into three subintervals Ω_1, Ω_2, and Ω_3. The variability of f over the entire interval $(0, 1)$ is greater than its variability over any subinterval. We expect each standard deviation σ_j of $f_j(\boldsymbol{X})$ to be less than the standard deviation σ of $f(\boldsymbol{X})$. This will help minimize the terms $p_j\sigma_j$.

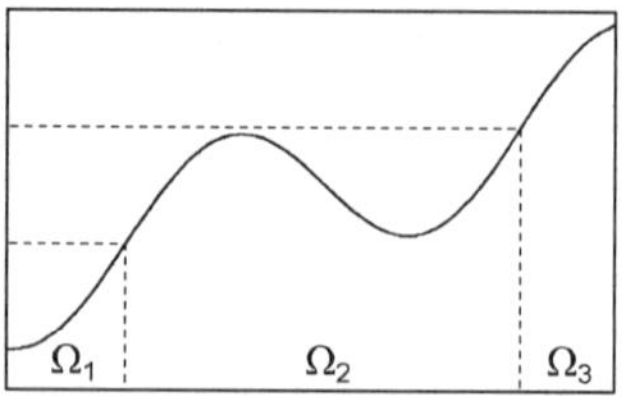

Exhibit 5.15 The variability of f over the entire interval (0, 1) is greater than its variability over any of the subintervals Ω_1, Ω_2, or Ω_3.

Formula [5.89] also suggests that we maximize each sample size m_j. If the total sample size $m = m_1 + m_2 + \cdots + m_w$ is fixed, we can increase one term m_j only at the expense of the others. An optimal choice of sample sizes is to set, for each j,

$$m_j = m \frac{p_j \sigma_j}{\sum_{i=1}^{w} p_i \sigma_i}. \qquad [5.90]$$

The preceding optimization techniques depend upon the quantities σ_j, which typically will not be known. Accordingly, optimizing a stratified sampling analysis is often a matter of trial and error. A simple solution is to employ a preliminary Monte Carlo analysis to estimate the quantities σ_j.

Exercises

5.8 Consider the definite integral

$$\psi = \int_{-1}^{1} \int_{-1}^{1} exp(\sqrt[3]{x_1} + \sqrt[3]{x_2}) dx_1 \, dx_2. \qquad [5.91]$$

Use the following steps to estimate the integral with stratified sampling:

a. Apply to the integral a change of variables

$$\begin{pmatrix} x_1 \\ x_2 \end{pmatrix} = 2 \begin{pmatrix} u_1 \\ u_2 \end{pmatrix} - \begin{pmatrix} 1 \\ 1 \end{pmatrix} \qquad [5.92]$$

to obtain an integral of form

$$\psi = \int_{(0,1)^2} f(\boldsymbol{u}) d\boldsymbol{u}. \qquad [5.93]$$

b. Stratify the new region of integration $(0, 1)^2$ into three subregions:

$$\Omega_1 = \{\boldsymbol{u} : u_1 \leq .5 \text{ and } u_2 \leq .5\}, \qquad [5.94]$$

$$\Omega_2 = \{\boldsymbol{u} : (u_1 \leq .5 \text{ and } u_2 > .5) \text{ or } (u_1 > .5 \text{ and } u_2 \leq .5)\}, \qquad [5.95]$$

$$\Omega_3 = \{\boldsymbol{u} : u_1 > .5 \text{ and } u_2 > .5\}. \qquad [5.96]$$

c. Sketch the three subregions.
d. Explain in your own words why these subregions are a reasonable choice for stratified sampling.
e. Estimate the standard deviations σ_j of each $f_j(\boldsymbol{u})$, where the f_j are the restrictions of f to each of the subregions Ω_j. Do so as follows:
   - Generate 50 $U_2(\Omega_j)$ pseudorandom vectors $\boldsymbol{u}_j^{[k]}$ for each subregion Ω_j.
   - For each subregion Ω_j, calculate sample standard deviations $\hat{\sigma}_j$ of the $f_j(\boldsymbol{u}_j^{[k]})$.
f. Based upon the estimated standard deviations $\hat{\sigma}_j$, apply [5.90] to determine a suitable sample size m_j to be used in each region Ω_j. Assume $m = 1000$.
g. Compare your three results m_1, m_2, and m_3 with the expected number of pseudorandom vectors $\boldsymbol{u}^{[k]}$ that would fall in each of Ω_1, Ω_2, and Ω_3 if stratified sampling were not used and crude Monte Carlo estimator [5.85] were used with the same total sample size of $m = 1000$.
h. Based upon your values m_j from item (f), specify an estimator for [5.93] of form [5.88].
i. Based upon your estimated standard deviations from item (e), estimate the standard error of your estimator as well as the standard error of the corresponding crude Monte Carlo estimator.
j. Based upon your results from item (i), how much would you need to increase the sample size for the crude Monte Carlo estimator in order for it to have the same standard error as your stratified sampling estimator from item (h)?
k. Apply your estimator from item (h) to estimate [5.93].

5.10. FURTHER READING

The classic text on the Monte Carlo method is Hammersley and Handscomb (1964). More recent texts are Rubinstein (1981), Morgan (1984), and Fishman (1996). Knuth (1997) is an excellent reference on pseudorandom number generation. See also the survey articles by Hellekalek (1998) and L'Ecuyer (1998). Park and Miller (1988) discuss the implementation of pseudorandom number generators.

Part III

Value-at-Risk

Chapter 6

Market Data

6.1. MOTIVATION

When we design a VaR measure, one of the first steps is to choose a key vector ${}^1\boldsymbol{R}$. We need this before we can design a mapping procedure that will construct portfolio mappings ${}^1P = \theta({}^1\boldsymbol{R})$. We also need it before we can design an inference procedure that will characterize the conditional distribution of ${}^1\boldsymbol{R}$.

There are various issues to consider in selecting what financial variables to represent with key factors ${}^1R_i$. One of these is the availability of historical market data. An inference procedure requires historical data related to all key factors. If there is no historical data relating to a particular financial variable, it makes little sense to model that variable as a key factor.

In this chapter, we discuss types of historical market data that may be used by VaR measures. We describe how data is collected over time, how it is filtered and cleaned of errors, and how it is converted into forms usable by an inference procedure.

6.2. FORMS OF DATA

Data can represent market prices, interest rates, spreads, implied volatilities, etc. Any of these may be directly quoted in the markets, or they may be inferred from other quantities that are directly quoted. All are, in some sense, prices. Price data can vary with respect to type, method of collection, and source.

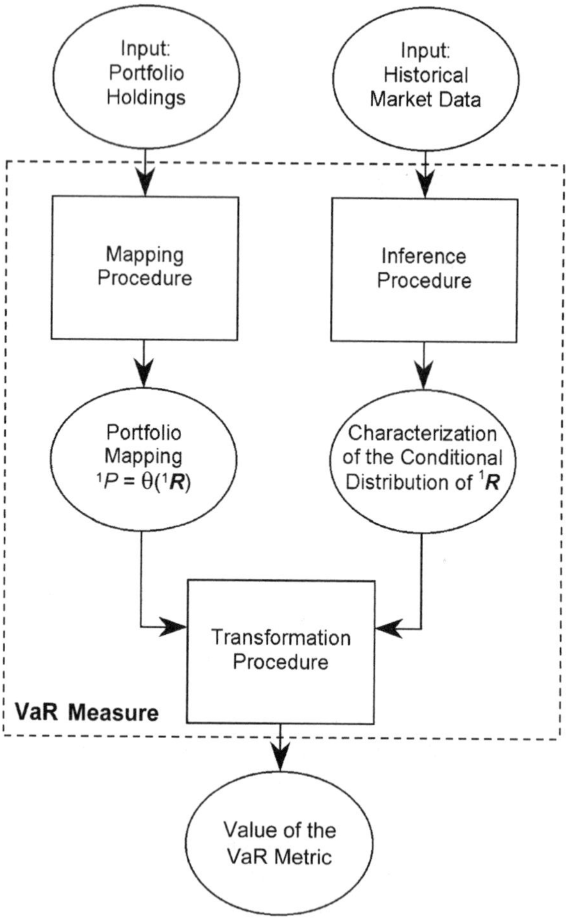

Exhibit 6.1 A reproduction of Exhibit 1.11, which is a general schematic for VaR measures. The availability of historical market data influences the selection of financial variables to be modeled with key vector $^1\boldsymbol{R}$. This, in turn, influences our design of both a mapping procedure and an inference procedure.

Types of Prices

There are essentially four types of prices:

- **Transaction prices** are prices at which actual transactions took place.
- **Firm prices** are bid or offer prices quoted by market participants, who are then obligated to transact at those prices if accepted by a counterparty. Firm bid and offer prices may be averaged to obtain firm mid-market prices.

- **Indicative prices** are bid, offer, or mid-market prices quoted by market participants—usually brokers or market makers—for informational purposes only. The quoting party has no obligation to transact.
- **Settlement prices** are prices specified by exchanges for purposes such as calculating daily margin requirements. Each exchange has its own rules for calculating settlement prices based upon transaction, firm, or indicative prices at the close of trading each day.

COLLECTING DATA

Time series of historical prices are constructed by recording prices at a regular interval—each day, each week, each month, etc. For settlement prices, collecting data is as easy as recording the daily settlement prices released by the appropriate exchange.

Transaction prices are more problematic. For actively traded instruments, there can be thousands of transactions spaced at irregular intervals throughout each day. Other assets trade less frequently and may fail to trade at all on some days. Four techniques for collecting daily transaction data are:

- **opening prices**, which comprise the first transaction price following the market open each day;
- **closing prices**, which comprise the last transaction price prior to the market close each day;
- **high prices**, which comprise the highest transaction price each day; or
- **low prices**, which comprise the lowest transaction price each day.

For VaR applications, closing prices are most commonly used. Irrespective of how they are collected, transaction prices tend to be **nonsynchronous**. This means that prices for different assets will reflect transactions occurring at different times. On a given day, the last trade in one stock might occur at 2:20 PM with the last trade in another occurring at 4:15 PM.

If trading in an asset is light, several days or weeks may transpire between transactions. If there are no transactions in a given day, a missing data indicator may be entered in the time series in lieu of a value. Alternatively, some rule may be applied for filling in missing values. On days when an asset doesn't trade, its closing price might be set equal to the previous day's closing price.

With exchanges implementing evening trading sessions and electronic trading sessions, it is important to clarify which trading sessions opening, closing, high, and low prices are based upon. For markets that trade around the clock, such as foreign exchange, the notions of market open and market close are not meaningful. In such cases, two times can be selected to represent "market open" and "market close." In certain OTC markets, high and low prices may be exaggerated by outliers—transactions at significantly off-market prices. Some rule may be employed to discard outliers when calculating high and low prices.

Firm or indicative prices are easier to collect synchronously than transaction prices. In inactive markets, indicative quotes may be solicited from brokers or dealers at a fixed time each day. In more active markets, firm or indicative quotes are distributed electronically throughout each trading day. Problems may arise during periods of active trading when dealers may be too busy to update indicative quotes. Lyons (1995) observes that, during periods of volatility in the foreign exchange market, indicative bid and offer prices on Reuters FXFX screens may fail to bracket transaction prices.

A shortcoming of indicative quotes is questionable quality. If a relationship exists with the quoting party, that party will want to provide quality quotes. However, market makers have no financial stake in indicative quotes, so they are unlikely to prepare them as carefully as they would firm quotes. A less common problem is indicative quotes being intentionally made off-market as a means of influencing markets.

One technique for addressing such problems is to obtain indicative quotes from multiple parties. The high and low quotes may be discarded and the remainder averaged. The British Bankers Association (BBA) uses such a formula in preparing its daily Libor indicative quotes.

The particular types of data we choose to use in a VaR analysis will depend upon the foregoing issues as well as availability. Transaction prices are generally available for exchange-traded instruments, but are more difficult to obtain in OTC markets. Settlement prices are only available for exchange-traded instruments such as futures and options. In some OTC markets, firm quotes may be available. In others, it may only be possible to obtain indicative quotes. Indeed, in many markets, data of any sort may be difficult to obtain.

Data Sources

There are many sources for data. The most common include:

- exchanges,
- broker or dealer quotes,
- data vendors,
- real-time data feeds, and
- trade tickets.

All exchanges record detailed information on transactions. This is used for various purposes, including:

- audit,
- dispute resolution,
- distribution of real-time price information via data feeds, and
- determination of settlement prices.

Not all information is available publicly, but most exchanges distribute price histories indicating, among other things, high, low, closing, and settlement prices for each trading day.

Indicative prices may be obtained directly from brokers or dealers. It is best to standardize this process so the operational definition of the time series remains stable over time. Quotes may be obtained from one or several parties. Be candid with quoting parties. Let them know that the quotes are for risk management purposes only, and seek their commitment to provide the quotes on an ongoing basis. Many brokers or dealers are happy to provide this service for institutions with whom they have a profitable business relationship.

Data vendors collect data from multiple sources, preprocess it, and distribute it as time series. Costs vary, but are generally modest compared to the cost of constructing and maintaining one's own time series.

It is important to understand what sources data vendors use for data as well as what preprocessing they perform. If possible, it is best to purchase data prepared specifically for risk analyses. Some data vendors distribute covariance matrices for key factors instead of time series. If possible, avoid using these. As we shall discuss in Chapter 7, different analyses may yield very different covariance matrices from a given time series. The choice of technique is a significant design decision for a VaR model that should not be left to a data vendor.

Most trading organizations purchase real-time data feeds for their traders. Values can be captured from these periodically—perhaps at an appointed time each day—and used to construct time series. Data collected in this manner may require extensive cleaning. Because the data is delivered in real time, quality controls are minimal. Even in liquid markets, data feeds may lag the markets. Also, most vendors place restrictions upon use of their real-time data, and these may prohibit the accumulation of historical databases.

If an institution is active in a particular market, it may capture transaction prices directly from its own trade tickets, or subsequently from its trade accounting system. This should be considered only as a last resort if alternative data sources are unavailable. It is feasible only for market participants who trade in volume—primarily market makers. Cleaning the data is expensive and labor intensive. There is the risk of losing the data source if, for some reason, the institution is forced to stop trading in a particular market for a period.

6.3. NONSYNCHRONOUS DATA

A time series $\{{}^{-\alpha}\boldsymbol{q}, {}^{-\alpha+1}\boldsymbol{q}, \ldots, {}^{0}\boldsymbol{q}\}$ is said to be **synchronous** if components ${}^{t}q_i$ for each term ${}^{t}\boldsymbol{q}$ are realized simultaneously. Otherwise, it is said to be **nonsynchronous**. Financial time series are typically nonsynchronous for one of two reasons:

- **Trading effects** relate to instruments that trade infrequently or fail to trade for a period of time. It also encompasses certain effects such as brokers failing to provide timely indicative quotes during a period of heavy trading volumes.
- **Timing effects** relate to instruments trading in different time zones or according to different schedules. Some exchanges—such as the Singapore Exchange—have different closing times for different instruments trading in the same time zone. This causes settlement prices to be nonsynchronous.

We have already mentioned trading effects. They primarily affect opening or closing transaction price data. As we indicated above, they may also affect firm or indicative quotes. High and low transaction prices are not expected to be synchronous since different assets will attain their high and low prices at different times each day. If instruments do not trade for a day or more, the resulting nonsynchronicity can be a serious issue. Trading effects generally do not affect settlement prices. Each exchange has its own methodology for determining settlement prices. Most are based upon some average of transaction prices occurring immediately prior to the market close. If trading is not active at the close, a common practice is to poll traders and base the settlement price on some average of the indicative quotes.

As an illustration of a timing effect, the Tokyo, London, and New York stock exchanges stop trading each day at 3:00 PM, 5:00 PM, and 4:00 PM, respectively, in their local times. Because of time zone differences, Tokyo actually closes 11 hours before London, and London closes 4 hours before New York.[1] Closing prices collected from the respective exchanges are nonsynchronous.

Impact of Nonsynchronous Data

Nonsynchronous data complicates the task of assigning a current value ${}^0p$ to a portfolio if the current value ${}^0\boldsymbol{r}$ of the key factors is collected nonsynchronously. Cross-hedged positions may appear to not be hedged. Arbitrage conditions that should hold may appear to not hold. The resulting value for ${}^0p$ may be misleading or even nonsensical.

If time series models are not implemented specifically to address nonsynchronous data, inferred correlations will be lower, in absolute value, than they would be if the data were collected synchronously. Spurious autocorrelations between different risk factors will also arise.

Consider the stocks of two companies that trade on the same exchange and tend to move in tandem. The first trades actively; the second does not. News arriving late in the day will not be reflected in the inactive stock's closing price if that stock fails to trade subsequent to the arrival of the news. This tendency

[1] Time differences reflect periods when daylight savings time is nowhere in effect.

will suppress the inferred return correlation between the two stocks and induce a positive autocorrelation between the stocks' returns lagged by one day. If the inactive stock sometimes fails to trade for a day or more, such autocorrelations may persist for several days.

Eurodollar futures are traded on both the CME in Chicago and the Singapore Exchange. The two contracts are essentially identical. For a given expiration date, we may treat closing prices in Chicago and Singapore as being for the same contract, but collected at different times.[2] By comparing these closing prices to closing prices of some other contract, we may assess the impact of nonsynchronous data.

We collect daily settlement price data from May 3, 1999, to February 1, 2000, for the following contracts:

- CBOT June 2000 Treasury bond future,
- CME June 2000 Eurodollar future, and
- Singapore Exchange June 2000 Eurodollar future.

The CBOT and CME are both in Chicago, so settlement prices for the CBOT Treasury bond contract and CME Eurodollar contract are synchronous.[3] The settlement price for the Singapore Eurodollar contract is set 8 hours earlier.[4] Also, 16 hours after the Chicago settlement prices are set, the subsequent day's Singapore Eurodollar settlement price is set (assuming this is also a trading day.) This is illustrated in Exhibit 6.2:

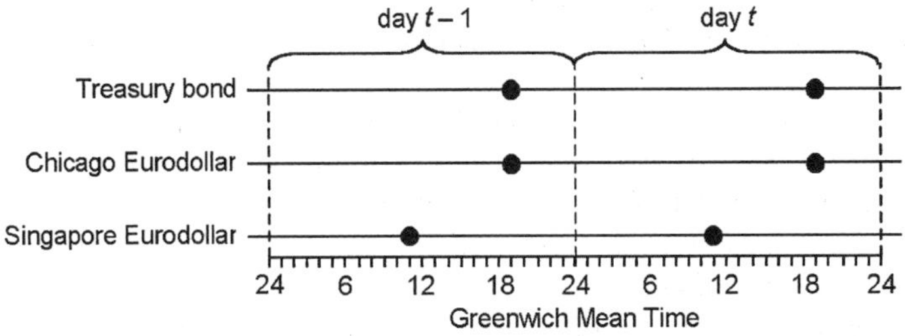

Exhibit 6.2 Time lines illustrate when prices for the three contracts are collected. The Chicago settlement prices are set 8 hours after the Singapore settlement prices. They are set 16 hours before the Singapore settlement prices for the subsequent day, assuming it is also a trading day.

We expect the Treasury bond contract to be positively correlated with both Eurodollar contracts, but because the Singapore Eurodollar contract is nonsynchronous, we expect its correlation with the Treasury bond contract to be lower.

---

[2]The two exchanges have an offset arrangement that allows an open contract on one exchange to be closed on the other, so the two exchanges' contracts are truly fungible.

[3]Open outcry trading for both contracts ends at 2:00 PM each day.

[4]Trading closes in Singapore at 7:00 PM local time.

The Treasury bond contract should also exhibit a modest autocorrelation with the Singapore Eurodollar contract. To test these hypotheses, we calculate return correlations and return autocorrelations as indicated in Exhibit 6.3:[5]

Daily Return Correlations

	Chicago Eurodollar settlement price for day *t*	**Singapore Eurodollar** settlement price for day *t*
Chicago Treasury bond settlement price for day *t*	.808	.142

Daily Return Autocorrelations

	Chicago Eurodollar settlement price for day *t*	**Singapore Eurodollar** settlement price for day *t*
Chicago Treasury bond settlement price for day *t* - 1	-.036	.634
Chicago Treasury bond settlement price for day *t* + 1	-.034	.043

Exhibit 6.3 The top table shows daily return correlations between the CBOT Treasury bond contract and the two Eurodollar contracts. The bottom table shows corresponding return autocorrelations with the CBOT Treasury bond contract either leading or lagging by a day.

Prices for Treasury bond and Eurodollar futures move in tandem, as indicated by the .808 correlation for the two contracts traded in Chicago. However, nonsynchronicity causes the Chicago Treasury bond future and Singapore Eurodollar future to have a correlation of just .142. If the Treasury bond future is lagged a day, the autocorrelation is .634.

The effect of nonsynchronicity on correlations tends to diminish if data is collected at longer intervals. If prices are collected monthly, the effect of the nonsynchronicity will be modest, as long as the prices are not too mean-reverting.

The most effective way to address nonsynchronicity is to avoid it in the first place. If transaction prices are highly nonsynchronous because of nontrading, consider using firm, indicative, or settlement prices instead. To the extent possible, try to collect prices in a single time zone. If this is impossible, consider collecting most prices in a particular time zone, and obtain prices from other time zones as broker quotes, which offer some flexibility in the timing.

[5]Log returns are used. Data from days when any of the exchanges were closed is omitted from the calculation. Results are inferred using the method of uniformly weighted moving averages (UWMA) discussed in Chapter 7.

6.4. DATA ERRORS

Data errors are data values that are, in some sense, erroneous. **Filtering** is any procedure for identifying data values as erroneous. **Cleaning** is any procedure that corrects erroneous data values or replaces them in the data series with some missing data indicator.

ERRORS

Data errors frequently arise when data is first placed in electronic form, either through manual keying or through a process of scanning and optical character recognition. With manual keying, forward prices may be entered for the wrong maturity. Bid and offer prices may be transposed. Exchange rates may be inverted or entered for the wrong currency pair. Decimal places can be omitted or shifted; digits can be transposed; incorrect digits may be entered; digits may be dropped or extra digits entered.

Optical character recognition software introduces different types of errors. Characters may be mistaken for other characters, with particular mistakes depending upon the font in which scanned data is printed as well as the quality of the printing. The letter O may be read as the number 0. In certain fonts, the numerals 6, 8, and 9 may be mistaken for one another, as may be 5 and 6. Stray marks may be interpreted as text or decimal points. Legitimate decimal points may be overlooked.

Even after data is in electronic form, software or hardware may introduce errors. If a real-time data feed fails, a user may misinterpret bid and offer prices at the time of the failure as being effective throughout the period when the system is down. A system might transmit only the third and fourth decimal places of a price except when the second decimal place changes. If the second decimal place changes during a period when the system is down, a user may be unaware of the change after the system is restored. Some systems may transmit dummy data when they are turned on or being tested. In some markets, automated quotation systems are designed to indicate "reasonable" prices as if they were actual prices during periods of trading inactivity.

Off-market prices are actual prices that are not, in our subjective opinion, reflective of markets at the time they are quoted. A broker may carelessly quote an indicative price. An unsophisticated market participant may accept an unreasonable price. A trader may mistakenly trade at an off-market price. Occasionally, a trader may transact at off-market prices to manipulate markets or distort his portfolio's mark-to-market value. **Wash trades** are identical offsetting trades between two counterparties, which can be performed at off-market prices. **Ramping** is the performance of very small transactions at off-market prices.

The pricing of one transaction may influence the pricing of other transactions with the same counterparty. If a trade accounting system cannot handle swaps, a trader may transact a swap as a strip of individual forwards, each at the same price. Recorded in a time series, the identical prices will appear to indicate a flat forward curve.

Data Filtering

Data filtering may entail one or more of:

- computer algorithms,
- human review, or
- data comparisons.

Many data errors—especially keying errors—are blatant. If the decimal point is accidentally dropped from 1.72, it becomes 172.00. If we mistakenly transpose the leading digits in 19.02, it becomes 91.02. Such blatant errors are easily identified in the context of a time series. Computer algorithms can sift through large volumes of data to locate such outliers. For more subtle errors, algorithms may employ statistical inference, pattern-recognition techniques, or arbitrage relationships—such as put-call parity or interest-rate parity—to identify suspect data values. Spreads or other price relationships can be checked to see if they conform to historical patterns.

Simple filtering algorithms are easy to construct, but more sophisticated algorithms require careful design as well as some fine-tuning over time. Seasonality and heteroskedasticity complicate designs. Tests relating to specific price relationships or patterns must be customized.

Subtle data errors can be identified manually by traders or other professionals who follow market developments. Such reviews should be performed soon after data is recorded, while a reviewer's memory is fresh. Also, if a computer algorithm identifies data values as suspect, humans may perform a final review to determine which of these are actual data errors.

Finally, if data for certain risk factors is available from several independent sources, the data from these sources can be compared for consistency.

Data Cleaning

Once data errors have been identified, they must be cleaned—either set equal to values we believe to be correct or deleted. Corrected values should be obtained from the same source from which the data originated. For keying errors, refer to the documents from which the data was keyed. If erroneous data is obtained from an exchange, the exchange should be able to correct it. If transaction prices are erroneous, contact the counterparties to the trade. If data is obtained from a data vendor, you won't have access to original sources, but you can request that the vendor obtain corrected values.

6.5. DATA BIASES

As market theoreticians, we like to think of historical prices as forming an unbroken series of numbers, each representing the price at which an efficient market cleared at a particular point in time. Data may contain errors, but we filter and clean it to eliminate these.

As practitioners, we accept a different view. While certain data values are clearly erroneous, others are not so easily categorized. From an operational standpoint, data is erroneous if our filtering procedure identifies it as such. Otherwise it is correct. Subjectively, things are not so stark. We perceive a continuum of gradations between erroneous and correct data. A filtering procedure discards certain values as erroneous, but the remainder may reflect a variety of modest biases or distortions. Isolated distortions, so long as they are minor, have little effect on VaR measurements. More problematic are modest biases of a systematic nature.

In any market, there are bid-ask spreads. These introduce a bias into transaction prices—biasing them upward/downward when a market maker is selling/buying. Such biases are inconsequential in liquid markets if daily price fluctuations dwarf bid-ask spreads. They are more problematic in illiquid markets, where bid-ask spreads can be large.

Transaction costs reduce arbitrage opportunities, which increases the potential for modest biases or discrepancies to persist in markets.

If an asset is credit sensitive, different transaction prices may reflect differing counterparty credit qualities or differing collateralization arrangements. Even if credit quality is not an issue, liquidity effects can introduce biases. Two bonds may be issued by similar credits—or both by the same credit—but one trades at a premium to the other because it has a more active secondary market. This is evident in the US Treasury bond market, where the most recently issued "on the run" bonds trade at a premium.

In most commodity markets, there is some choice as to the method of settlement, and prices vary depending upon which method is selected. Some standard methods are:

- free on board (FOB)—the commodity is cleared through customs and delivered on board the recipient's ship at the port of departure.
- free alongside (FAS)—FOB delivery, except the commodity is delivered alongside the recipient's ship.
- cost, insurance, freight (CIF)—FOB delivery as well as insurance and shipping. Essentially, the commodity is delivered to the destination port, but actual settlement is through delivery of the ship's bill of lading.
- ex-dock—the commodity is cleared through customs and delivered on the dock of the destination port.
- in-warehouse—the commodity is cleared through customs and delivered in a warehouse at the destination port.

- ex-warehouse—the delivering party provides in-warehouse delivery and pays the cost of moving the commodity to the warehouse exit.

In addition, transaction prices may reflect additional services such as storage, inventory management, or balancing fees. Payment terms may also influence prices.

The biases described above are all associated with transaction prices. As an alternative, firm or indicative prices may be available reflecting some standard settlement and payment terms, and mid-market prices can be calculated from these. Another solution is to apply standard adjustments to transaction prices to make them comparable. Prices reflecting different settlement methods might be adjusted to make them all consistent with, say, ex-dock settlement. If a market is active, it may be reasonable to use some average of prices, say recording each day's closing price as the average price of all transactions completed during the last minute of trading. Individual prices may reflect specific biases, but these will cancel somewhat in the averaged price.

Substituting the price of one asset for that of a closely related asset can introduce biases. Forward and future prices for the same underlier often move in tandem, especially if they have identical or similar settlement terms. However, they can diverge. One reason is market segmentation. If large transactions that would move the futures market are always transacted on the forward market, arbitraging between the two markets may be infeasible. Another reason is a phenomenon that has come to be known as **convexity bias**.

Cox, Ingersoll, and Ross (1981) and Jarrow and Oldfield (1981) suggest that daily margin payments on futures may cause forward and futures prices to diverge. If there is a correlation between daily futures prices and interest rates, one party to a futures contract will tend to receive margin payments on days when interest rates rise and make margin payments on days when interest rates decline. On average, she can expect to invest the margin payments she receives at interest rates that are higher than those at which she finances the margin payments she makes. The other party can expect the opposite experience. This should cause a divergence in forward and futures prices, with the effect depending upon the maturity of contracts, the magnitude of correlations, and the volatility of the future's prices.

Empirical studies by Cornell and Reinganum (1981), French (1983), and Park and Chen (1985) confirm a modest convexity bias in gold, silver, silver coins, platinum, copper, and plywood prices, but fail to find one for various currencies.

As we might expect, the effect is most pronounced when a future's underlier is an interest rate or fixed-income instrument that exhibits a high correlation with applicable interest rates. In this context, Burghardt and Hoskins (1995) coined the name "convexity bias." They and Gupta and Subrahmanyam (2000) discuss the convexity bias in the pricing of interest-rate swaps. The swap market traditionally priced swaps directly off Eurocurrency futures without recognizing any convexity bias, but this started to change in the early 1990s. Today, swap prices reflect a significant convexity bias relative to Eurocurrency futures.

Taxes may also introduce biases. Discrepancies can exist across jurisdictions or within a jurisdiction.

Between 1953 and 1963, the US Treasury issued a number of Treasury bonds with a special feature. If tendered as payment of federal estate taxes, the bonds would be valued at par, irrespective of their current market value. Because of their association with estate taxes and funerals, the bonds came to be called "flower bonds." When interest rates rose during the 1970s and 1980s, flower bonds traded at a premium. The last flower bond had a coupon of 3.5% and matured in 1998.

Many tax-related biases are unintentional. If they offer opportunities for tax arbitrage, they are likely to soon be legislated out of existence. Cornell (1981) and Viswanath (1989) describe one such effect that existed until 1981 in the US Treasury bill futures market.

6.6. FUTURES

Futures prices are generally collected as settlement prices. Because the contracts mature, and because multiple contracts usually trade simultaneously for a given underlier, futures prices do not form continual time series. Instead, they form multiple time series corresponding to different contracts. Each one begins when the corresponding contract starts to trade and ends when that contract expires. This is illustrated in Exhibit 6.4.

Time (month)	Contract (indicated by month of expiration)				
	Jan-00	Mar-00	May-00	Jul-00	Sep-00
Apr-99	241.2				
May-99	244.1				
Jun-99	243.6	248.8			
Jul-99	239.3	244.0	246.0		
Aug-99	245.7	248.5	251.5		
Sep-99	237.3	242.3	246.5	252.0	
Oct-99	230.0	235.0	239.0	243.0	
Nov-99	223.5	225.2	228.9	232.4	235.5
Dec-99	216.7	218.5	221.6	224.7	231.5
Jan-00		221.7	225.0	229.0	233.0
Feb-00		221.8	222.1	225.0	230.0
Mar-00			231.0	232.5	240.5
Apr-00			238.2	241.5	244.5
May-00				224.0	227.0
Jun-00				218.0	218.0
Jul-00					214.8
Aug-00					219.0

Exhibit 6.4 Monthly prices for flaxseed futures traded on the Winnipeg Commodities Exchange (WCE). Prices are quoted in CAD/ton and represent the last settlement price for the respective month. Source: WCE.

Techniques of time series analysis require data to be in continual time series. There are two ways to convert discontinual futures price data into continual time series. We can construct nearbys or constant-maturity price series.

Nearbys

The standard means of obtaining continual time series from futures prices is to use **nearby series** or simply **nearbys**. Consider futures trading on a particular exchange for a given underlier. At any point in time, there will be contracts trading for several expirations. A **first nearby** is a time series comprising the price, at each point in time, of the nearest-to-expiration contract. The **second nearby** comprises the price, at each point in time, of the second nearest-to-expiration contract, etc.

Exhibit 6.5 indicates monthly settlement price data for municipal bond index futures traded on the CBOT. Prices are in USD and reflect the last settlement price for each month. Data is provided for six contracts maturing between September 1998 and December 1999. Exhibit 6.6 presents a first and second nearby constructed from the data. To clarify how the nearbys are constructed, we have used shading in Exhibits 6.5 and 6.6 to indicate the prices used to form the second nearby.

Time (month)	Contract (indicated by month of expiration)					
	Sep-98	Dec-98	Mar-99	Jun-99	Sep-99	Dec-99
Jun-98	124.4688	124.0625				
Jul-98	124.0000	123.5625				
Aug-98	126.6250	126.4063				
Sep-98		128.3750	128.2188			
Oct-98		125.4688	125.0938			
Nov-98		126.4688	126.0938			
Dec-98			125.0000	124.5313		
Jan-99			126.7500	126.2813	125.8125	125.3438
Feb-99			124.6250	123.6875	123.2188	122.7500
Mar-99				123.5938	122.7188	122.2500
Apr-99				123.1875	122.3125	121.8438
May-99				121.9688	120.4688	119.5313
Jun-99					118.7813	117.7500
Jul-99					118.0625	116.4375
Aug-99					114.9688	114.0000

Exhibit 6.5 Monthly prices for municipal bond index futures traded on the CBOT. Prices are quoted in USD and represent the last settlement price for the respective month. The purpose of the shaded numbers is explained in the text. Source: CBOT.

Time months	Nearby First	Nearby Second
Jun-98	124.4688	124.0625
Jul-98	124.0000	123.5625
Aug-98	126.6250	126.4063
Sep-98	128.3750	128.2188
Oct-98	125.4688	125.0938
Nov-98	126.4688	126.0938
Dec-98	125.0000	124.5313
Jan-99	126.7500	126.2813
Feb-99	124.6250	123.6875
Mar-99	123.5938	122.7188
Apr-99	123.1875	122.3125
May-99	121.9688	120.4688
Jun-99	118.7813	117.7500
Jul-99	118.0625	116.4375
Aug-99	114.9688	114.0000

Exhibit 6.6 The first two nearbys constructed from the data of Exhibit 6.5. The first nearby represents, for each time *t*, the price of the future that was closest to expiration at that time. The second nearby represents, for each time *t*, the price of the future that was second closest to expiration at that time. To clarify the construction of nearbys, the futures prices used to construct the second nearby have been shaded in both Exhibits 6.5 and 6.6.

Nearbys and Distortions

Nearbys exhibit certain distortions related to contract expirations. Depending upon the underlying commodity, price standard deviations may rise or fall as the last trade date approaches. Correlations with other prices may also be affected. If the same commodity is traded on two geographically separate exchanges, the correlation between futures prices on the two exchanges will tend to decline as the contracts approach expiration. Localized supply and demand imbalances will become evident and it will become increasingly infeasible to transport the commodity from one location to the other in time for delivery. During the final days prior to a contract's last trade date, distortions can be pronounced as positions are closed out, open interest declines, and liquidity migrates to the subsequent contract.

If futures prices are formed into nearbys, such expiration-related behavior manifests itself as a cyclical pattern in each nearby. This may be especially pronounced in the first nearby. One way to mitigate this effect in the first nearby is to construct nearbys by rolling over contracts prior to each last-trade date.

The **rollover date** for a set of nearbys is the date when each nearby is switched to reflect prices of the subsequent futures contract. The last possible rollover date is the last trade date of the expiring contract, but earlier dates, such as the first day of the expiring contract's delivery month, are possible.

The earlier we make a rollover date, the more we can mitigate expiration-related distortions in the first nearby. If we set our rollover date 2 weeks prior to the last-trade date, prices during each contract's last 2 weeks of trading will be discarded. They will appear in none of the nearbys.

Early rollover of nearbys raises a problem if a portfolio holds futures contracts to expiration. We don't want to stop recording data for a soon-to-expire contract while it is still held by the portfolio! A simple solution is to track data right up until contracts expire. Only after they expire do we go back and modify nearbys to reflect the earlier rollover date.

The judicious selection of a rollover date is just one technique that addresses a specific form of distortion in the first nearby. Other distortions may remain across all nearbys. Exhibit 6.7 is a graph of the daily second nearby for IPE natural gas futures. The first trading day of each delivery month is used as a rollover date. The graph covers the second half of 1998.

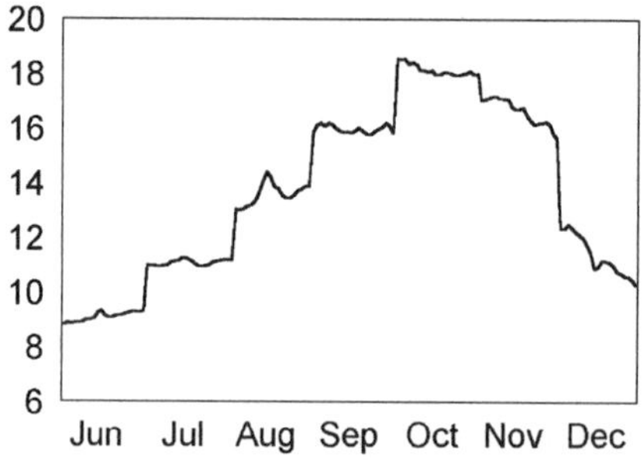

Exhibit 6.7 Second nearby for International Petroleum Exchange (IPE) natural gas futures for June 1998 through December 1998. Prices are settlement prices in USD. The first trading day of each delivery month is used as a rollover date.

The nearby prices exhibit a pattern. This is more pronounced in Exhibit 6.8, which shows daily returns for the same nearby. The six largest (positive or negative) returns in Exhibit 6.8 are evenly spaced in time. Indeed, each occurs on the first day of a month. These returns do not reflect market events. They are artifacts of how the nearby was constructed. IPE natural gas futures expire monthly. Every month, each nearby rolls over to the next contract. Because of seasonality effects, there is usually a price jump between consecutive contracts. These are incorporated into each nearby. The monthly price jumps are evident in Exhibit 6.7. They cause the large evenly spaced returns in Exhibit 6.8.

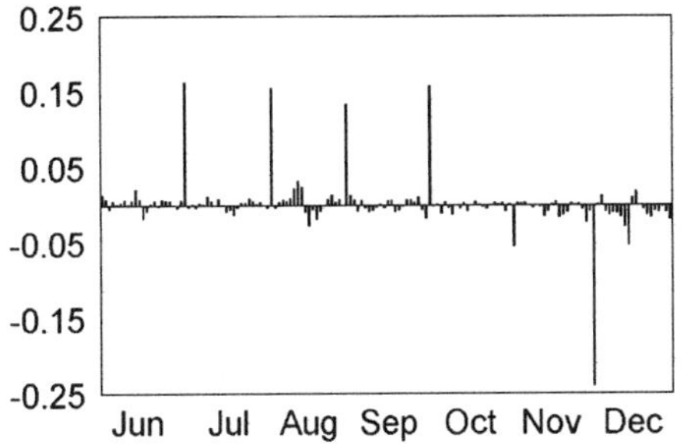

Exhibit 6.8 Daily log returns for the nearby price data of Exhibit 6.7.

Such artifacts can be addressed in various ways. One approach is to remove artifact price jumps by directly adjusting nearby prices upward or downward as needed prior to each rollover date. Prices prior to the most recent rollover date are adjusted by the price difference between the new and old contracts. Prices prior to the previous rollover date are adjusted by that amount plus the price difference between the new and old contracts for that rollover date, etc. Nearbys constructed in this manner are called **price-adjusted nearbys**. This solution eliminates artifact price jumps. However, the accumulation of price adjustments may cause older nearby prices to stray significantly from their true levels. Indeed, if we go back far enough, nearby prices may even become negative.

Alternatively, we may remove artifact returns by directly adjusting those returns that straddle a rollover date. The artifact returns arise because, when a return straddles a rollover date, it is calculated using a price from the old contract and another price from the new contract. The solution is to calculate such returns exclusively from the new contract's prices. Based upon these returns, and returns that can be calculated from the rest of the nearby's prices, we obtain a series of returns for the nearby. We then convert these into what is called a **return-adjusted nearby** by starting with the most recent futures price and applying the most recent return to obtain the previous price. Working backwards in this manner, we obtain an entire series of prices. Prior to the most recent rollover date, these may not reflect actual price levels or actual price changes. However, prices will not become negative, and historical returns will be correctly represented.

Through the judicious selection of a rollover date and the use of price-adjusted or return-adjusted nearbys, we can mitigate the most obvious distortions associated with nearbys. More subtle distortions can remain. Primarily, these will be cyclical patterns in standard deviations or correlations. If contracts expire frequently, say every month, these will be modest. With bimonthly or quarterly expirations, they may be more severe. Such distortions are not easily mitigated.

Constant-Maturity Futures Prices

As an alternative to nearbys, futures price data can be merged into continual time series as **constant-maturity** prices. A constant-maturity price series indicates, for each time t, an interpolated price reflecting a specific time-to-expiration that is constant over time.

To illustrate, let's construct monthly 60-day, 120-day, and 180-day constant-maturity prices from the CME random-length lumber futures prices of Exhibit 6.9. Data for contracts maturing between September 1998 and November 1999 are indicated. Prices are USD settlement prices for the last trading day of each month. The corresponding number of days to expiration is indicated for each contract at each time t.

Interpolation is performed with a cubic spline. Exhibit 6.10 illustrates the interpolation for the data of October 1998, which is shaded in Exhibit 6.9. Performing such an interpolation for each month yields the constant-maturity price series of Exhibit 6.11.

Constant-maturity prices are appealing because they don't exhibit some of the cyclical distortions of nearbys, but they have other limitations. One is the fact that forward contracts are typically quoted as spreads to specific "benchmark" futures contracts. This is done in oil, natural gas, coffee, cocoa, and other markets. For this reason, it is desirable to model the actual futures prices that are used as benchmarks. Converting data to a constant-maturity form is a step in the wrong direction.

Another problem is the availability of futures prices from which to interpolate constant-maturity prices. Active futures markets, such as the Eurodollar or Henry Hub natural gas markets, have numerous contracts trading simultaneously. Less active markets may offer just a handful of maturities—perhaps three, or sometimes only two. Futures curves may have irregular shapes. Supply and demand issues as well as seasonality effects cause them to rise and fall with irregular patterns. Trying to interpolate constant-maturity prices based upon two or three contracts is likely to be a unsettling experience!

The most useful application of constant-maturity futures prices is as a proxy for forward prices. As long as enough futures maturities are traded to facilitate reasonable interpolation, and there is no significant convexity bias, such use may be reasonable. For most purposes, nearbys are a better alternative.

Exercises

6.1 Use the data of Exhibit 6.9 to construct first and second nearbys for random-length lumber. Use last reported trade dates as rollover dates. Perform the calculations twice:

a. Calculate price-adjusted nearbys.
b. Calculate return-adjusted nearbys.

Time (month)	Contract (indicated by month of expiration)													
	Sep-98		Nov-98		Jan-99		Mar-99		May-99		Jul-99		Sep-99	
	days	price	days	price	days	price	days	price	days	price	days	price	days	price
Dec-97	258	317.8												
Jan-98	228	325.8	287	320.0										
Feb-98	200	317.4	259	312.0										
Mar-98	168	326.0	227	320.0	290	321.7								
Apr-98	138	313.0	197	312.5	260	323.0	319	333.9						
May-98	109	280.5	168	285.6	231	300.5	290	313.0						
Jun-98	77	292.9	136	294.9	199	302.2	258	307.5	318	305.1				
Jul-98	46	301.3	105	297.4	168	303.7	227	310.5	287	311.0				
Aug-98	15	287.9	74	275.9	137	284.5	196	291.5	256	300.0				
Sep-98			44	255.8	107	268.9	166	281.9	226	292.5	288	300.5		
Oct-98			14	260.7	77	270.0	136	282.0	196	286.2	258	292.7		
Nov-98					46	290.5	105	297.2	165	299.0	227	301.6		
Dec-98					15	305.6	74	309.2	134	307.0	196	307.1		
Jan-99							45	343.5	105	322.7	167	317.9	229	316.4
Feb-99							17	334.4	77	333.8	139	323.5	201	321.6
Mar-99									44	337.5	106	329.5	168	324.2
Apr-99									14	343.9	76	334.8	138	328.3
May-99											48	349.2	110	341.0
Jun-99											15	403.6	77	386.6
Jul-99													47	372.9

Exhibit 6.9 Monthly prices and days-to-expiration for random length lumber futures traded on the CME. Prices are quoted in USD and represent the last settlement price for the respective month. Source: CME.

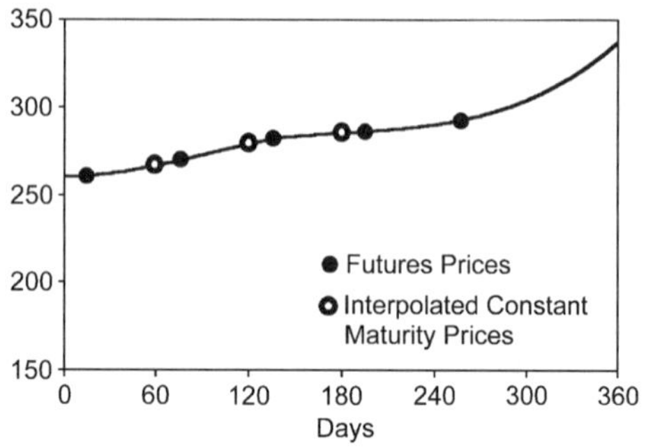

Exhibit 6.10 The interpolation of constant-maturity prices is illustrated. Random length lumber futures prices for October 1998 (shaded in Exhibit 6.9) are used to interpolate 60-day, 120-day, and 180-day constant-maturity prices. Interpolation is performed with a cubic spline.

Time	Constant-maturity Price		
(month)	60-day	120-day	180-day
Jul-98	299.05	298.28	305.25
Aug-98	276.21	281.33	289.57
Sep-98	258.85	271.82	284.62
Oct-98	266.62	279.06	285.31
Nov-98	292.83	297.90	299.33
Dec-98	309.16	307.62	306.35
Jan-99	336.11	320.49	317.77
Feb-99	335.65	326.62	320.16
Mar-99	334.99	328.19	323.20
Apr-99	336.72	330.19	323.05

Exhibit 6.11 Using the data of Exhibit 6.9, 60-day, 120-day, and 180-day constant-maturity random-length lumber prices are interpolated using cubic splines. Results are shown for July 1998 through April 1999.

6.7. IMPLIED VOLATILITIES

If a portfolio holds options, it is exposed to changes in implied volatilities. These can be modeled with key factors just like any other risk factors, but an inference procedure will require historical implied volatility data. Implied volatilities are rarely quoted directly in the market. An exception is the OTC currency options market, but in most markets, implied volatilities must be inferred from option prices.

A challenge in compiling historical data for implied volatilities is the sheer volume of data. For a single underlier, options may trade for multiple maturities and multiple strikes. Also, different implied volatilities may apply to different options structures. Put-call parity ensures close compatibility between put and call implied volatilities for a given underlier, but this is not true of other structures. Interest-rate caps and interest-rate swaptions ostensibly have the same underliers, but they are different instruments. Implied volatilities for one are remotely related to those of the other.

To provide a sense of the volume of raw data involved, consider put and call options traded on the Coffee, Sugar and Cocoa Exchange[6] (CSCE). On April 26, 2001, the exchange listed settlement prices for 536 distinct options on coffee futures, 247 options on sugar futures, and 328 options on cocoa futures. This is data generated in a single day for just three underliers! Faced with such an avalanche of data, we must find some means of organizing and synthesizing it into a form that is amenable to time-series analysis.

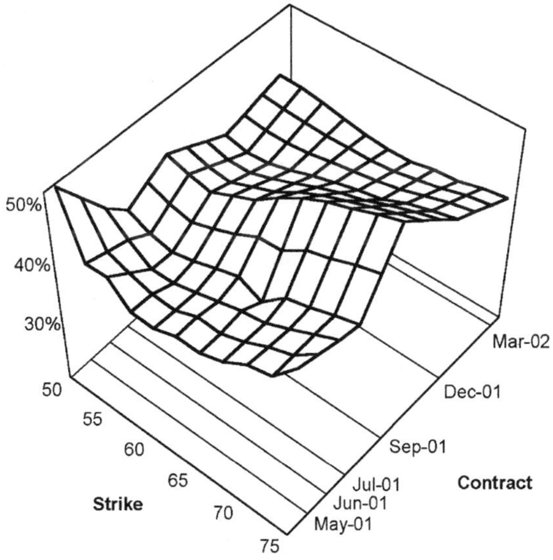

Exhibit 6.12 The implied volatility surface for CSCE coffee call options on March 12, 2001. Skew is apparent, as is a spike in volatilities for the September contract.

Implied volatilities vary by expiration. In most markets, they also vary by strike—a phenomenon that is referred to as **skew**. If data is to reflect both expiration and strike dependencies, it must comprise an entire **volatility surface** for each trading day. Such a surface is illustrated for options on coffee futures in Exhibit 6.12. A volatility surface is generally recorded as a set of implied volatilities for specific expiration-strike pairs. Below, we discuss how to choose those pairs for tracking historical implied volatility data.

[6]The CSCE is a subsidiary of the New York Board of Trade (NYBOT).

Expirations

If options are OTC, implied volatilities are generally tracked for constant-maturity expirations. For exchange-traded options, we may track implied volatilities either for constant-maturity expirations or as nearbys. Although there are exceptions, most exchange-traded options are either on equities or futures.

For exchange-traded equity options, as long as there are sufficient expirations to facilitate interpolation, it makes sense to track constant-maturity implied volatilities. This will avoid the nonstationarities and artifact returns associated with nearbys. Since equity markets exhibit no pronounced seasonalities, constant-maturity implied volatilities are generally well behaved.

For exchange-traded options on futures, it is usually best to treat options in the same manner as you do the underlying futures. If you track the futures as nearbys, track the implied volatilities as nearbys. Options on futures may expire as much as a month prior to the underlying future. Accordingly, rollover dates for implied volatility nearbys are likely to precede rollover dates for the futures. As long as a mapping procedure recognizes when an implied volatility from one nearby corresponds to the futures price of the *subsequent* nearby, this should present no problem. Another challenge is that there may be more options expirations than futures expirations. The CSCE has futures expiring on only certain months, but options on those futures expire monthly. Such issues can be addressed on a case-by-case basis through suitable construction of both nearbys and the mapping procedure.

Many of the distortions that arise with futures nearbys also arise with volatility nearbys. Analogous solutions generally apply.

Strikes

If options exhibit skew, we will want to track implied volatilities for multiple strikes. We might simply choose a few specific strikes—say GBP 40, GBP 45, and GBP 50—and track, for each expiration, implied volatilities at those strikes. Doing so raises two problems:

1. We need the strikes to bracket the current underlier price. Strikes that do so today may fail to do so in the future.
2. Because of skew, observed implied volatilities for a given strike will rise and fall as that strike moves in and out of the money.

A standard solution is to track implied volatilities for strikes corresponding to specific normalized[7] deltas. For call options, we might track implied volatilities

[7] A normalized delta is an option's delta divided by the option's notional amount. For vanilla options, normalized deltas are between –1 and 1.

for deltas of .25, .50, and .75. Over time, the corresponding strike prices will change, but the deltas will remain constant. We obtain time series for out-of-the-money, at-the-money, and in-the-money implied volatilities. Note that the .75 delta will correspond to a *lower* strike price than the .25 delta. Also, by put-call parity, call-option implied volatilities for deltas of .25, .50, and .75 should correspond to put implied volatilities for deltas of –.75, –.50, and –.25, respectively. In most markets, it is only necessary to track implied volatilities for only calls or only puts, as put-call parity will ensure close correspondence between the respective volatilities. Violations of put-call parity may occur for far in-the-money or far out-of-the money options. For options with significant time value, such violations may become apparent at call deltas of .25 and .75. A solution is to track implied volatilities for a more narrow range of deltas, say .35, .50, and .65. Corresponding put deltas would be –.65, –.50, and –.35, respectively.

6.8. FURTHER READING

See Davidson (1996) and Zangari (1996a) for issues related to sourcing of data. See Goldman Sachs and SBC Warburg Dillon Read (1998) for data issues primarily from a systems standpoint. Ma, Mercer, and Walker (1992) and Geiss (1995) discuss the construction of futures nearbys.

Chapter 7

Inference

7.1. MOTIVATION

In Section 1.8, we described three components of any VaR measure:

- an inference procedure,
- a mapping procedure, and
- a transformation procedure.

In this chapter, we discuss inference procedures. Unfortunately, the discussion will be somewhat tentative. Whereas many sophisticated techniques are available to support mapping and transformation procedures, techniques for inference procedures are less developed. Researchers are studying ways to extend traditional methods of time series analysis to the needs of VaR measures, but techniques currently used are largely ad hoc.

The purpose of an inference procedure is to characterize a distribution for key factors ${}^1\boldsymbol{R}$ conditional on information available at time 0. Although practice varies, the characterization typically takes one of three forms:

1. a fully specified conditional distribution;
2. a conditional mean ${}^{1|0}\boldsymbol{\mu}$ and conditional covariance matrix ${}^{1|0}\boldsymbol{\Sigma}$;
3. a realization $\{{}^1\boldsymbol{r}^{[1]}, {}^1\boldsymbol{r}^{[2]}, \ldots, {}^1\boldsymbol{r}^{[m]}\}$ of a sample for the conditional distribution.

In the following section, we discuss how to select key factors that will facilitate an inference procedure. We then describe current practice for constructing the first or second of the above three forms of characterizations. Next, we critique current

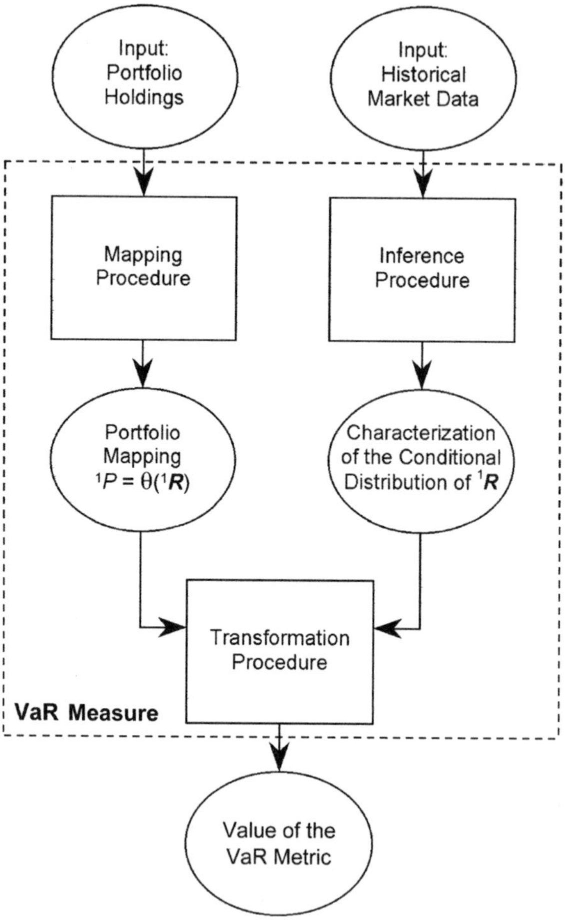

Exhibit 7.1 A reproduction of Exhibit 1.11, which is a general schematic for VaR measures. VaR measures comprise three essential components. In this chapter, we consider inference procedures.

practice, and identify avenues for further research. We close with a discussion of the third of the three forms just listed.

7.2. SELECTING KEY FACTORS

A judicious choice of the financial variables to be represented with key factors can simplify the task of designing an inference procedure.

Data Availability

We seek a key vector for which there is historical data: $\{{}^{-\alpha}\boldsymbol{r}, \ldots, {}^{-2}\boldsymbol{r}, {}^{-1}\boldsymbol{r}, {}^{0}\boldsymbol{r}\}$. We also consider the quality of data that will be available. Issues include:

- frequency and nature of data errors;
- frequency of missing data;
- synchronicity of data;
- nature of prices (transaction, firm, indicative, or settlement); and
- future availability of data.

Stationarity and Homoskedasticity

Time series modeling is facilitated if stochastic processes are covariance stationary and conditionally homoskedastic. We don't require that key factors exhibit these properties. If they don't, it is desirable that they be transformable into related risk factors that do. Given the nature of markets, conditional homoskedasticity may be unachievable.

We may reasonably insist that key factors not exhibit conditional heteroskedasticity that arises from structural causes. Two types of prices are susceptible to such structural conditional heteroskedasticity:

- prices of instruments that mature,
- prices of instruments that have optionality.

Bonds, futures, and options are examples of instruments that mature. As an instrument approaches maturity, its price behavior changes. The result is unconditional heteroskedasticity—and corresponding conditional heteroskedasticity. For example, a bond's duration declines as it approaches maturity. This causes the standard deviation of its price to diminish.[1] It also impacts the degree to which the price correlates with other financial variables. For this reason, we may model constant-maturity interest rates as key factors instead of bond prices.

Option prices experience structural conditional heteroskedasticity related to their nonlinearity. Exhibit 7.2 illustrates the price of a London Metals Exchange (LME) 3-month call option on copper as a function of the underlier price. Because of the "hockey stick" shape of the graph, we expect the option's price to fluctuate more when it is in-the-money than when it is out-of-the-money. This is confirmed empirically with historical data in Exhibit 7.3.

In Exhibit 7.3, price data is provided for copper and a (constant maturity) 3-month call option on copper struck at USD 2250 per ton. In June 1996, the price

[1] The effect is partially offset if short-term interest rates are more volatile than long-term interest rates.

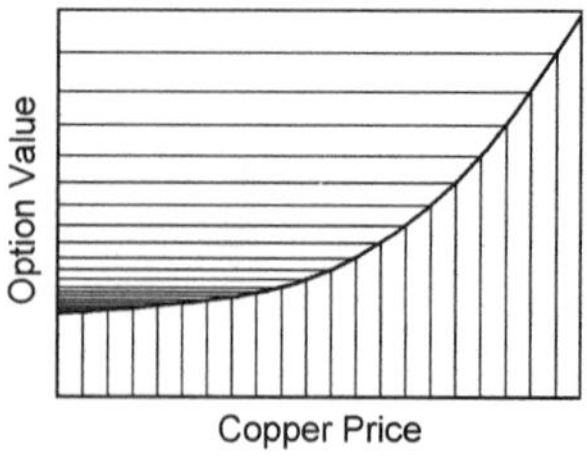

Exhibit 7.2 Price of an LME 3-month call option on copper as a function of the underlier price.

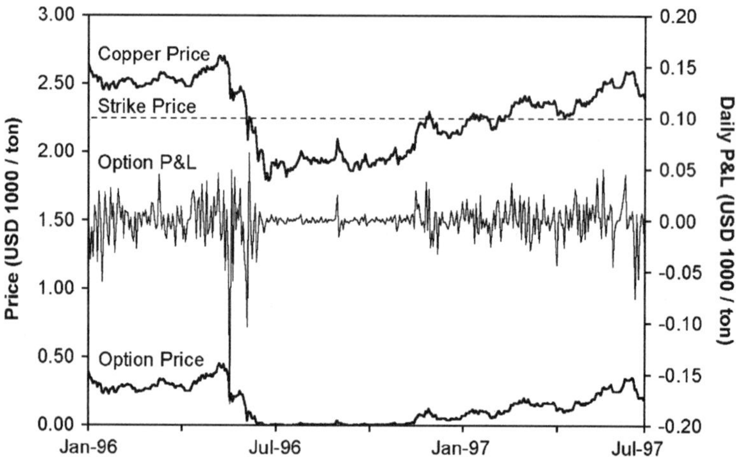

Exhibit 7.3 Price data for the LME 3-month call options on copper and the underlying copper. LME options are options on futures for 25 tons of copper. Prices are quoted in USD. Constant maturity 3-month option prices were determined using Black's (1976) pricing formula for options on futures. Historical copper prices are 3-month forward prices obtained from the LME.

of copper fell sharply. The conditional standard deviation of the option's price diminished as the price of copper fell below the strike price. This is apparent in the option's P&Ls.

Because of structural conditional heteroskedasticity, option prices are generally not modeled as key factors. If a portfolio holds options, underlier prices and implied volatilities are much better behaved as key factors.

Structural Relationships

Risk factors are more than disparate random variables. They may exhibit complex relationships that need to be captured in how we characterize their joint probability distribution. Our choice of key factors may facilitate this. Suppose a portfolio is exposed to both the 3-month US Treasury rate and 3-month USD LIBOR. We might model both as key factors, treating each as lognormally distributed. Doing so would not preclude the Treasury rate exceeding the LIBOR rate. An alternative approach that avoids a negative Treasury-Eurodollar (TED) spread is to model the Treasury rate and the TED spread as key factors. Now, if each is lognormally distributed, the TED spread cannot become negative.

Consistency over Time

We seek consistency over time in both:

- our set of key factors, and
- the definitions of those key factors.

We don't want to have to change our key factors to accommodate changes in the portfolio's composition. Accordingly, we seek a general set of key factors that can remain the same as a portfolio's composition changes.

We also prefer that definitions for key factors be as consistent as possible over time. Every data series is operationally defined by the specific operations by which it is gathered and/or calculated. Such operational procedures may change over time. The definitions of indices such as the S&P 500 or FT 100 change as specific issues are added or dropped. If a price series is constructed by averaging indicative quotes from five dealers, replacing one of the dealers with a new one represents a change in the operational definition of that risk factor.

7.3. CURRENT PRACTICE

Consider key vector ${}^{1}\boldsymbol{R}$, which is one term in a stochastic process $\boldsymbol{R}$. We have historical data $\{{}^{-\alpha}\boldsymbol{r}, \ldots, {}^{-1}\boldsymbol{r}, {}^{0}\boldsymbol{r}\}$. Assume the data is spaced at intervals of one unit of time, so the spacing of historical data equals the length of the VaR horizon.

In this section, we describe current practice for characterizing the distribution of ${}^{1}\boldsymbol{R}$ conditional on information available at time 0 where the characterization takes one of the two forms:

1. a fully specified conditional distribution;
2. a conditional mean ${}^{1|0}\boldsymbol{\mu}$ and conditional covariance matrix ${}^{1|0}\boldsymbol{\Sigma}$.

The first is used with quadratic and numerical transformation procedures. The second is used with linear transformation procedures. See Chapter 10. We discuss both forms of characterization together because constructing either entails largely the same steps.

Choice of Distribution

Various distributions are used to model key factors, including the normal, log-normal, mixed normal, and Student t distributions. By far, the most widely used assumption is that key factors are conditionally joint-normal: ${}^1\boldsymbol{R} \sim {}^0N_n({}^{1|0}\boldsymbol{\mu}, {}^{1|0}\boldsymbol{\Sigma})$. The assumption is necessary if a quadratic transformation is to be used, but it is also widely assumed with Monte Carlo transformations.

In practice, we do not attempt to empirically justify a joint-normal assumption for key factors. Empirically estimating a conditional covariance matrix ${}^{1|0}\boldsymbol{\Sigma}$ is challenging enough! Instead, we invoke standard financial models. If conditional marginal distributions of individual key factors ${}^1R_i$ can reasonably be assumed normal, we accept that ${}^1\boldsymbol{R}$ is joint-normal. In practice, this is usually reasonable.

There are various models for financial variables. These often assume that prices of primary instruments are conditionally lognormal, in which case their log returns are conditionally normal. If risk factors represent prices, interest rates, exchange rates, or implied volatilities, we might directly model them as lognormal key factors. Alternatively, we might model their log returns as conditionally normal key factors. A spread that is necessarily nonnegative (such as a credit spread) might be treated similarly. A spread that can be positive or negative (such as the price spread between two growths of coffee) might be directly modeled as a conditionally normal key factor.

Conditional Mean Vectors

The conditional mean vector ${}^{1|0}\boldsymbol{\mu}$ is specified component-by-component in a manner that depends upon what individual key factors represent. If key factor ${}^1R_i$ represents a price, interest rate, foreign exchange rate, implied volatility, or spread, it is common to assume

$${}^{1|0}\mu_i = {}^0r_i. \qquad [7.1]$$

This zero-drift assumption may be inappropriate for certain key factors, especially over longer horizons. Suppose our VaR horizon is 2 weeks and ${}^1R_i$ represents a stock price. If we assume stock prices rise on average 8% per year, then we might set

$${}^{1|0}\mu_i = \left(1 + \frac{.08}{26}\right){}^0r_i. \qquad [7.2]$$

Stocks going ex-dividend during the VaR horizon require special consideration. We may ascribe exchange rates nonzero drifts based upon interest rate parity. If prices, spreads, or implied volatilities exhibit seasonal rises and falls, this will induce short-term drifts that can also be reflected in ${}^{1|0}\mu_i$.

If key factors represent differences or returns, it is often reasonable to assume

$$ {}^{1|0}\mu_i = 0. \qquad [7.3] $$

Over longer VaR horizons, this may also be adjusted to reflect nonzero drifts, as appropriate.

In the same manner that conditional mean vector ${}^{1|0}\boldsymbol{\mu}$ is constructed, so can conditional mean vectors ${}^{t|t-1}\boldsymbol{\mu}$ be constructed for previous points in time. We use these hereafter.

White Noise

Whereas construction of conditional mean vector ${}^{1|0}\boldsymbol{\mu}$ is based largely upon financial arguments for how risk factors should evolve over time, construction of a conditional covariance matrix ${}^{1|0}\boldsymbol{\Sigma}$ relies more on empirical evidence. If we are to apply techniques of time series analysis, it is convenient to apply them to a process that we consider to be white noise. Depending upon what its components represent, $\boldsymbol{R}$ may not satisfy this criterion. Usually, we can transform $\boldsymbol{R}$ to a process $\dot{\boldsymbol{R}}$ that does. We require that the transformation comprise, at each time t, a linear polynomial

$$ {}^{t}\dot{\boldsymbol{R}} = {}^{t}\boldsymbol{b}\,{}^{t}\boldsymbol{R} + {}^{t}\boldsymbol{a}, \qquad [7.4] $$

where ${}^{t}\boldsymbol{b}$ is a diagonal $n \times n$ matrix, and ${}^{t}\boldsymbol{a}$ is a vector. Then, once we have estimated the conditional covariance matrix ${}^{1|0}\dot{\boldsymbol{\Sigma}}$ of ${}^{1}\dot{\boldsymbol{R}}$, we can obtain the conditional covariance matrix ${}^{1|0}\boldsymbol{\Sigma}$ of ${}^{1}\boldsymbol{R}$ as

$$ {}^{1|0}\boldsymbol{\Sigma} = {}^{1}\boldsymbol{b}^{-1}\,{}^{1|0}\dot{\boldsymbol{\Sigma}}\,{}^{1}\boldsymbol{b}^{-1}. \qquad [7.5] $$

We define transformation [7.4] component by component, depending upon what each component $\boldsymbol{R}_i$ of $\boldsymbol{R}$ represents. If a component $\boldsymbol{R}_i$ can already be considered white noise, then it requires no transformation. We set

$$ {}^{t}\dot{R}_i = {}^{t}R_i. \qquad [7.6] $$

If it represents a return or spread with nonzero conditional mean, it is generally reasonable to subtract the conditional mean

$$ {}^{t}\dot{R}_i = {}^{t}R_i - {}^{t|t-1}\mu_i. \qquad [7.7] $$

If a component represents a price, interest rate, exchange rate, or implied volatility, it is more often reasonable to set

$$ {}^{t}\dot{R}_i = \frac{{}^{t}R_i - {}^{t|t-1}\mu_i}{{}^{t|t-1}\mu_i}. \qquad [7.8] $$

If ${}^{t|t-1}\mu_i = {}^{0}r_i$, this is a simple return.

Having defined transformation [7.4], we apply it to data $\{^{-\alpha}\boldsymbol{r}, \ldots, {}^{-2}\boldsymbol{r}, {}^{-1}\boldsymbol{r}, {}^{0}\boldsymbol{r}\}$ to obtain data $\{^{-\dot{\alpha}}\dot{\boldsymbol{r}}, \ldots, {}^{-1}\dot{\boldsymbol{r}}, {}^{0}\dot{\boldsymbol{r}}\}$ to which we may apply methods of time series analysis. Note that $\dot{\alpha}$ may equal α or $\alpha - 1$. It will equal $\alpha - 1$ if the first data point $^{-\alpha}\boldsymbol{r}$ is used to define a conditional mean $^{-\alpha+1|-\alpha}\boldsymbol{\mu}$ for $^{-\alpha+1}\boldsymbol{R}$.

Assuming we can transform $\boldsymbol{R}$ to white noise $\dot{\boldsymbol{R}}$, then $\dot{\boldsymbol{R}}$ will be covariance stationary with (conditional and unconditional) mean $\boldsymbol{0}$. It will be unconditionally homoskedastic, with constant unconditional covariance matrix $^{t}\dot{\boldsymbol{\Sigma}}$.

Uniformly Weighted Moving Average Estimates

A standard approach for estimating $^{1|0}\dot{\boldsymbol{\Sigma}}$ is to treat the data $\{^{-\dot{\alpha}}\dot{\boldsymbol{r}}, \ldots, {}^{-1}\dot{\boldsymbol{r}}, {}^{0}\dot{\boldsymbol{r}}\}$ as a realization of a sample, and apply an estimator for a covariance matrix. For this purpose, we might use the sample estimator

$$\frac{1}{\dot{\alpha}+1}\sum_{t=-\dot{\alpha}}^{0}({}^{t}\dot{\boldsymbol{r}} - \bar{\dot{\boldsymbol{r}}})({}^{t}\dot{\boldsymbol{r}} - \bar{\dot{\boldsymbol{r}}})'. \qquad [7.9]$$

but we already know that $^{t|t-1}\dot{\boldsymbol{\mu}} = \boldsymbol{0}$ for all t, so a better estimator is

$$\frac{1}{\dot{\alpha}+1}\sum_{t=-\dot{\alpha}}^{0}({}^{t}\dot{\boldsymbol{r}} - {}^{t|t-1}\dot{\boldsymbol{\mu}})({}^{t}\dot{\boldsymbol{r}} - {}^{t|t-1}\dot{\boldsymbol{\mu}})' = \frac{1}{\dot{\alpha}+1}\sum_{t=-\dot{\alpha}}^{0}{}^{t}\dot{\boldsymbol{r}}\,{}^{t}\dot{\boldsymbol{r}}'. \qquad [7.10]$$

If $\dot{\alpha}$ is fixed from one VaR analysis to the next, $^{1|0}\dot{\boldsymbol{\Sigma}}$ will always be estimated from the same number of historical data points. We call this the **uniformly weighted moving average** (UWMA) method for estimating $^{1|0}\dot{\boldsymbol{\Sigma}}$.

Example: Aluminum Prices. Exhibit 7.4 indicates historical LME cash and forward prices for aluminum.

Date	Time	Cash	3-Month	15-Month	27-Month
12/3/01	-9	1418.0	1439.0	1480.0	1505.0
12/4/01	-8	1373.0	1392.0	1428.0	1455.0
12/5/01	-7	1358.0	1377.0	1418.0	1440.0
12/6/01	-6	1388.0	1404.0	1442.0	1462.0
12/7/01	-5	1365.0	1384.0	1420.0	1437.0
12/10/01	-4	1334.5	1353.0	1393.0	1415.0
12/11/01	-3	1335.0	1351.5	1392.0	1413.0
12/12/01	-2	1332.0	1352.0	1393.0	1415.0
12/13/01	-1	1317.5	1333.0	1378.0	1403.0
12/14/01	0	1311.0	1326.0	1375.0	1398.0

Exhibit 7.4 Historical LME prices for cash, 3-month, 15-month, and 27-month aluminum. Source: LME.

Let's estimate a conditional mean vector ${}^{1|0}\boldsymbol{\mu}$ and conditional covariance matrix ${}^{1|0}\boldsymbol{\Sigma}$ for key vector

$$
{}^{1}\boldsymbol{R} = \begin{pmatrix} {}^{1}R_1 \\ {}^{1}R_2 \\ {}^{1}R_3 \\ {}^{1}R_4 \end{pmatrix} \sim \begin{pmatrix} \text{cash aluminum price} \\ \text{3-month aluminum price} \\ \text{15-month aluminum price} \\ \text{27-month aluminum price} \end{pmatrix}. \qquad [7.11]
$$

For expositional convenience, we consider only the 10 data points of Exhibit 7.4. More data would be used in practice.

Denote the data $\{{}^{-9}\boldsymbol{r}, {}^{-8}\boldsymbol{r}, \ldots, {}^{0}\boldsymbol{r}\}$. Assume ${}^{t|t-1}\boldsymbol{\mu} = {}^{t-1}\boldsymbol{r}$ for all t, so

$$
{}^{1|0}\boldsymbol{\mu} = \begin{pmatrix} 1311 \\ 1326 \\ 1375 \\ 1398 \end{pmatrix}. \qquad [7.12]
$$

Transform ${}^{1}\boldsymbol{R}$ to white noise. Transformation [7.8] takes, for each term ${}^{t}\boldsymbol{R}$, the form of linear polynomial [7.4], where

$$
{}^{t}\boldsymbol{b} = \begin{pmatrix} \dfrac{1}{{}^{t-1}r_1} & 0 & \cdots & 0 \\ 0 & \dfrac{1}{{}^{t-1}r_2} & & 0 \\ \vdots & & \ddots & \vdots \\ 0 & 0 & \cdots & \dfrac{1}{{}^{t-1}r_n} \end{pmatrix}, \qquad [7.13]
$$

and

$$
{}^{t}\boldsymbol{a} = \begin{pmatrix} -\dfrac{{}^{t}\mu_1}{{}^{t-1}r_1} \\ -\dfrac{{}^{t}\mu_2}{{}^{t-1}r_2} \\ \vdots \\ -\dfrac{{}^{t}\mu_n}{{}^{t-1}r_n} \end{pmatrix} = \begin{pmatrix} -1 \\ -1 \\ \vdots \\ -1 \end{pmatrix}. \qquad [7.14]
$$

Applying the transformation to the data of Exhibit 7.4, we obtain white noise data $\{{}^{-8}\dot{\boldsymbol{r}}, \ldots, {}^{-1}\dot{\boldsymbol{r}}, {}^{0}\dot{\boldsymbol{r}}\}$, which is indicated in Exhibit 7.5.

Date	Time	Cash	3-Month	15-Month	27-Month
12/3/01	-9	–	–	–	–
12/4/01	-8	-0.0317	-0.0327	-0.0351	-0.0332
12/5/01	-7	-0.0109	-0.0108	-0.0070	-0.0103
12/6/01	-6	0.0221	0.0196	0.0169	0.0153
12/7/01	-5	-0.0166	-0.0142	-0.0153	-0.0171
12/10/01	-4	-0.0223	-0.0224	-0.0190	-0.0153
12/11/01	-3	0.0004	-0.0011	-0.0007	-0.0014
12/12/01	-2	-0.0022	0.0004	0.0007	0.0014
12/13/01	-1	-0.0109	-0.0141	-0.0108	-0.0085
12/14/01	0	-0.0049	-0.0053	-0.0022	-0.0036

Exhibit 7.5 White noise data calculated from the data of Exhibit 7.4.

Estimator [7.10] becomes

$$\frac{1}{9}\sum_{t=-8}^{0} {}^{t}\dot{\boldsymbol{r}}\,{}^{t}\dot{\boldsymbol{r}}'. \qquad [7.15]$$

Applying this to our white noise data, we estimate ${}^{1|0}\dot{\boldsymbol{\Sigma}}$ as

$$\begin{pmatrix} .0002818 & .0002780 & .0002632 & .0002485 \\ .0002780 & .0002776 & .0002624 & .0002469 \\ .0002632 & .0002624 & .0002540 & .0002390 \\ .0002485 & .0002469 & .0002390 & .0002288 \end{pmatrix}. \qquad [7.16]$$

Applying [7.5], we estimate ${}^{1|0}\boldsymbol{\Sigma}$ as

$$\begin{pmatrix} 484.4 & 483.2 & 474.5 & 455.4 \\ 483.2 & 488.1 & 478.5 & 457.7 \\ 474.5 & 478.5 & 480.2 & 459.4 \\ 455.4 & 457.7 & 459.4 & 447.1 \end{pmatrix}. \qquad [7.17]$$

Assumptions

Our description of the UWMA method for estimating ${}^{1|0}\boldsymbol{\Sigma}$ is operational. It describes how ${}^{1|0}\boldsymbol{\Sigma}$ is estimated without justifying the methodology in terms of a formal time series model. This is because the methodology is ad hoc. It is described by many authors and is widely used, but it has never been formalized.

A reasonable interpretation of the method is that it treats the white noise time series $\{{}^{-\alpha}\dot{\boldsymbol{r}}, \ldots, {}^{-1}\dot{\boldsymbol{r}}, {}^{0}\dot{\boldsymbol{r}}\}$ as a realization $\{{}^{1}\dot{\boldsymbol{r}}^{[1]}, \ldots, {}^{1}\dot{\boldsymbol{r}}^{[\alpha]}, {}^{1}\dot{\boldsymbol{r}}^{[\alpha+1]}\}$ of a sample $\{{}^{1}\dot{\boldsymbol{R}}^{[1]}, \ldots, {}^{1}\dot{\boldsymbol{R}}^{[\alpha]}, {}^{1}\dot{\boldsymbol{R}}^{[\alpha+1]}\}$ for the unconditional distribution of ${}^{1}\dot{\boldsymbol{R}}$. Estimator [7.10] is applied to the realization to estimate the unconditional covariance matrix ${}^{1}\dot{\boldsymbol{\Sigma}}$. This is used as a proxy for the conditional covariance matrix ${}^{1|0}\dot{\boldsymbol{\Sigma}}$.

In order for $\{{}^1\dot{\boldsymbol{R}}^{[1]}, \ldots, {}^1\dot{\boldsymbol{R}}^{[\dot{\alpha}]}, {}^1\dot{\boldsymbol{R}}^{[\dot{\alpha}+1]}\}$ to be a sample, terms ${}^t\dot{\boldsymbol{R}}$ must be unconditionally IID. In addition, using ${}^1\dot{\boldsymbol{\Sigma}}$ as a proxy for ${}^{1|0}\dot{\boldsymbol{\Sigma}}$ assumes that ${}^1\dot{\boldsymbol{\Sigma}} = {}^{1|0}\dot{\boldsymbol{\Sigma}}$. Accordingly, UWMA seems to entail three assumptions:

- terms ${}^t\dot{\boldsymbol{R}}$ are unconditionally identically distributed;
- terms ${}^t\dot{\boldsymbol{R}}$ are independently distributed;
- ${}^1\dot{\boldsymbol{\Sigma}} = {}^{1|0}\dot{\boldsymbol{\Sigma}}$.

Because $\dot{\boldsymbol{R}}$ is white noise, all terms ${}^t\dot{\boldsymbol{R}}$ have identical unconditional means and covariance matrices. It does not necessarily follow that they are unconditionally identically distributed; but it is reasonable to assume that they are.

The fact that $\dot{\boldsymbol{R}}$ is white noise does not ensure that terms ${}^t\dot{\boldsymbol{R}}$ are independent. Indeed, they likely are not. This is not a serious problem. As white noise, $\dot{\boldsymbol{R}}$ is assumed to have no autocorrelations or cross correlations. What dependencies may exist between terms ${}^t\dot{\boldsymbol{R}}$ are unlikely to seriously effect our estimate of the unconditional covariance matrix ${}^1\dot{\boldsymbol{\Sigma}}$.

Finally, while it is always possible that ${}^1\dot{\boldsymbol{\Sigma}} = {}^{1|0}\dot{\boldsymbol{\Sigma}}$ by coincidence, in order for it to be generally true, we require that ${}^t\dot{\boldsymbol{\Sigma}} = {}^{t|t-1}\dot{\boldsymbol{\Sigma}}$ for all t. Since $\dot{\boldsymbol{R}}$ is white noise, it is unconditionally homoskedastic, so ${}^t\dot{\boldsymbol{\Sigma}}$ is constant. Consequently, the condition ${}^t\dot{\boldsymbol{\Sigma}} = {}^{t|t-1}\dot{\boldsymbol{\Sigma}}$ requires that ${}^{t|t-1}\dot{\boldsymbol{\Sigma}}$ be constant. In other words, it requires that $\dot{\boldsymbol{R}}$ be conditionally homoskedastic. Most markets exhibit conditional heteroskedasticity, so this is unreasonable.

Consider Exhibit 7.6 indicating daily simple returns for the SGD/USD exchange rate during 1997. The returns exhibit conditional heteroskedasticity.

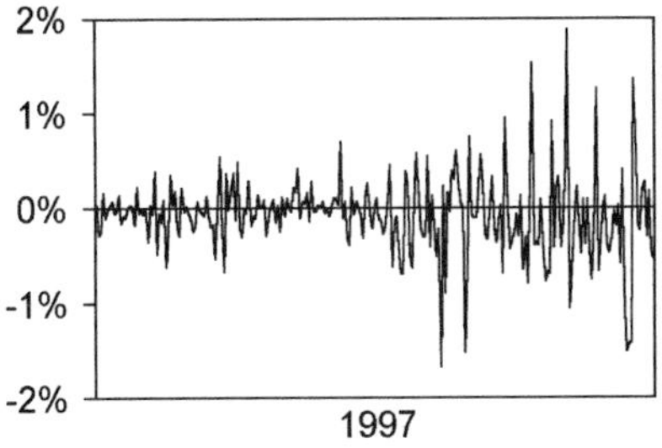

Exhibit 7.6 Daily simple returns for the SGD/USD exchange rate during 1997.

The second half of 1997 ushered in a period of turmoil for Asian markets, which came to be known as the Asian flu. This is evidenced in Exhibit 7.6 by an increase in the volatility of the SGD/USD exchange rate, commencing around July of that year.

Suppose today is January 1, 1998, and a US investor holds a USD 10MM spot position in the SGD. We want to calculate its 1-day 95% USD VaR. For this we need an estimate of the conditional standard deviation ${}^{1|0}\sigma_1$ of the SGD/USD exchange rate. We can calculate this using UWMA, but how much data should we use? If we use an entire year of daily return data, we obtain an estimate for ${}^{1|0}\sigma_1$

of .0043. If we use only the most recent 3 months of data, we obtain an estimate of .0066. These correspond to position VaRs of USD 71,000 and USD 109,000, respectively. A decision as to how much historical data to use with UWMA has a significant impact on the VaR result we obtain.

Exponentially Weighted Moving Average Estimates

To reconcile the assumptions of UWMA with the realities of market heteroskedasticity, we might apply estimator [7.10] to only the most recent historical data ${}^{t}\boldsymbol{q}$, which should be most reflective of current market conditions. Doing so is self-defeating, as applying estimator [7.10] to a small amount of data will maximize its standard error. Consequently, UWMA entails a quandary: applying it to a lot of data is bad, but so is applying it to a little data.

This motivated Zangari (1994) to propose a modification of UWMA called the **exponentially weighted moving average** (EWMA) method.[2] This applies a nonuniform weighting to data $\{{}^{-\dot{\alpha}}\dot{\boldsymbol{r}}, \ldots, {}^{-1}\dot{\boldsymbol{r}}, {}^{0}\dot{\boldsymbol{r}}\}$ so that a lot of data can be used, but recent data is weighted most heavily. As the name suggests, weights are based upon the exponential function. EWMA replaces estimator [7.10] with

$$(1-\lambda)\sum_{t=-\dot{\alpha}}^{0} \lambda^{-t}\, {}^{t}\dot{\boldsymbol{r}}\, {}^{t}\dot{\boldsymbol{r}}' \qquad [7.18]$$

where **decay factor** λ is generally assigned a value between .95 and .99. Lower decay factors tend to weight recent data more heavily. Note that

$$\lim_{\dot{\alpha}\to\infty} (1-\lambda)\sum_{t=-\dot{\alpha}}^{0} \lambda^{-t} = 1, \qquad [7.19]$$

but the weights do not sum to 1 for finite $\dot{\alpha}$. To remedy this, we may modify estimator [7.18] as

$$\frac{1-\lambda}{1-\lambda^{\dot{\alpha}+1}}\sum_{t=-\dot{\alpha}}^{0} \lambda^{-t}\, {}^{t}\dot{\boldsymbol{r}}\, {}^{t}\dot{\boldsymbol{r}}'. \qquad [7.20]$$

EWMA is widely used, but it is a modest improvement over UWMA. It does not attempt to model market conditional heteroskedasticity any more than UWMA does. Its weighting scheme replaces the quandary of how much data to use with a similar quandary as to how aggressive a decay factor λ to use.

Consider again Exhibit 7.6 and our example of the USD 10MM position in SGD. Let's estimate ${}^{1|0}\sigma_1$ using EWMA estimator [7.20]. If we use $\lambda = .99$, we obtain an estimate for ${}^{1|0}\sigma_1$ of .0054. If we use $\lambda = .95$, we obtain an estimate of .0067. These correspond to position VaRs of USD 89,000 and USD 110,000, respectively.

---

[2]EWMA had been used in time series analysis for some time. Zangari's contribution is to propose its use in VaR analyses.

Covariance Matrices That Are Not Positive Definite

Estimated either by UWMA or EWMA, the matrix ${}^{1|0}\boldsymbol{\Sigma}$ may fail to be positive definite. This typically occurs for one of two reasons:

1. If ${}^{1}\boldsymbol{R}$ has high dimensionality n, it is likely to be multicollinear. Roundoff error in applying UWMA or EWMA can cause the estimated matrix ${}^{1|0}\boldsymbol{\Sigma}$ to have one or more eigenvalues that are zero or slightly negative.
2. If $\dot{\alpha} + 1 < n$, any of estimators [7.10], [7.18], or [7.20] will produce a singular positive semidefinite matrix ${}^{1|0}\boldsymbol{\Sigma}$, assuming exact calculations. Roundoff error may cause the matrix to have one or more eigenvalues that are slightly negative.

We discuss covariance matrices that are not positive definite in Section 3.6. The Cholesky algorithm fails with such matrices, so they pose a serious problem. There are two ways we might modify such matrices to make them positive definite.

Principal component remappings can be used to replace estimated covariance matrices that are not positive definite with lower-dimensional covariance matrices that are. See Section 9.5.

Alternatively, ${}^{1|0}\boldsymbol{\Sigma}$ may be replaced with:

$$ {}^{1|0}\boldsymbol{\Sigma} + \varepsilon \boldsymbol{I}, \qquad [7.21] $$

where $\boldsymbol{I}$ is the identity matrix and $\varepsilon > 0$ is small. Generally, ε can be selected small enough to have no material effect on calculated VaR but large enough to make covariance matrix [7.21] positive definite.

Exercises

7.1 Reproduce the calculations of our aluminum example. Confirm that you obtain the same results.

7.2 Exhibit 7.7 indicates 30 days of data for 1-month CHF Libor. Let $\boldsymbol{R}_1$ be a stochastic process representing daily values of 1-month CHF Libor. Assume terms ${}^{t}R_1$ have conditional mean ${}^{t|t-1}\mu_1 = {}^{t-1}r_1$. Define white noise $\dot{\boldsymbol{R}}_1$ with [7.4].

a. Apply [7.8] to calculate historical data for $\dot{\boldsymbol{R}}_1$ from the data of Exhibit 7.7.
b. Apply UWMA to estimate ${}^{1|0}\dot{\sigma}_1$ and ${}^{1|0}\sigma_1$. Use all available data.
c. Apply UWMA to estimate ${}^{1|0}\dot{\sigma}_1$ and ${}^{1|0}\sigma_1$, but use sample estimator [7.9] in place of estimator [7.10]. Use all available data.
d. Apply EWMA to estimate ${}^{1|0}\dot{\sigma}_1$ and ${}^{1|0}\sigma_1$. Let $\lambda = .95$. Use [7.20] and all available data.
e. Compare your results from parts (b), (c), and (d).

Date	Rate	Date	Rate	Date	Rate
11/28/01	2.130	12/12/01	1.962	12/28/01	1.790
11/29/01	2.137	12/13/01	1.953	12/31/01	1.788
11/30/01	2.103	12/14/01	1.953	1/2/02	1.780
12/3/01	2.067	12/17/01	1.922	1/3/02	1.773
12/4/01	2.057	12/18/01	1.927	1/4/02	1.783
12/5/01	2.010	12/19/01	1.927	1/7/02	1.780
12/6/01	2.028	12/20/01	1.927	1/8/02	1.703
12/7/01	1.922	12/21/01	1.895	1/9/02	1.647
12/10/01	1.922	12/24/01	1.848	1/10/02	1.693
12/11/01	1.937	12/27/01	1.800	1/11/02	1.673

Exhibit 7.7 Data for 1-month CHF Libor. Rates are expressed as percentages. Source: British Bankers' Association (BBA).

7.3 Consider the covariance matrix

$$\begin{pmatrix} 0.99 & 0.78 & 0.59 & 0.44 \\ 0.78 & 0.92 & 0.28 & 0.81 \\ 0.59 & 0.28 & 1.12 & 0.23 \\ 0.44 & 0.81 & 0.23 & 0.99 \end{pmatrix}, \qquad [7.22]$$

which has one slightly negative eigenvalue. Select a value ε and apply [7.21] to construct a positive definite approximation for the matrix.

7.4. UNCONDITIONAL LEPTOKURTOSIS AND CONDITIONAL HETEROSKEDASTICITY

Exhibit 7.8 indicates a histogram of daily log returns for the Toronto Stock Exchange TSE-100 Total Return Index during the 5-year period 1995 through 1999:

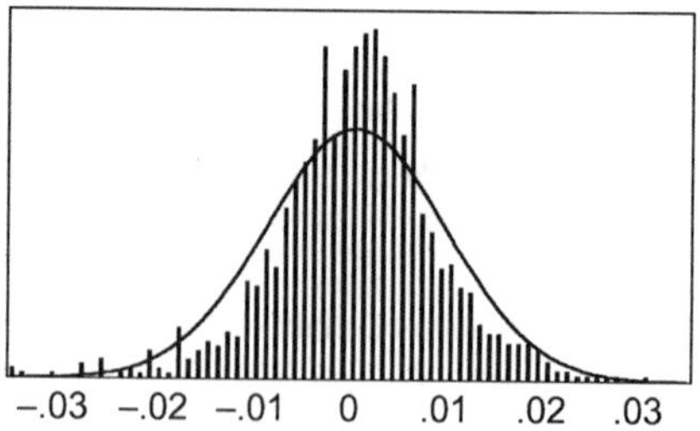

Exhibit 7.8 Histogram of daily log returns for the Toronto Stock Exchange TSE-100 Total Return Index during the 5-year period 1995 through 1999. A normal distribution has been fit to the data based upon its sample mean and sample standard deviation. Of 1259 data points, 8 in the left tail and 3 in the right tail are not displayed because they fall outside the range [–.035, .035].

A normal distribution has been fit to the data based upon the data's sample mean and sample standard deviation. Comparing the normal curve and the histogram in Exhibit 7.8, we see that the histogram is leptokurtic. Exhibit 7.9 compares the mean, standard deviation, skewness, and kurtosis of the normal curve and histogram.

	Normal Distribution	Histogram
Mean	0.0006	0.0006
Standard Deviation	0.0092	0.0092
Skewness	0.0000	-0.8278
Kurtosis	3.0000	9.4570

Exhibit 7.9 Parameters of the normal distribution of Exhibit 7.8 are compared with sample parameters of the histogram of returns from the same exhibit. The histogram of returns is highly leptokurtic.

This is not an isolated result. Histograms of log returns for financial assets often exhibit leptokurtosis. For commodities or energy products, such leptokurtosis is often extreme. It has prompted some authors to propose that log returns be modeled with leptokurtic distributions. For example, Wilson (1993) proposes that key factors for VaR measures be modeled with Student t distributions.

Replacing normal distributions with leptokurtic distributions complicates VaR measures. Furthermore, both theory and empirical evidence suggest that it is not necessary to do so. For measuring VaR, we are interested in modeling the conditional distributions of key factors, but histograms such as Exhibit 7.8 are more descriptive of unconditional distributions.[3] Is it possible for a stochastic process to have leptokurtic unconditional distributions but non-leptokurtic conditional distributions? Certainly; this is a common phenomenon with conditionally heteroskedastic processes.

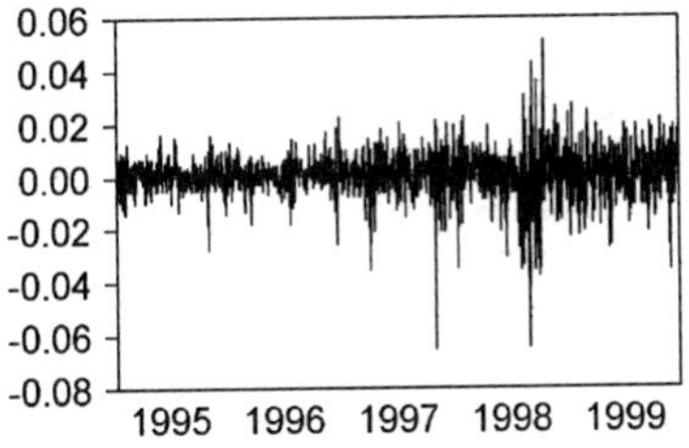

Exhibit 7.10 The same returns as in Exhibit 7.8 are presented chronologically as a time series. The returns exhibit conditional heteroskedasticity.

Soon, we describe how conditional heteroskedasticity can manifest itself as unconditional leptokurtosis. Before we do so, let's take a different look at the TSE-100 returns of Exhibit 7.8. In Exhibit 7.10, we graph them chronologically as a time series. They exhibit conditional heteroskedasticity.

[3] A histogram of a time series can be treated as a realization of a sample from the unconditional distribution of the underlying stochastic process if the process is strictly stationary.

An Experiment

Let's conduct an experiment. I will do it here, but I would like you to reproduce the same work on your own computer. Generate a time series of 1500 pseudorandom variates. Let the first 500 be $N(0,25)$. Let the next 500 be $N(0,9)$. Let the last 500 be $N(0,1)$. Graph your time series. Exhibit 7.11 shows my graph.

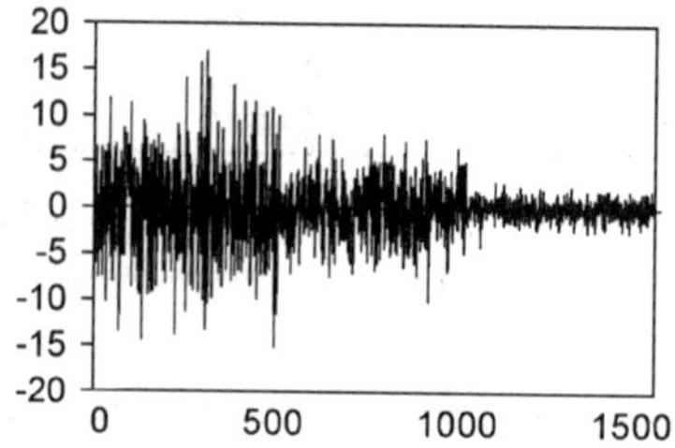

Exhibit 7.11 A time series constructed from 1500 pseudorandom variates. The first 500 are $N(0, 25)$. The next 500 are $N(0, 9)$. The last 500 are $N(0, 1)$.

Now calculate the sample mean, standard deviation, skewness, and kurtosis of the first 500 values of your time series. Do so for the second 500 values and the third 500 values. Finally, calculate the same parameters for the entire time series. My results are indicated in Exhibit 7.12.

	First 500	Second 500	Third 500	All 1500
Mean	0.02	0.04	0.09	0.05
Standard Deviation	5.01	2.94	0.99	3.40
Skewness	0.02	-0.11	-0.17	-0.02
Kurtosis	3.27	2.97	3.21	5.70

Exhibit 7.12 Sample parameters for sections of the time series as well as for the entire time series. Sample parameters for the sections are consistent with normal distributions. Sample parameters for the entire time series are not. In particular, the entire time series exhibits kurtosis that is almost twice that of a normal distribution.

A normal distribution has a kurtosis of 3. The first, second, and third sections of my time series each have sample kurtoses consistent with a normal distribution. The overall time series does not. This is illustrated in Exhibit 7.13 with a histogram of all the time series' 1500 values.

Each value in the time series was generated from a normal distribution, but the histogram of all values is distinctly non-normal. The sample leptokurtosis of the overall time series arises much as it can with a mixed-normal distribution, as discussed in Section 3.10.

This experiment is a warning for us. Conditional heteroskedasticity can manifest itself as unconditional leptokurtosis. Just because a histogram of time series

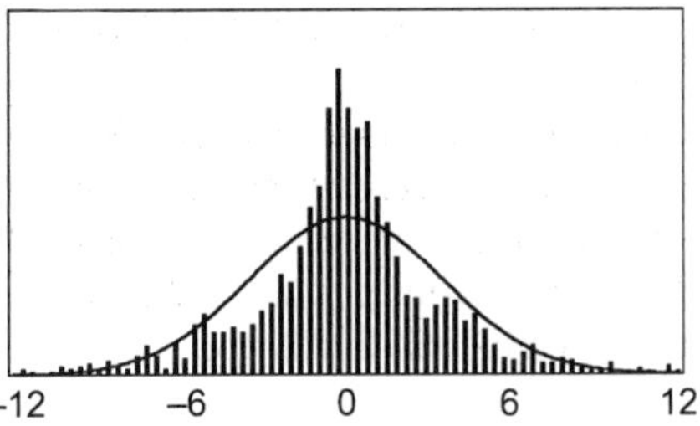

Exhibit 7.13 Histogram of time series values from the experiment. A normal distribution has been fit to the data based upon its sample mean and sample standard deviation. Of 1500 data points, 5 in the left tail and 5 in the right tail are not displayed because they fall outside the range [−12, 12].

values is leptokurtic does not mean that those values were drawn from leptokurtic conditional distributions. In the context of VaR, if a histogram of historical data for a key factor is leptokurtic, this does not mean that the key factor needs to be modeled with a conditionally leptokurtic distribution.

Modeling Unconditional Leptokurtosis

It is important to distinguish between markets and models for those markets. Markets generate data. There are various models we might fit to that data. Consider again Exhibit 7.8, which indicates a leptokurtic histogram of total returns for the TSE-100. Of the many models we might fit to that data, let's explore two competing white noise models:

1. Returns are conditionally homoskedastic and are drawn from a fixed conditional distribution that is leptokurtic. A Student t distribution might be used for this purpose.
2. Returns are conditionally heteroskedastic and are drawn from conditional distributions that are normal. A GARCH model might be used for this purpose.

Both models could produce the leptokurtic histogram of Exhibit 7.8. The first would do so directly with a conditional distribution that is leptokurtic. The second would do so indirectly with conditional heteroskedasticity. Both approaches are studied in the financial literature.

There is a characteristic of financial time series that makes us favor the second model over the first. This is **volatility clustering**. For the most part, extreme market moves do not occur in isolation. They cluster. Markets experience periods of turmoil and periods of tranquility. Our first model cannot reproduce this behavior. It will produce consecutive extreme market moves only by coincidence. The second model easily reproduces volatility clustering. Indeed, GARCH models are designed specifically for this purpose.

We have many options in how we model markets. We don't have to choose between a conditionally leptokurtic model and one that is conditionally heteroskedastic. Both of these properties might be combined in a single model. A regime-switching model might be implemented with conditional heteroskedasticity and leptokurtic mixed-normal conditional distributions.

Implications for VaR Measures

In Chapter 4, we discussed multivariate GARCH and multivariate regime-switching processes that can be used to model conditional heteroskedasticity. These are actively being researched, but cannot yet be recommended for production VaR measures. Some versions of these, such as orthogonal GARCH, have known shortcomings. Others hold promise, but require further study before they can be recommended.

Despite their shortcomings, the UWMA and EWMA methods are simple and reliable. They can be trusted to produce covariance matrices that, although imperfect, are reasonable. These are the standard methods used today.

This conclusion is necessarily tentative. We have described in detail the challenges of modeling financial markets. Yet, available solutions fall short of the needs we have identified. Still, our discussion is useful. If we find ourselves using a VaR measure that employs UWMA or EWMA, it is important to know the limitations of those methods. Also, our discussion may spur further research into alternative modeling techniques.

Exercises

7.4 If you have not already done so, perform the experiment described in this section.

7.5. HISTORICAL REALIZATIONS

We close by describing a technique that was popular during the mid-1990s, but is falling out of use today. In Chapter 1, we described Monte Carlo transformations. We will describe them again in more detail in Chapter 10. These apply the Monte Carlo method to a realization $\{{}^1\boldsymbol{r}^{[1]}, {}^1\boldsymbol{r}^{[2]}, \ldots, {}^1\boldsymbol{r}^{[m]}\}$ of a sample $\{{}^1\boldsymbol{R}^{[1]}, {}^1\boldsymbol{R}^{[2]}, \ldots, {}^1\boldsymbol{R}^{[m]}\}$ for ${}^1\boldsymbol{R}$ in order to value a given VaR metric. The realization is usually constructed using standard techniques of pseudorandom vector generation, but it does not have to be.

In this section, we describe how the realization can be constructed directly from historical data $\{{}^{-\alpha}\boldsymbol{r}, \ldots, {}^{-2}\boldsymbol{r}, {}^{-1}\boldsymbol{r}, {}^{0}\boldsymbol{r}\}$. With this approach, the inference procedure takes on a new character. Rather than employing techniques of time series analysis to construct a conditional covariance matrix, it works directly with historical data to convert it to a realization. Whereas most inference procedures characterize the distribution of ${}^{1}\boldsymbol{R}$ with parameters, these historical inference procedures characterize it with that realization.

If we feel it is reasonable to treat $\boldsymbol{R}$ as white noise, historical values ${}^{t}\boldsymbol{r}$ for ${}^{1}\boldsymbol{R}$ can be directly used as values ${}^{1}\boldsymbol{r}^{[k]}$ of the "historical" realization. Let $m = \alpha + 1$, and set

$$ {}^{1}\boldsymbol{r}^{[k]} = {}^{1-k}\boldsymbol{r} \tag{7.23} $$

for all k.

If we feel that it is unreasonable to treat $\boldsymbol{R}$ as white noise, historical values ${}^{t}\boldsymbol{r}$ of $\boldsymbol{R}$ cannot be directly used as elements ${}^{1}\boldsymbol{r}^{[k]}$ of the realization. The historical values are likely to be inconsistent with current market conditions. Suppose a key factor ${}^{1}R_i$ represents a stock price whose current value ${}^{0}r_i$ is EUR 120. If most of our historical data for the stock is from a period when it was trading near EUR 70, we would not want to directly construct a realization $\{{}^{1}r_i^{[1]}, {}^{1}r_i^{[2]}, \ldots, {}^{1}r_i^{[m]}\}$ from that data. The realization is supposed to reflect current market conditions, so its values need to cluster about EUR 120, not EUR 70!

In this circumstance, we employ the white noise transformation $\dot{\boldsymbol{R}}$ of $\boldsymbol{R}$, which we introduced in Section 7.3. This is defined for each term ${}^{t}\boldsymbol{R}$ of $\boldsymbol{R}$ with a linear polynomial:

$$ {}^{t}\dot{\boldsymbol{R}} = {}^{t}\boldsymbol{b}\,{}^{t}\boldsymbol{R} + {}^{t}\boldsymbol{a}. \tag{7.24} $$

We construct the "historical" realization in two steps. First, we convert historical data $\{{}^{-\alpha}\boldsymbol{r}, \ldots, {}^{-2}\boldsymbol{r}, {}^{-1}\boldsymbol{r}, {}^{0}\boldsymbol{r}\}$ for $\boldsymbol{R}$ into corresponding historical data for $\dot{\boldsymbol{R}}$:

$$ {}^{t}\dot{\boldsymbol{r}} = {}^{t}\boldsymbol{b}\,{}^{t}\boldsymbol{r} + {}^{t}\boldsymbol{a}. \tag{7.25} $$

Next, we apply to this data the inverse of transformation [7.24] for time 1,

$$ {}^{1}\boldsymbol{r}^{[k]} = {}^{1}\boldsymbol{b}^{-1}({}^{1-k}\dot{\boldsymbol{r}} - {}^{1}\boldsymbol{a}), \tag{7.26} $$

to obtain the desired historical realization $\{{}^{1}\boldsymbol{r}^{[1]}, {}^{1}\boldsymbol{r}^{[2]}, \ldots, {}^{1}\boldsymbol{r}^{[m]}\}$, where $m = \dot{\alpha} + 1$.

By composing the two steps, we can combine them into a single step:

$$ {}^{1}\boldsymbol{r}^{[k]} = {}^{1}\boldsymbol{b}^{-1}({}^{1-k}\boldsymbol{b}\,{}^{1-k}\boldsymbol{r} + {}^{1-k}\boldsymbol{a} - {}^{1}\boldsymbol{a}). \tag{7.27} $$

EXAMPLE. Today is January 11, 2002. Let $\boldsymbol{R}_1$ represent the value of 3-month CHF Libor. Exhibit 7.7 indicates 30 days of data, which you used for Exercise 7.2. Let's use the data to construct an historical realization of a sample for ${}^{1}R_1$.

It would be unreasonable to treat $\boldsymbol{R}_1$ as white noise. Its unconditional mean is not 0. Assume ${}^{t|t-1}\mu_1 = {}^{t-1}r_1$ for all t, and transform $\boldsymbol{R}_1$ to white noise $\dot{\boldsymbol{R}}_1$ with

$$
{}^{t}\dot{R}_1 = \frac{{}^{t}R_1 - {}^{t|t-1}\mu_1}{{}^{t|t-1}\mu_1}. \qquad [7.28]
$$

Applying the transformation to the data of Exhibit 7.7, we obtain the white noise data shown in Exhibit 7.14. We apply the inverse transform for time 1,

$$
{}^{1}r_1^{[k]} = {}^{1|0}\mu_1\left(1 + {}^{1-k}\dot{r}_1\right), \qquad [7.29]
$$

to obtain the historical realization indicated in Exhibit 7.15. A histogram of the historical realization is indicated in Exhibit 7.16.

t	${}^{t}\dot{r}_1$	t	${}^{t}\dot{r}_1$	t	${}^{t}\dot{r}_1$
-29	-	-19	0.0129	-9	-0.0056
-28	0.0033	-18	-0.0046	-8	-0.0011
-27	-0.0159	-17	0.0000	-7	-0.0045
-26	-0.0171	-16	-0.0159	-6	-0.0039
-25	-0.0048	-15	0.0026	-5	0.0056
-24	-0.0228	-14	0.0000	-4	-0.0017
-23	0.0090	-13	0.0000	-3	-0.0433
-22	-0.0523	-12	-0.0166	-2	-0.0329
-21	0.0000	-11	-0.0248	-1	0.0279
-20	0.0078	-10	-0.0260	0	-0.0118

Exhibit 7.14 White noise data calculated from the data of Exhibit 7.7 with transformation [7.28].

j	${}^{1}r_1^{[j]}$	j	${}^{1}r_1^{[j]}$	j	${}^{1}r_1^{[j]}$
30	-	20	1.695	10	1.664
29	1.678	19	1.665	9	1.671
28	1.646	18	1.673	8	1.666
27	1.644	17	1.646	7	1.666
26	1.665	16	1.677	6	1.682
25	1.635	15	1.673	5	1.670
24	1.688	14	1.673	4	1.601
23	1.586	13	1.645	3	1.618
22	1.673	12	1.632	2	1.720
21	1.686	11	1.630	1	1.653

Exhibit 7.15 Historical realization of a sample ${}^{1}R_1$. Interest rates are expressed as percentages.

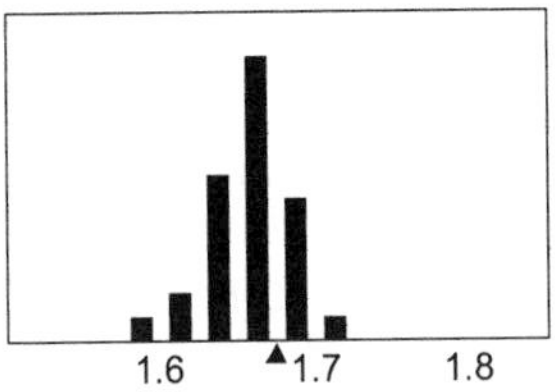

Exhibit 7.16 Histogram of the historical realization. The current CHF Libor rate of 1.673% is indicated in the exhibit with a black triangle.

Mirror Values

Histogram 7.16 highlights a problem. In the example, we assumed that the expected value of ${}^1R_1$ equals the current value ${}^0r_1$, which is 1.673%. However, this is not the sample mean of the historical realization. In the histogram, most values fall to the left of 1.673%. This results from the fact that the historical data from which we derived the realization was drawn from a period during which CHF Libor fell. It started the period at 2.130% and ended the period at the current value of 1.673%. On an average day during that period, Libor fell, and this is reflected in our historical realization.

A solution to this problem is to use "mirror" values in the historical realization. For each value ${}^1r_1^{[k]}$ of the realization, add another value:

$$2\,{}^{1|0}\mu_1 - {}^1r_1^{[k]}. \qquad [7.30]$$

This doubles the size of the realization and ensures that it has sample mean ${}^{1|0}\mu_1$. The solution assumes that the conditional distribution of ${}^1R_1$ is symmetric.

We add mirror values to the historical realization of our example. A histogram of the new realization is indicated in Exhibit 7.17.

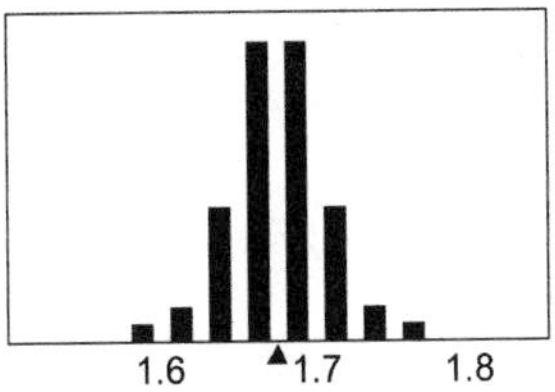

Exhibit 7.17 Histogram of the new historical realization obtained by adding mirror values to the historical realization depicted in the histogram of Exhibit 7.16.

Issues

Like UWMA and EWMA, the method of historical realizations is ad hoc. It does not address conditional heteroskedasticity. Also, its use of historical data to directly specify a realization of a sample for ${}^1\boldsymbol{R}$ is difficult to justify in light of our discussion of Sections 7.3 and 7.4. Such a historical realization might reasonably represent the unconditional distribution of ${}^1\boldsymbol{R}$, but not its conditional distribution. Conditional heteroskedasticity will introduce—or otherwise exaggerate—leptokurtosis in the historical realization, making it a poor representation of the conditional distribution of ${}^1\boldsymbol{R}$.

There are other problems with the methodology relating to sample sizes. We address these in Chapter 10 when we discuss Monte Carlo transformations.

7.6. FURTHER READING

Jarrow (1998), Mills (1999), Franses and van Dijk (2000), and Alexander (2001) discuss time series analysis for financial markets. Zangari (1996b) introduces the UWMA and EWMA methods. Hendricks (1996) provides a detailed empirical comparison of inference procedures that employ UWMA, EWMA and historical realizations.

Chapter 8

Primary Mappings

8.1. MOTIVATION

Risk comprises both uncertainty and exposure. In Chapters 6 and 7, we focused on the uncertainty component, compiling historical market data and designing inference procedures to characterize a conditional distribution for ${}^1\boldsymbol{R}$. We now turn to the exposure component, which is represented with a portfolio mapping. Portfolio mappings are specified with a mapping procedure.

When we specify a portfolio mapping, we may perceive this as somehow approximate. This perception is difficult to formalize. From an operational standpoint, a portfolio has no "true" portfolio mapping. How can a portfolio mapping be an approximation if there is no true mapping for it to approximate?

In Section 1.8, we distinguished between primary portfolio mappings and remappings. This distinction allows us to formalize approximations while acknowledging that all portfolio mappings are models.

We construct a portfolio mapping by first specifying a primary mapping ${}^1P = \theta({}^1\boldsymbol{R})$. We choose the mapping function θ and key vector ${}^1\boldsymbol{R}$ to reflect as accurately as is reasonable our perception of how the market value of a portfolio will depend upon market variables. For certain VaR measures, the primary mapping is all we need. These VaR measures use the primary mapping as a practical tool, applying a transformation procedure directly to it. Other VaR measures approximate the primary mapping with a remapping. For these VaR measures, the primary mapping has more theoretical importance. It is a point of departure for defining the remapping. By defining precisely what the remapping is intended to approximate, the primary mapping formalizes the approximation, rendering it suitable for analysis. This allows us to analyze errors the remapping introduces or to objectively assess alternative approximations.

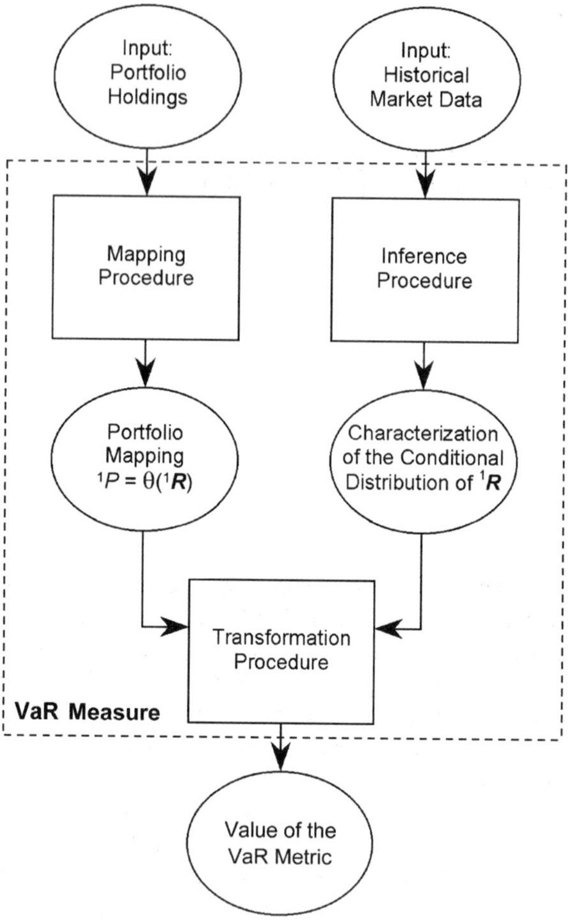

Exhibit 8.1 A reproduction of Exhibit 1.11, which is a general schematic for VaR measures. In Chapter 7, we described inference procedures. We now turn to mapping procedures in Chapters 8 and 9.

In this chapter, we describe how mapping procedures construct primary mappings. In the next chapter, we consider how they construct remappings.

8.2. DAYCOUNTS

If a VaR measure is to reasonably reflect such factors as the accrual of interest, theta effects, ex-dividend dates, or "riding down" the yield curve, it must accurately account for the passage of time during the VaR horizon. It is inexact to speak of an asset's value without specifying a point in time. Consider an at-the-money call option that has 8 calendar days to maturity at time 0. If we employ a 1-week VaR horizon, its price behavior will be quite different at time 1 than at time 0.

To avoid confusion, we label quantities with time superscripts. Both ${}^0p$ and ${}^1P$ denote a portfolio's value, but ${}^0p$ denotes it at the present time and ${}^1P$ denotes it at the end of the VaR horizon. In this section, we address some technical issues relating to the measurement of time. The material is more important for some portfolios than others. For a repo portfolio, settlement dates are precisely defined and should be recognized by a VaR measure. For a coffee portfolio, ex-dock settlement occurs when the ship arrives in port, whenever that might be.

Actual Days, Calendar Days, and Trading Days

We distinguish among:

- **actual days**, each comprising a 24-hour period;
- **calendar days**, counted on an actual, 30-day, or other basis, consistent with interest rate conventions, such as actual/actual, 30/360, or 30/actual; and
- **trading days**, which are any actual day during which a specified market conducts business.

If calendar days are calculated on an actual basis, then calendar days equal actual days. Trading days may be defined with regard to the days of operation of a specific market or more generally with regard to the business days of some collection of markets or geographic region. Consequently, trading days and nontrading days are not universally defined.

Today, it is common to measure VaR over short horizons of a day or a week. We might define such horizons in terms of actual days or trading days. To avoid having the end of a horizon fall on a weekend or holiday, we adopt the latter convention. A "1-day horizon" comprises 1 trading day. A "5-day horizon" comprises 5 trading days.

This convention is endorsed by empirical studies[1] indicating that market fluctuations from one trading day to the next exhibit little effect from intervening nontrading days. For this reason, VaR measurements provide a more consistent indication of risk if they are measured over a trading day than over an actual day.

We might feel inclined to measure time in trading days and not bother at all with calendar days. Unfortunately, things aren't so simple. In finance, some computations depend upon the passage of calendar days. Most obvious of these is the accrual of interest. As a practical matter, many VaR measures must account for time in both trading days and calendar days.

To facilitate writing formulas, we define the **calendar days function** τ. For integers $d > 0$, $\tau(d)$ indicates the number of calendar days from time 0 until trading

---

[1]Classic papers include French (1980), Gibbons and Hess (1981), and French and Roll (1986).

day d. There is no simple formula for $\tau(d)$. It depends upon the present date, the calendar, and our convention (actual, 30-day, etc.) for counting calendar days.

Count calendar days as actual days. If today is October 15, 2002, what is $\tau(5)$? Using the calendar in Exhibit 8.2, we count 5 trading days from October 15. Skipping weekends and other nontrading days, we conclude that trading day $d = 5$ coincides with October 22. There are 7 calendar days between October 15 and October 22, so $\tau(5) = 7$.

October 2002							November 2002						
S	M	T	W	T	F	S	S	M	T	W	T	F	S
		1	2	3	4	5						1	2
6	7	8	9	10	11	12	3	4	5	6	7	8	9
13	14*	15	16	17	18	19	10	11*	12	13	14	15	16
20	21	22	23	24	25	26	17	18	19	20	21	22	23
27	28	29	30	31			24	25	26	27	28*	29	30

Exhibit 8.2 Calendar for October and November 2002. US holidays (nontrading days) are indicated with *.

Suppose today is November 8, 2002, count calendar days as actual days, and assume a 1-day VaR horizon. How many calendar days are in our horizon? Because November 9, 10, and 11 are nontrading days, our VaR horizon ends on November 12. There are $\tau(1) = 4$ calendar days in the VaR horizon.

Time Versus Maturity

An important convention is that time is always measured from time 0, but the maturity of an instrument may be measured from any point in time. Measure calendar days as actual days and suppose today is October 11, 2002. Our VaR horizon comprises 1 trading day, which is 4 calendar days. The horizon ends on October 15. At time 0 a loan has 12 calendar days until it matures. As of time 1, that same loan has 8 calendar days until it matures. Maturity is relative, based upon the point in time at which it is measured. Time, on the other hand, is always measured from time 0.

Value Dates

When we value an instrument—a stock, deposit, swap, block of electricity, etc.—the result reflects our perception of the price the instrument might command in the market. The **value date** is the date on which the quoted price would be paid. If the instrument were delivered today for payment today, it would command a certain price. If it were delivered today for payment in a month, it would command a different price due to the time value of money.

Suppose an electricity generator sells electricity for payment in 30 days. It hedges its fuel costs with NYMEX natural gas futures, which settle (margin) daily. If the generator marks its positions to market, it cannot simply sum its receivables and the value in its margin account. The receivables have a value date 30 days in the future. Money in the margin account has a value date of today.

A value date does not have to be the actual date on which money will change hands. We can discount value or accumulate it to reflect some other payment date. Our electricity generator might discount its receivables back to today before adding them to the balance in its margin account. To mark a portfolio to market, it is reasonable to select a single value date and accumulate or discount all values to that date.

The simplest approach to valuation is **cash valuation**. Measure time t in trading days. With cash valuation, a valuation at time t reflects a value date of t—so asset value ${}^0s_i$ reflects value date 0, and asset value ${}^1S_i$ reflects value date 1. If, in a particular market, spot contracts settle in n trading days, cash valuation requires that spot prices at time 0 be discounted back $\tau(n)$ calendar days.

Alternatively, we might use $\boldsymbol{n^{\text{th}}}$**-day valuation**, where the value date occurs n trading days after the time a price is quoted. With this approach ${}^0s_i$ reflects a value date of n trading days, and ${}^1S_i$ reflects a value date of $n+1$ trading days. With n^{th}-day valuation, prices of spot contracts that settle in n trading days require no discounting.

Given the simplicity of cash valuation, why would we ever use n^{th}-day valuation? Doing so can be convenient. Suppose you hold 100 shares of a particular stock that is trading at USD 56. Based upon that price, you value the position at USD 5600. Because a sale of the stock today will not settle for 3 trading days, you have just employed 3rd-day valuation.

EXAMPLE: CASH VALUATION DISCOUNT CURVE. Consider the calendar of Exhibit 8.3. Today's date is May 10, 2001. Current USD Libor quotes for short maturities are shown in Exhibit 8.4.

May 2001						
S	M	T	W	T	F	S
		1	2	3	4	5
6	7	8	9	10	11	12
13	14	15	16	17	18	19
20	21	22	23	24	25	26
27	28*	29	30	31		

Exhibit 8.3 Calendar for May 2001. US holidays (nontrading days) are indicated with *.

Maturity	USD Libor
overnight	4.51
1-week	4.18
2-week	4.15

Exhibit 8.4 USD Libor quotes for overnight, 1-week, and 2-weeks on May 10, 2001.

USD Libor is quoted on an actual/360 simple basis, so calendar days are actual days. Let's construct a discount curve for daily maturities out to 15 calendar days. We employ cash valuation. Based upon British Banker Association (BBA) specifications, the overnight rate is for a loan commencing immediately and maturing on the next trading day. The 1-week and 2-week rates are for loans commencing in 2 trading days and maturing on the first trading day that is at least 1 week or 2 weeks later, respectively. Based upon the calendar of Exhibit 8.3, we determine the calendar day counts associated with these loans, which are shown in Exhibit 8.5.

Libor Maturity	Loan Commences	Loan Matures
overnight	0	1
1-week	4	11
2-week	4	19

Exhibit 8.5 Libor indicative interest rates, as compiled by the BBA, correspond to loans commencing and maturing on specific dates. This table indicates calendar days from the current date until commencement and maturity for loans corresponding to overnight, 1-week, and 2-week USD Libor quotes as of May 10, 2001.

Since we are using cash valuation, the discount factor for 0 calendar days' maturity is 1.0. We can calculate the discount factor for 1 calendar day from the overnight rate:

$$\frac{1}{1+.0451(1)/360} = .999875. \quad [8.1]$$

We don't have a tom-next[2] rate. Let's assume it equals the overnight rate. Because of the intervening weekend, a tom-next loan would commence in $\tau(1) = 1$ calendar day and mature in $\tau(2) = 4$ calendar days. If we multiply our 1-day discount factor [8.1] by the discount factor corresponding to the tom-next loan (which discounts 3 calendar days from May 14 back to May 11) we obtain a 4-day

[2]If there are no intervening nontrading days, a overnight loan is a loan that commences today and matures tomorrow. A tom-next (tomorrow-next) loan commences tomorrow and matures the next day. A spot-next loan commences in 2 days (spot) and matures the next day. Such loans are convenient for extending an existing loan by a day.

discount factor:

$$.999875\frac{1}{1+.0451(3)/360} = .999499. \qquad [8.2]$$

Note that this discount factor is for a loan maturing in 4 calendar days whereas the 1-week Libor rate is for a loan commencing in 4 calendar days and maturing in 11. If we multiply our 4-day discount factor [8.2] by the discount factor corresponding to the 1-week loan (which discounts 7 calendar days from May 21 back to May 14) we obtain an 11-day discount factor:

$$.999499\frac{1}{1+.0418(7)/360} = .998687. \qquad [8.3]$$

Similarly, we obtain a 19-day discount factor from the 4-day discount factor [8.3] and the 2-week Libor rate:

$$.999499\frac{1}{1+.0415(15)/360} = .997774. \qquad [8.4]$$

We have 5 discount factors—including discount factor 1.0 for 0 days' maturity. We linearly interpolate between values to obtain our discount curve. Results are presented in Exhibits 8.6 and 8.7.

Calendar Days	Discount Factor	Calendar Days	Discount Factor
0	1.000000	8	0.999035
1	0.999875	9	0.998919
2	0.999750	10	0.998803
3	0.999624	11	0.998687
4	0.999499	12	0.998573
5	0.999383	13	0.998459
6	0.999267	14	0.998345
7	0.999151	15	0.998231

Exhibit 8.6 The interpolated, cash valuation discount curve for May 10, 2001. Since we only required discount factors out to 15 actual days, the 19-day discount factor was used in the interpolation, but is not indicated.

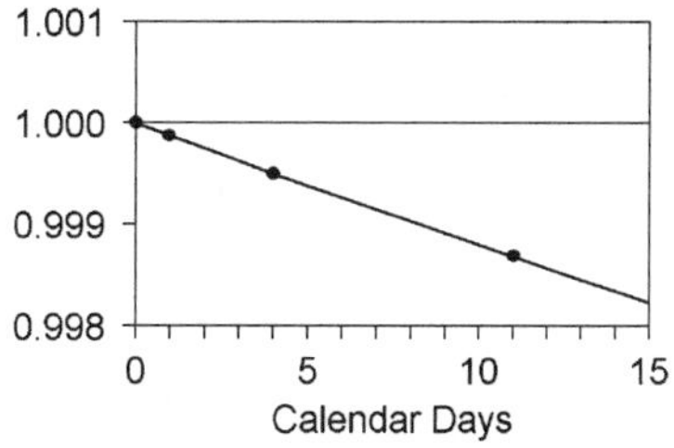

Exhibit 8.7 Graph of interpolated, cash valuation discount curve for May 10, 2001.

EXAMPLE: 2nd-DAY VALUATION DISCOUNT CURVE. Most Libor rates are quoted for 2nd-day valuation. For this reason, it may be convenient to employ 2nd-day valuation in certain VaR measures. In the last example, we constructed a discount curve based upon cash valuation. Let's now construct the same discount curve, but base it upon 2nd-day valuation.

We could start with the Libor quotes of Exhibit 8.4 and build the discount curve from there. Let's take a simpler approach. When we change from one value date to another, all we need do is accumulate forward or discount backward to the new value date. In this manner, we can construct our 2nd-day valuation curve from the cash valuation curve that we constructed in the last example. We accumulate all discount factors by $\tau(2) = 4$ calendar days by dividing by the 4-day discount factor [8.2]. Results are indicated in Exhibits 8.8 and 8.9.

Calendar Days	Discount Factor	Calendar Days	Discount Factor
0	1.000501	8	0.999536
1	1.000376	9	0.999420
2	1.000251	10	0.999304
3	1.000125	11	0.999188
4	1.000000	12	0.999073
5	0.999884	13	0.998959
6	0.999768	14	0.998845
7	0.999652	15	0.998731

Exhibit 8.8 The 2nd-day valuation discount curve for May 10, 2001.

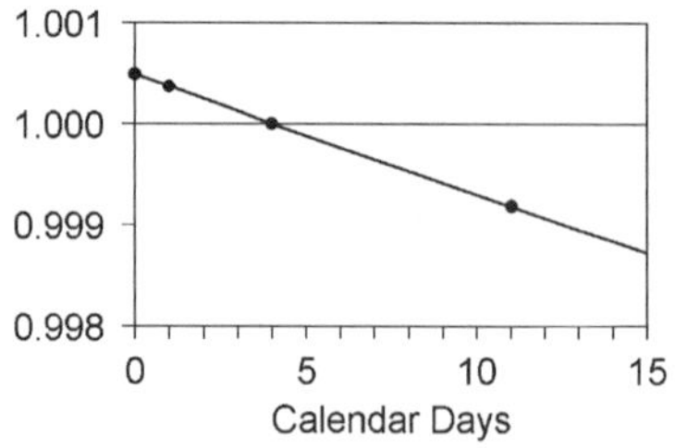

Exhibit 8.9 Graph of the 2nd-day valuation discount curve for May 10, 2001.

Because the 4th calendar day—May 14—is the value date, it has a discount factor of 1.0. Discount factors for shorter maturities exceed 1.0. They are actually accumulation factors. They accumulate cash flows forward to the value date.

EXAMPLE: RANDOM DISCOUNT CURVE. Measure time t in trading days. Suppose today is May 10, 2001, but now we want to construct the 2nd-day valuation discount curve for May 11. That's tomorrow! The discount curve we are about to construct is random. Tomorrow, just as we did today, we will observe USD Libor rates for overnight, 1-week, and 2-week loans. Denote these rates with random variables ${}^1R_1$, ${}^1R_2$, and ${}^1R_3$. From these we will be able to calculate 2nd-day valuation discount factors. Denote these random variables ${}^1Q_i$, corresponding to discount factors for i calendar days, $i = 0, 1, \ldots, 15$. Note that these are maturities, so we can measure them relative to any date. In this case, we measure them from the time the Libor rates will be quoted. This is time 1, which is May 11.

Based upon the calendar of Exhibit 8.3, we determine the calendar day counts for the loans associated with the three Libor rates. These are indicated in Exhibit 8.10:

Libor Maturity	Loan Commences	Loan Matures
overnight	0	3
1-week	4	11
2-week	4	18

Exhibit 8.10 This table indicates calendar days from May 11 until commencement and maturity for loans corresponding to overnight, 1-week, and 2-week USD Libor rates to be quoted on May 11, 2001.

We are using 2nd-day valuation. From May 11, 2 trading days will be 4 calendar days, so our value date is May 15. The discount factor ${}^1Q_4$ is not random; it will equal 1.0. Discount factors for maturities of less than 4 calendar days will be accumulation factors. They are random, but we know they will exceed 1.0. As before, we assume the tom-next rate equals the overnight rate ${}^1R_1$. We obtain discount factors by accumulating to the value date:

$$ {}^1Q_3 = 1 + {}^1R_1(1)/360, \tag{8.5} $$

$$ {}^1Q_0 = \big(1 + {}^1R_1(3)/360\big)\big(1 + {}^1R_1(1)/360\big). \tag{8.6} $$

We obtain the discount factor ${}^1Q_{11}$ from the 1-week Libor rate by discounting 7 days, from May 22 back to the value date May 15:

$$ {}^1Q_{11} = \frac{1}{1 + {}^1R_2(7)/360}. \tag{8.7} $$

We are only interested in discount factors for maturities out to 15 actual days. However, for interpolating some of the later maturities, we need the 18-day discount factor:

$$ {}^1Q_{18} = \frac{1}{1 + {}^1R_3(14)/360}. \tag{8.8} $$

Linearly interpolating between values, we obtain the remaining discount factors. With Exhibit 8.11 and the formulas it references, we have defined a mapping ${}^1\boldsymbol{Q} = \varphi({}^1\boldsymbol{R})$.

Calendar Days	Discount Factor	Formula	Calendar Days	Discount Factor	Formula
0	${}^1Q_0$	Formula [8.6]	8	${}^1Q_8$	$(3/7) + (4/7){}^1Q_{11}$
1	${}^1Q_1$	$(2/3){}^1Q_0 + (1/3){}^1Q_3$	9	${}^1Q_9$	$(2/7) + (5/7){}^1Q_{11}$
2	${}^1Q_2$	$(1/3){}^1Q_0 + (2/3){}^1Q_3$	10	${}^1Q_{10}$	$(1/7) + (6/7){}^1Q_{11}$
3	${}^1Q_3$	Formula [8.5]	11	${}^1Q_{11}$	Formula [8.7]
4	${}^1Q_4$	1.0	12	${}^1Q_{12}$	$(6/7){}^1Q_{11} + (1/7){}^1Q_{18}$
5	${}^1Q_5$	$(6/7) + (1/7){}^1Q_{11}$	13	${}^1Q_{13}$	$(5/7){}^1Q_{11} + (2/7){}^1Q_{18}$
6	${}^1Q_6$	$(5/7) + (2/7){}^1Q_{11}$	14	${}^1Q_{14}$	$(4/7){}^1Q_{11} + (3/7){}^1Q_{18}$
7	${}^1Q_7$	$(4/7) + (3/7){}^1Q_{11}$	15	${}^1Q_{15}$	$(3/7){}^1Q_{11} + (4/7){}^1Q_{18}$

Exhibit 8.11 Formulas for the random discount factors of May 11, 2001. The 18-day discount factor ${}^1Q_{18}$ is obtained from [8.8].

Exercises

Refer to the calendars of Exhibit 8.2 or Exhibit 8.3 as appropriate to answer the following questions. Measure time t in trading days, and treat US holidays as nontrading days.

8.1 If today is November 14, 2002, what is $\tau(10)$? Assume calendar days are actual days.

8.2 Suppose today is October 23, 2002, and we are employing a 1-day VaR horizon. How many actual days are in our horizon?

8.3 Suppose today is November 27, 2002, and we are employing a 1-day VaR horizon. How many actual days are in our horizon?

8.4 Suppose today is October 11, 2002, and we are employing a 1-day VaR horizon. How many actual days are in our horizon?

8.5 The month of February 2003 has 28 days. How many actual days are there between February 25 and March 5, 2003? How many 30-day basis calendar days are there?

8.6 Measure time t in trading days. The spot-next USD Libor rate for time 1 corresponds to a short-term loan commencing and maturing on specific dates (see footnote 2 of this chapter). Assume calendar days equal actual days. Use the day count function τ to represent:

a. the number of calendar days from time 0 until that loan commences and until it matures;
b. the number of calendar days from time 1 until that loan commences and until it matures.

8.7 Assume calendar days equal actual days. Use a 1-day VaR horizon and 2nd-day valuation. Represent discount factors as ${}^1Q_i$, where i is the number of calendar days from time 1 to the maturity of the cash flow being discounted. Suppose today is November 7, 2002. A USD 1MM cash flow will be received on November 15, 2002. You represent its value at the end of the VaR horizon with the formula

$$1{,}000{,}000\ {}^1Q_i. \qquad [8.9]$$

In this formula, what should the subscript i be?

8.3. PRIMARY MAPPINGS

The construction of a primary mapping always begins—explicitly or implicitly—with a row vector of holdings $\boldsymbol{\omega}$ and an asset vector ${}^1\boldsymbol{S}$. We define

$${}^1P = \boldsymbol{\omega}\,{}^1\boldsymbol{S}. \qquad [8.10]$$

We can let ${}^1\boldsymbol{S}$ be our key vector, in which case [8.10] is our primary mapping. More often, we select some other key vector ${}^1\boldsymbol{R}$. Using asset valuation formulas φ_i for each asset ${}^1S_i$, we specify a mapping ${}^1\boldsymbol{S} = \boldsymbol{\varphi}({}^1\boldsymbol{R})$. The composition $\theta = \boldsymbol{\omega} \circ \boldsymbol{\varphi}$ defines a primary mapping:

$${}^1P = \theta({}^1\boldsymbol{R}). \qquad [8.11]$$

Our discussion of primary mappings must address the four constructs: ${}^1\boldsymbol{S}$, $\boldsymbol{\omega}$, ${}^1\boldsymbol{R}$, and $\boldsymbol{\varphi}$.

Specifying ${}^1S$ and ω

Asset values ${}^1S_i$ represent the accumulated value at time 1 of one unit of some asset held at time 0. Selecting what instruments to represent with ${}^1\boldsymbol{S}$ entails a number of definitional issues.

Any institution that implements a VaR measure will link the system (directly or manually) to some portfolio accounting system. That system will define a universe of instruments it can account for. As a practical matter, it makes sense to define ${}^1\boldsymbol{S}$ to conform closely to this. However, the correspondence need not be identical. Assets do not need to conform to any legal or accounting notions of what might constitute an asset. In many cases, it makes sense to define assets creatively or break certain instruments into components, each of which is represented by a different asset. Doing so can minimize the dimensionality of $^1\boldsymbol{S}$—and possibly reduce the number of active holdings we need to model for a portfolio.

Asset values ^1S_i typically reflect mid-market valuations, but they can also represent bid or offer valuations. Since mapping [8.10] defines the portfolio ^1P in terms of $^1\boldsymbol{S}$, we must decide whether we wish ^1P to reflect mid-market, bid, or offer valuations. This depends upon our intended interpretation of our VaR measure, but it also depends upon the historical market data available to us. If the data we have is indicative offer prices, then it is practical to let assets ^1S_i—and hence our portfolio ^1P—represent offer valuations.

Another issue is valuation method. Should asset values—and hence portfolio values—reflect cash or some n^{th}-day valuation? It may be convenient to decide this issue based upon applicable settlement conventions. In foreign exchange and money markets, spot transactions tend to have 2nd-day settlement. Corporate bonds typically settle in 3 days. Futures settle (margin) daily, which facilitates cash valuation.

Specifying $^1\boldsymbol{R}$ and θ

If our primary mapping is to employ some key vector $^1\boldsymbol{R}$ other than $^1\boldsymbol{S}$, we must specify a mapping

$$^1\boldsymbol{S} = \varphi(^1\boldsymbol{R}). \tag{8.12}$$

The mapping function φ is a vector of component functions φ_i, each of which values some asset:

$$^1S_i = \varphi_i(^1\boldsymbol{R}). \tag{8.13}$$

From an implementation standpoint, the mapping φ corresponds to a library of financial engineering models—a **model library**. If a VaR measure is to be used in a fixed-income trading environment, the library will have models for valuing swaps, caps, floors, swaptions, bonds, etc. If it is to be used in an energy trading environment, the library will have models for valuing energy forwards, futures, options, etc.

The model library that defines φ requires various inputs in order to value assets, and these are the key factors ^1R_i. This does not mean that selecting key factors is as simple as selecting some model library and seeing what inputs it requires. Our choice of financial variables to represent with $^1\boldsymbol{R}$ will be determined by a number of considerations. To some extent, these must drive our selection of a model library.

To avoid $^1\boldsymbol{R}$ having a singular covariance matrix, it is desirable that key factors be linearly independent. If we model two prices as key factors, we should not model the spread between them as a third key factor. To avoid multicollinearity, it is desirable to avoid key factors that are highly correlated or are in some other sense "almost" linearly dependent. If we model interest rates as key factors, it does not make sense to also model the corresponding discount factors or forward rates. It is desirable that the dimensionality of ${}^1\boldsymbol{R}$ not be too great. Specifying 20 or 100 key factors is reasonable. Specifying 10,000 is not.

None of the above issues is critical. A subsequent remapping can tidy up problems, but we should not rely too heavily on one to do so. Applying a remapping can be computationally intensive or unstable. Fitting a quadratic approximation in 10,000 dimensions is not a task to be taken lightly!

An important consideration in selecting a model library for a VaR measure is the fact that its purpose is different from that of a model library that might support a front office. A front-office library—one that supports trading—is intended to calculate market values ${}^0s_i$ for instruments as of time 0. A middle-office library—one that supports risk measurement—is intended to calculate accumulated values ${}^1s_i$ for instruments as of time 1. If an instrument generates cash flows during the interval (0, 1], a middle-office library must accumulate these until time 1 and include them in its calculation of accumulated value for that instrument. If a VaR metric depends upon ${}^0p$, the middle office model library will also need to calculate current asset values ${}^0s_i$.

EXAMPLE. Consider a VaR metric of 5-day 95% USD VaR. Measure calendar days as actual days. Time 0 is May 29, 2001. Based upon the calendar of Exhibit 8.12, time 1 is June 5, 2002. A VaR measure is applied to a foreign exchange portfolio comprising:

- a forward contract to exchange USD 10MM for CAD 15.47MM on June 8, 2001, and
- a short European-exercise call option on CAD 30MM struck at 1.55 CAD/USD and expiring on May 31, 2001.

May 2001							June 2001						
S	M	T	W	T	F	S	S	M	T	W	T	F	S
		1	2	3	4	5						1	2
6	7	8	9	10	11	12	3	4	5	6	7	8	9
13	14	15	16	17	18	19	10	11	12	13	14	15	16
20	21	22	23	24	25	26	17	18	19	20	21	22	23
27	28*	29	30	31			24	25	26	27	28	29	30

Exhibit 8.12 Calendar for May and June 2001. US holidays (nontrading days) are indicated with *.

Our example is contrived, but it will illustrate some important concepts. In particular the short option expires prior to the end of the VaR horizon. This will be our first example of a portfolio mapping that must account for an intra-horizon event.

We adopt 2nd-day valuation and specify asset values:

$$^{1}\mathbf{S} = \begin{pmatrix} ^{1}S_1 \\ ^{1}S_2 \end{pmatrix} \sim \begin{pmatrix} \text{USD accumulated value per-CAD for the forward} \\ \text{USD accumulated value per-CAD for the option} \end{pmatrix}. \quad [8.14]$$

Holdings are $\boldsymbol{\omega} = (15{,}470{,}000 \quad -30{,}000{,}000)$, so we define

$$^{1}P = \boldsymbol{\omega}\,^{1}\mathbf{S} = (15{,}470{,}000 \quad -30{,}000{,}000)\begin{pmatrix} ^{1}S_1 \\ ^{1}S_2 \end{pmatrix}. \quad [8.15]$$

The option expires in $\tau(2) = 2$ calendar days. If it is exercised, CAD will be delivered against USD 2 trading days later, which is at $\tau(4) = 6$ calendar days. The VaR horizon ends at $\tau(5) = 7$ calendar days. Its value date is at $\tau(7) = 9$ calendar days. The forward contract matures at $\tau(8) = 10$ calendar days. These events are plotted on a time line in Exhibit 8.13.

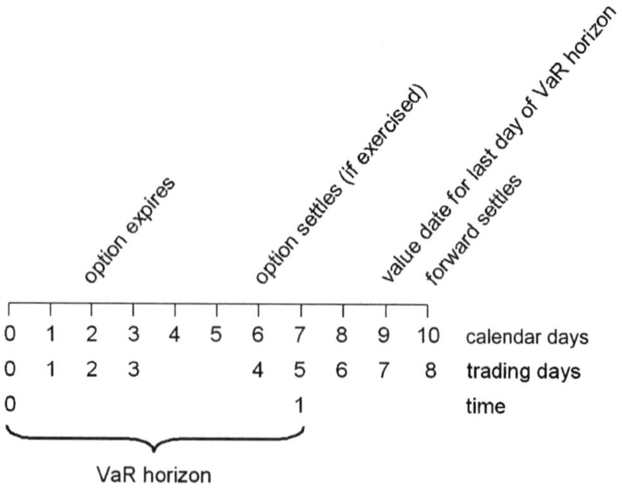

Exhibit 8.13 Time line for the example. The VaR horizon is 5 trading days. Valuation is 2nd-day.

Because of the option's expiration, the portfolio value ^{1}P depends upon market conditions on both May 31 and June 5—at $\tau(2) = 2$ and $\tau(5) = 7$ calendar days.

Specify risk factors as

$$
{}^1\boldsymbol{Q} = \begin{pmatrix} {}^1Q_1 \\ {}^1Q_2 \\ {}^1Q_3 \\ {}^1Q_4 \\ {}^1Q_5 \end{pmatrix} \sim \begin{pmatrix} \text{May 31 spot CAD/USD exchange rate} \\ \text{May 31 USD accumulation factor from actual day 6 to actual day 9} \\ \text{June 5 spot CAD/USD exchange rate} \\ \text{June 5 USD discount factor from actual day 10 to actual day 9} \\ \text{June 5 CAD discount factor from actual day 10 to actual day 9} \end{pmatrix}. \quad [8.16]
$$

The first risk factor will determine the value of the option at expiration. Because the option settles 2 trading days later, that value is realized at calendar day 6. The second risk factor will accumulate that value to the value date, calendar day 9. The last three risk factors will determine the value of the outstanding forward at the end of the VaR horizon, again for a value date at 9 calendar days.

Note that we do not use fractional time superscripts to indicate when values of risk factors will be realized. All five risk factors have time superscript 1, which is intended only to indicate that each is realized at some point in the time interval (0, 1]. Our convention is that a time superscript t indicates that a value ${}^tQ_i$ is realized at some point between times $t-1$ and t. Even over a 1-day horizon, risk factors are often realized nonsynchronously because of markets being in different time zones, etc. Nothing is gained by trying to identify the precise times at which each is realized.

To specify a mapping ${}^1\boldsymbol{S} = \varphi({}^1\boldsymbol{Q})$, we must specify two component formulas φ_1 and φ_2 for valuing the forward and option, respectively. Both must reflect value based upon information available at the end of the VaR horizon—actual day 7—but for value date 2 trading days later—actual day 9. Starting with φ_1, the forward comprises two cash flows. At actual day 10, for each CAD we receive, we will pay .6464 USD. Discounting USD .6464 back to actual day 9 yields a USD market value of $.6464\,{}^1Q_4$. Discounting a CAD back to actual day 9 yields a CAD market value of ${}^1Q_5$. To convert this to a USD market value, we divide by the CAD/USD exchange rate ${}^1Q_3$. Conveniently, ${}^1Q_3$ is a spot exchange rate for actual day 7, which means it settles on the value date, which is actual day 9. This isn't coincidence—we chose to use 2nd-day valuation for a reason! The value of the forward per CAD is

$$
{}^1S_1 = \varphi_1({}^1\boldsymbol{Q}) = {}^1Q_5/{}^1Q_3 - .6464\,{}^1Q_4. \quad [8.17]
$$

Turning now to φ_2, the option expires at actual day 2. If exercised, it settles as a spot foreign exchange transaction at actual day 6 for value $(1/1.55 - 1/{}^1Q_1)$ per CAD. We will know at actual day 2 that this value is to be realized, so financing from actual day 6 to actual day 9 can be arranged at that time. Accumulated to actual day 9, the option's value per CAD is

$$^1S_2 = \varphi_2(^1\boldsymbol{Q}) = -^1Q_2 max\big[\big(1/^1Q_1 - 1/1.55\big), 0\big]. \quad [8.18]$$

Together, [8.15], [8.17], and [8.18] define a portfolio mapping. We could let $^1\boldsymbol{Q}$ be our key vector and be done. However, the accumulation/discount factors $^1Q_2$, $^1Q_4$, and $^1Q_5$ make odd key factors, even for a contrived example such as this. To tidy things up, let's express $^1\boldsymbol{Q}$ in terms of key factors that are quoted in the market:

$$^1\boldsymbol{R} = \begin{pmatrix} ^1R_1 \\ ^1R_2 \\ ^1R_3 \\ ^1R_4 \\ ^1R_5 \\ ^1R_6 \\ ^1R_7 \\ ^1R_8 \\ ^1R_9 \\ ^1R_{10} \\ ^1R_{11} \end{pmatrix} \sim \begin{pmatrix} \text{May 31 spot CAD/USD exchange rate} \\ \text{May 31 USD overnight Libor rate} \\ \text{May 31 USD 1-week Libor rate} \\ \text{May 31 USD 2-week Libor rate} \\ \text{June 5 spot CAD/USD exchange rate} \\ \text{June 5 USD overnight Libor rate} \\ \text{June 5 USD 1-week Libor rate} \\ \text{June 5 USD 2-week Libor rate} \\ \text{June 5 CAD overnight Libor rate} \\ \text{June 5 CAD 1-week Libor rate} \\ \text{June 5 CAD 2-week Libor rate} \end{pmatrix}. \quad [8.19]$$

Using techniques similar to those of the previous section, we construct a mapping:

$$^1\boldsymbol{Q} = \dot{\varphi}(^1\boldsymbol{R}). \quad [8.20]$$

This completes our primary portfolio mapping:

$$^1P = \theta(^1\boldsymbol{R}) = \boldsymbol{\omega} \circ \varphi \circ \dot{\varphi}(^1\boldsymbol{R}). \quad [8.21]$$

This example is useful for two reasons. First, it illustrates the generality of our framework for modeling VaR. We have been developing VaR measures as single-period models. They characterize at time 0 a conditional distribution of a portfolio's value at time 1. It might seem that intra-horizon events—such as the expiration of an option, resetting of a floating interest rate or knocking out of a barrier option between times 0 and 1—might force us to employ multi-period models. Our example illustrates that this is not necessary. Key factors ^1R_i can represent quantities that will be realized at any point in the interval (0,1]. Timing issues do not prevent us from specifying a portfolio mapping $^1P = \theta(^1\boldsymbol{R})$. They will not prevent us from characterizing a joint distribution for $^1\boldsymbol{R}$ or from applying a suitable transformation procedure.

Second, the example illustrates how intra-horizon events can complicate VaR measures. They require the modeling of additional key factors and the construction of specialized model libraries. Such complexities are avoided if we use a 1-day VaR horizon—which is a compelling reason to do so!

Practical Examples

The example of this section was somewhat contrived. We were given a specific portfolio on a specific current date, which meant we could design a minimalist portfolio mapping based upon only the key factors necessary for that portfolio and based upon day counts applicable to that specific date. When we design a mapping procedure, we must be more general. The procedure must be able to specify a primary mapping for any portfolio that may be encountered. It must be able to apply day counts for any date.

In the remaining sections of this chapter, we consider practical, scalable examples. Because the emphasis is on practicality, these entail much "bookkeeping"—with numerous day counts, asset values, risk factors, and mappings carefully defined. The examples offer a clear sense of what it is like to specify practical primary mappings.

Exercises

8.8 Measure VaR as 1-day 95% USD VaR and employ cash valuation. A portfolio comprises 130 troy ounces of gold, which will be received in one trading day. The gold has already been paid for, so there is no offsetting cash flow. Construct a primary mapping for this portfolio based upon a single key factor:

$$^1R_1 \sim \text{cash price of gold in USD/ounce.} \qquad [8.22]$$

8.9 Repeat the previous exercise, but now use two key factors:

$$\begin{pmatrix} ^1R_1 \\ ^1R_2 \end{pmatrix} \sim \begin{pmatrix} \text{cash price of gold in EUR/ounce} \\ \text{cash EUR/USD exchange rate} \end{pmatrix}. \qquad [8.23]$$

8.10 Measure VaR as 1-day 95% USD VaR and employ cash valuation. NYMEX gold futures have a notional amount of 100 troy ounces. Today's date is March 2, 2001. A portfolio comprises 12 April contracts. The April contract's current settlement price is 263.50 USD/ounce. Construct a primary mapping for the portfolio based upon a single key factor:

$$^1R_1 \sim \text{settlement price of the April contract in USD/ounce.} \qquad [8.24]$$

8.11 Measure VaR as 1-day 95% USD VaR and employ cash valuation. Today's date is March 2, 2001. A gold portfolio comprises:

- 200 ounces of gold to be received in one trading day;
- a long position of 6 April contracts; and
- a short position of 2 June contracts.

Construct a primary mapping for the portfolio based upon three key factors:

$$\begin{pmatrix} {}^1R_1 \\ {}^1R_2 \\ {}^1R_3 \end{pmatrix} \sim \begin{pmatrix} \text{cash price of gold in USD/ounce} \\ \text{settlement price of the April contract in USD/ounce} \\ \text{settlement price of the June contract in USD/ounce} \end{pmatrix}. \quad [8.25]$$

8.12 Measure VaR as 5-day 95% USD VaR. Today's date is September 20, 1999. A portfolio comprises an OTC up-and-in barrier call option on 10,000 ounces of gold. The option expires on September 24, 1999. It has strike price 275 and barrier 300. If, at any time up to and including the expiration date, the price of gold (London afternoon fixing) reaches USD 300/ounce, the option will convert to a European call struck at 275. Otherwise, it will expire worthless. If exercised, the option settles for cash (as opposed to physical delivery) 2 trading days after expiration.

September 1999						
S	M	T	W	T	F	S
			1	2	3	4
5	6*	7	8	9	10	11
12	13	14	15	16	17	18
19	20	21	22	23	24	25
26	27	28	29	30		

Exhibit 8.14 Calendar for September 1999. US holidays (nontrading days) are indicated with *.

Employ 2nd-day valuation. Construct a primary portfolio mapping as follows:

a. Construct a time line for the problem similar to that of Exhibit 8.13.
b. Identify variables—quoted in the markets—to be modeled as key factors.
c. Specify a primary mapping in terms of these.

8.4. EXAMPLE: EQUITIES

Measure VaR as 1-week 95% USD VaR. Measure calendar days as actual days. Assume 2nd-day valuation.[3] A US fund manager runs a portfolio of Pacific Basin equities. The fund does not hedge foreign exchange exposures. Holdings are in actively traded stocks on the following exchanges:

- Jakarta Stock Exchange,
- Philippine Stock Exchange,
- Stock Exchange of Hong Kong,

[3] This is consistent with foreign exchange settlement, but not equity settlement, which is 3rd-day or longer in most countries.

- Stock Exchange of Singapore,
- Stock Exchange of Thailand,
- Taiwan Stock Exchange.

Let's construct a primary mapping ${}^1P = \theta({}^1\boldsymbol{R})$ of the form

$$\overbrace{{}^1P \xleftarrow{\boldsymbol{\omega}} {}^1\boldsymbol{S} \xleftarrow{\varphi} {}^1\boldsymbol{R}}^{\theta}. \qquad [8.26]$$

For each stock traded on one of the exchanges, define an asset value ${}^1S_i$ to represent the USD accumulated value of a single share. Accumulated value reflects the stock's price, dividends, stock splits, and the USD exchange rate versus the stock's local currency. For expositional convenience, we segment ${}^1\boldsymbol{S}$ and the holdings $\boldsymbol{\omega}$ into sub-vectors by country:

$${}^1\boldsymbol{S} = \begin{pmatrix} {}^1\boldsymbol{S}^{Indonesia} \\ {}^1\boldsymbol{S}^{Philippines} \\ {}^1\boldsymbol{S}^{Hong\ Kong} \\ {}^1\boldsymbol{S}^{Singapore} \\ {}^1\boldsymbol{S}^{Thailand} \\ {}^1\boldsymbol{S}^{Taiwan} \end{pmatrix}, \qquad [8.27]$$

$$\boldsymbol{\omega} = (\boldsymbol{\omega}^{Indonesia} \quad \boldsymbol{\omega}^{Singapore} \quad \cdots \quad \boldsymbol{\omega}^{Taiwan}). \qquad [8.28]$$

Then:

$${}^1P = \boldsymbol{\omega}\,{}^1\boldsymbol{S}, \qquad [8.29]$$

$$= \boldsymbol{\omega}^{Indonesia}\,{}^1\boldsymbol{S}^{Indonesia} + \boldsymbol{\omega}^{Philippines}\,{}^1\boldsymbol{S}^{Philippines} + \cdots + \boldsymbol{\omega}^{Taiwan}\,{}^1\boldsymbol{S}^{Taiwan}. \qquad [8.30]$$

We specify key vector ${}^1\boldsymbol{R}$ using component vectors:

$${}^1\boldsymbol{R} = \begin{pmatrix} {}^1\boldsymbol{R}^{FX} \\ {}^1\boldsymbol{R}^{Indonesia} \\ {}^1\boldsymbol{R}^{Philippines} \\ {}^1\boldsymbol{R}^{Hong\ Kong} \\ {}^1\boldsymbol{R}^{Singapore} \\ {}^1\boldsymbol{R}^{Thailand} \\ {}^1\boldsymbol{R}^{Taiwan} \end{pmatrix}, \qquad [8.31]$$

where the first component vector, ${}^1\boldsymbol{R}^{FX}$, is a vector of spot exchange rates, which settle in 2 days:

$$ {}^1\boldsymbol{R}^{FX} = \begin{pmatrix} {}^1R_1^{FX} \\ {}^1R_2^{FX} \\ {}^1R_3^{FX} \\ {}^1R_4^{FX} \\ {}^1R_5^{FX} \\ {}^1R_6^{FX} \end{pmatrix} \sim \begin{pmatrix} \text{spot USD/IDR exchange rate} \\ \text{spot USD/PHP exchange rate} \\ \text{spot USD/HKD exchange rate} \\ \text{spot USD/SGD exchange rate} \\ \text{spot USD/THB exchange rate} \\ \text{spot USD/TWD exchange rate} \end{pmatrix}. \qquad [8.32] $$

The remaining component vectors indicate, for each stock, accumulated value in local currency based upon 2nd-day valuation. If ${}^1S_{14}^{Thailand}$ represents the USD accumulated value of a share of Bangchak Petroleum, ${}^1R_{14}^{Thailand}$ represents the THB accumulated value of that same share. We map ${}^1\boldsymbol{R}$ to ${}^1\boldsymbol{S}$ with a simple currency conversion. For Bangchak Petroleum:

$$ {}^1S_{14}^{Thailand} = {}^1R_5^{FX}\, {}^1R_{14}^{Thailand}. \qquad [8.33] $$

More generally, expressed with component vectors,

$$ {}^1\boldsymbol{S} = \varphi({}^1\boldsymbol{R}) = \begin{pmatrix} {}^1R_1^{FX}\, {}^1\boldsymbol{R}^{Indonesia} \\ {}^1R_2^{FX}\, {}^1\boldsymbol{R}^{Philippines} \\ {}^1R_3^{FX}\, {}^1\boldsymbol{R}^{Hong\ Kong} \\ {}^1R_4^{FX}\, {}^1\boldsymbol{R}^{Singapore} \\ {}^1R_5^{FX}\, {}^1\boldsymbol{R}^{Thailand} \\ {}^1R_6^{FX}\, {}^1\boldsymbol{R}^{Taiwan} \end{pmatrix}. \qquad [8.34] $$

Combining [8.30] with [8.34], we obtain our primary mapping:

$$ {}^1P = \boldsymbol{\omega}\, {}^1\boldsymbol{S} = \boldsymbol{\omega} \circ \varphi({}^1\boldsymbol{R}) = \theta({}^1\boldsymbol{R}). \qquad [8.35] $$

Because exchange rates are multiplied by local-currency accumulated values, this defines ${}^1P$ as a quadratic function of ${}^1\boldsymbol{R}$.

EXERCISES

8.13 In our international equities example, the primary mapping [8.35] has a quadratic mapping function. It can be represented in matrix form as

$$ {}^1P = {}^1\boldsymbol{R}'\boldsymbol{c}\, {}^1\boldsymbol{R} \qquad [8.36] $$

using some symmetric matrix $\boldsymbol{c}$. In this exercise, you will construct such a representation. To simplify the task, consider a reduced asset vector

$$
{}^1\boldsymbol{S} = \begin{pmatrix} {}^1S_1^{Philippines} \\ {}^1S_2^{Philippines} \\ {}^1S_1^{Taiwan} \\ {}^1S_2^{Taiwan} \\ {}^1S_3^{Taiwan} \end{pmatrix} \sim \begin{pmatrix} \text{Ayala Corp.–AUD accumulated value of a share} \\ \text{Petron–AUD accumulated value of a share} \\ \text{Acer–AUD accumulated value of a share} \\ \text{Hotai Motor–AUD accumulated value of a share} \\ \text{Tatung–AUD accumulated value of a share} \end{pmatrix}. \quad [8.37]
$$

Assume portfolio holdings

$$
\boldsymbol{\omega} = (500 \quad 4500 \quad 3800 \quad 900 \quad 2400), \quad [8.38]
$$

and use key vector

$$
{}^1\boldsymbol{R} = \begin{pmatrix} {}^1R_1^{FX} \\ {}^1R_2^{FX} \\ {}^1R_1^{Philippines} \\ {}^1R_2^{Philippines} \\ {}^1R_1^{Taiwan} \\ {}^1R_2^{Taiwan} \\ {}^1R_3^{Taiwan} \end{pmatrix} \sim \begin{pmatrix} \text{spot PHP/AUD exchange rate} \\ \text{spot TWD/AUD exchange rate} \\ \text{Ayala Corp.–PHP accumulated value of a share} \\ \text{Petron–PHP accumulated value of a share} \\ \text{Acer–TWD accumulated value of a share} \\ \text{Hotai Motor–TWD accumulated value of a share} \\ \text{Tatung–TWD accumulated value of a share} \end{pmatrix}. \quad [8.39]
$$

8.14 In the last exercise, you expressed [8.35] in the matrix form [8.36]. Suppose we add US equities and a USD cash position to the portfolio of our example. How would we need to generalize [8.36] to reflect these additional holdings?

8.5. EXAMPLE: FORWARDS

Assume a 1-day 95% AUD VaR metric. An Australian foreign exchange trader holds forward positions in AUD, USD, and JPY. All contracts have maturities of less than 365 actual days. Measure calendar days as actual days. Because foreign exchange transactions typically settle in two trading days, adopt 2nd-day valuation. Count calendar days as actual days. We shall construct a primary mapping ${}^1P = \theta({}^1\boldsymbol{R})$ of the form

$$
\overbrace{{}^1P \xleftarrow{\boldsymbol{\omega}} {}^1\boldsymbol{S} \xleftarrow{\varphi} {}^1\boldsymbol{Q} \xleftarrow{\dot{\varphi}} {}^1\boldsymbol{R}}^{\theta}. \quad [8.40]
$$

Specify asset vector ${}^1\boldsymbol{S}$ as representing accumulated values at time 1 of 1 million units of particular currencies to be received on particular future dates. Using component vectors, specify

$$ {}^1\boldsymbol{S} = \begin{pmatrix} {}^1\boldsymbol{S}^{AUD} \\ {}^1\boldsymbol{S}^{USD} \\ {}^1\boldsymbol{S}^{JPY} \end{pmatrix} \sim \begin{pmatrix} \text{AUD time-1 present values} \\ \text{USD time-1 present values} \\ \text{JPY time-1 present values} \end{pmatrix}, \qquad [8.41] $$

where

$$ {}^1\boldsymbol{S}^{AUD} = \begin{pmatrix} {}^1S_1^{AUD} \\ {}^1S_2^{AUD} \\ \vdots \\ {}^1S_{365}^{AUD} \end{pmatrix} \sim \begin{pmatrix} \text{accumulated value, 1MM AUD payable on actual day 1} \\ \text{accumulated value, 1MM AUD payable on actual day 2} \\ \vdots \\ \text{accumulated value, 1MM AUD payable on actual day 365} \end{pmatrix}, \qquad [8.42] $$

and component vectors ${}^1\boldsymbol{S}^{USD}$ and ${}^1\boldsymbol{S}^{JPY}$ are similar. Because currencies generally won't be delivered on weekends or holidays, we have specified more assets than we need, but our choice of assets is notationally convenient.

Each forward contract comprises two "legs"—a long position in one currency and a short position in another. For example, a contract to deliver AUD 2MM in exchange for JPY 169MM on actual day 124 is represented as

$$ -2\,{}^1S_{124}^{AUD} + 169\,{}^1S_{124}^{JPY}. \qquad [8.43] $$

In this manner, each contract is broken into individual holdings in specific assets represented by ${}^1\boldsymbol{S}$. Summing such holdings across all contracts held by the portfolio, we obtain the portfolio holdings $\boldsymbol{\omega}$. We define ${}^1P$ with the vector product

$$ {}^1P = \boldsymbol{\omega}\,{}^1\boldsymbol{S}. \qquad [8.44] $$

We define ${}^1\boldsymbol{S}$ as a mapping of a key vector ${}^1\boldsymbol{R}$ in two steps. First we define a mapping ${}^1\boldsymbol{S} = \varphi({}^1\boldsymbol{Q})$ where ${}^1\boldsymbol{Q}$ represents two spot exchange rates and discount factors for daily maturities out to 364 days. Next, a mapping ${}^1\boldsymbol{Q} = \dot{\varphi}({}^1\boldsymbol{R})$ employs linear interpolation to obtain the daily discount factors of ${}^1\boldsymbol{Q}$ from discount factors corresponding to quoted Libor rates. This yields a primary mapping

$$ {}^1P = \theta({}^1\boldsymbol{R}) = \boldsymbol{\omega} \circ \varphi \circ \dot{\varphi}({}^1\boldsymbol{R}). \qquad [8.45] $$

Specify ${}^1\boldsymbol{Q}$ with component vectors

$$ {}^1\boldsymbol{Q} = \begin{pmatrix} {}^1\boldsymbol{Q}^{AUD} \\ {}^1\boldsymbol{Q}^{USD} \\ {}^1\boldsymbol{Q}^{JPY} \\ {}^1\boldsymbol{Q}^{FX} \end{pmatrix} \sim \begin{pmatrix} \text{vector of daily AUD discount factors} \\ \text{vector of daily USD discount factors} \\ \text{vector of daily JPY discount factors} \\ \text{vector of spot exchange rates} \end{pmatrix}, \qquad [8.46] $$

where

$$ {}^1\boldsymbol{Q}^{FX} = \begin{pmatrix} {}^1Q_1^{FX} \\ {}^1Q_2^{FX} \end{pmatrix} \sim \begin{pmatrix} \text{AUD/USD spot exchange rate} \\ \text{AUD/JPY spot exchange rate} \end{pmatrix}, \qquad [8.47] $$

$$ {}^1\boldsymbol{Q}^{AUD} = \begin{pmatrix} {}^1Q_0^{AUD} \\ {}^1Q_1^{AUD} \\ {}^1Q_2^{AUD} \\ \vdots \\ {}^1Q_{364}^{AUD} \end{pmatrix} \sim \begin{pmatrix} \text{AUD discount factor for 0-days maturity} \\ \text{AUD discount factor for 1-day maturity} \\ \text{AUD discount factor for 2-days maturity} \\ \vdots \\ \text{AUD discount factor for 364-days maturity} \end{pmatrix}, \qquad [8.48] $$

and the two other discount curves ${}^1\boldsymbol{Q}^{USD}$ and ${}^1\boldsymbol{Q}^{JPY}$ are similar. In total, ${}^1\boldsymbol{Q}$ comprises 1097 risk factors.

Foreign exchange professionals may wonder why we are modeling cash flows with 0 days to maturity, which would be physical cash. Since any cash position can be invested, at least overnight, shouldn't the minimum maturity be 1? At time 0, the answer is yes, but we are modeling the portfolio as of time 1. If cash is invested overnight at time 0, it will be returned and have 0 days until maturity at time 1. In a similar vein, we don't need to model discount factors at time 1 for maturities of 365 days because a cash flow with 365 days until maturity at time 0 will have $365 - \tau(1)$ days until maturity at time 1.

Since we don't know the present date—we are designing a mapping procedure that will apply for any date—we don't know the value date for time 1. Discount factors ${}^1Q_i^{AUD}$, ${}^1Q_i^{USD}$, and ${}^1Q_i^{JPY}$ for maturity on that date will all equal 1.0. For convenience, we treat them as risk factors, but they are not random. Discount factors for maturities prior to the value date are accumulation factors. Representing accumulation of value to the value date, they are random but will exceed 1.0.

Define the mapping ${}^1\boldsymbol{S} = \varphi({}^1\boldsymbol{Q})$ with

$$ {}^1S_i^{AUD} = \varphi_i^{AUD}({}^1\boldsymbol{Q}) = 1{,}000{,}000\ {}^1Q_{i-\tau(1)}^{AUD}, \qquad [8.49] $$

$$ {}^1S_i^{USD} = \varphi_i^{USD}({}^1\boldsymbol{Q}) = 1{,}000{,}000\ {}^1Q_{i-\tau(1)}^{USD}\ {}^1Q_1^{FX}, \qquad [8.50] $$

$$ {}^1S_i^{JPY} = \varphi_i^{JPY}({}^1\boldsymbol{Q}) = 1{,}000{,}000\ {}^1Q_{i-\tau(1)}^{JPY}\ {}^1Q_2^{FX}, \qquad [8.51] $$

where subscript terms $\tau(1)$ are used to account for the decline in the time-to-maturity of each cash flow over the VaR horizon.

We now reduce our 1097 risk factors to just 47 key factors with a mapping ${}^1\boldsymbol{Q} = \dot{\varphi}({}^1\boldsymbol{R})$ that linearly interpolates between discount factors corresponding to quoted Libor rates. Specify ${}^1\boldsymbol{R}$ with component vectors:

$$ {}^1\boldsymbol{R} = \begin{pmatrix} {}^1\boldsymbol{R}^{AUD} \\ {}^1\boldsymbol{R}^{USD} \\ {}^1\boldsymbol{R}^{JPY} \\ {}^1\boldsymbol{R}^{FX} \end{pmatrix} \sim \begin{pmatrix} \text{vector of AUD Libor discount factors} \\ \text{vector of USD Libor discount factors} \\ \text{vector of JPY Libor discount factors} \\ \text{vector of spot exchange rates} \end{pmatrix}, \quad [8.52] $$

where

$$ {}^1\boldsymbol{R}^{FX} = \begin{pmatrix} {}^1R_1^{FX} \\ {}^1R_2^{FX} \end{pmatrix} \sim \begin{pmatrix} \text{AUD/USD spot exchange rate} \\ \text{AUD/JPY spot exchange rate} \end{pmatrix}, \quad [8.53] $$

$$ {}^1\boldsymbol{R}^{AUD} = \begin{pmatrix} {}^1R_1^{AUD} \\ {}^1R_2^{AUD} \\ {}^1R_3^{AUD} \\ {}^1R_4^{AUD} \\ {}^1R_5^{AUD} \\ \vdots \\ {}^1R_{15}^{AUD} \end{pmatrix} \sim \begin{pmatrix} \text{spot-next AUD Libor discount factor} \\ \text{one-week AUD Libor discount factor} \\ \text{two-week AUD Libor discount factor} \\ \text{one-month AUD Libor discount factor} \\ \text{two-month AUD Libor discount factor} \\ \vdots \\ \text{12-month AUD Libor discount factor} \end{pmatrix}, \quad [8.54] $$

and the two other discount curves ${}^1\boldsymbol{R}^{USD}$ and ${}^1\boldsymbol{R}^{JPY}$ are similar. Define mapping ${}^1\boldsymbol{Q} = \dot{\varphi}({}^1\boldsymbol{R})$ by setting corresponding exchange rates equal to each other

$$ {}^1Q_i^{FX} = \dot{\varphi}({}^1\boldsymbol{R}) = {}^1R_i^{FX}. \quad [8.55] $$

and linearly interpolating between the discount factors of ${}^1\boldsymbol{R}^{AUD}$, ${}^1\boldsymbol{R}^{USD}$, and ${}^1\boldsymbol{R}^{JPY}$ to obtain the discount factors of ${}^1\boldsymbol{Q}^{AUD}$, ${}^1\boldsymbol{Q}^{USD}$, and ${}^1\boldsymbol{Q}^{JPY}$. The resulting mapping function $\dot{\varphi}$ is a linear polynomial

$$ {}^1\boldsymbol{Q} = \dot{\varphi}({}^1\boldsymbol{R}) = \boldsymbol{b}\,{}^1\boldsymbol{R} + \boldsymbol{a}. \quad [8.56] $$

where, $\boldsymbol{b}$ is a 1097×47 matrix, and $\boldsymbol{a}$ is a 1097-dimensional vector. The actual matrix $\boldsymbol{b}$ and vector $\boldsymbol{a}$ depend upon the day counts for the times-to-maturity of quoted Libor rates at time 1. Let's illustrate for an actual portfolio.

FOREIGN EXCHANGE EXAMPLE (ACTUAL PORTFOLIO). The current date is May 17, 2001. Based upon the calendar of Exhibit 8.3, a time line is plotted in Exhibit 8.15. The foreign exchange portfolio holds 17 contracts indicated in Exhibit 8.16. We calculate portfolio holdings $\boldsymbol{\omega}$ in Exhibit 8.17.

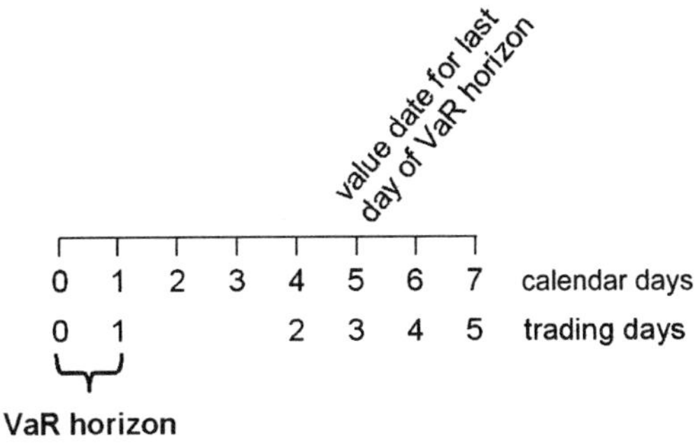

Exhibit 8.15 Time line for the example. Time is measured in trading days. Calendar days are actual days. Valuation is 2nd-day.

Contract	Cash Flows (millions) AUD	USD	JPY	Settlement (actual days)
1	12.00	-7.91		21
2	-80.00	53.02		21
3	8.88	-6.00		87
4	22.50	-14.83		87
5	-30.00	20.01		136
6	45.00		-3712	19
7	5.53		-450	19
8	12.75		-1039	20
9	-14.00		1148	20
10	12.60		-1041	20
11	-10.37		850	87
12	24.00		-1994	87
13	-2.25		184	136
14	14.00		-1137	136
15	-20.50		1680	136
16		-10.50	1311	87
17		-30.00	3740	136

Exhibit 8.16 Foreign exchange forward portfolio.

Contract	Settlement	Holdings											
	d	${}^1S^{AUD}_{19}$	${}^1S^{AUD}_{20}$	${}^1S^{AUD}_{21}$	${}^1S^{AUD}_{87}$	${}^1S^{AUD}_{136}$	${}^1S^{USD}_{21}$	${}^1S^{USD}_{87}$	${}^1S^{USD}_{136}$	${}^1S^{JPY}_{19}$	${}^1S^{JPY}_{20}$	${}^1S^{JPY}_{87}$	${}^1S^{JPY}_{136}$
1	21			12.00			-7.91						
2	21			-80.00			53.02						
3	87				8.88			-6.00					
4	87				22.50			-14.83					
5	136					-30.00			20.01				
6	19	45.00								-3712			
7	19	5.53								-450			
8	20		12.75								-1039		
9	20		-14.00								1148		
10	20		12.60								-1041		
11	20		-10.37								850		
12	87				24.00							-1994	
13	136					-2.25							184
14	136					14.00							-1137
15	136					-20.50							1680
16	87							-10.50				1311	
17	136								-30.00				3740
Total		50.53	0.98	-68.00	55.38	-38.75	45.11	-31.33	-9.99	-4162	-82	-683	4467

Exhibit 8.17 Calculating portfolio holdings for the foreign exchange forward portfolio. Only assets ${}^1S_i$ in which the portfolio has active holdings are indicated. Maturities are actual days as of time 0.

Based upon this analysis

$$\boldsymbol{\omega}' = \begin{pmatrix} \omega_{19}^{AUD} \\ \omega_{20}^{AUD} \\ \omega_{21}^{AUD} \\ \omega_{87}^{AUD} \\ \omega_{136}^{AUD} \\ \omega_{21}^{USD} \\ \omega_{87}^{USD} \\ \omega_{136}^{USD} \\ \omega_{19}^{JPY} \\ \omega_{20}^{JPY} \\ \omega_{87}^{JPY} \\ \omega_{136}^{JPY} \end{pmatrix} = \begin{pmatrix} 50.53 \\ 0.98 \\ -68.00 \\ 55.38 \\ -38.75 \\ 45.11 \\ -31.33 \\ -9.99 \\ -4162.00 \\ -82.00 \\ -683.00 \\ 4467.00 \end{pmatrix}, \qquad [8.57]$$

where only active holdings are indicated. Define ${}^1P = \boldsymbol{\omega}\,{}^1\boldsymbol{S}$. Tomorrow, May 18, is a trading day, so $\tau(1) = 1$. Our mapping ${}^1\boldsymbol{S} = \varphi({}^1\boldsymbol{Q})$ becomes

$${}^1S_i^{AUD} = \varphi_i^{AUD}({}^1\boldsymbol{Q}) = 1{,}000{,}000\,{}^1Q_{i-1}^{AUD}, \qquad [8.58]$$

$${}^1S_i^{USD} = \varphi_i^{USD}({}^1\boldsymbol{Q}) = 1{,}000{,}000\,{}^1Q_{i-1}^{USD}\,{}^1Q_1^{FX}, \qquad [8.59]$$

$${}^1S_i^{JPY} = \varphi_i^{JPY}({}^1\boldsymbol{Q}) = 1{,}000{,}000\,{}^1Q_{i-1}^{JPY}\,{}^1Q_2^{FX}. \qquad [8.60]$$

We obtain

$${}^1P = 1{,}000{,}000 \begin{pmatrix} 50.53\,{}^1Q_{18}^{AUD} + 0.98\,{}^1Q_{19}^{AUD} - 68\,{}^1Q_{20}^{AUD} + 55.38\,{}^1Q_{86}^{AUD} \\ -\,38.75\,{}^1Q_{135}^{AUD} + 45.11\,{}^1Q_{20}^{USD}\,{}^1Q_1^{FX} - 31.33\,{}^1Q_{86}^{USD}\,{}^1Q_1^{FX} \\ -\,9.99\,{}^1Q_{135}^{USD}\,{}^1Q_1^{FX} - 4162\,{}^1Q_{18}^{JPY}\,{}^1Q_2^{FX} - 82\,{}^1Q_{19}^{JPY}\,{}^1Q_2^{FX} \\ -\,683\,{}^1Q_{86}^{JPY}\,{}^1Q_2^{FX} + 4467\,{}^1Q_{135}^{JPY}\,{}^1Q_2^{FX} \end{pmatrix}, \qquad [8.61]$$

which is a quadratic polynomial. To express ${}^1P$ in terms of ${}^1\boldsymbol{R}$, we must specify matrix $\boldsymbol{b}$ and vector $\boldsymbol{a}$ that define mapping [8.56]. The linear interpolation is simple in principle. What complicates it is day counts. Let's illustrate for the AUD discount factors ${}^1Q_i^{AUD}$. Key factors ${}^1R_i^{AUD}$ correspond to the specific loan periods for which Libor will be quoted at time $t = 1$. Loans commence 2 trading days from the date they are quoted. Since May 18 is a Friday, those 2 trading days are 4 actual days. Based upon BBA specifications, the loan periods are indicated in Exhibit 8.18.

Libor Maturity	Loan Commences	Loan Matures
spot-next	4	5
1-week	4	11
2-week	4	18
1-month	4	35
2-month	4	66
3-month	4	96
4-month	4	129
5-month	4	157
6-month	4	188
7-month	4	220
8-month	4	249
9-month	4	280
10-month	4	308
11-month	4	339
12-month	4	369

Exhibit 8.18 Libor indicative interest rates, as compiled by the BBA, correspond to loans commencing and maturing on specific dates. This table indicates actual days from time $t = 1$ until commencement and maturity for AUD Libor quotes made at time 1, which is May 18, 2001. For AUD Libor, all loans commence spot. Because May 18 is a Friday, this is 4 actual days.

${}^1\boldsymbol{R}$ has 15 key factors corresponding to AUD discount factors. In addition, because May 22 is our value date for time 1, the discount factor for 4 actual days' maturity must be 1.0. Including this and our 15 key factors ${}^1R_i^{AUD}$, we have 16 discount factors to interpolate between.

To illustrate the interpolation, consider discount factor ${}^1Q_{136}^{AUD}$ for 136 actual days' maturity as of time 1. By Exhibit 8.18, key factors ${}^1R_7^{AUD}$ and ${}^1R_8^{AUD}$ for 4- and 5-month maturities correspond to 129 and 157 actual days' maturity. Linearly interpolating, we set

$$ {}^1Q_{136}^{AUD} = \frac{157-136}{157-129}\,{}^1R_7^{AUD} + \frac{136-129}{157-129}\,{}^1R_8^{AUD} = .75\,{}^1R_7^{AUD} + .25\,{}^1R_8^{AUD}. \quad [8.62] $$

Accordingly, components $b_{136,7}$ and $b_{136,8}$ of the matrix $\boldsymbol{b}$ are .75 and .25. Remaining components $b_{136,i}$ are 0, as is component a_{136} of vector $\boldsymbol{a}$. Now consider discount factor ${}^1Q_4^{AUD}$. For it, we know

$$ {}^1Q_4^{AUD} = 1.0, \quad [8.63] $$

so components $b_{4,i}$ are 0 for all i, but component a_4 of vector $\boldsymbol{a}$ is 1.0. For maturities of less than 4 actual days, we extrapolate backward from the 4-day and 5-day discount factors. For the 3-day maturity, we set

$$ {}^1Q_3^{AUD} = \frac{5-3}{5-4}1 + \frac{3-4}{5-4}\,{}^1R_1^{AUD} = 2 - {}^1R_1^{AUD}, \quad [8.64] $$

so components $b_{3,1} = -1$ with remaining components $b_{3,i}$ all 0. Component $a_3 = 2$. Continuing in this manner, we complete the matrix $\boldsymbol{b}$ and vector $\boldsymbol{a}$. Our mapping [8.56] is

$$\begin{pmatrix} {}^1Q_0^{AUD} \\ {}^1Q_1^{AUD} \\ {}^1Q_2^{AUD} \\ {}^1Q_3^{AUD} \\ {}^1Q_4^{AUD} \\ {}^1Q_5^{AUD} \\ {}^1Q_6^{AUD} \\ {}^1Q_7^{AUD} \\ {}^1Q_8^{AUD} \\ {}^1Q_9^{AUD} \\ {}^1Q_{10}^{AUD} \\ {}^1Q_{11}^{AUD} \\ {}^1Q_{12}^{AUD} \\ {}^1Q_{13}^{AUD} \\ \vdots \end{pmatrix} = \begin{pmatrix} -4 & 0 & 0 & 0 & \\ -3 & 0 & 0 & 0 & \\ -2 & 0 & 0 & 0 & \cdots \\ -1 & 0 & 0 & 0 & \\ 0 & 0 & 0 & 0 & \\ 1 & 0 & 0 & 0 & \cdots \\ .8333 & .1667 & 0 & 0 & \\ .6667 & .3333 & 0 & 0 & \\ .5000 & .5000 & 0 & 0 & \cdots \\ .3333 & .6667 & 0 & 0 & \\ .1667 & .8333 & 0 & 0 & \\ 0 & 1 & 0 & 0 & \cdots \\ 0 & .8571 & .1429 & 0 & \\ 0 & .7143 & .2857 & 0 & \\ & \vdots & & & \ddots \end{pmatrix} \begin{pmatrix} {}^1R_1^{AUD} \\ {}^1R_2^{AUD} \\ {}^1R_3^{AUD} \\ {}^1R_4^{AUD} \\ {}^1R_5^{AUD} \\ {}^1R_6^{AUD} \\ {}^1R_7^{AUD} \\ {}^1R_8^{AUD} \\ {}^1R_9^{AUD} \\ \vdots \end{pmatrix} + \begin{pmatrix} 5 \\ 4 \\ 3 \\ 2 \\ 1 \\ 0 \\ 0 \\ 0 \\ 0 \\ 0 \\ 0 \\ 0 \\ 0 \\ 0 \\ \vdots \end{pmatrix} \quad [8.65]$$

We often think of linear interpolation as an approximation, but [8.65] is not an approximation—it is not a remapping. Mathematically, [8.65] defines the random vector ${}^1\boldsymbol{Q}$ in terms of ${}^1\boldsymbol{R}$. There is no independent mathematical definition of ${}^1\boldsymbol{Q}$ to approximate, so this is a mapping. The relationship is indicated in schematic [8.40].

Composing, $\boldsymbol{\omega}$, φ, and $\dot{\varphi}$, we obtain

$${}^1P = 1{,}000{,}000 \begin{pmatrix} -8.548\,{}^1R_3^{AUD} - 7.942\,{}^1R_4^{AUD} + 18.460\,{}^1R_5^{AUD} \\ +6.474\,{}^1R_6^{AUD} - 8.304\,{}^1R_7^{AUD} + 39.803\,{}^1R_3^{USD}\,{}^1R_1^{FX} \\ +5.307\,{}^1R_4^{USD}\,{}^1R_1^{FX} - 10.443\,{}^1R_5^{USD}\,{}^1R_1^{FX} \\ -28.736\,{}^1R_6^{USD}\,{}^1R_1^{FX} - 2.141\,{}^1R_7^{USD}\,{}^1R_1^{FX} \\ -4239.176\,{}^1R_3^{JPY}\,{}^1R_2^{FX} - 4.824\,{}^1R_4^{JPY}\,{}^1R_2^{FX} \\ -227.667\,{}^1R_5^{JPY}\,{}^1R_2^{FX} + 3054.452\,{}^1R_6^{JPY}\,{}^1R_2^{FX} \\ +957.214\,{}^1R_7^{JPY}\,{}^1R_2^{FX} \end{pmatrix}. \quad [8.66]$$

Our portfolio mapping is quadratic. Note that it has more terms than our earlier mapping [8.61] in terms of ${}^1\boldsymbol{Q}$. This is only true because we considered a small portfolio. The dimensionality of ${}^1\boldsymbol{R}$ is 47 while that of ${}^1\boldsymbol{Q}$ is 1097. If we considered larger portfolios, our mapping [8.66] in terms of ${}^1\boldsymbol{R}$ would entail a maximum of 45 terms while the mapping [8.61] in terms of ${}^1\boldsymbol{Q}$ could entail as many as 1095.

8.6. EXAMPLE: OPTIONS

Measure VaR as 1-day 95% USD VaR. Measure calendar days as actual days. Assume cash valuation. A trader holds NYMEX Henry Hub natural gas futures and options with expirations out to a year. We shall construct a primary mapping of the form

$$\overbrace{{}^1P \xleftarrow{\boldsymbol{\omega}} {}^1\boldsymbol{S} \xleftarrow{\varphi} {}^1\boldsymbol{Q} \xleftarrow{\dot{\varphi}}}^{\theta} {}^1\boldsymbol{R}. \qquad [8.67]$$

Futures are for 10,000 MMBtu. Puts and calls are for a single future and expire on that future's last trading day. Out to a year, there are monthly expirations of futures, puts, and calls. A challenge in modeling exchange-traded options is the proliferation of strikes and expirations. We consider asset vector

$$
{}^1\boldsymbol{S} = \begin{pmatrix} {}^1\boldsymbol{S}^{Futures} \\ {}^1\boldsymbol{S}^{Calls1} \\ {}^1\boldsymbol{S}^{Calls2} \\ \vdots \\ {}^1\boldsymbol{S}^{Calls12} \\ {}^1\boldsymbol{S}^{Puts1} \\ {}^1\boldsymbol{S}^{Puts2} \\ \vdots \\ {}^1\boldsymbol{S}^{Puts12} \end{pmatrix} \sim \begin{pmatrix} \text{accumulated values, futures} \\ \text{accumulated values, } 1^{\text{st}} \text{ nearby calls} \\ \text{accumulated values, } 2^{\text{nd}} \text{ nearby calls} \\ \vdots \\ \text{accumulated values, } 12^{\text{th}} \text{ nearby calls} \\ \text{accumulated values, } 1^{\text{st}} \text{ nearby puts} \\ \text{accumulated values, } 2^{\text{nd}} \text{ nearby puts} \\ \vdots \\ \text{accumulated values, } 12^{\text{th}} \text{ nearby puts} \end{pmatrix}, \qquad [8.68]
$$

where

$$
{}^1\boldsymbol{S}^{Futures} = \begin{pmatrix} {}^1S_1^{Futures} \\ {}^1S_2^{Futures} \\ \vdots \\ {}^1S_{12}^{Futures} \end{pmatrix} \sim \begin{pmatrix} \text{accumulated value, } 1^{\text{st}} \text{ nearby future} \\ \text{accumulated value, } 2^{\text{nd}} \text{ nearby future} \\ \vdots \\ \text{accumulated value, } 12^{\text{th}} \text{ nearby future} \end{pmatrix}, \qquad [8.69]
$$

$$
{}^1\boldsymbol{S}^{Calls1} = \begin{pmatrix} {}^1S_1^{Calls1} \\ {}^1S_2^{Calls1} \\ \vdots \\ {}^1S_{106}^{Calls1} \end{pmatrix} \sim \begin{pmatrix} \text{accumulated value, } 1^{\text{st}} \text{ nearby strike 2.00 call} \\ \text{accumulated value, } 1^{\text{st}} \text{ nearby strike 2.10 call} \\ \vdots \\ \text{accumulated value, } 1^{\text{st}} \text{ nearby strike 8.00 call} \end{pmatrix}, \qquad [8.70]
$$

and other components are similar. When implemented, the VaR measure will need to be flexible to handle the actual strikes trading at any given time.

We determine holdings $\boldsymbol{\omega}$ and define

$$ {}^1P = \boldsymbol{\omega}\, {}^1\boldsymbol{S}. \tag{8.71}$$

We shall employ futures prices, implied volatilities, and Libor rates as key factors. To avoid a proliferation of such factors, it is natural to model just a handful and interpolate to obtain the rest. Because such interpolation represents an approximation, we defer it for a subsequent remapping. For now, we directly model implied volatilities corresponding to each option as well as monthly Libor discount factors.

Specify risk factors

$$ {}^1\boldsymbol{Q} = \begin{pmatrix} {}^1\boldsymbol{Q}^{Futures} \\ {}^1\boldsymbol{Q}^{Vols1} \\ {}^1\boldsymbol{Q}^{Vols2} \\ \vdots \\ {}^1\boldsymbol{Q}^{Vols12} \\ {}^1\boldsymbol{Q}^{Libor} \end{pmatrix} \sim \begin{pmatrix} \text{futures settlement prices} \\ \text{implied volatilities, } 1^{\text{st}} \text{ nearby options} \\ \text{implied volatilities, } 2^{\text{nd}} \text{ nearby options} \\ \vdots \\ \text{implied volatilities, } 12^{\text{th}} \text{ nearby options} \\ \text{interpolated cash valuation Libor rates} \end{pmatrix}, \tag{8.72}$$

where

$$ {}^1\boldsymbol{Q}^{Futures} = \begin{pmatrix} {}^1Q_1^{Futures} \\ {}^1Q_2^{Futures} \\ \vdots \\ {}^1Q_{12}^{Futures} \end{pmatrix} \sim \begin{pmatrix} \text{settlement price, } 1^{\text{st}} \text{ nearby future} \\ \text{settlement price, } 2^{\text{nd}} \text{ nearby future} \\ \vdots \\ \text{settlement price, } 12^{\text{th}} \text{ nearby future} \end{pmatrix}, \tag{8.73}$$

$$ {}^1\boldsymbol{Q}^{Vols1} = \begin{pmatrix} {}^1Q_1^{Vols1} \\ {}^1Q_2^{Vols1} \\ \vdots \\ {}^1Q_{106}^{Vols1} \end{pmatrix} \sim \begin{pmatrix} \text{implied volatility, } 1^{\text{st}} \text{ nearby strike 2.00 options} \\ \text{implied volatility, } 1^{\text{st}} \text{ nearby strike 2.10 options} \\ \vdots \\ \text{implied volatility, } 1^{\text{st}} \text{ nearby strike 8.00 options} \end{pmatrix}, \tag{8.74}$$

and other implied volatility components are specified similarly. Invoking put-call parity, we do not distinguish between put and call implied volatilities for a given strike and expiration.

The Libor component ${}^1\boldsymbol{Q}^{Libor}$ comprises interpolated cash-valuation Libor rates for maturities corresponding to the expiration dates of the NYMEX options.

We refer to these as the 1st through 12th nearby Libor rates:

$$^{1}\boldsymbol{Q}^{Libor} = \begin{pmatrix} ^{1}Q_1^{Libor} \\ ^{1}Q_2^{Libor} \\ \vdots \\ ^{1}Q_{12}^{Libor} \end{pmatrix} \sim \begin{pmatrix} 1^{\text{st}} \text{ nearby Libor rate} \\ 2^{\text{nd}} \text{ nearby Libor rate} \\ \vdots \\ 12^{\text{th}} \text{ nearby Libor rate} \end{pmatrix}. \qquad [8.75]$$

Define the mapping $^{1}\boldsymbol{S} = \varphi(^{1}\boldsymbol{Q})$ as follows. Since futures margin daily, current values $^{0}\boldsymbol{s}^{Futures}$ are zero and accumulated values $^{1}\boldsymbol{S}^{Futures}$ are the margin payments for time 1:

$$^{1}\boldsymbol{S}^{Futures} = \varphi^{Futures}(^{1}\boldsymbol{Q}) = {^{1}\boldsymbol{Q}^{Futures}} - {^{0}\boldsymbol{q}^{Futures}}. \qquad [8.76]$$

Options components are defined with Black's (1976) options pricing formula, which we denote $B^{Call}(\,)$ or $B^{Put}(\,)$, as appropriate. For example,

$$^{1}S_2^{Calls3} = \varphi_2^{Calls3}(^{1}\boldsymbol{Q}) = B^{Call}\left(^{1}Q_3^{Futures}, 2.10, {^{1}Q_2^{Vols3}}, {^{1}Q_3^{Libor}}, y_3\right), \qquad [8.77]$$

where y_3 is years until expiration, as of time 1, for third nearby options.

We could almost use $^{1}\boldsymbol{Q}$ as a key vector. Indeed, we almost will. The only reason we choose not to do so is the contrived nature of our Libor rates $^{1}\boldsymbol{Q}^{Libor}$, which are not quoted in the markets. USD Libor rates published by the BBA are for 2nd-day valuation and specific maturities. We specify key vector

$$^{1}\boldsymbol{R} = \begin{pmatrix} ^{1}\boldsymbol{R}^{Futures} \\ ^{1}\boldsymbol{R}^{Vols1} \\ ^{1}\boldsymbol{R}^{Vols2} \\ \vdots \\ ^{1}\boldsymbol{R}^{Vols12} \\ ^{1}\boldsymbol{R}^{BBALibor} \end{pmatrix} \sim \begin{pmatrix} \text{futures settlement prices} \\ \text{implied volatilities, } 1^{\text{st}} \text{ nearby options} \\ \text{implied volatilities, } 2^{\text{nd}} \text{ nearby options} \\ \vdots \\ \text{implied volatilities, } 12^{\text{th}} \text{ nearby options} \\ \text{BBA Libor rates} \end{pmatrix}. \qquad [8.78]$$

All component vectors of $^{1}\boldsymbol{R}$ are identical to the corresponding component vectors of $^{1}\boldsymbol{Q}$ except the last, which is

$$^{1}\boldsymbol{R}^{BBALibor} = \begin{pmatrix} ^{1}R_1^{BBALibor} \\ ^{1}R_2^{BBALibor} \\ \vdots \\ ^{1}R_{15}^{BBALibor} \end{pmatrix} \sim \begin{pmatrix} \text{BBA overnight USD Libor rate} \\ \text{BBA 1-week USD Libor rate} \\ \vdots \\ \text{BBA 1-year USD Libor rate} \end{pmatrix}. \qquad [8.79]$$

We define the mapping $^{1}\boldsymbol{Q} = \dot{\varphi}(^{1}\boldsymbol{R})$ by simply mapping each component vector of $^{1}\boldsymbol{R}$ to its counterpart in $^{1}\boldsymbol{Q}$. The only exception is the component mapping $^{1}\boldsymbol{Q}^{Libor} = \dot{\varphi}^{Libor}(^{1}\boldsymbol{R}^{BBALibor})$, which converts from 2nd-day valuation to cash valuation and interpolates to adjust maturities. It parallels techniques covered in Section 8.2, so we don't provide details. Note that the interpolation is not an approximation—it is not a remapping. Since components of ${}^{1}\boldsymbol{Q}^{Libor}$ are not observable in the market, the interpolation ${}^{1}\boldsymbol{Q}^{Libor} = \dot{\varphi}^{Libor}({}^{1}\boldsymbol{R}^{BBALibor})$ actually defines ${}^{1}\boldsymbol{Q}^{Libor}$.

8.7. EXAMPLE: PHYSICAL COMMODITIES

A difference between financial markets and physical commodities markets is the fungibility of what is traded. Japanese yen, Eurodollar futures, and shares of IBM are fungible. Coffee, oil, and electricity are not. Because of transmission costs, electricity in Quebec is worth a different price than electricity in Massachusetts. Because of marketing and perceived quality differences, coffee grown in Nicaragua commands a different price than coffee grown in Colombia. A VaR measure for a commodities portfolio must address different qualities, origins, or delivery locations.

In many commodities markets, futures contracts are used as a benchmark for pricing spot or forward contracts. A future is for a specific quality, origin, and/or point of delivery. Spot or forward transactions for other qualities, origins, and/or points of delivery trade at spreads to the future.

Assume cash valuation and measure VaR as 1-day 90% USD VaR. An international coffee wholesaler trades arabica coffee from its US headquarters as well as local offices around the world. Although coffee transacts in various currencies, each office hedges foreign exchange risk locally. Accordingly, our firm-wide VaR measure does not consider foreign exchange risk. All prices are in USD, and all transactions mature within a year. We shall construct a primary mapping ${}^{1}P = \theta({}^{1}\boldsymbol{R})$ of the form

$$\overbrace{{}^{1}P \xleftarrow{\omega} {}^{1}\boldsymbol{S} \xleftarrow{\varphi} {}^{1}\boldsymbol{R}}^{\theta}. \qquad [8.80]$$

Exhibit 8.19 indicates the specific arabicas traded by our firm.

Arabica Coffees		
Bolivia	Guatemala	Panama
Brazil	Haiti	Papua
Burundi	Honduras	Peru
Colombia	India	Rwanda
Costa Rica	Indonesia	Tanzania
Dom. Rep.	Kenya	Uganda
Ecuador	Malawi	Venezuela
El Salvador	Mexico	Vietnam
Ethiopia	Nicaragua	Zimbabwe

Exhibit 8.19 Growths of coffee traded by the firm. Our example does not consider specialty or "gourmet" coffees, which comprise a distinct segment of the market.

Although the VaR measure distinguishes between growths of coffee, it does not distinguish between delivery points. This is because the cost of shipping coffee is small compared to its value. This does not mean that coffee at one location is fungible with that at another—you can't deliver coffee at Rotterdam while it is afloat off the Horn of Africa. A VaR measure can only address market risk. Liquidity issues must be addressed with alternative means, such as careful scheduling of deliveries.

Because of the vagaries of shipping, forward contracts typically specify a delivery month, with delivery acceptable on any day during that month. For this reason, the precise day counts and discounting of our earlier examples will not be evident in this example.

NYBOT coffee futures are benchmarks for arabica coffees. Coffee forwards are priced at a spread to the first future maturing either during or subsequent to the forward's delivery month. That future's expiration month is called the forward's **cover month**. Cover months corresponding to specific delivery months are indicated in Exhibit 8.20.

Delivery Month	Cover Month
Jan, Feb, Mar	Mar
Apr, May	May
Jun, Jul	Jul
Aug, Sep	Sep
Oct, Nov, Dec	Dec

Exhibit 8.20 The cover month of a coffee forward is the maturity month of the coffee future that either matures during the forward's delivery month or is the first future to mature subsequent to the forward's delivery month. NYBOT coffee futures mature during March, May, July, September, and December.

There are two forms of forward contracts: **fixed** and **to-be-fixed**. Both forms specify quantity, quality, delivery point, and delivery month. A fixed contract indicates a fixed price. A to-be-fixed contract indicates a spread to be paid over the benchmark future. The actual price is determined on a subsequent **fixing date** by adding that spread to the benchmark future's settlement price on the fixing date. For this example, all prices are USD per pound of delivered coffee.

The practical difference between fixed and to-be-fixed contracts is that a fixed contract offers absolute price exposure to the physical coffee. A to-be-fixed contract offers, until its fixing date, exposure to only the spread between the physical coffee and the benchmark future.

A forward contract may provide some flexibility in the actual growth to be delivered. Such flexibility is called an **optional provision**. Standard optional provisions are presented in Exhibit 8.21. Optional provisions trade at spreads to benchmark futures just as growths do. Indeed, a forward on 4 Horsemen is similar to a forward on Guatemalan. The only difference is that, at delivery, the seller has more flexibility in the actual coffee delivered.

Name	Provision
2 Horsemen	Seller's option among Guatemala and Mexico
3 Horsemen	Seller's option among El Salvador, Guatemala, and Mexico
4 Horsemen	Seller's option among El Salvador, Honduras, Guatemala, and Mexico
5 Horsemen	Seller's option among coffees of 4 Horsemen and Costa Rica
6 Horsemen	Seller's option among coffees of 5 Horsemen and Nicaragua

Exhibit 8.21 Standard optional provisions specified in forward contracts provide flexibility in the actual growth to be delivered. In effect, the optional provision is the forward contract's underlier, so you would buy a forward on 4 Horsemen just as you might buy a forward on Colombian.

Our firm also holds NYBOT futures to hedge fixed forward contracts. Each NYBOT future is for 37,500 pounds of coffee.

To conform with our firm's accounting system, contracts are aggregated by delivery month. The following discussion speaks of 1-month, 2-month, . . . , 12-month contracts. These correspond to contracts for delivery in the current month, next month, etc. If today is October 28, 1-month contracts will deliver prior to November 1; 2-month contracts will deliver during November; etc.

As in our foreign exchange example of Section 8.5, it is convenient to split forwards into "legs" and model each as a separate asset. For a fixed forward, three legs correspond to:

1. component of coffee value due to the spread over its benchmark future,
2. component of coffee value due to the price of the benchmark future, and
3. discounted fixed purchase price to be paid on delivery.

The value of the forward is the sum of the first two less the third. For a to-be-fixed forward, there are two legs:

1. component of coffee value due to the spread over its benchmark future, and
2. discounted fixed spread to be paid on delivery.

The value of the forward is the first less the second.

Along these lines, we specify

$$
{}^1\mathbf{S} = \begin{pmatrix} {}^1S^{SpreadLeg} \\ {}^1S^{SpreadLegOpt} \\ {}^1S^{FutureLeg} \\ {}^1S^{CashFlowLeg} \\ {}^1S^{Future} \\ {}^1S^{SpreadLegPhy} \end{pmatrix} \sim \begin{pmatrix} \text{discounted spreads for 1 pound coffee} \\ \text{discounted spreads for 1 pound optional} \\ \text{discounted future prices, 1 pound coffee} \\ \text{discounted USD} \\ \text{futures' margins, 1 pound coffee} \\ \text{spreads for 1 pound physical coffee} \end{pmatrix}. \quad [8.81]
$$

The first component, ${}^1\boldsymbol{S}^{SpreadLeg}$, provides the discounted values of spreads on a pound of coffee. There are 30 growths of coffee and 12 delivery months out to a year, so it has 360 components:

$$
{}^1\boldsymbol{S}^{SpreadLeg} = \begin{pmatrix} {}^1S_1^{SpreadLeg} \\ {}^1S_2^{SpreadLeg} \\ {}^1S_3^{SpreadLeg} \\ \vdots \\ {}^1S_{359}^{SpreadLeg} \\ {}^1S_{360}^{SpreadLeg} \end{pmatrix} \sim \begin{pmatrix} \text{discounted Bolivian spread, 1 month} \\ \text{discounted Bolivian spread, 2 month} \\ \text{discounted Bolivian spread, 3 month} \\ \vdots \\ \text{discounted Zimbabwe spread, 11 month} \\ \text{discounted Zimbabwe spread, 12 month} \end{pmatrix}. \tag{8.82}
$$

The second component, ${}^1\boldsymbol{S}^{SpreadLegOpt}$, is similar. It provides the discounted values of spreads on optional provisions for a pound of coffee. There are 5 optional provisions and 12 delivery months, so it has a total of 60 components:

$$
{}^1\boldsymbol{S}^{SpreadLegOpt} = \begin{pmatrix} {}^1S_1^{SpreadLegOpt} \\ {}^1S_2^{SpreadLegOpt} \\ \vdots \\ {}^1S_{60}^{SpreadLegOpt} \end{pmatrix} \sim \begin{pmatrix} \text{discounted 2 Horsemen spread, 1 month} \\ \text{discounted 2 Horsemen spread, 2 month} \\ \vdots \\ \text{discounted 6 Horsemen spread, 12 month} \end{pmatrix}. \tag{8.83}
$$

The third component, ${}^1\boldsymbol{S}^{FutureLeg}$, provides, for each delivery month, the discounted value of the corresponding benchmark future's settlement price. For example, suppose today is June 10. Then ${}^1S_5^{FutureLeg}$ corresponds to October delivery. December is the cover month for October, so ${}^1S_5^{FutureLeg}$ represents the time-1 December futures price discounted from October back to time 1. ${}^1\boldsymbol{S}^{FutureLeg}$ has 12 components corresponding to 12 delivery months out to a year:

$$
{}^1\boldsymbol{S}^{FutureLeg} = \begin{pmatrix} {}^1S_1^{FutureLeg} \\ {}^1S_2^{FutureLeg} \\ \vdots \\ {}^1S_{12}^{FutureLeg} \end{pmatrix} \sim \begin{pmatrix} \text{discounted future price, 1 month} \\ \text{discounted future price, 2 month} \\ \vdots \\ \text{discounted future price, 12 month} \end{pmatrix}. \tag{8.84}
$$

The fourth component, ${}^{1}\boldsymbol{S}^{CashFlowLeg}$, represents the discounted values of a USD. Maturities are monthly out to a year:

$$ {}^{1}\boldsymbol{S}^{CashFlowLeg} = \begin{pmatrix} {}^{1}S_1^{CashFlowLeg} \\ {}^{1}S_2^{CashFlowLeg} \\ \vdots \\ {}^{1}S_{12}^{CashFlowLeg} \end{pmatrix} \sim \begin{pmatrix} \text{discounted USD, 1 month} \\ \text{discounted USD, 2 month} \\ \vdots \\ \text{discounted USD, 12 month} \end{pmatrix}. \quad [8.85] $$

These four components are for modeling the various "legs" of forward contracts. For modeling direct holdings in futures, ${}^{1}\boldsymbol{S}^{Future}$ represents per-pound accumulated values of the first six nearby futures. Because futures settle daily, they have 0 market value at time 0. Their accumulated values at time 1 are simply the margin payments for the futures at that time. To keep our units consistent, ${}^{1}\boldsymbol{S}^{Future}$ represents margin payments on a per-pound basis:

$$ {}^{1}\boldsymbol{S}^{Future} = \begin{pmatrix} {}^{1}S_1^{Future} \\ {}^{1}S_2^{Future} \\ \vdots \\ {}^{1}S_6^{Future} \end{pmatrix} \sim \begin{pmatrix} \text{margin payment, first nearby future} \\ \text{margin payment, second nearby future} \\ \vdots \\ \text{margin payment, sixth nearby future} \end{pmatrix}. \quad [8.86] $$

Finally, the last component, ${}^{1}\boldsymbol{S}^{SpreadLegPhy}$, represents the spreads to the nearby future at which physical coffee already held by the firm is valued:

$$ {}^{1}\boldsymbol{S}^{SpreadLegPhy} = \begin{pmatrix} {}^{1}S_1^{SpreadLegPhy} \\ {}^{1}S_2^{SpreadLegPhy} \\ \vdots \\ {}^{1}S_{30}^{SpreadLegPhy} \end{pmatrix} \sim \begin{pmatrix} \text{Bolivian spot spread} \\ \text{Brazilian spot spread} \\ \vdots \\ \text{Zimbabwe spot spread} \end{pmatrix}. \quad [8.87] $$

Together, the foregoing assets can represent any instrument held by our firm. Suppose today is October 29, 2001, and consider a fixed forward to pay USD 70,000 for 100,000 pounds of Brazilian coffee to be delivered during January 2002. This is represented as

$$ 100{,}000\ {}^{1}S_{16}^{SpreadLeg} + 100{,}000\ {}^{1}S_{4}^{FutureLeg} - 70{,}000\ {}^{1}S_{4}^{CashFlowLeg}. \quad [8.88] $$

A fixed forward to pay USD 74,000 for 95,000 pounds of 4 Horsemen during February 2002 is represented as

$$ 95{,}000\ {}^{1}S_{41}^{SpreadLegOpt} + 95{,}000\ {}^{1}S_{5}^{FutureLeg} - 74{,}000\ {}^{1}S_{5}^{CashFlowLeg}. \quad [8.89] $$

A to-be-fixed forward to pay a spread of $-.03$ USD per pound for 1.6MM pounds of Mexican coffee to be delivered during April 2002 is represented as

$$1{,}600{,}000\,{}^1S_{235}^{SpreadLeg} + 48{,}000\,{}^1S_7^{CashFlowLeg}. \quad [8.90]$$

Taking into account the fact that each NYMEX future is for 37,500 pounds of coffee, a short position in 14 March futures is represented as

$$-14(37{,}500)\,{}^1S_2^{Future}. \quad [8.91]$$

A physical position comprising 700,000 pounds of Zimbabwe coffee is represented as

$$700{,}000\,{}^1S_{30}^{SpreadLegPhy} + 700{,}000\,{}^1S_1^{FutureLeg}. \quad [8.92]$$

In this manner, all instruments held by the portfolio may be represented in terms of ${}^1\boldsymbol{S}$. Summing coefficients for each component, we obtain the portfolio's holdings $\boldsymbol{\omega}$ and define

$${}^1P = \boldsymbol{\omega}\,{}^1\boldsymbol{S}. \quad [8.93]$$

Our selection of key factors ${}^1R_i$ is driven as much by practical issues of data availability as by pricing theory. We model futures' settlement prices, spreads for individual growths, and interest rates. Futures prices for various nearbys define a term structure. Conceivably, spreads for each growth might also vary by maturity. As a practical matter, individual growths do not trade in sufficient volume for such spread term structures to be discernable. Market participants track cash spreads—spreads between cash prices and the first nearby future. Spreads for other maturities are treated as equal to these. This practice is common in a number of commodities markets.

We specify

$${}^1\boldsymbol{R} = \begin{pmatrix} {}^1\boldsymbol{R}^{Futures} \\ {}^1\boldsymbol{R}^{Spreads} \\ {}^1\boldsymbol{R}^{Libor} \end{pmatrix} \sim \begin{pmatrix} \text{futures settlement prices (USD/pound)} \\ \text{cash spreads (USD/pound)} \\ \text{USD Libor rates} \end{pmatrix}, \quad [8.94]$$

where

$${}^1\boldsymbol{R}^{Futures} = \begin{pmatrix} {}^1R_1^{Futures} \\ {}^1R_2^{Futures} \\ \vdots \\ {}^1R_6^{Futures} \end{pmatrix} \sim \begin{pmatrix} \text{settlement price, first nearby NYBOT future} \\ \text{settlement price, second nearby NYBOT future} \\ \vdots \\ \text{settlement price, sixth nearby NYBOT future} \end{pmatrix}, \quad [8.95]$$

$${}^1\boldsymbol{R}^{Spreads} = \begin{pmatrix} {}^1R_1^{Spreads} \\ {}^1R_2^{Spreads} \\ \vdots \\ {}^1R_{30}^{Spreads} \end{pmatrix} \sim \begin{pmatrix} \text{Bolivia coffee cash spread} \\ \text{Brazil coffee cash spread} \\ \vdots \\ \text{Zimbabwe coffee cash spread} \end{pmatrix}, \quad [8.96]$$

and

$$ {}^1\boldsymbol{R}^{Libor} = \begin{pmatrix} {}^1R_1^{Libor} \\ {}^1R_2^{Libor} \\ \vdots \\ {}^1R_{12}^{Libor} \end{pmatrix} \sim \begin{pmatrix} \text{1-month Libor rate} \\ \text{2-month Libor rate} \\ \vdots \\ \text{12-month Libor rate} \end{pmatrix}. \qquad [8.97] $$

We define the mapping ${}^1\boldsymbol{S} = \varphi({}^1\boldsymbol{R})$ by component vectors. Since the timing of forward deliveries is uncertain, we do not try to achieve a false sense of precision in our discounting. We simply discount from the last day of each delivery month using 1-month Libor for month 1 contracts, 2-month Libor for month 2 contracts, etc.

Set

$$ {}^1S_i^{SpreadLeg} = \frac{{}^1R_j^{Spreads}}{1 + (d_i/360)\,{}^1R_k^{Libor}}, \qquad [8.98] $$

$$ {}^1S_i^{FutureLeg} = \frac{{}^1R_l^{Futures}}{1 + (d_i/360)\,{}^1R_k^{Libor}}, \qquad [8.99] $$

$$ {}^1S_i^{CashFlowLeg} = \frac{1}{1 + (d_i/360)\,{}^1R_k^{Libor}}, \qquad [8.100] $$

where d_i is actual days from time 1 to the end of the delivery month; ${}^1R_j^{Spreads}$, ${}^1R_k^{Libor}$ and ${}^1R_l^{Futures}$ are applicable spreads, Libor rates, and futures settlement prices.

We model optional provision spreads as the minimum of applicable growth spreads. This is a crude but effective solution, which treats the optional provision's value as its intrinsic value:

$$ {}^1S_i^{SpreadLegOpt} = \frac{min(\text{applicable spreads})}{1 + (d_i/360)\,{}^1R_k^{Libor}}. \qquad [8.101] $$

As an example, for a 3 Horsemen contract,

$$ {}^1S_i^{SpreadLegOpt} = \frac{min\left({}^1R_9^{Spreads}, {}^1R_{11}^{Spreads}, {}^1R_{19}^{Spreads}\right)}{1 + (d_i/360)\,{}^1R_k^{Libor}}. \qquad [8.102] $$

For futures,

$$ {}^1\boldsymbol{S}^{Futures} = {}^1\boldsymbol{R}^{Futures} - {}^0\boldsymbol{r}^{Futures}. \qquad [8.103] $$

Finally, we define:

$$ {}^1\boldsymbol{S}^{SpreadLegPhy} = {}^1\boldsymbol{R}^{Spreads}. \qquad [8.104] $$

8.8. FURTHER READING

See Zangari (1996c) and Best (1998) for alternative treatments of mapping procedures. There is extensive literature on financial engineering techniques that can be used to construct primary mappings. Hull (1999) is an introductory text on financial engineering, with Wilmott et al (1993) and Baxter and Rennie (1996) offering more advanced treatments. Two edited collections of seminal papers on financial engineering are Hughston (1996, 1999), with the first focusing specifically on fixed income derivatives. Haug (1997) provides a catalogue of standard derivatives pricing formulas. For modeling interest rates and fixed income instruments, see Questa (1999) and James and Webber (2000). For foreign exchange, see Walmsley (2000). Kolb (1997) is an elementary text on futures. Reuters (2000) offers a general overview of commodities and energies markets.

Chapter 9

Remappings

9.1. MOTIVATION

Remappings take many forms. Before exploring some of these, let's first address the question: why remap?

There are many reasons that motivate us to replace one portfolio mapping function θ with an alternative function $\tilde{\theta}$ or to replace one key vector ${}^1\boldsymbol{R}$ with an alternative vector ${}^1\tilde{\boldsymbol{R}}$. Doing so may support one of three purposes:

1. to facilitate a transformation procedure;
2. to facilitate an inference procedure; or
3. to facilitate another remapping.

FACILITATING TRANSFORMATIONS

Transformations fall loosely into two categories:

1. linear and quadratic transformations, which are applicable if a portfolio mapping function is a linear or quadratic polynomial; and
2. numerical transformations—primarily Monte Carlo transformations—which entail repeated valuations of a portfolio mapping function.

If a primary mapping function θ can be approximated with a linear or quadratic polynomial $\tilde{\theta}$, this will facilitate a linear or quadratic transformation. If a numerical transformation is to be used, replacing a primary mapping function θ with another function $\widetilde{\theta}$ that is easier to value may reduce the processing time required to perform the many valuations numerical transformations require.

Quadratic remappings can also facilitate variance reduction in Monte Carlo transformations. Standard methods of variance reduction described in Chapter 10 employ control variates and stratified sampling. Both apply directly to a primary portfolio mapping ${}^1P = \theta({}^1\boldsymbol{R})$, but they employ a quadratic remapping ${}^1P = \widetilde{\theta}({}^1\boldsymbol{R})$ to facilitate the variance reduction.

Facilitating Inference

Inference procedures generally require historical data. If data is unavailable for the key vector ${}^1\boldsymbol{R}$ of a primary mapping, a remapping may introduce an alternative key vector ${}^1\widetilde{\boldsymbol{R}}$ for which data is available. Also, certain time series models can only be applied in low dimensions. For this reason, we may replace a high-dimensional key vector ${}^1\boldsymbol{R}$ with a low-dimensional key vector ${}^1\widetilde{\boldsymbol{R}}$.

Facilitating Another Remapping

Applying certain remappings can be computationally expensive. Computations to apply one remapping may be streamlined by first implementing another remapping. For example, applying certain global remappings requires multiple portfolio valuations. The computations for each portfolio valuation can be streamlined by first applying a holdings remapping. Global and holdings remappings are discussed later in this chapter.

Types of Remappings

In Section 1.8, we divided remappings into three broad categories:

1. function remappings,
2. variables remappings, and
3. dual remappings.

Within each category, remappings take various forms. We describe several in this chapter, but these are not exhaustive of what is possible.

Because it is an approximation, a remapping alters the output of a VaR measure. In most cases, we can design remappings to have a modest or even trivial impact. However, any decision as to what is reasonable must entail human judgment as well as careful consideration of the intended application for the VaR measure.

9.2. HOLDINGS REMAPPINGS

Often a portfolio has active holdings ω_i in numerous assets, but many of those assets are similar to each other. Two cash flows may be due 500 and 501 actual days from today. Technically, they represent distinct assets, but the two entail almost identical market risks. Two call options may both expire in 6 months. They both have the same underlier, but one is struck at 100 and the other is struck at 102.5. They represent distinct assets, but from a risk standpoint, they are similar.

With a **holdings remapping**, we identify active holdings in similar assets and model them with holdings in just one or a few representative assets. The goal is to dramatically reduce the number of active holdings that must be modeled. In many cases, $\boldsymbol{\omega}$ may have thousands of active holdings but can be replaced by some $\tilde{\boldsymbol{\omega}}$ with only a handful. The result is a portfolio mapping function $\theta = \tilde{\boldsymbol{\omega}} \circ \varphi$ that, with fewer active holdings, can be valued more rapidly than the original mapping function $\theta = \boldsymbol{\omega} \circ \varphi$. Schematically, a holdings remapping has the form

$$\begin{array}{c} \overbrace{{}^1P \xleftarrow{\boldsymbol{\omega}} {}^1\boldsymbol{S} \xleftarrow{\varphi} {}^1\boldsymbol{R}}^{\theta} \\ \uparrow \qquad\qquad\qquad \\ \underbrace{{}^1\tilde{P} \xleftarrow{\tilde{\boldsymbol{\omega}}} {}^1\boldsymbol{S} \xleftarrow{\varphi} {}^1\boldsymbol{R}}_{\tilde{\theta}} \end{array} \qquad [9.1]$$

Note that θ is affected by the remapping, but ${}^1\boldsymbol{R}$ is not. Holdings remappings are function remappings. We seek holdings remappings such that:

- ${}^1\tilde{P}$ reasonably approximates ${}^1P$,
- $\tilde{\boldsymbol{\omega}}$ has considerably fewer active holdings than $\boldsymbol{\omega}$, and
- the task of determining $\tilde{\boldsymbol{\omega}}$ from $\boldsymbol{\omega}$ is computationally inexpensive.

Holdings remappings are most attractive in situations where asset mappings ${}^1S_i = \varphi_i({}^1\boldsymbol{R})$ are complicated, making individual assets computationally expensive to value. This is often the case with exotic derivatives or mortgage-backed securities. Nevertheless, holdings remappings are used in a variety of situations. The following example illustrates concepts in the simple context of fixed cash flows.

EXAMPLE: HOLDINGS REMAPPINGS OF FIXED CASH FLOWS. Consider a 1-day VaR horizon. Suppose a portfolio holds AA-rated non-callable debt instruments. Because of the uniform credit quality, we treat cash flows settling on the same date as fungible for market risk calculations. Let assets represent individual cash flows. Specifically, each asset value ${}^1S_i$ represents receipt of USD 1000 on actual day i. A partial list of active holdings is shown in Exhibits 9.1 and 9.2.

i	ω_i
5	50
52	25
72	50
160	75
205	50
236	50
⋮	⋮

Exhibit 9.1 Partial listing of active holdings. Holdings are in units of thousands of USD.

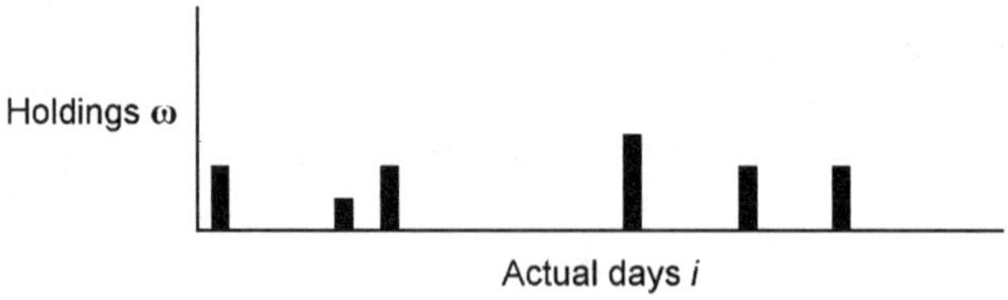

Exhibit 9.2 Graphical depiction of the holdings listed in Exhibit 9.1.

Let's start with a holdings remapping based upon a simple bucketing scheme. We divide assets into consecutive maturity "buckets," each of 91 actual days length. All holdings within a bucket are summed and assigned to a proxy asset at the center of that maturity bucket. The first bucket b_0 includes maturities between 1 and 91 actual days. As indicated in Exhibit 9.1, this bucket has three active holdings: 50, 25, and 50 thousand USD at maturities of 5, 52, and 72 actual days. Summed, these represent an active holding of 125 thousand USD, which is assigned to the proxy asset ${}^1S_{46}$. Similar analyses are performed on the remaining buckets. Results for the first three buckets are shown in Exhibits 9.3 and 9.4.

i	$\widetilde{\omega}_i$
46	125
137	75
228	100
⋮	⋮

Exhibit 9.3 Active holdings $\widetilde{\omega}_i$ obtained from a simple bucketing of the holdings ω_i of Exhibit 9.1.

In this example, bucketing reduced the active holdings in the first three buckets from six to three. If our portfolio had several thousand active holdings across all maturities, similar bucketing would reduce these to a single active holding for each bucket. The example also illustrates a problem with simple bucketing. The technique does not preserve average maturities within buckets. It does not preserve the portfolio's present value, duration, or other sensitivities to interest rates. The resulting approximation ${}^1\widetilde{P} \approx {}^1P$ may be poor.

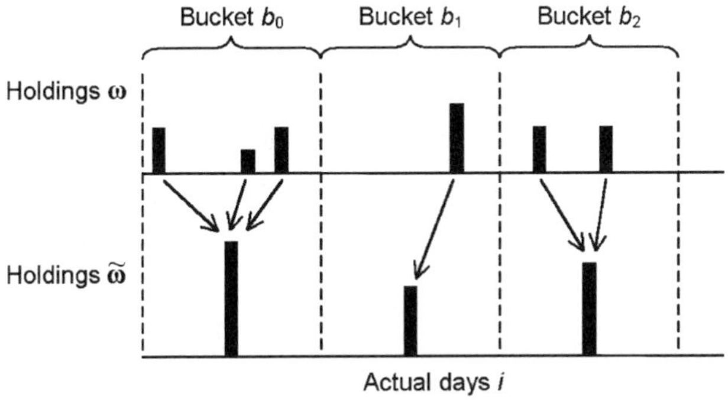

Exhibit 9.4 With simple bucketing, holdings within each maturity bucket are represented with a single aggregate holding in the asset at the center of that bucket.

Consider a more sophisticated holdings remapping. We segregate assets into the same consecutive maturity buckets. Instead of representing each bucket's cash flows with a single proxy cash flow at its center, we employ two proxy cash flows at either end of the bucket. Each cash flow in bucket b_0 is represented with proxy cash flows of maturities 1 and 92. Cash flows in bucket b_1 are each represented with proxy cash flows with maturities of 92 and 183, etc.

Consider from Exhibit 9.1 our maturity 160 cash flow for 75 thousand USD. We represent this with a position of a thousand USD at maturity 92 and another position of b thousand USD at maturity 183. We select the quantities a and b to satisfy the following two conditions:

- The combined present value of the proxy cash flows equals the present value of the original cash flow.
- The Macaulay duration of the proxy cash flows equals the Macaulay duration of the original cash flow.

Let ${}^0q_i$ denote continuously compounded (actual/actual) interest rates for maturity i at time 0. Our conditions require

$$75e^{-{}^0q_{160}(160/365)} = ae^{-{}^0q_{92}(92/365)} + be^{-{}^0q_{183}(183/365)} \qquad [9.2]$$

and

$$\frac{160}{365} = \frac{a(92/365)e^{-{}^0q_{92}(92/365)} + b(183/365)e^{-{}^0q_{183}(183/365)}}{ae^{-{}^0q_{92}(92/365)} + be^{-{}^0q_{183}(183/365)}}. \qquad [9.3]$$

Together, conditions [9.2] and [9.3] define two linear equations which we solve for a and b. Repeating this process for each cash flow and summing results, we obtain $\tilde{\omega}$. The process is illustrated in Exhibit 9.5.

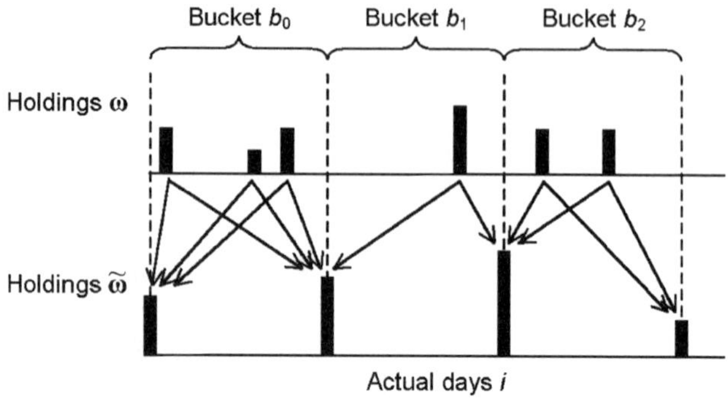

Exhibit 9.5 Within each bucket, holdings are each represented with two proxy holdings—one at the start of the bucket, and the other at the start of the subsequent bucket. The size of each proxy holding is selected to preserve present values and Macaulay durations.

Consider a third holdings remapping. All cash flows within a bucket are represented with a single cash flow whose magnitude and maturity are determined to satisfy the same two conditions. For example, our third bucket has two holdings of 50 thousand USD at maturities 205 and 236. We seek to represent these with a holding of a thousand USD in an asset of maturity c. The first of our conditions requires

$$ae^{-{}^0q_c(c/365)} = 50e^{-{}^0q_{205}(205/365)} + 50e^{-{}^0q_{236}(236/365)}. \qquad [9.4]$$

The second condition requires

$$\frac{c}{365} = \frac{50(205/365)e^{-{}^0q_{205}(205/365)} + 50(236/365)e^{-{}^0q_{236}(236/365)}}{50e^{-{}^0q_{205}(205/365)} + 50e^{-{}^0q_{236}(236/365)}}. \qquad [9.5]$$

Together, conditions [9.4] and [9.5] define two equations which we can solve for a and c. Repeating this process for each bucket, we obtain $\tilde{\boldsymbol{\omega}}$. The process is illustrated in Exhibit 9.6.

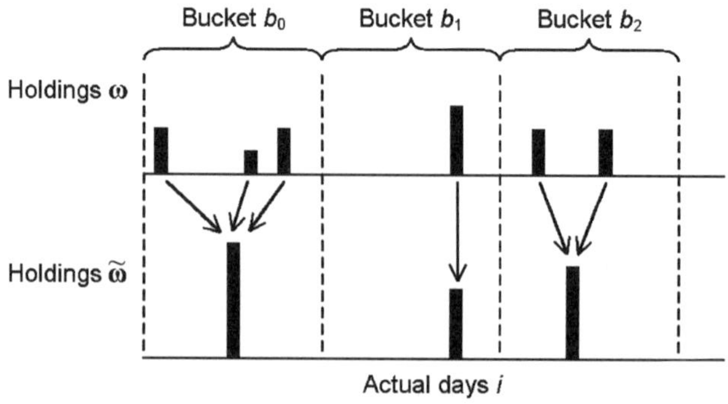

Exhibit 9.6 Holdings within each bucket are represented with a single holding within the bucket. Its size and maturity are selected to preserve present values and Macaulay durations.

Because conditions [9.4] and [9.5] are nonlinear, solving for constants a and c for each bucket will require a numerical solution such as Newton's method. Consequently, the mapping requires more computations than the previous one, but only modestly so.

Other holdings remappings might be employed. Longerstaey (1995) proposes a holdings remapping that, based upon certain interpolation assumptions, preserves the VaR of individual cash flows (but not of an entire portfolio).

EXAMPLE: HOLDINGS REMAPPING OF INTEREST RATE CAPS. Cárdenas *et al.* (1999) propose holdings remappings for portfolios of interest rate caps, floors, and swaptions. Consider caps.

Assume a 1-day VaR horizon. Today is March 23, 2000, and 3-month Euribor is 3.767%. A portfolio holds EUR interest rate caps. All are linked to 3-month Euribor, settle quarterly, and make payments in arrears. Contracts are detailed in Exhibit 9.7.

Strike Rate	Notional (MM EUR)	Next Rate-Reset Date	Final Rate-Reset Date
5.00%	100	4/21/2000	4/23/2001
5.25%	250	6/1/2000	6/2/2003
5.75%	50	5/1/2000	11/1/2004
6.25%	200	5/26/2000	5/26/2004
6.50%	100	6/1/2000	6/1/2004
6.75%	75	5/1/2000	5/1/2003

Exhibit 9.7 Contracts comprising the portfolio in the example. All contracts are interest-rate caps on 3-month Euribor. They settle quarterly in arrears.

Assets represent individual caplets with a notional amount of 1MM EUR.[1] Each asset is uniquely specified by a rate-determination date (settlement occurs 3 months later) and its strike rate. We determine holdings $\boldsymbol{\omega}$ and define

$$^{1}P = \boldsymbol{\omega}\,^{1}\boldsymbol{S}. \qquad [9.6]$$

Holdings are summarized graphically in Exhibit 9.8. Each caplet is represented with a dot positioned according to its rate-determination date and strike rate. Sizes of dots correspond to notional amounts. As indicated, caplets are aggregated into rectangular buckets according to both rate-determination date and strike rate.

We apply a holdings remapping as follows. Caplets with essentially no market value—those that are far out-of-the-money and whose rate-determination date is imminent—are discarded. Within each rectangular bucket, the total market value, delta, and vega of remaining caplets are calculated. The remapping represents

[1]For simplicity, we assume the portfolio is due to receive no fixed cash flows from caplets whose rate-determination dates have already passed.

those caplets with a single proxy caplet that has the same market value, delta, and vega. The process is repeated for each bucket.

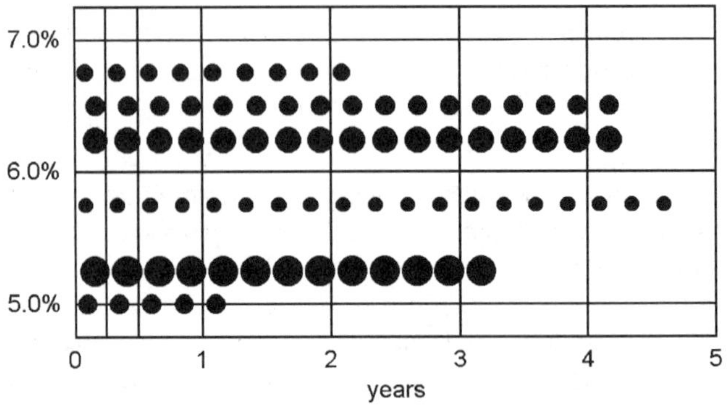

Exhibit 9.8 Portfolio holdings are illustrated graphically. Individual caplets are represented with dots positioned according to the number of years to the caplet's rate-determination date and its strike rate. The size of each dot corresponds to notional amount. Caplets are aggregated into rectangular buckets, as demarked by horizontal and vertical lines.

We don't attempt to match the net gamma of caplets within a bucket. This is because we have only three degrees of freedom to work with—rate-determination date, strike rate, and notional amount. Because vega is closely related to gamma, this is not a significant problem.

Determining a single caplet with a desired market value, delta, and vega is a nonlinear problem. We solve it for each bucket using Newton's method with line searches. Because there is no guarantee that this will converge, it is advisable to start with seed values for the rate-determination date, strike rate, and notional amount as close to the solution as possible. For this purpose, we use as seed values:

- the weighted average rate-determination date,
- the weighted average strike rate, and
- the sum notional amount

of all caplets in a bucket. Caplet market values are used as weights in the two averages.

Based upon the above analysis, remapped holdings are determined as indicated in Exhibit 9.9. With this holdings remapping, we have replaced 80 caplets with just 13 proxy caplets. If our portfolio held more caps, economies would be greater.

Let's assess how accurately our remapped portfolio value ${}^1\widetilde{P}$ approximates ${}^1P$. To facilitate the analysis, we first specify key factors. We define ${}^1\boldsymbol{S} = \varphi({}^1\boldsymbol{R})$, where ${}^1\boldsymbol{R}$ represents forward rates and implied volatilities. A joint distribution for ${}^1\boldsymbol{R}$ is constructed from historical data using techniques from Chapter 7. Schematically, we have

$$\begin{array}{l} {}^1P \xleftarrow{\omega} {}^1S \xleftarrow{\varphi} {}^1\boldsymbol{R} \\ \uparrow \\ {}^1\tilde{P} \xleftarrow{\tilde{\omega}} {}^1S \xleftarrow{\varphi} {}^1\boldsymbol{R} \end{array} \qquad [9.7]$$

Note that both ${}^1P$ and ${}^1\tilde{P}$ depend upon the same key vector ${}^1\boldsymbol{R}$. We generate 1000 pseudorandom realizations ${}^1\boldsymbol{r}^{[k]}$ for ${}^1\boldsymbol{R}$. Corresponding realizations ${}^1p^{[k]}$ and ${}^1\tilde{p}^{[k]}$ are calculated. Pairs $({}^1p^{[k]}, {}^1\tilde{p}^{[k]})$ are plotted to form the scatter diagram in Exhibit 9.10. All points fall near a line passing at a 45° angle through the center of the graph. This indicates that ${}^1\tilde{P}$ is an excellent approximation for ${}^1P$.

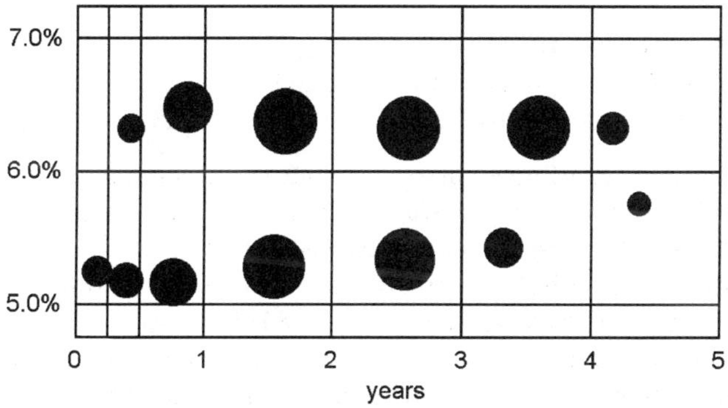

Exhibit 9.9 Remapped portfolio holdings are illustrated graphically. Proxy caplets for each bucket are represented with dots positioned according to the number of years to the caplet's rate-determination date and its strike rate. The size of each dot corresponds to notional amount. The upper left bucket has no proxy caplet. All caplets within that bucket were discarded for having essentially no market value.

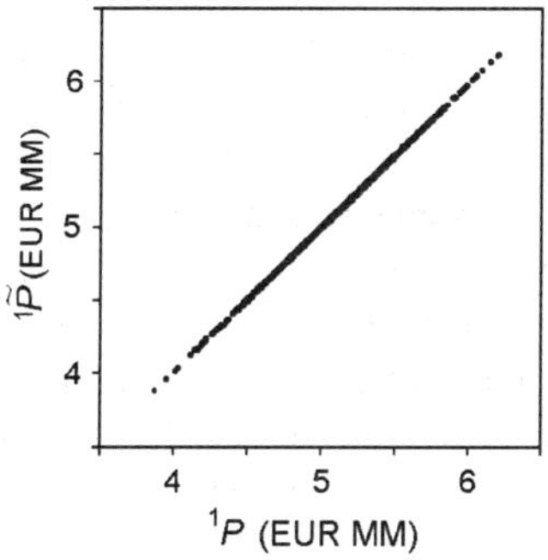

Exhibit 9.10 This chart illustrates how well the remapped portfolio value ${}^1\tilde{P}$ approximates ${}^1P$. It was constructed by generating 1000 pseudorandom realizations ${}^1\boldsymbol{r}^{[k]}$ for key vector ${}^1\boldsymbol{R}$. Corresponding realizations ${}^1p^{[k]}$ and ${}^1\tilde{p}^{[k]}$ were calculated. Pairs $({}^1p^{[k]}, {}^1\tilde{p}^{[k]})$ are plotted as a scatter diagram. The fact that all points fall near a line passing at a 45° angle through the center of the graph indicates that ${}^1\tilde{P}$ is an excellent approximation for ${}^1P$.

Designing Holdings Remappings

Our last example hints at the tremendous potential of holdings remappings. They:

- are applicable to a wide variety of instruments;
- can dramatically reduce the computations required to value a portfolio mapping function; and
- offer excellent approximations ${}^1\widetilde{P}$ for a portfolio's value ${}^1P$.

We have much flexibility in how we design a holdings remapping, and it is worth exploring several options to find which works best in any given situation. Decisions include:

- how to bucket assets,
- what assets to employ as proxy assets, and
- what characteristics of bucketed assets to match with proxy assets.

Bucketing can be performed in several dimensions, depending upon the assets. In our fixed cash-flow example, we bucketed according to a single dimension: maturity. In our cap example, we bucketed according to two: rate-determination date and strike. For a vanilla swaption portfolio, three dimensions would be appropriate: expiration, strike, and tenor of the underlying swap.

You can also vary the size of buckets. With options, gamma tends to be most extreme for contracts that are close to expiration and at-the-money. For this reason, it may be advantageous to use smaller buckets for options close to expiration and for those that are near-the-money. In our cap example, we varied bucket size by expiration, but not by strike. If options will expire during the VaR horizon, it may be appropriate to not bucket them. Simply include such holdings, unaltered in $\widetilde{\boldsymbol{\omega}}$.

Consider ignoring assets that contribute essentially nothing to market value or risk. In our cap example, we discarded from the analysis those caplets that had essentially no market value. In many cases, this will leave some buckets empty, which will further reduce the active holdings of $\widetilde{\boldsymbol{\omega}}$.

As our fixed cash-flow example illustrates, we can employ proxy assets in various ways. In the second approach of that example, we used cash flows at either end of each bucket as proxy assets. We could vary the size of each, allowing us two degrees of freedom to match both the market value and duration of bucketed assets. In the third approach of that example, we employed a single cash flow as a proxy asset for each bucket. We could select both its maturity and its size. This also afforded two degrees of freedom, allowing us again to match both total market value and duration.

Various characteristics of bucketed assets can be matched with proxy assets. It is desirable that market value be matched. Various sensitivities may also be matched: duration, convexity, delta, gamma, vega, rho, etc. Since the purpose of a remapping is to approximate ${}^1P$, it makes sense to match characteristics reflective of the portfolio at time 1. Consider time-1 sensitivities

$$\left.\frac{\partial\, {}^1P}{\partial\, {}^1R_1}\right|_{{}^0E({}^1\boldsymbol{R})} \quad\text{and}\quad \left.\frac{\partial^2\, {}^1P}{\partial\, {}^1R_1^2}\right|_{{}^0E({}^1\boldsymbol{R})}, \tag{9.8}$$

which are analogous to time-0 sensitivities delta and gamma. Time-1 market value, evaluated perhaps at ${}^0E({}^1\boldsymbol{R})$, might also be matched in lieu of time-0 market value.

In general, determining $\tilde{\boldsymbol{\omega}}$ from $\boldsymbol{\omega}$ entails solving a system of equations for each bucket. These may be linear or non linear. In either case, it is possible that a system will have no solution, but this is rarely an issue. If a system is nonlinear, it can be solved using Newton's method with line searches. To ensure convergence to a reasonable solution, it is important to identify seed values as close to the solution as possible. This is illustrated by our choice of seed values in our cap example.

Exercises

9.1 In our discussion of holdings remappings, we illustrated three approaches for fixed cash-flows and one for interest-rate caps. Of the three fixed cash-flow approaches, which is most analogous to the cap approach?

9.2 Consider a 1-day VaR horizon with 2nd-day valuation. A Canadian firm holds a portfolio of call USD put CAD options. The options' prices, deltas, and vegas can be determined with the Garman and Kohlhagen (1983) option-pricing formula as

$$\text{price} = n[s\, exp(-r_{USD}y)\Phi(d_1) - x\, exp(-r_{CAD}y)\Phi(d_2)], \tag{9.9}$$

$$\text{delta} = n\, exp(-r_{USD}y)\Phi(d_1), \tag{9.10}$$

$$\text{vega} = n\, s\, exp(-r_{USD}y)\phi(d_1)\sqrt{y}, \tag{9.11}$$

where

$$d_1 = \frac{log(s/x) + (r_{CAD} - r_{USD} + v^2/2)y}{v\sqrt{y}}, \tag{9.12}$$

$$d_2 = d_1 - v\sqrt{y}, \tag{9.13}$$

and

n = notional amount (USD);
s = CAD/USD exchange rate;
x = strike rate;
y = time to expiration in years;
r_{CAD} = continuously compounded CAD interest rate for maturity y;
r_{USD} = continuously compounded USD interest rate for maturity y;

v = implied volatility for strike x and maturity y;
Φ = CDF of the standard normal distribution;
ϕ = PDF of the standard normal distribution.

Define

$$^{1}P = \boldsymbol{\omega}\,{}^{1}\boldsymbol{S}, \quad [9.14]$$

where assets represent individual options with notional amount USD 1MM.

A holdings remapping

$$^{1}\widetilde{P} = \widetilde{\boldsymbol{\omega}}\,{}^{1}\boldsymbol{S} \quad [9.15]$$

is proposed. Options with essentially 0 market value are discarded from the analysis. Remaining options are aggregated into buckets for maturities 0–1 month, 1–3 months, 3–6 months and 6–12 months and strikes spaced at .025 increments. For each bucket, the total value, delta, and vega are determined. The options are represented with a single option having the same value, delta, and vega. The process is repeated for each bucket.

Consider the bucket for maturities 3–6 months and strikes 1.550–1.575. It contains the contracts indicated in Exhibit 9.11. In this exercise, you will represent the options of this bucket with a single option that matches their total value, delta, and vega.

Strike (CAD/USD)	Notional (MM USD)	Expiration (years)
1.550	10	0.334
1.550	15	0.375
1.550	10	0.479
1.560	20	0.271
1.560	5	0.384
1.565	10	0.449
1.570	15	0.263
1.570	15	0.301

Exhibit 9.11 Contracts in a single bucket.

a. Current values for CAD interest rates r_{CAD} at maturities $y = .25$ and $y = .50$ are .0393 and .0385. Use linear interpolation to obtain an expression for r_{CAD} of the form

$$r_{CAD} = by + a \quad [9.16]$$

for any maturity y between .25 and .50.

b. Current values for USD interest rates r_{USD} at maturities $y = .25$ and $y = .50$ are .0352 and .0354. Use linear interpolation to obtain an expression for r_{USD} of the form

$$r_{USD} = by + a \quad [9.17]$$

for any maturities y between .25 and .50.

c. Implied volatility v varies with both strike x and expiration y. Current implied volatilities are indicated in Exhibit 9.12. Use quadratic interpolation to obtain an expression for v of the form

$$v = cxy + b_1x + b_2y + a \tag{9.18}$$

for values x between 1.550 and 1.575 and values y between .25 and .50.

	y = .25	y = .50
x = 1.550	.079	.071
x = 1.575	.074	.068

Exhibit 9.12 Current implied volatilities v by strike x and expiration y.

d. The current exchange rate s is 1.559 CAD/USD. Substitute this and your results for items (a), (b), and (c) into [9.9] through [9.11] to obtain formulas for an option's value, delta, and vega that are applicable across a range of strikes x and maturities y.
e. Use your results from item (d) to determine the prices, deltas, and vegas of the options in Exhibit 9.11. Sum your results to obtain the total price, total delta, and total vega.
f. Calculate the weighted average strike, weighted average expiration, and total notional amount of the options in Exhibit 9.11. Use the options' values as weights in the first two items.
g. Employ Newton's method with line searches and your results from item (d) to find the strike, maturity, and notional amount of a single option whose value, delta, and vega match the total value, total delta, and total vega of the options of Exhibit 9.11. In your search routine, use your results from item (f) as seed values.

9.3. GLOBAL REMAPPINGS

Global remappings are function remappings that directly approximate a mapping function θ with some simpler function $\tilde{\theta}$ of a specified form. This is illustrated schematically as

$$\begin{array}{ccc} & \overbrace{\hphantom{\xleftarrow{\omega}\;{}^1\boldsymbol{S}\;\xleftarrow{\varphi}}}^{\theta} & \\ {}^1P & \xleftarrow{\omega}\; {}^1\boldsymbol{S} \;\xleftarrow{\varphi} & {}^1\boldsymbol{R} \\ \uparrow & & \\ {}^1\tilde{P} & \xleftarrow{\quad\quad\tilde{\theta}\quad\quad} & {}^1\boldsymbol{R} \end{array} \tag{9.19}$$

The function $\tilde{\theta}$ can take many forms. Linear or quadratic polynomials are most common, in which case the remapping is called a **linear** or **quadratic** remapping. A more general term, **polynomial remapping**, encompasses remappings that employ any polynomial form. Other terminology refers to how the mapping function $\widetilde{\theta}$ is constructed. We may speak of **interpolated**, **least squares**, **gradient**, or **gradient-Hessian** remappings.

If $\widetilde{\theta}$ is to have a nonlinear polynomial form and the dimensionality of ${}^1\boldsymbol{R}$ is high, constructing $\widetilde{\theta}$ can be computationally expensive. Two ways to streamline computations are:

1. precede the polynomial remapping with a holdings remapping, and
2. limit the number of quadratic or higher-order coefficients in the functional form of $\widetilde{\theta}$.

Compared to holdings remappings, which tend to provide excellent approximations, global remappings offer more varied results. Considerable care should be exercised when incorporating them into a mapping procedure. Regardless, linear and quadratic remappings are popular because they facilitate linear and quadratic transformation procedures.

Selecting a Polynomial Form

Consider portfolio mapping ${}^1P = \theta({}^1\boldsymbol{R})$ where ${}^1\boldsymbol{R}$ is n-dimensional. Linear and quadratic remappings have forms

$$ {}^1\widetilde{P} = \widetilde{\theta}({}^1\boldsymbol{R}) = \boldsymbol{b}\,{}^1\boldsymbol{R} + a \qquad [9.20] $$

and

$$ {}^1\widetilde{P} = \widetilde{\theta}({}^1\boldsymbol{R}) = {}^1\boldsymbol{R}'\boldsymbol{c}\,{}^1\boldsymbol{R} + \boldsymbol{b}\,{}^1\boldsymbol{R} + a, \qquad [9.21] $$

where a is a scalar, $\boldsymbol{b}$ is an n-dimensional row vector, and $\boldsymbol{c}$ is an $n \times n$ symmetric matrix. Linear remappings are used with portfolios comprising "linear" instruments such as forwards. Quadratic remappings are used with portfolios that hold options or other "nonlinear" instruments.

In the quadratic case, $\boldsymbol{c}$ has

$$ \frac{n^2 + n}{2} \qquad [9.22] $$

unique components. Assigning all of these values can be computationally expensive if n is large, so it is worth limiting the generality of a quadratic form where possible. This is done by fixing certain components $c_{i,j}$ and b_i equal to zero in advance.

Selecting which components to assign nonzero values requires experience and some experimentation. It is often reasonable to model all b_i terms and the single a term. Deciding which diagonal terms $c_{i,i}$ to model is a question of which key factors contribute significantly to nonlinearity. In an options portfolio, these are the key factors for the options' underliers. You might also permit nonzero diagonal coefficients $c_{i,i}$ for key factors representing implied volatilities, although these are less significant. Usually, most or all off-diagonal terms $c_{i,j}$ can be set equal to 0.

Linear Remappings

Linear remappings are widely used with portfolios composed exclusively of "linear" instruments—futures, forwards, spot or physical commodities positions, swaps, most non-callable bonds, foreign exchange, and equities. For such portfolios, linear remappings afford excellent approximations. They facilitate the use of linear transformation procedures.

If a portfolio holds even a single "nonlinear" instrument—such as an option—a linear remapping should not be used. Exhibits 9.13 and 9.14 offer a simple but dramatic example of why this is so. Exhibit 9.13 illustrates a portfolio mapping function θ of a portfolio with a delta-hedged, negative-gamma exposure to a single underlier, whose value is represented by key factor ${}^1R_1$:[2]

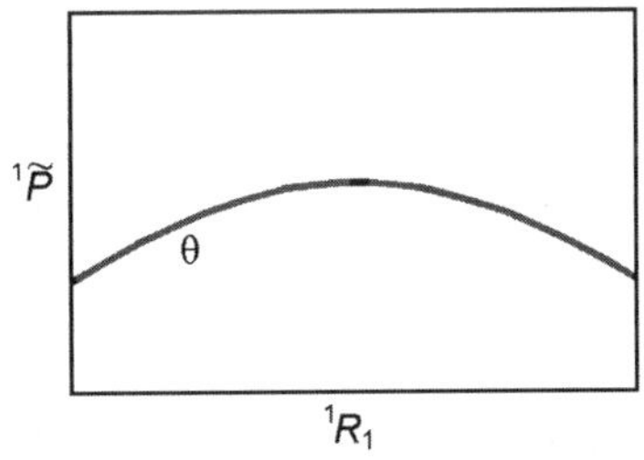

Exhibit 9.13 A portfolio's value ${}^1P$ depends upon a single key factor ${}^1R_1$ as shown.

Using a derivative approximation, we approximate ${}^1P = \theta({}^1R_1)$ with linear remapping ${}^1\widetilde{P} = \widetilde{\theta}({}^1R_1)$. The new mapping function $\widetilde{\theta}$ is graphed in Exhibit 9.14.

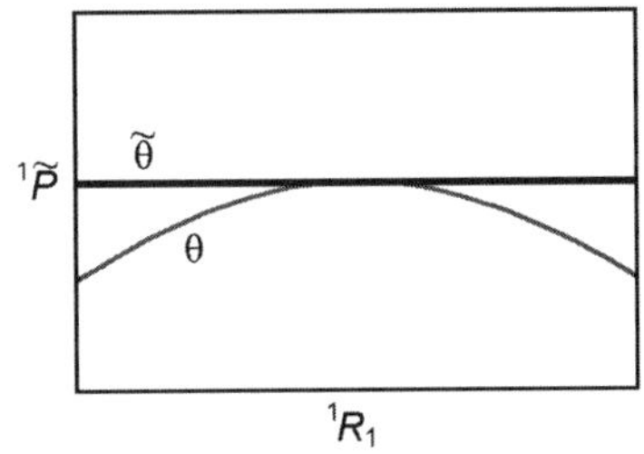

Exhibit 9.14 This linear remapping erroneously suggests an absence of market risk.

[2]In practice, such a position would also have implied volatility and interest rate exposures. For this example, we treat these as constant.

The new mapping function $\tilde{\theta}$ is a constant function, suggesting the portfolio has no market risk whatsoever. This ignores the—possibly substantial—risk due to the portfolio's negative gamma. In this example, a linear remapping does not provide a crude approximation. It is simply wrong. This example is not contrived. Derivatives dealers routinely delta hedge negative gamma positions.

Linear Remappings with Gradient Approximations

Linear remappings are usually constructed with gradient approximations. A gradient approximation can be constructed about any point, but the conditional expectation ${}^{1|0}\mu = {}^{0}E({}^{1}\boldsymbol{R})$ is a reasonable choice. The remapping then has form

$$\tilde{\theta}({}^{1}\boldsymbol{R}) = \theta({}^{1|0}\mu) + [\nabla\theta({}^{1|0}\mu)]'({}^{1}\boldsymbol{R} - {}^{1|0}\mu). \qquad [9.23]$$

Because pricing formulas for many financial instruments are easily differentiated, the gradient can usually be valued analytically. Otherwise, it may be valued with finite differences. This will require $n + 1$ valuations of θ.

Example: Gradient Approximations. In an example of Section 8.5, we constructed a primary mapping for an Australian trader's foreign exchange portfolio, as indicated in Exhibit 8.16. We obtained primary mapping [8.66], which is presented again here

$${}^{1}P = 1{,}000{,}000 \begin{pmatrix} -8.548\,{}^{1}R_3^{AUD} - 7.942\,{}^{1}R_4^{AUD} + 18.460\,{}^{1}R_5^{AUD} \\ +6.474\,{}^{1}R_6^{AUD} - 8.304\,{}^{1}R_7^{AUD} + 39.803\,{}^{1}R_3^{USD}\,{}^{1}R_1^{FX} \\ +5.307\,{}^{1}R_4^{USD}\,{}^{1}R_1^{FX} - 10.443\,{}^{1}R_5^{USD}\,{}^{1}R_1^{FX} \\ -28.736\,{}^{1}R_6^{USD}\,{}^{1}R_1^{FX} - 2.141\,{}^{1}R_7^{USD}\,{}^{1}R_1^{FX} \\ -4239.176\,{}^{1}R_3^{JPY}\,{}^{1}R_2^{FX} - 4.824\,{}^{1}R_4^{JPY}\,{}^{1}R_2^{FX} \\ -227.667\,{}^{1}R_5^{JPY}\,{}^{1}R_2^{FX} + 3054.452\,{}^{1}R_6^{JPY}\,{}^{1}R_2^{FX} \\ +957.214\,{}^{1}R_7^{JPY}\,{}^{1}R_2^{FX} \end{pmatrix}. \qquad [9.24]$$

The primary mapping is quadratic, which makes taking its gradient easy. All we need is a value for ${}^{1|0}\mu = {}^{0}E({}^{1}\boldsymbol{R})$, and we can apply [9.23]. Assuming ${}^{0}E({}^{1}\boldsymbol{R}) = {}^{0}\boldsymbol{r}$, we have

$${}^{1|0}\mu = \begin{pmatrix} {}^{1|0}\mu^{AUD} \\ {}^{1|0}\mu^{USD} \\ {}^{1|0}\mu^{JPY} \\ {}^{1|0}\mu^{FX} \end{pmatrix} = \begin{pmatrix} {}^{0}\boldsymbol{r}^{AUD} \\ {}^{0}\boldsymbol{r}^{USD} \\ {}^{0}\boldsymbol{r}^{JPY} \\ {}^{0}\boldsymbol{r}^{FX} \end{pmatrix}, \qquad [9.25]$$

where current discount factors are

$$
{}^{0}\boldsymbol{r}^{AUD} = \begin{pmatrix} .999861 \\ .999032 \\ .998068 \\ .995758 \\ \vdots \\ .951729 \end{pmatrix}, \quad {}^{0}\boldsymbol{r}^{USD} = \begin{pmatrix} .999886 \\ .999204 \\ .998409 \\ .996496 \\ \vdots \\ .958876 \end{pmatrix}, \quad {}^{0}\boldsymbol{r}^{JPY} = \begin{pmatrix} .999998 \\ .999988 \\ .999976 \\ .999941 \\ \vdots \\ .998899 \end{pmatrix}, \qquad [9.26]
$$

and current exchange rates are

$$
{}^{0}\boldsymbol{r}^{FX} = \begin{pmatrix} .527300 \\ .004298 \end{pmatrix}. \qquad [9.27]
$$

Taking the gradient of [9.24] at ${}^{1|0}\boldsymbol{\mu}$, and applying [9.23], we obtain a linear remapping ${}^{1}\widetilde{P} = \widetilde{\theta}({}^{1}\boldsymbol{R})$:

$$
{}^{1}\widetilde{P} = 1{,}000{,}000 \begin{pmatrix} -8.548\,{}^{1}R_3^{AUD} - 7.942\,{}^{1}R_4^{AUD} + 18.460\,{}^{1}R_5^{AUD} \\ +6.474\,{}^{1}R_6^{AUD} - 8.304\,{}^{1}R_7^{AUD} + 20.988\,{}^{1}R_3^{USD} \\ +2.798\,{}^{1}R_4^{USD} - 5.507\,{}^{1}R_5^{USD} - 15.152\,{}^{1}R_6^{USD} \\ -1.129\,{}^{1}R_7^{USD} - 18.221\,{}^{1}R_3^{JPY} - .021\,{}^{1}R_4^{JPY} \\ -.979\,{}^{1}R_5^{JPY} + 13.132\,{}^{1}R_6^{JPY} + 4.115\,{}^{1}R_7^{JPY} \\ +4.104\,{}^{1}R_1^{FX} - 459.716\,{}^{1}R_2^{FX} - .188 \end{pmatrix}. \qquad [9.28]
$$

To assess how well ${}^{1}\widetilde{P}$ approximates ${}^{1}P$, we generate 1000 pseudorandom realizations ${}^{1}\boldsymbol{r}^{[k]}$ of ${}^{1}\boldsymbol{R}$ based upon an assumed conditional distribution for ${}^{1}\boldsymbol{R}$. We determine corresponding realizations ${}^{1}p^{[k]} = \theta({}^{1}\boldsymbol{r}^{[k]})$ and ${}^{1}\widetilde{p}^{[k]} = \widetilde{\theta}({}^{1}\boldsymbol{r}^{[k]})$ for ${}^{1}P$ and ${}^{1}\widetilde{P}$. These are plotted in the scatter diagram of Exhibit 9.15.

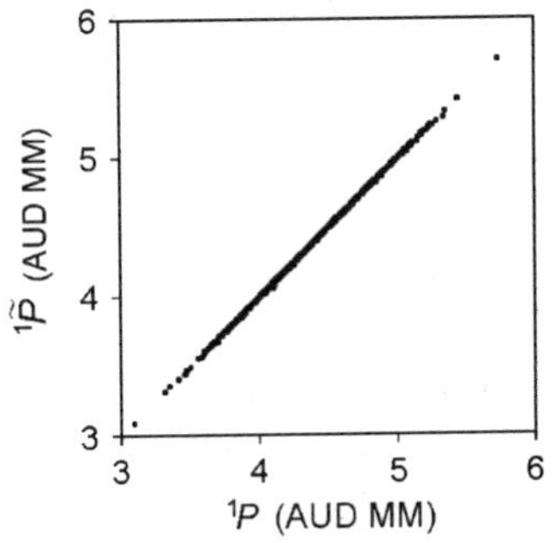

Exhibit 9.15 This chart illustrates how well the remapped portfolio value ${}^{1}\widetilde{P}$ approximates ${}^{1}P$. It was constructed by generating 1000 pseudorandom realizations ${}^{1}\boldsymbol{r}^{[k]}$ for key vector ${}^{1}\boldsymbol{R}$. Corresponding realizations ${}^{1}p^{[k]}$ and ${}^{1}\widetilde{p}^{[k]}$ were calculated. Pairs $({}^{1}p^{[k]}, {}^{1}\widetilde{p}^{[k]})$ were plotted to form the scatter diagram shown here. The fact that all points fall near a line passing at a 45° angle through the center of the graph indicates that ${}^{1}\widetilde{P}$ is an excellent approximation for ${}^{1}P$.

All points cluster near a line passing through the center of the chart at a 45° angle. The remapping provides an excellent approximation. Although primary mapping [9.24] is mathematically quadratic, its behavior is essentially linear over a region of likely realizations for ${}^1\boldsymbol{R}$.

Quadratic Remappings

Quadratic remappings are used with portfolios that hold one or more "nonlinear" instruments—options, interest-rate caps or floors, mortgage-backed securities, callable bonds, various derivative instruments, most structured notes, etc. These remappings are appealing because they facilitate quadratic transformation procedures as well as certain Monte Carlo transformation procedures that employ variance reduction. Despite such appeal, quadratic remappings should be applied with care.

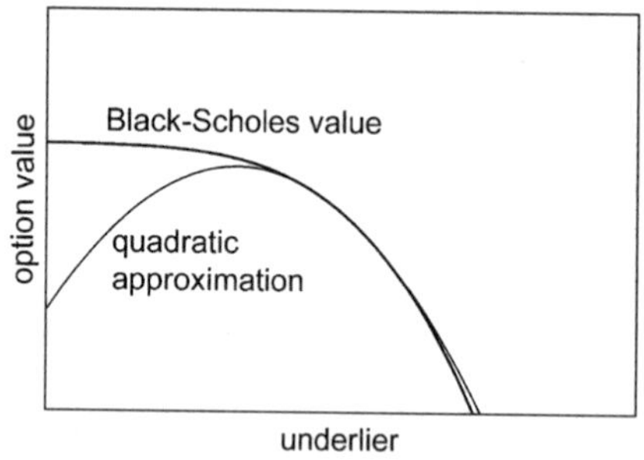

Exhibit 9.16 Quadratic remappings generally provide a good approximation over a certain region of values for ${}^1\boldsymbol{R}$. Outside that region, the approximation can be poor. This is illustrated with a quadratic polynomial used to approximate the Black-Scholes market value of a short call option.

Exhibit 9.16 illustrates a quadratic polynomial approximation for the Black-Scholes (1973) option pricing formula. The value of a short option is graphed as a function of underlier value. A quadratic polynomial approximation is fit to this based upon the first and second derivatives of the option's value. Over a region of underlier values, the approximation is excellent. Outside that region, the approximation is poor. Such behavior is typical of situations in which we might apply a quadratic remapping. The approximations are highly localized.

Before incorporating a quadratic remapping into a mapping procedure, we must assess whether that region of good approximation will be large enough for the needs of the VaR measure. The decision is complicated by the fact that we don't know in advance all the portfolios to which the VaR measure will be applied. We also don't know the distributions—especially their standard deviations—of applicable key factors. We want to be sure that a quadratic remapping will be reasonable for all portfolios and all distributions of ${}^1\boldsymbol{R}$ that may be encountered.

A region of good approximation will need to be larger for a 95% VaR metric than for a 90% VaR metric because the larger quantile encompasses more extreme market events. For reasons such as this, a quadratic remapping may be reasonable with one VaR metric but not with another. They are generally unreasonable for 99% or ETL metrics. Horizon is also an issue. Key-factor standard deviations tend to be larger for long horizons than for short horizons. A quadratic remapping's region of good approximation will need to be larger for a 1-week VaR horizon than for a 1-day horizon.

Quadratic remappings may poorly approximate discontinuous or non-smooth primary mappings. An obvious problem is put or call options expiring at time 1. Even worse are expiring digital options, which introduce a jump discontinuity into the primary mapping function. The existence of such instruments in a portfolio should not rule out the use of a quadratic remapping, but it does raise serious concerns. (Exhibit 9.17.)

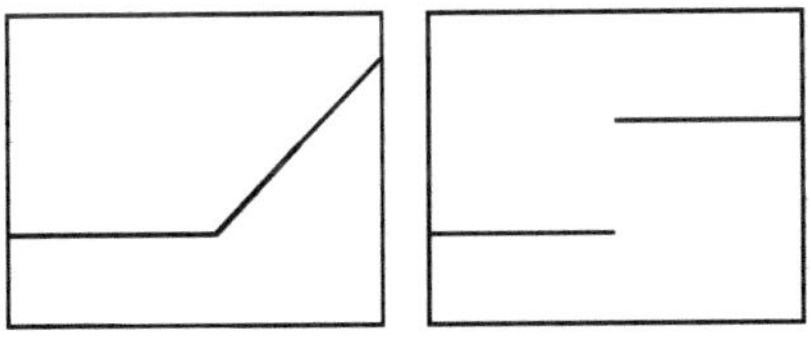

Exhibit 9.17 Price functions for an expiring call option and expiring digital option are indicated. If a portfolio mapping is discontinuous or non-smooth, a quadratic remapping may be inappropriate.

A final issue is the purpose of a quadratic remapping. If a quadratic remapping is intended to replace a primary portfolio mapping, it needs to be a good approximation. In Chapter 10, we will discuss how quadratic remappings can complement primary mappings to facilitate variance reduction in a Monte Carlo transformation. When used in this manner, the quadratic remapping doesn't have to be as good an approximation.

Quadratic Remappings with Gradient-Hessian Approximations

A quadratic remapping can be constructed with a gradient-Hessian approximation. Constructed about the point ${}^{1|0}\mu = {}^0E({}^1\boldsymbol{R})$, the remapping has form

$$\tilde{\theta}({}^1\boldsymbol{R}) = \theta({}^{1|0}\mu) + [\nabla\theta({}^{1|0}\mu)]'({}^1\boldsymbol{R} - {}^{1|0}\mu) + \frac{1}{2}({}^1\boldsymbol{R} - {}^{1|0}\mu)'[\nabla^2\,\theta({}^{1|0}\mu)]({}^1\boldsymbol{R} - {}^{1|0}\mu). \tag{9.29}$$

Quadratic remappings are rarely constructed in this manner. Because they are based upon first and second partial derivatives, the approximations are too localized.

Interpolation and the Method of Least Squares

To construct a quadratic approximation that is good over a larger region of values for ${}^1\boldsymbol{R}$, we may apply ordinary interpolation or ordinary least squares to fit a quadratic remapping:

1. select a set of realizations $\{{}^1\boldsymbol{r}^{[1]}, {}^1\boldsymbol{r}^{[2]}, \ldots, {}^1\boldsymbol{r}^{[l]}\}$ for ${}^1\boldsymbol{R}$,
2. value ${}^1p^{[k]} = \theta({}^1\boldsymbol{r}^{[k]})$ for each, and
3. either interpolate or apply least squares to the points $({}^1\boldsymbol{r}^{[k]}, {}^1p^{[k]})$.

Since ordinary least squares is a generalization of ordinary interpolation (see Exercise 2.16), we consider both approaches simultaneously. Suppose the form of quadratic polynomial we wish to fit has m unique potentially nonzero components $c_{i,j}$, b_i, and a. With interpolation, the number l of realizations ${}^1\boldsymbol{r}^{[k]}$ equals m. With least squares, l exceeds m.

If the dimensionality of ${}^1\boldsymbol{R}$ is large, l will also be large. Since we must perform l valuations ${}^1p^{[k]} = \theta({}^1\boldsymbol{r}^{[k]})$, it is desirable that θ be as easy to value as possible. It may be advisable to precede the remapping with a holdings remapping that simplifies θ.

Selecting Realizations for Interpolation or Least Squares

Realizations ${}^1\boldsymbol{r}^{[k]}$ for interpolation or least squares should be selected with care. A poor choice may distort results. The simple approach of generating pseudorandom realizations based upon the distribution of ${}^1\boldsymbol{R}$ is inadvisable, as it will cause most realizations to cluster near ${}^{1|0}\boldsymbol{\mu} = {}^0E({}^1\boldsymbol{R})$. If a quadratic remapping is to be a good approximation over a large region of values for ${}^1\boldsymbol{R}$, we need to apply interpolation or least squares to a dispersed set of realizations.

A general approach to specifying realizations is to let the point ${}^{1|0}\boldsymbol{\mu}$ be one realization ${}^1\boldsymbol{r}^{[l]}$, and select other realizations that are dispersed in some manner on the ellipsoid[3]

$$({}^1\boldsymbol{R} - {}^{1|0}\boldsymbol{\mu})' \, {}^{1|0}\boldsymbol{\Sigma}^{-1}({}^1\boldsymbol{R} - {}^{1|0}\boldsymbol{\mu}) = q^2, \qquad [9.30]$$

where ${}^{1|0}\boldsymbol{\Sigma}$ is the conditional covariance matrix of ${}^1\boldsymbol{R}$ and q is a constant. If ${}^1\boldsymbol{R}$ is joint-normal, this ellipsoid defines a level curve (surface) of its distribution—that

[3]Formula [9.30] defines an ellipsoid as long as ${}^{1|0}\Sigma$ (and hence ${}^{1|0}\Sigma^{-1}$) is positive definite.

is, a curve on which the probability density of ${}^1\boldsymbol{R}$ is constant. In practice, q can be set equal to 1, 2, or some value in-between. In a sense, it reflects the number of standard deviations from ${}^{1|0}\boldsymbol{\mu}$ at which realizations are placed, but this is precise only in one-dimension.

We may disperse $l - 1$ realizations on ellipsoid [9.30] by selecting points on the unit sphere centered at $\mathbf{0}$ and projecting these onto the ellipsoid. There are various ways this might be done. The following approach provides a good dispersion of realizations as long as ${}^{1|0}\boldsymbol{\Sigma}$ is not multicollinear.

Let ${}^{1|0}\boldsymbol{\sigma}$ be a diagonal matrix with diagonal elements equal to the conditional standard deviations of ${}^1\boldsymbol{R}$. Let ${}^{1|0}\rho$ be the conditional correlation matrix of ${}^1\boldsymbol{R}$. Given points $\boldsymbol{p}_k$ on the unit sphere centered at the origin $\mathbf{0}$, define corresponding realizations ${}^1\boldsymbol{r}^{[k]}$ as

$$
{}^1\boldsymbol{r}^{[k]} = \left(\frac{q}{\sqrt{\boldsymbol{p}_k' \, {}^{1|0}\rho^{-1} \boldsymbol{p}_k}}\right) {}^{1|0}\boldsymbol{\sigma}\boldsymbol{p}_k + {}^{1|0}\boldsymbol{\mu}. \qquad [9.31]
$$

This leaves the question of how to select $l - 1$ points $\boldsymbol{p}_k$ on the unit sphere centered at $\mathbf{0}$. We might randomly disperse them. Generate $l - 1$ pseudorandom vectors $\boldsymbol{v}_k \sim U_n((-1, 1)^n)$. Discard and generate replacements for any vectors that equal the zero vector $\mathbf{0}$ or have norm greater than 1. Then set

$$
\boldsymbol{p}_k = \frac{\boldsymbol{v}_k}{\|\boldsymbol{v}_k\|} \qquad [9.32]
$$

for all k. This approach has little to recommend itself other than the fact that it is easy. Distortions may result from points randomly clustering in certain regions and not in others.

If a quadratic remapping is to be constructed with interpolation, we may directly select points $\boldsymbol{p}_k$ based upon the coefficients $c_{i,j}$, b_i, and a to be determined. For each coefficient $c_{i,i}$, select a point $\boldsymbol{p}_k$ whose components are all 0's except the ith component, which is 1. For each coefficient $c_{i,j}$, $i \neq j$, select a point $\boldsymbol{p}_k$ whose components are all 0's except the ith and j^{th} components, which are $1/\sqrt{2}$. For each coefficient b_i, select a point $\boldsymbol{p}_k$ whose components are all 0's except the ith component, which is -1. This procedure will yield precisely $l - 1$ points unless your quadratic form has $a = 0$. In that case, the approach will yield l points. To reduce this to $l - 1$ points, discard two points, $\boldsymbol{p}_k$ and $\boldsymbol{p}_j$, and replace them with the single point

$$
\frac{\boldsymbol{p}_k - \boldsymbol{p}_j}{\|\boldsymbol{p}_k - \boldsymbol{p}_j\|}. \qquad [9.33]
$$

Obviously, discarded points $\boldsymbol{p}_k$ and $\boldsymbol{p}_j$ should be selected so that their replacement point is not the same as one of the other points already selected.

To construct a quadratic remapping of form

$$\theta({}^1\boldsymbol{R}) = c_{1,1}\,{}^1R_1^2 + c_{1,2}\,{}^1R_1\,{}^1R_2 + b_1\,{}^1R_1 + b_2\,{}^1R_2 + a \qquad [9.34]$$

we would select points $\boldsymbol{p}_k$ as indicated in Exhibit 9.18.

Considering this configuration of points, we may wonder if better results might be obtained with a symmetrical configuration, such as that in Exhibit 9.19:

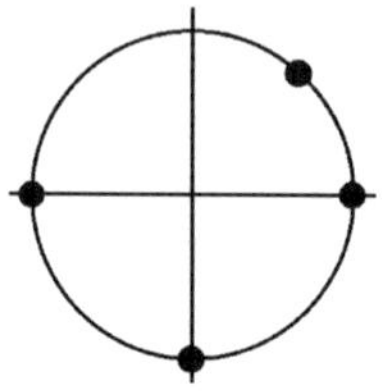

Exhibit 9.18 An arrangement of points $\boldsymbol{p}_k$ on the unit sphere suitable for use in interpolation of a quadratic remapping of form [9.34].

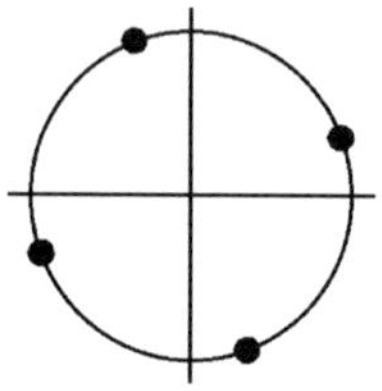

Exhibit 9.19 A symmetrical alternative to the configuration of Exhibit 9.18.

Such symmetrical configurations tend to work best if a remapping is to be constructed using least squares and the number of points l exceeds the number m of coefficients to be selected by a reasonable margin.

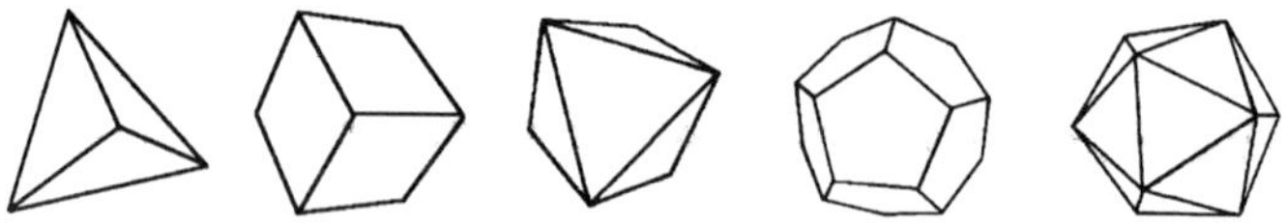

Exhibit 9.20 The Platonic solids.

Ignoring trivialities,[4] a perfectly symmetrical configuration of $l - 1$ points on a unit sphere in n dimensions is not always well defined. In three dimensions, such an arrangement is possible with 4, 6, 8, 12, or 20 points. These symmetrical configurations are achieved by inscribing one of the five Platonic solids within the sphere and placing a point at each of the solid's vertices.

[4] A trivial solution is to space the points at equal intervals about the equator of the sphere. This works in all cases and is perfectly symmetrical, but it is uninteresting for our purpose.

In three dimensions, five points cannot be distributed with such symmetry. Perhaps the most symmetrical configuration is the one illustrated in Exhibit 9.21. Here, points at the north and south poles of the sphere are symmetrical to each other, but are configured differently from those on the equator.

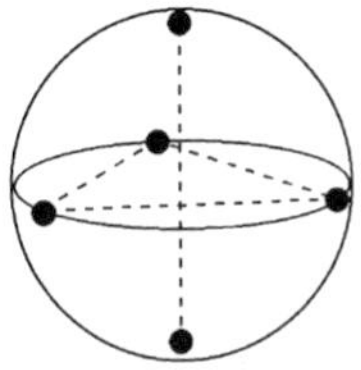

Exhibit 9.21 A nontrivial perfectly symmetrical configuration does not exist for five points on the surface of a sphere in three dimensions. Displayed here is a less-than-perfect solution. Points at the north and south poles are symmetrical to each other, but are configured differently from the three points on the equator.

In higher dimensions, the situation is similar. Certain numbers of points allow for perfectly symmetrical configurations, but for most numbers of points, any nontrivial configuration affords less-than-perfect symmetry.

Accordingly, we don't seek perfect symmetry, but only an arrangement of points that is as uniform as possible. A convenient solution is to distribute the points in the same manner in which $l - 1$ electrons would distribute themselves on the surface of a sphere based upon the mutual repulsive forces between them. This concept is defined[5] in three dimensions, and the mathematics generalizes to higher dimensions. Treated as electrons, $l - 1$ points $\boldsymbol{p}_k$ distribute themselves to minimize the sum

$$\sum_{k<j} \frac{1}{\|\boldsymbol{p}_k - \boldsymbol{p}_j\|}. \qquad [9.35]$$

The configuration of Exhibit 9.21 is such a "minimum energy" configuration. Minimum energy configurations for other values of n and $l - 1$ can be obtained by computer simulation. First generate a set $\{\boldsymbol{p}_k^{[0]}\}$ of $l - 1$ pseudorandom points on the surface of the sphere. A procedure for doing so was described earlier in this section. Next, shift the points around iteratively based upon applicable electrostatic forces to obtain subsequent point sets $\{\boldsymbol{p}_k^{[1]}\}$, $\{\boldsymbol{p}_k^{[2]}\}$, $\{\boldsymbol{p}_k^{[3]}\}$, ... Continue until the points stop moving discernibly from one iteration to the next—until $max(\|\boldsymbol{p}_k^{[i+1]} - \boldsymbol{p}_k^{[i]}\|) < \alpha_1$ for some suitable value α_1.

[5]It is not uniquely defined. Two stable arrangements of 16 electrons are possible. However, one of these has a lower potential energy as defined by [9.35].

At each iteration, the new point set $\{\boldsymbol{p}_k^{[i+1]}\}$ is obtained from the current one $\{\boldsymbol{p}_k^{[i]}\}$ as follows. For each point $\boldsymbol{p}_k^{[i]}$, calculate a vector-valued "force" $\boldsymbol{f}_k^{[i]}$,

$$\boldsymbol{f}_k^{[i]} = \alpha_2 \sum_{j \neq k} \frac{\boldsymbol{p}_k^{[i]} - \boldsymbol{p}_j^{[i]}}{\left\| \boldsymbol{p}_k^{[i]} - \boldsymbol{p}_j^{[i]} \right\|^2}, \tag{9.36}$$

where α_2 is a suitable scaling factor. Shift each point to obtain the subsequent point:

$$\boldsymbol{p}_k^{[i+1]} = \frac{\boldsymbol{p}_k^{[i]} + \boldsymbol{f}_k^{[i]}}{\left\| \boldsymbol{p}_k^{[i]} + \boldsymbol{f}_k^{[i]} \right\|}. \tag{9.37}$$

The algorithm may converge slowly; especially for large n and p. Values $\alpha_1 = .001$ and $\alpha_2 = 1/(20p)$ work well for most VaR-related applications.[6]

If n and l remain the same each time a VaR measure is used, the above algorithm only needs to be run once. The resulting point set $\{\boldsymbol{p}_k\}$ can be stored for reuse each time the VaR measure is applied. Of course, the points will have to be projected onto different realizations ${}^1\boldsymbol{r}^{[k]}$ on ellipsoid [9.30] each time because ${}^{1|0}\boldsymbol{\Sigma}$ will change.

With least squares, it may be advantageous to weight the realization ${}^1\boldsymbol{r}^{[l]} = {}^{1|0}\boldsymbol{\mu}$ more heavily than others. Our discussion of least squares in Section 2.9 does not mention nonuniform weightings of points. However, this is easily accomplished by considering additional realizations $\boldsymbol{r}^{[k]}$ and setting them all equal to ${}^{1|0}\boldsymbol{\mu}$.

EXAMPLE: COCOA OPTIONS. Today's date is September 28, 2001. Consider a 1-week VaR horizon. A cocoa merchant holds 39 call options struck at 1050 on the December 2001 future, which is trading at 1077 USD/ton. The options expire in 35 actual days. Each future is for 10 tons. A primary mapping is

$${}^1P = \theta({}^1\boldsymbol{R}) = 390B^{Call}({}^1R_1, 1050, {}^1R_2, {}^1R_3, 28/365), \tag{9.38}$$

where $B^{Call}()$ denotes Black's (1976) pricing formula for call options on futures and

$${}^1\boldsymbol{R} = \begin{pmatrix} {}^1R_1 \\ {}^1R_2 \\ {}^1R_3 \end{pmatrix} \sim \begin{pmatrix} \text{future's price} \\ \text{implied volatility} \\ \text{1-month Libor} \end{pmatrix}. \tag{9.39}$$

Based upon current and historical market data, assume ${}^1\boldsymbol{R} \sim {}^0N_3({}^{1|0}\boldsymbol{\mu}, {}^{1|0}\boldsymbol{\Sigma})$ where

$${}^{1|0}\boldsymbol{\mu} = \begin{pmatrix} 1077 \\ .2721 \\ .0263 \end{pmatrix}, \quad {}^{1|0}\boldsymbol{\Sigma} = \begin{pmatrix} 2414 & .6655 & -.009923 \\ .6655 & .004691 & 2.183 \times 10^{-6} \\ -.009923 & 2.183 \times 10^{-6} & 7.650 \times 10^{-7} \end{pmatrix}. \tag{9.40}$$

[6] The algorithm is not intended to reproduce the exact motion of $l - 1$ electrons. To the precision dictated by our stopping condition, the result will be a locally minimum-energy configuration.

Let's use ordinary least squares with 10 realizations ${}^{1}\boldsymbol{r}^{[k]}$ to construct a quadratic remapping of the form

$$ {}^{1}\widetilde{P} = \widetilde{\theta}({}^{1}\boldsymbol{R}) = c_{1,1}{}^{1}R_1^2 + c_{2,2}{}^{1}R_2^2 + b_1{}^{1}R_1 + b_2{}^{1}R_2 + b_3{}^{1}R_3 + a. \qquad [9.41] $$

Realization ${}^{1}\boldsymbol{r}^{[10]}$ is set equal to ${}^{1|0}\boldsymbol{\mu}$. We choose to weight this three times the other realizations in the least squares analysis. This is accomplished by adding two redundant realizations ${}^{1}\boldsymbol{r}^{[11]} = {}^{1|0}\boldsymbol{\mu}$ and ${}^{1}\boldsymbol{r}^{[12]} = {}^{1|0}\boldsymbol{\mu}$. The remaining nine realizations, ${}^{1}\boldsymbol{r}^{[1]}$ through ${}^{1}\boldsymbol{r}^{[9]}$, are selected using the minimum energy approach described above. We generate 9 pseudorandom points on the unit sphere and iteratively shift these until they achieve a minimum energy configuration. Computations employ $\alpha_1 = .001$ and $\alpha_2 = 1/180$. Results are indicated in Exhibit 9.22.

k	Points $\boldsymbol{p}_k$
1	(0.9388, –0.1063, 0.3276)
2	(–0.7978, –0.5527, 0.2408)
3	(0.7247, 0.0618, –0.6863)
4	(–0.8678, 0.4836, 0.1148)
5	(0.2337, –0.9515, 0.1999)
6	(–0.1950, 0.6626, –0.7232)
7	(–0.0262, 0.0239, 0.9994)
8	(0.2614, 0.9064, 0.3319)
9	(–0.2719, –0.5275, –0.8049)

Exhibit 9.22 Nine points distributed in a minimum energy configuration on the unit sphere.

The points are projected onto ellipsoid [9.30] with constant $q = 1$. The result is 9 realizations ${}^{1}\boldsymbol{r}^{[k]}$. These, with the three realizations ${}^{1}\boldsymbol{r}^{[10]}$, ${}^{1}\boldsymbol{r}^{[11]}$, and ${}^{1}\boldsymbol{r}^{[12]}$ at ${}^{1|0}\boldsymbol{\mu}$, are indicated in Exhibit 9.23. Corresponding portfolio values ${}^{1}p^{[k]} = \theta({}^{1}\boldsymbol{r}^{[k]})$ are also indicated.

k	${}^{1}\boldsymbol{r}^{[k]}$	${}^{1}p^{[k]}$
1	(1117.22, 0.2657, 0.02655)	29,616
2	(1033.38, 0.2300, 0.02653)	7,388
3	(1116.53, 0.2768, 0.02563)	29,770
4	(1038.42, 0.3021, 0.02639)	11,426
5	(1087.43, 0.2129, 0.02646)	18,744
6	(1068.53, 0.3122, 0.02574)	18,116
7	(1075.74, 0.2737, 0.02715)	18,149
8	(1090.27, 0.3362, 0.02660)	24,549
9	(1063.87, 0.2366, 0.02561)	13,668
10	(1077.00, 0.2721, 0.02360)	18,396
11	(1077.00, 0.2721, 0.02360)	18,396
12	(1077.00, 0.2721, 0.02360)	18,396

Exhibit 9.23 Ten distinct realizations ${}^{1}\boldsymbol{r}^{[k]}$ are employed. The realization equal to ${}^{1|0}\boldsymbol{\mu}$ is repeated three times so it will be weighted more heavily in the least squares analysis. Corresponding portfolio values ${}^{1}p^{[k]} = \theta({}^{1}\boldsymbol{r}^{[k]})$ are also indicated.

Applying ordinary least squares, we fit quadratic polynomial [9.41] to the points $({}^1\boldsymbol{r}^{[k]}, {}^1p^{[k]})$, obtaining coefficient values

$$\begin{pmatrix} c_{1,1} \\ c_{2,2} \\ b_1 \\ b_2 \\ b_3 \\ a \end{pmatrix} = \begin{pmatrix} .8771 \\ 13{,}405 \\ -1640 \\ 34{,}850 \\ 41{,}355 \\ 755{,}499 \end{pmatrix}. \qquad [9.42]$$

To assess how well ${}^1\tilde{P}$ approximates ${}^1P$, we generate 1000 pseudorandom realizations ${}^1\boldsymbol{r}^{[k]}$ of ${}^1\boldsymbol{R}$ based upon a conditional distribution for ${}^1\boldsymbol{R}$. We determine corresponding realizations ${}^1p^{[k]} = \theta({}^1\boldsymbol{r}^{[k]})$ and ${}^1\tilde{p}^{[k]} = \tilde{\theta}({}^1\boldsymbol{r}^{[k]})$ for ${}^1P$ and ${}^1\tilde{P}$. These are plotted in the scatter diagram of Exhibit 9.24. Although points cluster around a line passing at a 45° angle through the center of the graph, the fit is not as good as in previous examples. This behavior is typical of quadratic remappings.

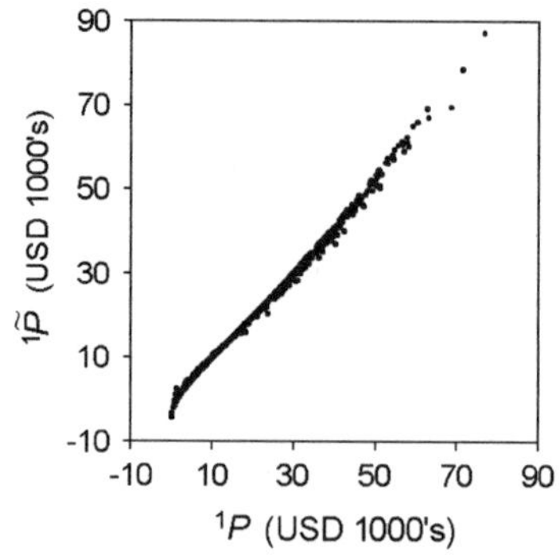

Exhibit 9.24 This chart illustrates how well the remapped portfolio value ${}^1\tilde{P}$ approximates ${}^1P$. It was constructed by generating 1000 pseudorandom realizations ${}^1\boldsymbol{r}^{[k]}$ for key vector ${}^1\boldsymbol{R}$. Corresponding realizations ${}^1p^{[k]}$ and ${}^1\tilde{p}^{[k]}$ were calculated. Pairs $({}^1p^{[k]}, {}^1\tilde{p}^{[k]})$ were plotted to form the above scatter diagram. Results are not as good as those we have obtained with other remappings.

Exercises

9.3 A forward portfolio has primary mapping

$${}^1P = \theta({}^1\boldsymbol{R}) = 10{,}000\, exp(-.25\, {}^1R_2)[{}^1R_1 - 76], \qquad [9.43]$$

where ${}^1R_1$ is a forward price and ${}^1R_2$ is an interest rate. Use a gradient approximation at point

$${}^{1|0}\boldsymbol{\mu} = \begin{pmatrix} 74 \\ .041 \end{pmatrix}. \qquad [9.44]$$

to construct a linear remapping of [9.43].

9.4 Prove that realization [9.31] is on ellipsoid [9.30].

9.5 Repeat our cocoa options example using ordinary interpolation to construct a remapping of form [9.41]. Do so according to the following steps:

(a) Based upon the coefficients required for form [9.41], select five points $\boldsymbol{p}_k$ on the unit sphere centered at $\mathbf{0}$.

(b) Use formula [9.31] with $q = 2$ to project the points from item (a) onto ellipsoid [9.30]. This will yield five realizations ${}^1\boldsymbol{r}^{[k]}$. Add to these realization ${}^1\boldsymbol{r}^{[6]} = {}^{1|0}\boldsymbol{\mu}$ for a total of six realizations.

(c) Use [9.38] to value ${}^1P$ at each realization to obtain six points for interpolation $({}^1\boldsymbol{r}^{[k]}, {}^1p^{[k]})$. Black's (1976) pricing formula for call options on futures is

$$B^{Call}(s, x, v, r, y) = exp(-ry)[s\Phi(d_1) - x\Phi(d_2)], \qquad [9.45]$$

where

$$d_1 = \frac{log(s/x) + (v^2/2)y}{v\sqrt{y}}, \qquad [9.46]$$

$$d_2 = d_1 - v\sqrt{y} \qquad [9.47]$$

and

s = underlying future's price;
x = strike price;
y = time to expiration in years;
r = continuously compounded (actual/actual) interest rate for maturity y;
v = implied volatility for strike x and maturity y;
Φ = CDF of the standard normal distribution.

We are assuming cash valuation. We use 1-month Libor in [9.45] out of convenience (despite the fact that USD Libor is for 2nd day settlement and the expiration for the option is only approximately 1 month). You do need to convert Libor rates from simple actual/360 to continuous actual/actual before using them in [9.45]. At time 1, there will be 28 actual days until the options' expiration.

(d) Apply ordinary interpolation to the six points $({}^1\boldsymbol{r}^{[k]}, {}^1p^{[k]})$ from part (c) to obtain a quadratic remapping of form [9.41].

9.6 Arrange 11 points in a minimum energy configuration on the surface of a sphere in four dimensions.

9.4. CHANGE-OF-VARIABLES REMAPPINGS

In VaR modeling, we frequently work with changes of variables. Every mapping is a change of variables. Consider a mapping that expresses a vector of discount factors ${}^1\boldsymbol{Q}$ as a function φ of corresponding interest rates ${}^1\boldsymbol{R}$. We describe it schematically as

$$ {}^1\boldsymbol{Q} \xleftarrow{\varphi} {}^1\boldsymbol{R} \qquad [9.48] $$

Here, mapping function φ reflects an exact relationship between ${}^1\boldsymbol{Q}$ and ${}^1\boldsymbol{R}$. A change of variables can also be an approximation—and hence a remapping. Suppose futures prices ${}^1\tilde{\boldsymbol{R}}$ are used to approximate forward prices ${}^1\boldsymbol{R}$. Based upon our convention that horizontal arrows denote exact relationships and vertical arrows denote approximations, we describe this relationship schematically as

$$ \begin{array}{c} {}^1\boldsymbol{R} \\ \uparrow \\ {}^1\tilde{\boldsymbol{R}} \end{array} \qquad [9.49] $$

Such approximations are employed in portfolio remappings in two ways. Sometimes, one key vector ${}^1\tilde{\boldsymbol{R}}$ can directly approximate another, ${}^1\boldsymbol{R}$:

$$ \begin{array}{ccccc} \multicolumn{5}{c}{\overbrace{\qquad\qquad\qquad\qquad}^{\theta}} \\ {}^1P & \xleftarrow{\omega} & {}^1S & \xleftarrow{\varphi} & {}^1\boldsymbol{R} \\ \uparrow & & \uparrow & & \uparrow \\ {}^1\tilde{P} & \xleftarrow{\omega} & {}^1\tilde{S} & \xleftarrow{\varphi} & {}^1\tilde{\boldsymbol{R}} \\ \multicolumn{5}{c}{\underbrace{\qquad\qquad\qquad\qquad}_{\theta}} \end{array} \qquad [9.50] $$

Other times, an approximating vector of risk factors ${}^1\boldsymbol{Q}$ must be constructed as a function $\dot{\varphi}$ of some other key vector ${}^1\tilde{\boldsymbol{R}}$:

$$ \begin{array}{ccccccc} \multicolumn{5}{c}{\overbrace{\qquad\qquad\qquad\qquad}^{\theta}} & & \\ {}^1P & \xleftarrow{\omega} & {}^1S & \xleftarrow{\varphi} & {}^1\boldsymbol{R} & & \\ \uparrow & & \uparrow & & \uparrow & & \\ {}^1\tilde{P} & \xleftarrow{\omega} & {}^1\tilde{S} & \xleftarrow{\varphi} & {}^1\boldsymbol{Q} & \xleftarrow{\dot{\varphi}} & {}^1\tilde{\boldsymbol{R}} \\ \multicolumn{7}{c}{\underbrace{\qquad\qquad\qquad\qquad\qquad\qquad}_{\tilde{\theta}}} \end{array} \qquad [9.51] $$

In schematic [9.50], key vector ${}^1\tilde{\boldsymbol{R}}$ replaces key vector ${}^1\boldsymbol{R}$, but portfolio mapping function θ is unaffected. Such remappings are variables remappings. In schematic [9.51], both key vector ${}^1\boldsymbol{R}$ and portfolio mapping function θ change. Such remappings are dual remappings.

EXAMPLE: COFFEE SPREADS. Consider our coffee wholesaler from Section 8.7. Based upon the primary mapping we constructed, the portfolio has exposures to a vector of coffee spreads:

$$ {}^{1}\boldsymbol{R}^{Spreads} = \begin{pmatrix} {}^{1}R_1^{Spreads} \\ {}^{1}R_2^{Spreads} \\ {}^{1}R_3^{Spreads} \\ \vdots \\ {}^{1}R_{30}^{Spreads} \end{pmatrix} \sim \begin{pmatrix} \text{Bolivia coffee cash spread} \\ \text{Brazil coffee cash spread} \\ \text{Burundi coffee cash spread} \\ \vdots \\ \text{Zimbabwe coffee cash spread} \end{pmatrix}. \qquad [9.52] $$

Many of these coffees trade inactively, so historical data is unavailable for their spreads. We address the problem by identifying eight coffees that are actively traded, and consider a vector of spreads for these

$$ {}^{1}\widetilde{\boldsymbol{R}}^{Spreads} = \begin{pmatrix} {}^{1}\widetilde{R}_1^{Spreads} \\ {}^{1}\widetilde{R}_2^{Spreads} \\ {}^{1}\widetilde{R}_3^{Spreads} \\ \vdots \\ {}^{1}\widetilde{R}_8^{Spreads} \end{pmatrix} \sim \begin{pmatrix} \text{Colombian UGQ cash spread} \\ \text{Guatemala SHB cash spread} \\ \text{Guatemala HB cash spread} \\ \vdots \\ \text{Brazil 4 cash spread} \end{pmatrix}. \qquad [9.53] $$

We cannot directly approximate ${}^{1}\boldsymbol{R}^{Spreads}$ with ${}^{1}\widetilde{\boldsymbol{R}}^{Spreads}$. The former has 30 components, whereas the latter has only 8. ${}^{1}\widetilde{\boldsymbol{R}}^{Spreads}$ offers among its components no reasonable proxy for many of the components of ${}^{1}\boldsymbol{R}^{Spreads}$. We solve the problem by approximating ${}^{1}\boldsymbol{R}^{Spreads}$ with a 30-dimensional vector ${}^{1}\boldsymbol{Q}$ comprising "blends" of the components of ${}^{1}\widetilde{\boldsymbol{R}}^{Spreads}$. Blends are specified by a knowledgeable coffee trader. The remapping has form

$$ \begin{array}{l} {}^{1}\boldsymbol{R}^{Spreads} \\ \uparrow \\ {}^{1}\boldsymbol{Q} \overset{\dot{\varphi}}{\longleftarrow} {}^{1}\widetilde{\boldsymbol{R}}^{Spreads} \end{array} \qquad [9.54] $$

The mapping function $\dot{\varphi}$ is a linear function that can be represented with a matrix:

$$ \begin{pmatrix} {}^{1}R_1^{Spreads} \\ {}^{1}R_2^{Spreads} \\ {}^{1}R_3^{Spreads} \\ {}^{1}R_4^{Spreads} \\ {}^{1}R_5^{Spreads} \\ \vdots \\ {}^{1}R_{30}^{Spreads} \end{pmatrix} \approx \begin{pmatrix} {}^{1}Q_1 \\ {}^{1}Q_2 \\ {}^{1}Q_3 \\ {}^{1}Q_4 \\ {}^{1}Q_5 \\ \vdots \\ {}^{1}Q_{30} \end{pmatrix} = \begin{pmatrix} 0 & 0 & 0 & 0 & 0 & .5 & .5 & 0 \\ 0 & 0 & 0 & 0 & 0 & 0 & 0 & 1 \\ 0 & 0 & 0 & 0 & .25 & .5 & .25 & 0 \\ 1 & 0 & 0 & 0 & 0 & 0 & 0 & 0 \\ 0 & .25 & .25 & .25 & .25 & 0 & 0 & 0 \\ & & & \vdots & & & & \\ 0 & 0 & 0 & 1 & 0 & 0 & 0 & 0 \end{pmatrix} \begin{pmatrix} {}^{1}\widetilde{R}_1^{Spreads} \\ {}^{1}\widetilde{R}_2^{Spreads} \\ {}^{1}\widetilde{R}_3^{Spreads} \\ \vdots \\ {}^{1}\widetilde{R}_8^{Spreads} \end{pmatrix}. \qquad [9.55] $$

For each row of the matrix, components sum to 1. This is a practical requirement, but it is not logically necessary. The remapping provides us with key vector ${}^{1}\widetilde{\boldsymbol{R}}^{Spreads}$ for which historical data is available.

Modeling Curves

Poorly designed VaR measures employ numerous key factors in an attempt to reproduce the actual shape of term structures or other curves. Consider the Euro swap curve for March 3, 1999, which is plotted in Exhibit 9.25.

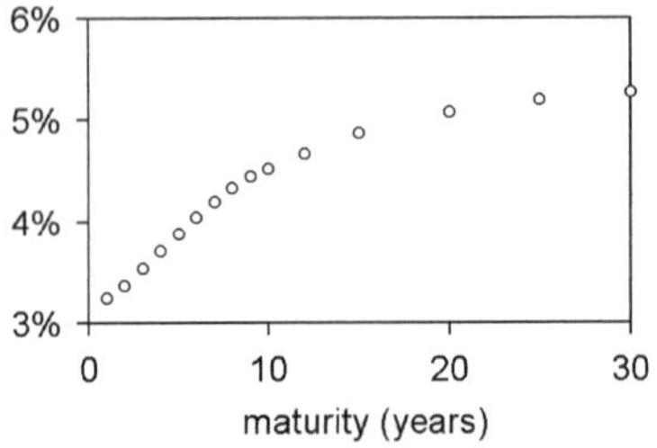

Exhibit 9.25 The Euro swap curve for March 3, 1999, is depicted with values for 15 maturities from 1 year to 30 years.

How many key factors are needed to model this term structure over time? In fact, it can be accurately reproduced with just three. The secret is to not model individual swap rates as key factors, but to model *changes* in individual swap rates. Exhibit 9.26 indicates the same swap curve as well as the swap curve from the previous week

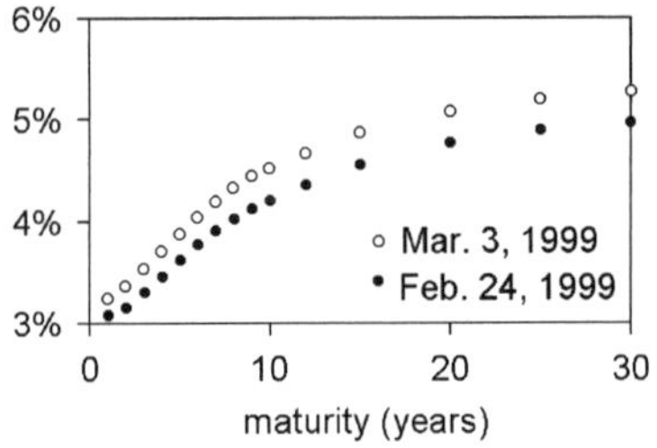

Exhibit 9.26 Euro swap curves for February 24 and March 3, 1999.

Over 1 week, the curve shifts upward with a slight tilt. Otherwise, its shape hardly changes. Exhibit 9.27 plots the change in the swap curve—swap rates for March 3 less corresponding swap rates for February 24.

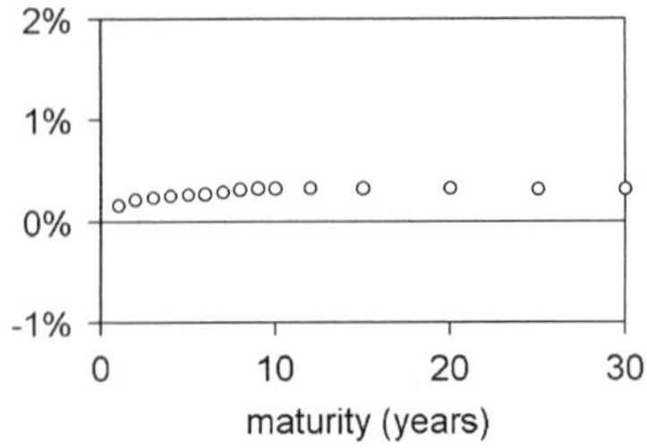

Exhibit 9.27 The change in the Euro swap curve going from February 24 to March 3, 1999.

This is a simple curve. We could easily model it with three key factors and interpolate for the rest. In this manner, we can accurately model the swap curve itself—it equals the change in the swap curve plus the previous week's swap curve. Let's formalize this.

Measure time in weeks. A primary mapping models the Euro swap curve with a 15-dimensional key vector

$$^{1}\boldsymbol{R} = \begin{pmatrix} {}^{1}R_1 \\ {}^{1}R_2 \\ {}^{1}R_3 \\ \vdots \\ {}^{1}R_{14} \\ {}^{1}R_{15} \end{pmatrix} \sim \begin{pmatrix} \text{1-year Euro swap rate} \\ \text{2-year Euro swap rate} \\ \text{3-year Euro swap rate} \\ \vdots \\ \text{25-year Euro swap rate} \\ \text{30-year Euro swap rate} \end{pmatrix}. \qquad [9.56]$$

We would like to implement a change-of-variables remapping that reduces the number of key factors. Consider a dual remapping of form

$$\begin{array}{l} {}^{1}\boldsymbol{R} \\ \uparrow \\ {}^{1}\boldsymbol{Q} \xleftarrow{\varphi} {}^{1}\dot{\boldsymbol{Q}} \xleftarrow{\dot{\varphi}} {}^{1}\widetilde{\boldsymbol{R}} \end{array} \qquad [9.57]$$

Let ${}^{1}\widetilde{\boldsymbol{R}}$ represent changes in the 1-, 10-, and 30-year swap rates

$${}^{1}\widetilde{\boldsymbol{R}} = \begin{pmatrix} {}^{1}\widetilde{R}_1 \\ {}^{1}\widetilde{R}_2 \\ {}^{1}\widetilde{R}_3 \end{pmatrix} = \begin{pmatrix} {}^{1}\boldsymbol{R}_1 - {}^{0}\boldsymbol{r}_1 \\ {}^{1}\boldsymbol{R}_{10} - {}^{0}\boldsymbol{r}_{10} \\ {}^{1}\boldsymbol{R}_{15} - {}^{0}\boldsymbol{r}_{15} \end{pmatrix}. \qquad [9.58]$$

We interpolate between these to obtain changes in the swap rates for other maturities y. We might quadratically interpolate, but an interpolation function of the form

$$cy + b\sqrt{y} + a \qquad [9.59]$$

tends to provide a better fit. The result is a vector ${}^{1}\dot{\boldsymbol{Q}}$ of changes in the swap curve at each of the 15 maturities modeled by ${}^{1}\boldsymbol{R}$. We add the current swap curve ${}^{0}\boldsymbol{r}$ to ${}^{1}\dot{\boldsymbol{Q}}$ to obtain

$${}^{1}\boldsymbol{Q} = {}^{1}\dot{\boldsymbol{Q}} + {}^{0}\boldsymbol{r}, \qquad [9.60]$$

which approximates ${}^{1}\boldsymbol{R}$.

This approach of modeling changes in a curve is invaluable for modeling yield curves, forward curves, volatility skews, and other curves. It is based upon an observation that changes in financial curves tend to have smoother shapes than the curves themselves. Hence, they can be accurately modeled with fewer key factors.

EXAMPLE: IMPLIED VOLATILITIES. In Section 8.6, we designed a primary mapping for a portfolio of natural gas options. This employed distinct key factors modeling implied volatilities for every strike/expiration pair. There were more than 1000 key factors! Let's reduce this number with a change-of-variables remapping.

In modeling volatility surfaces, we may either model separate volatility curves for each expiration or directly model an entire surface. The latter approach works well if implied volatilities for different expirations are closely related, which makes interpolation across expirations reasonable. In many markets, volatilities for different expirations are not so related. In agricultural markets, implied volatilities for options expiring before a harvest may have little relationship to implied volatilities for options expiring after the harvest. Natural gas implied volatilities for winter expirations may have little relationship to implied volatilities for spring expirations. For this example, we take the approach of modeling individual volatility curves for each expiration.

In the earlier example, our primary mapping depended upon a number of component vectors for implied volatilities. Let's focus this example on the one for second nearby options:

$$
{}^1\boldsymbol{R}^{Vols2} = \begin{pmatrix} {}^1R_1^{Vols2} \\ {}^1R_2^{Vols2} \\ \vdots \\ {}^1R_{106}^{Vols2} \end{pmatrix} \sim \begin{pmatrix} \text{implied volatility, } 2^{\text{nd}} \text{ nearby strike 2.00 options} \\ \text{implied volatility, } 2^{\text{nd}} \text{ nearby strike 2.10 options} \\ \vdots \\ \text{implied volatility, } 2^{\text{nd}} \text{ nearby strike 8.00 options} \end{pmatrix}. \qquad [9.61]
$$

${}^1\boldsymbol{R}^{Vols2}$ has 106 key factors. We shall reduce this to 3 with a change-of-variables remapping:

$$
\begin{array}{l} {}^1\boldsymbol{R}^{Vols2} \\ \uparrow \\ {}^1\dot{\boldsymbol{Q}}^{Vols2} \xleftarrow{\dot{\varphi}^{Vols2}} {}^1\ddot{\boldsymbol{Q}}^{Vols2} \xleftarrow{\ddot{\varphi}^{Vols2}} {}^1\widetilde{\boldsymbol{R}}^{Vols2} \end{array} \qquad [9.62]
$$

In Section 6.7, we discussed constant-delta implied volatilities—implied volatilities tracked over time for specific normalized deltas. Let's have ${}^1\widetilde{\boldsymbol{R}}^{Vols2}$ represent changes in three of these[7]:

$$
{}^1\widetilde{\boldsymbol{R}}^{Vols2} = \begin{pmatrix} \text{change in the } 2^{\text{nd}} \text{ nearby .25 call delta volatility} \\ \text{change in the } 2^{\text{nd}} \text{ nearby .50 call delta volatility} \\ \text{change in the } 2^{\text{nd}} \text{ nearby .75 call delta volatility} \end{pmatrix}. \qquad [9.63]
$$

[7] Corresponding put deltas are –.75, –.50, and –.25.

${}^{1}\ddot{\boldsymbol{Q}}^{Vols2}$ represents changes in implied volatilities for each of the strikes represented by ${}^{1}\boldsymbol{R}^{Vols2}$:

$$
{}^{1}\ddot{\boldsymbol{Q}}^{Vols2} = \begin{pmatrix} {}^{1}\ddot{Q}_1^{Vols2} \\ {}^{1}\ddot{Q}_2^{Vols2} \\ \vdots \\ {}^{1}\ddot{Q}_{106}^{Vols2} \end{pmatrix} \sim \begin{pmatrix} \text{change in the 2}^{\text{nd}} \text{ nearby strike 2.00 implied vol.} \\ \text{change in the 2}^{\text{nd}} \text{ nearby strike 2.10 implied vol.} \\ \vdots \\ \text{change in the 2}^{\text{nd}} \text{ nearby strike 8.00 implied vol.} \end{pmatrix}. \quad [9.64]
$$

We obtain ${}^{1}\ddot{\boldsymbol{Q}}^{Vols2}$ from ${}^{1}\widetilde{\boldsymbol{R}}^{Vols2}$ by quadratic interpolation. A complication is the fact that components of ${}^{1}\widetilde{\boldsymbol{R}}^{Vols2}$ correspond to specific deltas whereas components of ${}^{1}\ddot{\boldsymbol{Q}}^{Vols2}$ correspond to specific strikes. We must infer, based upon time-1 market variables, the specific strikes corresponding to normalized call deltas of .25, .50, and .75. Once we have these, we can interpolate to obtain ${}^{1}\ddot{\boldsymbol{Q}}^{Vols2}$.

Whereas ${}^{1}\ddot{\boldsymbol{Q}}^{Vols2}$ models changes in implied volatilities, ${}^{1}\dot{\boldsymbol{Q}}^{Vols2}$ models actual volatilities. It approximates ${}^{1}\boldsymbol{R}^{Vols2}$ and is defined as

$$
{}^{1}\dot{\boldsymbol{Q}}^{Vols2} = {}^{1}\ddot{\boldsymbol{Q}}^{Vols2} + {}^{0}\boldsymbol{r}^{Vols2}. \quad [9.65]
$$

EXERCISES

9.7 Measure time in trading days. Today is November 14, 2001. A portfolio holds IPE Brent oil futures. A primary mapping has key factors ${}^{1}\boldsymbol{R}$ for prices of the first 12 nearby futures. A change-of-variables remapping is applied:

$$
\begin{array}{c} {}^{1}\boldsymbol{R} \\ \uparrow \\ {}^{1}\boldsymbol{Q} \xleftarrow{\varphi} {}^{1}\dot{\boldsymbol{Q}} \xleftarrow{\dot{\varphi}} {}^{1}\widetilde{\boldsymbol{R}} \end{array} \quad [9.66]
$$

where ${}^{1}\widetilde{\boldsymbol{R}}$ represents changes in the first, second, sixth, and 12th nearby prices. ${}^{1}\dot{\boldsymbol{Q}}$ approximates changes in all 12 nearby prices. It is obtained from ${}^{1}\widetilde{\boldsymbol{R}}$ by setting ${}^{1}\dot{Q}_1 = {}^{1}\widetilde{R}_1$ and interpolating between ${}^{1}\widetilde{R}_2$, ${}^{1}\widetilde{R}_3$, and ${}^{1}\widetilde{R}_4$ to obtain the remaining components of ${}^{1}\dot{\boldsymbol{Q}}$. An interpolation function of form

$$
ck + b\sqrt{k} + a \quad [9.67]
$$

is used for this purpose, where k represents the number of a nearby, from 2 to 12. We do not include the first nearby in the interpolation because it tends to move independently from the rest. ${}^{1}\boldsymbol{Q}$ approximates ${}^{1}\boldsymbol{R}$ and is defined as

$$
{}^{1}\boldsymbol{Q} = {}^{1}\dot{\boldsymbol{Q}} + {}^{0}\boldsymbol{r}. \quad [9.68]
$$

Current values ${}^0\boldsymbol{r}$ for ${}^1\boldsymbol{R}$ are

$$
{}^0\boldsymbol{r} = \begin{pmatrix} 18.75 \\ 19.17 \\ 19.29 \\ 19.33 \\ 19.37 \\ 19.41 \\ 19.43 \\ 19.46 \\ 19.49 \\ 19.51 \\ 19.53 \\ 19.55 \end{pmatrix}. \qquad [9.69]
$$

A day goes by, and ${}^1\widetilde{\boldsymbol{R}}$ is realized as

$$
{}^1\widetilde{\boldsymbol{r}} = \begin{pmatrix} -1.07 \\ -1.84 \\ -1.55 \\ -1.23 \end{pmatrix}. \qquad [9.70]
$$

Determine the corresponding realization ${}^1\boldsymbol{q}$ of ${}^1\boldsymbol{Q}$.

9.5. PRINCIPAL-COMPONENT REMAPPINGS

If a portfolio mapping has many key factors, their covariance matrix is likely to be multicollinear. This affords an opportunity to reduce the number of key factors with a **principal-component remapping**.

Consider a portfolio mapping ${}^1P = \theta({}^1\boldsymbol{R})$, where ${}^1\boldsymbol{R}$ is n-dimensional with conditional mean vector ${}^{1|0}\boldsymbol{\mu}$ and multicollinear conditional covariance matrix ${}^{1|0}\boldsymbol{\Sigma}$. We can represent ${}^1\boldsymbol{R}$ in terms of its principal components:

$$
{}^1\boldsymbol{R} = \boldsymbol{v}\,{}^1\boldsymbol{D} + {}^{1|0}\boldsymbol{\mu}, \qquad [9.71]
$$

where $\boldsymbol{v}$ is the $n \times n$ matrix whose columns are orthonormal eigenvectors of ${}^{1|0}\boldsymbol{\Sigma}$, and ${}^1\boldsymbol{D}$ is an n-dimensional column vector of the principal components of ${}^1\boldsymbol{R}$. We convert [9.71] to an approximate relationship by discarding principal components ${}^1D_i$ that have variances close to 0.[8] Suppose we retain m principal components and discard $n - m$. Let ${}^1\widetilde{\boldsymbol{R}}$ be the m-dimensional vector of retained principal components. Let $\widetilde{\boldsymbol{v}}$ be the $n \times m$ matrix whose columns are the eigenvectors corresponding

[8] These may have negative or imaginary values due to roundoff error.

to those principal components. We obtain

$$^{1}\boldsymbol{R} = \boldsymbol{v}\,^{1}\boldsymbol{D} + {}^{1|0}\boldsymbol{\mu} \approx \widetilde{\boldsymbol{v}}\,^{1}\widetilde{\boldsymbol{R}} + {}^{1|0}\boldsymbol{\mu}. \quad [9.72]$$

Our portfolio remapping has form

$$\begin{array}{ccccc} ^{1}P & \xleftarrow{\theta} & ^{1}\boldsymbol{R} & \xleftarrow{\boldsymbol{v}} & ^{1}\boldsymbol{D} \\ \uparrow & & \uparrow & & \\ ^{1}\widetilde{P} & \xleftarrow{\theta} & \widetilde{\boldsymbol{v}}\,^{1}\widetilde{\boldsymbol{D}} & \xleftarrow{\widetilde{\boldsymbol{v}}} & ^{1}\widetilde{\boldsymbol{D}} \end{array} \quad [9.73]$$

When implementing a principal-component remapping, it is important to be aware of the scaling issue discussed in Section 3.7. This can be addressed by changing the units of measure for key factors as appropriate.

EXAMPLE: US TREASURY BONDS. Kenneth Garbade (1986) discusses VaR techniques developed by the Bankers Trust Cross Markets Research Group. His paper is historically important because it details sophisticated VaR research performed during the mid-1980s. It also represents the first published use of principal components in a VaR measure. The following example presents a principle component remapping similar to one proposed in that paper as well as those used in fixed income markets today. To make the example historically interesting, we employ the same covariance matrix used in the 1986 paper.

Measure VaR as 1-week standard deviation of return USD VaR. Today is May 27, 1986. A portfolio has holdings $\boldsymbol{\omega}$ in US Treasury securities. A primary mapping is constructed, and a linear remapping is applied:

$$\begin{array}{ccccc} & & \overbrace{\hphantom{xxxxxxxxxx}}^{\theta} & & \\ ^{1}P & \xleftarrow{\boldsymbol{\omega}} & ^{1}\boldsymbol{S} & \xleftarrow{\varphi} & ^{1}\boldsymbol{R} \\ \uparrow & & & & \\ ^{1}\widetilde{P} & & \xleftarrow{\hspace{3em}\widetilde{\theta}\hspace{3em}} & & ^{1}\boldsymbol{R} \end{array} \quad [9.74]$$

Key vector $^{1}\boldsymbol{R}$ represents basis point changes in constant-maturity Treasury yields for various maturities:

$$^{1}\boldsymbol{R} = \begin{pmatrix} ^{1}R_1 \\ ^{1}R_2 \\ ^{1}R_3 \\ ^{1}R_4 \\ \vdots \\ ^{1}R_{10} \end{pmatrix} \sim \begin{pmatrix} \text{Change in the 3-month constant-maturity yield} \\ \text{Change in the 6-month constant-maturity yield} \\ \text{Change in the 1-year constant-maturity yield} \\ \text{Change in the 2-year constant-maturity yield} \\ \vdots \\ \text{Change in the 30-year constant-maturity yield} \end{pmatrix}. \quad [9.75]$$

They have conditional mean vector ${}^{1|0}\boldsymbol{\mu} = \mathbf{0}$ and conditional covariance matrix[9]

$$ {}^{1|0}\boldsymbol{\Sigma} = \begin{pmatrix} 357.2 & 321.7 & 292.3 & 267.0 & & 173.9 \\ 321.7 & 372.5 & 360.1 & 346.0 & \cdots & 254.4 \\ 292.3 & 360.1 & 388.1 & 385.1 & & 305.0 \\ 267.0 & 346.0 & 385.1 & 412.1 & & 332.5 \\ & \vdots & & & \ddots & \vdots \\ 173.9 & 254.4 & 305.0 & 332.5 & \cdots & 349.7 \end{pmatrix}. \qquad [9.76] $$

Eigenvectors $\boldsymbol{v}_i$ of ${}^{1|0}\boldsymbol{\Sigma}$ comprise columns of the matrix

$$ \boldsymbol{v} = \begin{pmatrix} .2209 & .6867 & .5106 & .4074 & & .0036 \\ .2820 & .4595 & -.0897 & -.4907 & \cdots & .0556 \\ .3143 & .2252 & -.2428 & -.3582 & & -.0287 \\ .3312 & .0510 & -.3822 & .0056 & & -.0631 \\ & \vdots & & & \ddots & \vdots \\ .2881 & -.2792 & .4604 & -.4711 & \cdots & -.2335 \end{pmatrix}. \qquad [9.77] $$

These are graphed in Exhibit 9.28.

Recall from Section 3.7 that we likened eigenvectors $\boldsymbol{v}_i$ to "modes of fluctuation." The first three eigenvectors loosely correspond to parallel shifts, tilts, and bends in the yield curve. The mathematics has produced "modes of fluctuation" that our intuition might expect for a yield curve. The remaining eigenvectors reflect more complicated fluctuations that contribute modestly to actual fluctuations in the yield curve.

We have

$$ {}^{1}\boldsymbol{R} = \boldsymbol{v}\,{}^{1}\boldsymbol{D}, \qquad [9.78] $$

where components ${}^{1}D_i$ are respective principal components. By construction, the ${}^{1}D_i$ are uncorrelated random variables. Each has variance equal to the eigenvalue λ_i of the corresponding eigenvector. The covariance matrix of ${}^{1}\boldsymbol{D}$ is

$$ \boldsymbol{\Sigma}_{{}^{1}\boldsymbol{D}} = \begin{pmatrix} 3623 & 0 & 0 & 0 & 0 & 0 & 0 & 0 & 0 & 0 \\ 0 & 338 & 0 & 0 & 0 & 0 & 0 & 0 & 0 & 0 \\ 0 & 0 & 57 & 0 & 0 & 0 & 0 & 0 & 0 & 0 \\ 0 & 0 & 0 & 33 & 0 & 0 & 0 & 0 & 0 & 0 \\ 0 & 0 & 0 & 0 & 13 & 0 & 0 & 0 & 0 & 0 \\ 0 & 0 & 0 & 0 & 0 & 8 & 0 & 0 & 0 & 0 \\ 0 & 0 & 0 & 0 & 0 & 0 & 6 & 0 & 0 & 0 \\ 0 & 0 & 0 & 0 & 0 & 0 & 0 & 5 & 0 & 0 \\ 0 & 0 & 0 & 0 & 0 & 0 & 0 & 0 & 4 & 0 \\ 0 & 0 & 0 & 0 & 0 & 0 & 0 & 0 & 0 & 2 \end{pmatrix}. \qquad [9.79] $$

[9]If the basis point covariances seem large, remember that they are based on data from the 1980s.

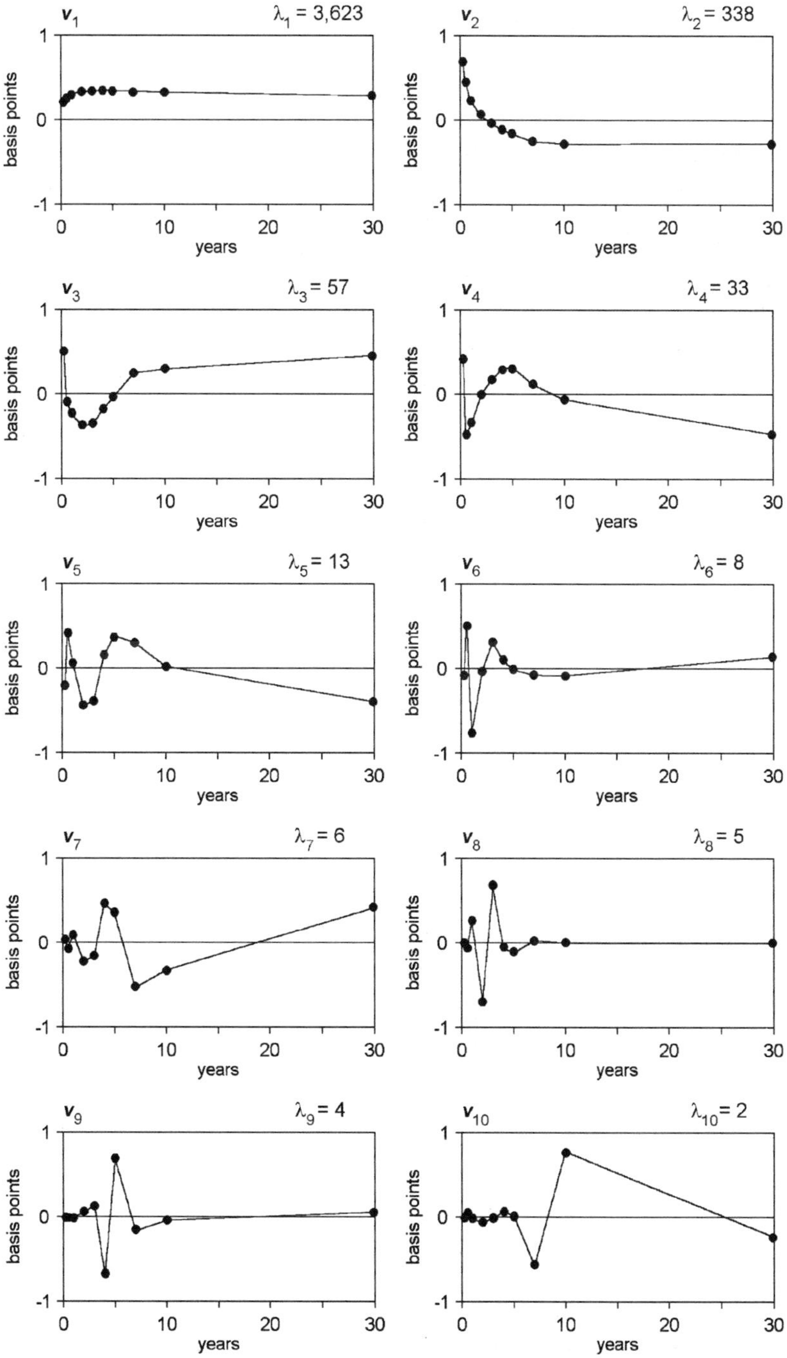

Exhibit 9.28 Orthonormal eigenvectors $\boldsymbol{v}_i$ calculated from covariance matrix [9.76] are ordered according to their respective eigenvalues λ_i. Eigenvalues equal the variances of corresponding principal components.

The variance for ${}^1D_1$ is 3623, which is far larger than the other variances. It contributes more to the variability in ${}^1\boldsymbol{R}$ than do any of the other principal components.[10] If we consider the variances of ${}^1D_1$, ${}^1D_2$, and ${}^1D_3$, together they account for almost all of the variability in ${}^1\boldsymbol{R}$. The remaining variances are all less than or equal to 33, which is less than 1% of the variance of ${}^1D_1$. Intuitively, this means that parallel shifts, tilts, and bends account for most of the variability in the Treasury yield curve.

For our principal-component remapping, we discard the contributions ${}^1D_i$ of the last seven principal components. We define a three-dimensional key vector ${}^1\widetilde{\boldsymbol{R}}$ comprising the first three principal components:

$$ {}^1\widetilde{\boldsymbol{R}} = \begin{pmatrix} {}^1\widetilde{R}_1 \\ {}^1\widetilde{R}_2 \\ {}^1\widetilde{R}_3 \end{pmatrix} = \begin{pmatrix} {}^1D_1 \\ {}^1D_2 \\ {}^1D_3 \end{pmatrix}. \qquad [9.80] $$

Let $\widetilde{\boldsymbol{v}}$ be the 10×3 matrix with columns equal to the first 3 eigenvectors $\boldsymbol{v}_i$ of ${}^{1|0}\boldsymbol{\Sigma}$:

$$ \widetilde{\boldsymbol{v}} = \begin{pmatrix} .2209 & .6867 & .5106 \\ .2820 & .4595 & -.0897 \\ .3143 & .2252 & -.2428 \\ .3312 & .0510 & -.3822 \\ & \vdots & \\ .2881 & -.2792 & .4604 \end{pmatrix}. \qquad [9.81] $$

We obtain

$$ {}^1\boldsymbol{R} = \boldsymbol{v}\,{}^1\boldsymbol{D} \approx \widetilde{\boldsymbol{v}}\,{}^1\widetilde{\boldsymbol{R}}. \qquad [9.82] $$

Our portfolio remapping has form

$$
\begin{array}{ccccc}
\multicolumn{3}{c}{\overbrace{{}^1P \xleftarrow{\;\omega\;} {}^1\boldsymbol{S} \xleftarrow{\;\varphi\;} {}^1\boldsymbol{R}}^{\theta}} & & \\
\uparrow & & & & \\
{}^1\widetilde{P} & \xleftarrow{\qquad\widetilde{\theta}\qquad} & {}^1\boldsymbol{R} & \xleftarrow{\;\boldsymbol{v}\;} & {}^1\boldsymbol{D} \\
\uparrow & & \uparrow & & \\
\multicolumn{5}{c}{\underbrace{{}^1\widetilde{\widetilde{P}} \xleftarrow{\qquad\widetilde{\theta}\qquad} \widetilde{\boldsymbol{v}}\,{}^1\widetilde{\boldsymbol{R}} \xleftarrow{\;\widetilde{\boldsymbol{v}}\;} {}^1\widetilde{\boldsymbol{R}}}_{\widetilde{\widetilde{\theta}}}}
\end{array}
\qquad [9.83]
$$

---

[10] Because all eigenvectors have length 1, it is meaningful to directly compare variances of corresponding principal components.

The first row of the schematic represents the primary mapping. The second represents the linear remapping ${}^1\tilde{P} = \tilde{\theta}({}^1\boldsymbol{R})$. The third represents the principal-component remapping ${}^1\tilde{\tilde{P}} = \tilde{\tilde{\theta}}({}^1\tilde{\tilde{\boldsymbol{R}}})$, which is the focus of this example.

To assess the quality of the principal component approximation, we consider a diversified portfolio of US Treasury bonds. We generate 1000 pseudorandom[11] realizations ${}^1\boldsymbol{d}^{[k]}$ of ${}^1\boldsymbol{D}$, and calculate corresponding realizations ${}^1\boldsymbol{r}^{[k]}$ for ${}^1\boldsymbol{R}$ and ${}^1\tilde{\tilde{\boldsymbol{r}}}^{[k]}$ for ${}^1\tilde{\tilde{\boldsymbol{R}}}$. From these, we calculate realizations ${}^1\tilde{p}^{[k]}$ and ${}^1\tilde{\tilde{p}}^{[k]}$ for ${}^1\tilde{P}$ and ${}^1\tilde{\tilde{P}}$. Pairs $({}^1\tilde{p}^{[k]}, {}^1\tilde{\tilde{p}}^{[k]})$ are plotted as the scatter diagram of Exhibit 9.29.

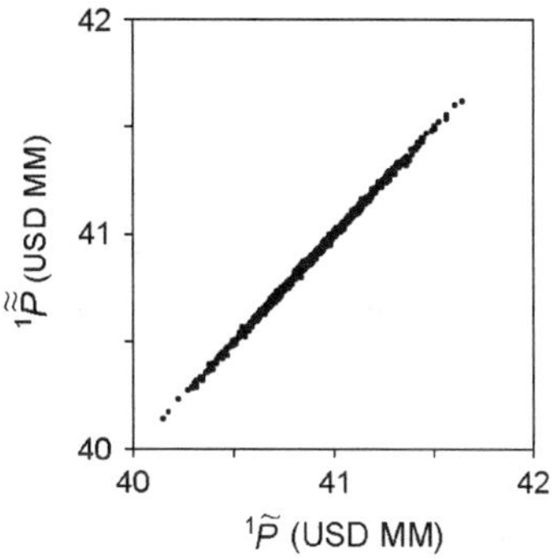

Exhibit 9.29 A scatter plot of realizations $({}^1\tilde{p}^{[k]}, {}^1\tilde{\tilde{p}}^{[k]})$ for ${}^1\tilde{P}$ and ${}^1\tilde{\tilde{P}}$.

The approximation is good, but not as good as those obtained in some earlier examples. Compare Exhibit 9.29 with Exhibits 9.10 and 9.15. The approximation could be improved by discarding fewer principal components.

Exercises

9.8 In our US Treasury bond example, which portfolio value will have greater VaR: ${}^1\tilde{P}$ or ${}^1\tilde{\tilde{P}}$?

9.9 In Section 8.7, we constructed a primary mapping for a coffee portfolio. In Section 9.4, we applied a holdings remapping, replacing a 30-dimensional vector of coffee spreads ${}^1\boldsymbol{R}^{Spreads}$ with an eight-dimensional vector ${}^1\tilde{\boldsymbol{R}}^{Spreads}$. Now let's apply a principal-component remapping to ${}^1\tilde{\boldsymbol{R}}^{Spreads}$, replacing it with a six-dimensional[12] vector ${}^1\tilde{\tilde{\boldsymbol{R}}}^{Spreads}$.

[11] We assume ${}^1\boldsymbol{D}$ is joint-normal for this purpose.

[12] In practice, we might not apply a principal-component remapping to eliminate just two dimensions. We apply the remapping here for practice.

Measure spreads in units of .01 USD per pound.[13] Assume ${}^{1}\widetilde{\boldsymbol{R}}^{Spreads}$ has conditional mean vector

$$
{}^{1|0}\widetilde{\boldsymbol{\mu}} = \begin{pmatrix} 8.5 \\ 7.0 \\ 3.0 \\ -4.0 \\ -3.0 \\ 0.0 \\ -10.0 \\ -14.0 \end{pmatrix} \qquad [9.84]
$$

and conditional covariance matrix

$$
{}^{1|0}\widetilde{\boldsymbol{\Sigma}} = \begin{pmatrix}
1.501 & 0.867 & 0.808 & 0.979 & 0.684 & 0.882 & 1.075 & -0.227 \\
0.867 & 1.519 & 1.053 & 1.061 & 0.958 & 0.983 & 0.855 & -0.326 \\
0.808 & 1.053 & 1.214 & 0.940 & 0.820 & 0.847 & 0.759 & -0.328 \\
0.979 & 1.061 & 0.940 & 0.946 & 0.772 & 0.824 & 0.827 & -0.296 \\
0.684 & 0.958 & 0.820 & 0.772 & 1.084 & 0.944 & 0.766 & -0.121 \\
0.882 & 0.983 & 0.847 & 0.824 & 0.944 & 1.681 & 1.157 & -0.229 \\
1.075 & 0.855 & 0.759 & 0.827 & 0.766 & 1.157 & 1.023 & -0.206 \\
-1.227 & -0.326 & -0.328 & -0.296 & -0.121 & -0.299 & -0.206 & 1.209
\end{pmatrix}. \qquad [9.85]
$$

(a) Calculate the determinant of the correlation matrix ${}^{1|0}\widetilde{\boldsymbol{\rho}}$ corresponding to ${}^{1|0}\widetilde{\boldsymbol{\Sigma}}$.

(b) Is ${}^{1}\widetilde{\boldsymbol{R}}^{Spreads}$ conditionally singular, multicollinear, or neither of these?

(c) Based upon its first six principal components, construct a principal-component remapping for ${}^{1}\widetilde{\boldsymbol{R}}^{Spreads}$. Denote your new key vector ${}^{1}\widetilde{\widetilde{\boldsymbol{R}}}^{Spreads}$.

(d) What are the conditional mean vector ${}^{1|0}\widetilde{\widetilde{\boldsymbol{\mu}}}$ and conditional covariance matrix ${}^{1|0}\widetilde{\widetilde{\boldsymbol{\Sigma}}}$ of ${}^{1}\widetilde{\widetilde{\boldsymbol{R}}}^{Spreads}$?

(e) Redraw schematic [9.54], adding your principal-component remapping.

9.10 Given a principal-component remapping [9.72], if ${}^{1}\boldsymbol{R}$ is non-singular and joint-normal, is ${}^{1}\widetilde{\boldsymbol{R}}$ necessarily joint-normal?

9.6. FURTHER READING

Saff and Kuijlaars (1997) discuss the arrangement of points on a sphere. Zangari (1996c) discusses holdings remappings for fixed cash flows. Wilson (1994) compares principal-component remappings and related remappings that employ factor analysis. Jamshidian and Zhu (1997) marry a principal-component remapping with a crude numerical transformation. Singh (1997) describes principal-component remappings for fixed income and foreign exchange portfolios.

[13] For expositional convenience, we change our units of measure from the earlier example.

Chapter 10

Transformations

10.1. MOTIVATION

Risk comprises uncertainty and exposure. A VaR measure represents uncertainty with a characterization of the conditional distribution of ${}^1\boldsymbol{R}$. It represents exposure with a portfolio mapping ${}^1P = \theta({}^1\boldsymbol{R})$, which may be a primary mapping or a remapping. To quantify market risk for a portfolio, we need to combine these two components. This is the purpose of a transformation procedure.

A transformation procedure—or transformation—represents risk with a characterization of the conditional distribution of ${}^1P$. It then uses that characterization to value a VaR metric. The value for that metric is the output of the VaR measure.

That characterization of the conditional distribution of ${}^1P$ may be a standard deviation, PDF, characteristic function, or some other representation. If the characterization is sufficiently general to support any reasonable VaR metric, we say the transformation is complete. Otherwise, it is incomplete.

In Section 1.8, we described three categories of transformations:

1. linear transformations,
2. quadratic transformations, and
3. Monte Carlo transformations.

Linear and quadratic transformations apply to linear and quadratic portfolios, respectively. Monte Carlo transformations apply generally to all portfolios. In this chapter, we describe all three types of transformations.

Linear transformations are most widely used. In practice, many portfolios are linear or so nearly linear that they can be accurately approximated with a linear remapping. Linear transformations are easy to implement, run in real time and are exact. The only reason to not implement a linear transformation is if a portfolio holds—or might some day hold—nonlinear instruments such as options or mortgage-backed securities.

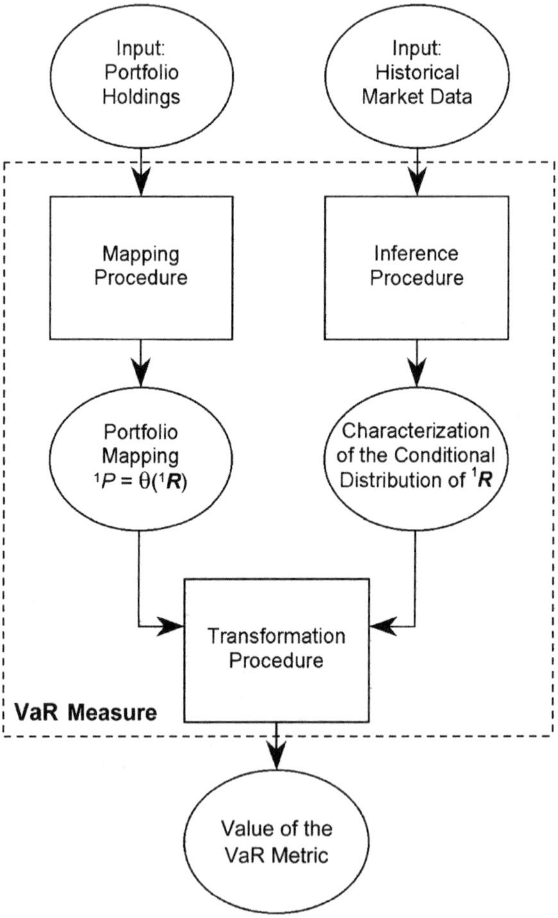

Exhibit 10.1 A reproduction of Exhibit 1.11, which is a general schematic for VaR measures. Risk comprises uncertainty and exposure. An inference procedure represents risk with a characterization of the conditional distribution of $^1\boldsymbol{R}$. A mapping procedure represents exposure with a portfolio mapping $^1P = \theta(^1\boldsymbol{R})$, which may be a primary mapping or a remapping. The topic of this chapter is transformation procedures. These combine the outputs of the inference and mapping procedures to characterize the conditional distribution of ^1P.

Quadratic transformations are used least. They are reasonably easy to implement, run in real time or near-real time, and can be exact. Their main problem is the fact that actual portfolios are rarely quadratic. Nonlinear portfolios can be approximated with quadratic remappings, but the approximations are often poor. Still, there is an allure to quadratic transformations. They offer the potential to calculate VaR for nonlinear portfolios in near-real time. Perhaps the most useful application of quadratic transformations is to facilitate variance reduction in Monte Carlo transformations. We discuss these important techniques in Section 10.5.

Monte Carlo transformations are part of a larger category of transformations called numerical transformations. These encompass the use of any technique of numerical integration. Conceivably a transformation might employ quadrature. Along these lines, various "grid" or "lattice" transformations have been proposed. All suffer from the curse of dimensionality, which limits their applicability. By far, the most widely used numerical transformations are Monte Carlo transformations. These are appealing because they are applicable to all portfolios and do not suffer from the curse of dimensionality. Two drawbacks are the standard error introduced by all Monte Carlo analyses and the fact that run times can be long—often several hours.

10.2. LINEAR TRANSFORMATION PROCEDURES

Linear transformations were pioneered by Markowitz (1952) and Roy (1952). Consider a portfolio $({}^0p, {}^1P)$ with linear portfolio mapping

$$ {}^1P = \theta({}^1\boldsymbol{R}) = \boldsymbol{b}\,{}^1\boldsymbol{R} + a. \qquad [10.1] $$

By [3.28], given a conditional covariance matrix ${}^{1|0}\Sigma$ for ${}^1\boldsymbol{R}$, the conditional standard deviation of ${}^1P$ is

$$ {}^0std({}^1P) = \sqrt{\boldsymbol{b}\,{}^{1|0}\Sigma\,\boldsymbol{b}'}. \qquad [10.2] $$

This defines an incomplete transformation that can be used to evaluate a ${}^0std({}^1P)$ VaR metric or related metrics, such as ${}^0var({}^1P)$ or ${}^0std({}^1L)$. On its own, a standard deviation is not sufficient to determine a quantile, so the transformation does not support quantile-of-loss VaR metrics.

To complete our transformation, we make additional assumptions. Various approaches are possible, but standard assumptions specify a value for ${}^0E({}^1P)$ and assume ${}^1P$ is conditionally normal. This fully specifies a conditional distribution for ${}^1P$, making it possible to value any VaR metric. By [3.82], a q-quantile-of-loss

VaR metric is evaluated as[1]

$$ {}^{1|0}\Phi^{-1}_{{}^1L}(q) = {}^0p - {}^{1|0}\Phi^{-1}_{{}^1P}(1-q) \qquad [10.3]$$

$$ = {}^0p - \left[E({}^1P) + \Phi^{-1}_Z(1-q)\,{}^0std({}^1P)\right] \qquad [10.4]$$

$$ = {}^0p - E({}^1P) + \Phi^{-1}_Z(q)\,{}^0std({}^1P), \qquad [10.5]$$

where $Z \sim N(0, 1)$. Specific values for $\Phi^{-1}_Z(q)$ corresponding to commonly used VaR metrics are (see Exhibit 3.15):

- $\Phi^{-1}_Z(.90) = 1.282$ for 90% VaR;
- $\Phi^{-1}_Z(.95) = 1.645$ for 95% VaR;
- $\Phi^{-1}_Z(.975) = 1.960$ for 97.5% VaR;
- $\Phi^{-1}_Z(.99) = 2.326$ for 99% VaR.

If our VaR horizon is short—say a day or a week—it may be reasonable to assume ${}^0E({}^1P) = {}^0p$. In this case, [10.5] simplifies to

$$ {}^{1|0}\Phi^{-1}_{{}^1L}(q) = \Phi^{-1}_Z(q)\,{}^0std({}^1P). \qquad [10.6]$$

This solution is widely used. Because [10.6] does not depend upon the value of ${}^0p$, there is no need to calculate ${}^0p$.

An assumption that ${}^1P$ is conditionally normal can be justified in various ways. If we assume ${}^1\boldsymbol{R}$ is joint-normal, by linearity condition [10.1], ${}^1P$ will be normal. If we can't assume ${}^1\boldsymbol{R}$ is joint-normal, we may still assume ${}^1P$ is normal based upon the central limit theorem. As long as ${}^1P$ has exposures diversified across multiple key factors that have modest correlations, conditions for invoking a central limit theorem should—at least approximately—be met.

Exercises

10.1 Measure VaR as 1-day 95% USD VaR. Consider a portfolio invested in four stocks. Holdings are 100, 250, –200, and 500 shares. Current market values for the stocks are USD 30, USD 45, USD 60, and USD 20 per share. Let ${}^1\boldsymbol{S}$ represent tomorrow's accumulated value (price plus any dividends since time 0) for the respective stocks. Assume ${}^1\boldsymbol{S}$ is conditionally joint-normal

[1] In Chapter 3, we adopted the inverse CDF notation $\Phi^{-1}(q)$ for quantiles. This was because, if a random variable has unique quantiles, they equal corresponding values of the inverse CDF. A random variable has unique quantiles for $q \in (0, 1)$ if it is continuous with a PDF that is nonzero on some interval (which can be unbounded or all of $\mathbb{R}$) and zero elsewhere. In essentially all VaR applications, random variables ${}^1L$ and ${}^1P$ have conditional distributions that satisfy this criterion. Contrived exceptions are possible; consider a portfolio composed entirely of expiring digital options.

with covariance matrix

$$^{1|0}\Sigma = \begin{pmatrix} 1.0 & 0.3 & 0.2 & 0.0 \\ 0.3 & 1.5 & 0.4 & 0.1 \\ 0.2 & 0.4 & 2.0 & 0.1 \\ 0.0 & 0.1 & 0.1 & 1.0 \end{pmatrix}. \qquad [10.7]$$

Assume tomorrow's expected accumulated value for each stock is its current value. Calculate the portfolio's 1-day 95% USD VaR by performing the following steps:

a. Specify ^1P as a mapping of $^1\boldsymbol{S}$. Is the mapping function a linear polynomial?
b. Calculate ^0p and $^0E(^1P)$.
c. Based upon your result from part (a) and the covariance matrix for $^1\boldsymbol{S}$, calculate the conditional standard deviation $^0std(^1P)$.
d. Based upon your results for parts (b) and (c), calculate the portfolio's VaR.

10.3. QUADRATIC TRANSFORMATION PROCEDURES

Quadratic transformations were pioneered by a number of researchers. The first complete published solution was Rouvinez (1997). Consider a portfolio (^0p, ^1P) with quadratic portfolio mapping

$$^1P = \theta(^1\boldsymbol{R}) = {}^1\boldsymbol{R}'\boldsymbol{c}\,{}^1\boldsymbol{R} + \boldsymbol{b}\,{}^1\boldsymbol{R} + a, \qquad [10.8]$$

where $^1\boldsymbol{R} \sim {}^0N_n(^{1|0}\boldsymbol{\mu}, {}^{1|0}\Sigma)$, $\boldsymbol{c}$ is a symmetric $n \times n$ matrix, $\boldsymbol{b}$ is an n-dimensional row vector, and a is a scalar. We assume $^{1|0}\Sigma$ is positive definite.

As described in Section 3.12, we may express ^1P as a linear polynomial of independent chi-squared and normal random variables. Based upon this representation, we can value various VaR metrics. To support a $^0std(^1L)$ VaR metric, we apply the techniques of Section 3.12 to calculate conditional moments $^0E(^1P)$ and $^0E(^1P^2)$ of ^1P. Then (see Exercise 3.15):

$$^0std(^1L) = {}^0std(^1P) = \sqrt{^0E(^1P^2) - {}^0E(^1P)^2}. \qquad [10.9]$$

Related metrics, such as $^0var(^1P)$, are calculated similarly.

Quantile-based VaR metrics are more difficult to calculate. Various solutions have been proposed. Zangari (1996c) approximates a solution using Johnson (1949) curves. Fallon (1996) and Pichler and Selitsch (2000) recommend approximate solutions based on the Cornish-Fisher expansion. Rouvinez (1997) uses the trapezoidal rule to invert the characteristic function. Britten-Jones and Schaefer (1997) use an approximation due to Solomon and Stephens (1977). Cárdenas *et al.* (1997) use the fast Fourier transform.

We shall focus on the Cornish-Fisher expansion, as described in Section 3.13, and on applying the trapezoidal rule to invert the characteristic function, as described in Section 3.16.

EXAMPLE. Measure time in trading days. A Japanese metals trading firm has exposure to forward and options positions in platinum. Some of the positions are USD-denominated. Treat interest rates and lease rates as constant. Model three key factors

$$^{1}\boldsymbol{R} = \begin{pmatrix} ^{1}R_1 \\ ^{1}R_2 \\ ^{1}R_3 \end{pmatrix} \sim \begin{pmatrix} \text{spot JPY price of platinum} \\ \text{a representative implied volatility for platinum} \\ \text{spot JPY/USD exchange rate} \end{pmatrix}, \qquad [10.10]$$

and assume $^{1}\boldsymbol{R} \sim {}^{0}N_3({}^{1|0}\boldsymbol{\mu}, {}^{1|0}\boldsymbol{\Sigma})$ where

$${}^{1|0}\boldsymbol{\mu} = \begin{pmatrix} 53{,}150 \\ 0.2670 \\ 107.80 \end{pmatrix} \text{ and } {}^{1|0}\boldsymbol{\Sigma} = \begin{pmatrix} 799{,}600 & 1.074 & -48.91 \\ 1.074 & 7.056 \times 10^{-5} & -3.875 \times 10^{-5} \\ -48.91 & -3.875 \times 10^{-5} & 0.4343 \end{pmatrix}. \qquad [10.11]$$

A primary portfolio mapping $^{1}P = \theta(^{1}\boldsymbol{R})$ is constructed based upon applicable forward and options pricing formulas. This is quadratically remapped as

$$^{1}\widetilde{P} = {}^{1}\boldsymbol{R}'\boldsymbol{c}\,{}^{1}\boldsymbol{R} + \boldsymbol{b}\,{}^{1}\boldsymbol{R} + a, \qquad [10.12]$$

where:

$$\boldsymbol{c} = \begin{pmatrix} 4.305 & 3921 & 257.1 \\ 3921 & 8.407 \times 10^{7} & 3.647 \times 10^{6} \\ 257.1 & 3.647 \times 10^{6} & -5673 \end{pmatrix}, \qquad [10.13]$$

$$\boldsymbol{b} = (-459{,}700 \quad -4.819 \times 10^{8} \quad -2.605 \times 10^{7}), \qquad [10.14]$$

$$a = 1.2210 \times 10^{10}. \qquad [10.15]$$

We set ${}^{0}\widetilde{p} = {}^{0}p =$ JPY 212.7MM. Let's calculate the remapped portfolio's VaR based upon the two metrics:

- 1-day standard deviation JPY VaR, and
- 1-day 90% JPY VaR.

For the purpose of illustration, we shall evaluate the latter metric twice, first using the Cornish-Fisher expansion and then by inverting the characteristic function.

Paralleling the techniques of Section 3.12, we construct the Cholesky matrix $\boldsymbol{z}$ of ${}^{1|0}\boldsymbol{\Sigma}$

$$\boldsymbol{z} = \begin{pmatrix} 894.2 & 0 & 0 \\ .001201 & .008314 & 0 \\ -.05470 & .003242 & .6567 \end{pmatrix}, \qquad [10.16]$$

and a matrix $\boldsymbol{u}$ with rows equal to orthonormal eigenvectors of $\boldsymbol{z}'\boldsymbol{c}\boldsymbol{z}$,

$$\boldsymbol{u} = \begin{pmatrix} .9990 & .0086 & .0449 \\ -.0325 & -.5582 & .8291 \\ -.0322 & .8297 & .5573 \end{pmatrix}. \qquad [10.17]$$

Define a mapping

$${}^{1}\boldsymbol{R} = \boldsymbol{z}\boldsymbol{u}'\,{}^{1}\dot{\boldsymbol{R}} + \boldsymbol{\mu} \qquad [10.18]$$

where ${}^{1}\dot{\boldsymbol{R}} \sim N_3(\boldsymbol{0}, \boldsymbol{I})$. We obtain

$${}^{1}\widetilde{P} = {}^{1}\dot{\boldsymbol{R}}'\dot{\boldsymbol{c}}\,{}^{1}\dot{\boldsymbol{R}} + \dot{\boldsymbol{b}}\,{}^{1}\dot{\boldsymbol{R}} + \dot{a}, \qquad [10.19]$$

with

$$\dot{\boldsymbol{c}} = \boldsymbol{u}\boldsymbol{z}'\boldsymbol{c}\boldsymbol{z}\boldsymbol{u}' = \begin{pmatrix} 3.432 \times 10^6 & 0 & 0 \\ 0 & -21{,}880 & 0 \\ 0 & 0 & 18{,}277 \end{pmatrix}, \qquad [10.20]$$

$$\dot{\boldsymbol{b}} = (2\boldsymbol{\mu}'\boldsymbol{c} + \boldsymbol{b})\boldsymbol{z}\boldsymbol{u}' = (5.047 \times 10^7 \quad -4.105 \times 10^6 \quad 4.400 \times 10^6), \qquad [10.21]$$

$$\dot{a} = \boldsymbol{\mu}'\boldsymbol{c}\boldsymbol{\mu} + \boldsymbol{b}\boldsymbol{\mu} + a = 2.103 \times 10^8. \qquad [10.22]$$

Multiplying [10.19] out

$${}^{1}\widetilde{P} = 3.432 \times 10^6\,{}^{1}\dot{R}_1^2 - 21{,}880\,{}^{1}\dot{R}_2^2 + 18{,}277\,{}^{1}\dot{R}_3^2 + 5.047 \times 10^7\,{}^{1}\dot{R}_1 - 4.105 \times 10^6\,{}^{1}\dot{R}_2 + 4.400 \times 10^6\,{}^{1}\dot{R}_3 + 2.103 \times 10^8. \qquad [10.23]$$

We "complete the squares" to obtain

$${}^{1}\widetilde{P} = 3.432 \times 10^6({}^{1}\dot{R}_1 + 7.353)^2 - 21{,}880({}^{1}\dot{R}_2 + 93.81)^2 + 18{,}277({}^{1}\dot{R}_3 + 120.4)^2 - 4.752 \times 10^7. \qquad [10.24]$$

We have expressed ${}^{1}\widetilde{P}$ conditionally as a linear polynomial of three independent random variables:

- $({}^{1}\dot{R}_1 + 7.353)^2 \sim \chi^2(1, 54.06)$,
- $({}^{1}\dot{R}_2 + 93.81)^2 \sim \chi^2(1, 8800)$,
- $({}^{1}\dot{R}_3 + 120.4)^2 \sim \chi^2(1, 14{,}490)$.

We calculate conditional values $g^{[k]}$ for ${}^{1}\widetilde{P}$, as defined in Section 3.12. These are indicated in Exhibit 10.2.

k	$g^{[k]}$
0	2.138×10^{8}
1	2.607×10^{15}
2	5.278×10^{22}
3	1.447×10^{30}
4	4.962×10^{37}

Exhibit 10.2 Using formula [3.167], conditional values $g^{[k]}$ are calculated for the remapped portfolio's value. Inputs for the calculations are obtained from [10.11], [10.13], [10.14], [10.15], [10.20], and [10.21].

From these, we calculate the conditional moments and central moments of ${}^{1}\widetilde{P}$ and the conditional central moments and cumulants of the normalization ${}^{1}\widetilde{P}^{*}$ of ${}^{1}\widetilde{P}$. Results are indicated in Exhibit 10.3.

r	${}^{0}E({}^{1}\widetilde{P}^{r})$	${}^{1\|0}\widetilde{\mu}_r$	${}^{1\|0}\widetilde{\mu}^{*}_r$	${}^{1\|0}\widetilde{\kappa}^{*}_r$
1	2.138×10^{8}	0	0	0
2	4.830×10^{16}	2.607×10^{15}	1	1
3	1.149×10^{25}	5.278×10^{22}	.3965	.3965
4	2.869×10^{33}	2.184×10^{31}	3.213	.2129
5	7.497×10^{41}	1.426×10^{39}	4.108	.1429

Exhibit 10.3 Conditional moments and central moments of the remapped portfolio's value as well as conditional central moments and cumulants of the normalization of the remapped portfolio's value are indicated. Computations are performed according to the discussions of Section 3.12. Inputs are the values of Exhibit 10.2.

Based upon its first and second moments, we calculate the conditional standard deviation of ${}^{1}\widetilde{P}$:

$$ {}^{0}std({}^{1}\widetilde{P}) = \sqrt{{}^{0}E({}^{1}\widetilde{P}^{2}) - {}^{0}E({}^{1}\widetilde{P})^{2}} = 5.106 \times 10^{7}. \qquad [10.25] $$

The portfolio's 1-day standard deviation JPY VaR is JPY 51.06MM.

To approximate the 1-day 90% JPY VaR using the Cornish-Fisher expansion [3.192], we apply the expansion to the normalization ${}^{1}\widetilde{P}^{*}$ of ${}^{1}\widetilde{P}$ based upon the conditional cumulants from Exhibit 10.3. We obtain the approximate .10-quantile of ${}^{1}\widetilde{P}^{*}$ as

$$ \begin{aligned} {}^{1|0}\Phi^{-1}_{{}^{1}\widetilde{P}^{*}}(.10) &\approx -1.2816 + .1071(.3965) + .0725(.2129) \\ &\quad -.0611(.1572) - .0346(.1429) + .1464(.0844) \\ &\quad -.1163(.0623) \qquad [10.26] \\ &= -1.233. \qquad [10.27] \end{aligned} $$

From [3.195],

$$ {}^{1|0}\Phi^{-1}_{{}^1\widetilde{P}}(.10) \approx 5.106 \times 10^7(-1.233) + 2.138 \times 10^8 \qquad [10.28]$$

$$ = 1.508 \times 10^8. \qquad [10.29]$$

The .10-quantile of ${}^1\widetilde{P}$ is JPY 150.8MM, and the remapped portfolio has approximate 1-day 90% JPY VaR of

$$ {}^{1|0}\Phi^{-1}_{{}^1\widetilde{L}}(.90) = {}^0\widetilde{p} - {}^{1|0}\Phi^{-1}_{{}^1\widetilde{P}}(.10) \qquad [10.30]$$

$$ = 212.7\text{MM} - 150.8\text{MM} \qquad [10.31]$$

$$ = 61.9\text{MM}. \qquad [10.32]$$

As an alternative, we can obtain an exact result by numerically inverting the characteristic function of ${}^1\widetilde{P}$. Based upon representation [10.24], as well as inversion theorem [3.212], the conditional CDF for ${}^1\widetilde{P}$ is

$$ {}^{1|0}\Phi({}^1\widetilde{p}) = \frac{1}{2} - \frac{1}{\pi}\int_0^\infty \frac{e^A sin(B + C)}{D} dw \qquad [10.33]$$

for

$$ A = -\frac{w^2}{2}\left(4\sum_{k=1}^{3}\frac{\gamma_k^2\delta_k^2}{1+4\gamma_k^2w^2}\right), \qquad [10.34]$$

$$ B = w\left(\alpha - {}^1\widetilde{p} + \sum_{k=1}^{3}\frac{\gamma_k\delta_k^2}{1+4\gamma_k^2w^2}\right), \qquad [10.35]$$

$$ C = \frac{1}{2}\sum_{k=1}^{3} tan^{-1}(2\gamma_k w), \qquad [10.36]$$

$$ D = w\left(\prod_{k=1}^{3}(1+4\gamma_k^2w^2)\right)^{1/4}, \qquad [10.37]$$

where $\alpha = -4.752 \times 10^7$; γ_1, γ_2, and γ_3 are 3.432×10^6, $-21{,}880$, and 18,277; and δ_1^2, δ_2^2, and δ_3^2 are 54.06, 8800, and 14,489. For this example, we employ approximation [3.219] with $u = 5 \times 10^{-7}$. We partition the interval $[0, u]$ into 100 subintervals to apply the trapezoidal rule.

To calculate 90% VaR, we require the conditional .10-quantile of ${}^1\widetilde{P}$. This is that value ${}^1\widetilde{p}$ such that ${}^{1|0}\Phi({}^1\widetilde{p}) = .10$. To find it, we employ the secant method. This requires two seed values—initial "guesses"—for the desired value for ${}^1\widetilde{p}$. If a portfolio has an established VaR limit, the seed values might reasonably be set equal to ${}^0\widetilde{p}$ and ${}^0\widetilde{p}$ minus .01 times the VaR limit. For this example, let's use seed values

- ${}^1\widetilde{p}^{[1]} = 200\text{MM}$,
- ${}^1\widetilde{p}^{[2]} = 190\text{MM}$.

Subsequent values ${}^{1}\widetilde{p}^{[3]}$, ${}^{1}\widetilde{p}^{[4]}$, ${}^{1}\widetilde{p}^{[5]}$, ... are obtained with the recursive formula

$$ {}^{1}\widetilde{p}^{[i]} = {}^{1}\widetilde{p}^{[i-1]} - \frac{\left[{}^{1|0}\Phi\left({}^{1}\widetilde{p}^{[i-1]}\right) - .10\right]\left({}^{1}\widetilde{p}^{[i-1]} - {}^{1}\widetilde{p}^{[i-2]}\right)}{{}^{1|0}\Phi\left({}^{1}\widetilde{p}^{[i-1]}\right) - {}^{1|0}\Phi\left({}^{1}\widetilde{p}^{[i-2]}\right)}. \quad [10.38] $$

The resulting sequence of values converges to the desired value for ${}^{1}\widetilde{p}$. Results are indicated in Exhibit 10.4

i	${}^{1}\widetilde{p}^{[i]}$	${}^{1\vert 0}\Phi({}^{1}\widetilde{p}^{[i]})$
1	200.00MM	0.41824
2	190.00MM	0.34030
3	159.17MM	0.13886
4	153.22MM	0.11053
5	151.01MM	0.10100
6	150.78MM	0.10003
7	150.77MM	0.10000

Exhibit 10.4 Results of applying the secant method to obtain the .10-quantile of the remapped portfolio's value. Each iteration of the secant method requires the evaluation of ${}^{1|0}\Phi({}^{1}\widetilde{p}^{[i]})$ using the trapezoidal rule.

The .10-quantile of ${}^{1}\widetilde{P}$ is JPY 150.8MM. This result matches, at least to the number of decimal places indicated, the approximate result we already obtained using the Cornish-Fisher expansion. Based upon calculations identical to [10.30] through [10.32], we obtain the same 61.9MM 1-day 90% JPY VaR.

EXERCISES

10.2 Consider a quadratic portfolio (53,600, ${}^{1}P$) that depends upon a single key factor ${}^{1}R_1 \sim {}^{0}N(25, 16)$:

$$ {}^{1}P = -80\,{}^{1}R_1^2 + 1120\,{}^{1}R_1 + 76{,}080. \quad [10.39] $$

In this exercise, you will use a quadratic transformation to evaluate the portfolio's VaR based upon standard deviation and 90% VaR metrics. You will calculate the 90% VaR twice: approximately using the Cornish-Fisher expansion and then exactly by inverting the characteristic function.

a. Express [10.39] as a quadratic polynomial ${}^{1}P = \dot{c}\,{}^{1}\dot{R}_1^2 + \dot{b}\,{}^{1}\dot{R}_1 + \dot{a}$ of a new risk factor ${}^{1}\dot{R}_1 \sim {}^{0}N(0, 1)$. What are your values for $\dot{c}$, $\dot{b}$, and $\dot{a}$?
b. Is what you did in part (a) a mapping or a remapping? Draw a schematic indicating the mappings and/or remappings that relate ${}^{1}P$, ${}^{1}R_1$, and ${}^{1}\dot{R}_1$.
c. Based upon your results from part (a) and the discussion of Section 3.12, determine conditional values $g^{[0]}$ through $g^{[4]}$ for ${}^{1}P$. (Hint: Formula

[3.167] for the $g^{[k]}$ is multidimensional, but you can easily interpret it for this one-dimensional problem.)

d. Based upon your results from parts (c) and the discussion of Section 3.12, determine conditional moments ${}^0E({}^1P)$ through ${}^0E({}^1P^5)$.

e. Use results from part (d) to calculate the portfolio's VaR based upon a standard deviation, ${}^0std({}^1L)$, VaR metric.

f. Based upon your moments from part (d), calculate conditional central moments of ${}^1P$ as well as the conditional central moments and cumulants of the normalization ${}^1P^*$ of ${}^1P$.

g. Use the Cornish-Fisher expansion to approximate the .10-quantile of ${}^1P^*$. Approximate the 90% VaR of ${}^1P$.

h. Complete the squares in your expression for ${}^1P$ from part (a). Doing so will express ${}^1P$ as a linear polynomial of a single chi-squared random variable.

i. What are the values of the parameters ν and δ_1^2 of the chi-squared random variable from part (h)?

j. Based upon your result from part (i), construct the characteristic function of ${}^1P$. (Note: We perform this calculation as a formality. We won't need the result for subsequent calculations.)

k. ▦ Based upon your representation from parts (h) and (i), calculate the .10-quantile of ${}^1P$ by inverting its characteristic function. Use seed values of ${}^1p^{[1]} = 25{,}000$ and ${}^1p^{[2]} = 50{,}000$ with the secant method. Calculate the 90% VaR of ${}^1P$.

10.3 Measure time in trading days and employ EUR as a base currency. A European investor has a portfolio with holdings in three United States stocks whose USD accumulated values we denote ${}^1R_1$, ${}^1R_2$, and ${}^1R_3$. Holdings are, respectively, 1000, 3000, and –2000 shares. Denote the EUR/USD exchange rate ${}^1R_4$. Consider the key vector

$$ {}^1\boldsymbol{R} = \begin{pmatrix} {}^1R_1 \\ {}^1R_2 \\ {}^1R_3 \\ {}^1R_4 \end{pmatrix}. \qquad [10.40] $$

Suppose:

$$ {}^0\boldsymbol{r} = \begin{pmatrix} 87.0 \\ 94.0 \\ 26.0 \\ 0.89 \end{pmatrix}, \quad {}^{1|0}\Sigma = \begin{pmatrix} .18923 & .06583 & .00543 & .00017 \\ .06583 & .43296 & .02327 & -.00045 \\ .00543 & .02327 & .04326 & .00022 \\ .00017 & -.00045 & .00022 & .00010 \end{pmatrix}, \qquad [10.41] $$

and assume ${}^1\boldsymbol{R} \sim N_4({}^0\boldsymbol{r}, {}^{1|0}\Sigma)$.

a. Calculate ${}^0p$.
b. Specify a mapping ${}^1P = \theta({}^1\boldsymbol{R})$. Is your mapping function θ a quadratic polynomial?
c. Express your mapping from part (b) in the form

$$\theta({}^1\boldsymbol{R}) = {}^1\boldsymbol{R}'\boldsymbol{c}\,{}^1\boldsymbol{R} + \boldsymbol{b}\,{}^1\boldsymbol{R} + a. \qquad [10.42]$$

Specify the symmetric matrix $\boldsymbol{c}$, row vector $\boldsymbol{b}$, and scalar a.
d. Construct the Cholesky matrix z of ${}^{1|0}\Sigma$.
e. ▦Construct the matrix $z'\boldsymbol{c}z$. Calculate its orthogonal eigenvectors. Normalize them (scale them so they each have unit length), and construct a 4×4 matrix $\boldsymbol{u}$ with rows equal to those normalized eigenvectors. (Hint: $z'\boldsymbol{c}z$ has 0 as a repeated eigenvalue, so its eigenvectors need not be orthogonal. Make sure the eigenvectors you select are orthogonal.)
f. Specify a mapping ${}^1\boldsymbol{R} = \varphi({}^1\dot{\boldsymbol{R}})$ such that ${}^1\dot{\boldsymbol{R}} \sim N_4(\boldsymbol{0}, \boldsymbol{I})$. (Note: We perform this calculation as a formality. We won't need the result for subsequent calculations.)
g. Specify a mapping ${}^1P = \theta \circ \varphi({}^1\dot{\boldsymbol{R}})$ of the form

$${}^1P = {}^1\dot{\boldsymbol{R}}'\dot{\boldsymbol{c}}\,{}^1\dot{\boldsymbol{R}} + \dot{\boldsymbol{b}}\,{}^1\dot{\boldsymbol{R}} + \dot{a}. \qquad [10.43]$$

Indicate the symmetric matrix $\dot{\boldsymbol{c}}$, the row vector $\dot{\boldsymbol{b}}$, and the scalar $\dot{a}$. (Hint: Work directly with formulas [3.147], [3.148], and [3.149].)
h. Based upon your results from parts (c) and (g) and the discussion of Section 3.12, determine conditional values $g^{[0]}$ through $g^{[4]}$ for ${}^1P$.
i. Based upon your results from part (h) and the discussion of Section 3.12, determine conditional moments ${}^0E({}^1P)$ through ${}^0E({}^1P^5)$.
j. Use results from part (i) to calculate the portfolio's 1-day standard deviation EUR VaR.
k. Based upon your conditional moments from part (i), calculate conditional central moments of ${}^1P$ as well as the conditional central moments and cumulants of the normalization ${}^1P^*$ of ${}^1P$.
l. Use the Cornish-Fisher expansion to approximate the conditional .05-quantile of ${}^1P^*$. From this, approximate the 1-day 95% EUR VaR of $({}^0p, {}^1P)$.
m. Multiply out your expression from part (g) and complete the squares to express ${}^1P$ as a linear polynomial of independent chi-squared random variables. What are the degrees of freedom and noncentrality parameters of the chi-squared random variables?
n. ▦Based upon your representation from part (m), calculate the conditional .05-quantile of ${}^1P$ by inverting its characteristic function. Use seed values

of ${}^1p^{[1]} = 280{,}000$ and ${}^1p^{[2]} = 290{,}000$ with the secant method. Calculate the 1-day 95% EUR VaR of ${}^1P$.

o. Retain your results, as we will refer back to them in Exercise 10.5.

10.4. MONTE CARLO TRANSFORMATION PROCEDURES

If a portfolio mapping is neither linear nor quadratic, we may apply a global remapping to make it such. If doing so would entail too large an approximation error, we resort instead to transformations that employ numerical methods of integration. Because of the high dimensionality of many VaR analyses, we focus on the Monte Carlo method. Numerical transformations based upon the Monte Carlo method were used as early as Lietaer (1971).

Consider a portfolio $({}^0p, {}^1P)$ with mapping ${}^1P = \theta({}^1\boldsymbol{R})$. Based upon a sample $\{{}^1\boldsymbol{R}^{[1]}, {}^1\boldsymbol{R}^{[2]}, \ldots, {}^1\boldsymbol{R}^{[m]}\}$ for ${}^1\boldsymbol{R}$, we define a sample $\{{}^1P^{[1]}, {}^1P^{[2]}, \ldots, {}^1P^{[m]}\}$ for ${}^1P$ with ${}^1P^{[k]} = \theta({}^1\boldsymbol{R}^{[k]})$. Any reasonable VaR metric may be estimated by applying a suitable sample estimator to $\{{}^1P^{[1]}, {}^1P^{[2]}, \ldots, {}^1P^{[m]}\}$. The result is a crude Monte Carlo estimator for the portfolio's VaR.

To apply the estimator, we need a realization $\{{}^1\boldsymbol{r}^{[1]}, {}^1\boldsymbol{r}^{[2]}, \ldots, {}^1\boldsymbol{r}^{[m]}\}$. The ${}^1\boldsymbol{r}^{[k]}$ may be pseudorandom vectors constructed as described in Chapter 5. They may also be constructed directly from historical data for key factors, as described in Section 7.5. In the former case, the transformation is called a **Monte Carlo transformation**. In the latter case, it is called an **historical transformation**.

Monte Carlo transformations offer flexibility, not only in the portfolio mapping function θ that may be modelled, but also in the conditional distribution that is assumed for ${}^1\boldsymbol{R}$. We mention historical transformations primarily for their historical significance—please pardon the pun. They were widely used during the early 1990s because they were intuitively appealing and easy to implement. They have a number of shortcomings that argue against their continued use. We have already mentioned, in Chapter 7, that conditional heteroskedasticity can render an historical realization $\{{}^1\boldsymbol{r}^{[1]}, {}^1\boldsymbol{r}^{[2]}, \ldots, {}^1\boldsymbol{r}^{[m]}\}$ a poor representation of a conditional distribution for ${}^1\boldsymbol{R}$. Another problem is the limited availability of historical data from which to construct realizations. Using 4 years of daily data will render a sample size of about 1000. As we shall see, this is barely sufficient to support a reasonable Monte Carlo analysis of portfolio VaR. Markets can change a lot in four years, so using more historical data may be inadvisable.[2] Finally, historical transformations are incompatible with some standard techniques of variance reduction.

---

[2]Pan and Duffie (1997), Holton (1998), and Hull and White (1998) propose techniques for addressing this issue, but these are primarily of theoretical interest.

Monte Carlo Standard Error

In implementing Monte Carlo transformations, an important issue is how large a sample size m to use. The standard error of the Monte Carlo analysis depends upon several factors:

- sample size m;
- the VaR metric being estimated;
- the conditional distribution of ${}^1P$, which depends upon both the conditional distribution of ${}^1\boldsymbol{R}$ and the portfolio mapping θ.

As with all Monte Carlo analyses, standard error is inversely proportional to the square root of sample size m but is unrelated to the dimensionality n of the problem. In the remainder of this section, we explore the effects of VaR metric and portfolio mapping on standard error.

A simple way to estimate the standard error of a Monte Carlo analysis is to perform the same analysis multiple times—using different pseudorandom vectors each time—and take the standard deviation of the results. For a given portfolio and VaR metric, employ a Monte Carlo transformation procedure with sample size $m = 1000$ to approximate the portfolio's VaR based upon that metric. Repeat the analysis 50,000 times, each time employing different pseudorandom vectors, to yield 50,000 independent approximations of the portfolio's VaR. Taking their sample standard deviation provides an estimate of the standard deviation of a single VaR analysis for that portfolio/metric pair based upon a sample size of $m = 1000$.

By performing this analysis for various portfolio/metric pairs, we may obtain a sense of how standard error varies for different portfolios and VaR metrics. Exhibit 10.5 indicates the results of such an analysis based upon five portfolios and three metrics—for a total of 15 portfolio/metric pairs.

Portfolio	Standard Deviation of ${}^1P$	90% Quantile of Loss	99% Quantile of Loss
a. Pure Delta	2.24%	4.21%	5.01%
b. Diversified Negative Gamma	2.75%	5.44%	6.60%
c. Diversified Positive Gamma	2.75%	2.83%	2.13%
d. Undiversified Negative Gamma	5.91%	8.89%	9.86%
e. Undiversified Positive Gamma	5.91%	0.31%	0.01%

Exhibit 10.5 Results of a Monte Carlo analysis of standard error for Monte Carlo transformation procedures. Monte Carlo transformation procedures employing a crude Monte Carlo estimator and sample size 1000 were applied to each of 15 portfolio/metric pairs a total of 50,000 times each. Standard errors were estimated for each portfolio/metric pair by taking the sample standard deviation of the 50,000 VaR results for each pair. The estimated standard errors are presented as a percentage of VaR for each portfolio/metric pair. Our first column lists the portfolios considered. The second column lists estimated standard errors for each assuming a standard-deviation VaR metric. The third and fourth columns indicate estimated standard errors for 90% and 99% quantile-of-loss VaR metrics.

We have given the five portfolios descriptive names. Their actual compositions are unimportant. What matters is their conditional PDFs for ${}^1P$.[3] These are graphed in Exhibit 10.6. The first three portfolios are most typical of what is encountered in applications. Portfolio (a) might correspond to diversified or undiversified linear exposures. It might also correspond to highly diversified nonlinear exposures. Portfolios (b) and (c) might correspond to a handful of positive or negative gamma positions. They might also correspond to delta and gamma exposure to a single underlier. Portfolios (d) and (e) might correspond to delta-hedged gamma exposure to a single underlier. These two portfolios are somewhat stylized. We include them in our analysis to illustrate how extreme standard errors might arrise. For all portfolios, ${}^0E({}^1P) = {}^0p$.

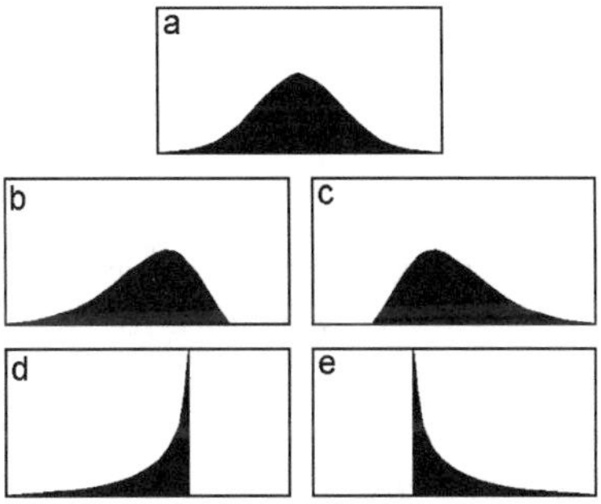

Exhibit 10.6 Conditional PDFs for ${}^1P$ are indicated for the five portfolios considered in the analysis of Exhibit 10.5.

Another way to look at our results is to determine, based upon [5.38], for each portfolio/metric pair the sample size that would achieve a 1% standard error. Results of this analysis are presented in Exhibit 10.7.

Portfolio	Standard Deviation of ${}^1P$	90% Quantile of Loss	99% Quantile of Loss
a. Pure Delta	5,100	17,800	25,100
b. Diversified Negative Gamma	7,600	29,600	43,600
c. Diversified Positive Gamma	7,600	8,000	4,500
d. Undiversified Negative Gamma	34,900	79,100	97,300
e. Undiversified Positive Gamma	34,900	100	100

Exhibit 10.7 Sample sizes required for a 1% standard error are indicated for the 15 portfolio/metric pairs. Values are obtained by applying [5.39] to the results of Exhibit 10.5.

[3] This is worth emphasizing. For a given sample size and VaR metric, standard error depends entirely upon the PDF of ${}^1P$. The Monte Carlo transformation procedure works by constructing a realization of a sample for ${}^1P$. The actual mechanics of how that realization is constructed are unimportant for standard error. Factors such as the composition of the portfolio, the number of key factors upon which it depends, or the portfolio mapping affect standard error only to the extent that they shape the PDF of ${}^1P$. If we know the PDF of ${}^1P$, we don't need to consider these other factors. Understand this, and you will understand why the Monte Carlo method does not suffer from the curse of dimensionality.

For standard deviation VaR metrics, a sample size of 8000 should ensure a standard error less than 1% for most diversified portfolios. Quantile-of-loss metrics require larger samples. For a 90% or 99% quantile-of-loss metric, consider sample sizes of 30,000 or 45,000, respectively.

Even if a portfolio mapping function θ is simple, performing such large numbers of valuations can be computationally expensive. If θ is more complicated, run times may become prohibitive. The worst situation occurs if a portfolio holds exotic derivatives, mortgage-backed securities, or other instruments that must be valued using numerical techniques such as binomial trees or the Monte Carlo method. If θ is a primary mapping, a single portfolio valuation ${}^1p^{[k]} = \theta({}^1\boldsymbol{r}^{[k]})$ might require minutes of processing time. The thousands of valuations required to estimate VaR would take days.

Exercises

10.4 A Monte Carlo transformation employs a sample size $m = 5000$. For a particular portfolio it has a 2.6% standard error. What sample size should be used to achieve a standard error of 1.0%?

10.5 ▤ Consider the portfolio of Exercise 10.3. Use a Monte Carlo transformation to evaluate the same VaR metrics:

- standard deviation EUR VaR; and
- 90% EUR VaR.

Do your calculations three times, using sample sizes m of 100, 1000, and 10,000. Compare your results for the different sample sizes, and compare them with the corresponding results you obtained for Exercise 10.3.

10.5. VARIANCE REDUCTION

Cárdenas *et al.* (1999) pioneered variance reduction techniques for Monte Carlo transformations. These can dramatically reduce the computational expense of applying a Monte Carlo transformation.

Standard variance reduction techniques employ a global remapping ${}^1\widetilde{P}$ to estimate the VaR of a portfolio $({}^0p, {}^1P)$. Rather than substitute ${}^1\widetilde{P}$ for ${}^1P$, they apply a Monte Carlo estimator directly to ${}^1P$, but use ${}^1\widetilde{P}$ to facilitate variance reduction. An obvious approach is to employ ${}^1\widetilde{P}$ as a control variate for ${}^1P$. We also may use ${}^1\widetilde{P}$ to implement stratified sampling. ${}^1\widetilde{P}$ may be a linear remapping, but best results are obtained if it is a quadratic remapping.

A shortcoming of these variance reduction techniques is that they place restrictions on the distribution of ${}^1\boldsymbol{R}$. We consider techniques that are suitable if ${}^1\boldsymbol{R}$ is conditionally joint normal.

CONTROL VARIATES

Consider a portfolio $({}^{0}p,\ {}^{1}P)$ with portfolio mapping ${}^{1}P = \theta({}^{1}\boldsymbol{R})$, where ${}^{1}\boldsymbol{R} \sim {}^{0}N_n({}^{1|0}\boldsymbol{\mu},\ {}^{1|0}\boldsymbol{\Sigma})$. We construct a quadratic remapping ${}^{1}\widetilde{P} = \widetilde{\theta}({}^{1}\boldsymbol{R})$ as described in Section 9.3. Set ${}^{0}\widetilde{p} = {}^{0}p$. We wish to estimate some VaR metric for ${}^{1}P$, which we denote ψ. Let $\widetilde{\psi}$ be the corresponding VaR metric for ${}^{1}\widetilde{P}$. Since ${}^{1}\widetilde{P}$ is a quadratic polynomial of a joint-normal random vector, we can value $\widetilde{\psi}$ using the techniques of Section 10.3.

Suppose

$$H\big(\theta({}^{1}\boldsymbol{R}^{[1]}), \theta({}^{1}\boldsymbol{R}^{[2]}), \ldots, \theta({}^{1}\boldsymbol{R}^{[m]})\big) \qquad [10.44]$$

is a crude Monte Carlo estimator for ψ. Define a corresponding estimator

$$\widetilde{H} = H\big(\widetilde{\theta}({}^{1}\boldsymbol{R}^{[1]}), \widetilde{\theta}({}^{1}\boldsymbol{R}^{[2]}), \ldots, \widetilde{\theta}({}^{1}\boldsymbol{R}^{[m]})\big), \qquad [10.45]$$

which is an estimator for $\widetilde{\psi}$. As described in Section 5.9, define a control variate estimator for ψ as

$$H - c[\widetilde{H} - \widetilde{\psi}]. \qquad [10.46]$$

Variance reduction depends on how well $\widetilde{H}$ approximates H, which depends on how well ${}^{1}\widetilde{P}$ approximates ${}^{1}P$. Often, the approximation is nearly perfect. In those situations, the control variate estimator has essentially zero standard error. Sample sizes m as low as 100 produce accurate VaR estimates, which match those obtainable using a stand-alone quadratic transformation as described in Section 10.3. If such instances can be identified, it makes sense to forgo a Monte Carlo transformation and use the computationally less expensive quadratic transformation.

The more interesting situation is if the approximation ${}^{1}\widetilde{P}$ for ${}^{1}P$ is not good enough to justify use of a stand-alone quadratic transformation. In this case, the approximation is usually good enough to achieve variance reduction as a control variate. In rare instances, it is inadequate even for this purpose. This is sometimes the case if a portfolio holds expiring options. Even this tends only to be a problem if a VaR metric has a long horizon and focuses on rare events, as do 99% or ETL VaR metrics.

If the VaR metric ψ is a quantile, $\widetilde{\psi}$ can be valued exactly by inverting the characteristic function or approximately by applying the Cornish-Fisher expansion. Any error associated with the Cornish-Fisher approximation will be incorporated into the control-variate Monte Carlo result.

EXAMPLE: CONTROL VARIATES. Results using control-variate estimator [10.46] tend to be excellent. In this example, we consider an extreme situation where a portfolio's value is dominated by several expiring options, which render a quadratic remapping an especially poor approximation for the primary portfolio mapping. Even in this extreme case, the control variate dramatically reduces standard error for a variety of VaR metrics. The one exception is a 99% VaR metric, for which the control variate increases standard error modestly.

Assume a 1-week VaR horizon. A portfolio $({}^0p, {}^1P)$ holds futures and options in several underliers. Its price behaviour is dominated by several options that expire at the end of the VaR horizon. Let ${}^1P = \theta({}^1\boldsymbol{R})$, where ${}^1\boldsymbol{R}$ is conditionally joint-normal. Using the method of least squares, we construct a quadratic remapping ${}^1\widetilde{P} = \widetilde{\theta}({}^1\boldsymbol{R})$ for ${}^1P$. We set ${}^0\widetilde{p} = {}^0p$. Exhibit 10.8 is a scatter plot of realizations for ${}^1\widetilde{P}$ and ${}^1P$.

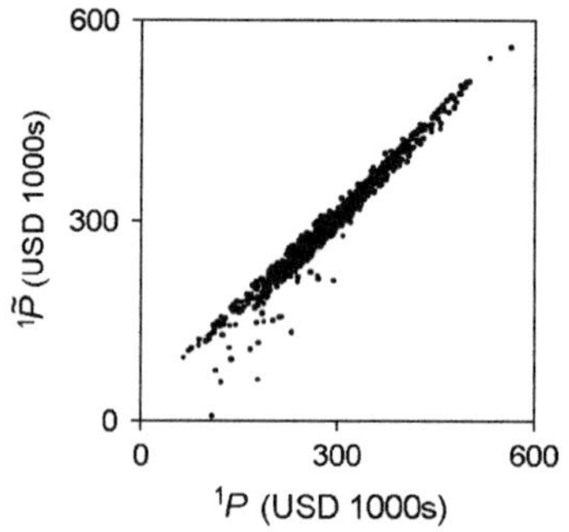

Exhibit 10.8 Scatter plot of realizations for ${}^1\widetilde{P}$ and ${}^1P$.

Because of the expiring options, the approximation ${}^1\widetilde{P} \approx {}^1P$ is not good enough to justify use of a stand-alone quadratic transformation. Instead, we use a Monte Carlo transformation with control-variate estimator [10.46] based upon ${}^1\widetilde{P}$. We do so for four metrics:

- standard deviation of loss;
- 90% quantile of loss;
- 95% quantile of loss; and
- 99% quantile of loss.

For each VaR metric ψ, we calculate the value of the corresponding VaR metric $\widetilde{\psi}$ for ${}^1\widetilde{P}$ using the methods of Section 10.3. Next, we generate a realization $\{{}^1\boldsymbol{r}^{[1]}, {}^1\boldsymbol{r}^{[2]}, \ldots, {}^1\boldsymbol{r}^{[20,000]}\}$ of a sample for ${}^1\boldsymbol{R}$, and calculate corresponding values ${}^1p^{[k]} = \theta({}^1\boldsymbol{r}^{[k]})$ and ${}^1\widetilde{p}^{[k]} = \widetilde{\theta}({}^1\boldsymbol{r}^{[k]})$. For each VaR metric ψ, we employ a sample estimator H, and set

$$h = H\left({}^1p^{[1]}, {}^1p^{[2]}, \ldots, {}^1p^{[20,000]}\right), \qquad [10.47]$$

$$\widetilde{h} = H\left({}^1\widetilde{p}^{[1]}, {}^1\widetilde{p}^{[2]}, \ldots, {}^1\widetilde{p}^{[20,000]}\right). \qquad [10.48]$$

Our crude Monte Carlo estimate for ψ is simply h. Substituting h, $\widetilde{h}$, and $\widetilde{\psi}$ into [10.46], and setting $c = 1$, we obtain our control-variate estimate for ψ:

$$h - [\widetilde{h} - \widetilde{\psi}]. \qquad [10.49]$$

Exhibit 10.9 indicates control variate and crude Monte Carlo VaR estimates for each of the four VaR metrics. It compares them with estimates obtained using a stand-alone quadratic transformation. It also indicates exact VaR results for each metric:

Metric	Control Variate	Crude Monte Carlo	Quadratic	Exact
std	76,719	77,062	76,639	76,780
90%	93,084	92,382	83,059	93,439
95%	123,687	122,521	110,475	123,610
99%	174,781	174,634	172,113	174,425

Exhibit 10.9 VaR estimates based upon four VaR metrics estimated using control variates, crude Monte Carlo, and a quadratic transformation. Results in the last column are exact.

Corresponding errors are indicated in Exhibit 10.10. Exhibit 10.11 illustrates for each metric how the control variate and crude Monte Carlo estimators converged to their respective results.

Metric	Control Variate	Crude Monte Carlo	Quadratic	Exact
std	0.1%	0.4%	0.2%	–
90%	0.4%	1.1%	11.1%	–
95%	0.1%	0.9%	10.6%	–
99%	0.2%	0.1%	1.3%	–

Exhibit 10.10 Realized absolute errors calculated from the results of Exhibit 10.9.

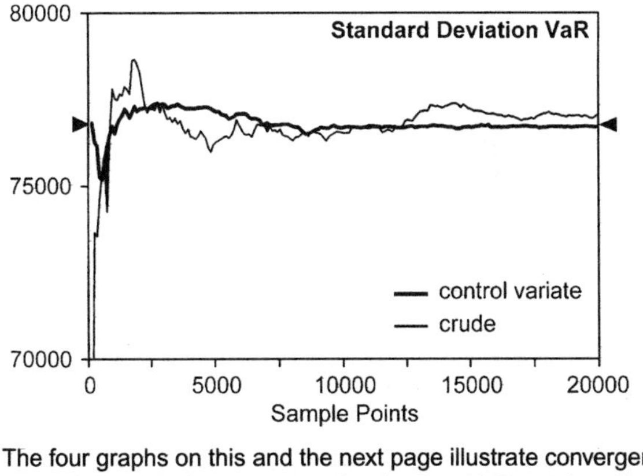

Exhibit 10.11 The four graphs on this and the next page illustrate convergence of the control variate and crude Monte Carlo estimators for the four VaR metrics. Each graph plots preliminary VaR estimates based upon partial sample sizes *m* ranging from just the first 100 sample points through the total 20,000 sample points used to construct the VaR estimates. Arrows on either side of each graph indicate the true VaR being estimated in each case.

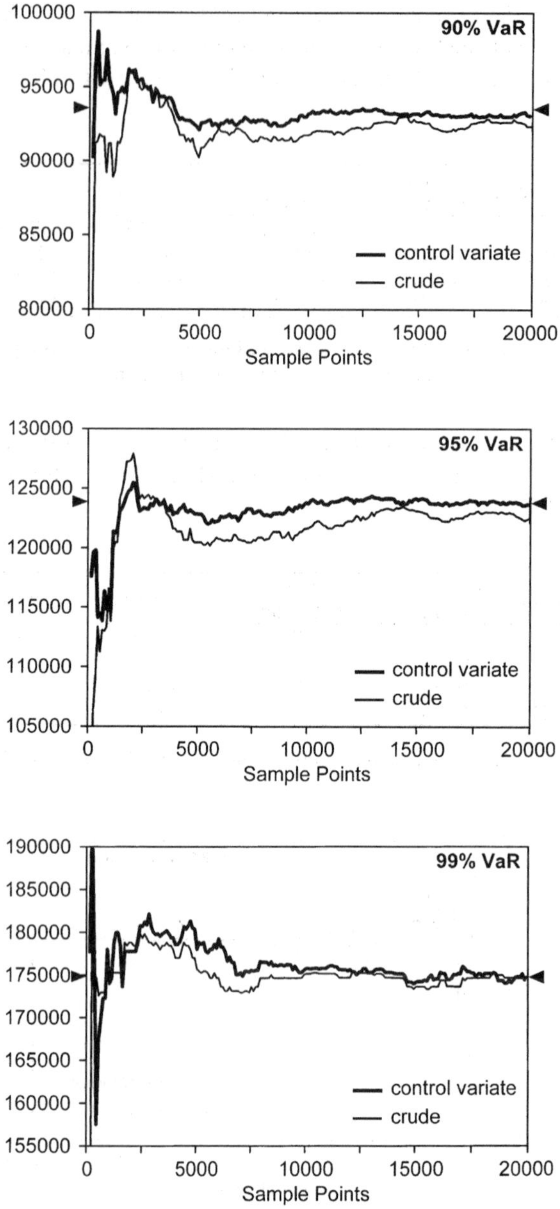

Exhibit 10.11 *Continued from previous page.*

Of more interest are the standard errors for each estimator. These are estimated by repeating each Monte Carlo analysis 500 times and taking sample standard deviations of the results.[4] Estimated standard errors are indicated in Exhibit 10.12.

Metric	Control Variate	Crude Monte Carlo
std	177	415
90%	508	909
95%	784	1280
99%	2353	1725

Exhibit 10.12 Estimated standard errors.

From these, we can calculate the sample size m required to achieve a 1% standard error. Results are indicated in Exhibit 10.13.

Metric	Control Variate	Crude Monte Carlo
std	1,062	5,857
90%	5,900	18,950
95%	8,040	21,440
99%	36,400	19,600

Exhibit 10.13 Sample sizes m required to achieve a 1% standard error.

For all metrics except 99% VaR, use of a control variate reduces the sample size m required to achieve a 1% standard error. Typical results are far better than these. For this example, we selected a portfolio for which a quadratic remapping is an especially poor approximation for the primary portfolio mapping.

Stratified Sampling for Standard Deviation VaR Metrics

Stratified sampling can also dramatically reduce the standard error of a Monte Carlo estimator for VaR. A quadratic remapping guides us both in specifying a stratification and in selecting sample sizes m_i for each subregion of the stratification. Our approach depends upon the VaR metric to be estimated. We consider standard deviation VaR metrics and later quantile VaR metrics.

Consider a portfolio $({}^0p,\ {}^1P)$ with portfolio mapping ${}^1P = \theta({}^1\boldsymbol{R})$, where ${}^1\boldsymbol{R} \sim {}^0N_n({}^{1|0}\boldsymbol{\mu},\ {}^{1|0}\boldsymbol{\Sigma})$. Construct a quadratic remapping ${}^1\tilde{P} = \tilde{\theta}({}^1\boldsymbol{R})$, and set ${}^0\tilde{p} = {}^0p$. To estimate a standard deviation VaR metric, ${}^0std({}^1L)$, we note that

$$ {}^0std({}^1L) = \sqrt{{}^0var({}^1P)}, \qquad [10.50] $$

[4]Each Monte Carlo analysis was performed with sample size $m = 1000$. Standard errors for a sample size of $m = 20{,}000$ were estimated by taking the sample standard deviation of the results and dividing by $\sqrt{20}$.

so it is sufficient to estimate ${}^0var({}^1P)$. We stratify $\mathbb{R}$ into w disjoint subintervals ϑ_j based upon the conditional PDF of ${}^1\widetilde{P}$ as follows. Since ${}^1\widetilde{P}$ is a quadratic polynomial of a joint-normal random vector, we may apply the methods of Section 10.3 to calculate its .01 and .99 quantiles, ${}^{1|0}\Phi^{-1}_{{}^1\widetilde{P}}(.01)$ and ${}^{1|0}\Phi^{-1}_{{}^1\widetilde{P}}(.99)$. Set

$$\vartheta_1 = \left\{{}^1\widetilde{p} : {}^1\widetilde{p} \leq {}^{1|0}\Phi^{-1}_{{}^1\widetilde{P}}(.01)\right\}, \quad [10.51]$$

$$\vartheta_w = \left\{{}^1\widetilde{p} : {}^1\widetilde{p} > {}^{1|0}\Phi^{-1}_{{}^1\widetilde{P}}(.99)\right\}. \quad [10.52]$$

Define intervening subintervals ϑ_j, each of length

$$l = \frac{{}^{1|0}\Phi^{-1}_{{}^1\widetilde{P}}(.99) - {}^{1|0}\Phi^{-1}_{{}^1\widetilde{P}}(.01)}{w - 2}, \quad [10.53]$$

so

$$\vartheta_j = \left\{{}^1\widetilde{p} : {}^{1|0}\Phi^{-1}_{{}^1\widetilde{P}}(.01) + (j-2)l < {}^1\widetilde{p} \leq {}^{1|0}\Phi^{-1}_{{}^1\widetilde{P}}(.01) + (j-1)l\right\}. \quad [10.54]$$

A stratification of size $w = 8$ is illustrated based upon a hypothetical conditional PDF for ${}^1\widetilde{P}$ in Exhibit 10.14. In practice, stratification sizes of between 15 and 30 may be appropriate.

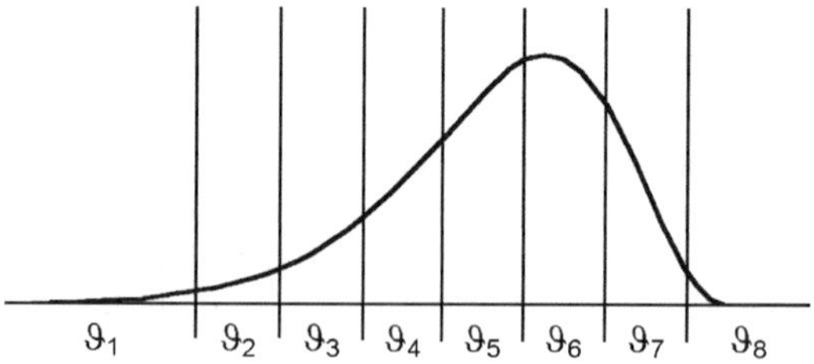

Exhibit 10.14 A stratification of $\mathbb{R}$ of size $w = 8$ constructed as described in the text based upon a hypothetical conditional PDF for ${}^1\widetilde{P}$.

Based upon stratification

$$\mathbb{R} = \vartheta_1 \cup \vartheta_2 \cup \cdots \cup \vartheta_w, \quad [10.55]$$

define a stratification

$$\mathbb{R}^n = \Omega_1 \cup \Omega_2 \cup \cdots \cup \Omega_w, \quad [10.56]$$

where

$$\Omega_j = \widetilde{\theta}^{-1}(\vartheta_j). \quad [10.57]$$

Specifically, Ω_j is the set of realizations ${}^1\boldsymbol{r}$ for ${}^1\boldsymbol{R}$ such that corresponding portfolio values ${}^1p = \widetilde{\theta}({}^1\boldsymbol{r})$ are in ϑ_j. In mathematical parlance, each set Ω_j is the **preimage** under $\widetilde{\theta}$ of the set ϑ_j.

Define w random vectors ${}^1\boldsymbol{R}_j = {}^1\boldsymbol{R}|{}^1\boldsymbol{R} \in \Omega_j$. That is, ${}^1\boldsymbol{R}_j$ equals ${}^1\boldsymbol{R}$ conditional on ${}^1\boldsymbol{R}$ being in Ω_j. Define ${}^1P_j = \theta({}^1\boldsymbol{R}_j)$ for all j. Then ${}^1P$ is a mixture, in the sense of Section 3.10, of the ${}^1P_j$. Applying [3.114] and [3.115],

$$ {}^0E({}^1P) = \sum_{j=1}^{w} p_j \, {}^0E({}^1P_j), \tag{10.58} $$

$$ {}^0std({}^1P) = \sqrt{\left(\sum_{j=1}^{w} p_j \, {}^0E\left({}^1P_j^2\right)\right) - {}^0E({}^1P)^2}. \tag{10.59} $$

Given samples for the ${}^1\boldsymbol{R}_j$, each of form $\{{}^1\boldsymbol{R}_j^{[1]}, {}^1\boldsymbol{R}_j^{[2]}, \ldots, {}^1\boldsymbol{R}_j^{[m_j]}\}$ and respective size m_j, we define an estimator for ${}^0std({}^1P)$:

$$ \sqrt{\sum_{j=1}^{w} \frac{p_j}{m_j} \sum_{k=1}^{m_j} \theta\left({}^1\boldsymbol{R}_j^{[k]}\right)^2 - \left(\sum_{j=1}^{w} \frac{p_j}{m_j} \sum_{k=1}^{m_j} \theta\left({}^1\boldsymbol{R}_j^{[k]}\right)\right)^2}, \tag{10.60} $$

where

$$ p_j = Pr({}^1\boldsymbol{R} \in \Omega_j) = Pr({}^1\widetilde{P} \in \vartheta_j). \tag{10.61} $$

Since ${}^1\widetilde{P}$ is conditionally a quadratic polynomial of a joint-normal random vector, we can apply the methods of Section 10.3 to value its conditional CDF, so values p_j can be calculated. Analogous to [5.90], sample sizes m_j are set equal to

$$ m_j = \begin{cases} \dfrac{mp_j w/3}{\dfrac{(p_1+p_2)w}{3} + \sum\limits_{i=2}^{w-1} p_i} & j = 1, w, \\[2ex] \dfrac{mp_j}{\dfrac{(p_1+p_2)w}{3} + \sum\limits_{i=2}^{w-1} p_i} & \text{otherwise,} \end{cases} \tag{10.62} $$

where the m_j sum to m. The formula for m_1 and m_w is reasonable based upon empirical analyses.

Generate realizations ${}^1\boldsymbol{r}_j^{[k]}$ simultaneously for all j by generating realizations ${}^1\boldsymbol{r}^{[k]}$ for ${}^1\boldsymbol{R}$ and allocating each to one of the ${}^1\boldsymbol{R}_j$ according to which set ϑ_j the corresponding realization $\widetilde{\theta}({}^1\boldsymbol{r}^{[k]})$ falls in. Stop when you have sufficient realizations for each ${}^1\boldsymbol{R}_j$. For some ${}^1\boldsymbol{R}_j$, you will have more than enough realizations, but extras can be discarded.

Stratified Sampling for Quantile VaR Metrics

Consider a portfolio $({}^0p, {}^1P)$ with portfolio mapping ${}^1P = \theta({}^1\boldsymbol{R})$, where ${}^1\boldsymbol{R} \sim {}^0N_n({}^{1|0}\boldsymbol{\mu}, {}^{1|0}\boldsymbol{\Sigma})$. We construct a quadratic remapping ${}^1\widetilde{P} = \widetilde{\theta}({}^1\boldsymbol{R})$ and set ${}^0\widetilde{p} = {}^0p$. We wish to estimate the portfolio's q-quantile of loss VaR, which we denote ψ.

The corresponding q-quantile of loss VaR for the remapped portfolio is denoted $\widetilde{\psi}$. It is calculated using the methods of Section 10.3.

To estimate ψ, we stratify $\mathbb{R}^n$ into two regions, Ω_1 and Ω_2. Optimally, realizations ${}^1\boldsymbol{r}$ for which portfolio losses exceed VaR should fall into one region, with the rest falling into the other region:

- $\Omega_1 = \{{}^1\boldsymbol{r} : {}^0p - \theta({}^1\boldsymbol{r}) \leq \psi\}$;
- $\Omega_2 = \{{}^1\boldsymbol{r} : {}^0p - \theta({}^1\boldsymbol{r}) > \psi\}$.

We will explain why this is optimal shortly. For now, we observe that the optimal stratification is impractical. Its definitions of Ω_1 and Ω_2 depend upon the portfolio's VaR ψ, which is what we are trying to estimate. As an alternative, we approximate the optimal stratification with one based upon the known VaR $\widetilde{\psi}$ of $({}^0\widetilde{p}, {}^1\widetilde{P})$:

- $\Omega_1 = \{{}^1\boldsymbol{r} : {}^0\widetilde{p} - \widetilde{\theta}({}^1\boldsymbol{r}) \leq \widetilde{\psi}\}$;
- $\Omega_2 = \{{}^1\boldsymbol{r} : {}^0\widetilde{p} - \widetilde{\theta}({}^1\boldsymbol{r}) > \widetilde{\psi}\}$.

Let's elaborate. To estimate a quantile of loss ${}^{1|0}\Phi^{-1}_{{}^1L}(q)$, it is sufficient to estimate the corresponding quantile ${}^{1|0}\Phi^{-1}_{{}^1P}(1-q)$ of ${}^1P$, since

$$ {}^{1|0}\Phi^{-1}_{{}^1L}(q) = {}^0p - {}^{1|0}\Phi^{-1}_{{}^1P}(1-q). \qquad [10.63] $$

Directly specifying a stratified sampling estimator for values of ${}^{1|0}\Phi^{-1}_{{}^1P}$ is difficult. We focus instead on devising a stratified sampling estimator for values of ${}^{1|0}\Phi_{{}^1P}$. If we can estimate ${}^{1|0}\Phi_{{}^1P}({}^1p)$ for suitable values ${}^1p$ based upon a single Monte Carlo analysis, we can estimate the quantile ${}^{1|0}\Phi^{-1}_{{}^1P}(1-q)$ based upon that same analysis.

Define the indicator function

$$ I(\textit{condition}) = \begin{cases} 1 & \textit{condition} \text{ is true,} \\ 0 & \textit{condition} \text{ is false.} \end{cases} \qquad [10.64] $$

For example, $I(x > 3)$ equals 1 if $x = 5$ but it equals 0 if $x = 2$. A crude Monte Carlo estimator for ${}^{1|0}\Phi_{{}^1P}({}^1p)$ is

$$ \frac{1}{m}\sum_{k=1}^{m} I\left(\theta\left({}^1\boldsymbol{R}^{[k]}\right) \leq {}^1p\right). \qquad [10.65] $$

Since $I(\theta({}^1\boldsymbol{R}) \leq {}^1p)$ can only take on values 0 or 1, it makes sense to stratify with just two subregions, Ω_0 and Ω_1, of $\mathbb{R}^n$ such that Ω_0 primarily contains values ${}^1\boldsymbol{r}$ for which the indicator function equals 0, and Ω_1 primarily contains values ${}^1\boldsymbol{r}$ for which the indicator function equals 1.

With such a stratification, define ${}^1\boldsymbol{R}_1 = {}^1\boldsymbol{R} \mid {}^1\boldsymbol{R} \in \Omega_1$ and ${}^1\boldsymbol{R}_2 = {}^1\boldsymbol{R} \mid {}^1\boldsymbol{R} \in \Omega_2$. Our estimator becomes

$$ \frac{1-q}{m_1}\sum_{k=1}^{m_1} I\left(\theta\left({}^1\boldsymbol{R}_1^{[k]}\right) \leq {}^1p\right) + \frac{q}{m_2}\sum_{k=1}^{m_2} I\left(\theta\left({}^1\boldsymbol{R}_2^{[k]}\right) \leq {}^1p\right). \qquad [10.66] $$

We equally weight realizations by setting

$$m_1 = (1 - q)m, \qquad [10.67]$$

$$m_2 = qm, \qquad [10.68]$$

for a suitable value m. The estimator becomes

$$\frac{1}{m}\left(\sum_{k=1}^{(1-q)m} I\left(\theta\left({}^1\boldsymbol{R}_1^{[k]}\right) \leq {}^1p\right) + \sum_{k=1}^{qm} I\left(\theta\left({}^1\boldsymbol{R}_2^{[k]}\right) \leq {}^1p\right)\right). \qquad [10.69]$$

This has standard error

$$\frac{1}{\sqrt{m}}\sqrt{(1-q)\,{}^0var[I(\theta({}^1\boldsymbol{R}_1) \leq {}^1p)] + q\,{}^0var[I(\theta({}^1\boldsymbol{R}_2) \leq {}^1p)]}. \qquad [10.70]$$

If $I(\theta({}^1\boldsymbol{R}_1) \leq {}^1p)$ always equals 1 and $I(\theta({}^1\boldsymbol{R}_2) \leq {}^1p)$ always equals 0, the standard error is 0. It is this observation that motivated the optimal stratification described earlier. Because that stratification is impractical, we resort to the related stratification based upon the remapped portfolio. Formally, we stratify $\mathbb{R}$ into two unbounded intervals:

$$\vartheta_1 = \left\{{}^1\widetilde{p} : {}^1\widetilde{p} \leq {}^{1|0}\Phi^{-1}_{{}^1\widetilde{P}}(1-q)\right\}, \qquad [10.71]$$

$$\vartheta_2 = \left\{{}^1\widetilde{p} : {}^1\widetilde{p} > {}^{1|0}\Phi^{-1}_{{}^1\widetilde{P}}(1-q)\right\}. \qquad [10.72]$$

This is illustrated based upon the hypothetical conditional PDF for ${}^1\widetilde{P}$ in Exhibit 10.15.

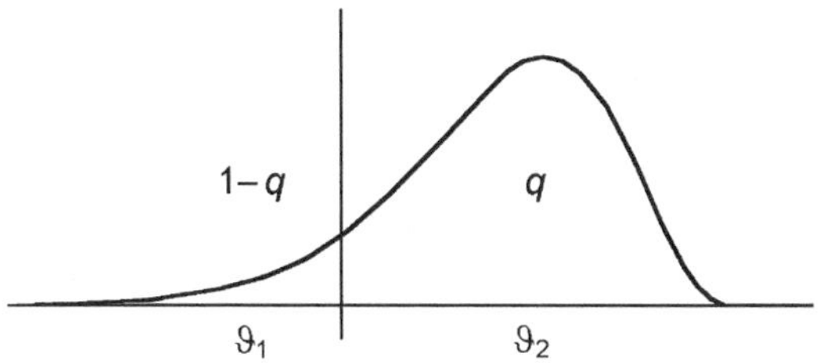

Exhibit 10.15 A stratification of $\mathbb{R}$ into two intervals divided at ${}^{1|0}\Phi^{-1}_{{}^1\widetilde{P}}(1-q)$.

Based upon stratification

$$\mathbb{R} = \vartheta_1 \cup \vartheta_2, \qquad [10.73]$$

define a stratification

$$\mathbb{R}^n = \Omega_1 \cup \Omega_2, \qquad [10.74]$$

where

$$\Omega_j = \widetilde{\theta}^{-1}(\vartheta_j). \qquad [10.75]$$

To estimate ${}^{1|0}\Phi^{-1}_{{}^1\widetilde{P}}(1-q)$, generate realizations $\{{}^1\boldsymbol{r}_1^{[1]}, {}^1\boldsymbol{r}_1^{[2]}, \ldots, {}^1\boldsymbol{r}_1^{[m_1]}\}$ and $\{{}^1\boldsymbol{r}_2^{[1]}, {}^1\boldsymbol{r}_2^{[2]}, \ldots, {}^1\boldsymbol{r}_2^{[m_2]}\}$. Apply θ to all points ${}^1\boldsymbol{r}_j^{[k]}$ to obtain $m = m_1 + m_2$ realizations ${}^1p^{[k]}$ of ${}^1P$. Estimate ${}^{1|0}\Phi^{-1}_{{}^1\widetilde{P}}(1-q)$ as that value ${}^1p^{[k]}$ such that $(1-q)m$ of the values are less than or equal to it.

Selective Valuation of Realizations

The computationally most expensive task in estimating VaR with the Monte Carlo method is performing m valuations ${}^1p^{[k]} = \theta({}^1\boldsymbol{r}^{[k]})$. As we have seen, variance reduction can dramatically reduce the number of valuations that must be performed. There is a complementary technique, which is applicable to VaR metrics that focus on a single tail of the conditional PDF of ${}^1P$. We describe the technique for quantile-of-loss VaR metrics, but it is applicable to others, such as ETL metrics.

For estimating a standard deviation of ${}^1P$, the precise value of every realization ${}^1p^{[k]}$ is important. Every one contributes to sample standard deviation. For estimating a quantile of ${}^1P$, the precise value of only one realization ${}^1p^{[k]}$ is important—the one equal to the quantile being estimated. Unfortunately, we only find out which one that is after we have valued all the ${}^1p^{[k]}$! We can avoid having to value every ${}^1p^{[k]}$ by employing a quadratic remapping ${}^1\widetilde{P} = \widetilde{\theta}({}^1\boldsymbol{R})$ to identify realizations ${}^1\boldsymbol{r}^{[k]}$ for which ${}^1p^{[k]} = \theta({}^1\boldsymbol{r}^{[k]})$ clearly exceeds the quantile. Since those values ${}^1p^{[k]}$ are unimportant, we may approximate them with values ${}^1\widetilde{p}^{[k]} = \widetilde{\theta}({}^1\boldsymbol{r}^{[k]})$. We now formalize the technique.

Consider a portfolio $({}^0p, {}^1P)$ with portfolio mapping ${}^1P = \theta({}^1\boldsymbol{R})$, where ${}^1\boldsymbol{R} \sim {}^0N_n({}^{1|0}\boldsymbol{\mu}, {}^{1|0}\boldsymbol{\Sigma})$. We construct a quadratic remapping ${}^1\widetilde{P} = \widetilde{\theta}({}^1\boldsymbol{R})$. Set ${}^0\widetilde{p} = {}^0p$. We wish to estimate the portfolio's q-quantile of loss VaR, which we denote ψ. The corresponding q-quantile of loss VaR for the remapped portfolio is denoted $\widetilde{\psi}$. It is calculated using the methods of Section 10.3.

We stratify $\mathbb{R}$ into w disjoint subintervals ϑ_j based upon the conditional PDF of ${}^1\widetilde{P}$ as follows:

$$\vartheta_1 = \left\{{}^1\widetilde{p} : {}^1\widetilde{p} \le {}^{1|0}\Phi^{-1}_{{}^1\widetilde{P}}(1-q+.05)\right\}, \qquad [10.76]$$

$$\vartheta_2 = \left\{{}^1\widetilde{p} : {}^{1|0}\Phi^{-1}_{{}^1\widetilde{P}}(1-q+.05) < {}^1\widetilde{p} \le {}^{1|0}\Phi^{-1}_{{}^1\widetilde{P}}(1-q+.10)\right\}, \qquad [10.77]$$

$$\vartheta_3 = \left\{{}^1\widetilde{p} : {}^{1|0}\Phi^{-1}_{{}^1\widetilde{P}}(1-q+.10) < {}^1\widetilde{p} \le {}^{1|0}\Phi^{-1}_{{}^1\widetilde{P}}(1-q+.15)\right\}, \qquad [10.78]$$

$$\vdots$$

This is illustrated for a hypothetical conditional PDF for ${}^1\widetilde{P}$ in Exhibit 10.16.

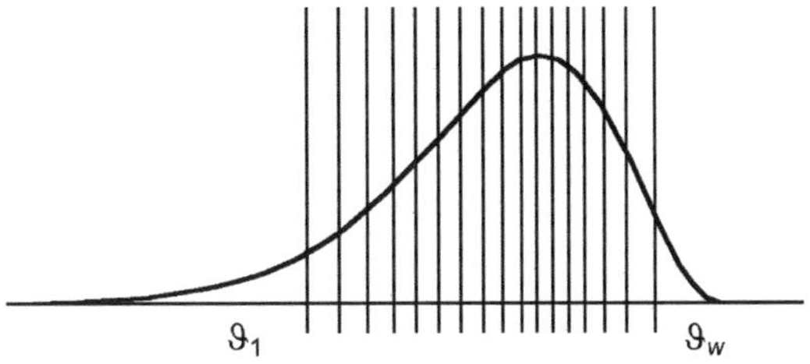

Exhibit 10.16 A stratification of $\mathbb{R}$ into w subintervals ϑ_j constructed as described in the text based upon a hypothetical conditional PDF for ${}^1\widetilde{P}$. With the exception of the first and possibly the last subintervals, all have probability .05 based upon the conditional PDF of ${}^1\widetilde{P}$.

Based upon stratification

$$\mathbb{R} = \vartheta_1 \cup \vartheta_2 \cup \cdots \cup \vartheta_w, \qquad [10.79]$$

define a stratification

$$\mathbb{R}^n = \Omega_1 \cup \Omega_2 \cup \cdots \cup \Omega_w, \qquad [10.80]$$

where

$$\Omega_j = \widetilde{\theta}^{-1}(\vartheta_j). \qquad [10.81]$$

The $1-q$ quantile of ${}^1\widetilde{P}$ is in ϑ_1 by construction. Based upon the approximation ${}^1\widetilde{P} \approx {}^1P$, we expect the $1-q$ quantile of ${}^1P$ to be in ϑ_1 as well; but we cannot be sure. Generate a realization $\{{}^1\boldsymbol{r}^{[1]}, {}^1\boldsymbol{r}^{[2]}, \ldots, {}^1\boldsymbol{r}^{[m]}\}$ and calculate corresponding values ${}^1\widetilde{p}^{[k]} = \widetilde{\theta}({}^1\boldsymbol{r}^{[k]})$. Based upon these, sort the ${}^1\boldsymbol{r}^{[k]}$ into regions Ω_j. For only those in regions Ω_1 and Ω_2, calculate ${}^1p^{[k]} = \theta({}^1\boldsymbol{r}^{[k]})$. For the rest, approximate ${}^1p^{[k]}$ with ${}^1\widetilde{p}^{[k]}$. Based upon the (exact or approximate) values ${}^1p^{[k]}$, estimate the VaR of $({}^0p, {}^1P)$.

The purpose of the region Ω_2 is to play a buffer role to protect against the possibility that the approximation ${}^1\widetilde{P} \approx {}^1P$ is poor. If the approximation is good, all realized losses ${}^1l^{[k]} = {}^0p - {}^1p^{[k]}$ for that region should be less than the estimated VaR. If this is the case, then you are done. If not, improve your VaR estimate as follows.

For all realizations ${}^1\boldsymbol{r}^{[k]}$ in region Ω_3, calculate exact portfolio values ${}^1p^{[k]} = \theta({}^1\boldsymbol{r}^{[k]})$. Based upon all values ${}^1p^{[k]}$ (which are exact in regions Ω_1, Ω_2, and Ω_3 but approximate in the other regions) estimate VaR again. Now letting Ω_3 play a buffer role, apply the same test as before. If all realized losses for Ω_3 are less than the new VaR estimate, you are done. Otherwise, repeat the same procedure again, but with Ω_4 playing the buffer role. Continue in this manner until an acceptable VaR estimate is obtained.

Technically, this is not a variance reduction technique, but by dramatically reducing the number of portfolio valuations ${}^1p^{[k]} = \theta({}^1\boldsymbol{r}^{[k]})$ that must be performed, it has the same effect.

Exercises

10.6 Consider a portfolio (89,700, ${}^1P$) with physical and options positions in two underliers whose values are represented by key vector ${}^1\boldsymbol{R} \sim {}^0N_2({}^{1|0}\boldsymbol{\mu}, {}^{1|0}\boldsymbol{\Sigma})$ where:

$$ {}^{1|0}\boldsymbol{\mu} = \begin{pmatrix} 1.2 \\ 1.6 \end{pmatrix}, \quad {}^{1|0}\boldsymbol{\Sigma} = \begin{pmatrix} .31 & .09 \\ .09 & .22 \end{pmatrix}. \qquad [10.82] $$

Active holdings $\boldsymbol{\omega} = (800 \;\; -300 \;\; -100 \;\; 250)$ are in four assets, where

$$ {}^1\boldsymbol{S} = \begin{pmatrix} {}^1S_1 \\ {}^1S_2 \\ {}^1S_3 \\ {}^1S_4 \end{pmatrix} \sim \begin{pmatrix} \text{physical position, 100 units of underlier 1} \\ \text{call, 100 units of underlier 1, strike 1.25} \\ \text{call, 100 units of underlier 2, strike 1.00} \\ \text{call, 100 units of underlier 2, strike 1.50} \end{pmatrix}. \qquad [10.83] $$

All options expire at time 1.

a. Specify a primary mapping ${}^1P = \theta({}^1\boldsymbol{R})$.

b. Value ${}^1P$ at the following nine realizations for ${}^1\boldsymbol{R}$ (the first equals ${}^{1|0}\boldsymbol{\mu}$, and the rest are arranged about an ellipse centered at ${}^{1|0}\boldsymbol{\mu}$. They were constructed as described in Section 9.3.):

$$ \begin{pmatrix} 1.200 \\ 1.600 \end{pmatrix}, \begin{pmatrix} 1.200 \\ 2.481 \end{pmatrix}, \begin{pmatrix} 2.113 \\ 2.369 \end{pmatrix}, \begin{pmatrix} 2.245 \\ 1.600 \end{pmatrix}, $$
$$ \begin{pmatrix} 1.837 \\ 1.063 \end{pmatrix}, \begin{pmatrix} 1.200 \\ 0.719 \end{pmatrix}, \begin{pmatrix} 0.287 \\ 0.831 \end{pmatrix}, \begin{pmatrix} 0.155 \\ 1.600 \end{pmatrix}, \begin{pmatrix} 0.563 \\ 2.137 \end{pmatrix}. \qquad [10.84] $$

c. Apply the method of least squares to your results from item (b) to construct a quadratic remapping

$$ {}^1\tilde{P} = \tilde{\theta}({}^1\boldsymbol{R}) = {}^1\boldsymbol{R}'\boldsymbol{c}\,{}^1\boldsymbol{R} + \boldsymbol{b}\,{}^1\boldsymbol{R} + a. \qquad [10.85] $$

Weight the realization (1.200, 1.600) five times as heavily as the rest.

d. Construct a scatter plot to assess how well ${}^1\tilde{P}$ approximates ${}^1P$.

e. Specify a crude Monte Carlo estimator for ${}^0std({}^1P)$. Use sample size $m =$ 1000. Estimate ${}^0std({}^1P)$.

f. Specify a control variate Monte Carlo estimator for ${}^0std({}^1P)$. Use sample size $m = 1000$ and the fact that ${}^0std({}^1\tilde{P}) = 38{,}150$. Estimate ${}^0std({}^1P)$.

g. Specify a stratified Monte Carlo estimator for ${}^0std({}^1P)$. Use sample size $m = 1000$ and stratification size $w = 16$. Use the values shown in

Exhibit 10.17 for the conditional CDF of $^1\widetilde{P}$ (calculated using the methods of Section 10.3) to construct your stratification. Estimate $^0std(^1P)$.

$^1\tilde{p}$	$^{1\|0}\Phi(^1\tilde{p})$	$^1\tilde{p}$	$^{1\|0}\Phi(^1\tilde{p})$
-14,730	0.01000	86,196	0.41572
-2,114	0.01792	98,811	0.54767
10,501	0.03123	111,427	0.68368
23,117	0.05280	124,043	0.80736
35,733	0.08635	136,659	0.90303
48,349	0.13621	149,274	0.96263
60,964	0.20653	161,890	0.99000
73,580	0.29997		

Exhibit 10.17 Selected values of the conditional CDF of $^1\widetilde{P}$.

h. Estimate $^0std(^1P)$ 10 times using each of your estimators of items (e), (f), and (g). Based upon the results, construct a (very crude) estimate of the standard error of each of the estimators.
i. Based upon the estimated standard errors from item (h), estimate for each of your estimators the sample size required to achieve a 1% standard error.
j. Specify a crude Monte Carlo estimator for the 95% VaR of portfolio (89,700, ^1P). Use sample size $m = 1000$. Estimate the VaR.
k. Specify a control variate Monte Carlo estimator for the 95% VaR of portfolio (89,700, ^1P). Use sample size $m = 1000$ and the fact that the .05-quantile of $^1\widetilde{P}$ is 21,770. Estimate the VaR.
l. Specify a stratified Monte Carlo estimator for the 95% VaR of portfolio (89,700, ^1P). Use sample size $m = 1000$ and the fact that the .05-quantile of $^1\widetilde{P}$ is 21,770. Estimate the VaR.
m. Estimate the 95% VaR of portfolio (89,700, ^1P) 10 times using each of your estimators of items (j), (k), and (l). Based upon the results, construct a (very approximate) estimate of the standard error of each of the estimators.
n. Based upon the estimated standard errors from item (m), estimate for each of your estimators the sample size required to achieve a 1% standard error.

10.6. FURTHER READING

See Morgan Guaranty (1996), Dowd (2002), or Marrison (2002) for an alternative treatment of transformation procedures. Pichler and Selitsch (2000) offer an empirical assessment of quadratic transformation procedures. Cárdenas *et al.* (1999) is the original paper on variance reduction techniques and related methods discussed in Section 10.5. Fuglsbjerg (2000) elaborates.

Appendix

Standard Normal Table

Cumulative Distribution Function

x	Φ(x)	x	Φ(x)	x	Φ(x)	x	Φ(x)	x	Φ(x)
0.00	0.5000	0.25	0.5987	0.50	0.6915	0.75	0.7734	1.00	0.8413
0.01	0.5040	0.26	0.6026	0.51	0.6950	0.76	0.7764	1.01	0.8438
0.02	0.5080	0.27	0.6064	0.52	0.6985	0.77	0.7794	1.02	0.8461
0.03	0.5120	0.28	0.6103	0.53	0.7019	0.78	0.7823	1.03	0.8485
0.04	0.5160	0.29	0.6141	0.54	0.7054	0.79	0.7852	1.04	0.8508
0.05	0.5199	0.30	0.6179	0.55	0.7088	0.80	0.7881	1.05	0.8531
0.06	0.5239	0.31	0.6217	0.56	0.7123	0.81	0.7910	1.06	0.8554
0.07	0.5279	0.32	0.6255	0.57	0.7157	0.82	0.7939	1.07	0.8577
0.08	0.5319	0.33	0.6293	0.58	0.7190	0.83	0.7967	1.08	0.8599
0.09	0.5359	0.34	0.6331	0.59	0.7224	0.84	0.7995	1.09	0.8621
0.10	0.5398	0.35	0.6368	0.60	0.7257	0.85	0.8023	1.10	0.8643
0.11	0.5438	0.36	0.6406	0.61	0.7291	0.86	0.8051	1.11	0.8665
0.12	0.5478	0.37	0.6443	0.62	0.7324	0.87	0.8078	1.12	0.8686
0.13	0.5517	0.38	0.6480	0.63	0.7357	0.88	0.8106	1.13	0.8708
0.14	0.5557	0.39	0.6517	0.64	0.7389	0.89	0.8133	1.14	0.8729
0.15	0.5596	0.40	0.6554	0.65	0.7422	0.90	0.8159	1.15	0.8749
0.16	0.5636	0.41	0.6591	0.66	0.7454	0.91	0.8186	1.16	0.8770
0.17	0.5675	0.42	0.6628	0.67	0.7486	0.92	0.8212	1.17	0.8790
0.18	0.5714	0.43	0.6664	0.68	0.7517	0.93	0.8238	1.18	0.8810
0.19	0.5753	0.44	0.6700	0.69	0.7549	0.94	0.8264	1.19	0.8830
0.20	0.5793	0.45	0.6736	0.70	0.7580	0.95	0.8289	1.20	0.8849
0.21	0.5832	0.46	0.6772	0.71	0.7611	0.96	0.8315	1.21	0.8869
0.22	0.5871	0.47	0.6808	0.72	0.7642	0.97	0.8340	1.22	0.8888
0.23	0.5910	0.48	0.6844	0.73	0.7673	0.98	0.8365	1.23	0.8907
0.24	0.5948	0.49	0.6879	0.74	0.7704	0.99	0.8389	1.24	0.8925

(Continues)

(Continued)

x	Φ(x)	x	Φ(x)	x	Φ(x)	x	Φ(x)	x	Φ(x)
1.25	0.8944	1.60	0.9452	1.95	0.9744	2.30	0.9893	2.65	0.9960
1.26	0.8962	1.61	0.9463	1.96	0.9750	2.31	0.9896	2.66	0.9961
1.27	0.8980	1.62	0.9474	1.97	0.9756	2.32	0.9898	2.67	0.9962
1.28	0.8997	1.63	0.9484	1.98	0.9761	2.33	0.9901	2.68	0.9963
1.29	0.9015	1.64	0.9495	1.99	0.9767	2.34	0.9904	2.69	0.9964
1.30	0.9032	1.65	0.9505	2.00	0.9772	2.35	0.9906	2.70	0.9965
1.31	0.9049	1.66	0.9515	2.01	0.9778	2.36	0.9909	2.71	0.9966
1.32	0.9066	1.67	0.9525	2.02	0.9783	2.37	0.9911	2.72	0.9967
1.33	0.9082	1.68	0.9535	2.03	0.9788	2.38	0.9913	2.73	0.9968
1.34	0.9099	1.69	0.9545	2.04	0.9793	2.39	0.9916	2.74	0.9969
1.35	0.9115	1.70	0.9554	2.05	0.9798	2.40	0.9918	2.75	0.9970
1.36	0.9131	1.71	0.9564	2.06	0.9803	2.41	0.9920	2.76	0.9971
1.37	0.9147	1.72	0.9573	2.07	0.9808	2.42	0.9922	2.77	0.9972
1.38	0.9162	1.73	0.9582	2.08	0.9812	2.43	0.9925	2.78	0.9973
1.39	0.9177	1.74	0.9591	2.09	0.9817	2.44	0.9927	2.79	0.9974
1.40	0.9192	1.75	0.9599	2.10	0.9821	2.45	0.9929	2.80	0.9974
1.41	0.9207	1.76	0.9608	2.11	0.9826	2.46	0.9931	2.81	0.9975
1.42	0.9222	1.77	0.9616	2.12	0.9830	2.47	0.9932	2.82	0.9976
1.43	0.9236	1.78	0.9625	2.13	0.9834	2.48	0.9934	2.83	0.9977
1.44	0.9251	1.79	0.9633	2.14	0.9838	2.49	0.9936	2.84	0.9977
1.45	0.9265	1.80	0.9641	2.15	0.9842	2.50	0.9938	2.85	0.9978
1.46	0.9279	1.81	0.9649	2.16	0.9846	2.51	0.9940	2.86	0.9979
1.47	0.9292	1.82	0.9656	2.17	0.9850	2.52	0.9941	2.87	0.9979
1.48	0.9306	1.83	0.9664	2.18	0.9854	2.53	0.9943	2.88	0.9980
1.49	0.9319	1.84	0.9671	2.19	0.9857	2.54	0.9945	2.89	0.9981
1.50	0.9332	1.85	0.9678	2.20	0.9861	2.55	0.9946	2.90	0.9981
1.51	0.9345	1.86	0.9686	2.21	0.9864	2.56	0.9948	2.91	0.9982
1.52	0.9357	1.87	0.9693	2.22	0.9868	2.57	0.9949	2.92	0.9982
1.53	0.9370	1.88	0.9699	2.23	0.9871	2.58	0.9951	2.93	0.9983
1.54	0.9382	1.89	0.9706	2.24	0.9875	2.59	0.9952	2.94	0.9984
1.55	0.9394	1.90	0.9713	2.25	0.9878	2.60	0.9953	2.95	0.9984
1.56	0.9406	1.91	0.9719	2.26	0.9881	2.61	0.9955	2.96	0.9985
1.57	0.9418	1.92	0.9726	2.27	0.9884	2.62	0.9956	2.97	0.9985
1.58	0.9429	1.93	0.9732	2.28	0.9887	2.63	0.9957	2.98	0.9986
1.59	0.9441	1.94	0.9738	2.29	0.9890	2.64	0.9959	2.99	0.9986

References

Alexander, Carol O. (2001). *Market Models*, Chichester: John Wiley & Sons.

Alexander, Carol O. and A. M. Chibumba (1997). Multivariate orthogonal factor GARCH, *working paper*.

Apostol, Thomas M. (1969). *Calculus*, Vols. I and II, 2nd ed., New York: John Wiley & Sons.

Baxter, Martin and Andrew Rennie (1996). *Financial Calculus: An Introduction to Derivative Pricing*, Cambridge: Cambridge University Press.

Bernstein, Peter L. (1992). *Capital Ideas: The Improbable Origins of Modern Wall Street*, New York: Free Press.

Black, Fischer (1976). The Pricing of Commodity Contracts, *Journal of Financial Economics*, 3, 167–179.

Black, Fischer and Myron S. Scholes (1973). The pricing of options and corporate liabilities, *Journal of Political Economy*, 81, 637–654.

Bollerslev, Tim (1986). Generalized autoregressive conditional heteroskedasticity, *Journal of Econometrics*, 31, 307–328.

Bollerslev, Tim (1990). Modelling the coherence in short-run nominal exchange rates: A multivariate generalized ARCH model, *Review of Economics and Statistics*, 72, 498–505.

Britten-Jones, Mark and Stephen M. Schaefer (1997). Nonlinear value-at-risk: the distribution of a quadratic approximation to portfolio value, *working paper*.

Burden, Richard L. and J. Douglas Faires (1993). *Numerical Analysis*, 5th ed., Boston: PWS Publishing Company.

Burghardt, Galen and Bill Hoskins (1995). A question of bias, *Risk*, 8 (3), 63–70.

Cárdenas, Juan, Emmanuel Fruchard, Etienne Koehler, Christophe Michel, and Isabelle Thomazeau (1997). VaR: One Step Beyond, *Risk*, 10 (10), 72–75.

Cárdenas, Juan, Emmanuel Fruchard, Jean-François Picron, Cecilia Reyes, Kristen Walters, and Weiming Yang (1999). Monte Carlo within a day, *Risk*, 12 (2), 55–59.

Chew, Lillian (1993). Made to measure, *Risk*, 6 (9), 78–79.

Cornell, Bradford (1981). A note on taxes and the pricing of Treasury bill futures contracts, *Journal of Finance*, 36 (12), 1169–1176.

Cornell, Bradford and Marc R. Reinganum (1981). Forward and futures prices: Evidence from the foreign exchange markets, *Journal of Finance*, 36 (12), 1035–1045.

Cornish, E. A. and Ronald A. Fisher (1937). Moments and cumulants in the specification of distributions, *Review of the International Statistical Institute*, 5, 307–320.

Corrigan, Gerald (1992). *Remarks before the 64th annual mid-winter meeting of the New York State Bankers Association*, January 30, Waldorf-Astoria, New York City: Federal Reserve Bank of New York.

Coveyou, R. R. and R. D. MacPherson (1967). Fourier analysis of uniform random number generators, *Journal of the Association for Computing Machinery*, 14, 100–119.

Cox, John C., Jonathan E. Ingersoll, Jr., and Stephen A. Ross (1981). The relation between forward prices and futures prices, *Journal of Financial Economics*, 9, 321–346.

Culp, Christopher (2001). *The Risk Management Process: Business Strategy and Tactics*, New York: John Wiley & Sons.

Dale, Richard (1996). *Risk and Regulation in Global Securities Markets*, Chichester: John Wiley & Sons.

Davidson, Clive (1996). The data game, *Firmwide Risk Management*, special supplement to *Risk*, 9 (7), 39–44.

Davies, Robert B. (1973). Numerical inversion of a characteristic function, *Biometrika*, 60, 415–417.

DeGroot, Morris H. (1986). *Probability and Statistics*, 2nd ed., Reading: Addison Wesley.

Dennis, J. E. and Robert B. Schnabel (1983). *Numerical Methods for Unconstrained Optimization and Nonlinear Equations*, Englewood Cliffs: Prentice-Hall.

Ding, Z. (1994). Time series analysis of speculative returns, *PhD thesis*, San Diego: University of California.

Doherty, Neil A. (2000). *Integrated Risk Management: Techniques and Strategies for Reducing Risk*, New York: McGraw-Hill.

Dowd, Kevin (2002). *Measuring Market Risk*, Chichester: John Wiley & Sons.

Dusak, Katherine (1973). Futures trading and investor returns: an investigation of commodity market risk premiums, *Journal of Political Economy*, 81, 1387–1406.

Eckhardt, Roger (1987). Stan Ulam, John von Neumann, and the Monte Carlo method, *Los Alamos Science*, Special Issue (15), 131–137.

Eichenauer, J. and J. Lehn (1986). A non-linear congruential pseudo random number generator, *Statistical Papers*, 27, 315–326.

Eichenauer-Herrmann, J. (1993). Statistical independence of a new class of inversive congruential pseudorandom numbers, *Mathematics of Computation*, 60, 375–384.

Engle, Robert F. (1982). Autoregressive conditional heteroskedasticity with estimates of the variance of UK inflation, *Econometrica*, 50, 987–1008.

Engle, Robert F. (2000). Dynamic conditional correlation—A simple class of multivariate GARCH models, *working paper*.

Engle, Robert F. and K. F. Kroner (1995). Multivariate simultaneous generalized ARCH, *Econometric Theory*, 11, 122–150.

Engle, Robert F. and Kevin Sheppard (2001). Theoretical and empirical properties of dynamic conditional correlation multivariate GARCH, *working paper*.

Evans, Merran, Nicholas Hastings, and Brian Peacock (1993). *Statistical Distributions*, 2nd ed., New York: John Wiley & Sons.

Evans, Michael and Tim Swartz (2000). *Approximating Integrals via Monte Carlo and Deterministic Methods*, Oxford: Oxford University Press.

Fallon, William (1996). Calculating value-at-risk, *working paper*.

Feller, William (1968, 1971). *An Introduction to Probability Theory and Its Applications*, 3rd ed. Vol. I and 2nd ed. Vol. II, New York: John Wiley and Sons.

Fincke, U. and M. Pohst (1985). Improved methods for calculating vectors of short length in a lattice, including a complexity analysis, *Mathematics of Computation*, 44 (170), 463–471.

Fishman, George S. (1996). *Monte Carlo: Concepts, Algorithms and Applications*, New York: Springer-Verlag.

Francis, Stephen C. (1985). Correspondence appearing in: United States House of Representatives (1985). *Capital Adequacy Guidelines for Government Securities Dealers Proposed by the Federal Reserve Bank of New York: Hearings Before the Subcommittee on Domestic Monetary Policy of the Committee on Banking, Finance and Urban Affairs*, Washington: US Government Printing Office, 251–252.

Franses, Philip Hans (1998). *Time Series Models for Business and Economic Forecasting*, Cambridge: Cambridge University Press.

Franses, Philip Hans and Dick van Dijk (2000). Non-linear Time Series Models in Empirical Finance, Cambridge: Cambridge University Press.

French, Kenneth R. (1980). Stock returns and the weekend effect, *Journal of Financial Economics*, 8, 55–69.

French, Kenneth R. (1983). A comparison of futures and forward prices, *Journal of Financial Economics*, 12, 311–342.

French, Kenneth R. and Richard Roll (1986). Stock return variance: the arrival of information and the reaction of traders, *Journal of Financial Economics*, 17, 5–26.

Fuglsbjerg, Brian (2000). Variance reduction techniques for Monte Carlo estimates of value-at-risk, *working paper*.

Garbade, Kenneth D. (1986). Assessing risk and capital adequacy for Treasury securities, *Topics in Money and Securities Markets*, 22, New York: Bankers Trust.

Garman, Mark B. and Steven W. Kohlhagen (1983). Foreign currency option values, *Journal of International Money and Finance*, 2, 231–237.

Gärtner, von Bernd (1999). Ein reinfall mit computer-zufallszahlen, *Mitteilungen der Deutschen Mathematiker-Vereinigung*, 2, 55–60.

Geiss, Charles G. (1995). Distortion-free futures price series, *Journal of Futures Markets*, 15 (7), 805–831.

Gentle, James E. (1998). *Numerical Linear Algebra for Applications in Statistics*, New York: Springer-Verlag.

Gibbons, Michael R. and Patrick Hess (1981). Day of the week effect and asset returns, *Journal of Business*, 54, 579–596.

Goldfeld, Stephen M. and Richard E. Quandt (1973). A Markov model for switching regressions, *Journal of Econometrics*, 1, 3–16.

Goldman Sachs and SBC Warburg Dillon Read (1998). *The Practice of Risk Management*, London: Euromoney Books.

Golub, Gene H. and Charles F. Van Loan (1996). *Matrix Computations*, 3rd ed., Baltimore: Johns Hopkins University Press.

Gridgeman, N. T. (1960). Geometric probability and the number π, *Scripta Mathematica*, 25, 183–195.

Group of 30 (1993). *Derivatives: Practices and Principles*, Washington: Group of 30.

Group of 30 (1994). *Derivatives: Practices and Principles, Appendix III: Survey of Industry Practice*, Washington: Group of 30.

Guldimann, Till M. (1995). Risk measurement framework, *RiskMetrics—Technical Document*, 3rd ed., New York: Morgan Guaranty, 6–45.

Guldimann, Till M. (2000). The story of RiskMetrics, *Risk*, 13 (1), 56–58.

Gupta, Anurag and Marti G. Subrahmanyam (2000). An empirical examination of the convexity bias in the pricing of interest rate swaps, *Journal of Financial Economics*, 55 (2), 239–279.

Hall, Asaph (1873). On an experimental determination of π, *Messenger of Mathematics*, 2, 113–114.

Hamilton, James D. (1993). Estimation, inference and forecasting of time-series subject to changes in regime, in G. S. Maddala, C. R. Rao, and H. D. Vinod (editors), *Handbook of Statistics*, Vol. 11, New York: North-Holland.

Hamilton, James D. (1994). *Time Series Analysis*, Princeton: Princeton University Press.

Hammersley, J. M. and D. C. Handscomb (1964). *Monte Carlo Methods*, New York: John Wiley & Sons.

Harvey, Andrew C. (1993). *Time Series Models*, 2nd ed., Cambridge: MIT Press.

Haug, Espen G. (1997). *The Complete Guide to Option Pricing Formulas*, New York: McGraw-Hill.

Hellekalek, P. (1998). Good random number generators are (not so) easy to find, *Mathematics and Computers in Simulation*, 46, 485–505.

Hendricks, Darryll (1996). Evaluation of value-at-risk models using historical data, *Federal Reserve Bank of New York Economic Policy Review*, April.

Hogg, Robert V. and Allen T. Craig (1995). *Introduction to Mathematical Statistics*, 5th ed., Upper Saddle River: Prentice Hall.

Holton, Glyn A. (1997). Subjective value-at-risk, *Financial Engineering News*, 1 (1), 1, 8–9, 11. Also published (1998) in *Risks and Rewards: The Newsletter of the Investment Section of the Society of Actuaries*, 31, 14–17.

Holton, Glyn A. (1998). Simulating value-at-risk, *Risk*, 11 (5), 60–63.

Hughston, Lane (1996). *Vasicek and Beyond: Approaches to Building and Applying Interest Rate Models*. London: Risk Books.

Hughston, Lane (1999). *Options: Classic Approaches to Pricing and Modelling*. London: Risk Books.

Hull, John C. (1999). *Options, Futures and Other Derivatives*, 4th ed., Englewood Cliffs: Prentice Hall.

Hull, John and Alan White (1998). Incorporating volatility updating into the historical simulation method for VaR, *Journal of Risk*, 1 (1), 5–19.

Imhof, J. P. (1961). Computing the distribution of quadratic forms in normal variables, *Biometrika*, 48, 419–426.

James, Jessica and Nick Webber (2000). *Interest Rate Modelling*, Chichester: John Wiley & Sons.

Jamshidian, Farshid and Yu Zhu (1997). Scenario simulation: Theory and methodology, *Finance and Stochastics*, 1 (1), 43–67.

Jarrow, Robert A. (1998). *Volatility: New Estimation Techniques for Pricing Derivatives*, London: Risk Books.

Jarrow, Robert A. and George S. Oldfield (1981). Forward contracts and futures contracts, *Journal of Financial Economics*, 9, 373–382.

Johnson, Dallas E. (1998). *Applied Multivariate Methods for Data Analysts*, Pacific Grove: Duxbury Press.

Johnson, N. L. (1949). Systems of frequency curves generated by methods of translation, *Biometrika*, 36, 149–176.

Judge, George G., R. Carter Hill, William E. Griffiths, Helmut Lütkepohl, and Tsoung-Chao Lee (1988). *Introduction to the Theory and Practice of Econometrics*. 2nd ed., New York: John Wiley & Sons.

Klaassen, Franc (2000). Have exchange rates become more closely tied? Evidence from a new multivariate GARCH model, *working paper*.

Knuth, Donald E. (1997). *The Art of Computer Programming*, 3rd ed., Vol. 2. Reading: Addison-Wesley.

Kolb, Robert W. (1997). *Understanding Futures Markets*, 5th ed., Malden: Blackwell.

Lad, Frank (1996). *Operational Subjective Statistical Methods: A Mathematical, Philosophical, and Historical Introduction*, New York: John Wiley & Sons.

Laplace, Pierre Simon, Marquis de (1878–1912). *Oeuvres Complètes de Laplace*, Paris: Gauthier-Villars.

Leavens, Dickson H. (1945). Diversification of investments, *Trusts and Estates*, 80 (5), 469–473.

L'Ecuyer, Pierre (1998). Random number generation, in Jerry Banks (editor), *Simulation: Principles, Methodology, Advances, Applications, and Practice*, New York: John Wiley & Sons.

L'Ecuyer, Pierre (1999). Good parameter sets for combined multiple recursive random number generators, *Operations Research*, 47 (1), 159–164.

L'Ecuyer, Pierre, F. Blouin, and R. Couture (1993). A search for good multiple recursive random number generators, *ACM Transactions on Modeling and Computer Simulation*, 3 (2), 87–98.

Lehmer, D. H. (1951). Mathematical methods in large-scale computing units, *Proceedings of a Second Symposium on Large-Scale Digital Calculating Machinery*. Cambridge: Harvard University Press, 141–146.

Leipnik, R. B. (1991). Lognormal random variables, *Journal of the Australian Mathematical Society, Series B*, 32, 327–347.

Lewis, P. A. W., A. S. Goodman, and J. M. Miller (1969). A pseudo-random number generator for the System/360, *IBM Systems Journal*, 8 (2), 136–145.

Lietaer, Bernard A. (1971). *Financial Management of Foreign Exchange: An Operational Technique to Reduce Risk*, Cambridge: MIT Press.

Lintner, John (1965). The valuation of risk assets and the selection of risky investments in stock portfolios and capital budgets, *Review of Economics and Statistics*, 47:13–37.

Longerstaey, Jacques (1995). Mapping to describe positions, *RiskMetrics—Technical Document*, 3rd ed., New York: Morgan Guaranty, 107–156.

Lyons, Richard K. (1995). Tests of microstructure hypotheses in the foreign exchange market, *Journal of Financial Economics*, 39, 321–351.

Ma, Christopher K., Jeffrey M. Mercer, and Matthew A. Walker (1992). Rolling over futures contracts: A note, *Journal of Futures Markets*, 12 (2), 203–217.

Mark, Robert (1991). Units of management. *Balance Sheet* (distributed in *Risk*, 4 (6)), 3–7.

Markowitz, Harry M. (1952). Portfolio Selection, *Journal of Finance*, 7 (1), 77–91.

Markowitz, Harry M. (1959). *Portfolio Selection: Efficient Diversification of Investments*, New York: John Wiley & Sons.

Markowitz, Harry M. (1999). The early history of portfolio theory: 1600–1960, *Financial Analysts Journal*, 55 (4), 5–16.

Marrison, Chris (2002). *The Fundamentals of Risk Measurement*, New York: McGraw-Hill.

Marsaglia, G. (1968). Random numbers fall mainly in the planes, *Proceedings of the National Academy of Sciences USA*, 61, 25–28.

Mathai, A. M. and Serge B. Provost (1992). *Quadratic Forms in Random Variables: Theory and Applications*, New York: Marcel Dekker.

Merton, Robert C. (1973). Theory of rational option pricing, *Bell Journal of Economics and Management Science*, 4 (1), 141–183.

Metropolis, Nicholas (1987). The beginning of the Monte Carlo method, *Los Alamos Science*, Special Issue (15), 125–130.

Metropolis, Nicholas and Stanislaw Ulam (1949). The Monte Carlo method, *Journal of the American Statistical Association*, 44 (247), 335–341.

Mills, Terence C. (1999). *The Econometric Modelling of Financial Time Series*, 2nd ed., Cambridge: Cambridge University Press.

Molinari, Steven L. and Nelson S. Kibler (1983). Broker-dealers' financial responsibility under the Uniform Net Capital Rule—a case for liquidity, *Georgetown Law Journal*, 72 (1), 1–37.

Morgan, Byron J. T. (1984). *Elements of Simulation*. London: Chapman & Hall.

Morgan Guaranty (1996). *RiskMetrics—Technical Document*, 4th ed., New York: Morgan Guaranty.

Mossin, Jan (1966). Equilibrium in a capital asset market, *Econometrica*, 34, 768–783.

Niederreiter, Harald (1992). *Random Number Generation and Quasi-Monte Carlo Methods*, Philadelphia: Society for Industrial and Applied Mathematics.

Ortega, James M. (1987). *Matrix Theory: A Second Course,* New York: Plenum Press.

Pan, Jun and Darrell Duffie (1997). An Overview of value-at-risk, *Journal of Derivatives*, 4 (3), 7–49.

Park, Hun Y. and Andrew H. Chen (1985). Differences between futures and forward prices: A further investigation of the mark-to-market effects, *Journal of Futures Markets*, 5 (1), 77–88.

Park, Stephen K. and Keith W. Miller (1988). Random number generators: good ones are hard to find, *Communications of the ACM*, 31 (10), 1192–1201.

Patel, Jagdish K. (1996). *Handbook of the Normal Distribution*, New York: Marcel Dekker.

Pichler, Stefan and Karl Selitsch (2000). A comparison of analytic VaR methodologies for portfolios that include options, *Model Risk: Concepts, Calibration and Pricing*, Rajna Gibson (editor), London: Risk Books.

Questa, Giorgio S. (1999). *Fixed Income Analysis for the Global Financial Market: Money Market, Foreign Exchange, Securities, and Derivatives*, New York: John Wiley & Sons.

Reuters (2000). *An Introduction to the Commodities, Energy and Transport Markets*, Singapore: John Wiley & Sons.

Rota, Gian-Carlo (1987). The lost cafe, *Los Alamos Science*, Special Issue (15), 23–32.

Rouvinez, Christophe (1997). Going Greek with VaR, *Risk*, 10 (2), 57–65.

Roy, Arthur D. (1952). Safety first and the holding of assets, *Econometrica*, 20 (3), 431–449.

Rubinstein, Reuven Y. (1981). *Simulation and the Monte Carlo Method*, New York: John Wiley & Sons.

Saff, E. B. and A. B. J. Kuijlaars (1997). Distributing many points on a sphere, *Mathematical Intelligencer*, 19 (1), 5–11.

Schrock, Nichols W. (1971). The theory of asset choice: simultaneous holding of short and long positions in the futures market, *Journal of Political Economics*, 79, 270–293.

Sharpe, William F. (1963). A simplified model for portfolio analysis, *Management Science*, 9, 277–293.

Sharpe, William F. (1964). Capital asset prices: A theory of market equilibrium under conditions of risk, *Journal of Finance*, 19 (3), 425–442.

Shirreff, David (1992). Swap and think, *Risk*, 5 (3), 29–35.

Singh, Manoj K. (1997). Value-at-risk using principal components analysis, *Journal of Portfolio Management*, 24 (1), 101–112.

Solomon, H. and M. A. Stephens (1977). Distribution of a sum of weighted chi-square variables, *Journal of the American Statistical Association*, 72, 881–885.

Spanos, Aris (1999). *Probability Theory and Statistical Inference: Econometric Modeling and Observational Data*, Cambridge: Cambridge University Press.

Stoyanov, Jordan (1987). *Counterexamples in Probability*, 2nd ed., Chichester: John Wiley & Sons.

Strang, Gilbert (1988). *Linear Algebra and Its Applications*, 3rd ed., Fort Worth: Harcourt Brace & Co.

Stuart, Alan and J. Keith Ord (1994). *Kendall's Advanced Theory of Statistics, Volume I: Distribution Theory*, London: Arnold.

Student (1908a). The probable error of a mean, *Biometrika*, 6, 1–25.

Student (1908b). Probable error of a correlation coefficient, *Biometrika*, 6, 302–310.

Thomas, George B., Jr. and Ross L. Finney (1996). *Calculus and Analytic Geometry*, 9th ed., Reading: Addison-Wesley.

Tobin, James (1958). Liquidity preference as behavior towards risk, *The Review of Economic Studies*, 25, 65–86.

Todhunter, Isaac (1865). *A History of the Mathematical Theory of Probability*, Cambridge: Cambridge University Press. Reprinted (1949), New York: Chelsea.

Treynor, Jack (1962). Toward a theory of market value of risky assets, *unpublished manuscript*.

Viswanath, P. V. (1989). Taxes and the futures-forward price difference in the 91-day T-bill market, *Journal of Money, Credit and Banking*, 21 (2), 190–205.

Walmsley, Julian (2000). *The Foreign Exchange and Money Markets Guide*, 2nd ed., New York: John Wiley & Sons.

Wilmott, Paul, Jeff Dewynne, and Sam Howison (1993). *Option Pricing: Mathematical Models and Computation*, Oxford: Oxford Financial Press.
Wilson, Thomas (1992). Raroc remodeled, *Risk*, 5 (8), 112–119.
Wilson, Thomas (1993). Infinite wisdom, *Risk*, 6 (6), 37–45.
Wilson, Thomas (1994). Debunking the myths, *Risk*, 7 (4), 67–73.
Zangari, Peter (1994). Estimating volatilities and correlations, *RiskMetrics—Technical Document*, 2nd ed., New York: Morgan Guaranty, 43–66.
Zangari, Peter (1996a). Data and Related Statistical Issues, *RiskMetrics—Technical Document*, 4th ed., New York: Morgan Guaranty, 163–196.
Zangari, Peter (1996b). Statistics of financial market returns, *RiskMetrics—Technical Document*, 4th ed., New York: Morgan Guaranty, 41–101.
Zangari, Peter (1996c). Market risk methodology, *RiskMetrics—Technical Document*, 4th ed., New York: Morgan Guaranty, 105–148.

Index

N

O

P